HISTORY AND FAMILIES · ANDERSON COUNTY, KENTUCKY ·

Turner Publishing Company

Turner Publishing Company

Created and designed by David A. Hurst, Publishing Consultant

Copyright © 1991 Anderson County Chamber of Commerce

Library of Congress Catalog No. 90-071717
ISBN 978-1-68162-446-4

LIMITED EDITION

Additional copies may be available directly from the Publisher.

Three sisters, Alice Utterback Johnson, Elizabeth Utterback Lynch Catharine Utterback and Harris Pleasant.

Old Lawrenceburg High School located on North Main.

2

James Garland, Marjorie Eloise, and Norman Earl Gudgel, children of Samuel and Verna Gudgel taken at the old homeplace in Alton.

CONTENTS

Beautiful waterfalls along Wildcat Pike

Civil War Veterans—Taken at the courthouse, Lawrenceburg. Seated, James Gee, Will York, James S. Coke, Dr. J.W. Speer, James Ripy, Charles Towles (Toll), Albert Sherwood. Second row, ?, Richard Johnson, Jad Frazier?, ?, ?, "Buck" Routt, John P. Vaughn, Edward J. Thacker, William H. Glass, Mitchell?. Back, John Shely, Green Baxter, ?, James Hawkins, James Long, ?, S.O. Hackley, Elijah Bowen, Charles Shely, Joe Waterfill, ?, Kleim, P.H. Farley, John Moffett, Charles Dawson. Some of the unknown are a Stucker, Ike Johnson and, maybe, Andy Akins.

Outside the Bond & Lillard Distillers, c. 1909.

FOREWORD

When the pioneers came into the part of Kentucky that is now Anderson County, they found a land of unique beauty and diversity. Some two hundred years later, people are still discovering Anderson County . . . and whether you are here for business, pleasure or have made your home here, I am sure you will enjoy the charm of Anderson County and the hospitality of its citizens.

This Family History of Anderson County preserves the proud heritage of our county and communities as well as many of our churches, businesses, organizations and families. Our intent is to record a picture of the people, organizations and activities for future generations.

No undertaking of this magnitude can be comprehensive. We regret that many families failed to submit a biographical sketch for this book, denying their descendants a written account of their heritage.

The Anderson County Chamber of Commerce gives special appreciation and thanks to those that submitted family histories, volunteered their services and/or financially supported this project.

It is hoped that this effort to preserve some of our past will motivate future generations to better preserve history as it is being made.

Robert M. Thompson, President
Anderson County Chamber of Commerce

Home of Tyler Burgin

Graduating Class, 1909, Lawrenceburg High School.

HISTORY OF ANDERSON COUNTY

Anderson County was the 82nd Kentucky county and was formed out of Franklin, Mercer and Washington Counties in 1827. Anderson County was named for Richard Clough Anderson, Jr., a Congressman and Speaker of the Hourse of Representatives and the first United States Minister to Columbia, South America. He died in 1826. His mother was Elizabeth Clark, sister of General George Rogers Clark.

Anderson County is situated on the west side of the Kentucky River and contains approximately 200 square miles. It is bounded on the north by Shelby and Franklin Counties, on the east by Woodford County, on the south by Mercer and Washington Counties and on the west by Nelson and Spencer Counties.

In 1873, James, Robert, and George McAfee led a party out of Virginia to explore and survey lands in Kentucky. In their exploration they came upon the spring at the head of Gilbert's Creek. They referred to it as either Cove or Cave Spring, later called Lillard's Spring from the pioneer Thomas Lillard, and presently called McCall's Spring. The spring is located in US 127 about five miles south of Lawrenceburg.

The territory of Anderson County was established by the Virginia Legislature of 1776, included in what was then called Kentucky County. In 1780 Kentucky County was divided into Jefferson, Lincoln and Fayette Counties. Anderson was included in Lincoln. Mercer was the first county formed out of Lincoln, and Anderson was then a part of Mercer County. Franklin County was carved out of Mercer County by the 1794 Kentucky Legislature and most of the present county of Anderson was included in Franklin. In 1827, Anderson became a county and was formed out of parts of Franklin, Mercer, and Shelby Counties.

Anderson County has a rolling to hilly terrain. The area along Kentucky River affords very beautiful and picturesque scenery. The soil is very productive in some sections, producing corn, tobacco, small grain and grasses. In early days, hemp was raised in abundance and Lawrenceburg possessed several hemp factories, or as they were called, "rope walks".

Anderson County has an abundant supply of water from the Kentucky River on the east, Salt River in the middle and several creeks and springs throughout the county.

Richard Benson, Nathan Hammond and William McBrayer are thought to be the first emigrants to come to Anderson County to locate their homes. They had spent some time at Harrod's Fort (Harrodsburg) in 1775,

and pushed north to stake their claims in what is now Anderson County. Richard Benson claimed four hundred acres on Kentucky River and left his name on four creeks. Hammond Creek was named for Nathan Hammond. William McBrayer was a surveyor and made several surveys to the north and east of Lawrenceburg and located north of Lawrenceburg.

In 1782, Thomas Baker settled west of Lawrenceburg on what is known as the Wash Farm. William Nelson and Peter Carr also located in that area.

Early settlers in the Alton area were Lynch, George, Mothershead, Marrs, Mountjoy, Thomas Gaines, Wafer Payne, and Thompson Thomason.

Settlers in the Hammond Creek area included Robert Elliott, Joshua Cummins, Samuel Burrus and Memucan Allen. Robert Elliott built a mill and distillery on Hammond Creek, thought to be the first in Anderson County.

In 1791, Charles Allen, Joshua Saffell, Samuel Marrs, Joseph McClure, Joseph Woods, Jacob Gudgel, Joseph Griffith, Daniel and Arthur McGaughey settled near each other.

To the east and south of Lawrenceburg were Jeremiah, Joseph, and James Mizner, Vincent Boggess, Robert Frazier, Berry Searcy, Nicholas Leathers, John Parker, Turner and Chichester Hanks, John Bond, Edward Wall, the Dawsons, McMichaels and Huffmans.

Near Salt River were David Egbert, John Odell, Samuel Butts, Jacob Middletown, Archie Parker, Joel Thacker, John Crossfield, Thomas Hackley, Mike Hockersmith, the Browns, Bells, Paxtons, Murphys, Wheats, Gillises, Benjamin Wash, Roadham Petty, Samuel Petty, Daniel Oliver, Thomas Buntain, John Jewel, John Morgan and the Franklins.

Anderson County has never failed to bear arms in time of war. During the war between the United States and Mexico, Anderson County furnished one company known as the Salt River Tigers, led by Captain John McBrayer.

During the Civil War, Anderson County sent about 400 to the South and about 200 to the North. The Confederates were led by Captains Utterback, Dedman, Dawson, and Jordan. The Union soldiers were led by Captain Searcy and Boston.

Anderson County responded with brave soldiers during the Spanish American War.

Monuments bearing the names of Anderson Countains that lost their lives

during World War I, World War II, Korean War and Vietnam War, for the "Ideals of Freedom", stand in the Court House Yard as a memorial to their gallantry.

Anderson County has been dependent upon the distillery industry as one of its sources of revenue. By 1818 there is said to have been more than 50 distilleries in operation. Anderson County's first distillery was established by "Old Joe" Peyton at Gilbert's Creek.

Anderson County is the home of The Anderson County Fair and Horse Show. The Anderson County Fair and Horse Show was established in 1872 and is said to be the second oldest county fair in the nation. This annual event draws some of the finest gaited and pleasure horses from all areas of the United States. Anderson Post #34 of the American Legion owns and operates the Anderson County Fair and Horse Show grounds. The grounds are available for community and family events when not being utilized by the American Legion.

Lawrenceburg/Anderson County Parks and Recreation Department maintains a community park, ballfields and swimming pool on the American Legion property under a lease agreement with Anderson Post #34 American Legion.

Lawrenceburg is the County Seat of Anderson County and is the only incorporated city in the county. Other unincorporated communities include:

Alton (formerly "Rough and Ready"), was established as a post office, (about 1840 - 1844), four miles north of Lawrenceburg.

New Alton (Alton Station), after the railroad was built through Anderson County a rail station sprung up about two miles from Alton.

Anderson City is in the exact center of Anderson County and was strongly suggested as the location for County govenment.

Lick Skillet

Sparrow (formerly Wardsville) was named for the number of Sparrows that lived in the vicinity.

Johnsonville is near the Washington County line.

VanBuren was located on Salt River about 17 miles from Lawrenceburg. With the impoundment of Salt River to form Taylorsville Lake, VanBuren was covered with water.

Glensboro was established as a post office in 1904. Prior to 1904 the community was known as Camden, Camdenville and Orr. Glensboro is located along Salt River, approximately 10 miles from Lawrenceburg.

Tyrone (formerly Streamville) is located

on the Kentucky River banks about three miles from Lawrenceburg. In 1868 a distillery was built at Tyrone by S. P. Martin. This distillery subsequently was owned by T. B. Ripy and was enlarged to a capacity of 4,000 bushel of grain per day, and was the largest "mash tub" distillery in the world. Tyrone was named for Tyrone County, Ireland. The Ripy's were orginally from Tyrone County, Ireland.

Sinai or Shiloh is a community approximately 10 miles west of Lawrenceburg with two names. The post office was established as Sinai while the church and school were known as Shiloh.

Ripyville was located about four miles south of Lawrenceburg. Fox Creek (Hawkins) is located approximately six miles west of Lawrenceburg.

Early Anderson County had an abundance of one room grade schools. Some of these schools that existed from the late 1800's to the 1930's were: Alexander, Alton, Anderson City, Antioch, Avenstoke, Bonds Mill, Buntain, Buck Lick, Cedar Grove, Champion, Fairview, Fox Creek, Franklin, Friendship, Glensboro, Goodlett, Gordon, Griffy, Hampton, Hebron, Herndon, Hickory Grove, Hughes, Johnsonville, Kays, Klondike, Long, Marlowe, Munday, McGinnis, Oak Grove, Peak, Pleasant Hill, Royalty, Rutherford, Salt River, Searcy, Shiloh, Stingy, Tanner, Tyrone, VanBuren, Wardsville, and Young.

In the late 1930's and early 1940's, the one room grade schools were consolidated into five elementary schools: Alton, Marlowe, Rutherford, Sand Spring and Western.

High schools were Lawrenceburg-City High, Kavanaugh and Western. Kavanaugh and Lawrenceburg-City High consolidated in 1950 forming Anderson County High School. By action of the Anderson County School Board, Western High School was closed in 1990 to join Anderson County High School. An elementary school remains at Western School, the only school outside the City of Lawrenceburg (1990).

Anderson County is emerging from an agricultural based economy to an industrial based economy. An industrial foundation has been formed and is developing an Industrial Park in the southeast quadrant of Lawrenceburg. This, along with the expansion of existing industries within the community, has contributed to Anderson County being rated as the fourth fastest growing community in Kentucky.

Anderson County's local government consists of a Judge/Executive and six magistrates that serve on the Anderson County Fiscal Court. Each is elected for a four year term. Jim Catlett, Judge/Executive; and Magistrates: Alton Warford, Stewart Gritton, Sherell Wells, Anthony Stratton, John Conway, and Jim Doss make up the 1990 Fiscal Court. Jerry Springate is the County Attorney.

The Erection of Anderson County

By an Act of the Legislature approved January 16, 1827, Anderson County was erected and established. By a supplemental Act approved January 18, 1827, the county was to go into effect and operation on the 20th of January, 1827. Willis Blanton and Peter R. Dunn were two of the Commisioners appointed by acts of General Assembly, January 18, 1827, to lay off by metes and bounds, the county. Up to this time the county had been a part of Washington, Mercer and Franklin Counties.

By the original Act all that part of the counties of Franklin, Mercer and Washington included in a boundry, beginning at the mouth of Little Benson Creek on Kentucky River in Franklin County; thence with the meanders of said creek, to Brooks spring, near the Harrodsburg Road; thence on a straight line to Caleb Tinsley's, leaving him in Franklin County; thence by a line due west to the line of Shelby County; thence along the same to the mouth of Crooked Creek on Salt River; thence along the dividing line of Washington and Nelson to the mouth of Beaver Creek, on Chaplin's fork on Salt River; thence up said creek to where the road from Springfield to Frankfort crosses the same; then with a line east so as to leave Vincent Morgan in Washington County, to the dividing line between Washington and Mercer; thence with the Washington and mercer line to a point from which a line due east will include the house of James Downy; thence a straight line to include the house of Thomas Hardesty on the Harrodsburg Road: thence a straight line to the Kentucky River at the ferry of Costello Dawson, Sr.; thence down the river to the beginning. By the same Act, the county was to be called and known by the name of Anderson, in honor of the late Richard C.

Anderson, Jr. The date of the county courts were fixed for the first Monday in every month, except the months when the circuit courts were held. The county was attached to the Fourth Judicial District, and the terms of the circuit courts were fixed on the fourth Mondays on January, July and November, with six day terms. 10 Justices of the Peace were allowed the county, and it was enacted that they should meet at the house of William Hudgins in the town of Lawrence (which name was changed to Lawrenceburg by the Act) on the first court day after the Act went into effect, at which time they were to appoint a clerk. The Governor was authorized to commission a sheriff.

William Trotter of Franklin County, R. D. Shipp of Woodford county, Joel P. Williams of Mercer County, Stephen Lee of Washington County, Wm. T. Webber, of Shelby County and Elias Kinchelo of Nelson county were appointed commissioners, any five of whom might act, to locate the county seat. They were ordered to assemble at the home of Wm. Hudgins in the month of March or April (1827) after the Act went into effect, and after being sworn, to select the seat of justice for the county, and make their report of their actions to the county court, for which they were allowed two dollars per day. The court was allowed five constables to be appointed by the court.

Arrangement was made for the levy and collection of taxes, and until the erection of public buildings, it was ordered that circuit and county courts be held at the house of Wm. Hudgins in Lawrenceburg. It was further enacted that Wm. Blanton, of Franklin county; Wm. M. Bell, of Washington County, and Peter R. Dunn, or Mercer County, be appointed commissioners.

(History of Anderson County, 1938)

DEVELOPMENT OF ANDERSON COUNTY

Anderson County, situated on the west side of Kentucky River, was established by an act of the Kentucky legislature on January 16, 1827.

In 1830, three years after the organization of the county, the first courthouse was built on the site of the present building. This was destroyed by fire in 1859 and in 1860, at the beginning of the War Between the States, the present structure was erected.

In 1905, the building was remodeled and so arranged that it is one of the most attractive and convenient courthouses in the state. In the courtyard are to be seen handsome monuments erected as a memorial to the famous Salt River Tigers and the other to Confederate soldiers who died on the field of conflict.

The territory of Anderson County was annexed by the Virginia legislature, in 1776, being included in what was called Ken-

tucky County which in 1780 was divided into Jefferson, Fayette and Lincoln Counties. Anderson was included in Lincoln. Mercer was the first county formed out of Lincoln, and Anderson became a part of Mercer.

Franklin was carved out of Mercer by the Kentucky legislature in 1794, and most of the present county of Anderson was included in Franklin, but in 1827 Anderson came into her own and was formed from parts of Mercer, Franklin and Shelby counties and was named for Richard Clough Anderson, who died the previous year while United States Minister to Columbia, South America. At that time, no native born Kentuckian had achieved greater political distinction.

Anderson County has a rolling surface and is almost mountainous in the eastern portion along the Kentucky River, thus forming picturesque scenery. Though its climate is fickle, the soil is very productive, in some sections producing fine tobacco and corn and all the small grains and grasses. In the early days, hemp was raised in abundance, and several hemp factories, or "rope walks" were located in Lawrenceburg.

No county has a better supply of water than has Anderson, as the Kentucky River borders its eastern shores and Salt River flows through its central part. The three Benson Creeks, Hammonds Creek and many other creeks and springs supply ample water for all purposes.

Richard Benson, Nathan Hammond and William McBrayer are thought to have been the first emigrants who came into Anderson to locate homes. They had spent some time at Harrod's Fort in 1775, and pushed on north to take up land claims.

Richard Benson took up a settlement claim of 400 acres on Kentucky River and impressed his name on four creeks, sold his claim and disappeared.

Nathan Hammond was a delegate from Boiling Spring to a convention which met at Boonesborough on May 23, 1775. Hammonds Creek perpetuates his name.

William McBrayer was a surveyor and made a number of surveys at the north and east of Lawrenceburg, and located two miles north of town. Another early settler was Thomas Baker, who in 1782 settled on what is now known as the George Wash farm. William Nelson and Peter Carr also settled in that neighborhood. A man named Lynch located on the farm now owned and operated by I. B. Bush and was surrounded by the Georges and Mothersheads. Families locating where Alton now is were the Marrs, Mountjoys, Thomas Gaines, Wafer Payne and Thompson Thomas.

On Hammonds Creek we find the names of Robert Elliott, Joshua Cummins, Samuel Burrus and Memucan Allen. Robert Elliott built a mill, thought to have been the first in Anderson County, on this creek. Charles Allen, Joshua Saffell, Samuel Marrs, James McClure, Joseph Woods, Jacob Gudgel, Joseph Griffith and Daniel and Arthur McGaughey also settled near each other on this stream in 1791.

On the east and south of town in pioneer days were the homes of Jeremiah, Joseph and James Mizner, Vincent Boggess, Robert Frazier, Berry Searcy, Nicholas Leathers, John Parker, Turner and Chichester Hanks, John Bond, Edward Wall, the Dawsons, the McMichaels and the Huffmans.

On Salt River lived David Egbert, John Odell, Samuel Butts, Jacob Middleton, Archie Parker, Joel Thacker, John Crossfield, Thomas Hackley, Mike Hockersmith, the Browns, the Bells, the Paxtons, the Murphys, the Wheats, the Gillises, Benjamin Wash, Roadham Petty, Senior and Junior and the Franklins.

Anderson never had failed to bear her part in time of war. When the war between the United States and Mexico broke out, she furnished one company known as the Salt River Tigers, led by Capt. John H. McBrayer. They served gallantly and, it is claimed, saved the day at the battle of Buena Vista.

During the War Between the States, Anderson County sent about 400 men to the South and about 200 men to the Northern forces. The Confederates were led by Captains Utterback, Dedman, Dawson and Jordan; the Unionists by Captains Searcy and Boston. No great battles were fought in this county, but there was a small skirmish at Fox Creek on October 8, 1862, besides others between guerillas and home guards, one of which was fought at Vandyke's Mill.

Anderson County sent a few soldiers to the Spanish-American War, but their service in actual warfare was limited. After the war ended, some of her sons saw services the Uncle Sam in the Philippine Islands.

In 1917, Anderson County rallied to the colors when the United States cast her lot with the Allied armies, and 293 of her sons were inducted into the service, 22 having volunteered before the draft. Under the selective draft law, there were 1,952 Anderson County men who registered. 14 men from the county lost their lives overseas: Jesse D. Lowen was the first Anderson County man killed in the service. Others were: Randolph Coke, William Cinnamon, Forrest Hayden, William Hansel, Delbert Riley, William Beasley, Charles Hillard, Jesse R. Morris, James N. Tucker, Henry Monroe, Vernon Watts, Nelson Woodward, and John Roy Carter, the latter a Negro. 18 were disabled in the fighting and service in the camps.

A bronze plated granite memorial, nine feet tall and five feet wide, has been erected to the county's World War dead. It occupies a space on Main Street directly in front of the county courthouse in Lawrenceburg. It was erected at a cost of $1,000, raised by popular subscription and supervised by Anderson Post, No. 34, American Legion. The dedication of the shaft took place on the morning of November 11, 1936, in the presence of a large audience. The address was delivered by Past State Commander Eldon S. Dummitt, of Lexington.

In 1827, when Anderson County was created and the act creating the county changed the name of the town from Lawrence to Lawrenceburg, it was natural through the creation of a new county, with Lawrenceburg a good prospect for the county seat, that a fresh boom would occur in town lots. A number of lots that had been lair off by the town trustees our of land conveyed to them by William Lawrence and Samuel Arbuckle in 1818 were sold by the trustees in 1827, 1828 and 1829, and there was quite a sale of the lots sold by the trustees in 1818 and built upon by the purchasers; in fact, there had been more than 40 transfers of town lots made in those year.

However, the growth of the town did not meet the anticipation of those who laid out the village in 1818. In 1830, the population of the town had increased to only 320 and of the county to 4,520. In 1830, and for some years previous, there has been as many as four tan yards and three rope walks and bagging factories. There also was one carding mill. One of these tope walks and bagging factories was working more than 40 slaves; yet, the growth of the town had not met the anticipations of the founders of the town.

Before 1830 a number of the leading citizens had sold out their holdings and left.

The county, with very few changes, has remained situated as at the time of its erection, except that its population was considerably enhanced by the cutting off from Mercer County of a large territory, including a population of about 400.

Thomas Prather built the first house in what is now Lawrenceburg. William Lawrence built the famous Galt House about the year 1815 on what is now the federal building (postoffice) site.

The first courthouse in Lawrenceburg was partly built by popular subscription and the name of the contributors are recorded in the office of the circuit clerk. It was erected in 1830, three years after the organization of the county.

The county's first circuit court convened in Lawrenceburg January 22, 1827 in the home of William Hudgins, where the building that houses a grocery now stands. Henry Daridge was the judge, and David White was appointed clerk. Chas. C. Bibb appeared as commonwealth's attorney.

The first county court was organized in Lawrenceburg February 5, 1827, when the following justices of the peace met at the home of Mr. Hudgins and took their seats according to seniority as follows:

Jesse Guess, presiding justice; James McBrayer, Dr. Dixon G. Dedman, John Wash, Andrew McBrayer, John Busey, Christopher Lillard, Reuben Boston, John C. Richardson and Thomas Phillips. David White, Jr. was named clerk of the court, with the permission of the court, he named John T. Daviess as his deputy; John F. Blackwell was named sheriff and George Morris jailer. The following gentlemen were permitted, by an order of the court, to practice as attorneys and counselors at law in the court: Louis Sanders, Jr., Nelson Cole Johnson, Washington Dorrell, John S. Greathouse, Preston Samuel Loughbrough and Thomas Triplett.

While Lawrenceburg does not and cannot claim to be the oldest or the largest city in the state of Kentucky, there are few other towns of any size whose people have more caused to congratulate themselves over the growth and prosperity which have attended their community from the earliest period of their history.

The first settlement on the land where the city now stands was made between 30 and 40 years before the incorporation of the town of Lawrence, the locality being first known as Kaufman's Station. Jacob Kaufman, a German, located 400 acres of land on a branch of Hammonds Creek, adjoining a claim held by a man named Bailey, and had his residence on the lot in the rear of the present home of Judge Stanley Trent, the claim being located in February, 1780, and in June of the same year he located another claim of 1,000 acres immediately adjoining the first.

A few months later a man by the name of Larue located a claim of 1,000 acres on a small creek emptying into Kentucky River near a tree bearing the name of Nathan

Randolph cut in the bark. Peter Asturgis located two claims, one of 200 acres and another of 1,000 acres, the first in 1780 and the last in 1783. Thomas Madison, for whom Main Street of the town was first named, located 1,000 acres in 1782 and in the same year Joseph Crockett located 1,000 acres. Thomas Madison, John Harvey, Cass Clark and John Payne located other lands, all near the first location of Jacob Kaufman's first settlement.

At the time of its incorporation in 1827 the town boasted one store, which stood on the lot now occupied by the Tinsley store-room on Main Street occupied by Turner and Brown and S. Rozen, a blacksmith shop where the Presbyterian church is now located, or just north of that lot, and a tailor shop, run by Anthony Miller.

The city has been visited by at least three disastrous fires. On March 15, 1873, a fire destroyed the entire business district of the city, as well as many of the residences. More substantial and commodious brick business houses were built in the burned district. In 1892, another disastrous fire broke out in the city work-house and destroyed 12 of 15 buildings and caused the death of an inmate of the prison.

Other smaller fires have burned almost every business house on Main Street between Court and Jackson, and many of the building further north. One of these fires caused the death of two small children who could not be saved from the second floor room in which they were sleeping. The last big fire was in 1898, when the Christian Church and some 15 business houses on Main and Court Street were destroyed.

Each of these fires was followed by the building of better houses than the city had known before, and today there are few cities of even larger size that can show visitors better, handsomer of more commodious business houses and dwellings than can Lawrenceburg.

Lawrenceburg, as she stands today, with her six miles of paved streets, including a brick paved Main Street, her splendid lighting system, her ice plant, her municipal water works plant, her thread factory and cheese factory, employing 150 people, her shipping facilities, both rail and bus, her up-to-date progressive business men in all lines, her low tax rate, her city delivery of mails, her religious facilities, her progressive city officials, her excellent schools, her two strong banks, her hospitable and properous people and her modern and commodius homes, may well claim to be, as she is one of the best of the good cities of the proud old Commonwealth.

Lawrenceburg lies at the crossroads of the nation. Down Main Street comes Taft Highway (once a deer trail), starting at Sault St. Marie, the northern point of Michigan, and continuing to the southern tip of Florida to Key West, the last ravelling of that state. Route 62, which unites the Atlantic and the Pacific, comes into town along Woodford Street, turns south on Main and west again at Broadway. The Midland Trail from Cumberland Gap to Louisville runs straight through the town. License plates for every state in the Union are seen as touring cars pass through. Over the $400,000 Tyrone bridge some day will be routed the air-line course from Lexington to Louisville, it is predicted.

The Public Works Administration has been busy the past year with projects which have improved the streets of the city. Many of the thoroughfares have been paved with rock asphalt, and concrete curbs and gutters have been built. Rights of way have been secured from property-owners in the North Main Street section preparatory to the building of a new concrete street by the State Highway Department, and this also will be fitted out with concrete curb and gutter.

Another improvement made possible by the PWA was the building of a sewage system throughout the city and the erection of a disposal plant that conforms to specification by the State Board of Health. *(c.1938)*

ANDERSON COUNTY NAMED FOR YOUNG MAN

Anderson County, the 82nd in order of formation, was organized in 1827 out of parts of Franklin, Mercer and Washington Counties and named after one of the most brilliant young men of Kentucky, Richard Clough Anderson, Jr., then recently deceased, according to Collins History of Kentucky, of 1846 and 1947.

It is situated in the middle portion of the state and is bounded on the north by Franklin County, east by the Kentucky River which separated it from Woodford, south by Mercer and Washington and west by Spencer County.

It is well watered by Salt River (which has many fine mills and good water power) by its tributaries, Crooked, Fox, Stoney and Hammond Creeks; and by the Kentucky River and its tributaries, Bailey's Run, Little Benson and Gilbert's Creek.

The surface is generally rolling, some portions level, rich, and very productive; the hills grow fine tobacco and grasses. Cattle and hogs, wheat, corn, whiskey, are the leading article of production and export. In the county are 13 distilleries, which have manufactured in a year 4,000 barrels of old fashioned, sour-mash, hand-made, copper distilled whiskey, of very fine quality.

Lawrenceburg was established in 1820 and called after Captain James Lawrence, U.S. Navy, whose last words on board the Chesapeake were "Don't give up the ship." It was first settled by an old Dutchman named Coffman. When his good wife first heard of his death, (he was killed by the Indians), she exclaimed in the bitterness of her affliction, "I always told my old man that these savage ingens would kill him, and I'd rather lost my best cow at the pail than my old man."

Lawrenceburg with a population of 400, is the county seat, 14 miles from Frankfort and 20 from Harrodsburg, on the turnpike road uniting them; has a substantial court-house, built at a cost of $18,000 in 1861—the old one, with many of the county records having been burned in 1860; it has a banking-house, a steam flouring mill, and four churches, Reformed or Christian, Methodist, Baptist, and a colored or African church established by the Freedmen's Bureau in its palmy days.

Homeplace of Porter and Eva Gibson.

COMMUNITIES

LAWRENCEBURG

Lawrenceburg, the county seat of Anderson County, is located in the rolling to hilly terrain of central Kentucky's famous Blue Grass Region. The 1986 estimated population of Anderson County was 13,800, with a 1984 estimated of 5,900 people residing within the Lawrenceburg city limits. Lawrenceburg is located 23 miles west of Lexington, Kentucky; 55 miles east of Louisville, Kentucky; and 101 miles south of Cincinnati, Ohio.

The Economic Framework - The total number of Anderson County residents employed in 1986 averaged 6,270. Manufacturing firms in the county reported 950 employees; wholesale and retail trade provided 650 jobs; 210 people were employed in service occupations; state and local government accounted for 430 employees; and contract construction firms provided 80 jobs.

Labor Supply - There is current estimated labor supply of 6,170 men and 8,880 women available for industrial jobs in the labor market area. In addition, from 1987 through 1991, 6,700 young men and 6,550 young women in the area will become 18 years of age and potentially available for industrial jobs.

Transportation - The Southern Railway System provides rail service, including daily stops for northbound and southbound freights. Major "AAA" - rated highways serving Lawrenceburg are U.S. Highways 127 and 62, and Kentucky Highway 151. In addition, Kentucky Highway 44, a "AA"-rated highway, serves the city. The Blue Grass Parkway is 4 miles south of Lawrenceburg, and Interstate 64 is accessible 10 miles north of the city. 31 common carrier trucking companies are authorized to serve Lawrenceburg. The nearest airport is located in Frankfort, 14 miles north, and the nearest scheduled airline service is available at Bluegrass Airport, 19 miles east of Lawrenceburg, near Lexington.

Power and Fuel - Electric power is provided to Lawrenceburg by Kentucky Utilities Company and to Anderson County by Fox Creek RECC, which is supplied by East Kentucky Power Cooperative. Natural gas service is provided by the Western Kentucky Gas Company, which is supplied by Texas Gas Transmission Corporation. There are two distributors of propane and five distributors of distillate fuel oil located within 15 miles.

Education - Primary and secondary public education is provided by the Anderson County School System in Lawrenceburg and Anderson County. There are 15 institutions of higher learning located within 65 miles. In addition, vocational training facilities are available at Frankfort, Harrodsburg and Lexington, all within 25 miles of Lawrenceburg.

ALTON

During the administration of President Taylor, a post office was established on the northern part of Anderson County, with Obediah Hawkins as postmaster. At that time offices of this kind were not so numerous and it was no mean honor to be conferred on a person. After serving many years as a good and efficient officer, Mr. Hawkins resigned and Hon. Fountain Crook, a man who has had quite a great deal to do with the education of the young and who resided in the western part of the county, was appointed to the place. The post office was named Rough and Ready in compliment to the President, who was so kind as to establish it.

In 1854, by special act of the Legislature, a town in the above name was incorporated with Robert Hollis, Judge, and G. H. Gaines, father of the writer, Marshal.

Situated on a public highway between Louisville and Crab Orchard, nine mils from the State Capitol, in the best and most productive part of the county, a dividing ridge between Salt and Kentucky Rivers; inhabited by honest and upright people, many of whom were from the best families of Virginia; possessed of successful merchants and the affairs of the town in the hands of efficient and trustworthy officers, assisted by a board of competent trustees, Rough and Ready continued to prosper and grow until it took the position of being the greatest business center in the county.

Between 1878 and 1882, during the time or while Dr. R. C. McQuiddy was in the State Senate, the name of the town was changed to Alton, its present name. During the thriving time of this prosperous town, it boasted of a large hotel, under the management of William Tracy, as good as any in the county, and which was a favorite stopping place for drummers over Sundays. Being between Lawrenceburg and Frankfort, it made a convenient place for the accommodation of travelers going to and from Frankfort, as it was the nearest railroad station to Lawrenceburg at that time. Its merchants were prosperous and it was not unusual to see people going from Lawrenceburg to Rough and Ready or Alton to purchase goods. The following are some of the name of the merchants who have sold goods there: Robert Collins, G. H. Gaines, Richard Taylor, Richard Parent, Ed Thomas, Horace Ragan, Jas. Wilson, J. B. Catlett, R. K. McClure, John T. Stout, and others. Alton has always had good schools and for more than 30 years the public school was taught by Prof. Isaac McAfee, a record to be commended in this day.

I wish that space was sufficient to give ample mention of the good and noble citizens who have ben instrumental in making this happy, quiet town, the most of whom have gone to join the "silent few", but I feel that the history of Rough and Ready would

Gudgel Garage 1939-1944, owned by Samuel M. Gudgel. It is located between the Alton Cemetery and the Sam and Verna Gudgel home.

be far from complete without mentioning the name of Rev. V. E. Kirtly, a man of God, practical, or remarkable physical strength and powers of endurance, who resided for many years on the Richard Miller farm and preached in all of the surrounding county. He was of the Baptist faith and his sermons and labors are remembered and felt to this day.

After Southern Railroad was built the business drifted away from this town and while most of the business portion has been destroyed by fire and the town not so large as it has been, yet its citizens are happy, quiet and hospitable, and there clings to the memories of her many former citizens recollections that time alone can erase. Alton has always been blessed with good churches and today it has a prosperous church, governed by a set of consecrated and Christian officers, and supported by up-to-date Sunday School. Dr. J. W. Speer is the only permanent physician that Alton has had in the writer's recollection.

I have written this article from information received from those, though quite old, who are still fighting the battles of life, and in talking with them, I find that as we grow older, retrospection becomes sweeter, and the things of the past tenderly cling to our minds, adding charm and pleasure to the passing days. Born, raised and having spent the greater part of my days in this community, I feel that there is an attachment to the old home and my many good friends there, that shall last until life becomes extinct. The associated of these good people has made my life sweeter, happier and better, and I feel that this article is feeble testimony to their honesty and goodness and the inexpressible kindness shown me.

BIRDIE

The Birdie Community is located in the northwestern part of Anderson County. No one really known of the origin of the name Birdie. Soon after the Civil War the community was called "Brown's Store" after a store located on the Browns Store Road, a gravel road about a quarter of a mile from the present Birdie Grocery. This original Brown's Store was moved in the late 1800's to the spot where the Birdie Store is now. William J. Brown started this store and handed it down to his son, Joseph Henry Brown. *(See Brown Family Article.)*

This country store had been an integral part of this community for over 100 years. In the late 1800's and early 1900-2, there was a U. S. Post Office located in the store. The Postmark read "Browns Store, KY." The earlier named Browns were perhaps the first postmasters in the community. In April of 1888, Edward D. Brown, another son of William J. Brown, became postmaster at Birdie. The Post Office was moved to the homeplace of John W. Humes in July of 1890 when he became postmaster. In December of 1900, James M. Marlowe took on the job. He was perhaps the last postmaster of Birdie because on November 4, 1903, the papers

were moved to Odell and the post office at Birdie, KY was discontinued.

An article on Birdie would not be complete if the Marlowe School wasn't included. The school began approximately in 1870 and was in operation until the end of the school term in 1962. At the time Marlowe was discontinued, Arthur Cooper was the principal and teacher of grades five through eight and Ruby Hardin taught the first four grades. Classes were held in a modern brick building but actually was still only two classrooms.

Marlowe began as a one room log building. It was replaced by a frame building in about 1905 consisting of two rooms. It remained a two room building until the mid 1950's when the old building was torn down and the brick replacement was constructed. Classes were conducted in this brick building until 1962 when the school was closed and the building was auctioned off and later renovated into a dwelling house by Elmer Hume.

The school bears the name of James M. Marlowe. Other bits of information include: the teacher at Marlowe in 1892 was J. T. Ragan, a minister, and the spelling bee winner was Joseph Edgar Hume, the father of the present owned Elmer Hume. In 1901, the school had 77 pupils. Next to the old Marlowe School building was an old house that stood in the schoolyard. The house was the Owen Bond House. Some older residents may remember that Poshe, Scott and Jesse Willard lived there in the 1920's. Scott Willard was a chairmaker.

A list of some of the teachers at Marlowe Graded School includes: Jordan Ragan, Oscar Adkins, Clarence Watts, Annia Casey, Etta Jelf, Stella Buntain, Etta Mae Marlowe Haden, Thelma Caudell, Evelyn Strange, Prentice Martin, Roxie Rogers, Onita Morgan, Dorothy Hutchinson, Agnes Lockhart, Stewart Shelburne, Marjorie Case, Sylvia Cox, Myrtle Perry, C. Marion Railey, M. H. Perry, Ruby Hardin, Mary Lou Booker, Lois Redmon Metcalfe, and Arthur Cooper.

In November on 1989 a reunion of Marlowe students, teachers, and friends was held. It was the first reunion in over 100 years. There was a Marlowe School for about 100 years in the Birdie Community. The people who lived in Birdie can attest what this school meant to them and their families. Perhaps Jim Boyd, past teacher and principal of Anderson County High School said it best when he attested to the quality education provided to the students from Marlowe. Boyd stated, "They knew how to spell, they spoke English well, and were great in math. And no one can forget the great athletes who came from Marlowe."

The Birdie Community is also blessed by having in its midst the Corinth Christian Church. A separate article in this book contains a history of this church.

Allie Hume owned and operated a store from the early 1920's until the 1950's. He was well-liked and prospered in his endeavor. As well as a store operator, he farmed and hauled livestock to and from Louisville

for people. His store building was located between the Corinth Church and the Marlowe School. He, like the other old-time store owners, let people charge all year long and they would repay him when they sold their crops at the end of the year.

But still, the most popular store in this community is the present "Birdie Store". It was mentioned at the beginning of this article and has been a grocery, post office, gas station, and perhaps most important, a meeting place of friends and neighbors. Past owners or operators include: William J. Brown, Joe H. Brown, James Suttley, Erastus Riley, Prentice Martin, Allie Carlton, Paul Baugh, Jim Allison, Tom Bagwell, David Botton, and present storekeeper in 1990, Tom Nation.

Throughout the years a few of the family names that appear in Birdie Community history are: Baugh, Brown, Burge, Carlton, Catlett, Cinnamon, Cooper, Cox, Gordon, Grace, Grugin, Haden, Hume, Lane, Marlowe, Melear, Palmer, Perry, Redmon, Siers, Tipton, Tracy, Thompson, Watts, and Willard. *Submitted By: Billy Joe Hume.*

ASHBROOK

In this day of progress and automation, we pause to recall a bygone day.

In the year of 1878 there came into existence a small country village. It was given the name of Ashbrook and was located about 12 miles southwest of Lawrenceburg on Beaver Creek, surrounded by hills.

A turnpike divided the village on either side of which were homes, stores, etc. A pike leading west over Beaver Creek bridge led to Leather's Store.

A post office was established June 6, 1890 with Thomas N. Calvert as postmaster who was followed by Jasper Bryant June 24, 1902, Elijah Case, February 10, 1904; Richard B. Tanner, May 26, 1905 (declined); Edgar Mayes, November 8, 1905; Walter Brawley, February 23, 1909, and Seastus Bryant, June 12, 1912. The post office was discontinued January 31, 1913 and moved to Sinai. Rural delivery was then established from Sinai which continues to date.

We remember Ashbrook as a thriving village. There were two general stores, a blacksmith shop and grist mill. There were several attractive homes, one of which was used as a sort of hotel for "drummers" or salesmen. A one-room country school (Royalty) sat high on a hill just above the village proper.

Thomas Calvert was one of the first merchants and at his store one could buy just about anything needed for the home and family. Richard Tanner, Walter Brawley and Grant Scrogham followed Mr. Calvert. There was a millinery shop connected with the store and we recall Miss Beulah Cole and Mrs. Florence Scrogham as operators. The other store across the road was operated by Walter Moore, then by William Bryant and Son, succeeded by Allen Cole and later by James Puckett.

Between the two stores to the right of

the road looking south were three houses identical in appearance, and what we now call "split level." Two rooms flush with roadway and stairs leading down to kitchen or lower levels, by which flowed a small brook and tiny gardens of vegetables and flowers grew in backyards.

Dr. E. V. Seay lived on a hill above the village and later Dr. Sidney Simpson hung out his shingle in the community. Dr. Seay moved to Salvisa.

Edgar Mayes ran the blacksmith shop and grist mill and we loved the sound of the hammer and anvil, when we were fortunate enough to make a trip to the village and we recalled Longfellow's "The Village Blacksmith."

Mr. Mayes sold his business and home to James Puckett and moved to Lucto. Later when Mr. Puckett bought the store, Walter Holt ran the shop and mill.

Today, only two of the original buildings are left, the Puckett home and store building. A blacktop highway was built during the 30's from Sinai to the Washington County line and although it has many curves, we are proud to claim a share of influence in obtaining road no. 53, and now after more than 30 years there is in the process of construction an elaborate east-west toll road or parkway about two miles south crossing road 53 neat the Rutherford School which will put no. 53 in commonplace. Such is progress.

Agriculture conditions have changed also. A few decades past larger acreage of corn and tobacco was grown, whereas now, more hillsides are in grass and hay crops and more dairy and beef cattle grown. Milk routes have been established for delivery to Kraft's cheese processing plant in Lawrenceburg. Tobacco acreage has been reduced and quality production rather than quantity has been encourages.

In the present day, Ashbrook is just a cherished memory to the older citizens. Memories of apricot candy from the store and the "clink, clank" of the hammer at the shop, the sounds of the horses hoofs of the wooden bridge floor and above all, memories of the lovely people who have passed on from this life. *(1974 Anderson News)*

CEDAR BROOK

The manufacture of whiskey is the most valuable interest in this county. In the period] of its earliest history when the settler had to war with savages, wild beast, cane brakes, and dense forests, where the bite of the rattlesnakes, and other venomous reptiles were of frequent occurence, whiskey was not only allowable, but was believed to be a necessity in every family. Each household possessed this antidote against the surrounding dangers and used it as a remedy, a preventative and sometimes - according to St Paul - "a little for their stomachs sake." The use of "bitters" was so prevalent among the country's pioneers that soon after the building of log cabins and clearing small patches of ground, distilleries appeared as

the first industries. With the passing years the business was increased until it became the greatest and most valuable commercial enterprise of the county. Cedar Brook with its world-wide reputation, was the most famous distillery in Anderson, the most prolific whiskey county. It is ideally situated between the Kentucky River cliffs where an abundance of the purest water flows from inexhaustible springs deep in the imbedded limestone and where the little brook bordered with cedar trees merrily carried into the still some of its sparkle and life.

Judge McBrayer, who made and established Cedar Brook in 1844, limited during his life the output of the distillery and this combined with his personal integrity, kept the brand at the highest notch of commercial value, and also elevated other Anderson County brands. At his death it became the property of his three minor grandchildren, and was run from 1888 to 1899 by their father, Col. D. L. Moore, of Harrodsburg, a man of superior business ability. At this date it was sold to the Kentucky Distilleries and Warehouse Company. At the time of the sale the mash house was a one story building made of stone taken from Kentucky River cliffs, and was in its day one of the most costly building of its kind in the country. The new firm of Julius Kessler and Co., wholesale liquor dealers of Chicago, one of the strongest whiskey firms in the world, with the vim and business acumen of the age, immediately began improvements on a most extensive scale. They added two stories of iron sheeting to the old mash house, and enlarged its capacity from 800 bushels per day to 1800 per day; they also built a bottling department, several new warehouses of enormous size, with all the modern appliances for aging whiskey, and put in a new pumping station, drawing water from Kentucky River, a distance of two and one-half miles, for cooling purposes only. For the spring, whose waters have been renowned since the first settlement of the county, and there has never been a time when they were not used for distilling purposes, has yet no rival. Cedar Brook is situated on the Southern Road, with switches and slides from the top of the cliff to the house below. The warehouses are on one of the highest points along the river cliffs, and keep the whiskey pure and of the highest quality.

In 1876, the Cedar Brook brand took the medal at the Philadelphia Centennial, and Newton Brown, the distiller, was given a gold watch by Judge McBrayer. For years James Levy and Bro., of Cincinnati, were the sole handlers of this brand, and made it their "leader," always selling it higher than any other brand, and never flooding the market.

The present proprietors, Julius Kessler and Co., recognizing the intrinsic value of Cedar Crook, are pursuing the same policy and today, from its high pinnacle of commercial fame, Cedar Brook heads their varied brands of bourbon whiskies.

Truly in the whiskey business there is no waste, after the beverage is drawn, the

residue has been proven to contain the most healthful nutriment for cattle, hence thousands are fattened annually at the slopping pens of Cedar Brook and shipped to the Eastern markets. In fact, this branch of the industry, has attained such a considerable magnitude that vast sums are made or lost each year, in this department alone. Kentucky and Anderson county are proud of the celebrity achieved by Cedar Brook, and in foreign lands it is a remedy, a beverage and a necessity, just as it is here.

Julius Kessler and Company, when the properties under the control of the Kentucky Distilleries and Warehouse Company were set aside, chose this famous plant and brand for their own personal management and control. They have not only enlarged the plant to it present tremendous capacity, but by their judicious advertising methods have placed it in all the markets in the world; until today it stands head and shoulders and pre-eminent above all other brands of whiskey. Fortunate indeed is that brand of whiskey that falls into the hands of honest man, such men as are willing to protect it as they do their own good name. Judge McBrayer during his lifetime did this, and Julius Kessler and Company being high-toned and honorable men, are pursuing the same policy and daily adding to their great name.

"As long as the hills of Anderson stand,
In the grandest spot on earth,
We wish success to the Cedar Brook brand,
And the place that gave it birth."

FOX CREEK

Fox Creek is located on U.S. Highway 62, five miles southwest of Lawrenceburg. Population in 1900 was 32; in 1950 it was 120 and now in 1964 if is 93. Fox Creek was named after the small stream flowing through it into Salt River.

Fox Creek's Post Office began in 1886, but was discontinued in 1904 when Rural Routes were established with H. L. Hutton, as carrier on No. 1.

The Baptist church served Fox Creek for about 20 years beginning in 1818. The Christian Church has been the only constituted congregation within the village since 1841. A new church was built in 1904, and in 1950 six Sunday school rooms and a basement were added to the main building.

Fox Creek had two blacksmiths, William H. Fall and Douglas Stevens, at one time. There has been none since Mr. Fall died in 1932.

At one time there was a mill for grinding corn on the bank of Fox Creek, near where Orbrey Wells now lives.

There have been six physicians in Fox Creek at different times. They were Dr. W. L. Miton, Dr. Richard L. Milton, Dr. Albert Wright, Dr. Albert Smither, Dr. Sidney Simpson, and Dr. Oscar F. Shewmaker. There are none at the present time.

Some of the merchants in Fox Creek were Douglas Simmerman, Ottenheimer, Gudgel, C. K. Crossfield, R. Calvert, Harrison

Baxter, James Sherwood and Lister Tinsley. There are now two general stores owned by A. E. Rogers and Hume and Ritchey. There are two garages owned by Earl Gordon, Sr. and James E. Dennis.

Fox Creek for many years had a one-room schoolhouse. Some of the early teachers were Miss Eddie Bickers, Mrs. Will Moffett, Mr. Lewis Sherwood, Miss Virgie Sweeney, Professor John Case, Mr. Wilkes Bond and Mrs. Ethel Crossfield.

In 1907 a large room was added to the structure and for a few years it was used as a high school. Serving the high school for brief periods each were: Prof. McGowan, Prof. Will Case, Mr. C. W. Harrison, and Mrs. Eula Cox Royalty.

An accredited county high school in Lawrenceburg soon made the teaching of high school subject impractical both at Fox Creek and other places throughout the county, and such work was discontinued.

However, by 1921, Fox Creek enrollment had increased and both rooms were again in use.

Some of the teachers in this school included Mrs. Effie Wilson Cox, Mrs. Frances Stevens Wilson, Mrs. Mollie Whitnack, Mrs. Hazel McKee Gash, Mrs. Grace Lloyd McKee, Miss Louella Roach, Mrs. Ethel Sweeney Baxter, Mrs. Cordie Case Royalty, Mrs. Lindsey Baxter, Miss Florence Champion, Miss Elizabeth Gibbs, Mrs. R. H. Toll, Mrs. Miriam Gerow, Miss Mary K. Moffett, Mrs. Frances Cox McGaughey, Mrs. Beulah Nevins, Mrs. Katherine Jamerson and Mrs. Faye Gash.

The school was discontinued in 1953, since which time pupils have been transported to Western.

U. S. Highway 62, which runs through the village, was begun in the fall of 1929 and completed in 1932. The work was done by a company owned by Mr. Speed Tye.

GLENSBORO

Beautiful, for situation, is Glensboro nestling at the feet of steep and rugged hills, skirted by the placid waters of "Old Salt River." There was a time within the memory of some of our oldest residents, when these hills were covered with the "giants" of the forest, but civilization is here, as elsewhere, and these wooded crests have been supplanted by pastures green. The magnificent and fertile soil in this locality if attributable to the limestone formation underlying it, and no richer land can be found in the county. The early settlers were quick to appreciate the power supplied by nature, through the waters of Salt River and a mill was the first public enterprise promoted and erected very near to the site of the present mill. The old mill was operated by and "undershot" wheel, the the water supply was so abundant that grinding would be continued almost throughout the entire years. In 1847 there were only three residences of the village, occupied by Elijah Orr, Brook Miller and Mrs. Edith Harris and her sons, John, Nat, and Green. Other families

residing near were W. A. Stevens, John Sherwood, Jas. Moore, the Minors, Jewels, Browns and others.

All honor to the stalwart, early settlers! They were a hardy race of men, who lived in log cabins, tilled the soil, and led simple, honest lives. Dr. J.C. Gibbs lays claim to having built the first frame house between Lawrenceburg and Van Buren, for which the lumber was sawed by hand. This house is still standing, and is at present occupied by W. L. Franklin and wife.

In 1853 a Christian church was erected. Among its first officers were W. A. Stevens, R. J. Milton, Silas Jones and Elijah Orr. One of the first pastors of this church, if not the first, was Elder Merritt, a man of saintly memory. The present pastor is D. W. Stone, of Lexington, Ky. Later on, a school house was erected by subscription, and one of the first teachers was Fountain Crook, who is still living in the county.

Among the teachers who succeeded him, were many gifted man and women, but the public points with special pride to Champ Clark, now a representative in the Congress of the United States from Missouri. A brilliant and ambitious man, who aroused the sleeping ambitions of many a girl and boy, who trudged over the hills and valleys to the village school, to absorb the essences of his proficient tutelage. In 1856, the wooden bridge which spans the river here, was erected by one Stephen Stone, and now on the threshold of the 20th century, this structure stands intact, a monument to his honest, sturdy handiwork. About 1868, a carding factory was erected by Thos. Montgomery, and operated by himself and heirs until in 1892 it was acquired by Franklin Bros. When weaving and knitting formed the principal occupation of many homes here, this institution did a thriving business, built in 1903, this old landmark succumbed to modern thrift and enterprise, and the Farmers' Bank now adorns this ancient site.

In 1881 the Baptist Church was erected by Capt. W. H. Bell, B. F. Franklin and wife, Warren Peters and wife, and others. Rev. S. S. Perry was the first pastor and held the charge for many years. The present pastor is Rev. W. T. Martin, of Louisville.

The roller mill was erected by Franklin Bros. in 1896 and was operated by them until September, 1905, when it passed to the present firm of Simpson and Elder. Its capacity is 40 barrels daily and controls the patronage of the large surrounding territory. The Farmer's Bank began business in February, 1904, with a capital of $15,000, Dr. O. L. Townsend, president and W. L. Franklin, cashier. The reports sent out from time to time, show that the institution is doing a steady, progressive business and that its interests are handled by safe, prudent and enterprising business men. Up to about 25 years ago, this town was known as Camden, but in the establishment of a post office, the name was changed to Orr, in honor of one of its pioneer settlers, and public spirited citizens. In the latter part of 1904 the name of

the place and post office was again changed, this time to Glensboro, and it is our hope that she may wear this name to the end of time. For many years the mail was brought here from Lawrenceburg by first one and then the other passerby. After the establishment of the post office a weekly mail was secured, but for some time past, two mails per day reach this thriving little village. Our only merchant is the wide-awake and hustling Tom N. Calvert. He is always to the front in anything that will rebound to the interest of the town of its citizenship. Dr. J. C. Gibbs hung out his sign here in 1847, with no opposition, and while many physicians of note have come and gone, the Doctor is still on hand, though not having been in active practice for many years. Dr. O. L. Townsend is the only practicing physician in the town. He is a man of sterling character, a fine practitioner, an enterprising gentleman, and a Mason. He enjoys a wide, increasing practice and holds the confidence of the public.

During the sale of ardent spirits, Glensboro held the reputation of being a tough place, but with this curse eliminated, there is nothing but peace and prosperity within our gates and the glad hand is ever extended to the stranger. Our men are brave, the women virtuous, and God has never ceased to smile upon us. *(1906 Supplement)*

JOHNSONVILLE

Johnsonville, a thriving little village in the western portion of Anderson County and in the midst of a fine agricultural community, was incorporated by the General Assembly of Kentucky during the session of 1855 and 1856, and was named in honor of David Johnson, who was the first settler, and who, about seventy years ago, built the first log house on the site of the residence now occupied by his son, William T. Johnson.

David Johnson was for many years one of the most prominent citizens of the county, and died full of years respected and honored by all who knew him. Judge Wade H. Morgan, the father of County Attorney Wilkes H. Morgan, removed to the village about 1864, and established a large general store, which he conducted successfully until a short time before his death, in October, 1892. Mr. J. W. Shouse, one of our Lawrenceburg merchants, conducted for some years a general store in the village and made many friends and some money. B. W. Ash, the father of John Ash, of Lawrenceburg, kept a grocery and tavern for several years on the site of the present department store of Lloyd Simpson, now a member of the Fiscal Court of Anderson County, and who is an enterprising, wide-awake, up-to-date merchant. Out present popular and efficient Deputy Sheriff, E. N. Johnson, and a grandson of David Johnson, the first settler, is a resident of this place. There are no more moral, law-abiding and prosperous people in the county, than those composing the present citizenship of

Johnsonville and the surrounding country.

RIPYVILLE

Our little village is situated about four miles south of Lawrenceburg, on the Louisville and Crab Orchard turnpike, and while she is small and unpretentious, she sits among her sister towns of the world and has a history. Away back in the 30's, two brothers, young men at the time, left their home in Tyrone, Ireland, seeking their fortunes in the new world. They were James and John Ripy, and brought with them a sister, who afterward became the mother of Robert and Jasper Lyons, well known business men of our county. These two brothers located in Lawrenceburg, KY. James embarking in the grocery business and John in the dry goods business. In 1855, John Ripy bought the "Bright" farm, where our energetic friend, R. E. Thacker, now lives, and in connection with John McMichael engaged in the mercantile business. The storehouse stood a little north of the Bright residence, and has just lately been removed by Mr. Thacker. This partnership continued about two years, during which Mr. Ripy continued to reside in Lawrenceburg. Mr. McMichael living in the storehouse.

Our village, therefore, gets its name from its first merchant, John Ripy.

TYRONE

In 1847, where the enterprising town of Tyrone now stands, was a dense forest, extending from Shryock's Ferry to the present site of the railroad bridge and about a half-mile in width, there being but three houses in all this vast wilderness, two of which stood back on the hill quite a distance from the river, one of which was occupied by John Cobb, the other by Robert Woldridge. Near the site of the post office stood a lone cabin of the Daniel Boone type, of round logs, mud chink, stick and clay chimney, board roof held down by weight poles. Such was the beginning of our busy little nestling city among the beautiful Kentucky river hills, when first remembered by our oldest citizen; and to this brief sketch we add the record of a few other important events of its history that have served to make it one of the best sixth-class towns in the whole Commonwealth.

In 1850 the first warehouse was built by W. H. Dawson, Joel Boggess and others, two having been built since the present one owned by our popular superintendent for Chess and Wyman, A. J. Nowlin, having been built y the late W. J. Waterfill, one of Tyrone's best friends.

Back in the 60's, S. P. Martin (whose name is probably more closely associated with the history of our little city than that of any other, because of his long and active life in our midst) built the first distillery, No. 112, in the town, which, after a few years passed into the hands of Martin, Walker and Co., and then to W. H. McBrayer, and a little later to the late T. B. Ripy, whose benevo-

Building of the Tyrone Bridge, 1931.

lence and charity to our people will be remembered for decades to come, and from him was transferred to the Kentucky Distilleries and Warehouse Co., for whom Col. S. E. Booth has been the popular superintendent from the first.In 1857 the first mile of pike (which is now Main Street), leading to Lawrenceburg, was built by Martin and Utterback, the whole road being finished the next year, just before the completion of the road leading to Versailles.

In 1879 our little city was incorporated, S. P. Martin, T. B. Ripy, J. T. Coke, G. M. Walker, W. M. Edmonson and H. M. Carter as trustees; N. T. Watson police judge; J. A. Wash, attorney; and John W. Wash, marshal. Judge Martin wrote the charter and afterward wrote its revision which has stood the test of the United States Courts is several suits. In 1885 the voting precinct was established.

In 1880 the first public school was established in the town. Judge Martin building the school house gratis. He has since, under contract, built two others, the present one having a capacity of 200, in which will be opened this fall a graded school, in charge of an efficient corps of teachers, offering an extended course of study, meeting a long-

felt need. Too much cannot be said in praise of our people and the faithful board, J. J. Lancaster, W. P. Frazier, W. T. Patterson L. R. Carter, and C. C. Tolls, who have labored so earnestly for this great and worthy cause.

In 1882 the post office was established. J. T. Coke was appointed postmaster and continued in office till 1898 to the very greatest delight of all our people and with the highest acceptability to the Department, when on his resignation the office passed into the hands of the present incumbent.

In 1880 S. P. Martin, J. M. Scarce, T. B. Ripy and a few other built the Methodist Church, which was destroyed by fire last year and which its members hope to rebuild between this and Conference. In 1890, J. N. Butts, R. S. Taylor, W. M. Carr and others built the Christian Church, in which through the courtesy of its membership, all religious services are now being held.

More than a quarter of a century ago J. N. Butts opened a general store, and is with us today with a complete line of goods, a good trade and the confidence of all. In 1890 J. A. Mountjoy opened with a full line of dry goods and groceries and has always had a good trade that he has served in the most delightful and clever way.

Somewhat later our old friend, G. W. Parker, established the People's Grocery and General Store, and through his business-like methods has enjoyed a splendid trade from the first.

About 1900 C. G. Bercaw opened in the way of a small grocery what seemed to be a very short-lived enterprise, but very must to the great, and yet no less agreeable surprise of all, he by diligent efforts and close application has enlarged his building from time to time till today he has a full line of groceries, confectioneries and notions, and enjoys a good trade with a long list of faithful customers.

Recently Miss Mary Carter opened a small grocery in which she is doing a good business.

This report would be very incomplete indeed were we to fail to say that we have two splendid blacksmith shops, one owned by John Nowlin, who has from the very opening has all the work that he could possibly do; the other owner by the Thomason Brothers is one of the most complete blacksmith and machine chops in the State, enjoying a large patronage throughout this and the adjoining counties.

While we have no great hotels whose ads are posted conspicuously, yet the wants of the stranger and traveler are by nor means forgotten. Mrs. J. N. Johnson has excellent accommodations in this line. Mrs. J. V. Patterson also keeps an excellent boarding house, which will be enlarged this fall.

Can you get a shave, did you ask? Well, I should say so, when John Smith, colored, is here three days in the week, and besides our own skilled hairdressers, Patterson and McGaughey, whose shop is open every day of the week except Sunday. Nothing open here in the way of business on the Sabbath.

L. Otley Pindar, M. D., has recently purchased the building in which he has opened the Riverview Hospital, having already treated several patients, his rooms all being engaged for the summer.

Perhaps no little city in the State represents so many fraternal orders and in a more worthy way than ours. In 1902 there was instituted an I.O.O.F. lodge of 11 members. It has continued to grow and prosper until today it has a membership of nearly 50, owns its own hall and is in a prosperous condition, having accomplished much good in our midst. In 1904 a splendid tent of K.O.T.M. was organized, which has trebled its membership, giving besides good social advantages to all worthy men, an excellent insurance within the reach of all. In connection with this tent an enthusiastic hive of the L.O.T.M. is now being organized by Mrs. Mary L. Anderson, of Louisville.

In 1904 there was also organized an aggressive little lodge of M.B.A.'s, that still thrives, offering in many respects some very fine advantages in the way of social features and cheap but good insurance to both men and women alike, which is a very commendable feature.

A little while ago was organized a strong lodge of Red Men, made up of the best and most energetic men of our town and community, who have been able in this short time to accomplish much good. They are preparing to erect a large lodge room and city hall and go right forward with their work on a still greater scale; they have also organized and established the Pocahontas Degree, made up of a score of more of our very best women, sweethearts, wives and friends of our hustling I.O.R.M.'s.

On the first day of January last the following gentlemen entered upon their duties as town officials: Trustees, J.J. Lancaster, chairman, who is also chairman of the school board, and who has been master mechanic for the Kentucky Distilleries and Warehouse Company since they took charge here, and who has been a citizen of our town for a number of years, enjoying the confidence and respect of our people and is thoroughly qualified for the position of honor that has been committed to him, standing for the rights of the people and the good of the town.

L.R. Carter, who is also master machinist of the Kentucky Distilleries and Warehouse Co., at the Blakemore Distillery is one of our very best citizens, always standing for the good of the people who have recognized his services as a faithful official by honoring him quite a number of times with their almost undivided support.

W.T. Patterson, Jr., is another worthy member of our council, who has had the supervision of the large warehouses for nearly 20 years, an excellent citizen with a host of friends who are proud of his record as an official and are always ready to cast their votes for him, he having been councilman for several years.

B. S. Hahn, the able distiller, is also a member of the board and enjoys the well-merited confidence and esteem of all our people, who have shown wisdom in selecting him for this position. He is a most excellent fellow, and has always stood for the advancement of our town and community along every line.

Recently W.N. Gibson, the faithful night watchman of the Kentucky Distilleries and Warehouse Co., at No. 112, has been made a member of the council, filling the place made vacant by the removal from the town of J.T. McGaughey, one of the best officials our town ever had. We believe Mr. Gibson will fill this place with honor, judging from his record in the past, the interest of the town is safe in his hands.

This new board has certainly acted wisely in retaining as city clerk our friend, J.A. Mountjoy, who is pre-eminently qualified for this position, which he has been filling for more than a decade. J.A. is all right, has friends without number, and no enemies at all.

Our new Marshal, Enos Nowlin, and his deputy, A.J. Nowlin, are well fitted for the work committed to their hands, and mean to see to it that the perfect order is maintained in the town, having no friends or pets, but enforcing the law, protecting the good, attending to the bad and giving every man a square deal. The people are standing by them too.

We doubt very much is any town in the State, regardless of size, has an abler attorney than we have in the person of Gov. L. H. Carter, a graduate of Vanderbilt University, a lawyer of very superior qualifications, an excellent gentleman and a warm friend of our little city, having brought her through some very trying days, but has at last established her on a financial basis that seems safe for all time to come.

Our new police judge, C. B. Bunter, a genial old gentleman, a splendid lawyer, has already made a record of which our people are justly proud. He is firm and true to his convictions in the proper interpretation of the law, giving both to the innocent and the guilt their portion in due season, and is in every way proving himself a worthy successor of the faithful men who have filled this office in the days gone by.

With a population of 600 people, good streets and pavements, great repairs now being made, splendid water supply, excellent lights, elegant court room and its adjunct commodious school house, six lodges, two churches (one to be built at once), two good Sunday Schools, six complete stores, two blacksmiths, two hotels, two barber shops, one physician, two pastors, resident minister, two teachers, bookkeepers, stenographers, etc., waterway and railroad facilities, great business enterprises giving employment to scores of men, reasonable rent and low taxes, and prospective street sprinkler, water works and fire department, electric lights and every other needed improvement forthcoming, we are fully persuaded that our little town will continue to grow and thrive until in no particular will it be excelled by that of any other of its size in the Commonwealth.

And now, in conclusion, we close with the words of one of the greatest American historians, "Our past has taught its lesson; the present has its duty; and the future its hope." (c. 1906)

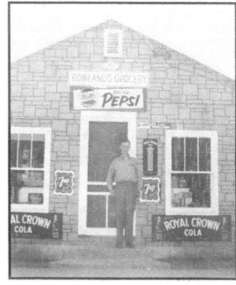

Rowland's Grocery, Easter, April 10, 1955

VANBUREN

On September 14, 1835, Edward Harris was granted a right to lay out a town on his land at the mouth of Crooked Creek on Salt River, and introduced a plat and survey which was ordered filed and recorded. John Busey, John Morgan, Thomas Harris and Bryce Ray were appointed trustees. Harris executed bonds for the deeds, but died before he had a chance to make the deeds. The town was re-chartered some years after, with one main street running through the center and three side streets. This town is 18 miles from Lawrenceburg. It was laid out during the Presidency of Martin VanBuren and named for him. In 1878 the population of VanBuren was 70. Today the little village has a population of 58. The lure of the larger towns and cities has a tendency to depopulate the smaller hamlets. Ashby and Co., in business for 40 years in VanBuren, is the only old-time country store in the entire county. A small grocery store, two blacksmith shops, Dadisman's truck line and the VanBuren bank constitute the other business enterprises of the place. C. F. Adkins, son of Rev. B. F. Adkins, is cashier of the bank. *(c. 1936)*

Old Van Buren Road now ends at boat ramp on Taylorsville Lake.

Foster Sale farm, c. 1910, near McCall's Spring.

LAWRENCEBURG

While Lawrenceburg does not and cannot claim to be the oldest or the largest city in the State of Kentucky, there are few other towns of any size whose people have more cause to congratulate themselves over the growth and prosperity which have attended their community from the earliest period of history.

The first settlements on the land where the city now stands were made between 30 and 40 years before the incorporation of the town of Lawrence, the locality being first known as Kaufman's Station. Jacob Kaufman, a German, located 400 acres of land on a branch of Hammond's Creek, adjoining a claim held by a man named bailey, and had his residence on the lot just in the rear of the present residence of L. J. Witherspoon, the claim being located another claim of 1,000 acres immediately adjoining the first.

A few months later a man by the name of Larue located a claim of 1,000 acres on a small creek emptying into Kentucky River near a tree bearing the name of Nathan Randolph cut in the bark. Peter Asturgis located two claims, one of 200 acres and another of 1,000, the first in 1780 and the last in 1783. Thomas Madison, for whom Main Street was first named, located 1,000 acres in 1782, and in the same year, Joseph Crockett located 1,009 acres. Thomas Madison, John Harvey, Cass Clark and John Payne located other lands, all near the first location of Jacob Kaufman's first settlement.

There is some disagreement as to the exact location of the first house in the new town of Lawrence, there being three sites mentioned in this connection. One claim is that the old hewed log house in the northern part of town where Judge T. J. Ballard now lives, which was built by Thomas Prather in 1791, and which was afterwards owned and occupied by the late Judge John F. Wills, was the first. Others say that a house which stood a few feet northeast of the building now occupied by the Anderson News, was built at an earlier date, but the name of the builder has been lost. Still others of the oldest residents of the county say that the first house was built on the ground now occupied by the residence of Prof. H. V. Bell and T. J. McMurray, and this double log house, which was successed by the old Anderson House, was built by William Lawrence, for whom the town was named, several years before the Prather house. William Lawrence ran a tavern in this house for some years, and then sold it to John Robertson, afterward building the house in which Capt. John H. McBrayer now lives.

Other early settlers were Captain W. B. Wallace, grandfather of Mrs.. W. H. McBrayer, William Robinson, Samuel Arbuckle, a son-in-law of Jacob Kaufman, and these were quickly followed by John Penny Sr., William Hudgins, Anthony Miller and Lewis Hyatt. Others came, among them the McBrayer family. It is recorded that Alexander McBrayer, with his wife, Susan, in 1820 sold a lot of ground on the corner of Madison (now Main Street) and White's Alley, to Phillip White for the sum of $50.

From this time, the little village grew more rapidly, and, in 1827, it became the county seat of the new county of Anderson, its name being changed by a special act, to Lawrenceburg. At the time of it incorporation, the town boasted of one store, which stood where the residence of Mrs. Maggie Gividen now stands; a blacksmith shop where the Presbyterian church is located, or just north of that lot, and a tailor shop, run by Anthony Miller.

Among those who came to the town soon after its organization may be mentioned John C. Richardson, George Morris, Cabel Fenwick, William McGinnis, David White, Drs. Dickson G. Dedman and L. J. Witherspoon, Jerry Beasley, Oliver Egbert, James Ashford, Thomas Hazlett, Samuel Lawrence, John Hudgins, John T. Daviess Jr., Thomas Q. Roberts, Charles Miles and John Draffen.

Ever since the first organization of the town, there has been a steady and healthy influx of people of good character and substantial qualities, which always give standing and tone to the community in which they live. At no time has there been anything ephemeral in the increase of population, and not much occurred to disturb the tranquility of the town until the Mexican war drew from its precincts many of the hardy and patriotic sons of the early settlers. Nearly all of these heroes have gone to their rewards, but there are still living, in Lawrenceburg, four of the survivors of this international struggle which ended almost 60 years ago: Capt. John H. McBrayer, who commanded Company D, 2nd Kentucky Infantry; Mr. W. F. Bond, Dr. J. H. Willis and Jackson Holmes, all of them far beyond the allotted span of human life, but all hale and hearty, spending their last days surrounded by their many friends and relatives, who leave nothing undone to make their last days their best.

In 1830, seven years after the organization of the county, the first Courthouse was built of brick, and occupied the same lot where the present one is now located. This building was used for all courts until 1859, when it, with many of the records, was destroyed by fire, and the present Courthouse was built in 1860, of stone from the Kentucky River cliffs, just at the beginning of the Civil War. This building was remodeled during the year 1905, and so arranged that it is one of the most attractive and convenient Courthouses to be found in the State. In the yard is to be seen a handsome monument erected to the famous "Salt River Tigers" in 1847, and one to the confederate soldiers who went from the county, erected in 1900, and unveiled in 1901.

During the Civil War, the people of Lawrenceburg, like those of the state at large, were divided in sentiment, and her sons did valiant service on both sides in that four years of fratricidal strife. Many of the survivors of that struggle are with us, and not a few of them have been repeatedly honored by their fellow citizens with positions of trust and honor. The sons of those who wore the blue and the gray have since united in defense of the stars and strips in foreign lands, and some of these, true to their patriotic traditions of their fathers, went out from Lawrenceburg and acted well the parts assigned them by their common country.

Aside from the usual Indian scares incident to the early days of Kentucky, the War of 1812, the Mexican Was, and the Civil War, in all of which the people of Lawrenceburg and Anderson County played their parts, as might have been expected from sons of the pioneer sires, there is little of a startling nature to relate. In 1833 and again in 1855, the growing settlement was visited by epidemics of that dread disease, the Cholera, during each day of which many of the people were carried off to their last resting places, and while no bard has sung the story of these dark days, there were many instances of self sacrifice and heroism which might well be taken for the foundation theme of a epic poem.

In the days when everybody wore boots and shoes manufactured at home, there was a tanyard located just below the present residence of Judge T. J. Ballard, where the leather was made for the necessities of the community. The first Presbyterian church was a frame building on a lot now owned by Mr. L. J. Witherspoon. This building was twice destroyed by wind. There were several general stores, the earliest being located at the corners of Main and Woodford Streets, near the first tavern. P. D. Brown, better known as Dan Brown, was a carpenter and cabinet maker and his shop was near the Courthouse.

William and Joe Hickman, W. H. Shipman, J. A. Witherspoon and W. H. McBrayer were dry goods merchants; Mort Walker and J. E. Collins kept groceries near where Toll's meat store now stands and Doctors Dixon Dedman, L. J. Witherspoon, John Witherspoon, R. I. McQuiddy, J. A. Witherspoon, James Chambers and O. H. Witherspoon ministered to the physical ills of their fellow citizens.

The people at an early date provided religious accommodations for the people of the new county seat, the Presbyterians and Baptists being the first to build suitable houses of worship, the first name building on Main Street, and the Baptist on the corner of the lot now occupied by the graded school building. The Methodists built some years later on the ground where their present home now stands, and the Christians or Disciples came many years afterward. All these old-time churches were of brick and have long since been removed, being replaced by most commodious and handsome structures which constitute the chief ornaments of the present city. There are now five white churches within the city limits: Presbyterian, Baptist, Christian, Methodist and Roman Catholic, beside three churches for the colored people. The total valuation of the property owned by these several denominations would closely approximate $30,000.

On March 15, 1873, a fire started which consumed the entire business district of the town and many of the best residences before it could be stayed in its progress, and at that time, but for the heroism of a man by the name of P. D. Brown, carpenter and undertaker, who stayed on the top of the Courthouse, while his own dwelling was destroyed, it must have gone up in smoke with all the priceless records of the town and county. After that time more substantial and commodious brick business houses were built in the burned district that had occupied the ground before the fire.

In 1892, another disastrous fire broke out in the city work-house, which consumed 12 or 15 buildings and caused the death of a man named King, who was confined in the work-house on a charge of drunkenness and disorderly conduct, and since then, almost every building on Main street between Court and Jackson Streets have been burned, and many of the buildings further north. One of these fires caused the death of two small children who could not be saved from the building in which they were sleeping.

The last great fire in our history, however, was that which, in 1898, started in a livery stable a few doors north of Court Street, and destroyed some 15 or 20 buildings, including the Christian Church, before it could be stopped, and the only one which approached this one in its magnitude since that time, was one which started in a grocery stores just opposite the depot and burned a number of dwellings and a good portion of the property of the Dowling Cooperage Company.

Each of there fires were followed by the building of better houses than the city had known before, and today there are few cities of larger size that can show the visitors better, more handsome of more commodious businesses, houses, and dwellings than can Lawrenceburg.

A few years since, the people of the city, by a overwhelming vote, authorized the City Council to put in a system of water works, for the better protection of the city in cases of fire, and this work was completed about three years ago, since that time, the people have been comparatively free from these terrible visitations. This plant cost the city about $25,000, and has paid for itself several time in the saving of property that was threatened with total destruction. The water supply, which is drawn from a number of wells belonging to the city, is inexhaustible, and is said by the National Geological Survey to be the purest to be found in the State. This water is furnished to private consumers at an average expense of $1.00 per month for the entire year.

In the legislative session of 1892, the government was changed from that of an incorporated village to that of a city of fifth class, and since that time the city has been governed by a Mayor and Board of Councilmen. It is doubtful whether there is any other fifth-class city in the State which has had a better of more economical administration of its affairs during that time than has Lawrenceburg. While all public interests have been efficiently cared for, the rate of taxation for city purposes has never exceeded thirty cents on each $100 worth of property, until since the installation of the water works, when thirty cents additional was levied for the purpose of paying the indebtedness incurred for this great public necessity. The present Mayor is Hon. John P. McWilliams, and the Council consisted of Messrs. J. P. Ripy, H. S. Carl, J. C. Vanarsdell, T. J. Ballard, W. Y. Spencer and W. B. Morgan, all of them among the most substantial and progressive businessmen of the city, and under their administration, the streets have been improved; Main Street has been paved with vitrified brick; the sidewalks have been graded and relaid to a great extent, many of them made of concrete; the water works have been installed, and an efficient fire department has been organized.

We regret that we are unable to give the population of the city for each decade since its first incorporation, but the best we can do is give it since 1890. The population in that year was, as shown by the United States Census, 1,308; in 1900 this number has increased to 2,006, and by a special census taken during last winter, the population was shown to be 3,329; and under this last showing, the Legislature of 1906 placed Lawrenceburg among the cities of the fourth class.

Lawrenceburg, as it stands today,, with its six miles of streets macadamized, its paved Main street, its electric lighting and ice plant, its splendid water works, its remarkably low death rate, its rapid but steady growth, its up-to-date and progressive business men in all lines, its low tax rate, its religious facilities, its magnificent graded school, its shipping facilities, its numerous mails, its two telephone exchanges, its first class banks, its Commercial Club, and its progressive and pushing city officials, its hospitable and prosperous people, and its handsome and commodious homes, may well claim to be, as it is, one of the very best of the cities of this proud old Commonwealth, and he who is seeking for a business location of a home combining the conveniences and advantages of the city with those of the country can do no better than to come here.*(c. 1906 Anderson News Supplement)*

Bond-Shouse Building, 1910.

Above, a bustling Lawrenceburg in 1915. West side of Main Street looking north to West Woodford. At right, 125 South Main Street, c. 1910.

SPECIAL FEATURES

OLD LANDMARKS CONNECTED TO IMPORTANT FACTS ABOUT LAWRENCEBURG

An Afterglow
"Gather we from the shadowy past
The straggling beams that linger yet,
Ere o'er those flickering lights are cast
The shroud that none can penetrate." -
Spencer

Old landmarks are passing away with those who reared them, and must be recorded, ere they are gone.

Many items of deepest interest have been neglected and allowed to disappear. There are many interesting and important facts connected with Lawrenceburg and her people, that have passed beyond the hope of recovery, but this golden opportunity shall not pass without recording a few of them.

The old stage coach! What sentiment and interest cluster around this old-fashioned and now obsolete mode of transit. 50 years ago it was the most popular way to travel, though many went by private conveyance or on horseback. A journey of 500 miles by the latter was not considered by our fathers any greater than the same distance now by rail. Lawrenceburg was among the last to give up the stage coach, for not until 1888 did the snort, smoke and rumble of the engine superseded the merry bugle blast and prancing steeds of the old stage coach. Its arrival in town created the excitement of the day. The people all gathered at the "post house" to see the passengers and hear the news of the outside world. The coach was of the pattern seen in old prints, and usually painted a fawn color profusely decorated with red. The body swung high above wheels on heavy leather springs. The mail was carried by these stages, and relays of horses were had at the various stopping places. Four horses were driven from the top of the coach by an expert whip. Mr. Hastings and Uncle Ben Townsend drove from Louisville to Crab Orchard. This line was owned by Dr. John Witherspoon and Mr. James Saffel.

The stage coach was so much a part of the turnpike, that we cannot speak of one without the other. The turnpike, which originally meant tollgate but now the road itself, is looked upon by the people of Central Kentucky with the deepest pride, and strangers coming from other states and countries are always impressed with our beautiful roads. A country's thoroughfares of travel stand pre-eminent among it internal improvements, and Anderson County had macadamized roads passing in every direction, to every point of importance. The first turnpike in the county, was the Frank-

fort and Crab Orchard, built in 1834-35. Tollgates were abolished in 1895, by "raiders" who taking matters in their own hands, destroyed the system, by intimidating the keepers and in case of resistance, dynamiting the gates. The Kentucky River was crossed by two ferry boats now - Shryock's Ferry at Tyrone and one at Clifton on the Woodford side. Far back of the pike, we find a branch in of the Old Wilderness road. A thread of pathos is interwoven with the sunshine and shadows that lie along the now almost obliterated traces pf this century-old thoroughfare, which in passing from the Painted Rock, (now Shelbyville) to Harrod's Station, passed through the outskirts of Lawrenceburg. Clearly defined evidences of this the link, connecting Virginia civilization with the impenetrable wilderness of Kentucky, are yet seen near the residence of Major Lewis McKee. To this road, teeming with life and people representing every element of the Anglo-Saxon race, Anderson County owes her civilization.

The White family came to Lawrenceburg in its earliest days. They had ten children, among them Joseph M. White, born in 1797, who was the first Governor of Florida, Ambassador to Italy, and married Eleen Adair, daughter of Kentucky's Governor.

Mary, the sister of Phillip White, married Robert P. Blackwell, a man of culture and wealth, of Virginia. To the day of his death, he wore silver buckles, silk hose and knickerbockers as he had been accustomed to in his youth in Virginia.

Two brothers, Edward and William Mountjoy, nephews of Governor Garrard, came from Virginia. Edward located near what is now the town of Alton, on the site of the home owned by Mrs. Sue Rhinehart, and his large tract of land extended almost to the limits of Lawrenceburg. He built what was then considered a fine house of logs, weather-boarded and plastered. Here he kept an old-fashioned tavern and his stricter neighbors were often shocked by the fiddling and dancing. This love of music and dancing was probably due to his French extraction. In his youth, when the Whiskey Rebellion occurred in Pennsylvania, he was a volunteer from Virginia. When General Washington reviewed the troops, he especially complimented Edward Mountjoy upon his fine stature and soldierly bearing, a characteristic still observed in many of his descendents.

These two brothers married and reared large families, so that their descendents here are very numerous. Nancy, a daughter of Edward Mountjoy, married Thomas Lillard, the representative of another pioneer family. He owned a farm two and one-half miles

from town. The house and a portion of it are now owned by Mr. Hal Carpenter. This family was noted for its zeal in religion. They had four sons, named Matthew, Mark, Luke and John.

The first Lillard who came from Virginia was John, who with his wife stopped at Harrod's Fort and afterwards came to Anderson, and chose a farm on Salt River. He is said to have introduced bluegrass into this county. The site of their old home, which was burned is now owned by the widow of William S. Bond. His oldest son, John Lillard, while carrying dispatches on our Canadian border in the War of 1812, caught cold, which resulted fatally. Another son, Christopher Lillard, became an acting General in the same War of 1812. He married Sallie Blackwell, daughter of Robert Blackwell, who were the parents of Mr. Marion Lillard of this place. The latter possesses a tomahawk and British pistol, captured by his illustrious father, at the battle of the Thames, when in a regiment of six hundred, under the command of Dick Johnson, in Jake Ellison's company, not one of which was killed on that memorable day, though hundreds of Indians were slain.

Ephriam Lillard, was an early settler of wealth from Virginia. He married Miss Margaret Prather and built his home on what is now West Woodford Street, as the place was fertile and well watered by many springs. He, too, had a large family - one of his daughters, Susan, marrying Dr. John Witherspoon, in 1836.

The McBrayers were another family whose history is closely identified with this county, William McBrayer and brother, James, having located in what is now Anderson County early in Kentucky's history. William McBrayer had eight sons and two daughters, and there is a large number of descendants now living. Among the grandsons were Captain Jno. H. McBrayer, who won glory on the Mexican battlefield, and James A. McBrayer, equally renowned in the field of letters.

James McBrayer had five sons, the youngest being Andrew McBrayer. Andrew McBrayer married Martha, daughter of Major Robert Blackwell, and wife, Mary White, and reared a large family of children, who were all an honor to their name. Martha McBrayer was early left a widow, and in the words of one of the loveliest old ladies in our midst, who knew her well, "she was a woman of remarkable strength of mind and many virtues, her fortitude, her Christianity, her intelligence, were far above the average. Her hospitality was noted and generous, and around the old homestead, yet standing, cluster fragrant memories of parties and picnics in the sugar grove, and all the refined and innocent merry-making of the times." Among their children were Wm. H., Sanford, and Dr. John A. McBrayer.

The Freemans, a name no longer heard in Anderson, although numerous in other counties of the State, and in other States, many of them having risen to distinction in politics and bell letters, were an illustrious Virginia family, who sent some members as early settlers to this county, notably, George Freeman, who owned a fine tract of land on Salt River, at Fox Creek, and built the log house, which still stands and is known as the old Freeman house. This was built in 1804. He also superintended the building of Freeman's bridge, which bears his name. He volunteered his services in the Revolutionary War, at the age of seventeen, but it was just before the battle of Yorktown, so his army life was a brief one. His oldest son, Dandridge Claiborne Freeman, was Sheriff of Franklin County, when Anderson was still a part of that county. His daughter, Elizabeth, married William Kavanaugh, the first of his name to enter Kentucky. He was descended from Charles Kavanaugh, one of three brothers who left Ireland in 1705. He emigrated to Virginia, where the Kavanaughs and Freemans intermarried, as they continued to do in Kentucky. The old Kavanaugh home yet stands overlooking the Salt River. In this house, all the lumber was sawed with a whip saw and an artisan from Lexington carved the wood work which is still beautiful. Judge George Kavanaugh, oldest son of William and Elizabeth Kavanaugh, was many time honored by his county, with positions of trust, being one of the Constitutional Committee in 1851. Three time this district gave him the Circuit Judgeship. He was an uncle of Dr. C. W. Kavanaugh and Mrs. Alleen Gilbert, they being the only descendants in this county of Freemans and Kavanaughs.

Robert Witherspoon and wife, Nancy Jordan, early came to Kentucky and settled on the Elkhorn. Their sons, Lewis and John, became physicians, and came to Lawrenceburg. Lewis was a surveyor of the county in 1837. They were both very successful in business, and Lewis Witherspoon died the wealthiest man in the county at age 54. The name has ever been the synonym for wealth in this community.

John Penny, Sr., exercised much influence in the formation of the early society of this county. His wife was a sister of Phillip White, as was Robert Blackwell's, all having married in Virginia. John Penny's residence was near Fox Creek pike. He raised six sons. Under his ministrations, the churches at Fox Creek, Salt River, Old Goshen and Little Flock, were built.

About 1971, George Jordan settled the farm adjoining the John Penny place, on which his son John G. Jordan for many years resided.

Randall and John Walker, located in the county in 1796. The first on the farm now occupied by Monroe Walker and the latter where Jordan H. Walker lived for many years. Both were prominent men in their time. John was sheriff of Franklin in 1826, and his son, Jordan, was deputy. Jordan H. Walker became a preacher of the old school Baptist church and was for many years clerk of the Anderson County Court, afterwards Presiding Judge of the county. His brother, Randall, was sheriff for a number of years, and represented the county in the Legislature in 1845. Monroe Walker yet lives on the farm where he was born, it having been the Walker homestead for more than 100 years.

William Bond was an Englishman and settled in the locality where William F. Bond, his grandson, and a Mexican Veteran, now lives. He had five sons, two of whom reared large families. Bond is the most extensive of all pioneer names in the county, having intermarried with the Hanks and McMichaels. They are noted for their thrift and industry. Some of the pioneers were Revolutionary soldiers, who received military land warrants or their services in the army, and sought the Western wilds for the purpose of finding homes. Among them was Captain William Brown Wallace, who came with his family from Virginia about 1795, he having 3,630 acres of land grants for services in the Revolution. Capt. Wallace's wife was Barbara Fox, a direct descendant of William Claiborne, Secretary, Treasurer, and Suveyor-General of the Virginia Colonies, and John West, her first governor. The Wallace family came from Scotland and can trace their ancestry to the time of the Scottish chieftain, they being descended from his brother, John. Major Robert Blackwell, was another Revolutionary soldier taking Kentucky land for his services. He first located in Woodford County, but exchanged his land to live in Anderson, on account of superior hunting and fishing.

Ere this sketch of the dawn passes into the noontime of the present, we must pause to refer to the courage and beauty of the Anderson women of a century ago.

Out on the Clifton Road stands an old dwelling built by a hardy pioneer over a spring to guard against attack from the dread "red-skins". As brave Susan Hutton descended the stairs for water, from the dim recesses sprang an Indian with tomahawk upraised, and with wildest whoop, exult over the scalp he was so confident of securing. Springing back, this courageous woman, to avert her fate, snatched an axe from the wall, and as the Indian in hot pursuit raised his head above the floor, down came the axe, cleaving the head from the body of the stalwart savage. And this is only one of perhaps hundreds of such deeds, that are now overgrown and hidden by the mosses of forgetfulness. Later we seen the "Salt River Tigers," as knights of old, gather in front of the old Blue Tavern, where, under an awning, stood Anderson fairest daughter, the fame of whose beauty has lingered with the years - Miss Henrietta Daviess, who, with words of courage and cheer, presented these bold warriors a silken banner of scarlet, with one large star of blue, made by the gentlewoman of Lawrenceburg. Each thread containing a thought, a blessing and a prayer, for the brave soldiers, who, amid the tears of nature, passed on to the battlesfields. *(c. 1906 Anderson News Supplement)*

COURTHOUSE

Commissioners of the May 1827 term of court were directed to draw up plans for a courthouse, but actual plans were not prepared for several months. By fall, 1829, a small two-story brick structure, costing approximately $3,000.00 was ready to use. The first court held in the new building was held in October 1829 though the building was not fully completed until July of 1830. The building was partly paid for by population subscription, some 50 or 60 citizens giving from $5.00 to $50.00 each. Some men donated their labor and one gave 36 gallons of whiskey—supposedly for personal use by the laborers. There were two two-room, one-story frame building on Main Street which were used as offices for the county attorney, sheriff and lawyers.

From the very beginning the court rooms were open for use to all religious bodies for regular services, to debating societies for civic meetings and at times for private schools.

The first courthouse was destroyed by fire about midnight October 26, 1859. Fortunately only a very few important records were destroyed.

Desire of many citizens to have the courthouse built near Glensboro or some other more central place was expressed and feelings became quite bitter as the contest continued. Nevertheless, the Lawrenceburg "faction" prevailed and within two years a larger stone structure was ready for use. In the meantime, court had been held first at the home of Mrs. Katherine Ransdell, later in the Methodist Church. January 1861, a new courthouse of stone with slate roof was built with two-story wings for the offices of sheriff, clerks and judges.

Courthouse, 1915-present

In the completed courthouse, which cost about $15,000.00, the court room was on the first floor with most offices upstairs. The only ornamentation consisted of four pillars in front with a cupola so tall that critics believed it would be blown off by the first strong wind.

Upstairs offices were entered by an iron stairway which was removed when the courthouse was remodeled in 1905.

At this time the court room was moved to the upstairs with most offices changed to the first floor, very much as they are today. The two front entrances were walled up and a hall through the center was constructed with offices on each side.

The remodeled courthouse burned during the night of April 13, 1915. Again most of the records were saved, though damage was estimated as high as $50,000.00 The front columns, erected in 1860, were deemed unsafe and were torn down.

Until a new building could be erected the court met in the Masonic Building on Main Street.

The clock installed in the new building (1916) is said to be the first self-winding tower clock built in America.

During the Civil War the courthouse was used as quarters for a company of union soldiers after Confederate troops evacuated Kentucky.

Courthouse after 1915 fire.

MCAFEE BROTHERS WERE AMONG EARLY PIONEERS IN COUNTY

Anderson County is situated on the west side of the Kentucky River and contains about 200 square miles. It is bounded on the north side by Shelby and Franklin Counties, on the west Side by Woodford County, on the south by Mercer and Washington Counties, and on the west by Spencer and Nelson Counties.

In the year 1773, the McAfee brothers, James, Robert, and George, led a party out from Virginia to explore and survey lands in Kentucky.

On the 16th of July, they surveyed lands at the present site of Frankfort. James McAfee says in his journal:

"Friday, the 16th, we left an axe and tomahawk and fish gig in the spring." This spring is about one and one-half mile northeast of the courthouse at Frankfort and is on the Franklin and Owen turnpike; it is still known as the McAfee spring. Again James says, "the 17th we kept the path on the east side of the river about eight miles in good land; we left the path, went to the southwest; in six miles we crossed the river at high hills and cedar banks." This must have been somewhere near what is known as Lover's Leap. Again, Sunday, the 18th, we camped on a small creek about five miles on the west side of the river." they traveled about eight miles which brought the to a spring, which is one of the heads of Gilbert's Creek. This spring is where the dawn of civilization for Anderson County began. It

Courthouse 1861-1915

was for a long time known as Lillard's Spring, from the pioneer, Thomas Lillard, but is now known as the McCall Spring. The McAfees called it either Cove or Cave Spring; there is some doubt about the spelling. It is a bold spring of clear, cool water located close to the old State Road between Lawrenceburg and Salvisa.

In the fall of 1862, a large part of the Confederate force under General Kirby Smith camped at this spring and found it equal to supplying their needs.

Robert McAfee related that while here they were surprised to hear the report of a gun. They immediately thought of Indians, as it was believed that no other white men

were in that part of the country; they never knew whether it was fired by an Indian or not.

When the McAfee part left this spring, they crossed over to what they called Crooked Creek or Salt River, and made several surveys; the exact point where they struck the river is not definitely known, but they continued open down the mouth of Hammond's Creek.

The territory of Anderson County was by the Virginia Legislature, in 1776, included in what was called Kentucky County, which in 1780 was divided into Jefferson, Fayette, and Lincoln Counties. Anderson was included in Lincoln, Mercer and was the first county formed out of Lincoln, and Anderson became a part of Mercer. Franklin was carved out of Mercer by the Kentucky Legislature in 1794, and most of the present county of Anderson was included in Franklin, but in 1827, Anderson came to her own, and was formed from parts of Mercer, Franklin and Shelby Counties, and was named for Richard Clough Anderson, who died the previous year while United States Minister to Colombia, South America.

At that time, no native born Kentuckian had achieved greater political distinctions.

Anderson County has a rolling surface, almost mountainous, in the eastern portion, along Kentucky River, thus forming picturesque and beautiful scenery. Though its climate is "fickle", the soil is very productive in some sections, producing hemp, tobacco, corn and all the small grains and grasses. In all early days, hemp was raised in abundance, and Lawrenceburg possessed several hemp factories, or as they were then called, rope walks. No county has a better supply of water than this, as the Kentucky River borders its eastern shore, and Salt River flows through its central part, the three Bensons, Hammonds, and many small creeks and springs supply the needs. Richard Benson, Nathan Hammond and William McBrayer are thought to be the first emigrants who came into Anderson to locate homes. They had spent some time at Harrod's Fort, in 1775, and pushed on north to take up claims. Richard Benson took up a settlement claim of 400 acres on Kentucky River, and impressed his name on four creeks, sold his claim and disappeared. Nathan Hammond was a delegate from Boiling Spring to a convention which met at Boonesborough, May 23, 1775. Hammond Creek perpetuates his name. Wm. McBrayer was a surveyor and made a number of surveys in the north and east of Lawrenceburg and located two miles north of town.

Another early settler was Thomas Baker who in 1782 settled on what is now known as the Wash farm. William Nelson and Peter Carr were also in that neighborhood. A man named Lynch located on the farm now owned by Miss Lucy Bush and was surrounded by the Georges, Mothersheads, Marrs, Mountjoys, and Thomas Gaines, Wafer Paynes and Thompson Thomason took up claims where Alton now stands.

Old Providence church on the Clifton Pike was built about 1825 when Rev. William Hickman was pastor. On Hammond's Creek, we find the names of Robert Elliott, Joshua Cummins, Samuel Burrus and Memucan Allen. Robert Elliott built a mill and distillery though to be the first in the county, on this creek. Charles Allen, Joshua Saffel, Samuel Marrs, James McClure, Joseph Woods, Jacob Gudgel, Joseph Griffith and Daniel and Arthur McGaughey, settled near each other in 1791. On the east and south of town were Jeremiah, Joseph and James Mizner, Vincent Boggess, Robert Frazier, Berry Searcy, Nicholas Leathers, John Parker, Turner and Chichester Hanks, John Bond and Edward Wall. The Dawsons,

McMichaels, and Huffmans.

On Salt River, David Egbert, John Odell, Samuel Butts, Jacob Middleton, Archie Parker, Joel Thacker, John Crossfield, Thomas Hackley, Mike Hockersmith, the Browns, the Bells, Paxtons and Murphys, Wheats, Gillises, Benjamin Wash, Roadham Petty, his son, Samuel B. Petty, Daniel Oliver, Thomas Buntain, John Jewel, John Morgan, Sr., and Jr., and the Franklins.

Anderson is known as No. 82 in Kentucky's list of fair counties.

She has never failed to bear her part in times of war. When the war between the United States and Mexico broke out, she furnished one company, known as the Salt River Tigers and led by Capt. John H. McBrayer. They did gallant service, and it is claimed saved the day at the battle of Buena Vista. Most of these old heroes have answered the last Roll Call and have gone to the land of "Eternal Peace," where the rattle of musketry and booming of cannon are never heard. There are only three of this company living in this county now: Capt. John H. McBrayer, Messrs. William F. Bond and John Tindall.

In the Civil War, Anderson County sent about 400 men to the Southern side and 200 hundred to the Northern forces. The confederates were led by Captains Utterbach, Dedman, Dawson and Jordan; the Unionists were led by Captains Searcy and Boston. No great battles were fought in this county, but there was a small battle fought at Fox Creek on October 8, 1862, besides many skirmishes between Guerillas and Home Guards, one of which was fought near Vandyke's Mill. Whether right or wrong in the principles which they advocated, no men ever fought more bravely, or suffered less complainingly than the Confederate soldiers, and when by force of overwhelming numbers, defeat came, they went back to their homes and with the same courage that sustained them on the battlefield, went to work to rebuild their fortunes; and the members of no secret order have a stronger feeling for each other than the Confederate soldier has for his comrade.

Anderson sent a few soldiers to the Spanish-American War, but I believe that the records would show they ate more tainted beef than they killed Spaniards; possibly because they had more opportunity in that line. Some of her sons are now in the United States Army in the Philippine Islands.

RAILROAD

The world's first locomotive was built in Lexington in 1826-27.

And it was Colonel Bennett H. Young who built the Southern railroad through Anderson county in 1888. It was during the spring of 1886 that the prospect of a railroad through the county engaged the attention of the citizens.

A former editor of the Anderson News, Judge Farris R. Feland, wrote many editorials pointing out the many benefits that would be realized from having this means of trans-

portation, by adding value to the land, bringing the cities close as markets for the farmer's produce., infusing new energy into the people, increasing the population, and he observed that other bluegrass counties, with only half the trade that Anderson County had in Kentucky, already have a railroad and that "the state coach must give way to the iron horse."

The L & N Railroad had the monopoly of the transportation of the county, it was said to haul the amount of nine or 10 thousand carloads per annum, which cost the county $60,000 or more to transfer this amount of traffic to and from the nearest depot. It was claimed that the L & N spent a large amount of money in the county to defeat voting the tax to procure the Southern railroad. They are said to have hired speakers who went throughout the county speaking in opposition and signifying the intention of the L & N to build a branch road through this territory.

According to the McKee Bond history of Anderson County, for two weeks prior to the voting in August, Col. Bennett H. Young, Judge Hoke and many local speakers, began at 10 o'clock in the morning and spoke all day in behalf of the new enterprise, while citizens in their respective neighborhoods furnished burgoo for the crowds. The election was held on August 14th, 1886 on a tax and the vote showed over 1,400 against the road tax, Lawrenceburg registered 556 for and 197 against, while the county showed 827 for and 1,300 against the tax. The friends of the road were undaunted and the question of a subscription to the capital stock of the Louisville Southern Railroad was pushed. It was pointed out those who were opposed to the tax could give voluntarily a sum commensurate with benefits derived from the road. The watchword was "Don't give Up the Road." Col. Young assured his friends the Southern would be built, and he expected Anderson County to cooperate.

The sense of right and the principle of progress became prevalent, and in a short time $35,000 was subscribed. Alton had voted 65 for the tax and 186 against, by before long her citizens had subscribed $3,000 to the fund. Other subscriptions were secured and on October 21, 1886, the contract to build the Southern road from Louisville to Lawrenceburg was let and in March 1887, 150 men were at work on the road in Anderson County. On the "Roll of Honor" of 1887, the names of those who gave the right of way through their lands in the county were: E. H. Reddish, John B. Mason, John R. Wilson, W. W. Satterwhite, G. H. Grimes, W. H. Tracy and William F. Bond. Others along the way sold the right of way at satisfactory prices.

By the first of April 1888 crowds of people from the surrounding country congregated daily at the scene of the track laying of the railroad ties near Lawrenceburg. Some parties brought dinner and remained all day. At 10 a.m. Thursday, April 15, 1888 the first passenger train to reach town pulled in with Judge W. H. McBrayer and family and a number of Harrodsburg people on board. The trains caused considerable commotion among the folk in the town as many of them had never seen a train of cars before. On May 28, 1888 the first excursion train to Louisville came through and many Anderson County folk were aboard. The longest freight train of that day went through Lawrenceburg on June 28, 1888 with 34 cars, mostly cattle.

In August 1889 the trains were run for the first time from Louisville to Lexington, over Young's High Bridge at Tyrone with more than 1,000 passengers every day.

At this time Lawrenceburg had 1,500 inhabitants, six churches, three schools, two banks, 12 business houses, three livery stables and three blacksmith shops.

Southern Depot, Lawrenceburg, as it looked in the early 1900s.

J. T. RIPY AND ANDERSON DISTILLING CO. DISTILLERIES

Within the corporate limits of the town of Tyrone, on the left bank in a graceful curve of beautiful Kentucky River, stand two distilleries, the property of the Kentucky Distilleries and Warehouse Company, one known as "The Anderson County Distillery Company" with the registered number 418, and the other called "The T. B. Ripy Distillery," with the registered number 112. The product of these distilleries is known throughout the length and breadth of the land, and Tyrone owes it existence to the distillery enterprise, which had it origin on the classic bank of the Kentucky River many years ago.

In the year 1868, in the flush times succeeding the Civil War, the distillery No. 112 of Walker, Martin and Co., with a capacity of mashing 100 bushels of grain daily, a very large enterprise for that day and time, was erected in what is now known at "Tyrone," but was then a wayside landing called "Streamville" by the streamboatmen.

The proprietors of this distillery were Mr. Monrow Walker, Mr. Sam P. Martin and Mr. James Ripy, all of Anderson County.

In the year 1869 the distillery property and the business were sold to Messrs. W. H. McBrayer and T. B. Ripy, son of Mr. James Ripy named above, and in 1870, Mr. T. B. Ripy, the junior partner, became the sole owner by the purchase of the interest of Judge W. H. McBrayer.

From that time the distillery has been known as the T. B. Ripy Distillery, the whiskey made therein has been tested and endorsed in almost every village and hamlet of the land.

In 1873 a new brick building was erected by the owner and the capacity increased to 600 bushels. In 1890 this building was torn down and a handsome new building erected, this time the capacity being increased to 1,200 bushels per day; subsequently an increase of capacity was made and the house was operated at a capacity of 1500 bushels daily until the Spring of 1889, when the property was sold by Mr. Ripy to the present owners, who in 1900 tore down the old

building and rebuilt with a capacity of 600 bushels per day, and at this distillery the famous T. B. Ripy Whiskey is now being manufactured.

The Anderson County Distilling Company distillery was built on its present site in 1881, by Waterfill, Dowling and Company, one member of the firm being Mr. T. B. Ripy. It was first operated in 1882, the mashing capacity being 300 bushels of grain a day.

In 1885, Mr. T. B. Ripy bought the interests of the other partners and operated the plant from that time until the date of its sale to Kentucky Distilleries and Warehouse Company in the spring of 1899. In the meantime, the building and machinery were several times enhanced, until, at the time of the sale, it was capable of mashing 1,500 bushels per day, and the daily output was about 150 barrels of whiskey.

When the present owners secured possession of the Anderson county distillery in the spring of 1899 the whole plant was renewed and enlarged; new machinery was put in and the capacity of the house was raised to the mashing of 4,000 bushels of grain per day. This house now enjoys the distinction of being the largest "mash tub" distillery in the world.

For the storage of the product of these distilleries, the Kentucky Distilleries and Warehouse Company had made ample provision by the erection of large, convenient warehouses constructed on the most approved plan and designed to insure the maturity of the whiskey to a mellow ripeness during the years it is permitted to remain in bond.

At the plant embracing these two distilleries there are employed, on an average, about 1250 workmen, in the various departments, nearly all of whom a resident of the thriving village of Tyrone. In addition, the bottling department employs the services of some 20 women.

The weekly pay-roll therefore foots a goodly sum, all of which goes into circulation in the immediate neighborhood; but this sum is small in comparison with that which is daily paid out to the Deputy Collector of Internal Revenue for taxes on whis-

key withdrawn from the bond. The monthly sum of these tax payments is in six figures.

MAIN STREET

Anderson County was formed in 1827 largely from Franklin County with smaller areas from Mercer and Washington Washington Counties. The county was named for Richard Clough Anderson Jr., lawyer, congressman, speaker of the State House of Representatives and the first American Minister to Columbia, South America. the town of Lawrence became Lawrenceburg in 1818, and was named for William Lawrence, who operated several successful businesses in the town. The population in 1830, just three years after the county was formed, was 320.

The railroad came through Lawrenceburg in 1888, greatly increasing the population. As a result, a sidewalk was built around the city. At that time Lawrenceburg was the most complete sidewalked town in Kentucky for a town of its size. Anderson County's economy is based on agriculture and industry. Some of the major industries today are tile, sausage, crushed stone, whiskey, and others. Early industries were a rope-walk, where twine was made; tannery, brick kiln, turkey pen and flour mill. Most of the early industries were operated out of homes or in buildings located on private property of residents.

Some other interesting facts of the town are: the courthouse clock is said to be the first self-winding tower clock built in America; the Pierian Clubhouse (connected to the public library) is the oldest building now standing in town; Main Street used to be called Madison Street; a hotel called The Galt House used to stand where the post office is now located; one of the first schools was a log schoolhouse located where Ninevah is today; and the water works, fire department and electric light plant were installed about 1904.

Some of the above information was gathered from the talk that Mr. Phil Spencer gave to a class at the public library.

From our interviews with our grandparents and friends, we learned what Lawrenceburg was like in the 1930's and 40's when they were in the third grade. Some remembered Lawrenceburg in the 1930's as being a very small town with around 1,800 to 2,000 people with the city limits being very close to the main part of town. There were very few automobiles in 1931 and most were Model A's. There were still a lot of horses and buggies.

There was a Lyric Theater, several grocery stores, restaurants, hardware stores, clothing stores, drug stores and pool rooms. In the 1940's a bowling alley and Newberry's 5 and 10 cent store were added.

There was an elementary school at the bus garage on Woodford Street, a high school on North Main Street where Anderson Middle School is now located and Kavanaugh High School on Woodford Street for the county children. There were also a number of elementary schools in the 1940's in the county. In the city, the children walked home for lunch and in the county they brought it with them. After school, children stopped at Ballards Drug Store or the general store close to the country school. Some of the games played were tag, tag football, horseshoes, jump-rope, marbles, kick-the-can, hopscotch, hide and seek, Annie over, Sugarloaf town and basketball.

In the 30's the children wore corduroy knickers, no blue jeans, leather high top shoes, no slacks for girls. If boys and girls misbehaved in school they were sometimes spanked in school and at home, were kept after school, stood in the corner, had recess taken away, wrote sentences, or put their nose in a circle on the board.

Most of the shopping was done in Lawrenceburg. It you went to Lexington, you had to take a ferry across the Kentucky River at Tyrone. Occasionally, some went to Louisville on an early morning train and came back on a late train. Both trips were long journeys. There were no TV's, but everyone had his favorite radio program he listened to after chores were completed. The chores were carrying in coal, kindling and water; taking out ashes, gathering eggs, cleaning the house, farm chores, and helping to care for younger brothers and sisters.

In the 30's there were no fast foods, pizza, tacos, TV dinners, frozen foods or yogurt. Holidays were spent with family and visiting neighbors.

MCCALL'S SPRING

This never-failing, ever-flowing spring of clear and sparkling water, (but condemned by the Board of Health) is always remembered by many people when they read "How dear to my heart are the scenes of my childhood."

Not gallons, but barrels and barrels, of refreshing water were required to quench the thirst of generations of school children who attended the nearby one-room Hebron School. Equally welcome for more than a century was the bucket of water which sat

Downtown Lawrenceburg, 1906-1910.

Main Street looking north, c. 1910

Lawrenceburg Hotel and Opera House, 1890s.

upon the stand near the pulpit at Old Hebron Church.

Long before sanitary drinking cups arrived on the scene, school kids stood in line to get their drink from the long handled dipper; and at church, children, parents and preacher though nothing of drinking from the common vessel.

McCall's Spring is one of the few remaining springs that served more than two score one-room schools of Anderson County. Anderson County has experienced many long, dry, and hot summers. We have seen our creeks run dry; we have seen Salt River down to just a few puddles; we have seen our springs cease their flow. Not so, at McCall's. Only once, at least in the past 140 years, has this spring shown even a sign of failure. That was on October 9, 1862, when swarms of retreating soldiers from bloody Perryville stopped at the sight of "clear, cool water." It is said that they "drank it dry" and waited impatiently for the spring to fill again.One elderly man in recalling years of drought says "There's just no telling how many wagon loads of water have been hauled from McCall's or how many horses and cattle have been saved from death by the old spring."

Several skirmishes occurred near McCall's during the Civil War, though no great battle was fought there. McCall's, so known because of its owners, was earlier known as Lillard's Spring because it was for many years owned by pioneer James Lillard who built his home there in 1795. The McAfee party in 1774 reached this spot and were happy to find a suitable site for camping a short while before moving on. They referred to this location in their journal. They called it the Cave of Cove Spring.

The spring was barely spared when Highway 127 was built and for some time it was, feared that it would be completely destroyed. Various efforts have been made to salvage what can yet be saved of it and perhaps even yet some organization can complete the park project, begun a few years ago, but never carried out. The Garden Cub is now considering restoration of the site as one of its projects.

Since Anderson County affords no restroom facilities for the traveling public, no roadside park with sufficient picnic equipment, and except for the fairgrounds, very limited recreational opportunities, it is hoped that the McCall's Spring project will meet with enthusiastic support from the general public, and that funds can be found to make of this site a place of great beauty and usefulness.

COUNTRY STORE

In the latter years of the last century Mr. Nimrod (called "Rod") Utterback and his wife Kate were owners of a prosperous grocery in the western part of Anderson County. Thursday was the big day at the store, for it was on this day that Mr. Reuben Casey met the mail coach at Leather's Store, four or five miles away, and brought mail

McCall's Spring

for customers congregated at the country store.

The small one-room building with its inevitable front porch and initialed benches, were farmers sat in quiet leisure and whittled away the hours, was on the old Delaney Road (now U.S. 62) about 15 miles west of Lawrenceburg.

Mail was later brought to the store by the Blakeman brothers, by George Sparrow, and others. They secured the mail at Sinai.

On mail day horses were hitched to nearly every tree for a half-mile in both directions. It would be 20 years before a horseless carriage would sputter past the quiet store to the amazement of 100 spectators and bewilderment of horses.

Finally is was suggested by some civic minded citizens that the community deserved a post office of its own. Accordingly, Mr. Utterback made the necessary request, and on January 22, 1890, a post office was established with "Rob" Utterback as postmaster. He named the office "Cora" in honor of Miss Cora Bond, whose family lived nearby.

Utterback was succeeded as postmaster by William F. Sutherland, John T. Hyatt, and Betis Ann Sparrow. In 1894 Mr. Joseph T. Hughes became postmaster. He held the position for four years. He was followed by Jim Utterback, Wood Blakeman, and Ed Blakeman. Hughes again served for a short time, but in 1902 Miss Una T. Gash secured her position until the Cora postoffice was discontinued in 1912.

Miss Gash (now Mrs. Dave Rogers) continued to work without pay until the Rural Free Delivery could be secured.

Increased services of the Sinai office made Cora and other small stations impractical. It was a great day for the community when Mr. Oscar Mayes delivered the first mail to a private box.

In the summer of 1913 Mr. Allen Wash became carrier, having passed the Civil Service examinations and received the appointment. He held this position until his recent retirement. Mr. Maurice Stratton, with C. V. McGuire assistant, now carries the mail on the Sinai route number one, which

passes through the community called Cora.

The old Utterback store, as well as the Joe Hughes store where the office was kept for a while, had long since disappeared.

Today only a few silver poplars mark the site of the one popular meeting-place. Mrs. Grace Cranfill, News Correspondent, keeps the public informed of current happenings in the neighborhood. *(From "Our Heritage" column of Wyatt Shely)*

ANDERSON COUNTY, KENTUCKY—HOME

Anderson County is a priceless gem set in the center of the crown of the state of Kentucky, firmly held in place by the prongs of Shelby, Franklin, Woodford, nelson and Spencer Counties.

From the large, gently winding, palisaded Kentucky, to the smaller, meandering Salt, her rivers are part and parcel of her. The multitude of creeks, sporting names such a Puncheon, Willow, Beaver, Hickory Nut, Benson and Little Benson and a wealth of other mellifluous names, trace glimmering lines through her, giving life and brilliance to her and her people.

A place where spring can come gaily traipsing, treading a wild flower strewn path, as the greening spreads up the hills and down the hollers. Where summer and fall are busy with the tasks, sights and sounds of a still largely agricultural society. Where winter can range from being simply cold to cold and wet to looking like a fairland when the occasional snow gently settles upon her.

Her people are her strength. I suppose it must ever be so. Honest, hard-working, cheerfully laboring to make their own lives, and the lives of those around them better. Her churches are many scattered to every point of her seven-sided border, and serve a multitude of people and beliefs, joining in the striving to keep their home county a good place to live.

It's where I was born. In a little house in Stringtown, a house still standing and still in use. It's where my father and his father before him were born. By and large, it seems we don't wander too far from our roots. My husband was also born in Anderson County. Though he has lived in five different homes in his lifetime, each of those homes have all been within a mile of the other!

Though, as a child, I seldom visited the larger towns and cities that surround us, now trips to Frankfort, Louisville and Lexington or other places between, are frequent excursions. Many of the residents of the county find the commute to jobs in these once removed towns and cities an easy, commonplace thing to do.

Wildlife abounds here. We have lakes and rivers and creeks that literally swarm with fish. Whitetail deer have made a monumental comeback and sighting one or several of these beautiful tawny critters while you're out driving around and they are endeavoring to cross to other territory is not out of the ordinary. Though these deer are probably the largest of our wild animals, there still persist tales and rumors of sighting of black bears, panthers, cougars or mountain lions, coy dogs and wild cats. This latter has nothing to do with the much touted University of Kentucky basketball team, though our county does have a large and healthy herd of fans of these Wildcats, too!

Anderson County is where my grandfather became a minor celebrity for developing a better turkey. There are multitudes of Strattons, which makes it difficult to differentiate between us, but when we used the appellation, "Turkey Ben," in reference to my grandfather, everybody knew, instantly, who we were.

Now, wild turkeys are making a comeback here. not because of my grandfather, but because the Kentucky Department of Fish and Wildlife began a re-populating program, a program which has flourished, just as did my grandfather's breeding program for domestic turkeys.

This is where I've spent most of my life. Though I didn't have the 'luxury' education offered by the typical one or two-roomed school, I did attend a small rural school, Sand Spring. I suppose we had 100 pupils, maybe a few more at times, in all eight grades. You could say when had a four-

room schoolhouse, as there were four teachers, each of whom taught two grades.

My children have all gone to school in this county and now my grandchildren are begining it all over again. No one more, two or four-room schools, but I do believe we have a good educational system.

Anderson County, Kentucky. A place of beauty, stability, permanence, history, future and now. An oasis in the center of the world's hustle and bustle. A touchstone of sanity in the midst of anarchy.

Anderson County, Kentucky. Home.
(By Kathleen Cooper)

Carnegie Library, 1936.

ANDERSON COUNTY PUBLIC LIBRARY

In 1906 the newly formed Pierian Club, with Mrs. Wallace Moore Bartlett as president, started a library club in two rooms over the Lawrenceburg National Bank. Within two years 2000 items were circulating throughout the county. The library club's success led Mrs. Ethyl G. Ripy, the second Pierian Club president, to contact Andrew Carnegie and ask for his aid in erecting a library building. Mr. Carnegie offered $5000.00 toward the new building if the community would contribute to its upkeep. The Lawrenceburg City Council agreed to help with a library tax. The Pierian Club's diligent work soon became reality on November 8, 1908. The Lawrenceburg Public Library was open.

Years of collection growth created the need for larger quarters and in 1973 a new library was started on the donated site of the Lawrenceburg Women's Club (formerly the Pierian Club). This property was said to be the oldest brick building standing in Lawrenceburg—erected prior to 1820. The new facility, now named the Anderson Public Library, was opened in July 1974 followed by a September 1974 dedication.

Since its founding the Public Library has had seven librarians and one acting librarian: Miss Susie Hooper, Miss Russell Chambers, Mrs. Allie Lyen Hiner, Mrs. Nell Marrs Board, Miss Joan Routt, Mrs. Mae Trent McKay (acting), Mrs. George McWilliam, Jr., and Mr. Jeffrey Sauer.

Groundbreaking for the library, 1906, by ladies of the library board.

EDUCATION

Mrs. Lee Campbell's private school, Woodford Street, 1912. First row, Marvin Wash, Miller McAfee, Ed Jones, Maurice Hagerman. Second row, Rice Mountjoy, Stewart McAfee, William Bond, Harold Buntain, Joe Rice, Mary Virginia Marrs Reynolds. Third row, Mary Searcy, Mattie Boggess, Margaret Lyons Spencer, Rhetta Farley, Seera B. Davenport, Mary Joseph Jones. Fourth row, ?, Marie Louise Myall, Mrs. Lee Campbell, Holly Martin.

Anderson County, KY has made a distinct contribution to early secondary education in Kentucky, according to information now in the process of compilation by the Bureau of Source Materials at the University of Kentucky, Lexington, under the direction of Professor Ezra L. Gillis, a former citizen of Anderson County.

The history of secondary education in Anderson County, so far as the Bureau of Source Materials has been able to ascertain, goes back as far as the year 1837 when Anderson Seminary was chartered.

There have been other private schools which were never chartered. Among them are the schools taught by Jessie Crook and the Central Normal College at Glensboro conducted by John C. Willis. This school was later transferred to Lawrenceburg and operated by Willis and Stewart.

According to the act to incorporate Anderson Seminary, which was approved January 28, 1837, the trustees were: Dixon G. Dedman, William McGinnis, John Howard, Lewis J. Witherspoon, William S. Hichman and Delancy Egbert. "It shall be the duty of said Trustee," said the act of incorporation; "to assemble at least once in three months, or oftener if they think proper, and make such examination into the progress of the students and management of the general concern of the institution-"

The act also stated that fines that accrued in the county would be appropriated for the benefit of the seminary. In February 1930, according to "Acts establishing Academies," the estate of the former slave was appropriated to the use of Anderson Seminary. This slave had formerly been a resident of South Carolina, according to information contained in the act. Anderson Seminary ceased to be a school in 1893.

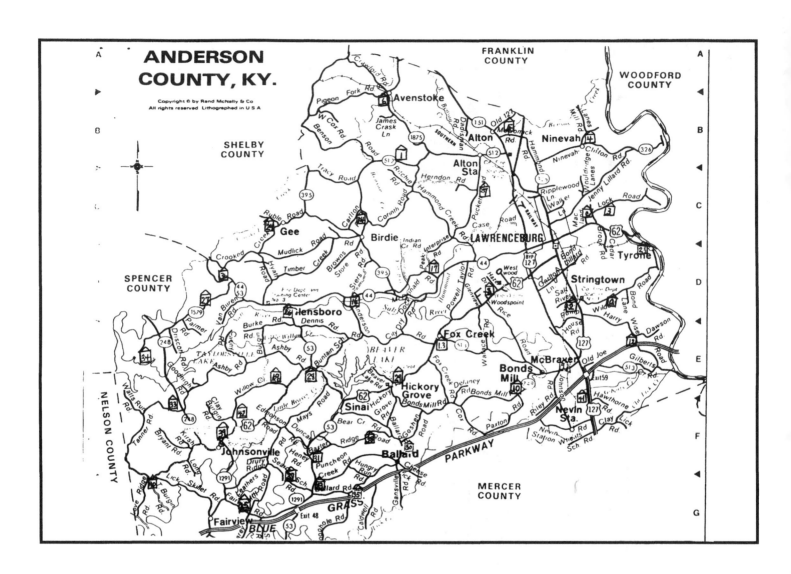

ANDERSON COUNTY SCHOOLS

ONE AND TWO(*) ROOM SCHOOLS
IN 1934-35

Alexander (10)
Pleasant Grove (27)
Alton (5)*
Pleasant Hill (36)
Anderson City (16)
Rutherford (43)
Avenstoke (6)*
Royalty (31)
Bonds Mill (9)
Salt River (2)
Cedar Grove (8)
Stingy (12)
Champion (38)
Searcy (37)
Fox Creek (13)

Tanner (33)
Friendship (19)
Tyrone (23)
Glensboro (26)
Union (0)
Goodlett (35)
Van Buren (34)
Gordon (24)
Wardsville (40)
Georgetown (c)
Young (30)
Hampton (1)
Hebron (41)
Herndon (7)
Hickory Grove (29)
Hughes (28)
Johnsonville (39)
Kays (25)
Klondike (42)
Marlowe (14)*

McGinnis (3)
Munday (17)
Ninevah (4)*

OTHER ONE ROOM SCHOOLS (not
in session in 1934-35)

Antioch
Buntain (on Buntain School Rd.)
Buck Lick (between Alton Station and
Avenstoke)
Fairview
Franklin
Griffy
Long (consolidated into Avenstoke)
Oak Grove (consolidated into
Avenstoke)
Peak (became Hampton)
Redmond (was on Mudlick Road)
Shiloh

CHURCHES

Members of the First Christian Church (Disciples of Christ), Lawrenceburg, KY. Picture made c. 1920. First row, Mollie Hyatt, Lulie Warren, Norma Hutton, Burdette Huffaker, Mrs. Gus Kington, J.W.B. Birdwhistell, Sue Wilson, Mrs. Matt Utterback. Second row, ?, ?, Mrs. John Walsh, Mrs. Mullins, ?, Zula Homes, Geneva Huffaker, Mrs. John Dawson. Third row, Mrs. Burford, Mrs. J. H. Farris, Mrs. Jasper Martin, ?, ?, ?, Lula Walker, Mrs. Cartinour, Mary Brown, Mary Bond, Lisle Bond.

CLAYLICK UNITED METHODIST

Claylick United Methodist Church is located on the Claylick Road in Anderson County, Kentucky, just north of the Anderson/Mercer County line. Claylick is a rural church but has a congregation made up of rural, urban and city residents and is fairly evenly composed of both Anderson and Mercer Countians.

This history is compiled from records and memories of many people, and may not be completely accurate in every detail, however, this recording will preserve a portion of the church history for future generations.

As far as can be learned, Claylick Church had its beginning in a log house behind the barn near the Hank Cornnor Farm, as it was known at that time. This old log house went by the name of The Mud Slide House. From this humble beginning the congregation grew and erected a log church on the Henry Parker Farm, near Claylick Creek, (approximately .5 mile east of the present location - 1990). This was probably the first church building to have the name of Claylick. It received its name from the fact that the clay soil contained salt. Deer and farm animals would lick the clay to satisfy their appetite for salt. Salt licks were common in this community in the early days.

Very little is known of the early history of this old church. It has been said that a local preacher and farmer by the name of Alec Chilton preached here. He was probably a layman. The story goes that one Sunday as he was preaching someone told him that his cows were in his cornfield. He immediately left the pulpit and congregation and went to his farm, known to us as the Jack Short place - 1990, adjacent to the church, herded his cows from the cornfield and came back and finished his sermon.

The Chilton name is still a prominent name in the community, with the sixth generation of descendents still active in the congregation.

In 1871, a Mr. Gill donated ground for a church site at what is presently known as the forks of Claylick and Hawthorne Roads. This is the present site of Claylick United Methodist Church.

Mr. Jake Kennedy was the building contractor for the first church at the present location. He with the help of the men of the church, erected a one-room building that served as both the Sunday School and worship services. It was constructed of native materials including poplar and oak. The sills were carved out of oak logs and the foundation was limestone. The rock possibly came from Kentucky River.

The Hawkins family of whom Mrs. Lillie Lyens was a daughter (wife of Dr. J. B. Lyens) was instrumental in building the original building. Mr. Jeff Robinson (deceased), as a youth, carried water, lunches and hot coffee to the workers on the church. Mr. Jeff Robinson was the father of the late Mrs. Bertis Currens. Mrs. Bertie was a Sunday School teacher for many years, and a prominent member. She was the wife of W. T. "Tucker" Currens. Mr. Tucker was the Church Treasurer for many years. They maintained some of the early records of the church.

Mr. Jake Kennedy also built the pews, pulpit and pillar stand for the church.

The old church was surrounded by beautiful oak, cedar, elm and walnut trees that served as hitching posts for the horses while their masters were in services. The old church was without an alter for many years. In later years, Mrs. Lena Short donated material from an old weaving loom, to build an alter. The work was done by Mr. Ezra Short, a member of the congregation and a talented craftsman and carpenter. Mr. Ezra short also built the pulpit chairs.

In the early days Sunday School was held in the afternoon and preaching services were only conducted one Sunday per month. Claylick was on a pastoral charge with the Methodist churches of Mount Edwin, Tyrone and Salvisa. In later years Claylick was assigned on a charge with Methodist Churches of Salvisa, Joseph Chapel and Mount Hebron.

The congregation of Claylick have always been generous with the donation of their time and talents to improve and maintain the church property. In the mid 1930's, the men of the church undertook and completed the project of replacing the wood steps at each of the front doors of the building. This project was supervised by Luther Robinson, a local carpenter and member of the church.

The early church was lighted by kerosene lights, later by new improved gasoline lamps similar to gas lanterns. These gave a very good light for that time. However, if the preacher was too lengthy they would begin to dim before his sermon was over. Later, a Delco System was installed that generated electricity for incandescent lighting. About 1940, electricity was made available to the rural area under the Rural Electrification Act. Claylick subscribed for this service and has remained a customer of Fox Creek Rural Electric Cooperative Corporation since that time.

The first addition to the church was a Sunday School facility and cistern. This addition included six Sunday school rooms and a basement. A kitchen with running water was constructed in the basement and that served as meeting place for social activities as well as a meeting place for the Methodist Men and Church Women's organizations. Hollie Warford, Sr. was the chairman of the building committee. Mr. Lon Dean, a black carpenter affectionately known as "Dummy Dean", was employed to oversee the building of this addition with the assistance of volunteers from the congregation. The second addition consisted of additional Sunday School rooms and was overseen by Mr. Lyndon Speaks, a Salvisa building contractor.

Following a mid-week Prayer Meeting, on January 10, 1962, with temperatures of -20 degrees, the church building was destroyed by fire from an overheated furnace. By the help of God and many volunteers fighting the blaze, the Sunday School addition was saved, though heavily damaged by water and smoke. The old sanctuary was torn down and a new one built.

Mr. Lois Short, a Lawrenceburg building contractor, was employed to construct a new modern sanctuary and full basement. The new facility included Claylick's first indoor bathroom facilities and was an all electric church including electric heat. Claylick was Kentucky's first all electric church.

During the interim between the destruction by fire and completion of construction, church services were held at the old Hebron Presbyterian Church near McCall's Spring.

The first service in the new church was October 14, 1962. Space will not permit the listing of all the people, churches and organizations that made contributions toward the construction of the new facility.

Claylick has a long heritage of providing a Sunday school for the community and its membership. In earlier days Sunday school was held in the afternoon. In addition to providing spiritual learning and guidance the Sunday school also provided a social event where members of the community could come together to visit and become acquainted.

Leadership of the Sunday School is under the direction of a superintendent chosen from the congregation by the Administrative Board.

Recorded Sunday School Superintendents at Claylick are: Lee Brandenburg, Frank Nichols, Dave Montgomery, W. T. "Tom" Overstreet, Hollie Warford, Jr., O. H. Gritton, Jr., Lynn Chilton and Juanita Gritton.

Claylick United Methodist Church is in the Franklin District of the Kentucky Conference of United Methodist Churches.

Claylick was selected "Church of the Year" by the Kentucky Conference in 1960.

Claylick encourages its members to became active participants in church sponsored organizations. Organization are available to accommodate all age groups. These organizations elect their own officers and are governed by the participants within guidelines set forth by the Administrative Board.

The youth of the church regularly meet on Sunday evening for a time of spiritual enrichment that includes an occasional business meeting to plan for fund raising events to support social activities and missionary giving.

Claylick has two women's organizations: Women's Society for Missionary Service and Women's Circle.

The Women's Society for Missionary Services was originally organized as The Ladies Aid and met monthly at the home of the members on a rotation basis. The meeting included a devotional, lunch and quilt making. Although the monthly meeting has been moved from the home to the church building, the purpose of the meeting remains the same, that being to raise funds for local church projects and missionary support through the sale of quilts which are hand quilted by the ladies.

Claylick's second ladies' organization is known as the Women's Circle. This organization was a spin-off of the Women's Society for Missionary Service by a group of women that were employed outside the home and were unable to meet during the day. The purpose of this organization is basically the same as the Women's Society however, they use various methods of raising funds for their projects.

Both organizations have had a positive influence on the church and community by their dedication to purpose and example as Christian leaders.

Claylick boosts of a men's organization that spans better than half a century. This group meets monthly at the church for an evening meal and devotional. A meeting may also include a work session that make repairs or improvements to the church property.

Annual projects of the Claylick United Methodist Men include an annual burgoo on the first Monday in October and a weekend revival at the old Hebron Presbyterian Church on the second weekend in July.

The annual burgoo is free and open to the public. Gospel singing entertainment is provided after the meal. Cooking of four to five lard kettles of burgoo over an open fire is an all day event. This outreach project is well over 50 years old.

The weekend revival at the old Hebron Presbyterian Church is a project that the Claylick Methodist men have sponsored for many years. The proceeds from this project are donated to the Hebron Cemetery Board to assist with financial requirements to maintain the cemetery grounds. Claylick does not have a church cemetery and many of its former members are buried in this community cemetery.

Claylick is well known as a friendly church with a congregation made up of several generations of the same families. Family names of early settlers in the community can still be found on the current membership roll.

Family names to be found in the archives of Claylick's membership roll, though probably not complete, include: Anderson, Baker, Beasley, Beckham, Bell, Bixler, Booth, Bottom, Bowen, Bowman, Brandenburg, Broce, Briscoe, Britton, Brown, Brooks, Burns, Chapman, Carter, Casey, Chilton, Coke, Combs, Conner, Cottrell, Coubert, Cox, Croslow, Crutchfield, Cunningham, Currens, Dailey, Davenport, Dawson, Delaney, Doyle, Drury, Earlywine, Eaves, Egbert, Ellis, Ervin, Freeman, Garrison, Gash, Goodlett, Gritton, Hall, Hamon, Hardin, Hawkins, Hawthorne, Hill, Hockersmith, Hockins, Holman, Howard, Huffman, Hutton, Ingram, James, Jeffries, Johnson, Lettridge, Lyens, Martin, Masters, McCoun, McCoy, Medley, Merriman, Moore, Montgomery, Mullins, Nichols, Orwig, Overstreet, Parker, Patterson, Phillips, Poulter, Proctor, Puckett, Pulliam, Redmon, Riley, Roark, Robinson, Rogers, Satterly, Sea, Searcy, Shelton, Shifflet, Short, Shouse, Simmons, Simpson, Smith, Soard, Sparrow, Spaulding, Spivey, Stinnett, Stewart, Stratton, Sullivan, Sutherland, Thacker, Thompson, Todd, Tolls, Votaw, Warford, Warren, Wayne, White, Wiley, and Wilham.

From its humble beginning in the early 1800's, Claylick Church had provided spiritual guidance to the Claylick Community, proclaiming and teaching the Gospel of Jesus Christ as recorded in the Holy Bible.

BUILT 1871
REBUILT 1962

FIRST CHRISTIAN

First Christian Church (Disciples of Christ)

In 1827 when Anderson County was carved out of parts of Franklin, Mercer, and Washington Counties, there were no church buildings within Lawrenceburg's boundaries. It is a fact that before the erection of buildings, the pioneers met under shade trees for their services. Homes were used for religious gatherings when the weather was inclement. On October 18, 1847, a lot of land on Allin (Court) Street was conveyed to the trustees of the Christian Church in Lawrenceburg. A frame building was erected on this lot with two front doors. The men and boys entered and sat on one side and the women and girls sat on the other side. It was the custom in those days for the men and women to be separated in religious services. This building was used until June 7, 1869, when it was sold to the Free Colored Church for $1,200.00.

W. H. Witherspoon donated a lot of land to the Christian Church and in 1872 a new church building was erected on the corner of Main and Court Streets. In June of 1876 a fire destroyed this building and in 1879 another building was used until June 7, 1869, when it was sold to the Free Colored Church for $1,200.00.

W. H. Witherspoon donated a lot of land to the Christian Church and in 1872 a new church building was erected on the corner of Main and Court Streets. In June of 1876 a fire destroyed this building and in 1879 another building constructed of brick was erected. In one corner of the square vestibule hung a rope tied to a bell in the church belfry. Time was when churches had bells calling parishioners to worship on time. A cottage organ was played by different member with musical talent. The pulpit was in an alcove reached by three or four steps, and the preacher literally looked down upon

his congregation. Two large coal stoves heated the sanctuary. This building burned on June 30, 1899. The building was fully insured and the congregation was able to begin the construction of another brick building on the same lot. The main entrance opened on Main and Court Streets. A pipe organ, pumped by hand, was placed in the church. The chore of pumping the instrument was given to one of the members of the official board. This building was dedicated in March, 1900. All congregations in town adjourned their meetings to join in this service. Officers of the Board in 1903 were J. R. York, Sr., J. W. Gaines, R. H. Lillard, and J. M. B. Birdwhistell, elders, and the deacons were R. S. Collins, W. H. Searcy, J. W. Waterfill, W. F. Lillard, Thomas McMurry, J. W. Shouse and B. L. Cox. Pastors serving the early church were Hastings, Haley, Lloyd, South, Polk, Stafford, Lampkin,

Reubelt, W. F. Grimm, W. C. Gibbs, and E. B. Bourland. During Mr. Bourland's ministry a house at 215 North Main Street was purchased for a parsonage. It was sold when the house at 302 South Main Street was bought from Mr. J. W. Shouse to be used for the parsonage in 1921.

After Mr. Bourland resigned, the Rev. Carl Agee was called to serve as pastor in 1919. On January 1, 1920, the church purchased two lots located on the corner of Main and Chautauqua Streets from J. W. Shouse. A new church building was erected at a cost of $110,000.00. This building was dedicated on August 28, 1921. The pipe organ was purchased by the Ladies' Aid Society at a cost of $5,200.00. There were 653 members on the church roll in 1921. At the time the church building was dedicated, the Board of Officers were J. M. B. Birdwhistell, chairman; W. H. Searcy, clerk; J. B. Ash, recording secretary; and J. B. Waterfill, treasurer. The elders were J. W. Gaines, B. L. Cox, J. M. B. Birdwhistell, Burdette Huffaker, R. H. Lillard, and J. L. Toll. Deacons were J. W. Shouse, Forest Ripy, J. W. Dawson, J. B. Waterfill, Alvin Major, Dudley Botts, J. E. Sweeney, H. S. Crossfield, John Gaines, W. H. Searcy, J. L. Sherwood, J. L. Cole, J. B. Ash, C. A. Routt, J. W. Rankin, E. B. Cartinhour, Sr., and Hugh Martin.

The new church building included a gymnasium, assembly room, rest rooms, Boy Scout room and a furnace room for a coal burning furnace in the basement. This gymnasium was the first of this kind in Lawrenceburg and was also used by the schools and community for games of basketball and other activities. The next floor consisted of the large sanctuary, pastor's study, two rooms and a foyer in the front of the church. The pipe organ was placed in the center of the pulpit area with the pulpit directly in front of the organ and the choir loft on the right side of the pulpit. The baptistry was under the extra choir loft on the left side of the pulpit. The floor was removed, along with the chairs, when the ordinance of baptism was administered. The communion table was in the center in front of the pulpit on the floor level with the sanctuary. There were three steps up to the pulpit and choir level. On the top floor were twelve rooms for classes for the youth. Some of there rooms were divided by wooden doors. The old church building on the corner of Main and Court was sold n 1922, and shortly thereafter it was destroyed by fire. The Lloyd Furniture Store is now located on that lot.

Mr. Agee resigned in 1923 and immediately the Rev. T. Hassel Bowen was called to be the pastor. He served only one year. The next pastor was the Rev. W. G. Eldred. He came to Lawrenceburg in 1924 and served the church until failing health caused him to resign in 1947. The Rev. Jack McCullough was the next pastor. He served the church for five years, resigning in 1953. Then the Rev. Jack M. Ervin was called. He began his ministry September 1, 1953 and served until his death in September, 1972. In 1973 the

Christian Church built in 1899.

Rev. Robert G. Parrish, III became the minister and served until his resignation on May 30, 1986. The Rev. Charles F. Brumley was called to minister to the church, beginning January 1, 1987. He is the minister at the present time. This church had been fortunate to call ministers who were truly servants of God, held in high esteem by the congregation, and committed to their calling. In addition to the above named pastors, the church has employed eighteen student ministers to serve the youth of the church. They have been students of the Lexington Theological Seminary and through their ministry at First Christian Church have received valuable training to prepare them for future pastorates.

Extensive renovation has been made to the church building since 1950. The old gymnasium is now a fellowship hall with chapel, library, offices and choir robing rooms over it. In 1969 the sanctuary was refurbished. A new baptistry was installed where the old organ was located, the communion table placed in front of the baptistry, and the pulpit moved to the right of the communion table. A new pipe organ was installed in 1972 and in located behind the pulpit. In 1986 the old parsonage was torn away and a meditation garden was built in memory of Jack Ervin and in honor of his wife, Jewell Ervin. Generous donations made this lovely garden, located on the south side of the church, possible.

As members of the Christian Church (Disciples of Christ), we believe that Jesus is the Christ, the Son of the living God, and the Lord and Savior of all humanity. This is our one major article of faith. Beyond this, we respect and expect varying understanding and interpretations of scripture. We believe that we are not the only Christians, and that God is at work in all churches, but we emphasize the universal name, Christian, because we wish to be known simply as Christians and Disciples of Christ. In keeping with the historical practice of the early Christian era and our denominational founders on the American frontier, communion is served each Sunday. It is presented, not as an obligation, but as a spiritual opportunity. It is a matter of personal conscience and decision. At First Christian Church, communion is not limited to our church members, but is open to all who believe in Christ and desire to follow his way.

The membership of First Christian Church is 775 at this time. The youth of the church are a very important group and includes Junior Fellowship (grades 4-6), Chi Rho (grades 7-8), and C. Y. F. (9-12_. The Christian Women's Fellowship has six circles: Eldred, Verna Bond, Lillard, Ervin, Christian Workers, and a new circle that has not yet been named. Music is a significant part of the worship service at First Christian. There is an Adult Choir, Youth Choir, composed of grades 7-12, Junior Choir (grades 4-6), Primary Choir (grades 1-3), and Cherub Choir (age 3-5). Handbell choirs are composed of Adult, Chi Rho and Junior Handbells.

The General Board is composed of chairman, vice chairman, secretary, treasurer, recorder, twelve elders, 45 members of the diaconate, Sunday school superintendent, and chairmen of the seven committees, which are Christian Education, Worship and Devotional Life, Membership, Evangelism, Buildings and Grounds, Stewardship and Finance, and World Outreach.

The purpose of this church shall be revealed in the New Testament. To win people of faith in Jesus Christ and commit them actively to the church, to help them grow in the graces and knowledge of Christ that they may known and do his will, and to work for the unity of all Christians in the common task of building the kingdom of God.

ALTON BAPTIST

Alton Baptist Church   Lawrenceburg, Kentucky
The Church on the Hill

"THE CHURCH ON THE HILL"

Alton Baptist Church was organized on October 7, 1945. 40 charter members purchased one acre of land and a 70 year old building from the Little Flock Baptist Church, whose eight surviving members sold the building and acre of land to the new church for the sum of $1000.00.

Today, the Alton Baptist Church is situated on 12 acres of land at 1321 U. S. Highway 127 By-pass North, identified by the building at the peak of the hill. Due to this, it is now known far and wide as "the Church on the Hill." Highlighting this new name is the recently added lighted cross which can be seen for miles in either direction. The current membership is nearly 700 and the value of the property is over $650,000.00.

The most important feature of the church is not the building or the cross, but the open door and warm welcome that has come to symbolize the close and caring fellowship which is the "church on the hill". It is a growing and dynamic arm of Christ which serves all needs from the youngest to the eldest member.

Alton Baptist has been served by seven pastors since the formation of the church. Reverend Sherley Woods was called on the day the church was organized and served until February, 1950. On May 7, 1950, Reverend David Lathrem came to the church and remained until May 22, 1955. The next pastor, Reverend Jerry Davis, joined the church as its leader on June 19, 1955. He remained until February 22, 1959.

Next was Reverend Ernest Cruise who served from June 8, 1959 through January 22, 1961. He was followed by Reverend Stratton Paxton who was here from April 1961 through March of 1964. In May of 1964, Reverend Neal Bowman, Jr. came to lead the church, staying through November 20, 1966.

On June 4, 1967, Tyre Denney assumed the pastorate. He is currently the pastor of the growing and dynamic congregation. In the 23 years since then, the church has grown from a small white frame building on Highway 151, with its education building that was added in 1962, to the present large, multi-purpose building at the Bypass 127 site.

The church has an aggressive, growing Sunday school, an active prayer ministry, active missions groups for all ages, an active and dynamic youth group, a strong music ministry, and a growing membership. This continued growth has caused the church to provide two worship services each Sunday morning. They are at 8:30 and 10:30 a.m. with the Sunday School hour at 9:30. The evening worship is at 6:30 p.m.

The worship services are televised on a taped-delay basis on cable channel 6 at 10:30 a.m. on Sunday and 7:00 p.m. on Monday. At 8:30 a.m. on Sunday and 8:00 p.m. on Tuesday, they can be seen on channel 22.

To support the many needs of the church, a number of seminary students have served the membership in staff positions. In 1966, Jim Buie served the summer as Youth Director and Al Legg served as Minister of Music. Donna Martin came as the fist Childrens Director in May of 1970 and was followed in 1971 by Nancy Felkel.

Music has been a growing and integral part of the worship experience of the church. Jerry Rice came to serve as Minister of Music in 1972. He was followed by Paul Adams in 1976, Marty Alexander and Buford Cox in 1978, Joel Walker in 1981, Matt Adams in 1983. Talmadge Hobbs followed in May of 1988. Ellery Milburn served as interim Minister of Music until the current Minister of Music and Education, Rick Fleenor, assumed the position in 1989.

The life blood of the growth of the church is its youth programs. Joel Waler was the first minister of Youth in 1981 and served in this position as well as the position of Minister of Music. Darryl Wilson assumed the position of Minister of Youth in 1983 when the positions were split. In 1985, Debbie Adams became Minister of Youth and Education. She was followed by the current Minister of Youth, Opal Phillips. The Youth Organization is growing in size and in its ministry to the church and the community.

In addition to the church staff, many hundreds have served their Lord in the church as teachers, ushers, musicians, deacons, committee members, and other workers. They have served countless hours, prayed countless prayers, visited and supported persons in need, and through the power and the direction of the Holy Spirit have been and will continue to be the "Church on the Hill."

ALTON CHRISTIAN

The list of ministers who have served Alton Christian Church is long, since the church has served as a training ground for ministers in conjunction with Lexington Theological Seminary. Most of these have gone on to larger churches and have become outstanding ministers. In the very early days, there was the Reverend Luther Stanley, father of Kentucky Governor and statesman A. O. Stanley.

In the past quarter-century, outstanding ministers have given of their time and talents to the church. Among them were Charles W. Riggs, J. R. Alderson, Bill Mounts, and Dr. Ivan Shelburne. The Reverend Christopher Whitehead presently serves as Pastor.

A complete list of past ministers is not available, but from the early part of this century, the following have served: G. Severance 1912-13; W. A. McPherson, 1914-15; James Barbee, 1920-21; John Greenwood, 1923-31; James Sparrow, 1931; A. E. Landolt, 1936-37; Wayne H. Bell, 1938-42; John Riley, 1943-44; A. T. Stanley, 1945; Arthur Digby, 1946; Everett Millard, 1947; A. M. Von Almen, 1948-49; Richard Sweeney, 1950-51; W. B. Apperson, 1953-54; Robert Whisler, 1955; Elmore Ryle, 1956-58; David Havens, 1960, William Guthrie, 1961-62; T. Morgan Hill, 1963-64; Rex Horne, 1964-66; Richard James, 1967-68; Joe Chenault, 1969-70; Charles Riggs, 1971-72; J. R. Alderson, 1973; Bill Mounts, 1974-78; Ivan Shelburne, 1978-88; Christopher Whitehead, 1988-present.

The members of the Alton Christian Church have been prominent in the community, serving in public office and working to improve the community. Three members of the church have been honored with the prestigious Farm-City Meritorious Service Award: George Cotton, Harry C. Towles, and Mary Jo Thacker.

The Alton Christian Church was built in 1872, having been moved from a site off present Highway 151, where it was known as Buck Lick Christian Church. When it was moved to its present location, the name was changed to the Christian Church of Rough and Ready, which was the name of Alton at that time. The name *Rough and Ready* was in honor of Zachary Taylor, a cognomen he acquired for his exploits as a general in the United States Army. Taylor later became the 12th President of the Unites States. The name of the town was changed to Alton in 1876, at which time the name of the church was changed also.

Not much is known about the Buck Lick church, but it was believed to have been a one-room structure. There was a

school nearby known as the Buck Lick School. The school teacher and minister at that time was named Josiah Shinn. The property on which the Buck Lick church was located was donated for that purpose by the Mountjoy Family. The site is near the present home of Paul Routt, on lane near a creek. The origin of the name is unclear, but it suggests that deer would congregate to lick salt at a nearby salt deposit.

At the time the church was moved to the town of Rough and Ready, it was a charter town with elected officers and a police force. The population was 150 which was about half the population of Lawrenceburg and which was about the same for Tyrone, an Anderson County town on the Kentucky River.

In addition to a grocery store, the town boasted of a city hall, a jail (painted red and located next door to the church), a hotel or tavern and a stage coach stop which was incorporated in the tavern. The tavern was on the northwest corner of the Crab Orchard Pike (Highway 151) and the present Frankfort Pike is known as U.S. 127.

About the time the church was moved, a Reverend Laban Merritt was active in this area in church expansion work and it is possible that he may have had something to do with the shifting the church to Rough and Ready. He was one of the ministers that Champ Clark, a U.S. Statesman and candidate for the Presidency, said had a great effect on him when he was growing up. The other was a Baptist minister, a Reverend Bruner. Clark was born in Lawrenceburg, taught school in Glensboro and at one time lived in the stone house on the Ninevah Road on the present Dr. George Gilbert property.

The stone from the foundation of the Buck Lick Church was moved by sleds and wagons to the new site by Joe Gordon and others of the area. Gordon was the father of Squire Gordon and they lived in Alton at the time. Working on the building was a Mr. Shryock and Felix Spencer among others.

The floor sill, still in use, are 197 years old and were hewn from white oak logs. They are 12" x 12" and some of them are 30' long. They are still in good condition and provide a solid foundation for the present church. The rafters also are of white oak but were sawed to the correct size. The floor joists are 3" x 12" and were sawed from poplar logs. The studs used in the wall are a full 2" x 5" and the original flooring was on one inch white asho boards. The present flooring is laid over the original boards.

Two pot-bellied Franklin stoves furnished the heat and originally burned wood, but later on coal was used.

The steeple was added in 1987 with memorial gifts.

CHURCH OF THE OPEN BIBLE

It all started in the fall of 1975, when Pastor Donald Frye, his wife Lee Ann and four daughter came to Kentucky with the dream of building a church for God, under the direction of Open Bible Standard Churches, Inc.

Sunday services were first held in their duplex off of Evergreen Road. Midweek worship and Bible study were moved around from home to home, and even the coonhunters club. Later Sunday morning worship was held at the Holiday Inn in West Frankfort, with the midweek being conducted in the home of Harold and Ritta Chrisman at the corner of B. Way and Bond St. in Lawrenceburg.

As God blessed and numbers grew, the church looked at property to purchase. The old Alton Baptist, the house close to the corner of 151 and Old Frankfort Road and the property close to Twilight Trail and 127 were considered. At a later date the property we eventually purchased at 1830 Old Frankfort Road, became available. Everyone was pleased with where the Lord was leading us to build His church.

On the second Sunday of February 1979 Pastor Frye and 70 charter members moved into their new church building. Reverend C. Russel Archer presided over the service. Later a Sunday School wing was added to the original building, with still future plans

consisting of a new sanctuary.

Brother Frye pastored for ten and a half year before being called to pastor in Springdale Pennsylvania. His vision and dream still lives on in the hearts of the people he directed for those ten years.

In August of 1986 Pastor Bill J. Barrett and his wife Carmen and son Ross were called to be the new pastors. Their second son was born in Frankfort that same fall. In 1987 the church was remodeled. Three new rooms were added at that time. In the coming years there are plans to add a new sanctuary, gym, and day school as the Lord Jesus directs. *Submitted By: Terry Chrisman.*

CORINTH CHRISTIAN

The Corinth Christian Church is a non-denominational church of the New Testament. It was organized in 1870 by Bro. Levin Merritt, after a revival meeting was held at the old Jordan Schoolhouse. For many years the congregation worshipped in the schoolhouse and in 1882 the place of worship was moved to a building situated on a dirt lane that extended from Akins Cemetery on Hammonds Creek Road to a location on the Herndon Road. Past names for that meeting house were "Bear Wallow" and "House of good Fellowship".

In November of 1885, Joseph H. Brown and his wife, Susan Redmon Brown, sold to the trustees of the church 3/4 of an acre more or less for the sum of $1.00. The deed for this plot is recorded at the Anderson County Clerk's office in Deed Book "S", page 374.

The first church building built on this plot of ground was erected in 1886 and this is the same plot where the present church building now stands. The minister when this building was raised was Brother Jackson Sims. The Elders then were Dawson Redmon, W. H. Glass, I. B. Peak, and Jordan Warford. The Deacons were Dawson Grace, Marion Cox, and A. G. Sherwood. In 1923 this building was torn down and in August of that year the minister of the Lawrenceburg Christian Church, T. Hassell Bowen, dedicated a newly constructed church building. The cost of this new building was small because most of the labor was donated by the members. On that occasion $355.70 was raised to pay off the existing debt on the building. At that time there were seven surviving members of the congregation meeting in the first building in 1886. They were Dawson Grace, Marion Cox, Joe Husband, James Akins, Mrs. Venie Melear, Mrs. Emma Cooper, and Mrs. Sallie Gordon. All seven of these members were present that day and sat on a special seat reserved for them in the "Amen Corner". Some of them made statements that day on what Corinth had meant to them through the years.

Electric lights were installed in 1939 to replace the old kerosene chandeliers and reflector window bracket lamps. In 1943 a parcel of land was purchased from Robert Baugh and laid off in lots for a cemetery by S. V. Gordon, a former member of the congregation. In 1948, four Bible School classrooms, the present pulpit area, vestibule and basements were built. The church, in 1952, purchased from Allie Hume a lot adjacent to the church and on this lot was built

a parsonage. In 1958, three additional classrooms were added and the entire building was covered in permastone. Since then at various intervals, minor and major construction projects have taken place that transformed the church building into the beautiful place of worship that it is today.

Some ministers and evangelists who have served over the years are: William

Morris, John Mahoney, Diamond Bentley, David Campbell, Perry Campbell, Aldolphus Mountjoy, Jordon T. Ragan, I. W. Rogers, William May, George Peel, Presley Herndon, Gilbert Easley, Forrest Mullins, Dan Murphy, Wesley Whitehouse, Cleo Purvis, Clarke Winkler, C. A. Van Winkle, Elbert Winkler, John Chambers, R. B. Baker, Frank Buck, Charles Buck, R. E. Stephenson, Terrill Riley, Leroy Tracey, Herbert Graham, W. I. Peel, Stanley Hicks, Thomas Bledsoe, Raymond Sparrow, E. Paul Perry, David Downey, Robert Whisler, William Miller, Don Nash, Metcalfe Miller, Ezra Sparrow, Melvin Styons, Homer Styons, Norman Miller, Roy McClain, James Simpson, Vernon Oakley, Ray Giles, Clyde True, Claude Waldridge, Nelson Lee, Bob Moulden, Lowell Thornton, and C. Marion Railey.

The present minister is Gene Koons. Elders are Earl Hume, Bernice Cinnamon, Vernon Perry, Connie Drury, and Maurice Cinnamon. Those serving as Deacons are Don Cooper, Bruce Willard, Stewart Brown, Alan Cooper, Clarence Pittman, Terry Cooper, Davis Boggess and Seth Jones.

Corinth Christian Church is located in the Birdie Community on Highway 512 about 10 miles from Lawrenceburg.

FAIRVIEW CHRISTIAN

Ninety-eight years ago on September of 1891, 39 persons gathered at the little hamlet of Fairview, located in the northern sector of Washington County, and organized the Fairview Christian Church. Organization of the church at Fairview in 1891 was directed by Brother John Marcum and Brother J. A. Sims. The plot of land contained two acres, on which the meeting house for the newly organized congregation was erected and acquired in October, 1889.

Old records indicate that it was originally intended that the congregation of worshippers at Fairview should be known as the Yawith Lick Christian Church, the name resulting from the fact that the church grounds were situated "on the waters of Yawith Lick Creek." However, by the time the sponsors of the project got around to the business of formally organizing the church, it had been decided they would be known as the Church of Christ at Fairview, Washington County, KY.

The land on which the Fairview Church building was erected, probably in the spring and summer of 1891, dedicated in 1894, was acquired from Thomas Welch Sr. and Mary Welch, his daughter, by N. S. Hahn, Thomas Brown and G. K. Mitchell, "trustees of the Yawith Lick Christian Church House."

The minutes of the first meeting of the sponsors for the Fairview church are very brief. They merely state that "The church of the Disciples of Christ was organized at Fairview, Washington County, KY. on September 9, 1891, by Bro. John Marcum, assisted by Bro. J. A. Sims, with total membership of 39 disciples.

Thomas, Brown, John T. Gillis and A. J. Moore were set apart by fasting and prayer and appropriate readings and commendations from the writings of the Apostles of Jesus Christ as Elders, after which the congregation was led in prayer by elder Thomas Brown and the meeting adjourned.

The original congregation of the Fairview Church included persons prominent in the northern sector of Washington County 90 years ago. Family names on the first roll of the congregation included: Wilham, Mitchell, Brown, Gillis, Dennis, Moore, Goff, Maddox, Brothers, Searcy, Hahn, Snider and Fenncil. Descendants of most of the charter members now attend services of the church.

There have been many wonderful ministers of God who have graced the pulpit of the Fairview Christian Church over the years, they are as follows:

Ezra Sparrow - Lawrenceburg, KY.	October 1942 - Jan. 1943
G. E. Roberts - Willisburg, KY.	Jan. 1943 - 1950
O.W. Baylor - Versailles, KY.	1950 1951
Jack McCommis - Louisville, KY.	1952 - 1953
Orvil Bean - Louisville, KY.	1954 - 1955
E. Paul Perry - Alton, KY.	1956 - 1959
James Mobley - Harrodsburg, KY.	1959 - 1962
George Martin - Freetown, Ind.	1962 - 1976
Paul R. Jackson II - Chillicothe, Ohio	Mar. 1977 - Mar. 1980
Billy D. Ford - Pikeville, KY	July 1980 - present

FELLOWSHIP BAPTIST

Not many years after the Civil War had ended, a Primitive Baptist Church was located on the Hammonds Creek Road. All that remains of its site now is a small cemetery located across the road from the home of Billy Akins.

John R. Major and his family were members of this church. Among the rules of this church there was a regulation forbidding its members from having problems resolved by court action.

Later, John R. Major, while serving as administrator in the settlements of an estate, was confused by a technicality in a will. All the heirs were in complete agreement. But in order to make the settlement valid, Mr. Major and the heirs asked the court to interpret the law involved.

For doing this the Primitive Baptist Church excluded Mr. Major for "going to the law". This action of the church created a division among its members. It was a friendly suit. The court procedure was taken only for the protection of the heirs benefiting from this estate.

The membership of this church became hopelessly divided. Some of its members contend that, since it was a friendly suit, (not a fight in court) John R. Major should not have been excluded. Other members insisted for enforcement of the rules of the church.

This division resulted in a complete split in the church. The group who supported Mr. Major decided to form another church organization. Mr. Major donated a lot in a corner, located on his farm, near a large pond, which according to tradition was wallowed out by bears. hence, the location became known as "Bear Wallow"

In the deed to the church lot a reverting clause existed. This provided that should the building erected on this lot cease to be used for church services, it would revert to John R. Major or his heirs.

A few years later the organization meeting in this church became completely inactive. And, for a time, no services were being held here.

About this time a young minister, W. D. Moore, began having regular services in this building. As yet, no organized church has been formed, but interest in regular church services developed in the community. The church building became known as the "Church of Good Fellowship". Eventually, some people living in the community took action toward the organizing of a Baptist church.

So, in the year 1882, a group of charter members met together. We are only able to recall the names of the following: Mrs. Jennie Jenson, Mr. and Mrs. James Long, Mr. and Mrs. John R. Hedger, Mr. and Mrs. James Grugin, Mr. and Mrs. W. J. Martin, Mr. and Mrs. E. A. Roberts, and Mr. and Mrs. Rowland Lane. The following ministers were present to form an Advisory Council: J. P. Sampson, J. T. Hedger, S. S. Perry, and John Morgan. Loss of records prevents us from having a complete list of members forming the organization of this church which took the name, "Fellowship Baptist Church".

The following pastors served this church during its early years: H. P. Hatchett, Gerret Reed, W. D. Moore, E. W. Summers, E. H. Blakeman, and W. T. Martin, Jr.

These ministers served under grave difficulties and genuine sacrifice. For example, E. W. Summers had to ride 65 miles on horseback from his home in Spencer County, every month, to give his pastoral services. The salary at that time was $25.00 a year. This is astonishing to us now, but money was hard to get then. Tobacco was bringing only five cents per pound on the market. Most of the members were share croppers with large families to support.

There was always a genuine spirit of hospitality among the people. Although their financial support was meager, they shared with their pastors of the produce from their farms. Their pastors were always welcomed in their homes.

In order to attend the services of this church the people rode in buggies, farm wagons, horseback, while many walked across fields and over dirt roads.

It was during the early years of this century, when they were finding it most difficult to continue, that Elmo Royalty became its pastor in the year 1909. He led the church to try a forward step. Under his leadership the members rallied from feelings of discouragement. Although facing attitudes of uncertainty, and often opposition, his work with the church proved to be effective.

The church building was needing repair, and the dirt road had bad places in it that often prevented attendance at the church. Mr. Royalty recruited voluntary help to make the needed repairs so that more people would attend church services. We are unable to know how many years this man of God spent in self-denying service for this church. He was a blessing to the church and the community.

Beginning in the year 1913, R. E. Booker served this church for two years as its pastor. Then, after 18 years of missionary work in mining camps. lumber camps, and destitute churches in the mountains of Eastern Kentucky, he and his family returned to Anderson County. He learned that Fellowship Church had not held any services for 10 years. When people tried to get to the church in automobiles, instead of the means of travel used in the past, they found the dirt road impossible. The dirt road was muddy most of the year.

So, most of the members lost interest in Fellowship church. All but 37 of its members moved their membership to churches more attractive to them. These 37 members at that time had only the church membership they used to have. They building had been sold, and the lumber in it used in the erection of a dwelling house.

R. E. Booker made visits in every home in the community, had prayer, and Bible reading with the families. At his own expense, he placed Bibles in 25 homes that were without reading matter of any kind.

This led to the organization of a Sunday school which met in the Hampton School House. New interest in re-building the church was being felt, but money was hard to get during those years of the depression. The Sunday school and church services had to be held for nine years in the school house.

Regardless of handicaps and discouragements, the members worked loyally with R. E. Booker as their pastor. Even with just the one room school building as its meeting place, a good Sunday school, training union, and workers' training courses, contributed to the development of a faithful church.

Finally, on November 29, 1941, the present house of worship was dedicated. It was built mostly with labor donated by members and friends of the church. Much of the money spent for materials came from members and friends of the church belonging to the churches nearby.

In the year 1958, R. E. Booker retired from the pastorate after serving the church for 25 years. Under the leadership of pastors who succeeded him, this church is proving to be well established in all phases of its work in its community.

The pastors from 1958 when Bro. Booker retired are: Jimmy Williams, Joe Loy, William Johnson, Bob Bottome, David Dean, Dale Huff, Bill Ivey, John Strange, Bob Mahan, James Kinney, Stephen Hoskins, Oscar Rose, Jim Hendricks, James Lee Fesler, and Gary Drury is the present pastor.

Our oldest member in 1989 is Rosie Thurman.

FIRST BAPTIST

In was a beautiful day in June 1834 that 85 brothers and sisters in Christ met to establish a Baptist Church in Lawrenceburg. A three week revival was conducted in June 1834, during which time there were many professions of faith. Dr. Silas M. Noel, one of the foremost ministers of Kentucky, having been among the founders of Georgetown College, assisted in the organization of the church and preached the sermon, using as his text Acts 2:41: " Then they that gladly received the word were baptized and the same day there were added unto them about 3,000 souls." He was assisted in the organizing of the church by Rev. Jordan H. Walker and Rev. E. Duval.

The first business session was July 5, 1834, with William Hickman serving as the first church clerk. The first moderator was J. Lancaster, and the first persons to join the church were Garland Lillard, Ephriam Lillard, Chris Lillard. Dicy Lillard, Eli Penny and Polly Penny. The first deacons were Eli Penny and Jame G. White.

Immediately after the organization the church appointed a building committee. It was June 15, 1835, that a lot was purchased on Woodford Street, about where the health Department is located. A small building was erected here to serve as the house of worship until 1862 when the property was sold.

Jordon H. Waler was called as the first pastor. Thomas Jefferson Fisher was called to be pastor, but for some reason failed to meet most of him monthly appointments, and Elder Eli Penny preached for the congregation. The present pastor, Bob C. Jones, has served as pastor longer than any other pastor. He came to First Baptist Church, from Northside Baptist Church, Mayfield, Kentucky on October 26, 1966.

In November 1870, Christopher M. Lillard and wife, Frances, conveyed to the trustees, the one-half acre of land upon which the present structure stands. The building was soon completed and a record of its appearance: "The church house is built of hard brick with a commodious basement with 8-foot ceilings, and admirably arranged for Sabbath school and committee rooms. The church house proper is 40 feet by 60 feet with high ceilings, well ventilated with vestibule and belfry 3 stories in height." The side walls and windows remain today. On Tuesday morning, January 8, 1924, a fire of unknown origin but believed to have started in the furnace room, did considerable damage to the church and destroyed the organ. The remodeled building was lacking the tall steeple and bells, but additional

Sunday School rooms were included. The present organ was installed.

A $60,000 Sunday School annex was built in 1953. In July, 1959, the church sold the parsonage at 118 North Main and purchased the present parsonage on Donna Drive. A new Sunday School unit with modern kitchen equipment and Fireside Room was built in 1960 at a cost of $91,000

In 1974, the church purchased the Simpson property adjacent to the church. Furloughing missionaries have lived in the house since that time. It was named the Zora Carter Memorial Missionary House as the purchase was made possible by her bequest.

The sanctuary was renovated in 1976. The balcony was enlarged to seat twice as many people, the seating capacity downstairs was increased by tearing out Sunday School rooms in the front, a ramp was built, the organ and piano were repositioned, clear shatterproof covering for the stained glass windows was installed and a public address system was installed.

Special ministries include Tele-News which began in 1976. By dialing 839-6977, church and community news and a devotional can be heard seven days a week, 24 hours a day. First Baptist began television ministry on cable channel 22 in 1984. The church has a bus ministry. A van was purchased in 1983 and the present bus in 1985.

The 150th Anniversary of First Baptist Church, Lawrenceburg, was celebrated

throughout the months of June through September in 1984. The Sesquicentennial Celebration Climax was on Sunday, September 30. A gospel concert and cutting of the birthday cake was held on Saturday evening. Approximately 735 persons were in attendance on Sunday for the worship service, dinner at the Anderson Middle School and for the afternoon ceremony. A special Box, "time capsule," containing historical items, has been placed in front of the church to be opened in 2034. Former pastors, staff members, federal, state and local officials, along with many distinguished guests and former members, were present.

A Prayer Room was completed in 1988. The room is beautiful decorated and furnished and was made possible through gifts given in memory of loved ones.

On Sunday, February 12, 1989, the church voted to build a Christian Life Center for approximately $550,000. $200,000 has to be raised before an architect is employed. As of May 10, 1989, $152,000 has been received and an additional $40,000 pledged making the total of gifts and commitments, $192,000.

The membership includes 915 resident members, 277 nonresident members - total membership of 1,192. The budget this year is $331,500. This past year the church gave over $84,000 through the Cooperative Program and other mission causes.

FIRST PRESBYTERIAN

Our history beings in the spring of 1828, just one year after Lawrenceburg was designated the county seat of Kentucky's 82nd county, Anderson The record indicated "for many years this place had been proverbial for its iniquity. Wickedness of almost every kind had reigned unmolested; and it was scarcely possible to induce the citizens to go and hear a discourse from a passing preacher. Those who were formerly accustomed to visit this place for its religious benefit had become discouraged and ceased their attendance here. A praying individual took up his residence in this place and while engaged in family worship he afforded amusement to many; and when he appointed prayer meetings none but slaves could be induced at first to attend. However, her persevered and their scoffing was turned into sighing and their sneer exchanged for supplication."

Just prior to the organization of the church in June 1828, a series of revival meetings, largely sponsored by Judge W. H. McBrayer, resulted in the winning of 23 confessions of faith. Charter members were, Thomas Q. Roberts, Mrs. Harriet Roberts, Mary Roberts, Mrs. Lydia Mizner, Susan Bush, W. K. Vanarsdale, Miss C. B. Roberts, Ann Dawson, Lucy Clark, T. Phillips, Sarah Boggess, Winny Phillips, Jane Fitzgerald, Sarah Ashford, Nancy Hudgins, Harriett Phillips, Martha McBrayer, Barbara Wallace, Jane Boston, Robert McMichael, Thomas Paxton, F. A. Olds, and Fielding L. Conner. The Rev. J. R. Moreland was moderator, and Mr. W. K. Vanarsdale and Mrs. F. L. Conner were first elders.

Also belonging to the church were the slaves of white members, and some of them reportedly were quite faithful not only in attendance, but participated freely in the services, not in our records as "a person of color."

Early in 1826 Fielding L. Conner bought a small plot of ground on the south side of Woodford Street from William Hudgins for $25. It was upon this quarter acre plot of ground that the Presbyterians built their small brick building some time in 1834. It fronted on Woodford Street, and as was the custom in all early churches, there were two front doors — one for men, the other for women and children. Trustees of this church were Dixon G. Dedmon, James B. Wallace and Robert McMichael. James G. Rannells, first sexton, was employed at ten dollars per year, and he was instructed to have the building in readiness for all services. Furthermore, the church offered the use of their new edifice to the Cumberland Presbyterians, the Methodists, and the Baptists at any time they might need it for special services.

The first church building was destroyed by windstorm, rebuilt, and suffered a second windstorm disaster in 1858 or 1859, It was never rebuilt at this location. The lot was sold to Mr. L. J. Witherspoon in 1879 for $250 in a trade that involved the purchase of a lot 50 feet by 75 feet at the corner of Main and Woodford Streets for $600. Due to windstorm damage, the Civil War, and resulting Reconstruction period, for about 20 years there was no church building and for 12 years no public services. It was presumed by many that the Presbyterian witness would be abandoned in Lawrenceburg. Then in 1880 after a year of construction a new brick building was dedicated. It was completely paid for when occupied.

It was just at the close of services on Palm Sunday morning 1905 that the church building caught fire and was completely destroyed. A new structure (our present building) was erected for the sum of $7000. It was freed of debt when dedicated just eight months after the fire. In 1906 a pipe organ, the first in Anderson County, was installed. The present building has been damaged at least twice by windstorms, the latest during a tornado which struck Lawrenceburg on November 2, 1965. Our church now has an annex building which was once a distillery warehouse. The annex now contains several Sunday school rooms, a fellowship hall, and a pastor's study.

Currently our membership numbers 75. At present the church has members of the families of three former pastors: Mrs. J. D. (Martha) Collins, the daughter of the Rev. D. T. Brandenburg, Mrs. J. T. (Alice) Cox, Jr., the daughter of the Rev. Tyler Davis, Mrs. Edward (Virginia) McCormick and Mrs. Larry (Charlotte) Harley, wife and daughter of the Rev. Edward McCormick.

Many fine pastors have graced our pulpit. A brief listing of the more prominent are: Rev. J. Hawthorne 1828-1846, Rev. M. Douglas 1870-1874, Dr. J. Sprole Lyons 1883-1890, Rev. W. J. Davis 1891-1895, Rev. J. W. Tyler 1896-1900, Rev. Llewellyn Humphrey 1903-1907, Rev. J. E. Parl 1912-1917, Rev. William McKay 1921-1928, Rev. J. Tyler Davis 1928-1930, Rev. D. J. Brandenburg 1932-1935, Dr. J.J. Rice 1935-1940, Dr. A. B. Rhodes 1940-1942, Dr. Edward Golden 1949-1950, and Rev. Edward McCormick serving our congregation as a seminary student 1948-1949 and returning to our church as pastor from 1977 to his retirement in 1987. Our present pastor, Rev. Peter Zinn came to us in 1988.

Truly our fine church has a rich history, steeped in tradition and faith. The sheer longevity of this fellowship is a testimony to our proud and strong heritage. Many fine citizens have pledged their steadfast loyalty and faith in our ministry to Anderson County. There have been times of hardship and hindrance, but we have continued to thrive. God willing, another 160 years will be graced upon our church.

GLENSBORO CHRISTIAN

The village of Glensboro is located on highway 44, approximately 10 miles west of Lawrenceburg, along Salt River. The village that is now called Glensboro was first founded in 1847 with three residences in the village at that time. The village has been called by several names - Camdenville or Camden, Orr, and finally Glensboro.

In 1853 a Christian Church was erected. Among its first officers were W. A. Stevens, R. J. Milton, Silas Jones, and Elijah Orr. The pioneer minister was Elder Eleven Merritt, who is buried at the Antioch Christian Church in Washington County.

A new church building to replace the original building was begun in August 1950. The first service in the new building was held on April 29, 1951. Homer McAfee was called in May of 1951 to be the first preacher in the new building. In 1984 an addition to the building included a multi-purpose room on the lower level, and a baptistry and two Sunday School rooms on the upper level. In 1988 a parsonage was built on the Steven property in back of the church. This is now occupied by the Youth Minister.

Several ministers, well-known in Anderson County, have served the church, including - Ezra Sparrow (Jan. 1925 - Dec. 1927), Raymond Sparrow (Feb. 1942 - Dec. 1945), and C. Marion Railey (Jan. 1947 - Mar. 1949).

The ministers since the new building was constructed in 1951 are:

Homer McAfee (May 1951 - Dec. 1953)
Jim Quisenberry (Jan 1954 - Nov. 1956)
Gene Welsch (Jan 1957 - August 1959)
Edgar Yates (Sept. 1959 - Aug. 1965)
Cleon Wright (Nov. 1965 - Sept. 1966)
Phillip Farnsley (Nov. 1966 - May 1968)
Donald G. Weldon (Nov. 1968 - Mar. 1970)
William A. Mounts (June 1970 - Oct. 1973)
David Johnson (May 1974 - Feb. 1977)
C. Truman McClain (June 1977 - Mar. 1989)

At present the church is without a minister but a call was extended in May, 1989 to Dale Parrish. He accepted the call and is to begin his ministry in September of 1989.

Glensboro Christian Church has an active youth program and at the present time, Heath Sherman, a student at Kentucky Christian College, is the youth minister. Glensboro Christian believes that the youth ministry is an important part of religious education, in order to equip and train our young people for life in the days ahead.

Serving as Elders for the congregation are:

Calvin Morgan
Jim Cattlett
Rick Boggs
Carlos Boggs
Randall Shouse

Serving as Deacons are:

George Ward
Harry Shely
Dick Wiedo
Gordon Catlett
Stanley Casey
Bill Shely
Don Shely
Elmer "Wig" Edmonson
Larry Armstrong
Albert Shely

Sunday School Superintendent is Rick Boggs, Assistant Sunday School Superintendent is Gordon Catlett. Song leaders are Calvin Morgan and George Ward. Organist is Lisa Brown and Pianist in Linda Shouse.

Custodians are Elmer W. and Irene Edmonson.

The Glensboro Christian Church is one of the many small churches found throughout this area, but its influence extends far beyond the immediate village of Glensboro. The church is proud of its past and look forwards to the future to proclaim the Gospel, teach the Word of God, and present the principles of Christianity to all who will hear.

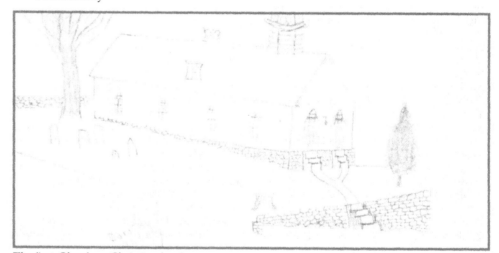

The first Glensboro Christian faced west.

The present church faces north.

GOLDEN PATHWAY FELLOWSHIP

Golden Pathway Fellowship Church has a very short history. It has only been in existence since April 23, 1989. Golden Pathway Fellowship is a non-denominational full gospel church. It is based on the inspired Word of God, the Holy Bible.

The pastor G. T. "Joe" Gay was called into the ministry in 1983, while still living in Frankfort. Joe in a 1985 graduate of Rhema Bible Training Center in Tulsa, Oklahoma.

The church began by having services on Sunday morning. When attendance increased, Thursday night Bible study began. Approximately three months later, Sunday night services began.

Golden Pathway Fellowship is located at 207 South Main Street. The building is approximately 100 years old. It is the former meeting place of Lawrenceburg United Methodist Church, which had moved to its new facility located on Carlton Drive.

Pastor Gay and his wife, Margaret are the parents of three children: Larry Gay of Frankfort, Danny Gay of Berea, and Misty Beasley of Lawrenceburg.

Pastor Joe, Margaret, and Misty began their pastorate at Golden Pathway Fellowship with high hopes and great expectations for spreading the good news of the gospel of Jesus Christ.

The first decisions for accepting Jesus Christ as their Savior was July 2, 1989. The decisions were made by Clydia Carpenter and her two daughters Crystal and Connie Carpenter and Tanya Thompson.

The first water baptismal service was September 17, 1989 at Fintville in Woodford County. The following were baptized: Clydia, Crystal, and Connie Carpenter, Michael Mitchell, Brian Pack, and Antonia Dials. Assisting Pastor Gay was Emory Dials.

Dedication services were conducted by Pastors David and Betty Lampkin, of Rivers of Life Teaching Center of Frankfort on May 20, 1989.

There were 50 people in attendance at this service.

The first guest speaker was Mary Frances Varallo from Nashville, Tennessee on June 30, 1989 for three days of evangelistic teaching.

October 7, 1989 was Golden Pathway Fellowships first gospel singing made up of several groups from Margaret's co-workers at GTE Fluorescent Lamp Plant in Versailles, Kentucky. There were 70 people in attendance.

Golden Pathway Fellowship donates its facility to Girl Scout Troop #722. It is a Brownie Troop lead by Peggy Jeffers Hatter,

assisted by her daughter Jennifer Jeffers, Brownies are: Shelly Cheuvront, Jillian Pence, Jessica Grigsby, Amanda Gibson, Natasha Alves, and Lucy Rucker.

The first service on April 23, 1989 was attended by Pastor Joe Gay, Margaret Gay, Misty Beasley and Misty's fiance, Christopher McGaughey.

Presently attending services are Pastor Joe and Margaret Gay, Misty Beasley, Christopher McGaughey, Ben and sharol Byrd, Michael Mitchell, Emory and Teresa Dials and their three children, Angie and Brian Pack and "Toni" Dials; Clydia, Crystal, and Connie Carpenter; Connie Tackett, her son Michaels and granddaughter, Kelsey; bobby and Betty Hatter and their grandchildren Jennifer and Casey Hatter.

Golden Pathway Fellowship's pastor's vision is to assist in producing strong, capable, ethical individuals in the body of Christ.

Our first wedding at Golden Pathway Fellowship was a renewal of vows for Ronita Osborn Leach and Earl C. Leach, Jr. on their eighth anniversary, Jan. 20, 1990.

Golden Pathway Fellowship, 207 S. Main Street. Pictured, front, Misty Beasley, Betty Lowe Hatter, Bobby Hatter, Peggy Jeffers Hatter, Casey Hatter, Denise Rice, Crystal Carpenter, Jason Nichols, Brian Nichols, Margaret Gay and Pastor Joe Gay. Center, Jennifer Jeffers, Brian Pack, Toni Dials, Connie Carpenter, Margaret Nichols. Back, Christopher McGaughey, Don Southworth, Robby Hatter, Beverly Chambers, Clydia Carpenter, John Nichols, Teresa Dials, Connie Carpenter, Darlene Rice, Sharol Byrd and Ben Byrd.

GOSHEN BAPTIST

Goshen Baptist Church's history cannot be separated from that of Salt River Church, constituted in 1798 with six members and one slave girl. John Penny, one of the founders of Salt River, was chosen pastor of that church in April 1799. He served the church continuously until his death in 1833.

In December 1811, 29 members from Salt River asked for a constitution which was granted. They formed Goshen Church, organized January 4, 1812 by John Penny, Sr. and William Heckman, Jr. The church consisted of 19 white members and 10 slaves. For more than a year members of the new church met in private homes.

On August 1, 1812, Jackson and Patsy Weatherford of Mercer County sold one acre of land located on Salt River in Mercer County to Nathaniel Burrus and Jesse Slaughter, trustees of Goshen Baptist Church, for fifty cents. In the spring of 1813 a small building of hewn logs was completed, and the first service was held in the meeting house in April 1813. An addition of 20 feet was made to the house in 1829, by which time the congregation had increased to 107. The building, in very bad repair, was sold in 1870 to F. M. Morris for $30.00. Logs were later sold for $50.00 and used in the construction of a barn.

Goshen Church met in Lyceum Schoolhouse from 1870 to 1889. In 1887 Bro. Dudley Moore began to promote a move to a new site. James H. and Nancy Hendricks deeded a parcel of land in Anderson County to Goshen on August 30, 1888. On the same date, J. B. and Nancy Case deeded a parcel of land to the church which adjoined that given by the Hendricks. Men of the community contributed logs for lumber, hours of labor, and helped in other ways. The new building was dedicated on September 29, 1889.

In 1910 James Gash, Verna Gash, Nora Gash, Bertram Gash, Charles Royalty, Ethel Royalty, Katie Vanarsdel, Lulie Robinson, and Mr. and Mrs. S.L. Edwards were dismissed to assist in the organization of Kirkwood Baptist Church.

In 1927 Bro. Dudley Moore was called for life. On August 5, 1935 he died from injuries received in an automobile accident.

The church voted in 1946 to remodel the church building and add Sunday School rooms. The Sunday School addition was dedicated in 1949. More remodeling was completed in the years 1987 - 1989.

Pastors who have served the church are as follows: John Penny, 1812 - 1822; W. W. Penny, 1822 - 1833; Jordan H. Walker, 1834 - 1839; John Dean, 1840 - 1844; B. F. Keeling, 1845 - 1847; S. S. Perry, 1848 - 1865; D. W. Case, 1865 - 1866; S. S. Perry, 1866 - 1867; David Bruner, 1867 - 1868; S. S. Perry 1869 - 1873; J. T. Hedger, 1873 - 1874; P. S. G. Watson, 1874; J. T. Hedger, 1874 - 1875; B. F. Adkins, 1876 - 1877; S. S. Perry, 1877 - 1880; J. T. Hedger, 1881 - 1884; H. P. Hatchett, 1885 - 1886; W. D. Moore, 1886 - 1909; Garrett Reed, 1910 - 1911; D. A. Dailey, 1912 - 1915; J. S. Kirby, 1916 - 1917; Elmo Royalty, 1918 - 1920; Garrett Reed, 1921 - 1922; O. R. Mosley, 1923 - 1924; Geffinger Judd, 1925 - 1926; W. D. Moore, 1927 - 1935; Gilbert Shely, 1935 - 1942; Young Gerrard, 1942 - 1944; Bill Watson, 1944 - 1945; John Schneider, 1945 - 1949; Wm. "Pete" Evans, 1949 - 1952; Walter Nolan, 1952 - 1955; Bill McCrary, 1955 - 1958; J. Alvin Hardy, 1958 - 1964; Richard Croft, 1964 - 1965; Herbert Gibson, 1965 - 1967; Edward Hankin, 1967 - 1969; Alan Woodward, 1969 - 1972; Robert Lewis, 1972 - 1975; Lawrence Tunks, 1975 - 1976; Tim Estes, 1976 - 1977; Fred Knickerbocker, 1977 - 1987, James L. Moon, Jr., 1987 - .

LAWRENCEBURG CHURCH OF CHRIST

In 1950 R. A. Craig, a preacher and realtor in Shelbyville, Kentucky, and his wife found several families and individuals in Anderson County who identified themselves as members of the Church of Christ. Then the Craigs, along with Cora Cheak, Raymond Cheak, Mary Mountjoy, Veril D. and Ruby Moore and their family, and Frances Royalty and her children began assembling on Sunday afternoons in the Anderson County Court House. They did not claim to be the only members of Christ's church in Anderson County, but they pledged allegiance only to Christ and admonished everyone to drop their denomination names and creeds and become united as one body in Christ. Thus, they called themselves the Church of Christ.

The Christians worked together to pattern their worship, doctrines, and lives after the teachings and examples designated in the Holy Scriptures, to grow in their faith, to stimulate one another to love and good deeds, and to proclaim the Gospel of Christ.

By 1952 the church had grown, so they purchased the house at 558 South Main Street from Mrs. Mayme Franklin for $10,000. The residence was used as a meeting place for the church, a home for the preacher, and a rented upstairs apartment. R. A. Craig, V. D. Moore, Raymond Cheak, Lee Gentry, and Clarence Eastham were named as trustees to sign for the loan. Before long they began meeting regularly on Sunday morning, Sunday evening, and Wednesday evening.

Charles Cheatham became the first designated preacher in 1958. Before this time R. A. Graig, Harding Lowry and several others taught and preached for the congregation.

In 1960 the group consisted of around 40 members and a more adequate facility was needed for the church's assemblies. Therefore, the trustees, Charles Lee Bertram and Glen Wooters, went to Garfield Heights Church in Indianapolis, Indiana and borrowed $15,000 to construct a brick building with seven classrooms and an auditorium which would seat 150 people. The members, their families, and friends worked along with the Paden Construction Company to tear down the old house and erect the new facility on the property. Members of the Baptist, Christian, Methodist, and Presbyterian churches helped with the construction. The dedication service was held October 9,

1960. Dr. Adrian Doran, president of the Morehead State College, and Harding Lowry were the dedicatory speakers.

Harold Driskell(1960), Glenn Wooters (1961 - 1962), John Moore (1963 - 1964), Stokley Hall (1965 - 1966), Oral Morgan (1966 - 1968) and Willie Long (1969 - 1970) were supported as ministers for the congregation during the 1960's. During this decade the congregation grew to an average Sunday morning worship attendance of 63. In the 1970's, Amos Gardner (1971 - 1973), Mike Withrow (1974 - 1976), and Mel Martin (1977 - 1979) were supported as ministers and the attendance grew to an average of 73. Mike Withrow was the first minister who received all of his financial support from the congregation. The other preachers had full-time secular jobs.

Howard Emerson (1980 -1 982), Darrell Simon (1984 - 1988), Ray Bertram (1988) and Burt Paden (present) were the regularly supported ministers in the 1980's. By the end of 1983 the average attendance had grown to 58 and it remained around 60 for the rest of the decade.

The Lawrenceburg Church of Christ has always been active in benevolent work and the spreading of the gospel of Christ. Members have actively provided financial assistance, food, shelter, clothing, bedding and cooking utensils to the needy. Some members went to Cherokee, North Carolina to proclaim the gospel, and some helped set up exhibits at two world fairs to share the good news. Also, the church has sent sup-

port to missionaries in India. But the congregation has primarily touched the lives of people here in Anderson County as they were taught of God's saving grace through Jesus Christ and the abundant life one finds in Him.

Although the Lawrenceburg Church of Christ has become recognized as one of the many denominations in Anderson County, the plea of the congregation is for all the disciples of Christ to be undenominational and to speak the same things in love. Since the Bible is the only source of truth revealed from God to man, those who claim to be His followers must search the scriptures diligently to know the truth, and put aside the teachings and practices of men. Then they will be able to be one body in one Spirit with one hope, one Lord, one faith, one baptism, and one God and Father of all who is over all and through all and in all.

Our Lord Jesus Christ earnestly prayed that his disciples might be perfected in unity so the world would come to know the love of God. However, many divisions prevail and the work of Christ's church is greatly hindered. The churches in Anderson County need to work together to pattern their worship, doctrines and lives after the teachings and examples designated in the Holy Scriptures. If the denominational walls can be torn down and the various congregations will unite as the churches of Christ in Anderson County, spiritual history will be made and God will be glorified through our Lord Jesus Christ.

NINEVAH CHRISTIAN

Ninevah Christian Church was established on 3-1-1871. The one-room building and property were purchased from Elizabeth Neal at the price of $10.00. The Trustees were: B. F. Watts, W. T. Taylor, and C. D. Neal. In the early years, the preacher was often paid with garden produce and chickens.

Over the years, many changes have been made to the original structure. In the 1940's, electricity was installed. During the 1950's, two Sunday school rooms were added to the building. In the 1960's, two more Sunday school rooms were built. Also, at this time, the coal oil stoves were replaced with electric furnaces. The minister at this time was Joe Wilhoite. The parsonage was also built in the 1960's. The minister at that time was Merle Farnsworth. In the early 1980's, while Ron O'Reilly was minister, a fellowship hall was added to the back of the original building. At this time, a baptistry was installed. Before this time, people were baptised in the Kentucky River and local ponds. In the late 1980's, air conditioning was installed and an outdoor shelter was built. Doug Martin was minister at the time.

Many of the ministers wee students from the Louisville Bible College, Cincinnati Bible College, and Kentucky Christian College. The present minister is Brother Truman McClain. The present elders are: Rudy Gay, Jim Sayre, and Warren Marshall. The deacons are: Bart Sayre, George Doss, A. L. Drury, and Terry Gash.

Although plans are underway at this time to build a new church building, services are still held in the original building. Even though it isn't used, the kerosene chandelier is still hanging in the sanctuary. The original communion set is in the possession of Mr. and Mrs. Jim Sayre. Many of the present members are descendants of the original charter members.

The kerosene chandelier is still hanging in the sanctuary. Holding the orginal communion set are Warren Marshall and Jim Sayre.

Bro. Truman McClain is the present minister.

PLEASANT HILL CHRISTIAN

The Pleasant High Christian Church was first located on Pleasant Grove Ridge and known as the Pleasant Grove Christian Church. The land for the first church was given by Mr. Bill Cook and was located next to the Pleasant Grove Baptist Church. The churches often opened their doors for the others use. Back then preaching was only once a month and there were large crowds. Joseph Best opened gates to his farm (across from the churches) and let people park cars here. George Best continued this practice after the death of his father, Joseph.

In 1927 the Christian church was in need of repairs and they decided to move it to a location on what is now Highway 44 across the road from the Best Cemetery. This location would make it convenient for funerals. The building was moved on wagons and one big truck. The workers were Zebedee Sutherland, George Best, Arch Shely, Jim Warford, and Henry Noel. Peyton Simpson couldn't help with the work because he operated a store in Glensboro but he furnished all the nails. Will Hazelwood was hired to lay the hardwood floor.

At the suggestion of Mrs. Owen Franklin, the name of the church was changed to Pleasant Hill Christian Church.

In 1961, lightning struck the church and destroyed it. The Board borrowed money to rebuild, and in a few years were debt free.

Some of the preachers at the Pleasant Grove Christian Church were Davie Campbell, William Bentley, Brother Sims, Lewis Cull, W. I. Peel, and Raymond Sparrow.

Some of the preachers at the Pleasant Hill Christian Church until 1977 were Raymond Sparrow, Elbert Winkler, W. I. Peel, Miner Bottoms, Paul Perry, Arthur Clark, Jack Hampton, Claude Waldridge, Van Hunt, and Richard Amerine.

The unincorporated Pleasant Hill Christian Church was founded as a Christian church only and not as a "Disciples of Christ" church. On March 24, 1969, this church was incorporated as the "Pleasant Hill Christian Church" with power to exercise certain duties consistent with the laws of the Commonwealth.

The incorporators were Jewell Casey, Charles D. Shely, Earl Sutherland, Lister C. Murphy, and Arch Shely.

Pleasant Hill Christian Church before being destroyed by lightning, 1961.

Pleasant Hill Christian Church after 1962.

ST. LAWRENCE CATHOLIC

St. Lawrence Church dedicated in 1952. (E. Garrison)

The first appearance of any active organization of the Catholic Church in Anderson County may be traced to the date of April 28, 1873 with the purchase of land for a possible church. The lot purchased was on the East side of Main Street, apparently just north of the present Klink's Store. Efforts were made to build a church. In reality, only a cornerstones and a possible foundation were accomplished. The reasons would appear, namely a priest caring for the congregation lived in Danville, and one would assume the financial means was not great.

A number of names appear in this early Catholic settlement. The names include John Dowling, and his wife, Mary Anne Murphy. Other name appearing were Rice, Foley, Shananhan, Chapman, Ware, McGrath, Horan and four families by the name of McCarthy, also name of Hughes and Lannon appear.

In 1894 under the efforts of Father Paul Volk, they bought on Gatewood a building formerly used as a school. The building was remodeled and converted to a church. For some reason the church became known at St. James the Less. A dedication ceremony

was held on July 15, 1894 with about 250 people from the town of Lawrenceburg and a number from Lexington attending.

The people noted earlier as a portion of the settlement simply disappeared from Anderson County with the exception of the Dowling family and most of those born to this family moved away. The result was only a very small group. The building fell into bad repair. One asks, why such a collapse? Perhaps it was due to lack of finance but also possibly the building was not too substantial. Its condition was so bad that it was abandoned around 1921 and eventually torn down around 1939.

The so called Dowling House built in 1886 occupies a prominent place in history because there were periods when Mass was said there and there were periods when the home of Mrs. Gilbert was used. Priests came at various times from Danville but at certain period from Harrodsburg and Rose Hill. In the period of 1925 to 1948, priests came from Versailles and Mass was said on the second floor room of the building now used as Klink's Drug Store.

The present church on Gatewood was completed in 1952 by the united efforts of the people and Father Gabriel Germann. Mass was said in this building for the first time on March 11, 1952 and was dedicated by Archbishop John A. Florsh on June 4, 1952. Incidentally the church once more was known as St. Lawrence. Father Gabriel was a resident in Harrodsburg and after him Father Julian Pank came from 1952 - 1960. Other priests, who would serve in years to come, would include Fathers Thomas, Caldwell, James Silver, French, Joseph F. Hayden, Bernard Boone, Henry Vessels, John Weyhing, Stanley Osborne, Joseph Miller and Robert DeWitt. Father Stanley Osborne, who had the spiritual care of St. Lawrence from 1974 - 1981, saw the erection of the Religion Education building and apartment for a priest. This is the brick building you see at 120 Gatewood.

In 1983, Father J. T. Blandford became a resident priest and still remains at St. Lawrence. He has seen a number of new families come here with the expansion of Lawrenceburg.

SAND SPRING BAPTIST

The Sand Spring story begins at the turn of the century with two revival meetings, one in a borrowed colored Baptist Church building in Ripyville, the other in the old Salt River Schoolhouse. On Monday, June 24, 1901, at Salt River School, Sand Spring Baptist Church was formed. B. F. Adkins, who had preached at the previous revival meetings, acted as moderator and Bro. W. D. Moore, a long-time farmer-preacher of Anderson county, acted as clerk. The minutes record that an opportunity was given for all those wishing to go into the congregation to do so and 37 presented themselves and were accordingly enrolled.

The new church was organized under the Articles of Faith and church Covenant found in J. M. Pendletone's Church Manual. They selected Bro. B. F. Adkins as pastor and Forrest Moore as clerk, and chose for the church name "Sand Spring." Mrs. Melissa Price, a charter member, suggested the name, which came from a spring on the plot of land donated by the Fallis family. This was the site of the first building and is where the church now stands. The congregation managed to put together $1600 needed to build the 36 x 30 foot building with a seating capacity for 250. The new building was dedicated debt free on June 29, 1902.

Bro. Adkins was pastor until late 1907 and in 1908 Bro. W. D. Moore accepted the call as pastor. He declined the call in 1909 and Bro. E. W. Summers became pastor in October, 1909. The church decided "if it suited the preacher, to have preaching twice a month during the year."

Bro. Summers resigned in August 1912 and Bro. Garrett Reed served the church through 1916. In 1917 Bro. E. W. Summers returned as pastor for two years, followed by C. T. Ricks (1920-21) and Zell Shaw (part of 1922).

A Sunday School annex was added to the original building in 1920 at a cost of $2800.

During the pastorate of J. E. Darter (1922-1925) the church grew to a membership of over 400 and began to have "full-time preaching."

Br. Darter was succeeded by Bert Gould (1926-1929). Under his leadership the church voted to build a basement under the existing structure.

In the first 30 years of existence, Sand Spring Baptist church grew from 37 members in 1901 to more than 10 time that membership in 1929.

The optimism that the Baptists of Sand Spring shared will all Americans in the period before 1929 was severely tested during the next 15 years. The men who led the church through this period of the Great Depression and World War II were H. H. McGinty (1930 - 1934) and M. D. Morton (1935 - 1945). During Br. McGinty's pastorate the membership passed the 500 mark.

M. D. Morton called in late 1934 served Sand Spring longer than any other pastor. It was he who led the church out of the Depression and the dark days of World War II. The main concern was for the young men of Sand Spring who went to war. During this time two service flags at the front of the church were decorated with stars, one for each man in the service. The weekly church bulletin kept members informed of those whom the church had nurtured through Sunday School and B.Y.P.U. This concern for servicemen continued during the wars in Korea and Vietnam.

During these trying times, the church continued to grow, the facilities were improved with electric lights and a furnace and a home was purchased for the pastor on the site of the present parsonage. Bro. Morton was recognized by the congregation through a resloution of appreciation for his untiring efforts and unfailing zeal.

The war was over in 1945, the boys came home and Bro. Roy A. Hamilton (1945 - 1948) became pastor. In 1948 the church was one of the largest rural churches in the Southern Baptist Convention. Bro. John W. Kruschwitz (1949-1955) became pastor in 1949. Under his leadership the church underwent extensive improvements in the structure, including the enlargements of the auditorium, additional Sunday School space, a choir loft, and a baptistry. The "new" church was dedicated on may 7, 1950. / On April 7, 1951, just 11 months after the dedication, the church building was destroyed by fire. Work began immediately on a new building due to the faith, courage, and determination of the people of the church. many friends gave encouragement and financial assistance.

On June 29, 1952, exactly one-half century from the dedication of the first building, the present Bedford stone structure was dedicated. Sand Spring later recalled its "debt of gratitude to Bro. John Kruschwitz for his faithful and loyal shouldering of the task of leadership in rebuilding."

Bro. Melvin E. Torstrick (1955 - 1957) became pastor in 1955. During his pastorate, on November 11, 1956, Sand Spring celebrated the retirement of the $40,000 debt on the new building.

Charles F. Jones was pastor from 1958-1959.

Pastor Hugh Brooks (1959 - 1961) began the Sand Spring Youth Choir program. The church's youth committee became active at this time. The youth ministers of the church, Jack Birdwhistell (1966-1970), David Smith, Jesse Gonzales, Hudson Slaughter, and David Charlton, the present youth minister, have also planned recreation programs.

After the pastorate of Hugh Brooks, the church turned toward a professional music ministry and music directors have included Bill Hawkins, Joe Slade, Bill Rideout, Bryan Burdette, Joe Hovater, Kevin Royalty, Gary Burton, Kirby Johnson, and presently Tony Whitfield.

Bro. Louis Twyman (1962 - 1965) continued the emphasis on Youth Ministry, taking the first group from Sand Spring to Ridgecrest Baptist Assembly. Under Bro. Twyman's leadership, the church started a direct mission endeavor to Eastern Kentucky. Also under his leadership, a new wing was added to the building.

Joseph W. Hinkle (1965 - 1967) added his own special concern for family centered ministry. By now a new generation of the "old families" was active, and the church had begun to benefit from a new influx of energetic and dedicated young couples.

Under Robert A. Hill (1968 - 1974) Sand Spring entered into a bus ministry. The details of this ministry involved a large number of men of the Brotherhood. A spacious new parsonage was built during Bro. Hills' pastorate.

Bill Messer (1974 - 1982) brought Eastern Kentucky to Sand Spring. Under Bro. Messer a Senior Adult Program was started and continues in full swing today.

In January, 1989, Dr. J. Terry Wilder, a native of North Carolina became the present pastor. Bro. Wilder's ministry continues to emphasize the mission heritage of Sand Spring. Annual giving to the Cooperative Program was increased to 21% of the church budget. Hands - on mission projects included sending teams of Baptist men and women to New Hampshire, Letcher County, Ky, and Pike County, Ky, to assist in the construction of new churches. The WMU observed the first Baptist Women's Day in 1988. The Brotherhood led in a project to place Bibles in the Soviet Union. In 1989, a new church bus was purchased for use by youth, senior adults, and mission teams.

In 1989, Sand Spring had 451 enrolled in Sunday School and a total membership of 983.

When each member asks himself the question, "What does Sand Spring mean to me?" The answer probably comes in the shape of persons who have touched his life. At Sand Spring many have encountered God, become Christians, courted future husbands and wives, received the church's comfort at a time of grief, and felt heart filled with pride at moments of accomplishment. For many longtime members, former pastors, and newcomers, Sand Spring, simply put, is "home."

SECOND CHRISTIAN

Pastor, Officers and Board members

When the Emancipation came, many new problems came, one of them related to their church affiliation. By then end of the War, 1865, there were four churches all white, they all had slaves in their congregation, yet altogether just enough for a small congregation. Nevertheless, Negro leaders encouraged by local pastors, decided to organize a separate group to be known as the Free Black Church, according to plans in 1869 formulated for organizing such a church.

The doctrinal difference so bitterly emphasized during 1880 made trouble for the Black Church. The First Christian Church located on the south side of Court Street decided to relocate and sold their meeting house to trustees of the newly organized Black Christian Church. Trustees were James Medley, Noah Hawkins, Simon Cabel and James Price. Price - $1,200 down with payment of $600, Book M., page 553 at Court House. Names of Charter Members are not available. However, members of the church in 1857 included Abraham Story, Milly Story, Squire Lillard, Absolom Mountjoy, Mariah Myers, Anna Bond, Aaron Bond, Susan Freeman, Nancy Myers, Joe Bond, Nancy Collins, Mariah Portwood, Katie Chambers, Martha Hickman, Mollie and William White. No doubt some of them were still living 12 years later to become members of the Free Church. The first meting house was destroyed by fire. The building was soon rebuilt before 1905. Mrs. Mary E. Gray (deceased) successfully solicited funds for the project. One of the ministers in the early Church was Elder Bowen.

In early days baptizings were conducted at Dowlings Pond, where large crowds gathered. The Church has had a number of leaders since then. The Rev. A. S. Gentry (deceased) was the pastor for 20 years. The pastor at this time in Reverend Ramon Smith.

SHILOH CHRISTIAN

The history of the Shiloh Christian Church dates back in the pages of time for over 100 years. The church actually began at the Brown School House located in the Sinai community in 1865 and continued meeting there until 1870. The church moved down the road to its current location in April of 1870. The land on which the church stands was donated by the George Searcy family. Brother Eleven Merritt was the pastor of the church.

The charter members of the Shiloh Christian Church, when organized on April 30, 1870, were: John Ackman, Margaret Ackman, George Bast, James Bast, Ann Baxter, Araminter Baxter, Elizabeth Baxter, George Ann Baxter, George F. Baxter, George W. Baxter, Green B. Baxter, Harriet Baxter, Harrison Baxter, Henry H. Baxter, James H. Baxter, John H. Baxter, Mariah Baxter, Mary Alice Baxter, Sally Baxter, Nancy Bently, William Bently, Mary Ann Best, V. B. Boston, Alice Brown, Elizabeth Brown, John Brown, Margaret Brown, Paralee Brown, Lucy Brown, E. H. Carrow, John Carrow, Ann M. Champion, Mankin Champion, William T. Champion, Mary A. Champion, Matt Cogine, Mary F. Devore, Mary Duncan, Hannah Gibson, William Gibson, Charles Gillis, Fannie Gillis, Hugh Gillis, Lucy Gillis, Martha F. Gillis, Nannie Gillis, Sara Gillis, William Gillis, Henry Gillis, Martha Grubs, B. H. Hall, Rebecca Hall, Lu Hamilton, Susan Hamilton, Benjamin Hawkins, Florida Hawkins, James Hawkins, Martha Hawkins, Betsy Hendrix, Viey Hilton, Sarah F. Hovvard, William Hovvard, George Hurt, Eliza Kays, Julia Kays, Letitia Kayes, Mary McCarty, Martha McMurry, Thomas McMurry, Tinsley McMurry, John Morgan, Thomas Morgan, William Morgan, Sarah Mullins, Thomas Mullins, Elizabeth Murphy, Riley Murphy, Eliza Payton, Ellen Payton, R. B. Petty, John Peyton, Nancy Powell, Agnes Samuels, Martha Searcy, George Searcy, John Searcy, Tobitha Searcy, Thomas Shouse, John Stephens, Burrel Strange, Jennie Strange, Martha Strange, Mary Strange, Benjamin Suel, Harriet Suel, Rebecca Suel, Eliza Sweeney, Martha Sweeney, Robert Sweeney, Polk Toll, Arietta Toll, Rachel Tunks and William Tunks.

Today, situated in a scenic valley, easy of access by U.S. Highway 53 passing in front, the friendly people that gather each week seem far removed from the hurry and turmoil of modern life; best of all, you feel that you are just a little closer to the Creator of all things when you come to this little country church where you are close to the beauties created by God.

Over the years, many improvements and additions have been made to this small church. During the Depression Days when ready cash for improvements and replacement of worn equipment was scarce, the members of Shiloh continued to provide not only for their families but for their church as well. The people of Shiloh were not satisfied with stopping with the addition of beauty and comfort to their homes; they were determined to do something about their church facilities that had remained the same since the days of their parents and grandparents. Livestock auction were held to raise funds for some of the improvements. The livestock were donated by local residents to help in the cause.

The first improvements were doing away with the unattractive plain glass window at the rear of the pulpit, and the building of a recess with stained glass windows with enlarged pulpit space and new pulpit furniture and communion table and chairs; next came the erection of a basement, three Sunday School rooms, and the installation of a new furnace. The determination of church members to improve their church facility has continued through the years with the installation of art glass memorial windows, new floor, carpet, a side entrance, covered way to the basement, choir loft, remodeling of the basement for a kitchen area, new roof, guttering, ceiling fans and vinyl siding. Shiloh Church reflects the love and sacrifice of many people, a number of which have passed on to their eternal reward.

The bell that now hangs in the spire of the Shiloh Christian church was used for many years as a "dinner bell" which was rung to call the farmhands to their noon meal. Mr. and Mrs. Polk Toll were the first owners of the bell, that we know of in this area. Several of the Toll descendants have had the bell in their possession through the years, the last being Mrs. Charles Jenkins. Mr. and Mrs. Jenkins presented the bell to the church in 1955 as a memorial to her grandmother, Mrs. Polk Toll (Arietta Toll) who was a charter member of the Shiloh Christian Church.

The members of the Shiloh Church have always been noted for their love and hospitality; this has been true from its beginning. Throughout the years many events have been part of the heritage of this small church. The homecoming days at Shiloh are filled with memories of "missing faces", fine fellowship, open-handed hospitality and an abundance of food spread on tables under the branches of old sugar maple trees for all comers.

Other events held during the years have been Sunrise Service/Breakfast, Annual Fish Fry, Annual Gospel Singing, and fellowship dinners. Special recognition services have been held for Mothers Day, Fathers Day and Graduation. Special activities such as church picnics, attending youth rallys, camp visits, participating in softball leagues, hayrides, cookouts, etc., are a part of the history of this small church.

The Shiloh Quartet was first composed of John Grace, Earldy Champion, Willis Shely and Lewis Young. This group sang at many neighboring churches, and was much in demand for funerals. After the death of Willis Shely, Hansford Gash became a member of the group in his stead. This group loved to sing, and were willing participants in every church and community program. One of the favorite numbers of this quartet was "Precious Memories". All of the members of this group are now deceased, but not forgotten. They left behind many "precious memories for Shiloh and the surrounding communities.

The Shiloh Church has, throughout the years, shared their loves through contributions/ donations to those in need. These contributions/ donations have been in the form of money, food, clothing or just a helping hand.

Ministers of this church are as follows: Eleven Merritt, Breen Perkins, Edgar Hume, William Yancy, John Perkins, Clinton Lockhart, Diamond Bently, Brother Havous, David Campbell, Daniel Case, Hallie Loyd, Eugene Clarkson, Herbert Campbell, G. J. Parrish, Clarence Harrison, Clyde Holder, Gabriel Banks, Reuben Steward, Carl Cheak, J. E. Wilson, Abe Anderson, Clark Winkler, Wilbur Davis, Henry Flemming, Hoke Dickerson, Ezra Sparrow, Robert Anderson, Karl Croel, William Corley, Doug Donavon, Harold Hively, Clyde Arnold, Gordon Reed, Bob McClain, Bob Sheffler, Tom Mobley, Bill Craig, John Willis, J. Hunter Jones, Howard Whitehouse, Bruce Barkhuer, Eldon Rucker and Joe E. Brown.

This small country church has been an inspiration to the Shiloh Community. The members of this church are family, with God as the head of the house. There is a feeling of love and warmth glowing from this small church in the valley. It is little wonder that one can sense a special feeling in one's heart when "Blest Be The Tie That Binds" is sung as the service's closing hymn.

View of Dam # 5, October 1, 1885.

Covered bridge over Salt River at Bond's Mill, Highway 513.

BUSINESSES, ORGANIZATIONS AND MEMORIALS

Champ Clark parade.

CITY OF LAWRENCEBURG

The land where the City of Lawrenceburg now stands was first known as Kaufman's Station. Jacob Kaufman, a German, located 400 acres of land on a branch of Hammond's Creek adjoining a claim held by a man named Bailey. Mr. Kaufman laid claim to an additional 1,000 acres adjoining the first.

Others claiming land in the area adjoining or near the Kaufman claims were a man named Larue, Peter Asturgis (2 claims - 200 acres - 1780; 1,000 acres - 1783), Thomas Madison, for whom Main Street was first named, 1,000 acres - 1782; Joseph Crocket 1,009 acres - 1782; John Harvey, Cass Clark, and John Payne.

William Lawrence, for whom the town of Lawrence was named, ran a tavern in the community for several years. Other early settlers to the community included Captain W. B. Wallace, William Robinson, Samuel Arbuckle, John Penny Sr., William Hudgins, Anthony Miller, Lewis Hyatt and McBrayer Family.

In 1820, by a special act of the Kentucky Legislature, incorporated the town of Lawrence. In 1827 it became the county seat of the new county of Anderson and its name was changed to Lawrenceburg by a special act. At the time of incorporation the town contained one store, a blacksmith shop, and a tailor shop.

Since the first organization of the town there has been a steady influx of people of good character and substantial qualities. The Mexican War drew several hardy and patriotic sons from this tranquil community.

In 1830 the first courthouse was built in Lawrenceburg on the present site (1990) of the Anderson County Courthouse. The first courthouse was built of brick and was the halls of Anderson County Government until it, along with many records, was destroyed by fire in 1859.

The second courthouse was built in 1860 using stone from the Kentucky River cliffs, just as the Civil War was beginning. This building was remodeled in 1905 and was one of the most convenient and attractive Courthouses in the stat. Attractive monuments erected to the "Salt River Tigers" in 1847 and one to Confederate soldiers from Anderson County unveiled in 1901, stood in the courthouse yard.

In 1833 and again in 1855 Lawrenceburg residents suffered from the epidemics of cholera. Several fell victim to this dreaded disease.

Lawrenceburg, at an early date, had religious accommodation for its people. The first houses of worship were built by the Presbyterians and Baptists, followed some years later by the Methodist and Christians. There are presently (1990) houses of worship for Baptists, Catholics, Christians, Churches of Christ, Churches of God, Jehovah's Witnesses, Methodists, Pentecostals, and Seventh Day Adventists.

On March 15, 1873 the entire business district and many of the residences were destroyed by fire. It is recorded that P. D. Brown, a carpenter and undertaker, stayed on top of the courthouse, while his own dwelling was destroyed, to prevent the courthouse and the records from burning. The business district was rebuilt with more substantial and commodious brick buildings.

In 1892 another disastrous fire broke out in the City Workhouse causing the death of a man named King that was confined on a charge of drunkenness and disorderly conduct. Again, 15 to 15 buildings were destroyed before bringing the fire under control.

In 1898 another disastrous fire started in a livery stable and destroyed 15 to 20 buildings including the Christian Church before it could be stopped. Shortly afterward the people of the city authorized the City Council to build a system of water works to enhance the protection against fire. The project was completed at a cost of approximately $25, 000.00. The water supply was from a number of wells belonging to the City and was believed to be an inexhaustible source of the purest water in the state according to a National Geological Survey. Water was furnished to private consumers for an average of $1.00 per month.

April 13, 1915 another destructive fire burned the courthouse. Again, most of the records were saved. In 1916 the courthouse was rebuilt with a clock tower said to be the first self-winding clock built in America.

In the Legislative session of 1892, Lawrenceburg was changed from an incorporated village to a city of the fifth class, presently (1990), Lawrenceburg is a fourth class. Since that time the city has been governed by a Mayor and Board of Council.

Lawrenceburg has grown from a small municipality, with all business being situated along Main Street and locally owned, to a municipality with shopping centers and corporation of international indistries. It is currently (1990) the 4th fastest growing community in the state but has maintained its rural small community atmosphere.

Lawrenceburg's residents are employed not only by local business and industries, but also by State government, business and industries in communities that are within commuting distance. As a result, Lawrenceburg has become known as a bedroom community.

Lawrenceburg City Government is organized as the Mayor/Council form of government. The six Councilmen are elected, at large, for two year terms. The Mayor is elected for a four year term. Each elected official may succeed themselves.

The following have held the Office of the Mayor:

1894 - 1906 John P. McWilliams
1907 - 1910 J.M.B. Birdwhistell
1911 - 1920 John P. McWilliams
1921 - 1925 J.W. Gaines
1926 - 1928 John P. McWilliams
1929 - 1944 Dr. J. L. Toll
1945 - 1952 William B. Nichols
1953 - 1960 Thomas Ripy
1962 - 1964 John Lyons
1965 - 1972 John Giles
1973 - 1976 Kenneth P. Hoskins
1977 - 1980 John Giles
1981 -   Kenneth P. Hoskins
Submitted By: R. M. Thompson

City Officers.—1906. Johnson, tresaurer; Vanarsdell, Councilman; Marrs, Clerk, Carl, Councilman; Dowling, City Judge; Ballard, Councilman; Stevens, Marshal; McWilliams, Mayor; F. L. Ripy, City Attorney; J.P. Ripy, Councilman; Dr. Lillard, Health; W.B. Morgan, Councilman; Lee Spencer, Water; W.Y. Spencer, Councilman; and James Holman, Assessor.

Lawrenceburg City Hall—1990.

ANDERSON NATIONAL BANK

The history of The Anderson National Bank reaches back to October 31, 1866 when John and John A. Witherspoon, two of the country's wealthiest citizens opened the J. and J. A. Witherspoon Bank. Its capital was $50,000. "With the management in the hands of these noted financiers and James A. McBrayer, a man of strong moral character, sound and liberal ideas, as the cashier, it soon became necessary to incorporate.." Twelve years later the Witherspoon's petitioned the Kentucky General Assembly to incorporate the bank. On February 14, 1878, the legislature enacted a bill creating the Anderson County Deposit Bank with capital of $50,000. The legislation allowed capital to be increased to $200,000, although there are no records to indicate this occurrence.

The charter names James R. York, William R. Bond, J. A. Witherspoon, Larken H. Penny, Gabriel H. Gaines, James McCall, A. C. Witherspoon and James A McBrayer to receive subscription for stock in the new bank at $100 per share. The state charter also authorized the bank, perhaps for the first time, to receive deposits from "minors and married women". On July 1, 1878 the doors of the Anderson County Deposit Bank were opened. Board members were J. A. Witherspoon, President, James McCall, A. C. Witherspoon, O. H. Witherspoon, J. R. York, Sr., Gabriel H. Gaines and John Witherspoon. Between 1878 and 1895, James A. McBrayer was employed as assistant cashier, clerk and teller on October 8, 1881. A five percent dividend was declared in July. L. B. McBrayer was employed at $600 per year and C. A. Witherspoon was employed at $500 per year. Also in July, James A. McBrayer resigned as assistant cashier but remained on the board. A 50 percent stock dividend was declared on January 19, 1884, and capital increased from $50,000 to $75,000. Doctor John W. Gilbert was appointed director on March 21, 1885. L. B. McBrayer was appointed assistant cashier on January 15, 1887 and authorized to sign drafts and the bank's correspondence. John William Gaines was employed by the bank on March 1, 1889 as a clerk on trial without pay. About a year later he was voted a salary of $600 per year.

James McCall and L. J. Witherspoon represented the bank at the organization meeting of the Kentucky Bankers Association meeting in Lexington. J. A. Witherspoon resigned as president August 20, 1892. Seven days later L. J. Witherspoon was appointed president. J. A. McBrayer, Sr. was made vice president. On July 1, 1895 the Anderson County Deposit Bank expired under the charter of 1878. The bank was promptly

reorganized under a new state charter with capital of $75,000. Directors are L. J. Witherspoon, James McCall, J. William Gaines, L. B. McBrayer, J. A. McBrayer, J. R. York, Sr., and A. H. Witherspoon.

Just after the turn of the century the Anderson County Deposit Bank reorganized into a national bank with capital of $100,000. It became known as The Anderson National Bank on April 9, 1907. The officers were J. William Gaines, President, and L. B. McBrayer, Cashier. Directors were: W. B. Morgan, J. P. McWilliams, L. B. McBrayer, J. William Gaines, A. H. Witherspoon, J. R. York and L. J. Witherspoon.

Original stockholders of the Anderson National Bank were W. G. Witherspoon, Dr. C. A. Leathers, A. B. McAfee, Louis McBrayer, H. C. Williams, Jr., G. B. Hawkins, T. J. Ballard, W. B. Morgan, J. P. McWilliams, Mrs. Mary M. Dowling, William E. Dowling, John H. Dowling, Leon McBrayer, L. E. Wilson, L. B. Young, John C. McBrayer, W. B. Sullivan, Dr. C. W. Kavanaugh, G. C. Speer, J. W. Cole, R. S. Gaines, F. R. Feland, L. B. McBrayer, G. H. Gaines, Mrs. Lou E. McKee, C. C. Trent, W. H. Smith, J. William Gaines, L. L. Moore, Jr., R. Paxton, Miss Emma Witherspoon, Mrs. L. E. Kavanaugh, J. A. McBrayer, Mrs. S. W. Boston, Mrs. Martha Abbott, Mrs. Elizabeth Bell, A. K. Gilbert, Mrs. A. H. Witherspoon, Mrs. Onie W. Moore, W. D. Moore, L. H. Witherspoon, Mrs. Sadie Ripy, James York Wallace, Mrs. Bell Rice, Mrs. Sallie Ripy, J. R. York, Mrs. Mary Adams, Mrs. Mattie Johnson, Mrs. Henryetta Dowling, Mrs. Ann E. Gaines and L. J. Witherspoon.

Deposits continued to increase including the years of World War I, until just before the stock market crash of 1929, but in 1930 the upward trend continued. The Anderson National Bank reached deposits of more than $1 million in 1941.

John William Gaines, who began his banking career in 1890, was largely responsible for the outstanding growth of the institution. He was elected president of the bank when it was reorganized into a national bank and served as its president until January 11, 1944. He resigned to become chairman of the board. Mr. Gaines, who was

also an attorney, continued to support the bank until his death June 9, 1959 at the age of 90.

Six presidents have labored in the bank: J. A. Witherspoon 1866 - 1892, L. J. Witherspoon 1892 - March 1907, L. W. Gaines March 1907 - 1942, Frank Routt 1942 - 1970, Allan S. Hanks 1971 - 1986 and James M. Stevens 1972 - present.

Vice presidents have been L. J. Witherspoon, J. A. McBrayer, J. W. Gaines, William E. Dowling, D. L. Moore, Jr., L. B. McBrayer, John A. Witherspoon, Frank Routt, John W. Dawson, Jr., R. York, L. W. McBrayer, Leon W. McBrayer, B. S. Grify, P. H. Crutcher, Allan S. Hanks, Euith Crossfield, Hilda D. Fallis, Gary B. Gaines and Dale Cinnamon.

Frank Routt was appointed president of the bank where he served until his death in December of 1972. During his term of office, from 1965 - 1966, a new home for the bank was purchased and construction completed for the new building.

Allan S. Hanks was appointed president January 1971. During his term as president he also served as Chairman of the Board, president of the Kentucky Bankers Association and member of the Board of Directors of the Federal Reserve Bank and a member of the Board of Directors of King Daughters Memorial Hospital. On November 2, 1982, a branch office of the Anderson National Bank was opened for business on the corner of U. S. 127 and Highway 62. This was to be Anderson County's first branch bank. Establishment of this branch began in July of 1981 when Anderson National Bank purchased the former Green Restaurant Building. The location was chosen because of the expansion of the community and for convenience to customers. Renovation and landscaping made the property one of the most attractive businesses in Kentucky.

The Anderson National Bank was purchased by Progressive Bancshares, Inc., a holding company, on July 1, 1986. Allan S. Hanks, having served the bank for 39 years, and Euith Crossfield having completed 65 years of service, tendered their resignations effective December 31, 1986.

James M. Stevens was appointed president and C. E. O. at the December meeting of the board of Directors to become effective January 1, 1987. Under his leadership, along with the present board, the bank now has achieved a level of $52,000,000. As we look to the future our aim is to be a high performance financial institution that is recognized as the "financial leader" in the Anderson County marketplace for our friendly and professional approach toward a total client relationship.

THE ANDERSON NEWS

In June 1877, a man by the name of C. A. Burton brought the first printing press to the county and was founder of the Anderson News. After a short time, he sold out to Judge John F. Wills, then one of Anderson County's most noted lawyers and eccentric citizens. The first plant was over the store of Frank Hickman, which was located in the Witherspoon Building.

Over the years, the Anderson News had many owners and editors. On December 1, 1921, Senator H. V. Bell sold to R. E. Garrison and Keen Johnson. In September 1925, Garrison bought out Johnson's half of The News. Russell McClure was managing editor. Garrison operated the paper 24 years until his death in February 1945. His son and daughter then took over the paper. R. Elliott Garrison, Jr. was publisher and Frances Garrison was the editor.

In 1950, a two-story brick building was purchased by the Garrisons with the idea of moving the operation at some late date. Fifteen days after the new building was bought, a fire destroyed its second floor apartments and heavily damaged the business below. The owners remodeled the burned out premises and several weeks later the entire plant was moved to its new and present location. The Garrisons brother, sister, and mother team operated the News for 21 years.

In 1966, the publishers of eight newspapers including The Anderson News agreed to the cooperatively-owned and operated publishing company, Greater Kentucky Publishers, and established a central printing plant. In September 1968, the company was incorporated and became Newspapers, Inc. with William E. Matthews serving as president. Soon the company owned and operated 20 newspapers and printed 10 other non-owned papers.

The merger of Newspapers, Inc. into Landmark Communications of Norfolk, Virginia was approved September 14, 1973. Matthews continued as president of Landmark Community Newspapers, a newly-created division of the diversified communications company.

Landmark Communications continues to be based in Norfolk, Virginia and has become a nation-wide communication company. A majority of the company's stock is held by Landmark's chairman, Frank Batten, and his family, and most of the remaining stock it owned by Landmark executives.

Landmark publishes nine daily newspaper, with 550,000 circulation, and 23 non-daily newspapers. It publishes a variety of special interest newspapers, magazines, and shopping guides. It owns and operates The Weather Channel, a cable television network serving more than 25 million cable subscribers in 50 states, and owns and operates two television and radio stations.

On April 4, 1977 , in the Anderson News' 100th year the newspaper for the first time became a semi-weekly publication. In the fall of 1978, the semi-weekly format was changed back to weekly and a new publication, The Anderson Advertiser, took the place of the Monday paper.

Other publications have appeared in Anderson County, but none continuing for a long period of time. The Anderson Republic, edited by Claude Cozine, appeared in 1896. In 1907, The Anderson County Herald was first published by Forrest Moore and Morton Green. Coleman Cox for a short while published a magazine-newspaper called "It". Only a few of these papers can now be found.

Over the years there have been a number of special editions. One of these, The Anderson News Supplement, appeared in 1906.

Don White, a native of Somerset, KY became managing editor of the Anderson News in June of 1978 and continues in that capacity today. Prior to coming to Lawrenceburg, the 41 year old editor was news editor of the daily, Somerset Commonwealth Journal, telegraph editor for The Lexington Herald-Leader and managing editor of the Casey County News at Liberty, KY.

The News has enjoyed a steady increase in circulation, growing along with the community from a 3,800 subscriber paper in 1978 to 5,500 today.

Down through the years the paper has been a strong supporter of community causes, including initiating efforts that led to the development of an upgraded community park at the America Legion property. Editor White was was recipient of the Landmark Community Newspapers Community Service Award for his personal efforts in this endeavor in 1987.

In the 80's, The News has won numerous Kentucky Press Association Awards for journalistic excellence including the coveted General Excellence Award on three occasions.

In addition to White, the News Staff as of April, 1989 includes the following personnel: E. W. "Bud" Garrison, advertising manager; Janie Buntain, reporter/photographer; Shirley Morgan, bookkeeper; Beverly McElwain, composing; and Mattie Cheak, typesetter and circulation record-keeper.

AUSTIN, NICHOLS & WILD TURKEY

Austin, Nichols started in 1855 under the name of Fitts, Martin and Clough, in New York City. The Company began as a wholesale grocery operation specializing in teas, coffees and spirits.

On January 1, 1879 the principle partners in the Company were Robert F. Austin and James E. Nichols. At this time, the name of the company was changed to Austin, Nichols and Company. The primary operation was still wholesale groceries and imported specialty items.

Upon the repeal of prohibition Austin, Nichols and Company began to engage in the wine and liquor industry. They applied for Federal Import Permit and a New York Wine and Spirits License. It was during this period that a group of New York businessmen would take an annual wild turkey hunting trip to North Carolina. Each person was given the responsibility of bringing different provisions on this trip. One year, Thomas F. McCarthy was to bring the spirits for the group. The men enjoyed the bourbon so much the only thing Mr. McCarthy was asked to bring in the future years was the bourbon for the hunt. After the success of the bourbon in a small group, a decision was made by Austin, Nichols and Company to market the brand using the Wild Turkey label.

The Company prospered through the years and in 1969 was acquired by Liggett Myers Tobacco Company. Liggett pur-chased the Lawrenceburg, KY. distillery in 1971 and the Wild Turkey Brand was removed from New York to Anderson County, Kentucky where it remains today.

In May of 1980, Austin Nichols was purchased from Liggett by the Pernod Richard Group of France. The decade of the 80s proved to be profitable and toward the end of the 80s, Pernod and Hublein joined forces and the name was changed to Boulevard Distillers and Importers.

The present location of Boulevard Distillers has a rich history in Anderson County.

In the 1890's this distillery was built by the Ripy Family and was operated under the name of Ripy Brothers. It was purchased in 1949 by Robert and Alvin Gould of Ohio and went under the name of J.T.S. Brown and Sons Company. In 1971, Austin Nichols moved to Anderson County and today employs close to 200 workers and covers some 850 acres of land. The plant supports the county through property taxes as well as contributing to various community functions. It is a main-stay of Anderson County and promises to be an asset for the future.

BIRDWHISTELL & PERRY

This prestigious firm was organized in the fall of 1944, when John Birdwhistell and Prentice Martin, farmers, became partners in real estate. Mr. Birdwhistell was the auctioneer and Mr. Martin was the clerk. Later, these two gentlemen served many years in county government, Mr. Birdwhistell as sheriff and Mr. Martin as tax commissioner. Mr. Martin was handicapped but this never came before his duties in office or real estate. Upon his victory as Judge, Mr. Birdwhistell passed away, never having the opportunity to serve in this capacity.

His son, Glenn Birdwhistell had worked several years with his father in the early 50's. Neighbors say Glenn could be heard in his dad's barn, practicing his auctioneer's chant, a natural born trait, for his son Randy

has the technique, too. Glenn became a partner with Mr. Martin in November, 1965.

After the retirement of Mr. Martin as tax commissioner, John Perry was appointed by Judge Hollie Warford. John worked with the real estate firm in the early 70's. When Mr. Martin passed away in 1974, John and Glenn became partners and the firm of Birdwhistell and Perry was established.

John works the crowd, taking bids and keeping the audience alert with his humorous comments and anecdotes.

Both Randy Birdwhistell and Tim Perry hold a vital interest in the firm and work in various capacities when called upon by their dads.

Hard work, cooperation, and a determination to serve the people of Anderson

county have helped to make the firm what it is today! The firm boasts of a team of the following: Larry Baker, Harold Reynolds, Billy Wellman, Betty Shryock, Jamie Elam, Claude Waldridge, Connie Ritchey, Kathy English, Renee Shelton, Kenton Bottoms, Dana Gash, Eddie C. Drury, Mary Lee Birdwhistell and Wanda Perry.

Full time associates are: Sharon Elliott, John Coffey, Cindy Crutcher, Ann Stansbury, and at nights Harold Ritchey.

List with us for three good reasons: We think our sense of values, our list of good prospects and our tireless efforts will make you glad!

Let this rich heritage become a part of you by letting us serve you!

First Place Winner, Bicentennial Parade, July 4, 1976. Left, John Perry, Children of employees and right, Glenn Birdwhistell.

DAVE DISPONETT

BUILDING CONTRACTOR, INC.

PHONE 839-4460

LOIS ANN DISPONETT

REAL ESTATE

FLORIDA TILE

James W. Sikes didn't plan to get into the tile business. After graduation from the University of Florida with a B.S. Degree in Business Administration, Jimmie returned home to West Palm Beach, Florida, and went to work for an insurance company. When his father, Leon R. Sikes, Sr., became seriously ill, Jimmie gave up his own career to run his father's tile contracting company.

Ceramic wall tile was in short supply. Looking about for a source, Jimmie found a small manufacturing company in Lakeland, Florida, which was in financial trouble. Leon R. Sikes, Jr., just released from service in the Air Force in Korea, stepped in to help.

On March 1, 1954, the young Sikes brothers and a few friends formed Florida Tile Industries , Inc. They had to borrow $8,000 for the down payment and assume $32,000 in debts to do it.

Jimmie took over the sales and business end of the company. Leon headed up manufacturing, engineering, research, and development.

It wasn't easy in the beginning, but the brothers held fast to principles, listened to the advice of their father, and worked hard.

The company began to grow.

In 1968 ground was broken for a new plant in Lawrenceburg, Kentucky. After

intensive research and analysis Lawrenceburg was chosen to put production facilities close to the population center of the United States.

Florida Tile, Lawrenceburg, began production in February of 1969. The plant that began with 16 original employees has grown to 350 today.

The Lawrenceburg plant manufactures glazed wall tile and is designed to produce a high volume, low cost, quality product. It is one of the largest volume producing 4 3/8" x 4 3/8" glazed wall tile plants in the world with annual production of approximately 38 million square feet.

FOX CREEK RECC

The 1930's! A time of privation..hunger..bankruptcy! Bread lines...men lined up at employment offices...families uprooted and wandering about the country-side in search of food and shelter...all symbols of the 1930s. It was the time of the Great Depression.

It was against this backdrop that a small group of farm folk gathered in the County Agent office in Lawrenceburg for the regular Farm Bureau meeting. It was November 16, 1937; the leaves had started to fall and the brisk winds bore the sting of the approaching winter. The warm glow of the wood stove was the only cheerful sight in the room. The people came in by ones and twos and took seats. These were the dreamers - the wishful thinkers - the ones who believed something could be done to improve the plight of man.

The discussion that night was on the new program being carried on by the government to bring electric power to rural areas...REA.

The farmers became excited...this could be an answer to their plight. Committees were named to go back to talk to the people. The response was good; the support was there for rural electrification.

Leaders in Mercer and Franklin Counties were also showing interest in the project. Floyd Watts, J. H. Hawkins, N. P. Green, W. H. Cunningham, H. B. Gardner and other were active in this phase of the planning.

The stage was at last set for this first organizational meeting of the Fox Creek R.E.C.C. It was held in Lawrenceburg, on March 22, 1938. J. R. York was named Acting Chairman of the meeting. He was elected to serve as the first president of Fox Creek RECC Board of Directors. Serving with him on the board were: W. O. Moffett, Elizabeth Toll Bailey, I. B. Bush, W. R. McRay, P. H. Crutsher, C. M. Cornish.

Much of the organizational work had now been completed. The task ahead was monumental...securing the sign-ups, obtaining rights of way and devising entire electric systems on rough country maps. At last, Fox Creek RECC was ready to move toward the day when work would actually begin on the lines.

October 1, 1938 was a "red letter" day in the history of Fox Creek R.E.C.C. On this date, the actual work began on the construction of lines. As the staking crews moved through the countryside, the rural families received their first concrete evidence that rural electrification was soon to become a reality.

The first section of line was energized on April 3, 1939, with Ernest Riley, on Bonds Mill Road in Anderson County, receiving the first service. There was great excitement when power first surged through the 172 miles of line. 50 rural families, for the firs time, saw the miracle of electric power light up their homes.

Since 1938, the cooperative has grown to a membership of approximately 7,500 serving in Anderson, Franklin, Henry, Mercer, Shelby, Spencer, Washington, and Woodford Counties.

The wires which tied the houses of rural people together also seemed to unite their spirits. Beginning in the early days, and growing through the years, there has been some unusual quality about the rural electrification program which has drawn people of diverse political and social views together in a common purpose.

Today in central Kentucky and throughout the country, virtually everyone who desires it had access to safe, dependable electricity to meet the needs of a modern lifestyle.

As of July 1989, the board of directors of the cooperative are Richard Crutcher and Jody Hughes from Anderson County, Gary Keller and Aubrey Morris from Mercer County, Kermet Gordon and Roy Smith from Franklin County, and Wayne Quisenberry from Woodford County. Serving as General Manager is Bob Kincer and Ralph Combs as Attorney.

The Back Supporter® mattress has been endorsed by a staff of orthopedic surgeons as an aid to healthful, proper sleep.

Spring Air® Back Supporter® mattresses... Rated No. 1 for comfort and support!

SPRING AIR

The exclusive 4-point comfort system provides unequalled surface comfort with deep down support. No other mattress can match the Back Supporter in sheer sleeping luxury.

SPRING AIR

Freeman-Mann Furniture
PHONE 839-3082

SOUTH MAIN STREET   LAWRENCEBURG, KENTUCKY

Beautiful New Homes,
 Designed & Built
 Especially For You

By

HAWKINS CONSTRUCTION

P.O. BOX 57
LAWRENCEBURG, KY 40342

329 COURT ST.
(502) 839-5140

CUSTOM RESIDENTIAL   COMMERCIAL   EXCAVATING

"Serving Lawrenceburg/Anderson County since 1972"

HERITAGE HALL CARE CENTER

Heritage Hall Care Center, located at 331 South Main, enters the decade of the nineties with a fresh look and a reputation for compassionate, quality care for the area's older residents.

Opened in 1973, by Stewart Gordon, Heritage Hall was a much needed facility and welcomed by the Lawrenceburg community.

Mr. Gordon sold the facility to Mike Owens in the summer of 1975. Seeing the need for additional beds, Mr. Owens added the back wing, known as "the hill", in 1976. Mr. Owens owned the facility until 1979.

EPI Corporation, a company already established in the health care field, purchased Heritage Hall in August, 1979. The 72 bed facility was kept filled to capacity and the demand for more beds continued to climb. The recognition of this need led to the addition of a new wing and the renovation of the existing building.

Ground breaking for this project was in January, 1985. Forty additional beds were completed in July, 1986. A celebration and open house was held on September 5, 1986. The community's support was overwhelming and has continued to grow.

The new facility contains: 80 intermediate and 32 personal care beds, 3 dining rooms, 5 patient lounge areas, a chapel, a large modern kitchen, a laundry, an activity room and a physical therapy room. The spacious hallways, in an aesthetic decor of blue and rose colors, add to the comfort and attractiveness of the facility.

The building surrounds an open courtyard with shade trees and also, an open park site in front of the building where resident are able to walk and enjoy the outdoors.

Fran Cole, the administrator of Heritage Hall, states; "There is a real need in this community for the services we provide and people place their trust in us. Families have come to expect something special from us and they have every right to. Our goal is to show this community that a care center can be a positive place to live."

With over 70 employees, Heritage Hall is a valued contributor to the Lawrenceburg economic community.

Heritage Hall had become an active part of this community and will strive to maintain the highest standards of excellence in quality care.

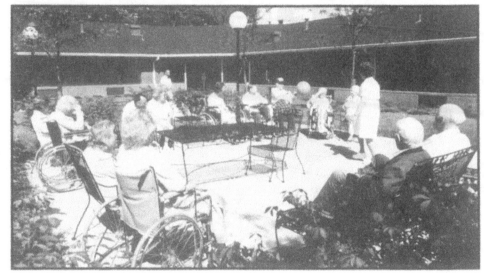

LAWRENCEBURG NATIONAL BANK

The Lawrenceburg National Bank was chartered by the Commonwealth of Kentucky on February 29, 1884, with a capital stock of $100,000. The charter named J. M. Johnson, A. C. Witherspoon and others on a committee to receive subscriptions for stock in the new bank at $100 per share. The original charter members and first stockholders were: Annie Woods, Frankie Saffell, A. C. Witherspoon, J. M. Johnson, F. M. Robinson, C. E. Bond, C. C. Lillard, W. B. Saffell, and W. F. Bond.

On January 24, 1885, these stockholders met and elected the first directors of the Lawrenceburg Bank. They were: W. F. Bond, Christopher C. Lillard, A. C. Witherspoon, F. M. Robinson, and W. B. Saffell. W. F. Bond was elected the first president at a salary of $500 per year.

W. B. Saffell was elected vice president (no salary recorded), J. M. Johnson, cashier, at a salary of $1200 per year, and R. H. Lillard, assistant cashier, at $400 per year. The president, cashier, and assistant cashier were required to post bonds of $10,000, $40,000 and $10,000, respectively, to insure the depositors of the reliability of the officials in the handling of deposited money.

The first Lawrenceburg Bank opened its doors for business at the corner of Main and Jackson Streets. In July 1885, the building was purchased from W. F. Bond and J. M. Johnson for the sum of $3,250, with possession given on January 1, 1885. The first vault was bought and installed for $1200. The bank declared its first dividend on December 10, 1887. This was a 4 percent dividend on the capital stock. The remainder of the net profit was credited to the surplus account. The bank passed through the panic of 1893 with strong resources unimpaired and was able to take care of all its customers and tide them over the hard times. The building was damaged by fire in 1894, but was rebuilt by C. E. Bond, who was then president.

Affairs at the bank ran smoothly for a number of years and prior to the expiration of its state charter, it was decided by the directors that the state bank should reorganize as the Lawrenceburg National Bank, under a national charter with capital assets of $100,000.

The Articles of Association were issued the on 20 October, 1904. The Articles appointed C. E. bond, W. B. Saffell, J. W. Rice, T. J. Ballard, and A. B. McAfee as directors. Mr. C. E. Bond was named President; W. B. Saffell, Vice-President; J. M. Johnson, Cashier; E. V. Johnson, Assistant Cashier; and Joe W. Waterfill and Herbert Crossfield, Bookkeepers. After six months, the bank showed a net profit of $515.60, which was, as stated in the minutes, unusually good for a bank of that size and age. On January 2, 1905, the bank building, supplies, furniture, and fixtures were sold to the newly organized Lawrenceburg National Bank for $6,500, which was twice the amount originally paid for it by the state bank. After the bank paid its first dividend in 1909, it has paid a dividend every six months since then, even during the Great Depression and bank holidays of the 30's.

In 1919, the Lawrencebug National Bank assumed the assets and liabilities of the Citizens Bank and Trust Company of Lawrenceburg. The following year, the shareholders approved a $25,000 increase in capital stock, bringing the total capital stock to $125,000.

On 27 June, 1935, the Lawrenceburg National Bank joined the Federal Deposit Insurance Corporation and subscribed to Class A stock in the organization. The F. D. I. C. insured each depositor in the bank for up to $10,000. In 1966, the amount of insurance was increased to $15,000 per account, and today each depositor is insured to $100,000. There have been very few changes in bank policy since joining the F. D. I. C.

The Lawrenceburg National Bank has grown continually through the years, as demonstrated by the following chart:

DATE	ASSETS
December 31, 1902	$470,708.10
December 31, 1915	$578,478.40
December 31, 1932	$1,049,058.82
December 31, 1967	$8,226,070.96
December 31, 1984	$42,403,543.00
June 30, 1985	$49,805,589.93
June 39, 1989	$63,289,272.31

There were no significant changes in the physical appearance of the bank until 1949, when the building was completely remodeled and redecorated. As the bank continued to grow steadily and began to show sings of outgrowing its building, the Board of Directors in August, 1965, entered into an agreement to purchase the adjoining Paul Routt and Fannie Leathers properties for the purpose of erecting a new building.

Demolition of the Routt and Leathers building was begun in November, 1966, and on November 16, 1967, the bank operation was moved into the new building on the site of the old Routt and Leathers property. The existing building on the corner of Main and Jackson Streets was then torn down and the addition to the new bank building was completed. On November 1, 1968, the bookkeeping department moved into its new quarters and drive-up banking was inaugurated.

The new bank has three office areas, three security and storage vaults, private coupon booths for lock-box customers, an executive area, a director's room, large community room for social occasions, large and modern bookkeeping department, safety deposit boxes, a night depository, and sufficient offices for private consultations. The spacious lobby, teller area, the small loan department, and the drive-in window are newly added features. The bookkeeping department contained an entire side featuring a Curion wall which was soundproof. A large customer parking area was provided at the rear of the bank. The building was fully air-conditioned at this time and a gas furnace was installed. A sound and public address system was developed throughout the entire building.

On Monday, October 24, 1983, the Lawrenceburg National Bank opened its new Branch Bank in the West Park Shopping Center. The attractive brick, colonial-style building, featuring the most modern equipment available, is located on the corner of the 127 By-pass and U. S. 62. Hettie Haye is the manager of the new facility, which features in-bank services, as well as a glass-enclosed, drive-in window completely under roof.

In further evidence of our changing world, the Kentucky Legislature passed a Multi-Banking Law, enabling multi-banking companies to purchase bank throughout the state. This law became effective in July, 1984, and in January, 1985, an offer was made to the stockholders of the Lawrenceburg National Bank by Farmers Capital Bank Corporation of Frankfort, Kentucky to purchase all 12,500 shares of stock at $500 a share. The offer was accepted by all the shareholders and on June 28, 1985, the Farmers Capital Bank Corporation assumed ownership of the Lawrenceburg National Bank.

The officers and directors on June 30, 1989 are as follows:

Officers:
William T. Bond, Chairman of Board
Charles L. Cammack, President, Chief Executive Officer
Paul Vaughn, Jr., Executive Vice President
Oneita M. Perry, Senior Vice President, Cashier, Head of Operations
Ben Birdwhistell, Vice President Clark Gregory, Assistant Vice President
Hettie E. Simpson, Branch Manager, Assistant Vice President
Frances Cox, Assistant Cashier
Selena Chilton, Assistant Cashier
William A. Barker, Loan Officer
Tim A. Perry, Loan Officer
Linda Hahn, Loan Operations Officer
Crystal Radcliffe, Assistant Cashier

Tellers:
Kathy Drury
Faye Wainscott
Jim Freeman
Carole Carlton
Vicki Walker
Sara Gash, Note Teller

Directors:
E. Bruce Dungan
Sam E. Blackburn
Tom D. Isaac
Donald F. Peach
Keith Freeman
Thomas H. Smith
William T. Bond
Charles L. Cammack
Paul Vaughn, Jr.
Oneita M. Perry

Advisory Directors:
Thomas B. Ripy
Ollie J. Bowen
Walter W. Major
Onita C. Cox, Receptionist and Safekeeping Clerk
Roberta Godby, Receptionist and Secretary
Drayma Holmes, Receptionist Consumer Loans
Barbara Markwell, Proof Operator, Assistant Cashier

Bookkeepers:
Ginny Robinson
Alberta Wiles

SPRINGATE & SPRINGATE

The law offices of Springate and Springate were established by Jerry L. Springate, attorney at law, in the winter of 1980-81. Jerry is a native of Sinai, Western Anderson County, and was a 1968 graduate of Western Anderson High School, a 1972 graduate of University of Kentucky and a 1979 graduate of the University of Baltimore School of Law. He originally established his offices at the old office of Dr. Boyd Caudill at 107 South Main Street in Lawrenceburg where he practiced solo. Jerry's wife, Betty, also an attorney, was then employed by the Kentucky Labor Cabinet.

In January of 1982, Jerry was appointed as Lawrenceburg's City Attorney, which position he held for four years. In 1985, he entered the race against opposition for the office of Anderson County Attorney. He was elected and took office in January, 1986. In 1989, he again faced opposition and was re-elected for another four year term which began in January, 1990.

In 1986, Betty Springate resigned her position as General Counsel for the state labor cabinet, and joined her husband, becoming Anderson County's first woman lawyer, and creating the husband and wife law practice of "Springate and Springate."

Betty was also appointed to be the Assistant County Attorney.

Betty is the former Betty Soeder, a Louisville native, and a 1970 graduate of Atherton High School. She received a bachelor's degree from the University of Kentucky in 1974, a masters degree from the University of Louisville in 1986 and a juris doctor (law) degree from the University of Baltimore in 1979. Betty and Jerry both worked paying their own way through school, Betty as a high school mathematics teacher, and Jerry as an aide in the office of one of Kentucky's United States Senators.

In 1982, Jerry and Betty purchased the building at 135 South Main Street where their offices are now located, from Elmer Maddox. Over the years, the building was used as a pharmacy, as a restaurant and as a pool hall and beer depot. When they took possession, the Springates eradicated all signs of the pool hall, changing the store front facade to a dignified brick federal style more suitable to a law office. They completely renovated the interior of the building creating four offices, a conference room and a reception area. Although they originally intended to expose at least some of the beautiful original tin ceiling in the building,

it became clear that it would not be practical to do so in the midst of an energy crisis. They did, however, incorporate 30 feet of beautiful cherry and mahogany bookcases and cabinets from the original building creating their law library in a long wide hallway. Because of inadequate space in the courthouse, the County Attorney's Office is also located in the private law offices of the Springates.

Since being elected as Anderson County Attorney, Jerry, with the help of a professional and talented staff, has expanded the services offered to Anderson County citizens, including an aggressive child support program. Jerry was elected and re-elected on his promise of tough but fair prosecution.

The Springates have a thriving private general law pactice in addition to their public duties. They belong to many local civic and community organizations volunteering their time for the betterment of the community.

As the Springates enter their second decade of service in this community, there is ever reason to believe that the future of Springate and Springate will be even more rewarding. Their most important, rewarding, and challenging job, however, is as parents to their two small children, Jay Bruce and Scarlett Lynn.

UNIVERSAL FASTENERS, INC.

In 1895, Mr. John Longyear and his brother, Dr. Howard Longyear formed the McKinney Button Fastening Company in Detroit, Michigan. The company manufactured a two-point fastener which was used for attaching buttons on men's and ladies' shoes. In order to provide a better method of attaching the shoe button, a semi-automatic machine was constructed. During the years of 1899 and 1900, a fully automatic machine was developed by the company.

Since shoe buttons were nearing their peak of popularity around the turn of the century, the company decided to produce a metal button for overalls. This product could be attached with their existing two-point fastener. A new fully automatic machine was designed for attaching the overall button. The new button with the automatic attaching machine was an immediate success. Several awards were received for the automatic machines at expositions held in San Francisco and St. Louis. A new building was built in 1906 for the company. At that time a new name was selected for the organization. This new name was Universal Button Fastening and Button Company.

Sales rapidly increased and many profitable years followed until the 1940's.

During the latter period, the company's button business suffered considerably due to diversification of products. In 1953, Rockwell Inc. purchased the company and, in turn, sold it to Talon, Inc. with this sale being completed on July 1, 1955. At that time, the company which was then known as Universal Button Company was moved to Lawrenceburg, Kentucky where a local plant building was made available by the Anderson County Industrial Corporation. The building and property which was leased for ten years, was purchased by Talon in 1965.

Textron Inc. acquired Talon including Universal button in 1968. In addition to the Lawrenceburg plant, a new manufacturing plant for Universal was built in Centerville, Tennessee in 1974. In 1981, Textron sold Talon and Universal to a capital investment company. At that time the name of the button company was changed to Universal Fasteners, Inc.

YKK, a worldwide leading manufacturer of zippers, purchased Universal Fastners in 1987. Besides manufacturing in Japan, YKK has approximately 50 operations in 40 other countries and has a worldwide employment of over 24,000 people. Fol-

lowing this purchase, a building addition was made in 1988 to the Centerville plant of Universal which doubled its manufacturing area. In the spring of 1989, a new manufacturing building consisting of 80,000 square feet was built in Lawrenceburg. This expansion doubled the manufacturing area of Universal's Lawrenceburg facility.

Universal Fasteners is a leader in the manufacturing of metal buttons, snap fasteners, rivets and burrs, hooks and eyes and plastic and metal Snapets. Along with these products, it continues to provide automatic machines to attach its products to the customer's garments. Numbered among the more than 750 firms that use its products are Levi Strauss, H. D. Lee, Wrangler, Haggar Slacks, Health-Tex, Osh Kosh B'Gosh, J. C. Penney, Sears Roebuck and Company, and Montgomery Ward. Products are also shipped to over forty foreign countries.

The Lawrenceburg location currently employs over 220 people and operates three shifts that produce over 3,000,000 fasteners a day. Universal Fasteners looks forward to continued growth in producing quality fasteners for the worldwide garment industry.

TURNER PUBLISHING COMPANY

Dave Turner reviewing a county book in the office complex at 412 Broadway, Paducah.

Established in 1977 as Dave Turner and Associates, Turner Publishing Company has earned a nationwide reputation as one of the most reliable and highest quality publishers in the United States, specializing in publishing histories on counties, military veterans' associations and other organizations. Turner Publishing Company has grown to more than sixteen full-time employees, approximately ten part-time employees and a host of freelancers. Originally located in Calvert City, Kentucky, Turner moved his offices to the Paducah Bank Building in 1986. In February of 1989, Turner purchased the Minnens Building in downtown Paducah at 412 Broadway.

Turner Publishing Company's dedication to the client's needs and to the quality of the final product has established the publisher as the leader in county history and military association history books.

The first county book published by Turner was Dent County in Missouri. Since then 80 county history books in Kentucky, Tennessee, Texas, Illinois, Missouri, and Indiana have been published with Turner's help. Along with the county books, many specialty books have been published, including: The St. Jude's Children's Hospital, International Shrine Clown Association, *Arkansas Quilts, Texas Quilts, Old Country Store Cookbook, Schmidt Museum Coke Book, Peoples First National Bank, Bank of Benton Centennial History, The Fabulous Fifties at WKU, CCC—The Way We Remember It, SunaKorn Drug Prevention Teaching Curriculum* and children's book, the *Indianapolis Zoo Guide* and the *Ft. Wayne Children's Zoo Guide.*

The first military veterans' organization history published by Turner was the *Hump Pilots Association of WWII.* That publication was soon followed by General Chennault's *Flying Tigers,* The *P-47 Thunderbolt, P.T. Boats* and many other titles. Turner Publishing Company has worked with more than 90 veterans' organizations and the list of the company's military titles keeps on growing, including *Trim but Deadly,* a history of Destroyer Escorts of WWII, *Guadalcanal Legacy, American Ex-Prisoners of War, The Legacy of Merrill's Marauders, Legacy of the Purple Heart, P-51 Mustang, P-38 Lightning, 98th Bomb Group, The Liberator Legend, 50th Anniversary—NAS Jacksonville, 17th Airborne Division, Chosin Few* (Korean War Veterans) and many other Navy, Air Force, Marine Corps, Armored and Infantry.

Turner is currently working on publications concerning Vietnam Fighter Pilots, Marine Corps Aviation (75th Anniversary), Naval Enlisted Reserve Association, US Merchant Marines, P-40 Warhawk, USS Fulton, Fleet Reserves, Korean War Veterans, Bataan/Corregidor, World War II Glider Pilots, American Battleships, Iwo Jima, Legion of Valor, Battle of the Bulge, Fiftieth Anniversary of Airborne, Ex-POWs of Canada and five titles in Canada including *Royal Canadian Air Force Association, Fighter Pilots of Canada, Harvard Airplane, 412 Transport Squadron* and one in England - *The Burma Star Association.* Specialty books include: *The National Press Club, International Shrine.*

The counties in Kentucky on which Turner has published books include: Caldwell, Calloway, Christian, Edmonson, Franklin, Fulton, Hickman, Hopkins, Marshall, McCracken, Simpson, Wayne and the city of Sturgis in Union County. Currently in progress are Floyd, Warren and Washington counties.

Turner Publishing Company would like to convey a special appreciation to the Anderson County Chamber of Commerce and the book committee for all the work they did on the Anderson County History book. The public is invited to visit the extensive military and county library located in the publisher's office complex at 412 Broadway.

EDWARDS SAUSAGE COMPANY

Mr. C. M. "Claude" Edwards opened a grocery store in Harrodsburg in 1935. The store was located on the corner of North Main and Price Avenue. He started killing hogs and making country sausage in the back of the store. People would come from around the state to buy this sausage. A good-sized room was built on the side of the grocery but soon they needed more room.

In 1940, the grocery store was sold and they all came to Lawrenceburg to build the plant on Lincoln St. next to the Kraft Cheese factory. They started selling in Lexington, Louisville and all the smaller towns around Lawrenceburg. When they started selling to Kroger, A and P,, and Winn-Dixie, Edwards Sausage and Edwards Hotdogs were pretty popular. Edwards Sausage was really gaining in popularity. Each year they had new growth and began to introduce new products. Edwards lard, bologna and Edwards weiners were popular with the public, especially the local school's lunchrooms. They had a slogan for their product that was catchy on the radio, "We don't want all the business in Kentucky, we just want yours."

While the Edwards family owned the company, several friends encouraged Marvin Edwards, the son of Claude and Dessie Lee Gritton Edwards, to run for the Senate seat in our district of Anderson, Spencer, Shelby, Franklin, and Scott Counties. He won and was elected to serve the term 1962 - 1966. If they had not had such loyal and good employees and a wonderful cooperative family, it would not have been possible for Marvin to devote that much time to politics.

The Edwards Sausage Co. was run as a "family affair". The family all helped when needed and the work force and employees were always loved and respected. The Company was sold in 1969 to Webber farm after the Edwards family had owned and operated it for 30 years. Mr. and Mrs. Claude Edwards retired and Marvin and his wife semi-retired, still keeping an interest in civic affairs and politics. They love the people of Anderson County and Lawrenceburg and they hope it shows.

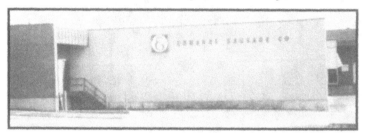

Above, Mr. and Mrs. C.M. Edwards, Mr. and Mrs. Marvin Edwards and son, Bobby, 1955. Below left, 1951. Below right, Edwards Sausage, 1990.

KLINK'S DRUG STORE, INC.

When Charlie and Ginny Klink opened the doors of Klink's Drug in November of 1947, little did they imagine that their store would still be in operation in 1990.

In 43 years, many changes have taken place in the store. Stocking the store for opening day 1947 required only $3000 in merchandise with Kleenex boxes covering the partially empty shelves. Now daily orders of $2000 are not uncommon. The stainless steel soda fountain, operated by Ginny's parents, Bonnie and Lee Waller, with it's .30 cent banana splits and .30 cent pimento cheese sandwiches has come and gone. Air conditioners, among the first in town, are here to stay - as are deliveries, charge accounts and computers. They have witnessed prescription compounded for .75 cents; and Sunday 3 a.m. calls for filling prescriptions have become a thing of the past. Older customers may remember when their son, Keith, who stood on a box and counted change for the customers. Upon his graduation from pharmacy college in 1977, he joined the firm. He is now chief pharmacist.

The Klinks owe the distinction of being the oldest business in Anderson County, run continuously by the original owners, to friendly, courteous service, fair prices, ethical business practices, superior employees and God's blessing.

LAWRENCEBURG IGA

The history of IGA (Independent Grocers Alliance) began in Chicago Illinois in 1926. Led by a visionary founder J. Frank Grimes, independent retailers all across America found a way to compete with the rapid growth of the corporate chain.

Most independent grocers found themselves left behind with outdated stores, limited services, and the inability to purchase their products as cheaply as the larger corporate chain stores. The formation of the voluntary chain organizations, where purchasing power was to be consolidated with over 3000 other stores, allowed IGA to buy products and equipment at a much more competitive price level. This, in turn, allowed independent stores the opportunity to sell their products at prices competitive to those

of the corporate chain, yet without the additional tremendous overhead often associated with such large scale organizations. These voluntary chains also provided leadership in store design, merchandising, and provided the latest in technology to its members. The word *foodliner* derived from the ultra modern trains and airplanes of the 1930's and 40's often referred to as Metroliners or Airliners.

The first IGA in Lawrenceburg was located on Main St. in 1937 and was managed by O. B. Goodlett. Lawrenceburg was without an IGA for several years until a new one was built in 1974 near the intersection of Broadway and the new 127 bypass. After a rocky beginning, the store was sold by the original owners and Jim Davis moved here

to manage the store. The store soon became very successful and when the new West Park Shopping Center with Wal-Mart was being developed, Jim and his partners knew they wanted to build in the center. In November of 1983, the new IGA opened, doubling the floor space of the old store. Building a reputation for low prices, friendly courteous service, and excellent meat, IGA soon became Lawrenceburg's leading supermarket.

In 1990 (as this article is published) the store began expansion to increase the floor space again by 50 percent. Additional departments and expanded variety will no doubt allow IGA to remain Lawrenceburg's largest supermarket.

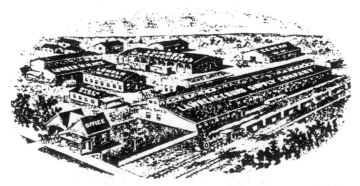

STANDARD OIL STATION

The Standard Oil Company opened the local station around 1925. Jasper Martin, of Anderson County, opened the station. Thomas Renfro had the bulk plant on Bush Ave. and made deliveries to all the small stores and gas stations in the county.

After one year, Robert Hanks bought the station from Mr. Martin. At first, Mr. Hanks hired local high school boys to work at the station. Therefore, lots of basketball games were discussed there, especially Lawrenceburg High versus Kavanaugh High.

The employees the last five years were Wilbur Roach, Cecil Cook, Jessie Thomas Sr., and Willie B. Two loyal employees on the Route Truck were Dudley Short and C. C. Fallis.

Mr. Hanks operated the station until he passed away in 1959. Richard Gash bought the station and ran it until the spring of 1989. It is presently closed.

Robert Hanks, 1926.

In Memory of
Phillip Scott Glass

Born: June 11, 1950, Shelby Co, KY
Died: May 14, 1971, Vietnam
Parents: Leon Glass (5/24/1921)
    Geraldine Marie (Best) Glass (8/30/1929)
Brother: Lonnie Wayne Glass (9/27/1952)
Education: Graduate of Shelby Co. H.S. 1968
Military Service: Entered US Army May 3, 1970, and went to Vietnam Dec. 28, 1970. May 14, 1971 was on combat operations when his platoon was mistaken for hostile forces and fired upon by friendly force.
Paternal Ancestors: Leon Glass (5/24/1921)
    Seibert Marion Glass (1873-1948), John C. Glass (1835-1908), Wakefield Glass (1801-1880)
Maternal Ancestors: Geraldine Marie (Best) Glass (8/30/1929), George Hudson Best (1880-1961), Joseph Best (1852-1914), Jack Best (1821-1893)

Servicemen like Mr. Glass fought for our freedom, and we owe them a debt that can never be repaid.

Submitted by: Juanita Glass, Geraldine Glass, Geneva Ruble, Joyce Murphy, Lucille Shouse and Mildred Rucker (Daughters of George and Ida Best)

ANDERSON CO.CHAMBER OF COMMERCE

Anderson County Chamber of Commerce
114 North Main
Lawrenceburg, KY 40342
(502) 839-5564

OFFICERS

Robert M. Thompson	President
Sandy Peggs	Vice President
Betty Springate	Secretary
Paul Vaughn	Treasurer

BOARD OF DIRECTORS

Bruce Royalty	Tom Bond
John Greer	Paul A. Drury
James M. Stevens	Garland Baxter
Wayne Richard	Stewart Gritton

It was January 23, 1959 that a meeting of businessmen, civic leaders, industrial representatives and farmers was called to order by the Hon. Thomas B. Ripy, Mayor of the City of Lawrenceburg.

The purpose of this meeting was to hear critiques from recognized experts of the unsatisfactory conditions of the community and for the further purpose of organizing a Chamber of Commerce.

Among those in attendance at the organizational meeting were visitors: W. H. Neal, Western Kentucky Gas Co.; E.B. Kennedy, Proctor-Engels, Inc.; James F. Zimmerman and Paul Grubbs, Kentucky Chamber of Commerce Directors.

By-laws as prepared by Walter Patrick were adopted and the following officers were elected: Walter Patrick, President; Ray T. Brown, Secretary/Treasurer; Harold Hanks, Vice President and Director representing Retail Merchants; Hollie Warford, Vice President and Director representing Agriculture; Thomas B. Ripy, Vice president and Director representing Civic Organizations; Joseph White, Vice President and Director representing Industry. Other directors elected were: Ed Grace, Walter Major, Charles Stewart and Frank Routt.

The minutes of the Anderson County Chamber of Commerce, May 1959, report a membership of 89 members in good standing. In 1987 the membership stood at 115 members in good standing.

The Chamber is actively promoting Lawrenceburg and Anderson County as a good place to visit, operate a business and call home.

The Chamber was instrumental in the formation of Lawrenceburg/Anderson County Industrial Foundation. The directors of the Industrial Foundation are members of the Anderson County Chamber of Commerce and serve as the Chamber's Industial Committee.

Projects of the Chamber include: Crime Stoppers program, Annual Christmas Banquet, Fourth of July celebration, Welcome signs at entrances to Lawrenceburg, Downtown flower and waste receptacles, Community maps, Community brochures, booths at Lawrenceburg Fair and Horse Show and Kentucky State Fair, etc., etc.

Membership is open to community minded citizens, businesses, industries, organizations, etc., for a nominal fee.

CHAMBER PRESIDENTS

Robert M. Thompson	1986-
Eugene Williams	1985
Jim Marquarde	1982-1984
Marvin Edwards	1966-1981
Ralph Homan	1965
Conway Smith	1963-1964
Thomas B. Ripy	1961-1962
Walter Patrick	1959-1960

AMERICAN LEGION

World War I Monument

World War II Monument

World War II continued, Korean and Vietnam War Monument

War Monuments on the Courthouse lawn.

ALTON RURITAN CLUB

On Aug. 12, 1960, the Alton Ruritan Club was chartered, becoming the first Ruritan Club in Anderson County. Charter members included David Caddell, Noal Cotton, Tom Cotton, Paul Crutcher Jr., Paul Drury, Raymond Franklin, Harry Towles, Earl Baxter, Cecil Cinnamon, W.E. Chowning, Stanley Crawford, Richard Crutcher, J.B. Gash, Maurice Gatewood, Ellis Hostetter, Frank Hostetter Jr., Schelma Meriwether, Harold Milburn, James Purvis, Kenneth Reed, Charles Sims, C. C. Toll and Urbane Wilson.

Over the 30 years, the Club has developed into a strong community minded center of action. In the 1960s, the Ruritan organized and immediately began to get involved in the community. The 1970s showed a continuation of the strong spirit within the club at a time when it worked to improve its facilities to make them more useful to all groups.

In 1960, when the club was founded, the first community action program initiated was to sell Christmas trees to finance the purchase of fruit baskets to be given to the needy. $50.00 purchased the makings for 14 baskets. Today, 30 years later, this project is still a main activity. The quality of life in Alton has improved directly from the actions of the Ruritan Club. From the bringing of city water to the community to the introduction of natural gas lines to, currently, the addition of a sewage treatment system, club members have been active in pushing these improvements. These improvements have brought new industry and increased the population of Alton.

Activities for the youth of the area have been a particular area of attention. In our own building and on our grounds, every popular sport has been sponsored: basketball tournaments, baseball and softball leagues. Additionally, support has been given over the years to help the various schools in the county fix and improve their facilities and aid in the Gatorade program for the Anderson County High School football team.

The Club has not forgotten its rural heritage. Past activities include soil conservation stewardship breakfasts, tobacco raising and various animal husbandry activities. We participate in the annual county Farm and City Days, County Fair and we serve Easter Sunday Sunrise Service breakfast for all the community and the Annual Labor Day Fish Fry.

The 1980s were as active and strong as in the past with most of the same activities plus Bingo each Tuesday night and Rook each Saturday and Monday nights. An average of $2,000 is donated to families in need from illness, burned out or any other need that may arise.

The Ruritan Club has an annual Family Pot Luck for members, a ladies' night each June and we honor wives and widows each Christmas. Each monthly meeting starts with a meal prepared by the Alton Christian Church ladies and Homemakers Club alternately, and we usually have a guest speaker.

Improvements to our facility as we go on into the 1990s have been a shelter over the picnic area and plans are being finalized for remodeling the kitchen. A walking track around the ballfield is in the planning for the community to use plus whatever need arises to help better the Alton area.

Help us continue in our desire to work for the betterment of the community and its quality of life.

Presidents of the Alton Ruritan Club since its charter are: 1960-1961, Harry Towles-1962, Tom Cotton-1963, George Cook-1964, Coy Davis-1965, Harley Stucker-1966, Dave Caddell-1967, Noal Cotton-1968, Paul Drury-1969, Jimmy Russell-1970, Ray Casey-1971, Gene Cinnamon-1972, Noal Cotton-1973, George Cook-1974, Charles Blackburn-1975, Harley Stucker-1976, Delbert Cox-1977, Delbert Cox Sr.-1978, Tom Cotton-1979, Delbert Cox Sr.-1980, Noal Cotton-1981, Paul Drury-1982, James Beasley-1983, James Beasley-1984, Noal Cotton-1985, James Doss-1986, Delbert Cox Sr.-1987, Johnny Aldridge-1988, Tom Cotton-1989, George Kinne-1990, George Kinne.

We dedicate this page to all the members past and present for the hard work and dedication that enables the Alton Ruritan Club to accomplish what has been done and what is to come.

For several years, Mr. Frank Hostetter, magistrate from the Alton District, and Mr. and Mrs. Earldy Champion of the Sinai Community, had been interested in a statewide organization, the Kentucky Extension Homemakers Association, whose main purpose was to better the quality of life for farm families. They persuaded the Anderson Fiscal Court to hire a Home Demonstration Agent to start the program here in cooperation with the County Agricultural Program. On August 11, 1937, Miss Helen Morgan arrived in Lawrenceburg to fill the position.

On August 31, 1937, Miss Morgan organized the first club at the home of Mrs. Earldy Champion. Other clubs followed in rapid succession in every part of Anderson County. Mrs. Champion signed a membership card, making her Anderson County's first Homemaker.

The Home Demonstration Agents have been, as follows:

Mrs. Helen Morgan Sherman (1937-1939); Miss Ruth Cash Price (1939-1941); Miss Louise McGoldrick (1940, assisted Miss Price 1942); Miss Elizabeth Donnell (1942-1946); Miss Louise Cosby (1946-1950); Miss Katherine Greenwood (1950-1954); Mrs. Margaret Cook Casey (1955-1960); Miss Dixie Grugin (1960-1966); Miss Jean Condor (1967-1968); Mrs. Susan Callahan Keen (1968-1970); Mrs. Ruth Meschko Ruggles 91970-1980)Mrs. Debra DeWitt Parrish (1981-Present).

Miss Martha Routt was County Chairman of the Homemakers from August 1937 to 1938, at which time a county-wide election of officers was held. People who have served as Presidents are as follows:

Miss Elizabeth Satterly (1938); Mrs. Charles Duncan (1938-1939); Mrs. A. H. Simpson (1939-1943); Mrs. James Goff (1941-1942); Mrs. A. H. Simpson (1942-1943); Mrs. Matt Birdwhistell (1943-1945); Mrs. C. E. Champion (1945- 1947); Mrs. John Wash (1947-1948); Mrs. Grace Cranfill (1948-1950); Mrs. Clarence Hoskins (1950-52); Mrs. J. W. Carlton (1952-1954); Mrs. June McKittrick (1954-1955); Mrs. John Dadisman (1955-1956); Mrs. Cecil Herndon (1956-1958); Mrs. J. D. Cook (1958-1960); Mrs. J. W. Carlton (1960-1962); Mrs. A. C. Overall (1962-1964); Mrs. Ollie Bowen (1964-1967); Mrs. J. W. Burge (1967-1969); Mrs. Jane Downey (1969-1971); Mrs. Joyce Cox (1971-1973); Mrs. Patsy McIlvoy (1973-1975); Mrs. Garnett Gibson (1975-1977); Mrs. Ann Crouch Cook (1977-1979); Mrs. Mae Hudson (1979-1981); Mrs. Pauline Cook (1981-1983); Mrs. Jackie Rice (1983-1985); Mrs. Mary Esther Brown (1985-1987); Mrs. Mattie Catherine Cheek (1987-1989); Mrs. Mary Jo Thacker (1989-Present).

The Homemaker Council, consisting of the county officers, the club presidents, and subject matter chairmen, meet several times each year and decide on major issues.

Each club meets once a month from September through June, at which time a lesson from the University of Kentucky Extension Service is given by local lesson leaders. Approximately 300 projects, covering every phase of family life, have been prepared and sent to each county by the Extension Service. Each project is the work of experts in that particular field.

The Bean soup and Cornbread Day is an annual affair, the proceeds from which enable Homemakers to take part in many community affairs. In the early forties, the Homemakers had a well-trained chorus, under the direction of Mrs. Evelyn Stamper, which sang for many important events both locally and state-wide.

Anderson County has a needle point square, depicting the Kentucky River Bridges at Tyrone, in the Kentucky Homemaker Tapestry which is on permanent display in the State Capitol Building at Frankfort. It was designed and made by Mrs. Bertha Grace.

Master Homemakers have been Mrs. Geneva Hoskins, Mrs. Katherine Dadisman, Mrs. Jean Spencer and Mrs. Elaine Corn.

Each year, the ACHA gives to Ovarian Cancer Research. The Homemakers have also helped in other drives, such as heart, polio, etc.

During WW II, the Homemakers responded to their country's call to help the Armed Forces by rolling bandages, soliciting Red Cross memberships, working in the blood canteen and donating blood. They also sent boxes of necessities to war-devastated countries. Wherever help was needed, the Homemakers were there, ready to serve.

Rooted in a past filled with accomplishments, and looking toward a bright future, the ACHA is an on-going organization, justly proud of its place in the educational and community life of Anderson County.

ANDERSON COUNTY SENIOR CITIZENS

The Anderson County Senior Citizens center opened on Main Street in Lawrenceburg, September 1973. A grant, under the Older Americans Act, and 25 percent from the local community supplied the funds. Helen Harris was hired as Director. This was a Socialization Center where games and crafts were enjoyed by the participants.

In January 1974 a bus was purchased through the Fiscal Court using Revenue Sharing Funds. Stanley Harris served as the Volunteer driver to provide transportation.

The Nutritional Program, serving lunches on Monday, Wednesday and Friday began in April 1977 and the Center moved to West Woodford Street

In July 1982, the center moved to 300 Lincoln Street, its present location. Services have expanded and now include Home Care, Homemaking, Recreation, Counseling, Health Screening and others.

Federal and State funding is supplemented by help from County and City Governments, United Way, donations and volunteers.

Directors have been—Helen Harris, Maggie Hanks, Steve Stivers and, presently, Judi Collin.

LAWRENCEBURG WOMAN'S CLUB

This historic landmark on North Main, long known as the Pierian Clubhouse and now the meeting place of the Lawrenceburg Woman's Club, was constructed around 1819. Through the efforts and hard work of the Pierian Club the Andrew Carnegie Library was built in 1909 on Woodford Street.

In 1962 the Younger Woman's Club and the Pierian Club were consolidated and the name changed to the Lawrenceburg Woman's Club.

On August 7, 1974 the building was donated and deeded by the Lawrenceburg Woman's Club to the Trustees of the Public Library with the consideration that the Lawrenceburg Woman's Club have use of the clubhouse for its meetings.

Each administration of the club has left monuments worthy of praise in its ability to promote the culture and fine arts that exist in the community today.

FAMILY HISTORIES

Above, James H. Baxter family, c. 1911. Behind, Greenberry Baxter. Back, Lindsey, Holly, Jim Elliott, Odena, Harrison, Rachel, Isaac Wilham, Rose Wilham, Jessie Champion, Nora and Homer Baxter. Second row, Tillie and Mabel, Martha Elliott and Jim Rose, Jim, Susan, Della Champion and Bernice, Tom Champion and Bruce, Earldy Champion. Front, Gertrude (Sanford), Opal, Blondella Elliott, Sally Elliott, Emma Elliott (Catlett) Wylna Wilham and Ruby Wilham. Below, members of the Leathers and Waterfill family, c. 1919.

SCOTT AND KATHY ADAMS Scott Adams is the second son of Dr. Townsel Lee and Donna Holthouser Adams. Dr. Adams and his family migrated to Lawrenceburg in 1961 when Scott was only a year old, to establish his dental practice. T. Lee, the youngest son of an Army officer, was raised in Whitesburg, KY and educated at the University of Louisville where he met Donna, a resident of Louisville.

Scott spent his childhood in Lawrenceburg where he was active in Little League, Boy Scouts, and school activities. He graduated from Anderson County High School in 1978, attended Transylvannia University in Lexington, KY from 1978-1980, and graduated with a BA in political science from the University of Kentucky in 1983. Scott joined the Kentucky National Guard in 1981 and pursued his military interests at UK by participating in ROTC and earning a A. S. Army Commission in May 1983 as an Infantry Officer.

Kathy is the daughter of John Allen and Wanda Hoskins Perry, both life long residents of Anderson County. Both the Perry and Hoskins families remain active in both civic and private sectors of Anderson County community. John currently serves as the Anderson County Property Valuation Administrator along with being a real estate broker and auctioneer. Wanda is a former teacher in the Anderson County School System and currently serves as a deputy in the PVA office.

Scott, Kathy and Ashlyn Adams

Kathy's childhood was spent growing up in different parts of Anderson County, to include both rural and urban, where she was active in Little League softball, First Baptist Church, and school activities. Kathy was the 1978 Miss Lawrenceburg Fair and Horse Show and 1980 Miss Fox Creek RECC. Kathy graduated from Anderson County High in 1980 where she earned academic, athletic, and social honors. Kathy remained active at the University of Kentucky where she graduated with High Distinction in 1983 earning a BA degree, majoring in Communications and minoring in Psychology.

Scott and Kathy were childhood sweethearts, falling in love in 1976 when Scott coached Kathy's softball team. Dating throughout high school and college, they base their fundamental principles on those taught by Beverly Stivers, Gladys Hutchinson, Larry Barnett, and Reverend Bob C. Jones.

Since their marriage in December 1983, Scott and Kathy have lived in Colorado Springs, Colorado, Osterholz-Scharmbeck, Germany, Ft. Benning, Georgia and currently Schofield Barracks, Hawaii. Scott is currently a captain serving with Third Battalion 21st Infantry Regiment. His military honors include two Army Commendation Medals, three Army Achievement Medals, Ranger Tab, Air Assault Wings, Airborne Wings, and two overseas ribbons. Kathy has obtained Civil Service status working for the Federal Government and is currently employed by the Hawaii Chapter of the American Red Cross where she serves as a caseworker for military soldiers and their families.

Scott and Kathy presently have one child, a daughter, Ashlyn Brooke, born March 8, 1988.

Upon Scott's retirement from the military, the Adams family plans to return to Anderson County.

DR. TOWNSEL AND DONNA ADAMS Dr. Townsel and Donna Adams were married August 25, 1956. They moved to Lawrenceburg in November 1961. At the time, he was one of only two full-time dentists here. They moved from Louisville where Donna left her job with U. S. Gypsum to become a full time mother and homemaker. Dr. T is the son of the late Townsel Carlisle Adams of Blackey, KY and Minnie F. Adams of Little Cowan , KY. Dr. T's father was a coal miner and his mother a postal clerk. Dr. T is an only child from their marriage but has four older stepbrothers and a stepsister. Donna grew up in Louisville. She is the daughter of Joseph M. Holthouser and the late Gladys Elizabeth Robinson. She has one sister and one brother in Louisville.

Dr. T. grew up in Whitesburg, KY. After Pearl Harbor, his father joined the U.S. Army at age 52 where he served as Captain. Dr. T. attended schools in Louisville, Camp Williams, Wisconsin and Salt Lake City, Utah. He graduated from Millersburg Military Institute in 1950. He attended the University of Louisville Arts and Science receiving his AB degree in 1954 and the University of Louisville Dental School, graduating in 1958. T, Donna, and their first son, Steven Townsel (born 1957) moved to Orlando, FL. He was stationed at the Orlando Air Forces Base for two years where he served as a dentist. Their second son, Scott Merrit was born there in 1960. During his college years, T. served in the KY National Guard for seven years in the 149th Regiment Combat team and the 240th Tank Bn.

Dr. Townsel Adams, Donna Adams, Dr. Steven Adams and Amy E. Adams

Dr. T. is active in the First Christian Church and is serving his first term on the Anderson County Board of Education this 1989. Other community service has been as Cubscout Packmaster, President of the Rotary Club and City Council member. He is a Master Mason and a member of the American Legion. As a member of the Blue Grass Dental Society, Dr. T serves as a delegate to the Kentucky Dental Association. He is a Fellow in the International College of Dentists.

Donna attended schools in Louisville, graduating from J. M. Atherton High School in 1954. She attended the University of Louisville for one year. She accepted a job as secretary to the Chief of Metallurgy in the Mettalurgical Laboratory at Reynolds Metals where andized and color andized aluminum were first produced. Donna's life had been her family. Although her formal training has been as a secretary, she always had a love of art and pursued it as a hobby - a gift from her Mother she says. She is a member of the choir at First Christian Church and serves on the Anderson County Junior Miss Committee.

Dr. T. and Donna are the proud parents of four children. Dr. Steven Townsel, age 32, is a graduate of ACHS (1975). He graduated Summa Cum Laude from Transylvania University (1979) and went on to graduate from the University of Louisville School of Medicine (1983). He participated in Operation Smile twice. Operation Smile is a medical mission where a team of plastic surgeons and anesthesiologists go into the jungles of the Philippines and perform cleft palate and facial surgery on severely deformed children and young adults. He lives in Louisville where he is an anesthesiologist on staff at St. Anthony's Hospital.

Captain Scott Merrit, age 29, graduated from ACHS (1978). He attended Transylvania University. He is a graduate of the University of Kentucky (1985), where he was a member of the ROTC and the Kentucky National Guard. He is now an Airborne, Ranger qualified, Infantry Officer stationed at Schofield Barracks, Hawaii. He is married to Mary Katherine Perry, daughter of John Allen Perry and Wanda Hoskins Perry, Lawrenceburg. They have one daughter, Ashlyn Brooke, 18 months, and are expecting again. Kathy is a full time case worker for the American Red Cross.

David Carlisle, age 25, graduated from ACHS (1982). He attended Transylvania University and is now a senior at the University of Kentucky Dental School. As a Marine Reservist, he completed basic training at Parris Island. He is now a 1st Lieutenant in the Army National Guard. He is married to the former Donna R. Tatum. Donna teaches French at the Lexington School.

Amy Elizabeth, age 19, graduated from ACHS (1988). She was selected as Anderson County's Junior Miss 1988. She was a Top 10 finalist in the state program where she received 2nd runner up in Scholastic Achievement. She was chosen as MISS ANDERSON her senior year - selected by the faculty. She was a Governor's Scholar. She is a William R. Young Scholar at Transylvania University. She is a sophomore is business and will graduate in 1992. *Submitted by: Donna Adams.*

ANDERSON - LAY James Burton Anderson was born on 9-26-1944 , in Woodford County. He is the son of Henry Clay Anderson and Beatrice West Anderson. He has one sister, Judith Ann, who married Thomas Lee Yann. James married Judith Ann Lay on 5-27-1967 in Versailles, KY. James and Judith are the parents of two children: Jamison C. Anderson, born 7-26-1969, and Jennifer Paige Anderson, born 2-27-1974. The family lived in Midway, Kentucky when Jennifer was born. She was two when her parents divorced. Her mother, brother, and Jennifer moved to Anderson County. Later, they moved to Versailles. She attended Simmons Elementary for half a year. Judith Lay Anderson married for the second time to Ed Spears. He was a car salesman and the family moved to Letcher County. This marriage did not work out and Judith and the children returned to Anderson County. They have lived in Anderson County for ten years. They currently reside on Fairview Street.

Jamison C. Anderson joined the Navy and resides in California. He is a graduate of Anderson County High School.

Judith Lay Anderson Spears is a nursing technician at King's Daughter Hospital in Frankfort. She has a close relationship with her daughter, because her own mother died when she was only fifteen.

James B. Anderson works at Rand McNally and is raising a son, Derrick Logan, born 7-19-1981, by a second marriage.

Judith Ann Lay was born on 1-4-1948 in Woodford County. She is the daughter of William Oscar Lay (3-20-1921 - 12-8-1974) and Lucille Croutcher Lay (11-8-1924 - 11-9-1967). She has a sister and brother: Helen Lee, born 1946, married Wayne Courtney; and Billy Alan, born 1949, married Janet Louise Lay. *Submitted by: Jennifer Anderson.*

GEORGE ARMSTRONG FAMILY George Jackson Armstrong was born on 4/13/52 in Louisville, Kentucky. He is the son of George Sheridan (1920-1981) and Ida Belle Montgomery Armstrong. He has one sister, Carol Jo, and one brother, James Sheridan.

George Jackson Armstrong married Holly Ann Hardy on 6/10/72 in Louisville. She is the daughter of Albert Leonard Hardy and Doris Nelson Briggs (1916-1989). She was born on 1/19/54 , in Schenectady, New York. She has three brothers: Albert Leonard, Jr., Robert Earl, and George Alan.

After the marriage of George J. and Holly Ann Armstrong, they moved from Louisville to Lexington, KY. This is where their first child, Carrie Ann, was born on 6/3/74. Ten years later, they had their second child, Chase Sheridan, on 1/28/84.

On 8/19/89, the Armstrong family moved to Anderson County and is currently living there today. *Submitted By: Carrie Armstrong.*

BALLOW The first of the Ballows to settle in Anderson County was William Ballow (1830-1905). He was the grandson of Charles and Elizabeth Marshall Ballow of Goochland County, Virginia. William Ballow was born in Shelby County and settled in Anderson County around 1848. He married Mary Egbert on the 23rd of September, 1849, and they were divorced around 1856. William then married Olive Jane Boston (1837-1916) on the 8th of July, 1857 and they moved to Mackville in Washington County.

William Ballow enlisted in the United States Army on July 15, 1861 and was assigned to Company F, 6th Regiment Kentucky Calvary. However, he spent most of the Civil War in hospitals in Lebanon and Louisville, KY. Upon his release from the hospitals he was assigned to the 49th Company, 1st Battalion Invalid Corps due to a functional heart disease. He and others in the 49th Company were captured by Confederate forces near Lipsy Mills, Alabama, three days before the surrender of the Confederacy on April 9, 1865. They were almost immediately paroled by the Confederates and sent to the U. S. garrison at Vicksburg, Mississippi.

After the war, William Ballow returned to Kentucky to raise his seven children: Melissa Ann, Lucy J., Louis, Luke, Margaret, Thomas, and George. All of the children except George and Margaret returned to Anderson County to marry and raise families of their own. The families they married into were the Bolton, Carlisle, Gordon, Morton, and Price families.

WILLIAM B. BARNETT, was born on 9/8/1816 and died on 9/7/1884. He married Elizabeth Robinson (1/22/1819 - 2/24/1902). They had a son named Fry Barnett (1863 - 1942). He was born in Washington County, Kentucky. Fry married Parlee Waldridge (1865 - 1937) on 8/19/1883 in Washington County. She was the daughter of Billy Pete Waldridge (1845-1904) and Maha Yocum (1842-1922). They had a son named Ellis Walter Barnett. He was born on 2/17/1885 in Anderson County and died on 4/27/1966 in Woodford County. He married Bessie Drury (1889-1938). She was the daughter of Jim Drury (1862-1934) and Almeda Wells (1866-1936).

Ellis Walter Barnett and Bessie Drury Barnett had a son named Leamon Barnett. He was born on 2/23/1911 in Anderson County and he died in 1980 in Lexington, KY. In 1938, he married Aileen Crouch, the daughter of Oliver Sanders Crouch (1866-1920) and Elizabeth Katherine Prather (1881-1957). Leamon and Aileen had their first child, Annie Bell, in 1939. She married Johnny Ledridge and they have three children.

Eleven years later, they had a second child, Bessie Katherine. She married Billy Wayne Gaunce on 12.20.1968. Billy was born in 1945 in Franklin County. He is the son of William Gaunce (1914-1976) and Clara Bell Friedly. Billy and Kay are the parents of three children, one of whom died at three days old. *Submitted By: Denise Gaunce.*

TOMMY AND JANETTE BARNETT Tommy and Janette Barnett, both of Anderson County, enjoy family, good friends, traveling, and entertainment. The two having so much in common has helped in having a successful marriage.

Truman Thomas Barnett is the only son born to

William Buel "Bill" Barnett and Juanita Corn Barnett. He was born on May 26, 1950 at King's Daughter Memorial Hospital in Frankfort, Ky. Tommy attended Western Anderson School for twelve years. He graduated high school in 1968, and now works at the General Electric Company.

Margaret Janette Yeager Barnett was the oldest of five children born to Royce Gilbert Yeager (who died on July 24, 1970) and Margaret Bell Hughes Yeager. Janette was born on March 30, 1955 and has three sisters, Ms. Rosanna Asay of Shelbyville, Ky., Mrs. Clark (Peggy) Peach, Mrs. Bryan (Tracy) Cammack. Both reside in Anderson County. She also has one brother, Royce Daniel (Danny) Yeager, also a resident of Anderson County.

Tommy and Janette Barnett with Billie Jo, Tracy Michele and William Thomas

Janette also attended Western Anderson School for twelve years. After high school graduation, she decided to put in her hours at Taylor's Beauty College in Frankfort, Ky., where she received her cosmetology license. She then worked in Lawrenceburg for three years at Edith's Beauty Shop, which was located in the top of the Feland Bldg. on Court Street.

Tommy and Janette fell in love and were married June 22, 1974. They have three beautiful children. Two daughters and one son: Billie Jo - born November 5, 1977; Tracy Michelle - born July 22, 1979; and William Thomas - born March 25, 1981.

Tommy and Janette have co-owned a retail, general merchandise and gasoline business since February of 1978, and reside at 4565 Bardstown Road in Lawrenceburg.

DARRELL AND JEAN BAKER Darrell and Jean Baker first moved to Anderson County in 1971. Jean was born in St. Mary's County, Maryland, the second child of Charlie and Betty Hurst Page of Hollywood, Maryland. Her father's family migrated to Maryland from the Buffalo, New York area to work at the Patuxent River Naval/Air Station located in Lexington Park, Maryland. Jean's mother, Betty Hurst, came to Maryland from Franklin, North Carolina, where she was raised by her aunt, Ethel Hurst Massey, of Macon County, North Carolina. Jean attended the Hollywood Elementary School in St. Mary's County, graduated from Chilhowee Baptist Academy, Seymour, Tennessee; and received her B. S. Degree from Frostburg State University, Frostburg, Maryland.

Darrell was born in Leslie County near the confluence of Jack's Creek and the Red Bird River. He was the second child of Esco and Martha Slusher Baker. Paternal grandparents were the Bakers who were farmers and loggers from the Stinking Creek area of Knox County, and the Hoskins, a pioneer family who were instrumental in the development of early education and religious institutions in Leslie County. Maternal grandparents were the Slushers who were merchants and educators who moved into Leslie County from Bell County and the Roarks, a pioneer family indigenous to the Red Bird Purchase area of Leslie and Clay Counties. The Esco Baker family moved from Clay County to Berea, Kentucky, in 1944, where Mr. Baker was employed at the Bluegrass Army Depot near Richmond. Darrell attended

Knapp Hall Elementary School and earned a B.S. Degree from Eastern Kentucky University. Darrell's mother, Martha, now lives in Leslie county and his father, Esco, lives in Florida. Ron, a younger brother, is an artist, teacher, and philosopher and now lives on Spring Creek in Clay County. Jessie, a sister, is an employee of the Kentucky Department of Highways and lives in Independence, Kentucky,

Following graduation from college, Darrel was employed in St. Mary's County, Maryland, for two and one-half years as a high school Business Education teacher. Darrell and Jean were married 5/17/1969, in St. Mary's County, Maryland, and moved to Alamance County, North Carolina, where Jean taught elementary school and Darrell earned a M. Ed. Degree from the University of North Carolina at Chapel Hill.

In 1971, the Bakers moved to Anderson County, where Jean was employed as a 4th grade teacher at Saffell Street School and Darrell was employed as a Training Officer by the Kentucky Department of Highways in Frankfort. In 1973, they moved from Lawrenceburg to a farm purchased from Gilbert and Goldie Thompson, located at Gee on Crooked Creek Road in Anderson County. The Bakers have two daughters, Emily and Laura, both are native Anderson Countians. Emily was born 4/11/1976, and Laura was born 8/16/1978.

Darrell was a charter member of the Glensboro Ruritan Club until his family moved to Campbell County, Kentucky, in 1980. While in Campbell County, Jean and Darrell studied at Northern Kentucky University. Jean received her M. Ed. Degree in 1983 and Darrell received a J. D. Degree in 1984.

Following the completion of their studies at Northern Kentucky University the Bakers returned to Anderson County in 1984. Jean resumed reaching in Anderson County and Darrell continued his employment as an Administrator with the Kentucky Transportation Cabinet in Frankfort. The Bakers now reside on Linden Drive in Lawrenceburg. *Submitted By: Jean Baker.*

JOHN BAXTER , married Mary Brown, who was a sister of Colonel Richmond Brown, who owned Brown's Island in the Ohio River near Stenbeville. Mary and John had eleven children.

Mary and John's second son, John, died when he was very young. They named their sixth son John as well. John married Elizabeth Sappington, and they settled in Bedford (now Somerset) County, PA. John served as a private in the company of his brother, Captain Edmund Baxter. It was the 8th Co. of the 4th Battalion under Lt. Col. John Marshall.

George Baxter, the third son of John Baxter and Elizabeth Sappington Baxter, settled in Madison County, Kentucky. He married Sallie Goodin. Their homeplace consisted of 148 acres on Otter Creek, Madison County. George and Sallie had ten children, the ninth of which was Harrison Baxter born in 1810.

Harrison Baxter married Rachael Hawkins on 1/31/1832 and moved to Anderson County in 1850. The fourth of their five children, Henry Hawkins "Hawk" Baxter, was born on 1/21/1841 and died 2/24/1917. He married Annie Smothers (1846-1889) on 10/25/1870. They lived in Anderson County and their children were: Albert Lee married Mary Scruggs; Minnie (1873-1894); twins, Nettie (1876-1895) and Lettie married Hanson Toll; Yancy married Mattie Champion; Hardin married Elizabeth Champion; and Stanley Hawkins (below).

In addition to farming, Hawk Baxter was also a finish carpenter and a great fiddler, as was his son, Stanley Hawkins Baxter. When a house reached a certain stage, they sent for him to come with his tools and do the finish work. When he grew older and came to live with his son, Stanley's family, they related that he could not sleep very well and that many mornings they would be awakened by his fiddling as he sat on the front porch steps, sometimes as early as 3 o'clock in the morning.

Stanley Hawkins Baxter was born 11/1/1885 in Anderson County. When he was in his twenties, he met a beautiful young girl, Sallie Payne Reed, who was the daughter of Rev. Garrett Reed and Cecil Perry. They had been seeing each other for a while when a handsome young visiting preacher, who was filling in for Sallie's father, offered her a ridse home after church. As she was getting out of the buggy, Stanley came down the road and stopped. He hitched his horse at the hitching rail and when he saw the stranger, he got mad and left in a hurry.; in such a hurry that he forgot his hitching strap. Sallie removed the strap knowing he would have to return for it and for her heart as well. She must have been right for they were married on 1/1/13.

Stanley and Sallie had four sons: Sidney Reed (1913-1989) married Elizabeth Hawkins; Bevin Lee married Juanita Long; Stanley Earl (below); and Cecil Hugh married Donna Hickey. Stanley died in 1948 and Sallie in 1975.

Stanley Earl Baxter was born on 12/11/26 in Anderson County. After his father's death, Earl returned home to help on the farm and lived with his mother. Earl taught 5th and 6th grades and coached basketball at Alton Grade School in 1948. In 1950, Earl went around taking the Government Census in this area. When he stopped at the home of Elvie and Walter Robinson, he noticed a picture on their mantle and thinking it was a younger picture of Mrs. Robinson, he commented on what a good picture it was. The Robinson's told him it was their niece, Gladys Pearl Robinson, who was named for Elvie Gladys. They promised to introduce them and did several months later at the annual REA Fair. Earl and Gladys continued to see each other and spent a lot of time square dancing. They were married on 12/31/54. They had two children: Joyce Lynn "Joy" married David Eugene Glass (wo sons - Chris and Brian) and Stanley Hawkins Baxter, named for his grandfather. Stanley married Brenda Gabbard - one son, Brandon Gabbard Baxter. *Submitted by: Chris Glass*

HARRISON BAXTER, (1809-1883) born in Madison County, Kentucky, and his wife Rachel Hawkins Baxter (1809-1866), moved to Anderson County before 1850. With them came five sons, ancestors of many Baxters who have lived or now live in Anderson County. The Baxters settled in the western part of the county in an area which came to be known as Baxter Ridge. The schools in this section always included many Baxter children from large families. Several Baxter descendents became outstanding teachers. Many of the early Baxters were charter members of the Shiloh Christian Church which was organized April 30, 1870.

The sons were as follows:

A) John H. Baxter (1833 - 1876), married George Ann Strange in 1867. Their Daughter, Hattie died unmarried in 1930.

B) George W. (1835-1914), married Ann Mary Samuels, daughter of Robert and Louisiana Samuels. Their family included thirteen children, five of whom became teachers.

C) Greenberry born 1837, died unmarried in 1919.

D) Henry H. (1841 - 1917), married Annie Smothers from Washington County, KY. Their family included nine children.

E) The youngest son, James Harrison (1844 - 1919), married Susan Elizabeth Mullins, daughter of William G. Mullins and Martha Jane Vandeventer of Anderson Co. in 1871. They had eleven children:

Holly, born in 1872, became a physician. After studying in Louisville, he came to Mercer County to practice medicine around the Dugansville community. Here he married Tillie Litsey in 1902. He was a well-known and well-loved doctor in Mercer County. One daughter, Gertrude Baxter Sanford, lives in Harrodsburg; Opal Tyler and Mabel Green are deceased.

2) Harrison, born in 1874, married Ethel Sweeney

in 1917. They lived at Fox Creek where they ran a store before moving to Lawrenceburg. Their foster daughter, Alice Duncan, is deceased.

3) Martha, born in 1876, married Jim Elliott in 1900. Their daughters were Emma, Sallie, Blondella, Gladys (who died young), and Jim Rose. All are deceased except Emma Elliott Catlett who, with her granddaughter Peggy, lives on Forest Drive. Her son, James Catlett, and daughter, Aileen Baker, also live in Lawrenceburg.

4) Another daughter, Rose, born in 1877, married Isaac Wilham of Mercer County in 1900. They had two daughters, Ruby Wilham, deceased, and Wylma Wilham McCray who lives in Lexington, KY.

5) The third daughter, Ardells "Della" (February 6, 1879-1959) married Thomas Davis Champion (August 29, 1879 - 1968) in 1906. Both Della and Tom taught school as did their four children: Bruce, Bernice, Grace, and Florence (all deceased).

6) An infant son (1881), is buried in the Sweeney Cemetery on Bear Creek.

7) Homer, born in 1882, married Nora Toll in 1911. They lived in Anderson County and later moved to Lexington, KY. Their son, Colonel Marvin Baxter, United States Air Force, Retired, died in 1986.

8) Jessie Baxter, born in 1885, married Earldy Champion. They lived at Sinai for many years before moving to Lawrenceburg where they lived on Chautauqua Street until their deaths. They adopted four children, three of whom are living in Anderson County: Jessie Mae Drury, Robert and Ralph Champion.

9) Odena Baxter, born in 1887, never married. She taught school and lived at the home place with her sister, Rachel.

10) Lindsey, born in 1889, married Mabel Toll. Their only daughter died in infancy.

11) Rachel (1891-December 22, 1975), never married. She is remembered in Anderson County where she was a much loved teacher. Her foster son, Davis Baxter, lives in Alamo, Texas.

(The history of the Baxter and Champion families is intertwined. Because they settled in the same general area of the county and many of them attended school and church services together, their social lives often led to a courtship and marriage between a Baxter and a Champion.) *Submitted By: Grace J. Champion.*

GEORGE W AND ANN MARY (SAMUELS) BAXTER In the mid 1800's the family of Harrison and Rachel (Hawkins) Baxter moved from Madison Co. KY. to Anderson Co. with their five sons: John H. (1833-1876), George W. (1835-1914), Greenberry (1837-1919), Henry H. (1841-1917), and James H. (1844-1919).

The following and the photo relate to the family of the above George W. Baxter and Ann Mary (Samuels) Baxter (1843 - 1928). They lived on Baxter Ridge Road and then in the log cabin (shown in the photo) which had originally been the Sinai post office and which was located at the junction of Salt Lick and Beaver Creeks - a point now below water level of Beaver Lake. The following are the children of this family: Robert H. (1860-1950) married Ora Morgan;

Front : Annie Elizabeth (Baxter) Sale, George Edward Baxter, Allen Wash, and Ruby Baxter. Second Row, Magdelena (Baxter) Hahn, the father of George W. Baxter, the mother Ann Mary (Samuels) Baxter, Susan Mary Baxter, and Martha Rachel (Baxter) Wash. Third row, James Hawkins Baxter, Silas Franklin Baxter, Robert H. Baxter, Fannin B. Baxter, Green Hardee Baxter, and Nancy Katherine Baxter, at rear is Greenberry Baxter. c. 1895.

Green Hardee (1862-1922) unmarried; James Hawkins (1864-1951) married Fannie Simpson. They had one daughter named Margaret who lives in Louisville; John William (1866-1918) unmarried, a school teacher and the superintendent of Anderson County schools; Martha Rachel (1868-1940) married George Wash. They farmed near Sinai, and their children were Allen (a county mail carrier) and Annie (a county school teacher); Magdelena (1870-1940) married Hade Hahn, They operated a boarding house on North Main St. near the post office for many years. They had one son Marshall (a physics teacher at University of Kentucky who later served in the military during WWII); Annie Elizabeth (1872-1960) married Henry Sale. They farmed near Bonds Mill. Their children were Lewis and John W. (retired employee of Bonds Mill distillery; Fannie Bette (1874-1932) married C. H. Holloway. they lived in Louisville and had three children - Harold, Hazel (who married E. Nachen), and Ralph; Silas Franklin (1877-1938) married Mary Etta Toll. They farmed in the county and he was Lawrenceburg water works superintendent. They had five children - Onita (married Charles Jenkins and is a retired county and city school teacher), Robert D. (married Katherine Healey, is retired from federal service and lives in Arlington, VA), Arietta Toll Baxter (a retired federal employee and lives in Lawrenceburg), Ruby (married Dr. John Schwab and lives in Louisville), William F. (married Glenna Stoner, is a retired engineer and lives in Huntsville, Alabama); Nancy Katherine (1879-1972) unmarried; Susan Mary (1881-1964) married Douglas Baxter. Lived in Utah and in Lawrenceburg. They adopted one daughter named Virginia who lives in Utah; Geroge Edward (1884-1966) was unmarried and farmed land now included in Beaver Lake; and Ruby (1886-1911) unmarried. *Submitted By: Arietta T. Baxter*

WILLIAM BAXTER William's ancestry begins with John Baxter (I) birth unknown. Will probated August 4, 1757 in Baltimore, Maryland. John Baxter (II), son of John (i) born February 17, 1746. Died 1783 in Ohio County, Virginia (now West Virginia). Married Elizabeth Sappington, daughter of John and Margaret Sappington. George Baxter, son of John (II) and Elizabeth born 1770 - 1780's, died in Bedford County, Pennsylvanio. Married Sallie Goodin. Emblem Baxter, son of George and Sallie, born December 23, 1803 in Madison County, KY. Died 1879 in Anderson County, KY. Married March 2, 1823 to Elizabeth Kennedy, the daughter of Arthur Kennedy, in Clark County, KY. Born September 10, 1805. Died December 20, 1885. They were living in Anderson County as early as 1837. Emblem was Justice of the Peace for 25 years and also was State Organizer for the Masonic Lodge in Kentucky for many years. All his sons were Masons. Emblem and

Elizabeth had 13 children of which one was John W., born November 23, 1835 in Fox Creek, Anderson County, KY. [This section is taken from the Anderson Newspaper.] OnNovember 3, 1859, he was united in marriage to Nancy Adams of Clark County, KY to whom four children were born - Thomas E., James W. and Mrs. Mildred E. Edgerton. In 1875 - 1882, John W. Baxter served as Deputy Assessor under Hary S. Wise. In 1883 - 1884 he was elected Sheriff under the Old Constitution and served 2 terms, 2 years each. In 1889, he was elected Assessor and served 5 years as the New Constitution and was in vogue then. On August 11, 1897, after the loss of his first wife, he was wed to Miss Ella Stone of Clark County, KY and to them one daughter was born, Miss Emma Lou Baxter. John W. Baxter died June 7, 1919 at the age of 83. He died of Brights Disease. Nancy Adams died March 4, 1897 buried in Lawrenceburg Cemetery. James W. Baxter (son of John W. and Nancy) born July 22, 1869. Died December 28, 1949. Married September 23, 1891 to Lucy Agnes Wise (daughter of William and Susan Mary Wise) born August 27, 1873. Died April 20, 1949. Buried in Lawrenceburg Cemetery. James and Lucy owned a farm on Case Road. To them one son, William E. born September 9, 1892. Died April 18, 1951. Married August 26, 1914 to Dovie Harvey (daughter of James and Leona Mastons Harvey) born August 24, 1897. Died November 8, 1965. William E. and Dovie had 2 children, Carl H. born September 22, 1915. Died December 6, 1982. Married April 1, 1937 to Lizzie Jane Willard (daughter of Allie G. and Exie J. Brown Willard) born February 18, 1923. Now he lives on Dove Dr. in Lawrenceburg. Mary Agnes, born March 28, 1922. Married May 21, 1947 to George Price. Now living in Louisville, KY. Carl and Lizzie Jane have six children: Betty Lois, born May 4, 1938, married October 14, 1961 to Billy Duncan and have one son, Todd; Joyce Lee, born October 7, 1939, married March 18, 1957 to Bobby Montgomery and have 3 children, Jimmy N., Wanda G. and Leonard S.; Lindia Lou, born November 23, 1940, married July 3, 1959 to James Montgomery and have three children, James M., Keith B. and Jamie Lynn; William Carl, born March 27, 1942, married to Rita Woodrum and have three children, Myron A., Gerald D. and Mary Elizabeth; Robert W., born July 18, 1943, married to Betty Cornish and have two children, Robert B. and Lisia Ellen; John Earl, born May 10, 1945, married June 6, 1964 to Frances Crowley and have two sons, John Estel and Jonathan Carl.

William attended Alton Elementary and Anderson County High School. Married Rita Woodrum formerly of Casey County, KY (daughter of Melvin T. and Mary Etta Wethington Woodrum) at St. Leo's Catholic Church in Versailles, KY on December 10, 1966. William worked for Southern Supply in the Service Department and Pepsi Cola Service Department until April 1976. He began his own business of Baxter Appliance Repair in April 1976 in Woodford County, KY. In June 1983, he moved to Lawrenceburg to the old Freeman Gilbert house on Woodford Street built circa 1880 by the Gilberts. William and Rita have three children: Myron Anthony, born November 2, 1967, married Belinda Driskell to them one child, Angel La Chelle born August 2, 1988; Gerald Douglas, born September 1, 1970; and Mary Elizabeth, born September 28, 1979. *Submitted By: William Carl Baxter*

CARL BEASLEY, the son of Jacki Beasley (1889-1965) and Susan Reed Beasley (1895-1978), was born on 11/28/1911 in Tyrone, Kentucky. Carl married Lilly May Bowman on 6/27/1931. She was born on 4/14/1917 in Tyrone. She is the daughter of Billy Bowman and Clara Rose Smith Bowman. Carl and Lilly May have nine children. they are: Clara Rose, Billy, Connie, Mary Lou, Morris, Johnny, Tommy, Marcus (died at age three), and Elbert.

Elbert W. "Junior" Beasley was born on 10/9/1950 in Tyrone. On 6/11/1971, he married Donna J. Brown in Shawnee Town, Illinois. Donna is the

daughter of Daily A. Brown and Oneida Casey Brown. Donna has one brother and one sister: Wayne and Sandra.

Junior and Donna are the parents of two children. They are: Adam Wayne, born 6/27/1974 in Louisville, Kentucky; and Jonathan Carl, born 11/2/1978 in Franklin County. *Submitted By: Adam Beasley.*

JAMES AND BONNIE BEASLEY James was born in Anderson County in 1913, one of seven children of John and Cynthia Norton Beasley. Brothers: Wesley, Virgil, Hansford, and Steve (killed in service). Sisters: Opal Murphy and Elizabeth Beasley. Jim attended Tyrone Elementary, joined C.C.C. and was sent to Stearns, Ky. where he married Bertha Koger. They had two sons, Donald and Virgil. They came back to Anderson County where Jim worked for Kentucky Utilities until he retired in 1978.

Donald attended Anderson High, joined the Navy and married Gene Godby. They had two children, Michelle and Anthony. Virgil now lives in Jefferson, Indiana.

On June 19, 1976, Jim remarried to Bonnie Brown Hahn. Bonnie was born in Anderson County in 1917, one of five children to Fred and Mary Sharp Brown. She graduated from Kavanaugh High and Lexington Beauty College. Married Alton Hawkins in 1934. They had two children, Alton Davis and Nancy. In 1952, Bonnie married Herbert Marshall Hahn (deceased) of Chaplin. They had one child, Marsha.

Davis, born 1936, graduated from Anderson High, joined the Marines, went to work at GE and married Betty Simpson. They had two sons, Stewart and Derric. Davis still lives at Chaplin, Betty teaches school and lives in Bardstown. Stewart graduated from University of Louisville and works for Bardstown Distillery. Derric graduated from Nelson High, served in the Marines and attended 2 1/2 years at Eastern University. Married Sharon Tate and they have one son, Justin. Derric is now employed by Kroger.

Nancy, born 1935, graduated from Anderson High, Campbellsville and Georgetown Colleges. She received her M.A. from the University of Kentucky and Education Specialist from EKU. She married Johnnie M. McQueary (deceased) of Russell Springs. She taught school 23 years in Kentucky, Japan, Germany, and Maryland. She married Donald Cheville in 1977 who retired from the Naval Research Lab in 1986 and now works for CSSC. Nancy is a Publications Editor for Unisys. They reside in California, Maryland.

Marsha, born in 1954, graduated from Anderson High School in 1972. Married Gary Briscoe and divorced in 1974. She married Earl B. Greaser of USAF. They have two sons, Brian, who was born in the Philippines and Eric, who was born in Las Vegas NV. Marsha worked at Nevada International Bank in Las Vegas and attended Clark Community College. Earl retired from the Air Force, August 1988 as Senior Master Sgt. He graduated from Embry Riddle University with a Bachelor Degree in Professional Aviation. He is a pilot flying for US Air based in Reading, Pennsylvania where he lives with Marsha and their two sons.

Bonnie retired as a beautician after forty years. She owned and operated the Nancy Davis Beauty Salon on Woodford Street and Hahns Beauty Salon on South Main Street. Bonnie and Jim live near Lawrenceburg. *Submitted by: Bonnie Beasley.*

JOHN BEASLEY is the son of Chesley Beasley and Rosie Fint Beasley. He married Elanor Akins. She is the daughter of Rowland Akins and Mary Elizabeth Watts Akins. John and Elanor are the parents of ten children: John P., Howard, Norman, Budger, Don, Rosemary Fint, Judy, Candy, Yonnie, and Naomie.

John P. Beasley married Shirley Grider. She is the daughter of Edward Grider and Ruby Blackburn Grider. John P. and Shirley are the parents of two sons, Johnny and Jason Beasley. The John P. Beasley family reside on Court Street in Lawrenceburg, Ky.

Edward Grider is the son of Mere Grider and Sally Sewell Grider. Edward married R[…] Blackburn. She is the daughter of Ambrose Black[…] and Mickey Hickman Blackburn. Edward and […] are the parents of five children: Myrtie, Shirley, Carol, Janice Harlow, and Nancy Lunsford. *Subm[…] By: Johnny Beasley.*

PAUL BECKLEY was born on 9-14-1944, in Frankfort, Ky.. He is the only son of Paul Raymond Beckley (born 10-5-1924) and Melba E. Wilhoite Beckley (12-4-1924 / 10-5-1989).

Paul married Pamela A. Sheffer on 8-8-1970. Pamela was born on 10-22-1946 in Henderson, KY. She is the daughter of Wayne Samuel Sheffer (3-19-1919 / 1-19-1982) and Jimmie Nell Carden Sheffer (born 4 - 19-1922). Pamela has one brother, Dennis.

Paul and Pamela are the proud parents of two children: Paul Marshall Beckley, born 7-24-1972 in Frankfort; and Gwyn Kerry Beckley, born 10-10-1974 in Henderson.

The Beckley family has lived in Anderson County only about three or four years. They currently reside on Court Street in Lawrenceburg. *Submitted By: Gwyn Beckley*

BEST CEMETERY In 1891, Jack "John" Best deeded 69 + acres of land to his son, Joseph Best. When Jack died in 1893, he was buried on this property. By 1908, a number of other family members were buried here. People other than family wanted to be buried here. So on 3-28-1908, Joseph and his wife, Minnie Best, gave about 3/4 acre of land to a Board of Trustees made up of J. D. Oliver, H. H. Elder, and W. Z. Best, to be used for a public cemetery, then under wire fence. This property lies on the south side of the Wayside and Glensboro Turnpike Road (This road is now called the Mt. Eden Road - U.S. 44).

Graves of Fredric and Luranah Whitehouse - in Best Cemetery Pleasant Hill Christian Church in Background

Lots in the cemetery were to be sold to parties desiring same by the Board of Trustees and their successors in office and all moneys received to be used in keeping the cemetery in nice repair at the direction of the Trustees.

On 7-28-1909, Board of Trustees - John D. Oliver of Glensboro, H. H. Elder of Waddy, and William Z. Best of Wayside - incorporated this cemetery as the "Best Cemetery Company" with the three named persons constituting the first Board of Directors. They had power to acquire more land (not to exceed five acres) and to make other improvements. The principal office of business was at the residence of W. Z. Best. J. D. Oliver was President and W. Z. Best was Secretary and Treasurer.

Joseph Best owned the surrounding property until 1915 when he sold 30 acres to Z. C. Sutherland and in 1919 sold the remaining 40 acres to W. C. Best. *Submitted By: Juanita Best Glass.*

GEORGE HUDSON BEST George Hudson Best was born in Anderson County, KY on 9-8-1880. He died on Good Friday, 3-31-1961, and buried Easter Sunday, April 2. He was 80 years old and is buried in the Best Cemetery on Highway 44.

George is the son of Joseph and Almarinda (Young)

...t from Washington County, KY. George's father ... a son of Jack and Sallie (Whitehouse) Best. All ...ied in Anderson County and are buried in the ...Cemetery. George married Ida Mae Whitehouse ...(1886 - 11-12-1977) at the home of Ida's parents ... ...ensboro on 12-29-1909. They have eleven chil-d...n, nineteen grandchildren, and twenty-seven great-grandchildren (only one great-grandson to carry on the "Best" name.)

Their children are: 1. Lorine (11-1-1910 / 4-11-1981) married Estill Peak - three children. 2. Wilma Kathleen (4-24-1912 - 11-20-1931) married Marshall Williams - no children. 3. Naomi (9-2-1913 - 10-24-1921). 4. Cecil (4-19-1915 - 10-25-1982) married Ada Elberta Kennedy and Jean Pfeiffer - two sons by Ada. 5. Lucille (4-12-1917) married Roston Shouse - Two children. 6. Ellis (1-20-1919 - 1-31-1919). 7. Joyce Mae (2-3-1920) married Lister Murphy - two sons. 8. Geneva (4-23-1923) married Paul Ruble - Three children. 9. Minnie Mildred (3-29-1925) married Kenneth Rucker - two daughters. 10. Juanita (3-16-1927) married Carl Glass - three children. 11. Geraldine Marie (8-30-1929) married Leon Glass - two sons. Carl and Leon Glass are brothers.

George Best is one of four children (See story of Joseph Best). George's father, Joseph Best, was in bad health most of his life and for a period of time operated a store which was located near what it now U.S. 44 and Crooked Creek Bridge.

On 11-26-1895, George's father bought a 104 acre farm on the Pleasant Grove Ridge Road from Mr. and Mrs. William Carter for $1500. George was now 15 years of age and he, his mother, and other children did the farming. George married in 1909 and in 1915 bought 5 acres from his father known as the old Pleasant Grove School House lot and built a house. This is next door to his parents and he is once again seeing that his parents needs are met.

After the death of George's father, Joseph Best, in 1920, he and his family moved in with his mother to take care of her. On 2-26-1923, George sold his School House lot to George Louis Martin of Mt. Eden, KY.

George's mother, Almarinda "Minnie" Best died in 1929, and George bought the homeplace and died there in 1961.

Back row: Lucille and Roston Shouse, Lorine and Estill Peak, Joyce and Lister Murphy, and Ada and Cecil Best. Center: George and Ida Best. Front Row: Geneva, Juanita, Geraldine, and Mildred Best (before marriage).

George and Ida made their living by farming. This wasn't easy since most of their children were girls. They always managed to make a good living; and when they retired, Social Security was certainly a blessing.

George's mother, Almarinda (Young) Best is the daughter of John Pendleton Young and Martha (Gabhart) Young, both of Washington Count, KY. When John P. Young came to Anderson County to live with his daughter, he brought with him a solid walnut bed that his father had made for him as a wedding present and put together with wooden pegs (now about 150 years old). George's daughter, Juanita Best Glass, heired this bed after George's death and Juanita has given it to her daughter, Alisa Glass Edwards, to enjoy. Just think she can say, "My great, great, great-grandfather made this bed." *Submitted By: Juanita Best Glass.*

JACK "JOHN" BEST

Jack Best of Garrard County, KY married Sallie Whitehouse of Boyle County, KY on 2-11-1840 in Washington County, KY. They owned property and lived most of their lives in Anderson County, KY along U.S. 44 near the Best Cemetery and the Pleasant Hill Christian Church.

Jack (1821-1893) and Sallie (1821-1914) Best had eight children: Malissa, Alfred, Joseph, Mattie, W.Z. "Billie", Nannie, Sallie, and Bettie.

1) Malissa (1842-1919) married William Harris and had a son, William.

2) Alfred (1850-1907) married Sallie Warford and had three girls - Hattie, Minnie, and Nannie. Alfred's wife died and he married Becky Elder. They had two children - Charlie and Lola.

3) Joseph (1852-1920) married Almarinda Young and had four children - Johnny Pendleton, George Hudson, Orvil Clive, and Martha Bell.

4) Mattie (1854-1924) married John Edwards and had three children - Sallie, George, and Charley.

5) W.Z. "Billie" (1856-1930) married Edna Bentley and had five children - Bettie, Roscoe, Ollie, Clarence, and Ruby.

6) Nannie married Tommie Sutherland and had three children - Ezra, Dud, and a daughter who died young.

7) Sallie (1860-1932) married Ham H. Elder and had three children - Edd, Oscar, and Claude.

8) Bettie married Ben Sutherland and had four children - John Walker, Frank, Hattie, and Zebedee.

One of Jack Best's grandchildren, Edd Elder, had six children. Four of these children (ages 10,13,15, and 17) died within two weeks with the awful WWI flu. They are buried in a row at the Best Cemetery.

Jack Best willed his land to his three sons. Jack and his wife, Almarinda "Minnie", are buried in the Best Cemetery, Anderson County, KY. In fact, many of the people named in this article are buried in the Best Cemetery. *Submitted By: Janice Best Glass from handwritten record of her mother Ida Mae Whitehouse Best (Mrs. George H. Best).*

JOSEPH BEST

Joseph Best (born in Washington County, KY on 11/11/1852) married Almarinda "Minnie" Young (born Washington County, KY 3-19-1856) in Washington County on 11-4-1874. They had four children - Johnnie Pendleton, George Hudson, Orvil Clive, and Martha Bell.

1) Johnnie (1875-1926) married Emma Newton. They had two children - Joe Bob and Gilbert Truman.

2) George (1880-1961) married Ida Mae Whitehouse. They had eleven children - Lorine, Wilma Kathleen, Naomi, Cecil, Lucille, Ellis, Joyce Mae, Geneva, Minnie Mildred, Juanita, and Geraldine Marie.

3) Orvil Clive (1882-1949) married Verna Grace. They had eight children - Lindsay, Lalah, Gertrude, Wilbur, Forest, Ira, Carl C., and Winfrey.

4) Martha Bell married George W. Pilcher. They had one daughter (10/17/1910) who died at birth.

When Joseph and Almarinda married they came to Anderson County to live. They had been married just a short time when one day Joseph came in from the field where he had been working and his sister, Sallie, about 12 years old was sick. He made the remark to her that with all the medicine she had on the mantel she ought to get well. Hie picked up a bottle and said, "Wonder what this would taste like?" He did not shake it up and all the poison had settled on top. Before they could tell him not to taste it, he had touched just a little to his tongue. He almost died. It ruined his stomach and thereafter in poor health was just able to go about but do no work. He was a big stout man prior to this incident.

Joseph Best moved to Washington County to live with his wife and Almarinda's father. (Almarinda's mother had died when she was a young girl.) In about five years they returned to Anderson County.

Joseph started a little store with his brother-in-law, Ham Elder, near what is now U.S. 44 and

O. Clive Best, Martha B. Pilcher and George H. Best

Crooked Creek Bridge. They started with a few loaves of bread, twists of tobacco and sacks of tobacco. The profits from these sales were used to purchase more merchandise and they didn't have to go into debt. In 1895, Joseph was able to buy a 104 acre farm on Pleasant Grove Ridge Road. His wife and children did enough farming to make a living.

Joseph Best became heir to 69 Acres of his father's property and from this property he gave 3/4 acre where the Best Cemetery is located as a public cemetery on 3/28/1908. Joseph gave each child six free graves.

Joseph's wife, Almarinda (Young) Best, is the daughter of John Pendleton (1829-1914) and Martha (Gabhart) Young. Almarinda had only one brother who died young and her mother died not too old. Almarinda had no playmates and was awfully lonesome sometimes. In a few years John P. Young came from Washington County to Anderson County to live with his daughter, Almarinda Best.

John P. Young died on 2-1-1914 and is buried in the Best Cemetery; his wife was buried in Washington County before he (John) came to live with Almarinda. John said not to take him to Washington County when he died because he would be just as close to her down here in Anderson County. Of course, this was horse and buggy days.

Joseph died on 08-11-1920 and Almarinda died on 10-5-1929. After the death of Joseph, his son, George Best, moved to the home place and cared for Almarinda until her death.

Joseph and Almarinda had many hardships in life but they never faltered in going to church as long as they were able. *Submitted By: Juanita Best Glass .*

JUANITA BEST-GLASS

daughter of George H. and Ida Mae Best, was born 3-16-1927, the tenth of eleven children (see article titled George H. Best).

Juanita's siblings are Lorine Peak (11-1-1910 - 4-11-1981); Wilma Kathleen Williams (4-24-1912 - 11-20-1931);Naomi (9-2-1913 - 10-24-1921); Cecil (4-19-1915 - 10-25-1982); Lucille Shrouse (4-12-1917) ; Ellis (1-20-1919 - 1-31-1919); Joyce Mae Murphy (2-3-1920); Geneva Ruble 4-23-1923); Minnie Mildred Rucker (3-29-1925); Geraldine Marie Glass (8-30-1929).

1st Row, Erin, Wesley, Martha, Juanita, and Carl Glass, and Alisa and Michael Edwards. 2nd row - David, Brian, Joyce, and Chris Glass

Juanita was born and reared in Anderson County,

KY, Pleasant Grove Ridge vicinity. She attended Pleasant Grove Grade School, Kavanaugh High School, and completed a business course.

Juanita married Jessie Carl Glass on 3-1-1947. They resided in Shelby County for three years; then in 1950, they bought a farm in Franklin County, KY. They still live on this farm. Juanita and Carl have three children. 1. David Eugene Glass (7-27-1948) married Joyce Lynn Baxter (2-12-1956). They have two sons - Christopher David (1-8-1975) and Brian Baxter (11-15-1977). 2. Wesley Carl Glass (9-23-1952 married Martha Sue Roberts (2-7-1951). They have one daughter - Erin Renee (6-14-1979). 3. Alisa Joy Glass (12-10-1960) married Michael Enos Edwards (7-4-1961)

Their son, David, served two years in the Vietnam War. Juanita's fond memories of her childhood are the every Sunday family gatherings and a home full of Christian love. Her mother's admonition was "Never let the sun go down upon your wrath."

Juanita has enjoyed the happiness of her three children with their love for milk shakes, banana sandwiches, and pillow fights. Four grandchildren are now a great joy and their favorite food at Grandmother's house is also the milk shakes.

Juanita's husband, Carl Glass (1888-1973), is the youngest of six children born to Seibert Marion (1873-1948) and Nancy Kate (Holmes) Glass (1888-1973). Carl was reared on a farm in Shelby County, KY near the vicinity of Mt. Eden. His siblings are Hubert (1907); Holmes (1910); Martha Pauline (1913-1933); Seibert M., Jr. (1917-1981); and Leon (1921).

Carl attended Cat Ridge Grade School, Waddy High School, and graduated from Mt. Eden High School in 1942.

Juanita and Carl's children are employed with State Government. One daughter-in-law is a school teacher and the other daughter-in-law is employed with the U.S. Post Office. Their son-in-law is employed by Winn-Dixie.

Carl has always farmed and is now semi-retired. Juanita retired October 1988 with 32 years of employment with State and County Governments. Call it retired if you wish, but their farm keeps them busy.

Carl loves to fish, but Juanita says this is worse than work for her.

Ancestors: Juanita Best (Glass), George Hudson Best, Joseph Best, and Jack Best.

Ancestors: Juanita Best (Glass), Ida Mae (Whitehouse) Best, Frederic Riley Whitehouse, and John Whitehouse. *Submitted by Juanita Best Glass.*

BIRDWHISTELL The root of this well known Anderson County family go back at least to the thirteenth century in Yorkshire, England. The name, the spelling of which has varied through the years, was evidently Briddestwysil (meaning "bend of the river') in the medieval period. Modern English spellings include Birdwhistle, Birtwhistle and Birtwistle.

Representatives of this family appear in parish records in Maryland in the late 1700's. One of their number, Thomas (1780-1864), made his way to Northern Kentucky in the early 1800's, moving later to Woodford County, where he married his third wife, Sarah (Sallie) Scearce, his previous spouses having died. In September, 1818, this couple acquired a farm on Salt River, then in Mercer County, now in Anderson

All of the Birdwhistells of Anderson County are descendants of Thomas and Sallie. Their children were: James S. (1817-1870); William Nathan (1819-1908); John (1825-1860); and Henrietta (1821-1854).

Of the four, the most significant for the Anderson County Birdwhistells was William Nathan, who married Mildred Smith of Mercer County in 1847. In 1897, The Anderson News carried an interesting account of their fiftieth wedding anniversary, celebrated on the family property on Salt River. William Nathan's five children were: Sarah Alice (b. 1847); William Ezra (1849-1916); Mahulda K. (1852-1864); Robert Nathan (1853-1863); and James Madison Bell (J.M.B.) (1855-1945), better known as "Mr. Matt".

Birdwhistell Homestead

J. M. B. Birdwhistell was probably the most influential member of the family in the late nineteenth and well into the twentieth century. An 1880 graduate of Centre College, "Uncle Matt" was an educator in several schools in Lawrenceburg, including the "Birdwhistell Academy for Males and Females" in the late 1800's. Located on Woodford Street, this school served both elementary and high school students. J. M. B. Birdwhistell was also a long-time elder and teacher in the Lawrenceburg Christian Church, and a vice-president of the Lawrenceburg National Bank. It was probably also "Uncle Matt" who insisted on the current spelling name: Birdwhistell (the spelling varies in the older documents.)

William Ezra Birdwhistell, married to Annie M. Nevins in 1871, fathered twelve children, from whom most of the Birdwhistells now living in the county are descended: Maranda Katherine (married A. J. Rice); Alvin H. (married Seenie Bell Yost); John William (married Maggie York); Phillip T. (married Addie Thacker); Ezra Cleveland (married Nellie M. Phillips); Alice (married Cecil Phillips); Viola (married Ford Dailey); James Madison Bell II (married Beulah Meaux); Robert Nevins (married Hattie Hughes); Wallace (married Hazel Phillips); Price (died young); and Stanley (died young.)

Having lived in Anderson County going on seven generations now, the Birdwhistells have certainly made their contribution to the community. In recent years, the descendants of Thomas Birdwhistell and Sallie Scearce have served in business, in civic clubs, in political office, in churches (mostly Baptist), in the military, in education, in the professions, and in public service. Many of the family have remained in the county, while others have moved to other places, where our name fails to draw comment. We always say, "When you pass through Anderson County, check the phone book! There are a lot of us there!" And may there always be! *Submitted By: Ira V. (Jack) Birdwhistell.*

JULIAN AND IRENE BIRDWHISTELL, are lifelong residents of Anderson County. Irene was born in Mercer Co. and moved to Anderson Co. at the age of six. The daughter of the late Oscar and Athena Royalty Monroe and the youngest of five children. Two brothers, Harold and Kisle of Anderson Co. and two sisters, Mrs. Volney (Josephine) Elam, Anderson Co. and Vora Hicks of Chattanooga, TN.

Julian, the son of the late Cleveland and Nellie Phillips Birdwhistell was born at Nevins Station in Anderson Co. and later moved to the Pump House Rd. where he lived until he entered the Army during WW II. Julian is the fourth of five children, being the youngest of four boys and one girl. Brothers, Carl and William Ezra, of Anderson Co. and sister Mrs. Harry (Annelle) Owens of San Antonio, TX. Lewis the eldest of the children, lived in Franklin, KY and died in Dec. 1987.

Julian and Irene both attended Salt River Elementary School and Kavanaugh High School. Julian later went to work as a delivery boy for the Oscar Cammack Grocery and from there he was called into the Army where he served three years of military service with 14 months spent in England with the 159th General Hospital.

After returning from overseas, he and Irene were married at Sand Spring Church parsonage by the pastor Rev. Roy Hamilton. He returned to work for Oscar Cammack but later he and his two brothers-in-law bought the Stringtown Grocery which they operated for twenty and a half years.

In 1969, Julian and the late J. W. Carlton ran for the office of County Clerk. Due to his ill health, Mr. Carlton resigned two months before his term was up and Julian was appointed clerk until he retired Dec. 31, 1988 due to ill health.

Julian and Irene are the parents of two children. David, 39, a graduate of Georgetown College, lives in Lexington and works for IBM. He is married to the former Beverly Boggs of Woodford, Co. and they have two children—a daughter Kelly, 11 and Scott, 4.

Julian and Irene Birdwhistell

Kay, 30, is a graduate of Transylvania University, lives in Lexington and works for the Comprehensive Care Center and is not married.

The Birdwhistells have been residents of Stringtown for 40 years and members of Sand Spring Baptist Church since a very early age, where they are regular attendants every week unless providentially hindered.

TRUMAN BIRDWHISTELL was born in Anderson County on July 4, 1909 to Phil Birdwhistell and Addie (Thacker) Birdwhistell both of Anderson County, Kentucky. Mary Lawrence was born to Will King and Lucy (Jones) King of Spencer County, Kentucky on August 30, 1914.

Truman and Mary Lawrence were married on May 29, 1932. They have three children: William Thomas; Janice Lea; and Nathan King. William Thomas is a graduate of the University of Kentucky and currently is a practicing CPA working for Cooper and Lybrand in Louisville, KY. He is married to the former Cynthia Clarks from Northern Indiana and has two children: David, 24 and Amie, 21. Janice Lea is currently a Customer Service and Order Entry Clerk at Rell Farming Corp. in Shelbyville, KY. She is married to John Riggs and has two children: Christy, 15 and Christopher, 12. Nathan is a graduate of Morehead State University and currently the Regional Manager for Dale Carnegie Courses in Lexington. He is married to the former Kathy Davis from Connorsville, Indiana, a teacher in Anderson County. They have one son - Clay, 12.

Truman and Mary Lawrence Birdwhistell

Truman graduated from Kavanaugh High School and was President of his Senior Class. He worked for Dean and Sherk Thread Mills as a Shipping Clerk. Truman later put in 12 years with the State Highway Department and 10 years as a clerk at the Old State Capitol Gift shop in Frankfort, KY. He also worked for the City of Lawrenceburg for 28 years as City Manager. Later, as a clerk for A & P Tea Grocer for 2 years. Truman is interested in politics, but never ran for an office in Anderson County (only for City Council in Lawrenceburg). He served as Red Cross Blood Program Chairman, giving nine gallons of blood, for 35 years. He has also served 5 years as Chairman of the Anderson County Red Cross.

Truman is interested in religious activities at the First Baptist Church of Lawrenceburg. He has served as a Sunday School teacher most of his life, teaching one class, Adult Men 61 Years and Up, for 35 years at this writing. He has spent most of his life working in the Baptist Training Union with all ages. He has been a Mason for 49 years at this writing, a Rotarian 21 years, 13 years perfect attendance at this writing.

Mary Lawrence graduated from Shelbyville High School. She worked for the City of Lawrenceburg for a short time and now is a loving housewife. She also has spent many hours in the Red Cross Blood Program in Anderson County. She had given much of her time to church activities and other volunteer community activities. *Submitted By: Truman Birdwhistell.*

HERMAN AND RHODA BLAKEMAN were

both born and raised in Anderson County. Born to Roy and Mittie Brumley Blakeman on March 24, 1919, Herman was the oldest of four boys: John Leroy (deceased, 1976); Eugene (deceased, 1975) and Arthur (San Antonio, Texas). Their father died in 1928 and their mother brought the family to a farm on Hammonds Creek Road where they lived with their mother and grandmother, Elizabeth Blakeman, and attended Anderson County Schools. Herman worked for Joe Rucker and Powell Hackney Grocery Companies in Lawrenceburg until the beginning of World War II, when he entered the Signal Corps (later attached to the Air Corps). All three of his brothers were in World War II. Arthur returned to service and is now a Retired Major.

Rhoda was born January 30, 1920 near Van Buren, the seventh child of seven, to Curtis and Ada Johnson Whitehouse. Her brother and sisters were: Ezra and Alvin (deceased as infants); Charlie, Lawrenceburg (deceased, 1983); Mollie, Mrs. Charlie Simpson, Glensboro; Manson, near Glensboro (deceased, 1977) and Mary, Mrs. Albert Thorson, Kenyon, Minnesota. Their parents are deceased, Curtis in 1943 and Ada in 1965. Rhoda attended Anderson County Schools through the eighth grade. She graduated from high school while living with her brother Manson's family in Jefferson County. She attended EKU, NCU, and graduated from U of L. She taught in Spencer County, Jefferson County, Salisbury in North Carolina, and a short time in Glensboro during World War II.

Herman and Rhoda Blakeman

Herman and Rhoda were married on November 24, 1943. They traveled to Warner Robins Air Force Base in Georgia and on to Boca Raton Air Force Base in Florida where Herman taught radar for eighteen months. Their son, Daniel Lynn, was born there on September 11, 1944. He now works for Sam Swope Autocenter in Louisville and has been married to Mary Sherrard since 1964. Mary is a kindergarten aide. They have three daughters: Melissa, Mrs. Jim McGrath; Tammy Sue, Mrs. Darren Goodlett and Stacey Lea, 13. A grandchild, Kaitlyn Elizabeth was born to Melissa on September 17, 1989.

When Herman was sent to the Pacific in 1945, Rhoda and Daniel returned to Glensboro.

After the war, Herman took a job with the Veteran's Administration in Lexington. In 1946, he was transferred to Louisville where he served in an administrative position in Veteran's Hospitals. Except for a three year transfer to Salisbury, North Carolina, he remained in Louisville until retirement in 1975.

In 1947, their oldest daughter, Rebecca, Mrs. Edward Nipp, was born. She is now a Respiratory Care Therapist in the Veteran's Administration Medical Center in Lexington. She has two sons — Jason, 11 and Joe, 7.

June, Mrs. Phillip Myers, was born in 1948. In 1971, she married and moved to Dayton, Ohio. They have two children - Phillip David, 16 and Susan, 13. June works for a shelving company and Phillip works for Gem City Engineering, both in Dayton.

Carol Ann, Mrs. Charley Amos, was born in 1951. She teaches at Mill Creek Vocational School in Jefferson County. They have two children - Carla, 11 and Matthew, 8. Charley works at Edgecomb Metals in Okolona.

Herman and Rhoda returned to Anderson County in 1976. They brought Herman's mother with them. She died in 1985. They had built a house at 2700 Glensboro Road and are still living there. They are members of Glensboro Baptist Church. *Submitted By: Herman and Rhoda Blakeman.*

JOSEPH BOGGESS Joseph Boggess and his

wife, Jemmiah Taylor Boggess are in Woodford County, Kentucky as early as 1796. They were members of the Salt River Baptist Church in 1798. Joseph and Jemmiah had five children: Jane (married Anthony Bond); Vincent (1781-July 1853) below; John (married Nancy Coffman in January 1806); Martin (married Rebecca Haynes in 1798; and William Henry (married Mary "Polly" Searcy in 1808).

Vincent Boggess, son of Joseph and Jemmiah Boggess, married Francies Walker on April 7, 1800 in Woodford county. Francies was born April 28, 1782 and died in May 1840. They are both buried in the family graveyard on Lock 5 Road. Vincent and Francies had ten children: Henry (married Lucinda Walls); Sarah (married Randol Walker in 1831) ; Alice (married John Mothershead in 1834); Argyle (married Eva Biles in 1834); Maria (married Nathaniel Watson in 1846); John W. (married Margaret McMichaels (or Michael) in 1845); Randolph (married Charlotte Dawson in 1847); Joel (never married - died of T.B.); Rebecca (married Thomas McGinnis in 1851) They moved to Ray County, Missouri as well as brother Argyle Boggess.; and Nancy (1821-1897) below.

Nancy Boggess, daughter of Vincent and Francies Boggess, was born on January 11, 1821 and died on July 3, 1897 She married Noah Cook on March 14, 1840 in Anderson County, Kentucky. He was born on January 11, 1822 and died on January 6, 1886. They are both buried in the Old Salt River Baptist Church Graveyard. Nancy and Noah had six children: Lucy (1841 - ?) married John Price; Sarah (1843-?) never married; John (1846-?) married Martha ?; Frances (1847-?) married Levy Thompson; Susan (1850); and Nancy (October 16, 1854 - January 5, 1928) married Elijah Crossfield on October 16, 1878 in Anderson County. *Submitted By: Mrs. Willie Crossfield.*

BOND-HAWKINS-COX William Bond, Sr. was

the first Bond in Anderson County. He was born in Hanover County, Virginia, and fought in the Revolutionary War, moving to Anderson County in the early pioneer days. He married Frances Ballou in Cumberland County, Virginia. She died before the move to Kentucky.

One of their sons, William, Jr., was the father of the Reverend Preston Bond (1824-1896), a Methodist minister, farmer and teacher. In 1847, Preston Bond married Belinda Arthur (1825-1909), daughter of Capt. Ambrose Arthur (1776-1859) and Jan Fletcher Arthur. They lived in the old Bond homestead five miles from Lawrenceburg.

Their daughter, Capitola Elizabeth (1859-1942) married Ballard DeWilton Hawkins (1845-1912) on September 19, 1877. His parents were Sheridan Bond Hawkins (son of Andrew and Melinda Shelton Hawkins) and Mary Ann White Hawkins, who married in 1832.

Capitola and Ballard Hawkins had eight children. One daughter, Leva Ann (1890-1965) married John T. Cox, Sr. (1876-1942), son of Burton (1846 - 1912) and Mary Jane Bond Cox (1852-1936).

John T. Cox, Sr. was a farmer and store owner until he was elected County Judge of Anderson County in 1933, serving until his death on October 7, 1942.

John T. and Leva Hawkins married August 12, 1913, and were the parents of three children: Mary Elizabeth Cox Hensley, Mildred Ann Cox Hodson and John T. Cox, Jr., all of whom still reside in Lawrenceburg.

Burton and Mary Jane Bond Cox, parents of John T. Cox, Sr. were large land owners in Anderson County. Burton was the son of Thurston Cox, who came from Mercer County, KY, and Henrietta Birdwhistell Cox.

Mary Jane's parents were John Wilkerson Bond (1820-1877) and Margaret Penny Bond (1824-1888) married in 1844.

John Wilkerson Bond's mother was Melinda Frances Hackley Bond. Margaret Penny Bond's mother was Nancy Burrus Penny.

BOND Probably the first Bond to enter Anderson County was William Bond who was born in Hanover County, Virginia in 1740. He was a Revolutionary War soldier for three years. He enlisted in September 1777 in the First Virginia Regiment. He fought in several battles. In about 1779 William married Frances Ballou They had four children: William Jr. married Rebecca Marshall, Anthony married Jane Boggess, James married Polly Griffey, and Sarah married James Arbuckle.

William Bond Jr. and Rebecca Marshall had seven children. Among the most well-known of these was perhaps Preston, who was a minister in local Methodist Churches.

James and Polly Griffey had eight children. One of their daughters, Sallie married Silas Ragan. Silas and Sallie were the parents of Jordan T. Ragan, a popular minister and school teacher in Anderson County.

Sarah Bond and James Arbuckle married on 7-16-1808 and they moved to Ray County, Missouri.

Anthony Bond married Jane Boggess on 6-17-1805. Jane was the daughter of Joseph and Jemmiah Taylor Boggess. Anthony Bond was a leading and prominent citizen when Anderson County was formed in 1827. He was one of the County's early settlers and took an active part in molding this county's history. There were thirteen children born to Anthony and Jane Boggess Bond, nine boys and four girls. The children are: William Bond, III; Joseph - killed by a sawmill; James married Malinda Frazier; Henry Harrison married Lavina Riley; Lydia Ann married John Dawson; Andrew Jackson; George Washington; Nancy married John W. Humes (See Hume article); Susannah married John W. Humes; Mary Ann married Simeon Taylor; Benjamin Franklin married Mollie Woodward; John H. married Sarah Johnson; Jordan W. married Mildred Martin.

The above is an account of the children of William Bond and Frances Ballou. Frances never left Virginia as she died and is buried there. William migrated to Kentucky with his children.

In present day Anderson County on 12-2-1790, William Bond married his second wife, Sarah Cranson. There were five children born into this union. There are countless descendants living in Anderson County today deriving from William Bond's marriages. He is buried on the Old Mary Jane Hanks Farm. *Submitted By: Billy Joe Hume* .

OLLIE J. BOWEN was born in Anderson County, May 20, 1906, the son and only child of G. C. and Nettie Shryock Bowen. His mother died when he was two years old, and when he was six years old, his father was shot and killed, and the killer was tried and convicted on murder and sentenced to life imprisonment. Therefore, he lived with his paternal grandparents, Charlotte Royalty Bowen and E. H. Bowen, who was a long time member of the Anderson Fiscal Court and was County Judge for a time in 1893. He was a Civil War Confederate Veteran, having served in the division commanded by General Price, later Governor of Missouri. After his grandfather's death when Ollie was 14, he lived with his paternal aunt and uncle, Mrs. Addie Hawkins and Chester Hawkins, until his graduation from Kavanaugh High School in 1926. He then attended and graduated from the University of Kentucky in 1929, and therefore went to Washington D.C. where he graduated from the George Washington University Law School and was admitted to the bar of the District of Columbia in 1932. He then returned to Anderson County and was elected and served two terms in the Kentucky House of Representatives and one term as State Senator from the district composed of Anderson, Franklin, Spencer and Mercer Counties. He was then the youngest member of the Senate. About two months after the close of his last Senate session, County Attorney William E. Dowling died and Bowen was then appointed and served continuously without opposition as County Attorney of Anderson County for 37 consecutive years. He was then elected and served eight years as District Judge of the district composed of Anderson, Shelby, and Spencer Counties. He has also had a successful career in general law practice and was elected and served one term as President of the Kentucky State Bar Association in 1967-1968. He has been a director of the Lawrenceburg National Bank and of the Kentucky Growers Insurance Company for more than 25 years. He is a veteran of World War II with one year of service in the Central Pacific Theater.

He was married to Louise Peak who died in 1977, and they had one daughter, Charlotte, a high school teacher, who is married to attorney and former County Attorney, Dale Wright, and they have two children, James Everett Wright, 14 years of age, and Kristen Louise Wright, 12 years of age.

Bowen's father's people came to this county from Washington County, and his mother's people came from Woodford County. His mother's brother Hugh E. Shryock, died while serving in the Spanish American War in 1898. His great grandfather Shryock was a cousin of the famous architect, Gideon Shryock,

who designed our state capital and the old state capital of Arkansas and Transylvania University's old Morrison Chapel and numerous other well known historic buildings.

Ollie J. Bowen passed away on December 16, 1989. He will be missed by many. During his lifetime, he touched many peoples lives. *Submitted By: Ollie J. Bowen*

THOMAS LEE BOWEN Thomas Lee Bowen, born 5-11-1871, was the son of the Elijah and Charlotte Royalty Bowen. He lived all his early life in the Ashbrook community. He married Frances Bunch and they were the parents of five children - Revie, Roy, Madel, Guy, and Hansford.

Revie married Arthur Drury. They lived most of their life on farms in Anderson County and moved into Lawrenceburg when they retired. They were the parents of eight children - Evadna, A.L., Evelyn, Juanita (deceased), Elwood, Alvin, Lois, and Phyllis.

Roy married Sally Woodard and their married life was spent on farms in Anderson and Mercer Counties. They had one son, William Everett Bowen, now deceased.

Thomas Lee Bowen

Mabel married W. E. (Ed) Phillips and is now the only living child of the Thomas Bowen family. Their married life was spent in Anderson County. They were the parents of two children - Woodrow and Pauline.

Guy married Edith Houchin. He lived in Anderson County all of his life. Their children were Onita, Frances (deceased), Herbert, and Allen. His wife, Edith, died in 1933 and he later married Rebecca Crouch. They had one son, Ralph Bowen.

Hansford, the youngest child, moved to Detroit, Michigan, when he was a young man and spent his life there. He married Agnes Lieber and they had three children - Jane (deceased), Phyllis, and Roy Martin Bowen.

Frances Bunch Bowen died early in life and Thomas later married Addie Thomas and still later Edna Utterback.

Thomas "Tom" Bowen lived his later life in Lawrenceburg and was a familiar figure around town during the 1930's. He died 5-2-1938 and is buried in the Hebron Cemetery. *Submitted By: Onita Morgan.*

BOWEN BROTHERS The Civil War (1861-1865) was a struggle between the North and South of this great country of the United States. It was something called "The War Between the States." It not only divided states, but families. Tragic is any quarrel that causes brother to rise against brother or causes father to be enmity with son. Sons of pioneer Bowens in Washington County found themselves in opposing camps during the War Between the States. Appomatox (April 9, 1865) brought the final surrender of Lee's army, but it by no means brought an end to hostilities. Bitterness, harsh accusations and bloodshed continued for years.

William G. Bowen was a 2nd Lieutenant of the Union Army and a younger brother, Elijah H. Bowen , fought for the Confederacy. William G. Bowen was stationed at Headquarters Camp Cumberland Gap. Nineteen Reg't Kentucky Volunteers, in Camp I (his

Standing: J. F. Bowen, Jr., Pauline Bowen Devine, Irene Bowen Stine, and William Edgar Bowen. Sitting: Margie Sea Bowen and James Frank Bowen.

granddaughter, Mrs. Pauline B. Devine, has a letter he wrote to his wife on Union Headlines). Second Lt. William G. Bowen was sent from Cumberland Gap with his men to Harrodsburg, where further orders would be given to him. The orders got mixed up and he was sent to meet a general in Louisville. It was a maracle for him and his men that he did not receive the orders. As they marched from Harrodsburg to Louisville, some family members met by the way side to see their sons, fathers, husbands, and friends.

William G. Bowen's younger brother, Elijah H. Bowen, when still in his teens, joined the trek to Missouri and was there at the outbreak of the war. He had two brothers living in Missouri and was probably visiting them and decided to stay there for a longer time. He entered under Gen. Price, serving with Confederate forces largely in Missouri and Arkansas.

William G. Bowen was married to Mary Jane Cornish before going into the war. Their children: George Washington, William Thomas, Calvin Hunt, Nancy Susan, Lenora, Oratha Surena Isabell, and James Frank. William G. Bowen "Button" worked as a clerk in a general store and as post office clerk at Sharpsville Post Office and managed his farm at Sharpsville. He died at the age of 67 in 1903. His wife died two years later. They are buried at Antioch Christian Church Cemetery in Washington County.

Their homeplace, where their children were born and reared, is on the Old Sharpsville Road. Most of the land is owned by his great grandson, James Frank Bowen, III, some by Charles Cornish, a plot of ground consisting of the house where the Bowens lived, the yard and garden belongs to Danny Stine, and a small lot, near the land that the Old Bowen School was located belongs to his daughter, Pauline Bowen Devine. The Bowen land is a landmark in the community.

Elijah Hunt Bowen married Charlotte Royalty and lived in Anderson County near Ashbrook, where his seven children: Enoch, Green, Thomas, Lillie Blakeman, Elizabeth Blake, Addie Hawkins, and a baby who died in infancy. He was buried in the Royalty Graveyard on the Gary Case farm near Ashbrook. *Submitted by: Pauline Bowen Devine.*

ELIJAH H. BOWEN was born in Washington County, Kentucky on September 4, 1842. At the outbreak of the Civil War he enlisted, serving with the Confederate Forces. As was often the case during the war, Elijah had a brother, William "Button" Bowen, who served with the Union Forces. Another brother, Martin Van Buren "Dock" Bowen, a jailer in Harrodsburg, was a Union sympathizer. In June of 1865, because of his continuing condemnation of the Confederates and their principles, a group of angry Confederate sympathizes proceeded to go to the jail, capture "Dock", and hang him. Elijah Bowen happened to be in the vicinity, and going to the jail, found his sister-in-law in tears. She told Elijah that the men were taking "Dock" to the woods to hang him. Forgetting past quarrels, Elijah hastened to the familiar woods, arriving just in time to save Martin Van Buren "Dock" from the noose. He made good

...ed gun for he wounded two of the men ...ers fled into the shadows of the forest. ...war, Elijah found employment with Mr. ...lty, a large land owner. On July 5, 1866, ...ied Charlotte Royalty, a daughter of Enoch ... For the greater part of their married life ...and his wife, Charlotte, lived near Ashbrook ...derson County. Elijah, better known as "Lige", ...ed many years as Magistrate from his district. ...received a license to practice law and was con ...ered quite exceptional in his ability to handle ...ficulties arising in his district or county. At one ...ne, he was appointed County Judge to finish a term of James M. Posey. Elijah died in March 1921, and his wife, Charlotte, died in January 1929. They are buried in the Royalty graveyard near Ashbrook.

Elijah and Charlotte Bowen had seven children. They were: Enoch, Thomas, William, Green, Elizabeth, Lillie, and Addie. Enoch Bowen died at age nineteen and William Bowen died at age ten months.

Thomas Bowen married Fannie Bunch. Their children were: Revie Bowen Drury, Roy Bowen, Guy Bowen, Mabel Bowen Phillips, and Hansford Bowen. Thomas' later marriages were to Addie Thomas and Edna Utterback.

Green Bowen married Nettie Shryock. They had one son, Ollie J. Bowen. Nettie Bowen died when Ollie was a small child. Green Bowen later married Nannie Royalty.

Elizabeth Bowen married Wood Blakeman. Their children were: Ramie Blakeman Robinson, Charlotte Blakeman, Haskel Blakeman, Buford Blakeman Knott, and Grace Blakeman Pock.

Lillie Bowen married Thomas Blakeman. Their children were: Gilbert Blakeman, Lillian Blakeman McGuire, and Lillard Blakeman.

Addie Bowen married Chester Hawkins. Their children were: Edna Hawkins York, Ethel Hawkins Thompson, and Mary Lois Hawkins Hanks.

Great grandchildren of Elijah and Charlotte Bowen living in Anderson County are Herbert Bowen, Ralph Bowen, Onita Morgan, Woodrow Phillips, Pauline Stucker, Charlotte Wright, Jane Gritton, Dudley Hanks, Evelyn Stinnett, Elwood Drury, A. L. Drury, Lois Ann Scott, Joy Spencer, Buddy Thompson, Marilyn Robinson, and Charlotte Robinson.

RALPH AND NANCY BOWEN were born and reared in Anderson County. Ralph was born on December 3, 1935, the only child of Guy and Rebecca C. Bowen. Ralph had two half-brothers, Allen and Herbert Bowen, and a half-sister, Onita B. Morgan.

Ralph has been a lifelong resident of Anderson County except for two years spent in the U.S. Army, with sixteen months being spent in Korea. Ralph attended Sand Spring School in Stringtown. In 1954, he graduated from Anderson County High School.

Ralph started employment, October 13, 1958 at IBM Corporation, Lexington, KY. He remains employed there today as a Financial Analyst. Ralph enjoys basketball, football, watching TV and reading.

Ralph married Nancy Perry on March 8, 1960. Nancy is the daughter of the late John W. and Ruby Franklin Perry. Nancy was born on September 20, 1940. She has three brothers, Arnold, John A. and William R. Nancy has been a lifelong resident of Anderson County.

Nancy attended Marlowe and Sand Spring Schools. In 1959, she graduated from Anderson County High School. After high school, she was employed by R.M. Lawson and L. E. Wash, MD's for five years. On March 16, 1969, she began employment with Boulevard Distillers and Importers. She remains employed there today as a lab technician.

Ralph and Nancy are the parents of two children: Natalie, 25, a registered nurse at Central Baptist Hospital. She lives in Lawrenceburg. Natalie is married to Tim Norton and they have one child, Heather, four months; and Jan, 22, a registered nurse at Central Baptist Hospital. She lives in Lawrenceburg. She is married to Tim Thompson.

Ralph and Nancy are members of the First Baptist Church, where Ralph serves as a Trustee. They reside at 1031 Macland in Lawrenceburg. *Submitted by: Ralph Bowen.*

WILLIAM GEORGE AND MARY JANE CORNISH BOWEN The Bowen family originated in Wales. After much migrating, they came to the United States and settled in Culpepper County, Virginia.

William George Bowen was the descendent of William Thomas Bowen and Nancy Ann Hunt. Nancy came to Kentucky in 1790.

William George Bowen was the Second Lieutenant of the Union Army during the Civil War and was stationed at Cumberland Gap. He was the postmaster of the Sharpsville Post Office. He was born 9-4-1836, and died 8-9-1903.

William George "Button" Bowen married Mary Jane Cornish on 4-9-1863. Mary Jane was born 11-7-1843, and died 5-12-1906. Both were born and reared in Washington County.

To this union was born seven children: George Washington, William Thomas, Calvin Hunt, Nancy Susan, Lenora, Oratha Surena Isabelle and James Frank.

George married Victoria Bryant. Their children were Bessie Lee Robinson, Nara Alice Richard, and William Thomas, who died in childhood.

Standing, J. F. Bowen, Jr., Pauline B. Devine, Irene B. Stine, W. E. (Bill) Bowen. Sitting, Margie Lee Sea Bowden, James Frank Bowen

Thomas married Mary Catherine "Molly" Sallee. Their children were: William Edgar Richard Sweeney, Calvin Hunt, Nara Ethel Ingram, Anna Bell Drury, Mary Elizabeth Evelyn Brown, Ida Lillian Thurman Logsdon, and James George Thomas.

Nancy married William "Billy" Erastus Robinson. Their children were: Hershell Bridge, Verna Beatrice Goodlett, Wade Litsey (died in childhood), Thomas Russell, William Cecil, Mary Edith Hacker, Roy Jackson, and Lena Frances Harlow.

Oratha married George Uriah Robinson. Their children were: Hazel Lillian, William Thomas, and Eliza Jane (twins) Elma Inell, Homer Bowen, Margie Fay and Gladys May (twins). All died in early childhood except Homer and Gladys May Miracle.

Frank married Margie Sea. Their children were: Mildred Pauline, Mabel Irene, James Frank, Jr., and William Edgar.

Pauline married Frank Eugene Corley. Their children were: Linda Joyce and Danny Eugene Corley. The grandchildren are: George Donald Mattingly, Jr., Dianna Lynn Mattingly Nally, Donna Lee Mattingly Beavers, Debra Gayle Mattingly Hillard, Jill Lynette Corley Liles, Jennifer Charlene Corley Houston and Amy Kathaleen Corley. Their great-grandchildren are: Angela Marie Beavers, Deanna Nicole, George Donald, III, and John Matthew Mattingly, Nikita Gayle Hillard and Christopher Ray Houston.

Irene married James Carl Stine. Their children are: Brenda Carlene Jenkins, James Carl, Carroll Bowen, Sandra Gayle Wilson, Gerry Dale, Mildred Ann Moore and Starlette Lee Drury.

James Frank Bowen, Jr. married Nila May Darnell.

Their children are: James Frank, III, Steven Ray and Jackie Curtis.

William Edgar married Mary Lena Brown. Their children are: Barbara Carolyn Berry, William Edgar, III, Rishell Brown, and Windell Gaylord.

William G., Mary Jane, George, Victoria, Thomas, Mary Catherine, Calvin Hunt Bowen, Nancy and William, Oratha and George Robinson were buried at the Antioch Christian Church Cemetery in Washington County. Frank and Margie Bowen were buried in the Lawrenceburg Cemetery in Anderson County. Those of the Bowen family who have served under the "American Flag" were: Civil War - William George Bowen; World War I - William Edgar Bowen; and World War II - James Frank Bowen, Jr.

William Edgar Bowen, James George Thomas Bowen, Homer Bowen Robinson, Hershell Bridge Robinson, Jr., William Thomas Robinson, James Dee Robinson, Joseph William Goodlett, William Franklin, Harold Dudley and James Russell Robinson, Bernice Bowen Richard, Roger D. Thurman, William Thomas, Charles Theodore and Belwood Ingram. They all came home from the battlefield but one - James Dee Robinson, son of Hershell and Elizabeth Robinson, was killed on his last mission. Danny Eugene Corley served a year in Vietnam and James Carl Stine, Jr., in Korea. May the new generation be as honorable and patriotic as those of the past. *Submitted By: Pauline Devine.*

FROM M. V. BOWEN TO W. G. BOWEN Dear Brother,

I avail myself of this opportunity to inform you that we are very well at this time, except Paralee. Fortune has favored us with a baby girl.

The war is now over, and peace is settling down over the land, and all points fair to a prosperous future. The rebellion is gone. It is suppressed. But there is a great work yet to be done. Civil law will have to be restored and take the lead in place of military law, and states reorganized to suit the age in which we live. Free government is about to take the lead among the foremost nations of the earth. But something yet will have to be done before the government can be permanently established upon a basis that will never crumble.

Then the cause of the war will have to be removed. The question than is, "What was the cause?"

I believe that all parties agree as to the cause. Then why not remove the cause and act the part of wise men?

The South started slavery and the war. The war faded, and consequently they lost slavery. The Union men of the border states, slave owners also, were forced into the issue, not with their own consent, but from the force of circumstances. Slavery went down with the Rebellion. Wise men predicted it, time has proven it, and we will have to admit it, and fix ourselves to receive it. No man can say that it would be wise in us as a nation to build up an institution that would finally bring about another collision. God forbid it, and may the people be wise enough to regret slavery, but whether we shall or shall not have a government based on a solid foundation. Then let us be capable of the duty imposed upon us. Let us settle the question forever, and the best way to do so is to amend the Constitution in regard to slavery. Is there anything wrong about that? There certainly is not. Everybody says it is dead. Then let us do it right and legal according to the Constitution. The proposed amendment ought be carried out.

Yours,
M. V. Bowen

Submitted By: Pauline Bowen Devine

BROWN FAMILY The Brown's were a family that immigrated to America from Ireland in 1786. They settled awhile in Rhode Island. In 1810, John Brown and his family moved inland to Hartford, Connecticut. In 1846, a grandson of John Brown,

Jacob Brown began moving west in hope of prospecting, but stopped in Indiana when his wife, Laura, began suffering from throat hemorrhages that soon killed her. Jacob himself later fought and was killed in the Civil War.

The Brown family lived in Indiana until 1876, when they moved to Ohio and again to Kentucky. Luther Brown moved from Adair County to Estill to Franklin and finally settled in Anderson County. Joe L. Brown, the son of Luther and Maime Brown, was born on 7/13/1902 and died on 6/27/74 in Lawrenceburg, KY. Joe farmed in Anderson County. He married Susan Mary Shouse. She was born on 5-15-06, the daughter of John D. and Susan Shouse. Susan Mary died on 6/4/76 in Versailles, KY.

Joe L. Brown and Susan Mary Brown were the parents of seven children: Blondella married Eddie Smith; twins, Collis (deceased) and Hollis married Mildred (?); Mina Ray married Thomas Perry; Evelyn married Carlos Boggs; Joseph Earl (below); and Mary Jo Brown.

Joseph Earl Brown was born on 9-8-38 in Lawrenceburg. He married Patricia Ann Roach on 9-24-54. She is the daughter of Wallace Errol Roach (1902-1976) and Ethel Susan Reynolds (born 1907). Patricia Ann has one sister, Linda Faye. She married Norman Casey. Joseph Earl later became a minister. They are the parents of four children: Charles Edward (below); Kenneth G. married Eunice Sowers; Donald Joseph married Donna Barnett; and Larry David.

Charles Edward Brown married 1st Sandra Lee Howard, the daughter of John Wilfred Howard and Zelma Irene Todd. They have two children - Charles Douglas and Michael Patrick. Charles Edward and Sandra Lee were divorced. He remarried to Edith May Shryock. They have a son, Matthew Christian. Charles Edward became a car dealer several years ago, and later was called to be a minister of the Church of Christ. *Submitted By: Charlie Brown.*

WILLIAM J. BROWN was born on 3-4-1831 and passed from this world 6-3-1899. He married Elizabeth "Betty" Gordon. Betty was born circa 1838. They lived in the Birdie area of Anderson County where William started a store. (See Birdie Community Article). These two raised several children among them Joseph Henry Brown. Joe was born in September 1857 in Anderson County, Ky. He helped his dad on the farm and later took over the Brown's Store that William started earlier. He married Susan Redmon, daughter of Dawson Northern Redmon and Ann Marie Shaddock Redmon. Joe and Susie had five daughters: Ann Elizabeth married Joe Hume, Hattie married Hollie Perry, Beulah married Albert Catlett, Exie Jane married Allie Willard, and Pearlie who died young. Susan died at 35 years of age when Beulah, the youngest, was only three years old.

About this time, Joseph Henry Brown was deputy sheriff and a confrontation took place between the Birdie Store and the entrance of Brown's Store Road. When Joe Brown attempted to arrest Polk Moffett, a gun fight erupted. Moffett shot Brown in the stomach and with the bullet burning his intestines, Brown drew his revolver and he shot and killed Moffett. Brown was taken in a residence where he was bleeding very badly. A doctor was summoned and Brown recovered.

Joseph Henry Brown

He later married Belle Buttner and they moved to Mercer County where they had several children. To Joe and Belle were born: Ollie, Oscar, Raymond, Ira, Hobert, Ester, Ruby, Cora, Vester, and Dewey. As this article is written only one child of Joe Brown's remains living. She is Ruby Brown who married Lawrence Adamson. They live in Hamersville, Ohio. After a stay in Mercer County, Joe and Belle took their family and moved to Brown County, Ohio where they farmed. Joe died in 1934 and is buried in the Brown Cemetery along side his first wife, Susan, and near his parents, William and Betty Brown. The Brown Cemetery is on the Corinth Road in Anderson County.

This article would not be complete if it did not contain the story that has been handed down throughout the William Brown descendants. When William Brown was a storekeeper in the Birdie Community, seems as if a gentleman came by the store peddling his goods to country storekeepers. It also seems that William "Billy" Brown wanted more than the peddlers wares. Legend has it that Brown killed the traveler, took his money and goods, and disposed of the body. The story is still told today of how the blood stains remained in the old wooden floor of Brown's Store. Is the story fact or fable? No one is left alive to attest either way, but the tale of how Billy Brown got his start in the store business is still told when family descendants get together. *Submitted By: Billy Joe Hume.*

FRED BROWN (son of Mason Brown and Sallie Hedges Brown) and Mary Sharp (daughter of George and Eliza Sharp) were married December 24, 1914 and lived most of their lives in Anderson County.

Five children were born to this union: 1) Wilbur W. Brown, Lawrenceburg, KY; 2) Bonnie Beasley, Lawrenceburg, KY; 3) James E. Brown, Durham, North Carolina; 4) Nora McMichael, Lawrenceburg, KY; and 5) Jesse Brown, Senerna Park, Maryland. Wilbur W. and James E. Brown are deceased.

Wilbur Brown had four sons: 1) James Brown, Owensboro, KY; 2) Jesse Brown, Somerset, KY; 3) Wilbur, Brown, Jr. Lawrenceburg, KY; and Gary Wayne Brown, Frankfort, KY.

Bonnie had three children: 1) Davis Hawkins, Chaplin, KY; 2) Nancy Cheville, California, Maryland; and 3) Martha Greaser, Reading, Pennsylvania.

Fred and Mary Brown

James had three children: 1) Lawrence Brown, Lawrenceburg, KY; 2) Faye Billings, Durham, North Carolina: and 3) Sherry Botts, Durham, North Carolina.

Nora has two children: 1) John L., Middlesboro, KY and Betty Heinemann, Chattanooga, Tennessee.

Jesse has one son, Scott of Senerna Park, Maryland.

Fred farmed several years, after their marriage, then he worked for the railroad for several years, later working in a store in Lawrenceburg until ill health forced him to retire at age 64.

Fred and Mary lived to celebrated their Golden Wedding Anniversary. Mary died in 1966 and Fred died in 1968. Both are buried in the Lawrenceburg Cemetery. *Submitted By: Nora L. McMichael.*

LUTHER AND SALLIE BE[L] **BROWN** lived in Anderson County [near?] Camden, which is now known as Glensb[...] lives. Their ancestors came to this area i[n?] from Virginia.

Luther was born December 15, 1868. He [was?] son of George and Mary Chainie Brown. Sallie [Belle?] Riley Brown was born in 1866. She was the daug[hter?] of Israel and Martha Wayne Brown. Her matern[al] grandparents were William and Melissa Wayne.

Sally Belle Riley Brown - Luther Brown

Luther was a farmer and Sallie Belle was a housewife. Sallie enjoyed cooking, spinning, knitting, and working with children. She often made home remedies from herbs and plants to tend the sick in the area.

Luther and Sallie Belle were the parents of eleven children: George, Mary, and Martha died in their childhood years and another daughter, Ola, died as a young woman; Emma Brown Searcy, Calpernia Brown Curtsinger, Erastus, Charlie, Joe, and Robert, all married, raised their families and died in Anderson County; and Woodrow Wilson "Dick" lived here most of his life, but moved to Mercer County for a few years preceding his death.

Robert's wife, the former Vurvie Peach, still lives in Anderson County at 549 South Main. Sallie Belle died May 4, 1928 from pneumonia. Luther died January 24, 1949 from cancer. They have several great-grandchildren and great-great-grandchildren still living in Anderson County. *Submitted By: Diane Poole.*

MASON "MACE" BROWN and Sallie Hedges were married in 1883, in Anderson County, KY. They had five children: 1) Fred; 2) Edna Rucker; 3) Elvie Scarce; 4) Nell Boggess; and 5) Taylor. Nell Boggess is the only surviving child. She resides in Jeffersonville, Indiana.

Mace farmed most of their married life, but moved to Bell Street in Lawrenceburg in the early 1920's and was on the Police Force.

After Mace died in 1926, Sallie lived with her children, but her later years were spent in the Masonic Widow's and Orphan's Home in Louisville, KY, dying there in 1940. Both are buried in the Lawrenceburg Cemetery. *Submitted By: Nora L. McMichael.*

BRUNK FAMILY This may be a bit of unknown history about a former merchant of Lawrenceburg who had been in business on Main Street for fifty years.

An ancestor from Switzerland, Jonas Von Bronck, was a wealthy land owner. He had three sons, Christopher, John and Jacob, to which he gave a sizeable amount of money each and sent them sailing to America to "seek their fortunes". He advised them to buy lands when they reached their new country and this they did, buying the entire island on New York City, now known as "The Bronx." They Americanized their name, dropping the Von and spelling Bronck as Brunk. Many friends would say they were going up to see the Broncks, thus the island got its name.

The families grew and multiplied, some moving

to Maryland, Pennsylvania, Virginia, and other states.

One descendent, Christopher III, settled in Harrodsburg, Virginia in the Shenandoah Valley, where he too became a large land owner. He had six children, one being a son, John, also a Virginia landowner. John, also had six children. One son, Frederick, had three sons and three daughters. One son, John, the oldest, came to Lawrenceburg and bought the jewelry store of Mr. Roger Meriwether on Main Street. John's younger brother, Enos, died at an early age and the mother made John promise he would always take care of his youngest brother, Harry. He sent Harry to the Elgin College of Watchmaking in Elgin, Illinois (his old alma mater) and to the Illinois School of Ontology and Ophthalmology, also his alma mater. When Harry finished his education, he joined his brother John in business and they became the firm "Brunk Brothers, Jewelers and Optometrists". Harry later moved to Louisville and became associated with the firm of "Vic Lorch, Jewelers".

John retained the business, helped by his wife, Mae, who did the book work for the firm and also helped in the store.

They had one daughter, Ruth, who married Otis Melbourne Hawkins, son of Hurd Hawkins, of the county. Ruth and Melbourne had five children. The two eldest sons, Johnny and Joe Kelly are deceased, but they left five sons and one daughter, and two grandchildren between them. Joe Kelly's eldest son, Kelly was killed in an automobile wreck. Ruth and Melbourne's oldest daughter, Betty Beryl Sudduth Robbins, now lives in Shelbyville, near her daughter and two granddaughters. The son, Jerry, lives in Lexington and has two sons. The youngest child, Lana Anne, is married to Steve Trent, also of Anderson County. They reside in Alton, have three children and one grandchild.

Ruth remarried eight years after Melbourne's death, to Stanley C. Moore, a cousin of her late husband. They lived in Sanibel Island, Florida for eight years before returning to Lawrenceburg where Mr. Moore died three years ago.

BURGIN FAMILY

The earliest ancestor that is recorded is William Burgin who was the grandfather of David Burgin. He was born in Virginia. Later he moved to Kentucky. He first settled in Madison County, then came to Anderson County, and settled on Big Willow Creek (about one mile from its entrance into Salt River) where he resided on a farm until his death. He left a large family of boys and girls on the farm, which all lived and died in Anderson County. David Burgin, father of David G. Burgin, lived and died on this farm. David G. Burgin's sons, down through Edgar Burgin, who was the last to settle there till death. On his death the house was auctioned off. Stephen W. Burgin, a grandson of Edgar, bought the house and property to save as a family heritage that the Burgin's have. The family is quite proud of having such a great, old heritage in the family.

David Graves Burgin was born on 4-28-1857 and died on 7-22-1926, the son of David Burgin. He married on 8-31-1881 to Sallie Jane Cranfill, the daughter of Abe Cranfill. She was born on 3-2-1860 and died on 8-29-1925. They were the parents of seven children: Grace Chairmane (1882-1916); Maud S. (1884 - 1969); Preston H. Thomas (1887-1919); David Graves (1889-1965); Edgar Marion; Sallie Jane (1896-1901); and Walter Ambrose (1899-1901).

Edgar Marion Burgin was born on 5-23-1894 in Sparrow KY. He died on 5-11-1978 in Louisville. He married Nina F. Franklin on 1-6-1918. She was the daughter of Charles Lewis Franklin (1878-1961) and Sarah Elizabeth Tindall Franklin (1881-1968). Nina was born on 12-6-1901 in Pleasant Valley, KY and died on 10-10-1981. They were the parents of eight children: Cecil Marion - three children - Wayne, Charlotte, and Kindra; Nina Pearl (1920-1960); Ambrose Waldo; Herman Bethel - four children-

Teresa, Sherry, Mark, and Kelly; Leah Dane - two sons - Greg and Michael Maynor; Ervin Thomas (1932-1938); Alvin Eugene - two sons - Jeff and David; and Bernice Lee (1941-1944).

Ambrose Waldo Burgin was born on 2-27-24 in Glesboro, KY and he died on 5-19-81. He married Stella Elizabeth Carter on 12-1-45 in Lawrenceburg. She was born on 7-19-24 in Lawrenceburg. She is the daughter of Willis Herford Carter (1881-1977) and Bessie Estelle Gibson Carter (1889-1962). Ambrose Waldo and Stella Elizabeth Burgin were the parents of four children: Sharon Elizabeth married William L. Parrent - one daughter, Sarah M. Parrent; Stephen Wayne married Christy G. Brown - two children - Stephen Bradley and Carrie Graham Burgin; Kela Michelle married Rodney A. Simpson - two children - Jennifer L. and Eric A. Simpson; and Kevin Neal married Delores R. Riley - one daughter, Andrea S. Burgin. *Submitted By: Stephen Burgin.*

TYLER PRESTON BURGIN

TYLER PRESTON BURGIN (1882-1976) married Truman Frances Case (1884-1954) on December 22, 1909. He was farming and she was teaching school. In 1905, one of her students was R. Ezra Sparrow. Both were residents of Anderson County. He was the son of David Graves Burgin (1853-1910) and Martha Jane Long Burgin (1856-1931). She was the daughter of Silas Newton Case (1854-1939) and Lamer Elizabeth Overstreet Case (1860-1894).

The Burgins lived for nine years in the western part of the county. Then in 1919, they bought the Crossfield farm near Fox Creek between Highway 62 and Anderson City Road, about 130 acres. They raised cattle, sheep, hogs, chickens, and turkeys. They also had horses for farming and riding. They had several fruit trees and every year raised a large garden. Much canning was done, the cellar was filled, and the smokehouse had cured meat. Much wood was cut and the woodshed was filled for cooking and heating the house in the winter. Crops were hay, tobacco, and corn.

Twice the home was almost destroyed by fire. Once the fire was in the wall between the kitchen and the dining room, caused by a faulty flue, but was extinguished without doing extensive damage. Again when a catalog was put in the grate, part of it was carried up the chimney and landed on the wooden shingles on the roof still burning. Before a ladder could be brought from the barn and water from the cistern, a big hole was burnt in the roof. That was an exciting time for all and they were thankful the children were playing outside and saw the fire.

Mr. and Mrs. Tyler Burgin

There were four children in the family: Truman Elwood, Maurice Marie, Garnett Glenn, and Preston Case. All attended Fox Creek School, all graduated from Kavanaugh High School. Maurice Marie graduated from Georgetown College, Georgetown, KY and got a Masters Degree from the University of Louisville. Garnett Glenn attended Easter University in Richmond, KY and graduated from Georgetown College, Georgetown, KY. Preston Case served in the Navy for two years during World War II.

Truman Elwood was born October 7, 1910. He married Elizabeth Dennis and was self-employed in

Harrodsburg, KY. They have one son and two grandchildren.

Maurice Marie was born March 19, 1915. She was teaching school at Avenstoke in Anderson County when she met and married James Ritter. They moved to Louisville, KY. She taught school in Anderson and Jefferson Counties for more than thirty years. They have one daughter and two grandsons.

Garnett Glenn was born March 26, 1919. She married Garvice Gibson. They bought and built a home on part of the Burgin farm. She taught school in one room schools: Young at Ballard, Hughes, Searcy, Rutherford, and Hickory Grove. When schools were consolidated she went to Alton School and taught until retirement in 1974, a total of 31 years. They have two children, six grandchildren and two great-grandchildren.

Preston Case was born March 5, 1924. He married Doris Ransdell and they live in Harrodsburg, KY. They have one daughter and three grandchildren.

The Burgins were regular attendants at Goshen Baptist Church. He was a Deacon, held several positions in the church, and she taught Sunday School classes. They were buried in the Lawrenceburg Cemetery. *Submitted By: Garnett Gibson.*

RUBIN BUTLER

RUBIN BUTLER, known to everyone as "Uncle Rube" was born in Franklin County, Kentucky on October 3, 1843. He was a slave to the "Blakemore", at Alton where he lived until his death on July 13, 1933. He joined the Army as a volunteer after the Civil War. Rubin was enrolled the 28th day of May 1865 at the age of 21 years. His brother, Nathan, was a slave to the "Neals" at Alton. Rubin was made Corporal of Company F 119th Regiment on November 5, 1865 at Camp Nelson Infantry.

Rubin Butler

Rubin Butler was married to Louisa Utterback. Rubin and Louisa raised a large family of eight children: Laura Butler (Carter); Alice Butler (Hayden); James Butler; William Purse Butler; Mary Butler (Gant); Nathan Linden Butler (Mason); Pearl Butler (Mason); and Beaulah Butler.

Rubin was denied an Army pension until June 5, 1912, because his service was rendered subsequent to the war of the rebellion. A grandson, John Ray Carter, lost his life during World War I, being the only black soldier killed from Anderson County. A granddaughter, Daisy Carter, lost her life when State Normal Dormitory burned in Frankfort. Rubin has grandchildren, great-grandchildren, and great-great-grandchildren in Anderson County and the adjoining counties. *Submitted By: Gertrude Cunningham.*

BUSEY-GLASS

BUSEY-GLASS The Busey family arrived in Maryland in 1660. Matthew Busey moved from Maryland to North Carolina, probably Rowan or Rockingham County, where he married Edith Philpot Wilcoxson in 1767. Matthew brought his family to Kentucky about 1788 in one of the Boone parties, stopping first at Boonesboro. Later, they came to Franklin County where, his son, John remained.

John Busey, very well educated and one of the most influential men of his time, was one of the Justices of the first court held in the newly formed county of Anderson, 2-5-1827. He took an active interest in county affairs, and also served as a constable in Franklin County. Minutes of the convention of delegates of the Baptist Churches held at Glenn's Creek meeting house in Woodford County list John Busey as a delegate for the Fox Creek church. John was married to Martha Adams, and they had five children: Sarah, Lydia, Edith, John Holmes, and Rebecca.

In 1831, Wakefield Glass married Rebecca Busey, and they raised ten children. After Rebecca's death, Wakefield married her sister, Edith, who was at the time fifty-five years old. They had no children.

Rebecca and Wakefield's son, John C., was born on 6-28-1835 and died 3-10-08 in Shelby County. John moved to the Mt. Eden area in Shelby County when he married Martha Jane Ware (1835-1901). The majority of the Glass family still reside in the Mt. Eden locale. John and Martha Jane were the parents of four children - Arch, Wakefield, Sebert, and Ellen "Fannie".

Sebert Marion Glass was born on 1-1-1873 in Shelbyville, KY and died on 1-29-1948 in Shelby County. He married Nancy Kate Holmes (1888-1973), the daughter of Wolford Holmes and Susie Bently. They raised six children: Hubert married Anna Jane Shouse; Holmes married Onita Tinsley; Martha Pauline Briscoe; Leon married Geraldine M. Best; and Carl (below). Prior to his death, Nancy and Sebert purchased a home in downtown Mt. Eden. Nancy lived there until her death in 1973.

Nancy and Sebert's youngest son, Jessie Carl, was born on 9-16-23 in Shelby County. Carl married Juanita Best in 1947. She is the daughter of George Hudson Best (1880-1961) and Ida Mae Whitehouse (1886-1977). Juanita was born on 3-16-1927 in Anderson County. Both her parents and all her brothers and sisters were also born in Anderson County.

Carl and Juanita are the parents of three children: David Eugene, Wesley Carl, and Alisa Joy. David met Joyce Lynn Baxter at the Alton Ruritan Field where she was playing softball in 1972. They married later that same year. They lived at Alton Station when their children, Chris and Brian, were born. Shortly after the birth of Brian, the family moved to a larger home on Old Lawrenceburg Rd. In 1988, the family moved to Westwood Dr. where they currently reside. *Submitted By: Chris Glass.*

MR. AND MRS. WILLIAM C. CAHILL were

lifelong residents of Anderson County, KY. William, who everyone liked to call "Willie" or "Bill", was the son of Caleb and Ophelia Munday Cahill, born July 6, 1886, married September 12, 1912 to Ruby Alice Young, daughter of Jasper Newton and Nancy Ann Patterson Young, born September 3, 1891. They only had one child, a daughter Wilma Cahill Davenport, who still resides in Anderson County.

William C. Cahill and Ruby Young Cahill

William will always be remembered spreading good humor and cheer among all he met along the way as he liked people. He was quite a noted painter and one long hot summer during the depression days painted about every house on South Main Street, which was then known as a very fashionable area in the town of Lawrenceburg. He later was a

painter for over nine years at the George T. Stagg Company in Frankfort from where he retired in 1951. Ruby was always a housewife, mother, and good neighbor to anyone that needed her and very devoted to her family. They both loved their country home on Highway 44, where they resided for 46 years before moving to town at 228 Woodford Street in 1956. They celebrated their 50th wedding anniversary in 1962. William departed this life on January 3, 1963. Ruby followed on November 7, 1967. Their daughter, Wilma married Robert Case, son of Clyde T. and Alla Sale Case, who passed away in 1956. Thirteen years later she met and married Gilbert Davenport, son of Add and Mae Davenport, who departed this life in 1979. All were very devoted residents of Anderson County. *Submitted By: Wilma Davenport.*

OSCAR CAMMACK, now deceased, was a

merchant in Lawrenceburg and Anderson County for 40 years. The oldest son of Levi and Emma Yocum Cammack, Oscar was born October 9, 1904 in Western Anderson County. He had an older sister, Reva Ellis of Harrodsburg, KY, and two brothers, Homer and Robert "Hick" Cammack of Lawrenceburg.

Oscar attended Young School at Ballard in Anderson County and later owned his first grocery there. Oscar decided to "test his wings" and he came to Lawrenceburg and bought out the partnership grocery of Charlie Marlowe and J. E. Blackburn. This store was located on the corner of Court Street and Waterfill Avenue, and it was known as Oscar Cammack's Grocery.

After a time this move led to another big move as Oscar married Mary Alpha Marlowe, daughter of Charlie and Virginia Hanks Marlowe. Mary Alpha was born on November 23, 1914 on the Old Glensboro Pike in Anderson County. She attended Salt River and Lawrenceburg Elementary Schools. She graduated from City High School in Lawrenceburg. Mary Alpha has a younger brother, Charles F. "Hooter" Marlowe, who resides in Frankfort.

Oscar and Mary Alpha were married at the home of Reverend M. D. Morton, who was pastor at Sand Spring Baptist Church on March 12, 1939. They were the parents of three children: Donna, wife of Raymond Freeman from Salvisa, is a teacher's aide in the Anderson County School System. They are the parents of two sons, Keith Martin Freeman of Versailles, a graduate of the University of Kentucky, and James Marlowe Freeman, a graduate of Milligan College, Tennessee, and lives in Lawrenceburg.

Oscar and Mary Alpha Cammack

Charles Cammack, a graduate of the University of Kentucky, is married to the former Patsy Ann Conway of Frankfort. They have one daughter, Stephanie Lynn Cammack, a student of Anderson County High School. Charles is President and C.E.O. of the Lawrenceburg National Bank.

Mary Jane is a graduate of Fugazzi Business College and is employed by Boulevard Distillers and Importers in the Traffic Department.

After World War II, Oscar took on a partner, his brother "Hick" and the grocery became known as Cammack Brothers. In 1950, he sold his interest in the business to Carl Birdwhistell and moved his

family to Winchester, KY, where he had purchased a jewelry business.

After moving back to Lawrenceburg, Oscar and Mary Alpha bought Carlton's Grocery on North Main Street in 1954 and once again went into the grocery business, known as Cammack Shopworth Supermarket.

Oscar passed away October 12, 1965 and Mary Alpha remained in the grocery until May 1967. She sold the grocery to the late Winfrey and Virginia Best. After selling the grocery, Mary Alpha went to work for the State of Kentucky in the Revenue Department in Frankfort. She worked there until her retirement at July 31, 1980.

Oscar was a member of the Beaver Creek Masonic Lodge in Anderson County. He served on the Lawrenceburg City Council and served on many other committees in the community. The Cammacks and their family have been active members in the Sand Spring Baptist Church, where Oscar was a deacon and trustee. Mary Alpha remains faithful serving in many capacities. *Submitted By: Mary Alpha Cammack.*

EMMETT CAMMUSE, JR., the son of Emmett

Cammuse Sr. and Lenora Harmon Cammuse, was born on 10/20/20 in Springhill, Tennessee. After dating for three months, Emmett Jr. asked Emma Dungy to marry him. Emma was only seventeen years old at the time, so they decided to take his car to a minister in a small town. On the way to Franklin, TN, their car broke down, but it was soon fixed, and they continued their plans. They arrived at the minister's house quite late and had to awaken him. Though frightened and scared Emma managed to lie and tell the minister she was eighteen. For nearly a week after the wedding, they continued living with their respective parents and told no one.

Emma Dungy Cammuse was born on 9-13-22 in Elkmont, Alabama. She is the daughter of Thomas Dungy (dec.) and Gracie Williams Dungy Clark (1898-1986). She has four sisters: Elizabeth, Joy, Margaret, and Ruth.

Emmett and Emma Cammuse were married on 6-22-40 in Tennessee. They soon came to Kentucky after their marriage. Emmett Jr. couldn't get work in Tennessee. After the move to Kentucky, he got a job at National Distillery where he worked for 38 years.

Emmett and Emma were the parents of four children: Gretchen; Leroy married Linda Maggert - four children - Missy, Michael, Marcus, and Brandon; Stephen; and Sandra married Kenneth Perkins, Jr. - two daughters - Jennifer and Kim - divorced - Sandra remarried. (Kenneth Perkins Jr. remarried and has one son, Joshua M. Perkins - they live in Franklin County.)

At the age of fourteen, Emma Cammuse started attending a Baptist church, and a few years following she taught a Sunday School class. Shortly after that her father decided he wanted her to attend the same church as her mother. Having to leave her church upset her greatly, but she attended her mother's Methodist Church. After marrying and moving to Kentucky, she didn't attend church for a long while. Eventually, she did go to a Pentecostal Church with a neighbor and began attending regularly. She became an ordained minister in the Pentecostal faith and started her own church in Lawrenceburg where she remained until a stroke impaired her in 1978. *Submitted By: Kim Perkins.*

ROBERT CARLTON was born in Virginia on

September 20, 1814. On April 21, 1836 in Anderson County, KY, he married Elizabeth B. Morning (1819-1891). She was the daughter of John and Nancy Ann Morning. They had one child, John H. Robert died on December 10, 1897 in Anderson Co.

John H. was born June 1, 1838 in Anderson County and died October 19, 1866. He married Martha Ann Watts (1841-1890), the daughter of Buford Watts. They had two sons: Robert Buford (who married Rose Lee Champion and had twelve children) and John Wesley (1866-1952). John Wesley married Nancy Elizabeth Hammond (1876-1930) on October 17, 1894 in Anderson Co. She was the daughter of Joseph Hutson III and Sarah Elizabeth Boyer Hammond. Nancy had eight brothers and sisters: Eliza Ann, Sarah B., M.D., William H., Josephine, Stella, John T., and Richard. John Wesley and Nancy had one son, John Hazzel.

John Hazzel Carlton was born on September 9, 1902 in Anderson County. On December 28, 1921, he married Laccie Thomas Baugh in Anderson County. She is the daughter of the late Robert and Betty Kent Baugh. Hazzel and Laccie had one daughter, Juanita Frances, who married Ellis Leon Sutherland. Laccie Baugh Carlton still resides in Anderson County. *Submitted By: Mrs. Gary Sutherland.*

WILLIAM AND JANE CAREY owned a farm
on Beaver Creek in Southwestern Anderson County. They built a grain mill on Beaver Creek which they operated for several years. The road to their farm and mill was called Carey Mill Road. They had eight sons and one daughter. The sons were Leander, Alexander, Oliver, Thomas, George, Wade, Clarence, and Joseph; their daughter was Daisy.

Alexander "Alex" Carey was born 10-23-1873 and died 12-22-1953. Alexander married Hester Gritton, born 11-28-1877 and died 12-19-1961. They lived for a short time on the Bard Peach farm, which joined the William Carey farm. Later they built a home on Beaver Creek, which was part of his father's farm. Later Alexander bought the Leathers farm, which was located at the corner of Carey Mill Road and what was then called Kays Road. They had four children, one son, and three daughters. The son, Guy Hurdle Carey, married May Hoskins, the daughters, Lola Carey married John Drury, Gillie Carey married Claude Satterly, and Era Anderson married Claude Anderson. All of Alex and Hester's children lived in Anderson County and died there, except Era Anderson, who moved to Beech Grove, Indiana after her marriage, and still resides there. All of William Carey's descendents were and have been well known throughout Anderson County. I am proud of my ancestors and also Anderson County. *Submitted By: Earl B. Anderson*

EDWARD LYNN AND RACHAEL COLLINS
CARLTON have lived in Anderson County since birth. They were united in marriage on 3-30-89, and currently reside at 117 Marrs Avenue in Lawrenceburg.

Lynn was born to John Willie and Marjorie Jefferies Carlton on 6-8-47. He attended Anderson County High School prior to joining the United States Marine Corps on 7-22-66. Before receiving his honorable discharge on 7-21-69, Lynn served two tours of duty in Vietnam. After returning to civilian life, he went to work for Austin Nichols Distillery and now has twenty years of service with them.

Rachael Ann was born to James David Jr. and Martha Brandenburg Collins on 6-8-49. She also attended Anderson High School. She began employment with Kentucky State Government in March, 1971, and she has nineteen years of service. Rachael has two sons: David Wayne Hawkins, born 1-6-69, and is married to the former Barbara Walling of Versailles, KY; and Anthony (Tony) Tyler Hawkins, born 4-12-77. *Submitted By: Rachael Carlton.*

JOHN WILLIE CARLTON and Majorie Jefferies
were both born in Anderson County, married 2-5-28, in Jeffersonville, Indiana and are members of the First Baptist Church.

John Willie was the son of Rose Champion and Robert Carlton. He was the eldest of twelve children, grew up on a farm on Crooked Creek and attended Marlowe School. From 1948 to 1951, he operated a grocery in Fox Creek, and in 1960 he was appointed to fill the position of Deputy Sheriff after the death of Herb Phillips, and was elected the Deputy Sheriff,

with John Birdwhistell in 1965 and was elected Sheriff in 1966. After this term, he was elected County Clerk with Julian Birdwhistell and Rosalie Yocum as Deputies. John Willie served as County Clerk from 1970 to 1973 until he had to resign because of ill health. He was elected magistrate of the South Lillard District in 1978 and served until his death in April, 1979. John Willie was instrumental in getting Carpenter Lane widened and blacktopped, and after his death it was renamed Carlton Drive, in his honor, where Majorie still resides.

Marjorie Jefferies was born on 9-26-10, to Lula Shely and Edward R. Jefferies, who was the County's first veterinarian in 1913, Deputy Sheriff, with Oscar Walker Sheriff, in 1930, and Sheriff from 1934 to 1938. Marjorie had three brothers and grew up in the western part of the county where she attended the first class of Western High School in 1925. She has been active in the Homemakers and is a 50 year member. Her hobby is piecing quilts and sharing her knowledge of crafts with others.

Marjorie and John Willie have five children: William Bert Carlton, who died in February, 1975; Twyla Trisler, Harrodsburg, KY; Jean Spencer, Lawrenceburg; Judy Bailey, Frankfort; and Lynn Carlton, Lawrenceburg. They have nine grandchildren and thirteen great-grandchildren. *Submitted By: Billy Spencer.*

CARTINHOUR The Cartinhour name has been
identified with Anderson County, its business, religious and civic affairs, for more than three generations.

Emmett Benjamin Cartinhour (1876-1947), a native of Scott County whose great grandfather came to Kentucky from Maryland, settled in Lawrenceburg in 1908. Some two years before, on December 27, 1905, he married Mabel Major, of Anderson County, who was the daughter of John William Major and Mary Ann Gaines. At the time, Mr. Cartinhour was in business in Chicago. When they returned to Kentucky, he opened a livery stable in Lawrenceburg which he operated until it was destroyed by fire. Later, he went into the retail grocery business which came to be known as E. B. Cartinhour and Son. His son, Emmett B. Cartinhour, Jr., and his grandson, William David Cartinhour, succeeded him and managed the business until 1978 when it was closed.

First Row, Mabel and Benjamin; Second Row, Emily and Keri; Third Row, Minnie Cartinhour, Emmett Benjamin and Linda Cartinhour.

Mabel Major, born 1884, was a descendent of Littleton Major and Richard Henry Gaines, men who immigrated to Anderson County from Culpeper County, VA. Early tax records indicate Littleton Major acquired land near Alton by the year 1800. Richard Henry Gaines, grandson of Revolutionary War veteran William Henry Gaines, was the father of Gabriel Hansford Gaines, of Lawrenceburg, who was Mrs. Cartinhour's uncle. J. W. Gaines (1869-1959) was an attorney, former mayor of Lawrenceburg, past president of the Anderson National Bank, and a prominent member of the First Christian Church (Disciples of Christ). Mrs. Cartinhour's brother, Walter W. Major, is past president of the Lawrenceburg National Bank. Mrs. Cartinhour died in 1989 at the age of 104 years.

Emmett and Mabel Cartinhour had two children, Mary Gaines Cartinhour, and Emmett B. Cartinhour, Jr., who was known as Buzz. Mary Gaines Cartinhour married John Clement Hearne of Ashland, KY, in 1931

They had two children, Nancy Major Hearne, the wife of Dennis Harry Jones of Louisville and Joseph Clement Hearne of Wilmington, NC. John Hearne was in the building material business in Catlettsburg, KY for many years. He died in 1982. Mary Gaines Hearne continues to live in Ashland.

Buzz Cartinhour graduated from Tennessee Military Academy in 1934 and then joined his father in the grocery business. In 1939, he married Minnie Mae Jones, a native of Mississippi, who came to Anderson County in 1937 as a public health nurse. Buzz Cartinhour died in 1972. Their children are E. Ben III, who is now a resident of Woodford County, and William David Cartinhour, of Lawrenceburg.

The Cartinhour's of Lawrenceburg have all been members of the First Christian Church (Disciples of Christ). *Submitted By: William Cartinhour.*

JOHN BRUNER CASE was born around 1842 in
Anderson County. He married Nancy Mae Shely. They were the parents of several children: Mary (married John Shely); Maggie (married John McCown); Clyde T.; John H. (married Cora Case); Sarah (married Charles Martin); Cordy (married Elmo Royalty); and Robert (married Emma ?). There may have been more children born to John and Nannie Case. John was a farmer in Anderson County.

Clyde Talmadge was born on 2-6-1881 in Anderson County and died on 1-2-1974 in Anderson County. On 8-20-1903, he married Alla Sale, the daughter of John and Emma Alexander Sale. She was born on 7-14-1884 in Anderson County and died on 3-6-1970 in Anderson County. They were the parents of at least eight children: Wallace B. married Rosa Bowles; John H. married Louise Case; Carl; Fred Toll married Edna McGurk; Roy (below); Richard Allan (below); Maggie Mae married Joseph Hartley; and Mrs. Paul Pate and Robert Sale.

Roy Case (1919-1972) married Ruby Leathers Case (Evans) on 8-12-38. She was born on 1-13-20 and is the daughter of Grover Ray (1882-1982) and Otha Blockson Leathers (1909-1982). Ruby has one sister, Virginia Leathers Kirsh, and one brother, Thomas (born and died 1923). Roy and Ruby were the parents of six children: Roy Kidwell (1940-1942); Steven married Ruby Mathis Case; Mike married L. A. Case; Alla married Ron Combs - two daughters - Kristel, born 1972, and Ronda Sue, born 1975; William "Bill" (1953-1988) married Sharon Case; and James "Jimmy" married Cathy Matz Case.

Richard Allan Case was born on 2-21-23 in Anderson County. He married Joyce Moore on 9-20-47. She was born on 8-20-30 in Anderson County to Ernest and Bessie Casey Moore. They are the parents of three children: Rickie, born 1948, married Mike Faust - four children - Kim, Lee, Len, and Micah; Jennifer, born 1958, married Larry Hays - four children - Josh, Sarah, Rebecca, and Andrew; and Richard Case II, born 1964, married Jennifer Sutherland. *Submitted By: Josh Hays and Ronda Combs.*

WILLIAM H. CASE was born 8 March 1808 in
Washington County, Kentucky. The names of his parents are still unproven, but according to the Anderson County 1880 Census, his father was born in Tennessee and his mother was born in West Virginia. He married, about 1827, to Margaret Burgan, born 16 April 1812 in Washington County, KY, the daughter of William and Margaret (Graves) Burgan, originally from Virginia. The Case and Burgan families were both in Anderson County at its formation in 1827, and many of their descendents remain in the area.

There were several children born to William and Margaret (Burgan) Case, of which, seven were known to have survived childhood: Nancy J., born 1828; Dennis, born 1829; Seperate, born 1831; John, born

1838; Elijah, born 1841-43; Margaret E., born 1847; and Sarah F., born 1850. Margaret (Burgan) Case died in Anderson County, Kentucky on 10 May 1880, William H. died there 12 October 1884, both are buried in the New Liberty Churchyard in Anderson County.

Dennis Case, born circa 1829 in Anderson County, Kentucky, son of William H. and Margaret (Burgan) Case, married in Anderson County on 4 January 1850 to Elizabeth Davis, born circa 1830, daughter of Allen Davis and Sarah (Shoemaker). Dennis and Elizabeth spent a few years in Texas, leaving Anderson County in a covered wagon, sometime after 1875. According to family lore, Elizabeth (Davis) Case died during the return trip and was buried along the trail. Dennis married second, in Anderson County, Kentucky, on 10 November 1892 to Mrs. Elizabeth Spratt, born 1 February 1853, daughter of Lloyd and Lucinda (Franklin) Simpson.

Lebon Merritt Case and Fida Hahn Case

There is little doubt that some of Dennis and Elizabeth's children married in Texas and most likely remained there when their parents decided to return to Kentucky. Dennis died in Anderson County on 22 August, 1896.

Lebon Merritt Case, born 13 July 1875 in Anderson County, Kentucky, son of Dennis and Elizabeth (Davis) Case, was in his mid-teens when his parents decided to return to Kentucky. He married in Nelson County, Kentucky on 22 March 1893 to Fida Hahn, born 31 Jan 1878 in Anderson County, daughter of Jordan Hahn and Sallie Bentley. Lebon died there in late 1960. Both are buried at the Fairmont Christian Church Cemetery. Five children: Rome Gardie Case, born 23 Jul 1894 in Anderson County, married Malinda Ellen Simpson; Louis Case; Sam Case; Ethel Case; and Georgia Case. *Submitted By: William R. Walls.*

SILAS NEWTON CASE was born in Anderson County on July 6, 1854 and died January 7, 1939 in Cocoa, Florida at the home of a daughter. He was the son of John Case (1814-1889) and Frances Franklin Morris (1813-1893). He married Almer Elizabeth Overstreet (1860-1916), daughter of Thomas Bonaparte Overstreet (1827-1916) and Sarah Elizabeth Baker Overstreet (1831-1916). They were the parents of ten children. Cora Lee (1881-1971) married Clyde Melrose Strange (1880-1972) and celebrated their sixty-fifth wedding anniversary in 1968. Twins, Thomas Walter and John Victor, were born in 1882. Thomas Walter never married and died in 1927. John Victor (1882-1959) married Georgia Davenport (1900-). They had five children and lived in Mercer County. Susan Elizabeth (1886-1870) and Lillian Mae (1885-1890) both died at an early age. William Stanley (1888-1976) married Bessie Goodlett and they had one son. Later he married Mary Cox and had three children. Frances Truman (1884-1954) married Tyler Preston Burgin (1882-1976) and they had four children. Alice Downey (1890-1980) never married and lived in California. Amy Estelle (1892-1983) married Oscar Cooper (1893-1967) and had two daughters. They lived in Alabama and Florida. James Guy (1893-1976) married Letitia Peach and had three daughters.

Later Silas Newton married Sara Elizabeth Hardwicke (1868-1925) and they had four children. Nell Gertrude (1898-1981) married Joe Griggs and moved to Florida. They had two children. Mabel Marie (1900-1983) married Gee Lancaster and they had four children. Ruth and Edith both died at an early age.

The Case family lived on a farm between Goshen and Ballard. They were faithful attendants at Goshen Baptist Church. The parents were buried in Goshen Cemetery. *Submitted By: Garnett Gibson.*

CATLETT The name Catlett is English, derived from Catt's Lot upon which the first of the name was settled.

John Catlett died before 1626 in England and left a widow, Sarah, age 24. Their son was: Col. John Catlett I, immigrant, b-1622, d-1670, came to Virginia with two sons: Thomas and Nicholas. He was Presiding Justice, Burgess, Sheriff, Col. of Militia and of the Vestry. He was one of three Commissioners to settle the boundary line between Virginia and Maryland. Married - 2nd Elizabeth Underwood Slaughter, b-1657, d-1673. He was killed by Indians, defending the fort at Port Royal. His home was on the Rappannock River and was called Green Hill.

Col. John Catlett II, the first son of John I and Elizabeth, b-1658, d-1724, married Elizabeth Gaines. He was Burgess, Justice, Coroner, President of the Court and Sheriff. He was father of seven children.

One of whom was: John Catlett III d-1739, married 2nd Mary Grayson. He was of the Vestry of St. George in 1738. He was father of seven children by his second marriage, one of whom was: Reuben Catlett d-1794, married Elizabeth.....The will of John III left a tract of land to his son Reuben called Magnum Oaks. He was a Patriot in the Revolutionary War. He was father of nine children.

One of whom was: Francis Catlett b-1777, d-1835, married Elizabeth Munday Robinson, 1801-4, b-1787, d-1870. Francis was born in Caroline County, Virginia, came to Franklin County, now Anderson, and built their home on the Hammonds Creek Road, on a 150 acre farm. The family attended the Little Flock Baptist Church. They were the parents of thirteen or more children, one of whom was:

Francis M. Catlett b-1827, d-1900, married 1st Nancy Jane Young, 1849. Married 2nd Martha Ann Watts Carlton, January 7, 1872. Children by first husband: John W. Carlton married Nannie Hammonds and Robert Buford Carlton married Rose Champion. Francis M. served in the Mexican War.

Children by Nancy Jane Young were: James William b-1850, married Margaret...; Thomas Berry b-1852, married Kate...;John Washington b-1854, married Amanda Jane Briscoe; Martha Elizabeth b-1856, d-1951, married John Harrison Ruble, 1875; Susan Mary b-1858, d-after 1900, single; George E. "Bose" b-1859, d-1904, married Alice W. Parmer, 1882; Sarah Ellen b-1862, d-1931, married Edward W. Briscoe, 1880; Robert Lee b-1864, d-1893, married Gertie Hawkins, 1892.

Children by Martha Ann Watts Carlton were: Henry Francis b-1873, d-1902; Hollie C. b-1875, d-1948, married 1st Lillian J. Gee, 1897 and 2nd Lena J. Husband; Ezra Thomas b-1877, d-1940, married 1st Nannie Burk, 1900 and 2nd Elizabeth E. Perry, 1918; Lillie b-1878, d-1962, married Charles Brown.

The youngest child was: Charles Herbert Catlett b-1882, d-1935, married Susan Mary Perry, b-1881, d-1935, three children - Charles Eunice Catlett b-1905, d-1971, married Corinne Driskell, 1928, b-1909. Children: Joyce Marie Soards, Louis Eldon Catlett, and Linda June Gilbert.

Lorene Catlett Murphy b-1913, married Robert Murphy, 1938, b-1911, d-1983. Children: Patsy M. Panella b-1939, married 1st Bruce Gash, 1959, 2nd Charles N. Panella, 1965. Children - Leslie Beth Panella b-1967; Melinda Marie Panella b-1969. Suzanne M. Duncan b-1943, married David Duncan, 1961. Children: David Bradley Duncan b-1961;

Stephen Eric Duncan b-1965; Laura Jeanette Duncan b-1968. William Robert Murphy b-1945, married Faye Kincannon, 1965. children: Amy Rene Murphy b-1968; Mark Robert Murphy b-1970.

Sidney Earl Catlett b-1921, d-1986, married Fannie Dearing, 1943. b-1923. Children: Kenneth Earl, Charles Larry, Gary Wayne, Danny Ray, Sidney Earl Jr., and Donna Sue Smith. *Submitted By: Lorene Catlett Murphy.*

CATLETT The Catlett family of French origin was well-established in Virginia long before the Revolutionary War.

Francis Catlett, taxpayer in Caroline Co., Virginia in 1798, was born there in 1777 or earlier. He was a son of Rueben and Elizabeth Catlett.

Francis Catlett was married to Elizabeth Munday Robinson about 1801. As early as 1808 this family is found in Fayette County, where in 1810 Francis listed four horses and four slaves. A few years later he appears in Franklin County (now Anderson) as owner of a 150-acre Farm. This land was on the Hammond Creek and it was here that Francis and Elizabeth Catlett built their home and lived until Francis' death in the 1830's.

The Catlett's attended the nearby Little Flock Baptist Church. They reared a large family including six sons and five daughters, most of whom lived to be married and have many descendents still residing in Anderson County. Among these descendents are teachers, ministers, public officials, and leaders in many walks of life.

The children of Francis and Elizabeth Catlett are: George Washington (below); Benjamin (1806-1877) married 1st Elizabeth Spears, 2nd Mary F. Cinnamon. Twelve or more children; Lawrence (1808-?) little is known of this family. They apparently left Anderson County disposing of their share in the parent's estate in 1840; Sarah "Sally" (ca 1814 - ?) married Lawrence Samuel in 1849; Martha (1821 - ?) married Jack B. Richard in 1840 - Six children; Elizabeth (1822 - ?) married Wesley Melear in 1855. Little is known of this family, but it is believed that Elizabeth was widowed not long after her marriage, probably one child; Andrew Jackson (ca 1824 - ?) served in the Mexican War. He was living in Anderson Co. in 1850; Louisa Ann (ca 1826-ca 1898) married 1st Robert Garnett Samuel in 1840, 2nd Woodson Munday. There were eight children by the first marriage; and Francis M. (1827-1900) married 1st Nancy Jane Young in 1849, 2nd Martha Ann Watts Carlton in 1872. Twelve or thirteen children.

In 1854, Elizabeth, widow of Francis, sold to her oldest son George Catlett, her farm and stock for one dollar. In return, he was to care for her for the remainder of her life.

George Washington Catlett (1804-1890) married Nancy Cole in 1832. They had ten or more children. One of which was Elijah "Lite" Catlett. He married Susan Mary Herndon, the daughter of Pressley Fisher Herndon and Elizabeth Jane Cole. They had five children: Valeria Alma (married Oscar Young Walker); Nora (married John Phillips); Nancy Jane "Nannie" (married John "Tuck" McCormick); Ernest Francis (married Jessie Bixler Catlett); and John Earl (married Carrie Meeks Stevens).

George was a successful farmer and maintained a keen interest in civic affairs. He was several times a magistrate from his district and records show that he was one of the most progressive justices. George was appointed county judge serving from September to December 1866.

There are many descendents of the Catlett family living in Anderson County today. *Submitted By: Jane Walker Wyatt Puhr.*

CHARLES EUNICE CATLETT Catlett's, English, (descendent's of immigrant Col. John Catlett) and Driskell's (derivative of Eiderscoil, Irish) have been in America over three hundred years and in Kentucky and Anderson County over two hundred.

Charles Eunice Catlett (b. 7-19-1905 d. 2-17-71), eldest of three children of Charles Herbert Catlett and Susan Mary Perry, was married to Corinne Driskell on May 26, 1928.

Eunice and Corinne Catlett

They resided in Glensboro for three years as he was a cashier of the Farmer's Bank of Glensboro. The charter expired in 1931, the depression was taking its toll, so an agreement was reached with the Lawrenceburg National Bank to take over the accounts and as a result of early dissolution nothing was lost by the depositors or stockholders.

Eunice then started as a salesman for the Lawrenceburg Motor Co. Inc., a Chevrolet dealership, soon becoming Dealer and part owner. While no cars were available during World War II and a long strike at General Motors, he negotiated with partners, bought their share and remained there until retirement on December 31, 1966.

He was a graduate of Kavanaugh High School, active member and deacon of First Christian Church, the City Council, School Board and a Business Mens Organization that worked diligently to bring what is now Universal Fasteners back to Lawrenceburg.

He was an energetic person, loved to tease and lived life to the fullest. His hobbies were fishing, fishing, and more fishing. Due to the early death of their parents, his brother, Sidney, and sister, Lorene (Murphy) came and lived with them several years.

Corinne (b. 9-25-1909) is an Anderson native but was raised in Spencer County and attended Mt. Eden High School. She is the third of eight children born to Charles Lewis Driskell and Frances Moriah (Fanny) Simpson.

While living in Glensboro, substituting for her husband alone in the bank one day, she received the alarming news that the Van Buren State Bank had just been robbed at gun point, leaving the cashier gagged and tied up.

She is a member of the Lawrenceburg First Christian Church, Christian Women's Fellowship and Lawrenceburg Woman's Club. She worked in their business office when needed. Her hobbies were traveling and antiquing. They had three children:

Joyce Marie (b. 5-31-29), a graduate of Lawrenceburg High and Transylvania College, married Otis Lee Swords, Jr. They have lived in Charlotte, N.C. for the last twenty years. Otis is the minister of South Park Christian Church and Joyce works as assistant secretary at Shedgefield Junior High. They have three children and six grandchildren.

Louis Eldon (b. 4-12-31), a graduate of Lawrenceburg High and the University of Kentucky in Engineering, married Joyce Fisher. They have three children and two grandsons. They divorced and he married Erma Fienburg. After spending seven years in the Air Force, Louis worked at Rand Corporation in Los Angeles for twenty years and is now renovating property in Hollywood and Los Angeles.

Linda June (b. 10-29-33), is a graduate of Anderson High School and attended Christian College in Columbia, Missouri. She married George Freeman Gilbert, M.D., a family practitioner, here in Lawrenceburg for many years. They have eight children and eight grandchildren. *Submitted By: Corrine D. Catlett.*

CHAMPION Davis Champion lived in Washington County, KY, where he married Mary Sweeney Rudd (1822-1897) on October 10, 1841. Soon afterward they moved into western Anderson County near Baxter Ridge where Champion School later stood. With them came Mary's father and sister, William and Susan Sweeney.

A) Willie Champion (1845-1927) married Ann Mariah Peyton (1849-1915). They had thirteen children: 1) Elvore married Jim Switzer, 2) George, 3) Edd 4) Rose married Robert Carlton. Their children Mabel and Margie live on Center Street; Annie Brown on Carlton Drive (named for her brother, John Willie, deceased); Sheila Rucker, Raymond, Marvin, and Rex Carlton within Anderson County. 5) Mary Eliza married Sam Brumley, 6-7) twins, Schuyler (lived a few days) and Tyler, 8) Tom married Essie Grace, 9) Emma married Albert Perry. Their daughter, Mrs. Will Brown lives in Lawrenceburg, 10) Ebon married Laura Lancaster and moved from Anderson County but returned to live with his niece, Mabel Carlton, until his death. His son, Billie Carlton Champion, lives in Houston, Texas. 11) Davis married Mary Brown. Their daughter, Louise Richardson lives on North Main. 12) Louis died in Florida, and 13) Jessie.

B) Arietta, and her husband, Polk Toll, were the parents of 1) Dr. Leslie Toll, a well-known Lawrenceburg doctor had three daughters: Elizabeth (deceased), Nancy Toll Smith who lives on Village Drive, and Leslie Hollingsworth. 2) Hanson Toll married Lettie Baxter and lived in Louisville. 3) Mary Toll married Frank Baxter. Their daughters, Arietta Baxter and Onita Baxter Jenkins, live in Lawrenceburg; Ruby, Robert, and William live elsewhere. 4) Verna Toll married Wilkes Bond and lived in Anderson County at the time of their deaths. 5) Nora Toll, married Homer Baxter. Their son, Marvin, USAF, Retired, died in 1986. 6) Mabel Toll married Lindsey Baxter. Their daughter died in infancy.

C) Mankin C. Champion, born 1853, married Sarah Frances Mullins, daughter of Thomas Mullins and Susan Utterback Mullins. Sarah died in 1891 at 36, leaving him seven children to raise. His grandchildren lovingly called him "Pa Champion". Mankin was elected to the Kentucky House of Representatives 1904-1906. Mankin and Sarah's children include: 1) Susan Mary Champion married James B. McMurry. They had four sons; Stanley, Roger, Davis, and Clellan, and two daughters; Sally Lynn and Helen Moss. Clellan lives on Meriwether Drive. 2) John F. Champion (1877-1878) is buried in the Sweeney Cemetery. 3) Thomas David Champion (1879-1968) married Della Baxter (1879-1959), and lived in Mercer County. Both were teachers who had four children, all college graduates who entered the education field. James Bruce was a teacher and principal for 37 years, mostly in Mercer and Anderson Counties; his widow, Grace James Champion, taught for 32. Bernice taught in Mercer County, Northern KY and Deer Park High School, Ohio. Bernice's widow, Matilda McClanahan Champion, is a retired teacher in Fort Thomas, KY. Grace taught in Mercer County, then became a Louisville teacher and supervisor. Florence taught in Anderson County, and was a Louisville teacher and principal.

Mankin C. Champion - "Pa"

Jeanette Champion Cole, daughter of Bruce and Grace James Champion, lives in Anderson County. Her sister, Jane Champion Norman, teaches in Louisville. Many Champions were active in Shiloh and Fox Creek Christian Churches and were musically talented. Tom and Della Champion were singers and encouraged their children who formed a quartet which won music contests and sang in churches throughout Anderson County.

4) Mattie Champion married Yancey Baxter, son of Henry H. Baxter. Their daughter, Elizabeth, died before adolescence. 5) Elizabeth "Lizzie" Champion who married Hardin Baxter; also a son of Henry H. Baxter. 6) Charles Earldy Champion who married Jessie Baxter was well known throughout Anderson County where he served many years as a magistrate. (Adopted Children, see Baxter History). 7) Etta Bell Champion married Eugene Hedger and moved to West Virginia. John Clark Hedger lives in Huntington, West Virginia; Robert (deceased); Charles (deceased); and Edwin in Austin, TX. 8) Walter Raymond Champion (1891-1975) taught in Clark, Boone, Rockcastle, and Garrard Counties and was Superintendent of Lancaster High School. He married Lois Pearl and was living in London, KY, at his death in 1975.

D) Adolphus Champion who married Phoebe Belle Mullins worked as a revenue officer in Lexington. Their children were Joe, Everett, and Sally Champion Bishop. A granddaughter, Mary Jo Bishop Jones, lives in Florida. *Submitted By: Grace J. Champion.*

CHEAK Although they were born and raised in Anderson County, Ruby Stratton and W. B. Cheak did not meet each other until the fall of 1947, after his return from World War II. They were an unlikely pair - she was a short 5'3" in height and he was a tall, lanky 6'6" tall. But they both knew they were meant to be together, so they were married on May 15, 1948, in a small private ceremony.

W. B. was the youngest child born to W. D. and Carrie Perry Cheak. His two sisters, Mrs. Robert (Edna) Wash and Mrs. Gertie Lyen, and his brother, Presley, have always lived in Anderson County.

Ruby was the third child and only daughter born to Willie and Margie Cammack Stratton. Two of her brothers, Garland and Sylvester, are now deceased, but her oldest brother, J. W., lives next door to her.

In early 1954, W. B. and Ruby bought and moved to the farm, which was to be their home for the next 23 years. In addition to operating the dairy farm, W. B. somehow found the time to do carpentry work, helping build many barns and houses throughout the years. They also raised tobacco, corn, soy beans, all types of hay, and had the usual farm animals - pigs, chickens, dogs, cats, pony, and even a white rabbit, in addition to the dairy cattle. Farm work, especially milking the cows twice every day (365 days a year), was very hard and confining, but there was never any complaining, even when the temperature dipped way below zero and snow covered the ground.

W. B., Ruby, Vickie, David, and Carroll Cheak

W. B. and Ruby raised their three children on that farm and worked together as a family in the tobacco patch, the hayfield, the garden, etc. Those years were the busiest, but the happiest of their lives, being together and working together to make a living.

In the late 1970's, after the death of Ruby's parents, W. B. and Ruby built a new home on Hwy. 62 on her father's farm. They continued farming, but bought beef cattle, rather than dairy cattle and W. B. once again started carpentry work, building new houses. Their new, less busy life was a wonderful change for them and they made plans to travel and see parts of the country they had always longed to see. Those plans were never to be - W. B. was tragically killed while bailing hay on June 30, 1982. Ruby continues to live in the house they built and operates the farm.

Their oldest child and only daughter, Vickie, graduated from Centre College, and now is the principal and director of the work program at the Stewart Home School. She and her husband, David Sellwood, are the parents of a three-year old daughter, Shelley. David also is the principal and recreation director at the Stewart Home School. They make their home in Frankfort now.

Their oldest son, David, graduated from the University of Kentucky and now is an accountant and supervisor in Corporation Income Tax with the Department of Revenue in Frankfort. He and his wife, the former Gloria Steele, have four children, Micah, 9, Nathan, 8, Brandon, 6, and Lydia, 4. Their home adjoins David's parents farm, and Gloria owns and operates a day-care there for children of all ages.

William Carroll, the youngest of W. B. and Ruby's children, currently works at Hoover Manufacturing Co., in Georgetown. He and his wife, the former Susan Flynn, recently built a log cabin on the rear of his parents' farm. Carroll helps his mother with many of the farm chores, such as cutting the hay and helping with the beef cattle. Susan works at Frankfort Habilitation, Inc. in production. *Submitted By: Vickie Cheak Sellwood.*

CHEEK - PHILLIPS Alfred Bertram Cheek married Ethel Mae Carter on 6-23-1934. She was born on 12-20-1910 in Lawrenceburg. She is the daughter of Jesse Elwood Carter (1891-1972) and Newell Perkins Carter (died 1923). She has five brothers and sisters: Wallace L., born 1913, married Marie Riley; Verna, born 1916; Gilbert W., born 1918; Roy E., born 1920, married Margaret Adams; and Louise, born 1921, married Marshall Gash.

Alfred and Ethel Mae Cheek had four children: Alfred Bruner; Roland F., born 1937, married Wanda J.; Annabelle, born 1938, married Jerald T. McElroy; and William C., born 1940, married Mary V. Bryan. Alfred Cheek died in January of 1977.

Alfred Bruner Cheek was born on 5-20-1935 in Frankfort, KY. He married Mattie Catherine Phillips on 4-21-1973 in Lafollette, Tennessee. She was born on 12-19-1952 in Lawrenceburg. She is the daughter of Stanley Phillips and Frances West Phillips. Alfred Bruner and Mattie C. Cheek have one daughter, Kellye, born on 2-17-1974 in Frankfort. They reside on Wildcat Road in Anderson County.

Stanley Phillips was born on 6-18-1922 in Mercer County. He is the son of David Phillips (1889-1956) and Mattie Kurtz Phillips (1887-1919); Ruth, born 1914; Sarah, born 1916; David W., born 1920; Carl, born 1924; Lena, born 1925; Albert, born 1926; Raymond, born 1928; and Alvin (born and died in 1931.)

Stanley married Frances West on 6-18-1938 in Lawrenceburg. She was born on 2-20-1921 in Lawrenceburg. She is the daughter of Robert T. West (1889-1927) and Annie L. Martin West (1892-1966). She has nine brothers and sisters: Lester Thomas (born and died 1911); William Earl, born 1912, married Alval Kelvy; Robert T., born 1915, married Elberta Chapeman; Jenevieve, born 1917, married Earl Gregory; Nora Bell, born 1918, married Harold Knight; Rose, born 1923, married Chester Sutherland; Joe, born 1925, married Jimmy Rogers; Elzie, born 1927, married Phillis Knox; and Leona, born 1930, married Harold Flynn.

Stanley and Frances Phillips are the parents of seven children: Frances Lucill (born and died 1939); Mary, born 1940, married James Hawkins; Stanley Jr., born 1941, married Sue Lollis; John Robert, born 1943, married Sue Ann Driscoll; Mattie Catherine; and Ruth Ann, born 1960, married Gary Carpenter. *Submitted By: Kellye Cheek.*

BURSE CHESTER or Cheshire (some say) married Sara Elizabeth Hamilton. They were the parents of two children: Thomas Louis and Nannie Frances Chesher.

Tom married Myrtie McMillin (1-12-1886 - 2-12-1974). Born to this union were three children: Paul, Edna, and Blondella Frances. Paul and Edna were both born in Lawrenceburg and Blondella was born in Anderson County.

Tom Chesher left his family when the children were: Paul, age seven; Edna, age three; and Blondella, age ten months. Tom was not heard from again. The children went to live with their Grandfather McMillin. *Submitted By: Edna Bernhardt.*

ONITA CHILTON COX and Ralph Coleman Cox of 403 Greenview Drive were married in Anderson County 8-29-1952 and have lived here all their lives except while Ralph served in the Armed Forces two years and they lived in Shelbyville, KY for two years due to their jobs.

Ralph worked at IBM in Lexington, KY for 31 years with 18 years in management. Onita is employed at Lawrenceburg National Bank.

They have two sons named Kent Coleman Cox and Kelly Conrad Cox. Kent is married to Teresa Adams Cox, who lives on a farm in Anderson County on Benson Creek Road and works at IBM. Kent has three boys, Jeremy Coleman, Jacob Kent, and Jonathan Thomas Cox. Kelly lives on Djeddah Drive in Lawrenceburg, works at Mathews-Conveyer Company in Danville, KY and has a fine friend, Tina Holt.

They are members of Claylick United Methodist Church as the Chiltons have always been in the south end of the county near Mercer County line. The Coxes have always been in the Western part of the county. With their heritage each family began with farming the most important source of making a living.

Onita's parents are Horace Chilton and Sadie Shelton Chilton with two sisters, Frances Lucille (Mrs. William Pearson) and Lillie Mae (Mrs. Billy Bottom). Frances with three children: Musial, Reva Lucille, and Mary Manita Pearson. Lillie with two boys, Donald Leon and Ronald Levan Bottom.

Onita Chilton Cox and Ralph Coleman Cox

Onita's grandparents are Fred Chilton and Minnie Robinson Chilton with eight children: Horace, Melvin, Evert, Linwood, Onieda, Allie Bell Coke, Elisie Ray (Mrs. Alonzo Roark), and Catherine (Mrs. R. V. Jeffries).

Onita's paternal great grandparents are Berryman Chilton and Belle Robinson Chilton with six children: Fred, Coy, Took, Bud, Sabe (Mrs. John Thompson) and Minnie (Mrs. Charlie Holman). Cynthia Sutterfield was second wife.

Onita's paternal great grandparents are Robert (Bob) Robinson and Rachael Spaulding Robinson with eight children: Minnie (Mrs. Fred Chilton), Fannie (Mrs. Lee Baker), Lela Belle (Airie Baker), Roy, Raymond, Luther, Herman, and Willie Robinson.

Onita's maternal grandparents are Vernon Shelton and Ida Mae Watts Shelton with six children: Sadie Mae (Mrs. Horace Chilton), Beatrice (Mrs. Oscar Newby), Dolly (Mrs. Chick Huffman), Ada (Mrs Carl Etherington), Burton, and Morris Shelton.

Ralph's parents are John Thomas Cox and Thelma Ward Cox with two sisters, Volita (Mrs. R. M. Thompson), Donna Rhea (Mrs. Daniel Tipton) and one brother, Leon Cox.

Ralph's paternal grandparents were Robert (Bob) Cox, and Cora McGinnis Cox with six children: John Thomas, Pete, Dallas (Mrs. Sam Curtsinger), Clara (Mrs. Dorsey Hall), Kenneth and Cecil Cox.

Ralph's paternal great grandparents were Rial McGinnis and Martha Burgin McGinnis.

Ralph's maternal grandparents were Newton Ward and Trent Adams Ward with six children: Thelma (Mrs. John Thomas Cox), Hester (Mrs. Cecil Wells), Rhea (Mrs. Silva Stoner), Cora (Mrs. Bob Darnell), Woodrow, and Bernice Ward.

Ralph's maternal great-grandparents were Newton Ward and Margaret Durr Ward.

As each Thanksgiving draws near, it always reminds us to be thankful for everything and thankful to be settled in such a nice county as our ancestors started for us. *Submitted By: Onita Chilton Cox and Ralph Coleman Cox*

TERRY AND ALICE CHRISMAN have been residents of Anderson County since they moved here from Lexington in 1974. He bought a farm here in Anderson County in 1972, called the Old Collins place on Buckley Lane.

Terry was born in 1941 to Vernon and Josie Chrisman, a graduate of McKee High School 1959. He is the eldest of nine children. Brothers: Harold and Robert, Lawrenceburg, KY; Rodney and Philip, McKee, KY; and David, Xenia, Ohio. Sisters: Mary Alice Revel, Richmond, KY; Brenda Gabbard, Wawetta, KY; and Evelyn Bowman, Lawrenceburg, KY.

The Terry Chrisman Family

Alice Chrisman was born in 1941 to the late Everette and Lena Toler of Lee Co., was raised in Jackson County and attended McKee High School. The third daughter of six girls: Marie Newsome, Virma Hobbs, and Barbara Toler, Lawrenceburg, KY; Betty Tussey, Blue Ash, Ohio; and Ernestine Poor, Oak Ridge, Tennessee.

They married in 1958 in McKee, KY. They moved to Lexington, KY and both went to work for Square D Company. Alice left the job when her second child was born. Terry worked his way up to manager. Then went to McLean's Trucking Company, he again worked up to a managing position. He established his own business of Chrisman Brothers Contractors. He then went to Lexington Fire Department where he has been for 20 years.

Terry and Alice have three children: Rhonda Kay, born in 1960, is a 1978 graduate of Anderson High and a 1980 graduate of the Appalachian School of

Nursing. She now works for Daniel and Morrow PSC of Frankfort, KY. She is married to Rick Courtney and lives in Frankfort.

Randy Keith, born in 1962, is a 1980 graduate of Anderson High and has completed studies to be a paramedic in 1989. He works for the Lexington Fire Department, where he rides an Emergency Care Unit. He is also a partner with his father in Chrisman Brothers Contractors. He married Dawn Lynn Adams in 1983 and they have two children: Emily Kay, born 1987, and Evan Kyle, born 1988. They live on a farm on Buckley Lane in Lawrenceburg.

Ryan Kraig, born 1971, is still in High School and resides at home with his parents on Buckley Lane. *Submitted By: Alice Chrisman.*

MARK CINNAMON

MARK CINNAMON, the son of Alfred Bruner Cinnamon and Mary Elizabeth Divine Cinnamon, was born on 5-10-1870 in Lawrenceburg, KY and died on 8-20-1910. He served in World War I and returned uninjured. He married Betty Lane on 6-15-1888 in Lawrenceburg. She was born on 4-10-1872 and died in 1890. She was the daughter of Edger Lane. Mark and Betty had one son, Hubert, born on 8-19-1890 in Lawrenceburg. He married Mintie Thomas Willard on 4-20-1920. She was born on 3-9-1890 in Lawrenceburg and was the daughter of Edward Gideon Willard and Bitty Bickers. She had four brothers and sisters: Nell married Willie Hill; Effie married Walter Bright; Horace married Hattie Sutherland; and Sherman married Virginia Leigh.

Hubert and Mintie Cinnamon were the parents of six children: Laura Alice married John Hellard; Clara Goldie married Thomas Hellard; Bernice Bruner (below); Albert Brice married Verna Lois Simpson; Horace Stanley married Virginia Busby; and Nellie Dean married Richard Barnes. Hubert and Mintie lived in Frankfort, KY at the time of their deaths. He died on 11-15-1985 and she died on 10-4-1988.

Bernice B. Cinnamon was born on 7-20-1920 in Frankfort. He married Mary Elizabeth Webb on 12-22-1941. She was born on 10-12-1920 and is the daughter of Willie Sam Webb and Clellie Aldridge Webb. Bernice and Mary are the parents of four children: Carolyn, born 8-11-1944, married James Durham; Maurice, born 7-18-1946, married Brenda Rucker; Eileene, born 3-28-1949, married 1st Johnny Boggess, 2nd Roy Moore; and Denise, born 5-16-1957, married David Stringfellow.

Willie Sam Webb, the son of William Thomas Webb and Mary Lee Rucker Webb, was born on 2-1-1903 in Lawrenceburg. He has one brother, James Harvey, born 4-8-1900, who married Bertie Lane. Willie Sam married Clellie Aldridge on 12-23-1921. She was born on 8-23-1904 in Lawrenceburg and died on 6-2-1976 in Gatlinburg, Tennessee. She was buried in Frankfort, KY. She was the daughter of Benjamin Franklin Aldridge and Mary E. Harlow Aldridge. She had eleven brothers and sisters: Leurs married Maude Cummins; Pearl married George Hellard; Stella married Ezra Cummins; Alex; Elizabeth married Earnest Murdock; Ora; Chester married Edith; Jessie; Effie; Bessie; and Floyd.

Willie Sam and Clellie had nine children: Mary Elizabeth; Bertie Mae married Vernon Eades; Pauline married Carl Johnson; James Richard married Jerri Taylor; Winset Samuel; Betty Joyce; David Gene married Dixie McKee; Linda married William Hillard; and William Benjamin married 1st Bessie Cubert, 2nd Barbara; 3rd Mildred. *Submitted By: Matthew Cinnamon.*

GENE CARLTON CINNAMON

GENE CARLTON CINNAMON lived in Mercer Co. during his adolescent years and attended twelve years of school at Salvisa, KY, where he lived with his parents, Mr. and Mrs. John Cinnamon. Although living in Mercer County, his roots ran deep into Anderson County, as his mother was the former Nellie Norris Hanks, daughter of Mr. and Mrs. Dandridge Hanks of Wildcat Road. His father was John Alvin Cinnamon who moved from Franklin

County to Anderson County and settled in the community of Stringtown, as a boy.

Gene was the third child in a family of five children. The eldest child is Mrs. Nell Cinnamon Lawrence of Williamstown, KY, a brother, Kenneth Cinnamon, deceased, two sisters, Mrs. Betty Lou Cinnamon Sanford of Salvisa and Mrs. Mary Nevins "Blondie" Cinnamon Warford of Anderson County.

After high school, Gene worked for a short time for the Shields Transfer before entering the U.S. Marine Corps in 1951. Upon release from the service in 1953, Gene met and married his wife of 35 years, the former Mary Ruth Clark, who moved to Anderson County with her family in 1954. They were married on 9-3-1954 at the Buck Run Baptist Church in Franklin County, by Dr. Bryant Hicks of the Southern Baptist Seminary in Louisville, KY.

Gene Carlton and Mary Ruth Cinnamon

He went to work in the office of the Old Joe Distillery in 1955 and went to the bottling house office at J.T.S. Brown Distillery when the Old Joe Distillery closed down in 1958. In 1967, Gene quit his job to go into business for himself. He bought a restaurant and operated it for five years before selling and going to work for the Lawrenceburg Transfer in 1972, at which time he also started another business, the C and C Sport Shop, which his wife managed until the summer of 1989, for a total of 22 years in business.

Gene and Mary Ruth have two children, a son, Gene Gregory Cinnamon, and a daughter, Julie McKee Cinnamon Milburn. Greg is married to the former Denise Flygstad and has three children - Derek Gregory, age 9; Brittney Elizabeth Cinnamon, age 7; and Jamie Lee, age 5. Greg was active in Little League sports programs and played high school football. He now helps with the Anderson Middle School Football Program. Greg completed 2 1/2 years of college and is employed at the U.S. Postal Service in Lexington. Julie is married to Mr. Ellery Milburn who owns and operates Milburn's Shoes and Repair in downtown Lawrenceburg. Julie worked with the Farm Bureau Insurance Co. for five years before getting a Bachelor of Arts Degree in Elementary Education and graduating Summa Cum Laude. She is presently employed by the Board of Education in Anderson County.

Gene worked with the Little League programs and was Commissioner of Baseball for Anderson County in 1971. He was active in the Alton Ruritan Club, serving as President, and also as a member of the Grand Masons of Kentucky, Anderson Lodge No. 90, for thirty years. Gene and Mary Ruth are active members of the Alton Baptist Church and live at 213 Whitney Avenue. *Submitted By: Gene and Mary Ruth Cinnamon.*

ANN MAC CLARK

ANN MAC CLARK was the first black woman, from Lawrenceburg, to attain the rank of first lieutenant. She was born June 20, 1919, in Anderson County. She graduated from the high school here in 1937, the most outstanding student. She graduated from Kentucky State College, Frankfort, in 1941. Here she became a member of Delta Sigma Theta Sorority in which she was an outstanding member and officer.

Ann Mac Clark

In 1942, she entered the Women's Army Auxiliary Corps on which she received her commission February 16, 1943. Immediately she was placed as Platoon Commander. A few months later she was sent to Washington D. C. with the classification section where she soon received promotion to First Lieutenant.

Following her promotion she attended Classification School at Camp Meade, Maryland. After completion of her training at Camp Meade, she returned to Fort Des Moines and later was sent to Chico, California. At the time of her death she was commanding officer of a WAC detachment of the air corps at the Douglas Army Air Field in Arizona. So ended 24 years for one who has achieved. *Submitted By: Gertrude Cunningham.*

WILLIAM NEVILLE CLAXON AND EMMA OSBORNE CLAXON

WILLIAM NEVILLE CLAXON AND EMMA OSBORNE CLAXON came to Anderson County in 1981 and lived for a year in the Zora Carter Missionary Residence of the First Baptist Church, Lawrenceburg. The Claxons are members of this church.

Neville and Emma came to Lawrenceburg after retirement from 33 years of service as Southern Baptist missionaries in West Africa. They worked in Nigeria, Ghana, Benin and BurkinaFaso.

The Reverend Claxon is a native of Franklin County and son of the late Elmer Stephens Claxon and Frona Stigers Claxon of Switzer, KY. The family included two sisters. When Neville was six, his father died, so he grew up with many responsibilities on the farm. After high school, he attended Georgetown College and received the A. B. Degree in 1942. During the years before he finished college, he taught in the elementary grades in Franklin County and coached basketball at Elkhorn High School.

Having sensed a call to the ministry, Neville left teaching and became pastor of Long Lick Baptist Church, Stamping Ground, KY. During the first eighteen months there he also served as pastor of the Berry Baptist Church, near Cynthiana.

In 1942, Neville and Emma Osborne were married. Her parents Henry Watterson Osborne and Cora Ledford Osborne lived in Winchester. Emma received the B.S. Degree in Business Education from Eastern Kentucky University where she also served on the Administrative Staff. She taught in elementary schools in Menifee County, at Elkhorn High School, Anchorage High School and Seneca High School (Louisville).

The Claxons have two children: Carol Claxon Polsgrove, who teaches at the University of Indiana, and William N. Claxon, Jr., who teaches at the University of South Carolina at Aiken.

Neville received the Master of Theology Degree from Southern Baptist Theological Seminary in 1946 and the following year he became Associational Director in the Kentucky Baptist Church Training Department. In 1948, he and Emma were appointed to Africa.

Neville was made responsible for church training in the 1500 Baptist churches of Nigeria for 20 years. In West Africa, he also preached and taught and led in Sunday School, radio, television, missions, and evangelism work.

Foreign Mission Board honors Neville and Emma Claxon (right), being presented a certificate of retirement, Dr. Keith Parks. August 1981

Mrs. Claxon did various tasks in the church, taught their own children, did accounting and secretarial work, wrote church training literature, etc.

Together, Neville and Emma established and organized the first French-speaking Baptist Church in Benin, where they opened Southern Baptist work in 1970.

Earlier experiences previewed the Claxons' coming to Lawrenceburg. Neville as a boy of twelve had visited his uncle, Duane Stigers and his aunt Edna Wilson Stigers at Alton. There he enjoyed a trip to the Lawrenceburg Fair in a "go-cart" behind a fine horse with the well-known Anderson citizen Ben Wilson at the reins.

Neville, with his bride, came as a young minister to Lawrenceburg to preach for Dr. Paul Horner at the First Baptist Church and after morning services enjoyed a good dinner and fellowship with the Dr. Overall family.

From Lawrenceburg, the Claxons have conveniently traveled to Florida, Canada and California to do volunteer work with the Haitian people and to various states to preach and to promote missions. The First Baptist Church had provided opportunity for local ministry. As a moderator of the Anderson Baptist Association the Reverend Claxon had had an addition privilege for service.

These two late-comers to Anderson County hope that they can make a worthy contribution to the people of this community and to peoples of the world in years yet to come. *Submitted By: Neville and Emma Claxon.*

COLE FAMILY (From the Bond - McKee History of Anderson County): "Elijah Cole was the pioneer of this family who came here during Indian depredations and helped carve a civilization out of a wilderness. His wife was Aquilla Hooker and they migrated from Maryland to Missouri in 1790, then shortly afterward came to Kentucky and settled near Lawrenceburg. His grandson William Cole was a substantial citizen of the Fox Creek neighborhood. His wife was Martha Sherwood and they were the parents of seven children: James Ed, Presley F., John William, Mary Belle (Crossfield), Lulie (Cox), Thomas Merritt, and Louis Edgar. John William Cole was born in 1860 and died in 1924. He was an upright citizen, a successful businessman and farmer, and a member of the Fox Creek Christian Church, who was highly regarded by the citizens of the county. In 1881, Mr. Cole was married to Miss Annie R. Bond (1862-1948), a member of the pioneer Bond family. To them was born one son, William Burton Cole (1881-1983), who was a well-to-do farmer and land owner. In 1901, he was married to Lula Roach (1880-1964), a gracious lady who was held in high esteem by all who knew her. They were the parents of five children:

Julian Burton (1902-1984) was a fifty-year employee of The Lawrenceburg National Bank, retiring as vice-president. He was married to Kathleen Phillips (1902-1983).

John William (J.W.) (1905-), a farmer and trucker who married Stella Mae Gash (1905-1986). They had

William Burton Cole and Lula Roach Cole

two foster sons, John Allen Gash and Bruce Cole Gash. After Mrs. Cole's death, he married Dorothy Perry Wiggington, formerly of Fox Creek.

Mary Louise (1911-1988) was married to Fred Ransdell of Salvisa, Mercer County. Mr. Ransdell died in his thirties. Mrs. Ransdell worked for the Commonwealth of Kentucky for many years. They had one daughter, Jane Cole (Ross), who has been a teacher in Anderson County for many years. Jane has two sons, Steve, a civil engineer living in Philadelphia, and James Cole, an employee of Delta Air Lines in Cincinnati.

Allen Carroll (1916-1987), a well-known farmer who lived in the Fox Creek neighborhood much of his life, was married to Evelyn Royalty of Salvisa, Mercer County.

Robert Bond (1922-), was employed by Eastern Air Lines in Lexington thirty years. He married Louise Ruth Hudson in 1958. They have one son, Robert Bond II, who is employed by USAir in Lexington; and a daughter, Julie Ann, who is married to Jay Bradley Wilson and lives in Versailles. They have one daughter, Lauren Ashley, born in 1989. Mrs. Cole has one son, Ronald Gene Hudson, by a previous marriage, who is employed by Delta Air Lines in Lexington. *Submitted By: Robert B. Cole and J. W. Cole.*

CHARLES TERRILL COLE (1875-1954) and Gracie Lee Riley Cole (1879-1956) were lifelong residents of Anderson County. They lived and farmed near Rutherford School. On their farm they had chickens, turkeys, sheep, cattle, and horses. They used horses to help raise corn, hay and tobacco. They also had a big garden from which she canned for the winter.

Mr. and Mrs. Charlie Cole

Charles was the son of Martha Beasley Cole (1852-1933) and Thomas Allen Cole (1843-1910). He had five brothers and one sister. They were Jess, John Will, Sarah Jane, Allen, Thomas Ulysses, and Malone.

Gracie was the daughter of Frances Satterly Riley and Joseph P. (Dode) Riley, who died in 1944. She had one brother, Alonzo Riley and two sisters, Effie Yates and Hallie Drury.

Charles and Gracie had three children. Gertie died four days before her fifth birthday, (1899-1904). Mary Eva (1897-1973) and Malone Marvin born 1908, resides in Owensboro, Ky.

Both Charlie and Gracie attended Anderson County School and were regular attendants of Mt.

Pleasant Baptist Church where both served in various positions in the church. They often kept evangelists and pastors in their home overnight and on weekends.

They were buried in Fairview Cemetery in Anderson County. *Submitted By: Garvice Gibson.*

MARY W. COLEMAN, a native of Anderson County and a teacher in Anderson County for over 45 years, also taught music in her home. Mary died on October 16, 1969, at the age of 85.

Mary W. Coleman

She began her career with only an eighth grade teacher's certificate. She later continued study in summer school and extension classes until she graduated from college, plus four hours toward a Masters. She never aspired for other than the lower grades, because she believed that the first years of a child's life were the most important; their characters are shaped, their habits molded. In her last speech, she asked her pupils to continue in school. Pleasure flies, fortune soon fades away, but education cannot be taken from you. Education will prove invaluable to you, to the end of your life.

Mary had one son, the late Charlie Coleman, a teacher and he was in the cast of "Porgy and Bess". *Submitted By: Gertrude Cunningham*

MARYLAND CONN and Mary Madeline Brahnan Conn lived in Eastern Kentucky. They married and had ten children: Margie, Fred, Polly, Maryland, Jr., Issac, Susie, Alberta, Artie, Virgil, and Garmi. Their fourth daughter, Alberta, was born on 9-26-26 in Printer, KY. Alberta grew up, moved to Martin, KY and met a man named Halbert. By this man she had her first child, James "Bud" Halbert, born 11-11-47 in Martin, KY. Something happened and her relationship with Halbert ended. She then met Walter Blackburn and had a daughter, Brenda, born 5-1-49. Alberta split up with Walter for a while, at this time, she met Fred Miller and had another son, Jack Conn, born 1-18-53. Later Alberta and Walter got back together. They had six more children: Ronald, Mike, Frieda, Linda, and twins, Terry and Sherry. Alberta and Walker stayed together after that and saw all their children grown and married. Walker died not long ago, but Alberta is still living in Martin.

Fred Miller left and was not heard from again after the birth of Jack. Alberta was having financial trouble so Jack moved in with his grandparents, Maryland and Mary Conn (called "Mam" and "Pap" by the children). He was raised by them through all of his childhood.

When Jack was around the age of 20 he met Marleen Coe in Iowa. She is the daughter of Neal Coe and Clairbelle Smith Coe (Erickson). She has one sister, Marilyn Coe Meilick. Neal and Clairbelle were divorced and she remarried to Donald Erickson. They have four children: Norman, Denise Erickson Merritt, Marsha Erickson Brooks, and Alan.

Jack and Marleen were married in Clintwood, Virginia on 11-3-73. Jack and Marleen moved from Iowa, where her family lived, to Martin, KY. Their only child, Jared, was born there on 2-7-75. About two years later they moved back to Iowa and lived there awhile. They then moved back to Kentucky again, this time to Lawrenceburg, KY where they have lived ever since.

Jack and Marleen were divorced. Marleen met Terry Burns and they were married on 3/18/89. Jack met a woman named Myra Tackett, who has three children of her own. They are currently expecting a son anyday. *Submitted By: Jared Conn.*

THE CORN FAMILY originated in or around the area of Ireland. Harrison Corn was born on 4-10-1891 in Mercer County, Kentucky. He was the son of Obie Corn. Harrison married Nina Mae Robinson, the daughter of Thomas L. Robinson (1874 - 1924) and Louisa J. Satterly Robinson (1876-1966). She was born on 4-16-1895 in Anderson County. Nina has nine brothers and sisters: Hattie Rae; Sanford Lee; Mary Eva; James Alonzo; Chesley Bee; Virtie Zyrrl; Willie Dee; Roy Lee; and Annie. Harrison and Nina were the parents of ten children: Vila Faye married (?) Satterly; Wesley H. married Onita Drury; Lesley A.; Presley K. married Callie Drury; Kesley Clay married Margaret (?); Clesley Nay married Geniva (?); Eula Mae married Wallace Wilson; Lida Lae married Frank Schuler; Ida Cae married Norman Gudgel; and Beulla Rae married Arthur Walls.

Presley K. Corn (1923-1946) married Callie Mildred Drury, the daughter of Charley W. Drury and Annie Robinson, on 3-16-46 in Lawrenceburg. She was born on 10-3-23 in Lawrenceburg. Callie has one brother and four sisters: Mary Onita married Wesley Corn; Blondella Marie married Dee Goodlett; Aline Agness married Douglas Drury; Frank Marce married Jesse Mae Champion; and Margaret Ann married John Tyler Broyhers.

Presley and Callie Corn have six children: Mildred Ann married Bernice Rogers; James Presley married Tami Garland; Mary Elizabeth married Stephen Driskell; Floyd Wayne married Nadine Hays; Wanda Louise married 1st Donnie Warner, 2nd Danny Edwards, 3rd Gerald Riley; and Chelsey Thomas married 1st Teddy Reinile, 2nd Donna Robinson.

James Presley Corn was born on 6-6-48 in Lawrenceburg. He married Tami Joyce Garland on 11-19-70. She is the daughter of Weldon G. Garland (1917-1977) and Mary Frances Lane Garland (1918-1983). Tami has five brothers and sisters: John L. Green married 1st Connie Hood, 2nd Virginia Jenkins; Lester Burnett; Atha Pearl married John Wesley Corn; Bobby Richard married Lula Estess; and Betty Ann married Charles Sutherland. James and Tami have two children: Melissa Ann and Sandy Bernice.

The Corn family once held family reunions regularly, but at the last known reunion a fight broke out among two people. One pulled a gun on the other and Presley K. Corn had to take the gun away. He told them to stop fighting. After this happened, no known reunion has been held. *Submitted By: Sandy Corn*

MAURICE AND ELAINE CORN have been dairy and tobacco farmers in the same area of Anderson County for 31 of their 37 years of marriage.

They were married on 6-28-1952 and in February of 1953 they moved to the farm of Brother and Mrs. Ezra Sparrow in the Western part of the County. Brother Sparrow sold his farm in the fall and they quit farming and went to DeKalb, Illinois for a visit. While there, Maurice went to work for Diamond Wire and Cable Co. and working part time on a farm. In January of 1958 they returned to the farm of Mr. and Mrs. Claude Davenport in Franklin County, KY and were there until December of 1958 at which time they came back to Anderson County and the farm of Mrs. Charles Vaughn and Ms. Mary Searcy on the Versailles Road. In 1966, Mrs. Vaughn and Ms. Searcy sold their farm to the distillery and Maurice continues to manage their farm which he operates today.

Maurice is the oldest of five living children of Lucille Matherly and the late William Euell Corn. He was born in the western section of Mercer County,

KY and at the age of fourteen his family moved to the Birdie section of Anderson County. He has two brothers that died in infancy. James William was born in 1931 and lived six months. Harold was born in 1939 and was two years old when he died. Ronald Clay (R.C.) lives in Sycamore, Illinois and Donald Ray lives in Lawrenceburg. His sisters are Mrs. Vernon (Imogene) Perry of Forrest Drive and Mrs. Paul (Wanda Gayle) Waldridge lives in Mercer County. His paternal grandparents were the late Mr. and Mrs. Troyher (Mary E. Foster) Corn of Mercer County. His maternal grandparents were the late Mr. and Mrs. Booker (Maude Lowery) Matherly of Washington County, KY, but they lived in DeKalb, Illinois in their later years. Maurice attended schools in Mercer County and Marlowe School in Anderson County.

Elaine is the oldest of four children of John Alvin and Hazel Duncan McGaughey. She was born at Alton, KY in the white house that stands today by the Alton Cemetery. She has two brothers and one sister. Mrs. Dale (Wilma) Flygstad, John Alvin, Jr., and Leslie Joe of Anderson County. Her paternal grandparents were the late Mr. and Mrs. John (Margaret Thurman) McGaughey. Her maternal grandparents were the late Mr. and Mrs. Henry (Lutie Ockerman) Duncan.

Elaine attended Munday, Glensboro, and Sand Spring, and Anderson County High School of Anderson County. She attended Forks of Elkhorn and Bridgeport of Franklin County for third and fourth grades.

Maurice and Elaine have five children. Patricia Elaine Alsabrook lives in Anderson County and is a nurse. She has three children: William Troy 14, Anita Gail 13, and Jason Roc. 11. Pamela Susan lives in Lexington and is employed at Magna Graphic and has one son, Austin. Marla Jo is married to William Smith and has one son, Robert Tyler, and one daughter, Tasha. She is employed at G. E. in Frankfort. Larry Maurice is married to the former Tina Cook, daughter of Mr. and Mrs. Leroy Cook of Woodford County. He is employed at Rand McNally of Versailles. John Michael is married to Lynette Willard, daughter of Mr. and Mrs. Bruce Willard of Anderson County. They have three children: Marisha Leicole 4, Ashton Deneen 3, and Jerica Laine 23 months. Mike is employed at Topy in Frankfort.

Maurice and Elaine are members of Sand Spring Baptist Church where they attend services regularly. *Submitted By: Elaine Corn*

COX - MCGINNIS   Robert L. "Bob" Cox and Cora Jane McGinnis were married December 12, 1894 in Anderson County, Kentucky.

Bob and Cora lived in the Old Friendship area of western Anderson County (Ashby Road), where Bob was a blacksmith and farmed.

Bob and Cora were the parents of five daughters: Verlie (died prior to 1900); Mary Dallas, August 14, 1899 - September 5, 1969, married Richard Samuel Curtsinger; Cora Elizabeth, March 6, 1907 (resides in Cincinnati, Ohio), married 1.? Hudson and 2. Charles J. Hines; Clara Kate, January 1, 1909 - October 9, 1983, married Dorsey Hall; and Edith Mabel, died as an infant - date unknown; and four sons: Charles, died prior to 1900; James Albert Cox, May 9, 1901 - 1965, married Lola Dennis; John Thomas Cox (June 29, 1903 - January 18, 1989), married Thelma Florence Ward; and Robert Dalton "Pete" Cox (April 14, 1905 - October 15, 1971) married Laura Harley.

After the death of his wife, Cora Jane McGinnis Cox, Bob married Ollie Sutherland. They were the parents of two sons: Cecil Cox, killed in combat during WWII; and Kenneth Cox, (resides in Cincinnati, Ohio).

Robert L. "Bob" Cox, (1868-1946) was the son of James Turner Cox, February, 1843 - May 28, 1919 and Susan Jane Burgin.

Bob's paternal grandparents were Preston Cox and Mariah Martin.

Robert L. "Bob" Cox is buried in the Highview Cemetery near Chaplin in Nelson County, Kentucky.

Cora Jane McGinnis (1869- July 8, 1912) was the daughter of Edward Riley McGinnis, August 2, 1832 - May 26, 1912, and Martha A. Burgin, May 14, 1840 - June 3, 1908. Cora's paternal grandparents were John McGinnis and wife (unknown).

Cora Jane McGinnis Cox is buried in the Chaplin Fork Cemetery near Chaplin in Nelson County, Kentucky. *Submitted By: Robert M. Thompson.*

JOHN T. COX, JR. (J.T.) was born June 24, 1919 in Lawrenceberg, son of the late Judge John T. Cox, Sr. (1876-1942) and Leva Ann Hawkins Cox (1890-1965). He is a life-long resident of Lawrenceburg as are his sisters, Mary Elizabeth Cox Hensley and Mildred Ann Cox Hodson. He is a member of the Lawrenceburg United Methodist Church and Anderson Lodge #90 F. and A. M.

He attended Lawrenceburg City Schools, graduating in 1937 from Lawrenceburg High School.

He retired in 1975 after 36 years of state service, 30 of which were with the Kentucky Department of Fish and Wildlife Resources. From 1958-1975, he served as Assistant Commissioner. He initiated and developed the small-lake fish-stocking program for farmers throughout the state and served on the Governors Committee for development of lakes in the state. He was instrumental in procuring a major lake (Beaver) in Anderson County.

First Row: Charisse and Stacey Umbaugh, Sarah, Benjamin, and Nathan Cox; Second Row: John III, Alice, J.T., Davis and Tyler Cox; Third Row: Sandy (Mrs. John III), Alison, Mary Jane Briscoe, Brandon, Sandy (Mrs John IV) and Kathie Cox; Fourth Row: Tracy, Davis and Douglas Briscoe and John IV

In January 1941, he married Alice McDowell Davis, daughter of the late Rev. James Tyler Davis, pastor of the Lawrenceburg Presbyterian Church in 1929-30, and Stella Dawson Davis Geiger. She has one brother, Dawson Young Davis, Middleton, Ohio. She attended schools in Morganfield and Lawrenceburg, graduating from Sayre School in 1939 in Lexington, and attended Centre College. She has been active in the Presbyterian Church, serving in many offices and is an ordained Elder. She has been active in the community, serving as Post Matron of Hamilton Chapter #239 O.E.S., former president of the Lawrenceburg Woman's Club and Parent Teachers Association, and worked with Red Cross, March of Dimes, Heart Association, and others.

They have three children. John T. Cox III (m. Sandra Umbaugh, Mason, Ohio), lives in Mason, Ohio and is manager of Florida Tile Ceramic Center in Ohio. Mary Jane Cox (m. Davis Briscoe, Lawrenceburg), is Branch Manager of the Anderson National Bank. Tyler Davis Cox (m. Kathryn Oakley, Louisville), lives in Westboro, Massachusetts, and is Program Manager of WBZ Radio Station in Boston.

Their eight grandchildren are: John T. Cox IV, Douglas, Tracy, and Alison Briscoe, all of Lawrenceburg; Benjamin Tyler, Nathan, and Davis Cox, Westboro, Mass.; and Sarah Cox, Mason, Ohio. Two great-grandchildren: Brandon Tyler and Courtney Marie Cox, live in Lawrenceburg. *Submitted By: Mrs. J. T. Cox.*

COX - WARD John Thomas Cox and Thelma Florence Ward were married October 11, 1924 in Jeffersonville, Indiana

John and Thelma were the parents of four children: Leon Thomas Cox, September 13, 1925 (resides in Nelson County, KY.) married 1. Roxie Ockerman and 2. Wilanna Barnes Hood; Volita Ruth, July 13, 1930 (resides in Lawrenceburg, KY.), married Robert Martin Thompson; Ralph Coleman Cox, April 20, 1933 (resides in Lawrenceburg, KY.), married Onita Chilton; and Donna Rhea, January 10, 1945 (resides in Lawrenceburg, KY.) married Daniel Tipton.

John attended the Old Friendship one room School and Thelma attended school at Fairview, Anderson County. They were members of the Friendship Baptist Church, Anderson County, Kentucky.

John and Thelma share cropped on various farms in Shelby and Anderson County prior to purchasing the Cox home place on Ashby Road, Anderson County, from John's father. They continued farming until their retirement and moving to Lawrenceburg, Kentucky in 1985.

John and Thelma Cox

John Thomas Cox is buried in the Highview Cemetery, Nelson County, Kentucky.

Thelma resides in Lawrenceburg, Kentucky.

John Thomas Cox, June 29, 1903 - January 18, 1989, was the son of a blacksmith, Robert L. "Bob" Cox, (1868-1946) and Cora Jane McGinnis (1869-July 8, 1912). Cora is buried in the Chaplin Fork Cemetery, Nelson County, Kentucky and Robert is buried in the Highview Cemetery, Nelson County, Kentucky.

John had five sisters: Verlie (died prior to 1900); Mary Dallas, 8-14-1899 - 9-5-1969, married Richard Samuel Curtsinger; Cora Elizabeth, 3-6-1907 (resides in Cincinnati, Ohio), married 1. ? Hudson and 2. Charles J. Hines; Clara Kate, 1-1-1909 - 10-9-1983, married Dorsey Hall; and Edith Mabel, died as an infant - date unknown: and three brothers: Charles, died prior to 1900; James Albert Cox, 5-9-1901 - 1965, married Lola Dennis; and Robert Dalton "Pete" Cox (4-14-1905 - 10-15-1971) married Laura Harley.

John had a stepmother, Ollie Sutherland Cox, and two half-brothers: Cecil, killed in action during WWII; and Kenneth, (resides in Cincinnati, Ohio).

See Cox - McGinnis for prior generations.

Thelma Florence Ward, August 4, 1910, was the daughter of a farmer, Newton Laurel Ward, October 25, 1881 - January 13, 1963, and Emily Tranquil Miller Adams, March 16, 1882 - February 28, 1962. They are buried in the Mount Freedom Cemetery, Washington County, Kentucky.

Thelma had four sisters: Margaret Z., 6-23-1903 - 6-30-1903; Cora Elizabeth Annfield, 3-17-1905 - 1941, married Robert Darnell; Hester A., 7-23-1907 - resides in Lawrenceburg, KY., married Cecil Wells; and Alma Rhea, 5-6-1913 - 1985) married 1. Silva Stoner and 2. Dillard Koger; and two brothers Woodrow Ward, 4-14-1918 - 5-20-1982, married Gertrude Cornish; and Bernice Edward Ward, 9-19-1921 - 1937, buried in Fairview Cemetery.

See Ward - Adams for prior generations. *Submitted By: Robert M. Thompson.*

ROGER COX, the son of Kenneth Cox and Edna Redman Cox Dennis, was born on 6-3-1950 in Shelby County, KY. He has one half-brother, Doug Dennis, born 2-16-1960 in Louisville, KY. Doug is married to the former Terri Durr.

Roger Cox married Connie Whitaker on 7-24-1970. She is the daughter of Carl Whitaker and Marie Brewer Whitaker of Spencer County, KY. She was born on 10-31-1954 in Louisville, KY. She has one sister and one brother: Betty Whitaker, born 10-19-1943 in Louisville, married Ted Goodlett; and Galewood Whitaker, born 10-10-1948 in Louisville, married Judy Bently.

Roger and Connie are the proud parents of three daughters: Rebecca Cox, born 4-17-1973; Lori Cox, born 7-9-1976; and Tiffany Cox, born 12-28-1984. All were born in Louisville. The Roger Cox family currently resides in Mt. Eden, KY. *Submitted By: Rebecca Cox.*

COX - WAGONER Marion Cox was born in Lawrenceburg, KY on 4-11-1855. He died on 4-11-1931 in Lawrenceburg. He married Susan Mary Searcy on 12-24-1882. She was born in Lawrenceburg on 4-24-1866 and died on 11-8-1908. They had a son, A. D., born 9-20-1884 in Versailles, KY. He married Willi Jane Eaves on 6-15-1897. She was born on 10-10-1893 in Woodford County and died 11-5-1978. She was the daughter of William Eaves (1868-1942) and Sara Cox Eaves (1865-1902). A. D. and Willi were the parents of two sons, Delbert and James (who married Louis Tincher). A. D. Cox died on 2-22-1963 in Anderson County.

Delbert Cox was born on 10-13-1914 in Anderson County. He married Dorothy "Dot" Howard on 5-15-1935 in Versailles. She was born on 3-24-1915 in Woodford County. She is the daughter of H. G. Howard (1889-1978) and Grace Weber Howard (1900-1979). She had eight brothers and sisters: Starlene married Frank Wizick; H. G. Jr., married Pauline McAm; Doris married Pete Troplois; Eda married Morise Harley; Betty married Bill Stourgham; Faye married Don Keeling; Gertrude married Tom Smith; and Patsey married Pete Turner.

Delbert and Dot are the parents of four children: Delbert Cox, Jr., born 1936, married Joyce Aldridge; Lois Jane Cox, born 1938, married Gilbert Tinsley; Robert K. Cox, born 1940, married Charlene Brown; and Roger Holt Cox, born 1942.

Roger Holt Cox was born on 11-21-1942 in Woodford County. He married Linda Kaye Wagoner on 1-19-1962 in Anderson County. She was born on 5-4-1945 in Franklin County, KY. She is the daughter of Sam Wagoner and Juanita Drury Wagoner. Roger and Linda are the proud parents of three children: Roger Thomas Cox, born 1963, married Kaye Moss; Christopher Samuel Cox, born 1973; and Anita Michelle Cox, born 1974.

Sam Wagoner was born on 11-25-1916 in Anderson County. He was the son of Thomas Wagoner and Margaret Murphy Wagoner. He married Juanita Drury on 9-26-1942. She was born on 5-21-1925 in Anderson County. She was the daughter of Arthur Lee Drury and Revie Bowen Drury. She had seven brothers and sisters: Alvin, Arthur, Elwood, Evadena, Evelyn, Phyllis, and Lois. Sam and Juanita had one daughter, Linda. Sam died on 7-2-1971 and Juanita died on 12-27-1987.

Thomas Wagoner was born on 4-14-1881 in Washington County, Ky and died on 7-14-1942 in Anderson County. He was the son of Lewis Wagoner (1841-1903) and Catherine Montgomery Wagoner (1849-1919). He married Margaret Francis Murphy on 2-7-1892 in Nelson County, KY. She was born on 3-18-1876 in Nelson County and died on 12-12-1929 in Anderson County. She was the daughter of John Logan Murphy (1820-1883) and Louisana Harmon Murphy (1830-1924). Thomas and Margaret had only one son, Sam. *Submitted By: Anita Cox.*

CLIFTON CRABB was born on 8-21-1912 in Taylorsville, Kentucky. He is the son of Collins Crabb

and Ela Jewel. Clifton has a sister and a brother: Jewel Crabb married Mort Hunley; and William B. Crabb. On 11-28-1936, Clifton married Thelma Humphrey in Ele Creek, KY. She was born on 7-26-1914 in Nelson Co., KY. She is the daughter of Simon and Grace Humphrey. She had four brothers and one sister: Lelind married Kitty Razor; Junior married Margaret Reynolds; Buster: Virgil (died in 1989); and Elner married Tyler Downs. Clifton and Thelma were the parents of five children: Gail (1952 - 1977) married Wayne Morris - two children, Robert and Thelma; Thomas (deceased); William (below); Anna Lee (1940 - 1940); and Allen married Barbara Rogers - three children - Connie, Denise, and Eva Lee. Clifton and Thelma are both retired and residing on Ballard Road.

William Crabb was born on 2-9-1943. On 3-16-1963, he married Carole Goodlett. She was born on 3-2-1947 in Chicago, Illinois. She is the daughter of Carl Goodlett and Frances Jefferies Goodlett (1924-1952). William and Carole are the parents of three children: Randy married Deanna Drury - one daughter, Alisha; Ronnie married Donna S. (?); and have one daughter, Chrissy. Chrissy is currently attending the Anderson County High School. *Submitted By: Chrissy Crabb.*

JOHN H. CRAIN was born on January 5, 1843 and passed from this world on March 23, 1927. He married Mollie Prewitt who was born on April 29, 1855. and died July 10, 1943. Children born from this union were Eddie Oran Crain, born May 22, 1875, died April 2, 1903; Emma Crain, born October 20, 1878, died January 16, 1969; Malcolm Clinton Crain, born February 18, 1881, died August 18, 1957; Ollie Crain (Champion) born September 13, 1890, died December 6, 1918. Also born to John and Mollie Crain was Bessie M. Crain who was well-known in Anderson County. She was born on October 27, 1886 and was a lifelong resident of Lawrenceburg. For many years she was a school teacher at the Lawrenceburg Elementary School. She later was engaged in the insurance business with her brother, Malcolm. She was a member of the First Presbyterian Church and a member of the Hamilton Chapter, # 293, Order of the Eastern Star.

The said John Crain was the son of Sida H. Crain, born 1812, died 1860 and Margaret McGohan, born 1821, died 1891. Margaret McGohan was the daughter of Andrew McGohan and Hanna Van Dyke. Andrew McGohan was the son of Mark McGohan, born 1755, died 1822, and Elizabeth Dunn, who was born in Pennsylvania and died in the year of 1882. *Submitted By: Billy Joe Hume.*

LUCILLE AND CHARLES W. CRAIN, SR. returned to Anderson County in 1960 to make their home. Frances Lucille Hughes Crain was born in Anderson County as the eldest daughter of the late Albert Marion and Loraine Smith Hughes. She is the grand-daughter of the late Robert and Fanny Ingram Hughes and John and Ophelia Bickers Crossfield Smith. Her great-grandparents were the late James and Mary Crossfield, Albert C. and Susan Robinson Hughes, and James and Mary Sagarcy Ingram, all former residents of Anderson County. Lucille has one brother, Albert Walter (Bud) Hughes of Anderson County. She has five living sisters, Thelma Taggart of San Diego, California; Mrs. James (Edith) Gatewood of Louisville, KY.; Mrs.. Herbert (Mildred) Bailey of New Albany, Indiana; Mrs. George (Virginia) Gerlach of Kissimmee, Florida; and Mrs. Alice Hoon of Crestview, Florida. Her sister, Beulah Mae Hughes is deceased.

Charles William Crain, Sr. is a native of Hart County, KY. He is the son of the late Elzia and Gertie Logston Crain. He and his twin brother, James W. Crain, were the tenth and eleventh of thirteen children, which also included a set of twin girls.

Charles and Lucille are the parents of five children. Charlotte Frances is a teacher with the Anderson County School System. She is married to Earl J.

Lucille and Charles W. Crain, Sr.

Puckett, Jr. and they have three children, Jonathan Christopher, Jennifer Leann, and Joseph Bradley.

Their daughter, Donna Hughes, is a Public Inquiry Coordination/Supervisor with State Government in Frankfort. She is married to Larry E. Drury and they have two children, LaStacya (Stacy) Lynn Headen and Derek Christopher Drury.

Their son, Charles William Crain, Jr., is the assistant principal at Grayson High School in Leitchfield, KY. He is married to the former Marsha Dunn of Clarkson, KY., and they have a daughter, Jenna Brooke.

Daughter Jeanne Evelyn teaches computer science in the New Jersey School System. She is married to Rick Puckett and they have three sons, Jason Earl, Charles David, and Nicholas Shaun. They reside in Hillsborough, New Jersey.

Their youngest child, Brenda Lois Cummins, is a career state employee with the Kentucky State Police. She resides in Anderson County with her two daughters, Laura Lee Bates and Stephanie Nicole Cummins.

CRANFILL

It is not known when the first Cranfill immigrants came to America, but some time prior to 1794 three brothers - Hezekiah, Isaiah, and Moses - had left their home in England and had settled in what is now Winston-Salem, North Carolina. Many of their descendants can still be found there. Abraham Cranfill, when only twelve years of age, came with his parents David and Mary Cranfill, from England to join relatives in North Carolina. There were several children in this family. Some remained in Carolina while others including Abraham set out for Kentucky. It is told that they cut wheels from large trees to make wheels for their ox carts.

Abraham soon came to Anderson County and in 1852 was married to Mary Jane Travis, daughter of Moses and Pollie Travis. Abraham died in 1897 and Mary Jane died in 1905. This couple reared a large family and many of their descendants remain in Anderson County today.

Their first child, Susan Alice, married Horace Tanner, whose children included Lester, Albert, Alpha, and Mamie (Mrs. Ezra Sparrow). The next child met a tragic death at age two when it fell into a kettle of hot grease. Sallie Jane, married David Burgin and their children included Preston, David Jr., Edgar, Grace, and Ess. Dovie Ann, married Arch Sparrow and raised Alice, Lena, Jessie, Willie, Viola, Betty, Clarence, Charlie, Icy Pearl, and Harry. William Truman married Nannie Cook and they had one child, Pearl. Miles H. married Mary Nutgrass and their children included Cordie, Ramie, Mary Frances, Ethel, and Earl. Sidney married Estella Martin and raised Mit, Othel, and Oneita. Margaret Elizabeth married William Stinnett and had children: Charlie, Hal, William, Truman, Margaret, Arch, and Herman. Minnie married Ed Cook. Abe Jr. married Minnie Martin. Mary Ellen married David Johnson and they had three children: Ezra, Ada and Samantha.

Samantha, daughter of David and Mary Ellen Johnson, married Zack Franklin and had eight children. They include Ibra, William Truman, Ollie Townsend, Mary (Mrs. Tullie Morgan), Ruby, (Mrs. John Willie Perry), Bruce, Virginia (Mrs. Ernest Brown), and Bonnie (Mrs. Raymond Carlton).

Coming to Kentucky with Abraham Sr. was his brother Issac, father of George Cranfill who married Fanny DeWitt and had children: Elmo, Thomas, Calvin, Issac, and Elliot. Issac also in addition to George raised Greenberry, Mary and Martha.

Sisters of Abe Sr. and Issac who made the immigration to Kentucky included: Kate (Mrs. Will Morgan), Martha (Mrs. Jim Cozine), Lizzie (Mrs. Walter Stone), and Margaret (Mrs. Henry Moore). *Submitted By: Billy Joe Hume.*

SILAS FOUNTAIN CROOK

(1826 - 1907) came to Anderson County in the early 1800's with his parents, Hezekiah and Sallie Johnson Crook. The family, consisting of eight children, had previously lived in Madison and Franklin Counties having migrated to Kentucky from Virginia.

Silas Fountain, later known as "Uncle Fount" by all who knew him, taught schools throughout the county. At one time, he taught "blab" schools. In this type of school the students studied and recited aloud so the alert teacher knew when work was being done. "Uncle Fount" was recognized as an outstanding mathemetician, poet, and master of English grammar. He enlisted in the army during the Civil War and fought at Shiloh, Vicksburg, and Jackson. He was captured in July, 1862, and spent considerable time in a federal prison.

"Uncle Fount" was married to Sarah Jane Thacker. They settled in the Penny's Chapel area of Anderson County, and to this union were born eight children: Edgar, Joseph Hanks, James Henry, Jesse, Bettie Ann, Melissa, Kate, and Lizzie. Three of the eight children remained in Anderson County and their families are as follows:

Bettie Ann married George Sparrow and lived in the western part of the county near Johnsonville. They had two children, Sidney and Nell, neither of whom married. Sidney was a farmer, Nell a school teacher. All of this family were deceased by the mid 1950's.

Joseph Hanks (Dick) Crook (1858), pictured above, also taught school in Anderson County but is better remembered for his four terms as County Clerk. He was married to Eddie Moore and they had six children (all deceased): Joe, Margaret (McGreevy), Bruce (married Bettie Lois Chilton), Ethel (Milliken), Kenneth (married Mattie Satterly), and Marshall, who died at the age of sixteen. Bruce was an employee of the Lawrenceburg Post Office for many years. His widow, Bettie Lois, still resides in Lawrenceburg. "Uncle Dick" died in 1957 at the age of ninety-nine. It is said that until the last two years of his life he was still making daily treks to the Court House, shuffling along and speaking to everyone he met. The Dick Crook farm and residence were located a mile or so out of Lawrenceburg on the Tyrone Road.

James Henry (Cutter) Croo, was a farmer and taught old-fashioned singing schools in the county. He was married to Ollie Bell (McGaughey) in 1905 and they lived in the Penney's Chapel area at the old Crook home place. In 1917, they moved to a farm in the Gilbert's Creek neighborhood near Lawrenceburg. After an illness which left "Cutter" unable to do heavy farm work, the family moved to Alton. "Cutter" died in 1949 at the age of 81. Ollie continued to live in Alton until her death in 1954.

Children of the "Cutter" Crook family are as follows: Robert (1906 - 1986) married Ethel Literal of Anderson County, and settled in Indiana; Silas (1908) married Gotha Johnson of Lawrenceburg. They live in Collegedale, TN.; Oneta (1910) married James Cogswell and resides in Franklin County, Sally (1915) married Rev. Gilbert Shely (now deceased), and is now living in Harrodsburg; Evelyn (1918), who chose to remain a Crook, lives in Danville; and Frona (1923) married Eugene Billiter of Anderson County, and they live in Campbellsville, KY.

A standing joke in the Crook family is ...that, at one time, there was a "crook" in the Post Office, (Bruce), a "crook" in the Lawrenceburg National Bank, (Frona), and a "crook" in church work, (Evelyn). And, the late Rev. Gilbert Shely often remarked that he was the only preacher he knew of who married an admitted "crook", (Sally). *Submitted By: Evelyn Crook and Oneta Crook Cogswell.*

CHARLES KAVANAUGH "C.K." CROSSFIELD,

the second son of Richard Henry and Elizabeth Ann Nee Jackson Crossfield, was born on 6-9-1863 at the Fox Creek plantation. C.K. married Ada Lee Hackey (born 7-27-1865), a daughter of Dairus and Susan M. Hackley in September 1887. C.K. and Ada had seven children who are named as follows: Mary C. (b. 1888) married Palmer McDairmid; Madie Bell (b. 1890) married Lloyd Redwine; Sarah Golden "Goldie" (b. 1892); Charles Louis (b. 1893) married Minna Dowling; Annie Ritchie (b. 1895); Lady Wallace (b. 1896) married John W. Mitchell; and Julia (b. 1900) married Henry G. Harp. C.K. was a successful farmer and livestock trader in the Fox Creek area. He also purchased his father's estate near Fox Creek some years before the latter's death. In the first decade of this century, C.K. and family moved to Lexington where he was also successful as a realtor and stock trader. Circa 1917, the family moved to Gadsen, Alabama where C.K. purchased an ice plant which proved very lucrative under his management. In January, 1934, he and Ada with two daughters, Ritchie and Goldie, were vacationing in Florida where on the morning of January 12 they were involved in an automobile collision at Live Oak, Florida. C.K. and Ritchie died from the accident and Ada Crossfield, seriously injured, was taken to a nearby hospital where she remained for some time. Ada suffered physical impairment from the accident and experienced a long illness before she died at her home in Tuckahoe Heights, at Gadsen, Christmas Eve, 1943. *Submitted By: James S. Pope.*

GEOBEL AND MYRTLE CROSSFIELD

lived most of their lives in Anderson County. Geobel, the son of Ernest and Sally Carter Crossfield, came from Fox Creek. Myrtle, the daughter of C.L. and Minnie McCoy Overstreet, came from Gilbert's Creek. They both attended Kavanaugh High School. They married on December 23, 1924. They had three children: Virginia, Billy, and Elizabeth Ann. Geobel was a barber and owned his shop from 1923 to 1950 when he retired. He kept his chair and barbered from his home until 1980. He also owned a furniture store in 1930 and a grocery store in 1938. In the 20's he played the fiddle with three other men for musical events and the tuba in the Town Band. In 1943, Geobel and Myrtle belonged to the Lawrenceburg Baptist Church. Geobel went out from the church with Bro. Booker to work in mission churches. Myrtle was a staunch worker in W.M.U. and at one time held a state position. In 1950, they decided to retire and go full time in Mission Work. In preparation, Geobel took courses from Dr. Paul Horner and attended a year at Baptist Seminary in Louisville. They spent 30 years in Boyle, Mercer, and Anderson Counties, building or adding on to churches as well as pastoring.

Geobel and Myrtle Crossfield

In 1970, the Crossfields decided to retire again and built a home on Beaver Lake. A committee from Ballard Church, where Geobel, Bro. Booker, and Virginia, used to have Sunday School and Church on Sunday afternoons in the 40's., wanted him to come and help build a church building. This he did, and stayed and pastored this church till his illness in 1980 forced him to retire. Geobel died in 1983. Myrtle lives on Chautauqua St. and is still teaching a Sunday School Class at Ballard Baptist Church.

Their oldest daughter, Virginia graduated from Lawrenceburg High School in 1946 and married Leon Carey in 1947. Leon died in 1962. She later married Frank Holbrook and has two sons, John Geobel and Samuel. Billy was drafted into the Army during World War II while a Junior. His grades from Medical Schooling were sent back and he graduated in 1946 from Lawrenceburg High School. He married Ruth Peyton in 1953. They have a son, Douglas, and a daughter, Deborah. They have two grandsons, Andy and Dustin. Elizabeth Ann graduated from Lawrenceburg High School in 1948 and is a graduate from Bethel Women's College. She married Paul Hanks in 1950 and have two sons, George and Brent, and two grandsons, Ryan and Cory. They have been life long residents of Lawrenceburg. Paul retired in 1987 from a Manager position at Kentucky Utilities and Elizabeth Ann is retired in 1990 from the City Water Works.

JOHN CROSSFIELD (1770-1842), son of James and Sarah Crossfield, married Lucy Gardiner on March 20, 1783 in Virginia. They had eight children: George (married Patsy Campbell); Polly; twins Elizabeth and Lucy (married James Stevens); William M.; John "Jack" (married Elizabeth Lott); Elliott (married Elizabeth Jones); and James.

In 1808, Lucy died and John married Polly Goode on July 1, 1809 in Middlesex County, Virginia. Polly was the daughter of John Goode. They had six children: Sarah "Sally" 1801 - 1871 (married Travis Brown); Morgan Goode 1812 - 1890 (married Katherine Samuels); Juliann, 1814 - 1885 (married Willis Jones); Woodford 1816 - 1890 (below); Sophronia 1818- ? (married William Mullins); and Richard Henry 1821 - 1908 (married Martha Bell Gudgel).

In 1812, John Crossfield came to Kentucky with his pregnant wife and children. They first came to Woodford Co., KY and later settled in Anderson County. John built a log house near Fox Creek. On the site where the log house once stood, now stands a large two-story white frame house built in the late 1800's by his son Richard. This house, presently owned by the Partlow family, is listed in the National Register of Historical Buildings. The property is located off the Anderson City Road. On this same road is a Crossfield family cemetery where Woodford and Richard Crossfield are buried along with several family members.

Woodford Crossfield, son of John and Polly Crossfield, married Amanda Gudgel (1820 - 1893) on October 20, 1840 in Anderson County. Amanda was the daughter of Elijah Gudgel and Lydia Bell. They had eleven children: Mary Elizabeth 1843 - 1935 (married James Smith); William Henry 1844 - 1860; John Thomas 1845 - 1929 (married Harriet Sweasy); Lydia Ann 1848 - 1929 (married Douglas Stevens); Elijah Gudgel 1850 - 1897 (below); Susan Arminto 1850 - 1908 (married James Walker); Lucy Bell 1854 - 1882; infant son 1856 - young; Amanda Ellen 1860 - 1909 (married James Johnson); Martha Sophrona 1863 - 1889 (married Joseph Mizner); and an infant son 1864 - 1864.

Elijah Gudgel Crossfield, son of Woodford and Amanda Crossfield, married Nancy Cook on October 16, 1878 in Anderson County. Nannie was the daughter of Noah Cook and Nancy Boggess. They had six children: Ernest 1879 - ? (married Sarah Elizabeth Carter); Martha Ellen 1881 - 1942 (married Harry Hendricks); Etta May 1884 - 1972 (married W.W. Bowman); Edward 1886-1956 (married Maggie

Stratton); John Eldred 1888 - 1963 (below); and Minnie Walker 1890 - 1969 (married Charlies Phillips).

John Eldred Crossfield, son of Elijah and Nannie Crossfield, married Iva Myrtle Stratton (1892 - 1968) on January 27, 1909 in Anderson County. Myrtle was the daughter of William Jackson Stratton and Samantha Belle Kays. They had five children: Herman Evart married Ina Mae Porter; Edward Roy (1911 - 1955) married Alice Summers; Willie Walker married Helen Smith McMurtry; Nell Mae married Billy Robinson; and Margaret Helen married Charles Marlowe. John was a tool and die maker for Old Stagg Distillery in Frankfort, KY for many years. Later, he owned and operated a successful plumbing and heating firm until his death on February 6, 1963. Both John and Myrtle were members of the Lawrenceburg Disciples of Christ Christian Church.

There are many descendants of John Crossfield in the area. Some collateral lines include the names: Gudgel, York, Cook, Pope, Cole, Walker, Baxter, and Boggess. *Submitted By: Willie Walker Crossfield and Helen McMurtry Crossfield.*

MATISSON M. CROSSFIELD, the third son of Richard Henry and Martha Crossfield, was born on 12-12-1852 in the old cabin erected by his grandparents in the years when Anderson County was still included as a part of Franklin County. As he was too young to see service in the Civil War, we assume that his childhood days were spent in helping his father with the duties on the plantation. Mat, as he was familiarly known, followed in the footsteps of his father as he was a constable for a period of time and later was a deputy sheriff of Anderson County. He was elected sheriff in his own right for a term of 1876 - 1878. On 9-11-1878, he married Sarah Bell McMurry, the oldest daughter of Thomas and Elizabeth McMurry. Sarah Bell's father was a cousin of Mat's stepmother, Elizabeth Ann and was cousins also with Henry Nathan and Squire Martin Ware. Before a decade had passed, Mat became seriously ill and died on 4-20-1887. There was no issue from this union. *Submitted By: James S. Pope.*

RICHARD HENRY (R.H.) CROSSFIELD, the youngest child of John and Polly Crossfield, was born on 10-15-1821. Five days later Polly died and to his half-sisters fell the duties of surrogate mother for the next four years, then to his stepmother, Elizabeth (Saffell) Crossfield nee Middleton, until her death 6-10-1827. His work duties began soon after 1827 as his adult brothers were married and had left home. By then he and his brothers, George and Woodford, were expected to assume duties on the farm at the head of Fox Creek. At the time of the Civil War he had become a successful farmer and stock trader.

In his last will, John specified that his lands be sold as units as originally acquired. R.H. and Woodford purchased two of the units with the former buying the original farm with the cabin that John built. R.H. married Martha Gudgel, a daughter of Elijah and Lydia Gudgel, on 11-16-1843. Woodford had married Martha's older sister Amanda in 1840; undoubtedly, Richard had ample opportunity to fall in love with the younger sister. He and Martha had nine children before her death on 3-22-1858. The children in order of birth are: George Washington, born 10-6-1844. Little is known about him except that he died 1-4-1871 and is buried in the Crossfield graveyard at the head of Fox Creek.; Thomas Jefferson; Susan Mary - included with the William H. York family; Julia Ann; Sarah Frances; Matisson M.; and Martha Belle.

Minnie Ella was born 2-29-1856. She married James L. Bond on 1-2-1877. A daughter, Mary, was born to this union. Ella Died 3-12-1892.

America Alice, the last daughter, was born 2-11-1858. She married Bryant O. Jones of Mercer County, Kentucky on 11-10-1886. They had three sons: Cleveland, Plummer and Bryon. Alice died in Fayette County on 11-5-1927.

Richard's second marriage occurred on 8-23-1860

when he married Elizabeth A. Golden nee Jackson whose mother was Thursa Hill, an aunt of Squire M. and Henry N. Ware. By this union three sons: William Hanson, Charles Kavanaugh, and Richard Henry, Jr. were added to R.H.'s family.

Many of Richard Henry, Sr.'s children became well known in their own right, but he also had an illustrious career. He was appointed as sheriff of Anderson County 1874 - 1875 and elected sheriff 1881 - 1882. In 1885, he was County Judge of Anderson County. R.H. served as Representative of Anderson County in the Kentucky State Legislature 1889 - 1890. His family were members of the Fox Creek Christian Church where for many years he was an elder of that congregation. In his later years, he was affectionately known as "Uncle Dick". His wife, Elizabeth A. died on 2-12-1908 and was buried on a cold, rainy day in the family graveyard. As a result of illness from exposure that day, Richard H. Crossfield, Sr. died the next month on March 15, at age 87. The following day he was interred into the family graveyard with his two wives who had shared his life for 63 years. *Submitted By: James S. Pope*

RICHARD HENRY CROSSFIELD, JR., the youngest son of Richard Henry Crossfield, Sr. and his wife, Elizabeth Ann, was born on 10-22-1868. Richard Henry attended school at Anderson County Seminary and later obtained his A.B. degree at Transylvania University in 1889. Continuing his studies at the College of the Bible he received an English Diploma in 1892. In addition, he later received M.A. and Ph. D. degrees from the University of Wooster in 1900. He also taught in Kentucky Normal College at Lawrenceburg and served as principal of the Classical and English Academy at Harrodsburg. In 1896, he became the pastor of the Christian Church at Owensville where he held that position until 1907. Later, he was to receive LL.Ds from Georgetown College, the University of Kentucky and Transylvania College.

He married Annie Ritchie Terry in February, 1895 at Glasgow, Kentucky. They had a son, Terry (1907 - 1957), who became Executive Vice-President of the Commercial Credit Co. in Baltimore, Maryland, and a daughter, Dorothy (1901 - 1981), who married a Mr. Atkins.

In June 1908, Dr. Crossfield became president of Transylvania University and remained in that position until 1921. He was also named President of the College of the Bible from 1912 to 1921. Afterwards he served one year as Executive Secretary of the Federal Council of Churches of Christ in America at New York, NY. He served three years as President of William Woods College, at Fulton, Missouri in the 1930's. From there he accepted a pastorate at Birmingham Christian Church. He returned to Transylvania College in September, 1938 on an interim basis for one year while the college searched for another president. Afterwards he resumed his pastorate at the Birmingham Christian Church and when he retired he had been with that congregation for over 10 years. For some years Dr. Crossfield traveled the Chautauqua circuit as a lecturer. After his retirement he traveled extensively in Mexico, Latin America, Alaska, Europe, and Asia. Dr. Richard Henry Crossfield died in Birmingham on 1-30-1951 and two days later was buried in Glasgow, Kentucky next to his wife who preceded him in death. *Submitted By: James S. Pope.*

THOMAS JEFFERSON CROSSFIELD Richard Henry Crossfield's second son, Thomas Jefferson Crossfield, was born near Fox Creek on 12-31-1845. As a boy he worked on the family plantation until the Civil War. During the War, he enlisted as a cavalryman in Co. F Fifth Kentucky Calvary, a unit of General John Hunt Morgan's command. He returned to Anderson County at the close of the War and resumed farming with his father on the old plantation. After his return he married Josephine Colter, a daughter of the Colter family who, by tradition, were relatives of the Lillard family by marriage, on 9-20-1866. Three children were born of this union: Rosa Jane in 1867; Alfred S. in 1869; and Thomas Vestal on 12-8-1875. Later, before 1880 the family moved to Kansas and then to Montague County, Texas where they lived for several years. On the afternoon of 4-22-1889, Thomas J. made the "Race" with many others from the southern border of Oklahoma Territory in the "Opening" of that area for homesteads. He was successful in staking claim to 160 acres and the family moved in December 1889 to his claim one mile north of what is now the town of Piedmont, Canadian County, Oklahoma. Before that time the daughter, Rosa, returned to Kentucky where she attended school to obtain credentials for teaching. At completion she returned to Montague County, Texas where she taught school for a number of years and later married a Mr. Cagle of that area. Thomas J. remained in Canadian County the rest of his life and died in July 1915 where he is buried near Piedmont. Josephine Crossfield died in 1928 and is buried with her husband. *Submitted By: James S. Pope.*

WILLIAM HANSON CROSSFIELD,

the first son of Richard Henry and Elizabeth Crossfield, was born 1-14-1862. To him was the honor of being the first of R.H.'s children to be born in the new home that replaced the old cabin erected by his grandfather, John Crossfield. William married Mary Bell Cole (1863 - ?), a daughter of Elijah and Martha (Sherwood) Cole, on 1-30-1883. William and Mary were the parents of four sons and two daughters, herein listed: Herbert Spencer (1884 - 1976) married Florence Waterfill; Raymond Cole (1886 - 1974) married Esther Houchin; William Richard (1892 - 1978) married Estelle May; Henry Charles (1898 - 1989) married Marian Hentz; Lelia May (1888 - 1965) married Dr. Iscar Shewmaker of Louisville; and Mayme Bell (b. 1894) married Addison Briggs. William was a farmer and owned farms and property in Anderson County.

The son, Herbert Spencer, had bottling plants for the sale and manufacture of soft drinks. His brother, Raymond Cole, was a farmer in the Fox Creek area and a resident of the town of Fox Creek. Brother, William Richard, as his uncle C. K., was in the ice manufacturing business and was an owner of plants in South Carolina. He lives in Griffin, Georgia.

Henry Charles, the youngest son, studied for the medical profession in Kentucky and New York. Dr. Henry C. Crossfield and his family lived in New Jersey where he established Heart Service at Orange Memorial Hospital. He was active in the New Jersey Academy of Medicine and was president of that organization for two years. Dr. Crossfield cooperated with a project at Princeton University for four years. He is the author of the books "Living with all your Heart" and "Ultimate Man." He retired after a very successful career and enjoyed many "golden years" before his death.

William Hanson died 1-26-1931 and his wife, Mary Bell died in 1919. Both are buried in the Fox Creek Cemetery. *Submitted By: James S. Pope.*

WILLIE WALKER CROSSFIELD,

third son of John Eldred and Iva Myrtle Stratton Crossfield and the great great grandson of John Crossfield was born in Lawrenceburg, Anderson County, Kentucky on June 11, 1913. Willie attended Lawrenceburg Grade School and graduated from Lawrenceburg High School in 1931. During the Second World War he served in the U.S. Army Air-Force from 1942 until 1945. After the war, he married Helen Smith (Smitty) McMurtry on February 2, 1946. Smitty was born on August 30, 1922 in Hardin County, Kentucky, the only child of Joseph Samuel McMurtry and his wife Mable Kathleen Bell (1893 - 1980). Smitty attended school in Vine Grove, KY. and graduated in 1941. She graduated from the University of Kentucky in Lexington, Kentucky in 1945 and taught for a brief

time before her marriage. Smitty returned to teaching in 1962 at Western Anderson High School in Anderson County. She taught five years before becoming the school librarian, a position she held until she retired fifteen years later. Willie worked for the old State Highway Department - later the Kentucky Department of Transportation for twenty-three years until his retirement in 1977.

Mr. and Mrs. Willie Walker Crossfield

Willie and Smitty have three sons: John McMurtry, Stephen Walker, and Robert Woodford. There are two daughters-in-law: Donna Katherine Paul and Carla Kaye Durham. Willie and Smitty also have six grandchildren: Matthew Paul, Sara Renee, Elizabeth Bell, Emily Lois, Lesly Ann, and Samuel Mefford.

The Crossfields still reside in Lawrenceburg, Kentucky on Village Drive where they have lived since 1951. They travel in the summer and spend the winter months in Punta Gorda, Florida. Willie is an active member of the Benevolent and Protective Order of Elks, the Veterans of Foreign Wars, and the Charlotte County, Florida Society of the Sons of the American Revolution. Smitty is a volunteer at the Punta Gorda Library and is an active member of the Charlotte County Genealogical Society, the Huguenot Society of Florida, the C. C. Democratic Women;s Club, Daughters of the American Revolution, the Anderson County Historical Society and the Magna Carta Dames. Willie and Smitty are also Kentucky Colonels and are both members of the Lawrenceburg Presbyterian Church.

There was many descendents of the original John Crossfield of Middlesex County, Virginia in this county. They can be found in most all the continental United States from Virginia to California, from Indiana to Florida. Their professions and occupations cover a wide range including preachers, teachers, doctors, lawyers, engineers, and members of the Armed Forces. It is a family of which its members can be proud.

CUMMINS

Upon arriving in America, William Cummins, settled in Kentucky. William and his wife had one child, who's name was Thomas. Thomas Cummins married and had one child, William. He was named after his grandfather. William Cummins lived in Woodford County where he met his wife, Alice Updike. They were married and had nine children. Seven are known: Sam Thomas, Regis, Jimmy, Jeff, Lucille Bryant, Laurie Ayres, and Frankie Neil.

Sam Thomas Cummins was born on 8-25-1885 in Versailles, KY. He met and married Cora Lee Toles, the daughter of Joseph Toles and Susie Powell. She was born on 2-10-02 in Versailles. Sam and Cora lived on a farm in Frankfort, KY. From this marriage fifteen children were born. They were: Alice M. married George Bryant - one child, Linda; Charles F. married Betty McClease - six children - Charles, Bryan, Teresa, Mike, Darla, and Tawanna; Mary A. married Gene Doss - three children - Glenn, Lloyd, and Wanda; Martha M. married Donald West - two daughters - Sharon and Angela; Edward L. married Lois Gerald - three children - Linda, Edward, and George; Evert T. married Ann Gerlads - three children - Kim, Dana, and Evelyn.; George G. married

Brenda Cook - three children - Lisa, Dwayne, and John; John C. married Ruth Violet - three children - Nelson, John, and Ruth; William T. married Lola Wilson; Racheal M. married Herman Snow - four children - Donald, Mike, Ned, and Tracey; Sam T. (died at birth); Susie F. married Morris Crawford - six children - Nancy, Mark, Thomas, Bea, Donnie, and Ronnie; Joseph R. married Sharon Mitchell - two children - John and Lisa; Regis married Ruth Stogner - three children - Jimmy, Judy, and Janey; and Jeff Curtis (below). Sam and Cora raised their children in a small two bedroom home. The Cummins family attended Victory Chapel Church of God. In the summer of 1952, the church was having a revival. Sam's son, Jeff attended the services. When he arrived that night he noticed a lady visiting that he had never seen. Her name was Gladys Mae Robinett. One thing led to another and they ended up going back to Arkansas to get married. They married in Lawrence County, Ark. on 4-13-52 and returned to settle in Kentucky. Jeff was born on 2-25-28 in Franklin County. Gladys was born on 4-1-20 in Kennsett, Ark. She is the daughter of Alvin Robinett and Nancy Melissa M. Russell.

After returning to Frankfort, a child was born to them, Alvin T., who married Janice Edwards - two sons - Alvin and Josh. Later they moved to St. Claris County, Michigan to help a close relative. They had three more children born to them while in Michigan: Nancy Lee (below); Jeff M. married Teresa Gay - two children - Christy and Mike; and Joseph R. married Annette Noble - two children - Joe and Tash. Later they moved from Michigan back to Arkansas where they remained for thirteen years.

Nancy Lee Cummins met Scotty Lee Goodon as he was leaving for bootcamp. The Cummins family then moved back to Anderson County. After returning from bootcamp, Scotty moved to Kentucky where he wed Nancy on 2-5-71. One child came from this marriage, Justin Scott, born on 12-26-72. They lived in Frankfort for two years until their divorce. After the divorce, Scotty Goodon moved back to Arkansas where he married Nancy Scarbough in 1977. She has a daughter from a previous marriage, Melissa Anderson. Some years later his job forced him to move to Mississippi for two years. His job then moved him to Texas where he remained for four years. The company he works for recently moved him back to Arkansas, where he lives today.

Nancy and Justin remained in Kentucky where in 1979, Nancy married Gary Wayne DeRossitt. From this marriage two children were born: Andrea and Chad. Gary has two children from a previous marriage, G. W. and Kevin. Gary and Nancy live in Anderson County. *Submitted By: Justin Goodon.*

THOMAS ALONZA CUNNINGHAM

was born in October 1917 in Mercer County. He was the son of Tom Cunningham and Minnie McAfee. Thomas served in the Army from 1942 - 1945. After the war in 1948, he married Virginia L. Waite. She was born on 4-27-1922 in Cincinnati, Ohio. She is the daughter of Ed McKee and Maggie Waite.

Thomas and Virginia had six sons: Thomas, born 12-3-1948, married Linda Biglesly; Arthur, born 1-5-1949, married Debra Thompson - one child; Kevin L., born 12-4-1950, one daughter, Stacy McKee; Perry, born 12-23-1952, married Debbie - one child; James, born 3-7-1953, married Ann McDuffey - one child, James; and Waymond C., born 5-18-1954, married Marcella Washington - one son, Waymond Jr. - divorced. All six sons were born in Anderson County.

Thomas was a farmer. He worked on houses and cemented walls and floors. Thomas died on 1-19-1962 in the Veteran's Hospital. *Submitted By: Stacy McKee.*

JOHN CODY CUNNINGHAM

was born on 6-16-1895 in Anderson County and died on 7-12-1979 in Lexington. He was the son of Edward Cunningham and Betty Hawkins Cunningham. He married Etha Meaux in April of 1915. She was born on 7-27-1894 in

Mercer County and died on 5-23-1979 in Vermont. She was the daughter of Vance Meaux Sr. and Lucinda Baldwin Meaux. They had a son, Oliver Cunningham, born in Salvisa. He married Gertrude Bean in 1935. She is the daughter of the late Lee Bean and Mary Hayden Bean. She was born on 5-6-1916 in Anderson County. They were the parents of three children: Johnny, born 1937, married Martha Shy; Merle, born 1940, married Rose Washington- four children- Merle Jr., Stacie, Jeneen, and Elizabeth; and Clifforda, born 1944, married C. B. Moore - one child, Darron. Oliver Cunningham died on 8-31-1980.

Lee Bean, the son of Noah Bean and Mary Thurman Bean, was born in Anderson County. He married Mary Hayden. She was born on 12-6-1895 in Anderson County and died on 2-12-1929 in Ohio. She was the daughter of George Hayden and Alice Butler Hayden. Lee and Mary Bean were the parents of two daughters: Gertrude Ray and Alice Pearl married Kenneth Vance - two sons, Travers and Ronald. *Submitted By: Jeneen Cunningham.*

PAUL ALLEN CURRY, the son of Paul Dedrick Curry and Madeline Renfro Curry, was born on 9-18-1953 in Madison County, KY. He has four brothers and sisters: Ronnie Curry, born 1950, married Katherine Stinnette; Donna Sue Curry, born 1951, married John Cobb; Gregory Lee Curry, born 1961, married Robin Carter; and Pamela, born 1963, married Ray Montgomery.

Paul Allen Curry married Julia Carol Spears on 6-6-1974 in Lexington, KY. She was born on 10-10-1955 in Lexington. She is the daughter of Raymond Cox Spears and Pearl Cornette Spears. Her parents currently reside on Bond's Mill Road. She has one sister and one brother: Donna Rae Spears, born 1952, married Doug Craig; and Rell Cox Spears, born 1953, married Pamela Buscher White.

Paul Allen and Julia Carol Spears are the proud parents of two daughters: Olivia Ann Curry, born 11-24-1974 in Lexington; and Belinda Carol Curry, born 1-16-1981 in Frankfort, KY. The Curry family currently resides on Bond's Mill Road. *Submitted By: Olivia Curry.*

JAMES PORTER (JIM) AND NANCY (NANNY) DADISMAN were born in Nelson County and moved to Anderson County at an early age. They resided near New Liberty until September 29, 1979 when they moved to Chaplin, except for two years (1920-1921) when they lived in Louisville, KY.

James P., son of Thomas K. Dadisman and Eliza Frances Greer, was born June 9, 1895, near Green's Chapel in Nelson County, and died June 6, 1981, and is buried at Highview Cemetery, Nelson County. He was a farmer and liked to fish and hunt.

Nancy A., daughter of W. Thomas Baxter and Minnie Lee Cammack, was born August 15, 1897, and died on May 18, 1990 at Federal Hill Manor Home, Bardstown, KY. She was buried at Highview Cemetery, Chaplin, Kentucky. She attended Tanner School.

James Porter and Nancy Ann Dadisman

James P. and Nancy are the parents of two children. Dorothy, born April 14, 1918, a graduate of Western High School, lives near Bloomfield, KY and

is married to Porter Bunch. They have two children: Glenna Bunch Simpson and Darrell Porter Bunch. James Quillan, born August 15, 1925 and died December 15, 1976 and is buried at Mt. Washington Cemetery. He served with the Army in Italy during World War II. He married Aileen Shouse and resided near Bardstown, KY. They have two children: Linda Dadisman Rogers and James Ronald Dadisman.

James P. and Nancy have twelve great-grandchildren: Douglas Simpson, Gregory Simpson, Deborah Bunch Avritt, Teresa Bunch Milam, Shawna Bunch, Julia Greenwell, Mark Greenwell, David Greenwell, Angela Dadisman, Brandy Dadisman, James Ryan Dadisman and Nicole Dadisman. They also have two great-great-granddaughters, Victoria Milam and Elizabeth Milam (who was born on April 29, 1990.)

James P. was a member of the New Liberty Christian Church and Beaver Creek Masonic Lodge. Nancy was a member of the New Liberty Christian Church. She was active in the Homemakers Club. *Submitted By: Glenna Simpson.*

ROBERT LEE "BOB" DARNELL and Cora Elizabeth Annfield Ward were married April 18, 1930. They lived and farmed in the western section of Anderson County on the Kays Road near Fairview.

Bob and Cora were the parents of two children: 1. Norva Lee Darnell born January 29, 1931, resides in Anderson County Kentucky; and 2. Almira Jane Darnell born July 12, 1937, married Boyd Douglas Rogers and resides in Lexington.

Norva is the father of three children: Cora Beth Darnell, Brenda Ann Critchfield and Tony Lee Darnell (deceased).

Jane is married to Douglas Boyd Rogers. They have three children: Douglas Rogers, Debra Profit and Donna Rogers.

Robert Lee Darnell (September 21, 1892 - May 7, 1969) was the son of David Bruner Darnell and Menervia Jane Waldridge.

Robert and Cora Darnell

Robert had two sisters: Mahala Gillis (Lexington, KY.) and Matha Satterly (Anderson County, KY.) and three brothers: Roscoe, Elester, and Sleet Darnell. (all 3 deceased).

After the untimely death of Cora, Robert remarried Opal Stratton.

Cora Elizabeth Ward Darnell (March 17, 1905 - April 9, 1940) was the daughter of Newton Ward and Tranquil Adams Ward. Cora was the sister of: Margaret Z., June 23, 1903 - June 30, 1903; Hester A., Jule 23, 1907 - May 1990, married Cecil Wells; Thelma Florence, August 4, 1910 - resides in Lawrenceburg, KY., married John T. Cox; and Alma Rhea, May 6, 1913 - 1985) married 1. Silva Stoner and 2. Dillard Koger; and two brothers: Woodrow Ward, April 14, 1918 - May 20, 1982, married Gertrude Cornish; and Bernice Edward Ward, September 19, 1921 - 1937, buried in Fairview Cemetery.

Cora and Robert are buried in the Fairview Christian Church Cemetery, Anderson County, Kentucky. *Submitted By: Robert M. Thompson.*

WILLIAM HENRY DAWSON was the son of John and Elizabeth Mothershed Dawson.

John Dawson was born 1-14-1792 to William Dawson and his wife, probably in Anderson County. William, a native of Caroline County, Maryland, married in Virginia and soon thereafter moved to Kentucky where he and his wife settled on a farm in Anderson County. His will dated 4-8-1819 named his wife, Elizabeth, and children, George, Rebecca Drew, Peter, Elizabeth Higgins, Joseph, Charlotte Miller, John, Charles, and Anna.

The farm of William and Elizabeth was left to John, who married Elizabeth Mothershed, daughter of John Mothershed, on 1-2-1823, in Franklin County, KY. John died 3-17-1869 and was buried on the Dawson Farm. Their children were William Henry, John, Wade, Charles, Charlotte, and Margaret.

William Henry was born 11-10-1823 in Anderson County and died 3-11-1877 at Hardin in Ray County, Missouri. He married Sarah Ellen McGinnis at Lawrenceburg, KY in 1845. She was the daughter of John and Sally Riley McGinnis. Sarah Ellen was born 3-15-1830, and died 9-3-1889, in Ray County, Missouri where she and William H. are buried at Lavelock Cemetery.

William Dawson, Sarah McGinnis Dawson

William H. and Sarah Dawson left Anderson County after the Civil War following the path of many Kentuckians, including Sarah's McGinnis relatives, and settled in Hardin, Ray County, Missouri with their children, James Elias, Sara Elizabeth (Beth), Wade Thomas, Louise Frances, John McGinnis, Charles Wallace, Malinda Catherine, William Riley, Rebecca Octavia (Tavia), and Edward Forest. Their last child, Mary Lurena was born in Missouri in 1869 and died in 1870.

Sara Elizabeth (Betty) married 1st James Houchens, with whom she raised three children and 2nd William Mosby. Charles Wallace married Maria Simmerman. He was in banking in Oklahoma, although they resided in Richmond, MO. They had four children. William Riley married Ollie Cline and raised six children in Weatherford, OK, where he was a stockman. Edward Forest became a Baptist minister where he preached in Carroll Co., MO. He married Linea Moore and they raised three children.

The descendents of these children of William and Sarah Dawson are now spread around the globe from Okinawa to England and the Mid-East where great-grandsons of Edward T. Dawson are serving in the U.S. Army and Navy (graduates of both West Point and Annapolis). *Submitted By: Robert L. Dawson.*

DORAN KAVANAUGH AND BERTHA MAE DAVENPORT, were residents of the southeastern part of Anderson County. Doran was born October 6, 1889, in Mercer County to Edward and Katherine Baker Davenport. He was the eldest of 13 children. He died April 17, 1969, and was buried in Hebron Cemetery in Anderson County. Bertha McCoy was born September 2, 1892 in Anderson County to Zackary Taylor and Mary Alice Robertson McCoy. She was the youngest of four children. She lived from birth until her death, September 23, 1984, in the same house. She too was buried in the Hebron Cemetery. The homeplace and about 190 acres of land was purchased by Zackary McCoy and his bride Mary Alice Robertson around

1874. It was a two story, one room structure used as a council house, similar to the courthouse, and over the years has been added to and remodeled. Zackary McCoy died December 23, 1922 and Mary Alice McCoy died November 29, 1949, at the age of 92. They were both buried in the Hebron Cemetery.

Doran Kavanaugh and Bertha Mae Davenport

Doran and Bertha were married July 20, 1919, by the Reverend Baker of Salvisa, Kentucky. They were members of the Claylick United Methodist Church. They were the parents of six children, all living in Anderson County. Delbert B., born July 17, 1922, died July 7, 1988, and buried in the Lawrenceburg Cemetery. He was married to Edna Disponett of Versailles. They have two sons Richard Dale and John Kavanaugh. Cecil McCoy, born January 11, 1924 is married to Marie Wayne of Anderson County. They have one daughter, Beverly Dianne. Elgeather, born July 23, 1928, is married to Clarence Sharp, Jr. from Taylorsville, Kentucky. They have one son, Wesley Doran, and one daughter, Patricia Lynn. Elgeather graduated from Kavanaugh High School in 1948. J.T. born June 11, 1930, is married to Shirley Hyatt of Anderson County. They have two sons, James Dudley and Luther Allen. Aubrey D., born May 17, 1932, died November 4, 1936, and was buried in Hebron Cemetery. Mary Anna, born November 23, 1933, was married to the late Oscar Drury of Anderson County. They have one daughter, Barbara Ann. Mary Anna was a member of the first graduating class of Anderson High School in 1953.

Doran and Bertha continued the farming of the land, after the death of Zackary. To supplement the income, Doran was a blacksmith and carpenter, both trades learned from his father. He was a World War I veteran. Delbert and Cecil were World War II veterans. J. T. served in the Korean War. Delbert, until his death, and J. T. tend their farmland on the Bonds Mill Road. Cecil still farms the homeplace on Claylick Road. Elgeather and Mary Anna work for the State Government in Frankfort. *Submitted By: Elgeather Sharp and Mary Anna Drury.*

LEWIS DECKER

LEWIS DECKER was the son of Robert Decker and Rose Grubbs Decker. He married Virginia Meryman. She was the daughter of B.L. Merryman and Effie Nichols Merryman. She had seven brothers and sisters: Eddie, Jimmy, John, Annie, Ada, Edward, and John. Lewis and Virginia were the parents of four children: Myrtle, Edith, William, and Ronnie. Virginia later remarried to Leonis Cox.

William Decker was born on 9-20-1947 in Anderson County. He married Linda Barnett Morgan. She was born on 5-15-1951 in Anderson County. She is the daughter of W. T. Barnett, Jr., and Lucille Sparrow Barnett. Linda was first married to Jimmy Morgan. William and Linda are the parents of three children: Heath Stacey (6-15-1970 - 5-7-1983) buried in the Hebron Cemetery; Kerry Grace, born on 6-19-1974; and Misty Dawn, born 1-26-1982.

W.T. Barnett Jr. was born on 7-21-1923 and is the son of W. T. Barnett Sr. and Carrie Whitaker Barnett. He has three sisters: Ethel, Maryalice, and Ruby. He married Lucille Sparrow. She was born on 4-9-1926 and is the daughter of Willis Sparrow and Gracie Ashby Sparrow (1897-1971). She has three sisters and one brother: Dora married Forrest Brown; Ruby married Willis Brown; Corinne married Earnest Cook; and Thomas married Myrtle.

W. T. Jr. and Lucille are the parents of four children: Wanda Francis, born 1942; Wilma Rachell, born 1945; Linda Kathryn, born 1951; and William Albert, born 1954. *Submitted By: Kerry Decker.*

JOHN CLAYTON DRAKE

JOHN CLAYTON DRAKE was born on 4-25-1906 in Bloomfield, Kentucky. He is the son of Coleman Elsberry Drake (1876 - 1948) and Cordie Green (died 1972). On 2-14-1936 in Bloomfield, he married Lula Mae Freer. She was born on 5-5-15 in Wakefield, KY. She is the daughter of Samuel B. Greer and Ida James. John and Lula Mae are the parents of eight children: Sam married Candy Jones; Ida Lee married Ken Baxter; John Clayton Jr.; Martha; Mary married Jim Simpson; Eva married Wally Waldridge; David married Beverly V. Drake; and Delton married Debbie Ford. John and Lula Mae live in the homeplace of his grandparents, John Clayton (1825 - 1890) and Melvina Snider Drake (1835 - 1907) in Nelson County.

John Clayton Drake, Jr. was born on 6-8-1941 in Bloomfield, KY. On 8-16-1969 in Rowan County, KY, he married Carolyn Stephens. She was born on 7-22-1947 in Piqua, Ohio and is the daughter of Ballard Stephens (1923 - 1988) and Bonnie Mumford Stephens. She has two sisters: Brenda Lee Stephens and Linda S. Stephens Stamper; and one brother, Charles Stephens. John Jr. and Carolyn are the proud parents of two children: John Clayton III, born 4-18-1973, and Jennifer Carol, born 8-12-1975. The Drake family currently resides at 240 Morningside Drive in Lawrenceburg. *Submitted By: John Clayton Drake III.*

LARRY E. AND DONNA C. DRURY

LARRY E. AND DONNA C. DRURY have lived in rural Anderson County most of their lives. Donna Crain Headen Drury was born in Louisville, KY, and moved to Anderson County from Hardin County with her parents, sisters and brother in 1960. At that time her family resided in the Fox Creek community. She is the second oldest of five children born to Charles William and Frances Lucille Hughes Crain, Sr. Two of her sisters, Mrs. Earl (Charlotte) J. Puckett, Jr. and Brenda Crain Cummins, reside in Anderson County. Her sister, Mrs. Rick (Jeanne) Puckett, lives in New Jersey and brother, Charles William Crain, Jr., resides in Leitchfield, Kentucky. Donna graduated from Western Anderson County High School in 1970 and attended Eastern Kentucky University and Kentucky State University. Since 1973 she has been employed with the state government in Frankfort, where she works in the Natural Resources and Environmental Protection Cabinet.

Larry E. and Donna C. Drury with Derek and Stacy

Larry Eugene Drury, the son of Lois Shackelford Drury and the late Everett Joseph Drury, was born in Anderson County. He is the youngest of three children. His older brother, William Edward Drury, resides in Salisbury, Massachusetts, and sister, Irene Drury Hicks, is deceased. Larry is a 1969 graduate of Anderson County High School. He was employed for many years in the grocery business in Lawrenceburg, but is now employed with GTE Sylvania in Versailles.

Donna and Larry were married June 2, 1979, at Fox Creek Christian Church by Reverend David Cornish. They are the parents of two children. LaStacya (Stacy) Lynn Headen was born December 27, 1977, and Derek Christopher Drury was born July 20, 1981.

The Drurys are active in community youth activities. In 1982, they organized Anderson County's TWIGS #14 (Together With Important Goals Shared), a charity organization that aided young patients at Kosair Children's Hospital, Louisville. They work with youth clubs and athletic leagues. They are members of Sand Spring Baptist Church and reside at 1600 Fox Creek Road with their children.

JAMES EDWIN EARNEST JR.

JAMES EDWIN EARNEST JR. was born on 4-6-1946 in Paducah, KY. He is the son of James Edwin Earnest, Sr. and Edwin Trevol Martin Earnest. They reside in Kevil, Ky. James Jr. had one sister, Dorothy Ann, born 1949.

James Earnest Jr. grew up in Kevil, KY. He attended the University of Kentucky, where he met Deveria Jill Ewell. She grew up in Lexington, KY. She also attended the University of Kentucky. They married on 6-2-1967 in Lexington. James Jr. joined the Army. He was stationed in San Antonio, TX. Later they moved to Winchester, KY. He then finished college and one year later they moved to Danville, KY. Later they moved to Anderson County.

James Jr. and Deveria Jill are the parents of four sons: Jonathan Edwin, born 5-24-1972; Jason Ewell, born 7-1-1975; James Elliott, born 3-5-1978; and Joshua Earl, born 11-2-1979.

Deveria Jill Ewell Earnest was born on 9-6-1948 in Lexington. She is the daughter of Stanley Clay Ewell Sr. and Minnie Christine Turpin Ewell. She has one brother, Stanley C. Ewell Jr., born 12-11-1942. Stanley Jr. married Doris Elaine Eades in 1961. They have three children: Rick, Kelly, and Chris. *submitted By: Jason Earnest.*

WILLIAM ROBERT EDWARDS

WILLIAM ROBERT EDWARDS was born on 4-8-1853 and died on 1-9-1917. He married Susan Margaret Hendren Carter on 3-31-1881. She was previously married to C. A. Carter on 11-17-1876. He died on 5-14-1877 before their only child, Emma Love, was born. Emma married Dud Thompson of Anderson County and they served several years as jailer in Lawrenceburg.

William Robert and Susan Edwards were the parents of two children: Walter (1882 - May 1931) married Stella ? (1882 - 1966); and C. M. (below)

C. M. "Claude" Edwards (11-26-1884 - 8-9-1962) married Dessie Lee Gritton (1-17-1885 - 3-20-1965). They had six children: James Shively (May 1912 - June 1913), Rev. William Bruce Edwards (6-30-1907 - December 1936), Nellie Mae Edwards Asher (born 10-17-1905, living in Harrodsburg), Hazel Lee Edwards Walker (born 2-15-1914, living in Lawrenceburg), and Marvin Edwards (living in Lawrenceburg).

Dessie Lee Gritton was the daughter of James Newton Gritton (12-6-1859 - October 1901) and Nancy Ann Kays Gritton (3-27-1859 - March 1947). She had ten brothers and sisters: Ora Bell married Willie Brown; James T. Lester married Lillian Taylor; Ovie Ethel married Frundy Brown; Minnie M. married Louis Chambers; Noma Ann married Jas. Patterson; ? married Hobert Wheeler; Elizabeth Lou "Lizzie" married Garnett Noel; Nellie Bly married Roy Kennedy, 2nd Jack Frank; William married Etha Sanford; and still living in Harrodsburg. Nancy Ann Kays Gritton was the daughter of James William Kays Sr. and Lucretia King Kays.

Marvin Edwards was born September 9, 1915 in Mercer County, Ky. He married his high school sweetheart, Edyth May Hanks on May 3, 1936. She was born February 26, 1917 in Anderson County. She is the daughter of the late Robert Hanks and Lucy Moore Hanks. Although Marvin was born in Mercer County, he attended Lawrenceburg High School and learned to love Lawrenceburg. They

Claude and Dessie Edwards

have one son, Robert Bruce, who was born on May 9, 1946.

Robert Bruce "Bob" Edwards graduated from Anderson County High School, attended Georgetown College and a business school in Lexington. He then joined the Air Force. After serving four years in the Air Force including a year in Vietnam during the Vietnam War, he was happy to "come home" to Lawrenceburg. Bob married Angela Catherine Sparrow (born on January 4, 1949). She is the daughter of Clinton and Audrey Sparrow of Lawrenceburg and the granddaughter of Brother Ezra Sparrow. They have two daughters: Michelle Renee born April 11, 1970. She is attending Eastern Kentucky University. Katherine Suzanne born July 15, 1976. Katie is currently in the 8th grade at the Anderson County Middle School.

Bob worked for the City Police Department until 1972. He and his father then opened Travel World and Sport Center on Woodford St. with the help of his wife, Angela Edwards, Steve Shryock and Wayne Morris. They operated the business for ten years. Lots of fishing and hunting were discussed there.

In 1982 or 83, Bob went off to work for our current sheriff, Harold Cornish as deputy sheriff. In 1989, Bob was given the job as Police Chief of Lawrenceburg under the current Mayor Kenneth Hoskins and the current City Council.

Mr. and Mrs. Marvin Edwards are retired and reside in Lawrenceburg. Mr. and Mrs. Bob Edwards and family also reside in the county. *Submitted By: Mrs. Marvin Edwards.*

CHARLES JOSEPH ELDER JR.

CHARLES JOSEPH ELDER JR. was born on 8-8-1936 in Louisville, Kentucky. He is the son of Charles Elder Sr. (1-5-1912 - 7-20-1976) and Ruby Shehan. He has two sisters and one brother: Diana Marie, born 7-2-1938; Theresa May, born 7-3-1939; and Martin Anthony, born 1-13-1951. He had two sisters that are deceased, Mary Ann and Clara.

Charles Elder Jr. married Norma Jane Miller on 5-9-1964 in Louisville. Jane was born on 10-23-1942 in Louisville. She is the daughter of Willie Miller and Elizabeth Layman Miller. She has one sister and one brother: Verna Dean, born 6-25-1926; and William Leonard, born 7-17-1929.

Charles and Jane are the proud parents of three children: Joseph Todd, born 7-12-1966; Christopher Dean, born 3-15-1970; and Lesley Elizabeth "Beth", born 7-19-1974. The Elder family currently resides at 1019 Melody Lane in Lawrenceburg. *Submitted By: Beth Elder.*

JOB AND CHARLOTTE ELDRIDGE

JOB AND CHARLOTTE ELDRIDGE traveled the wilderness road into Kentucky and settled in Nelson County in the late 1770's. After Job's death in 1795, sons Abraham and Levi tended the family farm near Bloomfield.

Abraham married Elizabeth Woodsmall on 10-26-1806. Their children: Walter, John Bradford, Francis, Harriet, and Zipporah. They moved to a 245 acre farm purchased for $6 per acre on Broad Creek in Jefferson County in 1835.

John Bradford (born 1818) married Mary Ann Wheeler, 1-13-1842. A farmer and stone mason by trade John and his family lived in Indiana for a

number of years, but returned to their native Kentucky settling again in Jefferson County. During the 1860's many of the Eldridge kin loaded up their covered wagons and headed westward. John and his family chose to remain in Kentucky. Known children: Elizabeth, William Franklin, Mary, and Cordelia.

William Franklin (1857 - 1944) married Minnie Rebecca Shake (1864 - 1932) on 12-27-1881. They had six children: Nannie Leotia (1884 - 1970), Clyde Vernon (1886 - 1983), Maude May (1888 - 1989), John William (1890 - 1980), James Cleveland (1892 - 1985) and Katie Edith (1899 - 1978). Their family farmed in the Jefferson and Bullitt County area.

Paul Wayne, Joshua Adam, Shirley Mattingly and James Cleveland Eldridge II

James Cleveland married Geneva Baete, daughter of Belgium immigrant Phillip Baete, 11-23-1916. They had four sons: James Calvin, Vernon Floyd, Paul Raymond, Leo Alton. All four boys served with the Army during World War II. Their home place was a 100 acre farm on Back Run in Jefferson County. In his youth, Cleve raced mules on Sunday afternoon at Fern Creek Fairgrounds. He owned and worked horses all his life and belonged to Bullitt County Saddle Club. He made the trail ride from Shepherdsville to Kentucky State Fairgrounds in Louisville well up into his eighties.

Paul Raymond (born 1923) married Blanche Davenport, the daughter of Rebie and Blanche Davenport, 12-26-1944. They had three sons: Rebie Cleveland, Paul Wayne, Barry Jay. Paul Raymond worked for 23 years making Oertel's 92 Beer, then for General Electric until his retirement. Their family home is located outside Jefferstown.

Paul Wayne (born 1950) graduated from Fern Creek High School, enlisted in the Air Force, met Shirley Mattingly, daughter of Felix and Daisy Mattingly of Raywick, Marion County. They were married 8-30-1969, lived in South Carolina and Indiana, except Shirley lived in Louisville while Paul Wayne was in Vietnam. After the Air Force, they moved to Lawrenceburg where they resided when their eldest son, James Cleveland II, was born in 1974. They moved to Fern Creek later that year and resided there when their second son, Joshua Adam, was born in 1976. In 1977, the family moved back to a small farm on Benson Creek Road in Anderson County they call Varmit Hill. *Submitted By: Paul Wayne Eldridge*

ELGIN LEE EMMONS

ELGIN LEE EMMONS was born on 4-15-1948 in Maysville, KY. He is the son of Lowell Lee Emmons and Teresa Alice Fay Emmons. He has one sister and four brothers: Janice Kay, born 1945, married 1st Bill Mineer - divorced - 2nd Danny Carpenter; Jerry Wayne, born 1950; Dale Clifton, born 1952, married 1st Marilyn Benge - divorced - 2nd Allison Lobb; Lowell Lewis, born 1953, married Tammy Smith; and William Scott (1954 - 1954).

Elgin married Kathy Ann Whisman on 9-30-1972. She was born on 9-1-1954 in Hillboro, KY. She is the daughter of Woodrow Wilson Whisman and Mary Hazel Harding Fry Whisman. She had two half-brothers: Kenneth Joe Fry, born 1950, married Ellin

Walling Ford; and Gary Lee Fry, born 1952, married 1st Louise Myner, 2nd Brenda Emmons.

Elgin and Kathy are the parents of three children: Lee Ann, Jared Scott, and Christopher David. The Emmons family currently resides on Evergreen Dr. in Lawrenceburg. *Submitted By: Lee Ann Emmons.*

HIRAM ESTES JR.

HIRAM ESTES JR. was born on 8-27-1944 in Clark, KY. He is the son of Hiram Estes Sr. and Luesinday Stamper Estes (1915 - 1988). He has four brothers and sisters: Kenneth Estes married Addie; Katherine Estes married Vernon Hatton; John Estes married Regian Hunt - he has been married three times; and Brenda Estes married Jerry Reynolds.

Hiram Estes Jr. married first to Shirley Like on 10-19-1962 in Saliana, Tennessee. She was born on 7-11-1949. She was the daughter of Dale Like and Paulien Young Like. Hiram Jr. and Shirley had two children: Roland J. Estes, born 8-19-1964, married Vanessa Smith; and Gary W. Estes, born 9-28-1965, married Patricia Walker. Shirley Like Estes died on 1-22-1972 in Louisville, KY. She was buried in Louisville.

Hiram Estes Jr. remarried Sandra Rosmarie Boylan on 6-3-1972 in Louisville. She was born on 10-19-1946 in Louisville. She is the daughter of the late Charles Austion Boylan (10-13-1909 - 11-11-1985) and Dolars Anna Mayer Boylan. She has eight brothers and sisters: Charles C. Boylan married Florencia Bembo; William Boylan married Laveran Goodman; Linda A. Boylan married Jerry L. Roth; Marylou Boylan married Richard Butler Schnitz; James J. Boylan married Nancy; and John Boylan married Alma Dressing.

Hiram Estes Jr. and Sandra Estes are the parents of two children: Lue Ann Estes, born 6-18-1973 in Louisville; and Charles Jr. Estes, born 1-8-1978 in Lexington. The Estes family currently resides on Birdie Road in Anderson County. *Submitted By: Lue A. Estes.*

ROBERT ETHERINGTON

ROBERT ETHERINGTON, (9-9-1873 - 11-10-1942) and Nina Lee Stratton (3-2-1878 - 8-15-1948) were married July 15, 1896.

Robert and Nina farmed and raised their family in the Nevins Station area of Anderson County along the banks of Salt River. They were the parents of six sons: John Hart Etherington, (5-30-1897 - 9-12-1965) married Ruby Phillips; Hiram Bronston (8-11-1900 - 1-30-1923); Robert Overton (1-31-1906 - 9-9-1980) married Hazel Hahn; Willard Aubrey (1-25-1908 - 8-19-1988) married Grace Camic; Carl Beryl (4-7-1917 - resides in Anderson County, KY.) married Ada Shelton; Clyde Darrel (4-7-1917 - 4-7-1917); and six daughters: Pearl Thelma (5-19-1899 - 12-23-1959) married Powell Hackney; Nannie Lee (5-20-1903 - 10-6-1925); Viola Madgalene (8-2-1909 - resides in Lawrenceburg, KY.) married B.R. Thompson; Mary Bird (4-30-1911 - resides in Jefferson County, KY.) married William Wesley Chilton; Mattie Bell (11-13-1913 - resides in Anderson County, KY.) married Presley Cheek; and Nina Moore (8-14-1923 - resides in Jefferson County, KY.)

Robert Etherington and Nina Lee Stratton Etherington

Robert Etherington was the son of Hartwell Etherington (10-12-1829 - 11-17-1905) and Hettie Thomason (7-12-1842 - ???). Both parents are buried in the Etherington Cemetery near Ballard in Anderson County, Kentucky.

Robert's sisters and brothers included: Ed Etherington and Mary Etherington Leathers.

Nina Lee Stratton was the daughter of John Corbin Stratton (1-17-1846 - 8-28-1921) and Elizabeth "Mollie" Sanders (9-30-1848 - 3-20-1915). John and Elizabeth were married August 2, 1870. They are buried in the Sand Spring Church Cemetery in Anderson County, Kentucky.

Nina's paternal grandparents were John Dogad Stratton (9-28-1815 - 10-11-1863) and Almira Brown (8-27-1824 - 2-14-1910). They were married January 22, 1844. They are buried in the Stratton Cemetery near Ballard in Mercer County.

Nina's paternal great grandparents were John Stratton (1790 - 2-2-1873) and Elizabeth Sorrel (1793 -1-9-1878). They were married in 1809 in Spotsylvania County, Virginia. *submitted By: Robert Martin Thompson.*

REUBIN ETHINGTON, born c. 1785 in Culpepper County, Virginia - resident of Anderson County, Kentucky.

In 1741, One William Ethington (various spellings) was transported from a Surry England jail to Patapsco, Maryland. Evidence indicates that this is possibly the same man who six years later settled across the bay in Spotsylvania County, Va, where he is the probable father of at least five sons: William, Joseph, James, John and Francis. Of these sons, James (married Lucy Peterson) died early in Spotsylvania County, Francis was killed in the American Revolution, John and Joseph raised families in Spotsylvania and Culpepper Counties, and William and his wife, Caty, settled in Culpepper County where they raised a family of ten children.

We find that between 1800 and 1815 many of the third generation of the American Ethington Family left Virginia for the West and South. Joseph's children passed through Woodford County, KY to settle in Henry County where the spelling of the name settled into ETHINGTON. Some of John's children remained in Spotsylvania County, VA where they became known as the EDENTON family, while others moved to Tennessee - also known as the EDENTON's. Most of William's ten children left Culpepper County. Some went to the Carolinas and Georgia, others went to Owen County, KY and then on to Indiana in the 1820's (known as ETHERINGTON). However, his son Reubin, and Reubin's Virginia wife, Eleanor McDonald found their way to Woodford County, KY, spent time in Versailles, then settled in Anderson County some time in the early 1820's.

We find no record of Reubin buying land in Anderson County, although he did mortgage some personal property to Allen Rowland in October of 1832 (Deed Book B page 261). Perhaps he followed the trade of saddle, harness, and shoe maker as did his Grandfather Ethington, Uncle Joseph, and Cousin William. We do know that he and Eleanor were the parents of at least three daughters as follows: 1) Mary Ethington, born about 1830. Mary married John McKenney on 5-12-1824. Her descendants have not yet been traced.

2) Elizabeth Ethington, born about 1819. Elizabeth married Robert Casey on 12-29-1836 in Anderson County. They had the following children: 1. Thomas Casey, born 1838 2. James W. Casey, born 1840. 3. Martha A. Casey, born 1846. 4. Reuben W. Casey, born 1848. Married Lucy L. about 1866 Their children: Alonza (Lonzo) Casey, born 1867/68; Jerusha Casey, born 1869; Bustonia Casey, born 1872; Nettie Casey, born 1874; John Casey, born 1875; Elza Casey, born 1877; and Lilly Casey, born 1880. All the Caseys were residents of Anderson County.

3) Susan Ethington, born about 1820, married Charles Gill 12-14-1844 in Anderson County. Her descendants have not yet been traced, but she and her husband, Charles, are found in Owen County, KY. (Montgomery Dist.) in 1883.

At Reubin's death in 1845 (will filed 6-9-1845), he asked that no inventory be taken of his estate, and that it all be given to his wife, Eleanor, who survived him. Witnesses were Turner Hanks and James McLearce. Eleanor was found living with the Caseys in later censuses.

For more information of the Ethington Family, contact: Harold Ethington, 9802 Chylene Drive, Sandy, Utah 84092. *Submitted By: Harold Ethington.*

GEORGE W. FALLIS was born August 29, 1841 in Mercer County, KY and died January 10, 1913 in Anderson County. He was the son of William M. and Rebecca Davis Fallis. He moved to Anderson County with his family, when he was just a child. He had six brothers and sisters: Samuel C. (married 1st Mary Ann Stipes, 2nd Louiza McQuinley, 3rd Sarah Gillis); - died young; Elizabeth (never married); Nancy J. (married Frederick Stripes); Rebecca; Sarah T. (married Henderson Stipes). George and his brother, Samuel, were expert stonemasons and worked on many houses in Anderson County. They probably learned their craft from their father, who was also a stonemason.

George's fist wife was Elizabeth Stipes. She was the daughter of Fredrick and Catheron Stipes. she was born on March 2, 1837 in Anderson County. They had five children: Mary W. (married William Houchin); Martha C. "Mattie" (married George T. Brown); James Francis (married Eliza A Colvin); Mary L. (born March 8, 1868 - died August 20, 1868); and George W. (born June 25, 1869 - died May 21, 1871). Elizabeth Stipes Fallis died of consumption on March 17, 1876. She is buried in the Old Salt River Church Cemetery with two of her children: Mary L. and George W.

On June 11, 1879 in Anderson County, George married Martha Ellen Gillis. She was born July 1, 1848 in Anderson County and died May 16, 1924 of pneumonia. She is buried in the Lawrenceburg Cemetery with her husband. Martha was the daughter of William and Frances Hedges Gillis. The Gillis family has been living in the area since before the county was formed.

George and Martha had two sons; Charles Lewis and Grover Cleveland. Charles was born June 21, 1883 and died November 16, 1953. He married Nancy Cordonia Norton on May 28, 1903 in Lawrenceburg, KY. She was the daughter of Andrew Jackson and Mary Elizabeth Wright Norton. They had five children: Charles Curtis (1904 - 1954) married 1st Mary Hutton (1906 - 1926), 2nd Naomi Goldie "Noma" Kays (1909 - 1984) They had two children: Charles Curtis, Jr. "C.C." (married Hilda Lucille Dawson) One daughter; Gus Dedman (1906 - 1954) married Helen Montgomery (1909 - 1972) They had one daughter, Wanda Mae (married Thomas Shelton - Three children) Ruth Gladys (1908 - 1979) married Thomas Hayes, they had four children: Louise Fallis (stepdaughter), James Thomas, Martha Ruth, and Dorothy Marie; Mary George (1910 - 1951) married Willard Dennis (divorced) They had one daughter, Mary Ann; and Nora Lee (1911 - 1985) never married.

Grover Cleveland was born June 1888 and died in 1964. He married Olive Key on August 28, 1907 in Lawrenceburg, KY. She was the daughter of W. H. and Maggie C. Key. They had five children; Margaret E., Grover Robert, Daviess Leonard, Nellie Francis, and Olive Anne.

George and Martha were both well-respected members of the community. George served as one of the first trustees of the Sand Spring Baptist Church. They even donated the land that the church was built on. *Submitted By: Denise Wilder.*

JAMES HARVEY FARRIS AND MARY CATHERINE PEARL, was a 7th generation American, his progenitor came from Scotland to the Albemarle Colony in 1663. Jimmy was born in Laurel County, Kentucky on 21 October 1851. His parents died of typhoid fever when Jimmy was 15 years old. To keep their four children together, his sister,

18, ran the house while Jimmy became a full time farmer. Jimmy was married in 1875 to Mary Catherine Pearl. She was born 23 September 1853 in Laurel County, Kentucky. Jimmy and Kittie moved to Madison County, Kentucky and became quite successful in farming. Jimmy accepted a position with the Internal Revenue Department as a Storekeeper-gauger, and after working in Madison County at the Silver Creek Distillery, was transferred to Lawrenceburg, Kentucky to work the distilleries in Anderson County. They bought a house and lot on East Woodford Street in 1906, from Mr. Bolzan for $2,850. In 1912, Jimmy, in addition to his Storekeeper-gauger work, was farming 800 acres of owned and rented land. Jimmy made a trip to Madison County to sell the last of his land. On 7 October 1912, he was murdered on the street in Richmond, Kentucky by a previous neighbor who held a grudge against Jimmy. Her sons helping, Kitty stayed at their home on Woodford Street until her death on 23 April 1925. Jimmy and Kitty had three sons: Hansford Lee Farris born 15 February 1876 in Laurel County, KY who married Edna L. Buckey. They had one son who died single. Hansford was the Chief Surgeon for the McDonald Douglas Aircraft Company in Tulsa, OK when he died 10 April 1953. Randall Farris was born 19 January 1880 in Laurel County, Kentucky. He married Lydia Estelle Lackey on 2 November 1908. They had five daughters, all had families. Randall was a minister with the First Christian Church, Disciples of Christ, for 55 years before he died 22 November 1977. Alex Pearl Farris was born 14 April 1892 in Madison County, Kentucky. He married Flonnie Evelyn Huffaker in Lawrenceburg, Kentucky 30 May 1916. They had three sons and one daughter, all married, and three had families. Alex was a Sergeant of Police for the Southern Railroad for 34 years. After retirement he died of a massive heart attack on 18 April 1961. James Harvey Faris used the single "r" in his last name, but his three sons added a second "r", believing the correct spelling to be with two "r"s. Both James Harvey Faris and Mary Catherine Faris are buried in the Lawrenceburg Cemetery.

Clockwise from top left: Mary Catherine Pearl, James Harvey, Stella Lackey, Randall, Hansford Lee and Alex Pearl Farris

ALEX PEARL FARRIS AND FLONNIE EVELYN HUFFACKER. Alex was born 14 April 1892, in Madison County, Kentucky, near the Kingston Community. His father was James Harvey Faris, his mother was Mary Catherine Pearl. The first school he attended was adjacent to his father's farm. He would ride his horse across the field to the fence dividing the farm and the school, then turn the horse loose to find its way back to the barn. His father secured a position with the Internal Revenue Service as a storekeeper-gauger, and was transferred to Lawrenceburg, KY to work the distilleries in Anderson County. In 1912 his father returned to Madison County to sell the last of his farm land, and was killed on the streets of Richmond, Kentucky, by a previous neighbor who held a grudge. Alex's parents had planned for Alex to become a pharmacist, but at age 20 he had to go to work to help support his mother. At the time of his father's death, they were farming

some 800 acres of owned and rented land. Most of the farms had to be sold to satisfy debts. After some bad farming seasons he invested in confectionery. At this he was not successful. He lost some money by investing in sugar futures. On 30 May 1916, Alex married Flonnie Evelyn Huffaker, born 18 April 1892, in Wayne County, Kentucky. She had completed two years at Eastern Kentucky State Teacher College. She had taught school for several years before marriage. Her parents, Burdette and Helen Huffaker, lived on North Main Street in Lawrenceburg. After marriage, Alex and Flonnie lived with Alex's mother on Woodford Street in Lawrenceburg. In the early 1920's, Alex was hired as a Special Agent with the Southern Railroad Company, and sent to Cincinnati, Ohio, to help break a machinists' strike. Flonnie stayed in Lawrenceburg with her 3 children and to help with Alex's mother. When Alex's mother died in 1925, Alex moved his family to Danville, Kentucky. Flonnie's mother was now alone with a grandson, born in 1919, so in January of 1927, Alex moved his family back to Lawrenceburg, and into Flonnie's mother's house. After Flonnie's mother died in 1946, Alex bought out the other heirs, and acquired the house for his family. In 1944 Alex and Flonnie took two grandsons into their home. In 1957, after 34 years, Alex retired from the Southern Railroad. He did a little farm work, raised a large vegetable garden, and did a little travelling. He suffered a heart attack, was moved to St. Joseph's Hospital in Lexington, Kentucky, where he died of a subsequent massive heart attack on 18 April 1961.

Flonnie stayed in her home until cancer was discovered. She was moved to a nursing home in Lexington, KY where she died on 28 May 1980. Alex and Flonnie were members of the First Christian church (Disciples of Christ) in Lawrenceburg. Both Alex and Flonnie are buried in the Lawrenceburg Cemetery.

Alex and Flonnie have four children:

James Burdette Farris born 30 August 1917, Lawrenceburg, KY, married first, August 1939, to Margaret Nancy Hance, second, 17 February 1945, to Anita Louise Tracey.

Mary Ann Farris, born 24 February 1920, Lawrenceburg, Kentucky, married 8 May 1942, to Hal Martin Haller.

Randall Lee Farris, born 19 May 1921, Lawrenceburg, Kentucky, married 31 August 1944, to Hildreth Creswell Cole.

William Pearl Farris, born 31 July 1925, Danville, Kentucky, married to Connie Sue Rowland of Tyrone, Kentucky.

JAMES BURDETTE FARRIS is a 9th generation American. He is the son of Alex Pearl Farris and Flonnie Evelyn Huffaker, born August 1917 in Lawrenceburg, KY. He attended school in Danville, Kentucky, and in Lawrenceburg, graduating from the Lawrenceburg High School in 1935. He attended the University of Kentucky in 1935 - 1936 and in 1937 - 1938. He worked with REA in Anderson County, and the Morganfield, Kentucky areas. He married Margaret Nancy Hance in August 1939 in Frankfort, KY. Nancy was born 23 January 1920 in Shelby

County, KY. James went to Gilmer and Bonham, Texas with REA work. August 1940 saw him back in Kentucky working with the Southern Railway. In September 1941 he moved to Cincinnati, Ohio with the Southern. He and Margaret Nancy had divorced and on 17 February 1945 in Covington, KY, he married Anita Louise Tracey, born 14 June 1923 at Washington Court House, Ohio. In 1946 They moved to Macon, Georgia and in 1967 moved to Marietta, Georgia, with the Southern Railroad at Atlanta. In 1980 he became Engineer Geotechnical Services for Southern Railway, a position he held after Southern became Norfolk Southern Corporation.

James Burdette Farris

He retired 30 April 1985 and became a part time consultant with Riley, Park, Hayden and Associates, Inc. in Atlanta. James is a Registered Civil Engineer and Registered Land Surveyor in Kentucky. He is a Life Member of the American Railway Engineering Association and Member Emeritus and former Chairman of Committee 1. James and Anita are active members of First Christian Church (Disciples of Christ) in Marietta, Georgia, where they reside. He has two sons by his first marriage. James Lee Farris born 24 February 1940 at Bonham, TX. He married first, Francis Marie O'hara June 1963 in Temple, TX. They had one son. Jimmy married a second time, 21 May 1955 in Leavenworth, Kansas to Hae Ja Song born 11 February 1955 in Seoul, Korea. They have one daughter. John Randall Farris was born 17 September 1943 in Shelby County, Kentucky. Johnny married Billie Joyce Shepherd-Moss 9 July 1970 in Georgetown, Kentucky. Joyce had two sons from her first marriage, then John and Joyce had one daughter. James and Anita had Jean Ann Francis born 13 March 1946 in Cincinnati, Ohio. She married and divorced, no children. Joseph Samuel Farris born 7 March 1952 in Cincinnati, Ohio married Margaret Geraldine Murphy at Frankfort, Kentucky on 28 April 1984. Jeri had two daughters from her first marriage, Joe and Jeri have no children. Judith Evelyn Farris born 9 July 1955 in Cincinnati, Ohio. She married 11 October 1980 in Marietta, Georgia to John Allen Northington, Ill. They have one son.

MARY ANN FARRIS was born 24 February 1920 in Lawrenceburg, Kentucky. Her parents were Alex Pearl Farris and Flonnie Evelyn Huffaker. She attended schools in Lawrenceburg, graduating from Lawrenceburg High School in 1938. She attended Mary Washington College in Fredericksburg, Virginia for two years. She worked at the telephone switchboard in Lawrenceburg until she married 8 May 1942 in Lawrenceburg, to Hal Martin Haller (Bud) born 14 August 1914 in Louisville, KY. In June of 1941 Bud was drafted into the Army. Mary Ann went with Bud to his training schools until he was shipped overseas to Iran for two and a half years. Mary Ann lived with Bud's parents in Miami and helped in the Mart Haller, Ins. Import and Export business.

Bud returned in 1946 and worked with his brother and father in Export until retiring 31 December 1988. Mary Ann is still working part time as bookkeeper in Mart Haller Company. They still live in Miami, Florida. Mary Ann and Bud had two children: Hal

Mary Ann Farris

Martin Haller, Jr. (Hal) born 29 January 1943 in Miami, Florida married 6 August 1945 in Miami, Florida to Susannah Elizabeth Houseman who was born 13 February 1945. They have one son and two daughters. Hal is the Academic Dean at the Florida Bible College in Kissimmee, Florida. Alan Farris Haller, born 19 January 1948 in Miami, Florida, married 24 July 1976 in Miami, Florida to Suzanne Veronica Pihera, born 27 July 1950 in Chicago, Illinois. They have three daughters. Alan carries on the Export Company with his cousins.

RANDALL LEE FARRIS AND HILDRETH CRESWELL COLE Randall is a ninth generation American. His parents were Alex Pearl Farris and Flonnie Evelyn Huffaker. He was born in Lawrenceburg, Kentucky, 19 May 1921. He attended all the Lawrenceburg schools, graduating from the Lawrenceburg High School in 1939. He attended Mrs. Rhoda Kavanaugh's intensive training for Service Academy appointment. Joined the Army, 17 October 1940 at Ft. Knox, KY. Was accepted into the Aviation Student Pilot Training Program, and received his wings on 10 November 1942, graduating as a Flight Officer. He transitioned during WWII, completing his missions on 6 May 1944. He was married by his "Preaching Uncle", Randall Farris, in Waycross, GA. His wife, Hildreth Creswell Cole was born 21 December 1922 in Three Notch, Alabama. She was a registered nurse working at the hospital in Brunswick, GA. Randall became an instructor in the B-17a and B-29s. He flew the refueling tanker, KB-29 and the KC-97. His last four years were spent with the U.S. Air Force Markmanship School, as a member of the High Power Rifle Team. He also worked with the research and Development branch during the Air Force search for sidearms for the Air Force, resulting acceptance of the AR-15 rifle and the S and W Combat Masterpiece .38 Cal revolver.

Randall Lee Farris

He served several tours outside the United States, mostly England and Okinawa, and numerous assignments within the States. After 21 years of active service he retired as a Mayor, Command Pilot. He was awarded the Distinguished Flying Cross, Air Medal with four Oak Leaf Clusters, Good Conduct Medal, American Defense Medal, American Theater Medal, European African Middle East Medal with one battle star, World War II Victory Medal, Occupation Medal, National Defense Service Medal, Air

Force Reserve Medal with Four Oak Leaf Clusters, and the Distinguished Rifleman Badge. He chose Troy, Alabama as his retirement home, and accepted a position as Coordinator of Civil Defense in Pike County, Alabama. In 1967 he left the Civil Defense and attended Troy State College, graduating with a BS Degree in 1971. He then worked as a Photo Lab Technician for 11 years. Still resides in Troy, Alabama, pursuing an avid interest in genealogy. They had two children: Margaret Catherine Farris (Kitty), born 26 Jun 1945 in Roswell, New Mexico. Kitty teaches Special Education. She married and divorced, no children. Randall Lee Farris, Jr. born 2 December 1946 at For Eustis, Virginia. He married Marilyn Elaine Kelley, born 23 Oct 1953 in Pike County, Alabama on 3 Jul 1970, in Troy, Alabama. He is an environmentalist, working in the State Health Department in Montgomery, Alabama. Now divorced, he supports his three children; Brandy Michele Farris, Kellie Page Farris, and Justin Randall Farris.

WILLIAM AND CONNIE FARRIS

WILLIAM AND CONNIE FARRIS reside at Poplar Dr. in Lawrenceburg, KY. They were married a little over 18 years ago at Connie's father's home by the Rev. Raymon Leake of the Tyrone Baptist Church.

William, called Bill and sometimes Moose, was born in Boyle County, Ky. and came to Anderson County with his parents at the age of 1 year old. He graduated from Lawrenceburg High School in 1943.

Bill worked six years for the Southern Railroad, moved to Miami, Florida in 1950 and worked for Mart Haller, Inc. till 1964 when he returned to Lawrenceburg. He then worked for the state government in Frankfort for the Finance and Administration Cabinet. where he served as Contracting Manager for 22 Years. He was presented with a plaque from the Office of the Adjutant General in appreciation of his 22 years of service. He was further presented with framed certificates from: The National Resources and Environmental Protection Cabinet commissioning him as "Admiral"; the City of Frankfort appointing him as a "Honorary Citizen"; the commission of "Kentucky Colonel" from the Governor's Office; a service award from the Kentucky State Park; and an appointment of "Colonel, Aide de Camp, commissioner's Staff" from the Kentucky State Police. Letters were read and presented from the House of Representatives; the Director of the Division of Telecommunications; and the Commissioner of the Kentucky State Police.

Bill is the youngest of four children born to Alex Farris and Flonnie Huffaker Faris. One brother, James Farris resides in Georgia, another brother, Randall Farris resides in Alabama and a sister, Mary Ann Farris Haller resides in Florida.

Bill 's father worked as a special agent for the Southern Railroad, and his mother was a school teacher until she married Bill's father.

Connie is the youngest daughter of Virgil Taylor Rowland and Myrtle Searcy Rowland. Connie has one sister, Myrtle Louise Rowland McGaughey who resides in Lawrenceburg, and a brother Marion Luther Rowland living in Florida.

Connie is a graduate of Anderson County High school. She then attended and graduated from Fugazzi Business College in Lexington. Connie

worked for the state government for about 13 years. She was working as a Clerical Section Supervisor of the Amendment Unit in Vital Statistics, Department of Human Resources when she left state government.

HAROLD K. FINK

HAROLD K. FINK was born on 1-19-1955 in Newark, Ohio. He is the son of Richard Kenneth Fink (1913 - 1962) and Florence Katherine Schwartz Fink (1917 - 1982). He has three brothers: Phillip Kenneth married Linda Winters - four children - Brian, Kyle, Aaron, and Melanie (who married Larry Hays - one son and one daughter); Vic married Carol Reed - three children - Kelli, Jill, and Kent - divorced; and Jan Eugene married Christine Gerber - three children - Tyrone, Thadeus, and Trina Marie.

Harold K. Fink married Alice Ann Wood Hatter on 6-10-1978 at Rosemont Baptist Chruch in Lexington, KY. She was born on 11-26-1952 in Frankfort, KY. She is the daughter of Kelly Samuel Wood, Jr. (1928 - 1985) and Helen Ruth Page Wood (born 1931). She has one brother, Larry Scott Wood.

Harold K. and Alica Ann Wood Fink are the parents of four children: Michael Keith Hatter Fink, born 5 -8-1973 (Alice Ann's son by a previous marriage); Richard-Neil Joseph Fink, born 3-12-1981; Shawn Phillip-Scott Fink (7-7-1982 - 7-16-1982); and Jon-Paul Kristian Fink, born 12-3-83. The Fink family currently resides in Lawrenceburg, KY. *Submitted By: Michael Fink.*

GREGORY ANDREW FITZWATER

GREGORY ANDREW FITZWATER was born on 7-19-1946 in Hamilton, Ohio. In Richmond, Indiana, he married Paula Sebald on 3-4-1967. Paula is the daughter of John Edwin Sebald and Paulene Manning Saunders Sebald (1923 - 1989). Greg has two daughters from a previous marriage. They are: Rhonda Fitzwater Hart and Tonya Fitzwater Durcoltz - two sons, Nick and Zack. Greg and Paula have two children of their own: Matthew G., corn 12-28-1970 in Hamilton, Ohio; and Megan Rebekan, born 2-22-1974 in Cynthiana, Kentucky.

Greg and Paula moved to Falmouth, Kentucky in 1972 when Greg was looking for a job. He later found a better job and the family moved to Versailles, Kentucky. Then later they found a house in Anderson County and they have lived here since. *Submitted By: Megan Fitzwater.*

JOHN AND GLADYS FLYNN

JOHN AND GLADYS FLYNN arrived in Lawrenceburg in September 1958. They chose the old McKee estate on McKee Lane to rear their eleven children.

Gladys was a native of Shelby County, Kentucky. John was from Waltham, Massachusetts. They met and married during World War II where they were serving in a Mobile Army surgical Unit in North Africa. They lived in Georgetown, Massachusetts, from 1945 to 1958.

John graduated from Boston College in 1934. He was employed by the Federal Department of Transportation until 1972, when poor health forced his early retirement.

Gladys graduated from Kentucky Baptist School of Nursing in 1940. She practiced nursing for 44 years until her retirement in 1983. In her last nursing position, she served as director of nursing at Heritage Hall in Lawrenceburg from 1979 to 1984.

The Flynn children all attended Anderson County schools, and all are college graduates.

Mary Elizabeth was born on July 13, 1945. She was a 1964 graduate of Anderson County High School and received her nursing degree from Albert Einstein School of Nursing in Philadelphia, Pennsylvania. She later received a bachelor's degree in psychology from St. Joseph College in Maine. Mary and John Joseph Uhrin were married on August 12, 1968. They have three sons, John Edward, Robert, and David. The Uhrins reside in Pottsdam, Pennsylvania.

Margaret Lillian was born on September 1, 1946. She graduated from Anderson County High School in 1965 and from the Good Samaritan School of Nursing in Lexington, Kentucky, in 1968. She mar-

ried Douglas Crucet on June 29, 1973, and they have four children, Mark Douglas, Courtney, Liat, and Hillary. The Crucet family resides in Atlanta, Georgia.

John James Jr. was born on February 22, 1948. He graduated from Anderson County High School in 1966 and obtained his bachelor's degree from Bellarmine College in Louisville, Kentucky, in 1970. He co-founded Flynn Brothers Construction Company. He married Linda Giovenco on July 2, 1972. John and Linda have two sons, John Jame III and Aron, and reside in Louisville.

George Jesse was born on May 24, 1949. He graduated from Anderson County High School in 1967 and from Bellarmine College in 1971. He co-founded Flynn Brother Construction. He married Elaine Dawson in November of 1974. Elaine and Jesse have two chiidren, Patrick and Kathleen, and reside in Louisville.

Anne Ruth was born on November 16, 1950. She graduated from Pinkerton High School in Midway, Kentucky, in 1968. She earned a master's degree in education from the University of Kentucky in 1974 and then taught school for nine years before returning to school in 1984 to earn a nursing degree from Spaulding College, Louisville, Kentucky. She currently co-owns the family property on McKee lane.

Joan Claire was born on April 29, 1952. She is a 1970 graduate of Anderson County High School and a 1972 graduate of Kentucky State University's nursing program. In 1975, she obtained a nurse practitioner degree from Emory University in Atlanta, Georgia. Joan has one daughter, Heather Leann Carmickle, by her first marriage to Robert Taylor Carmickle. She married Lawrence Girarg on January 1, 1983. The Girards reside in Aurora, Colorado.

Susan Janet was born on July 16, 1953. She graduated from Anderson County High School in 1971 and received her master's degree in speech pathology from the University of Louisville in 1982. Susan and Robert Staggs were married on December 21, 1974. They have four sons, Eric, Robert, Matthew, and Nicholas. The Staggs family lives in Jefferstown, Kentucky.

Daniel Stevens was born on August 1, 1955. He was a 1972 graduate from Anderson County High School and received a law degree from Columbia University in 1980. Daniel married Margaret Goodzeit on August 12, 1979. Daniel and Maggie had a son, Jess Farrell, who died in infancy, and have a daughter, Jamie Anne. They reside in Verona, New Jersy.

Edward Matthew was born on April 18, 1956. He graduated from Anderson County High School in 1974 and Berea College in 1979. Edward married Mary Richards on December 23, 1977. Ed and Mary have three children, Benny Lois, Arno, and Mindy Rae. They live in Waterfill, Kentucky.

Patricia Ellen was born on October 27, 1958. She graduated from Anderson County High School in 1975 and received a nursing degree from Berea College in 1980. Patricia and Barry Allen McKenzie were married on August 9, 1980. They have a daughter, Aileen Rose, and live in Lexington, Kentucky.

Nancy Gladys was born on March 26, 1960. She is a 1978 graduate of Anderson County High School and a 1988 graduate of Arizona State University where she received a master's degree in counseling. She married Joseph Davis on August 8, 1986. they have twins, a son, Martin Alexander and a daughter, Colleen Kelly. The Davis family lives in Sylva, North Carolina. *Submitted By: Anne Flynn.*

STEPHEN FRANKLIN

STEPHEN FRANKLIN (1761 - 1835) married Elizabeth ? and was a Revolutionary War soldier in Virginia. After the war, he moved to Fayette County, Kentucky. He had two sons - Benjamin (1800 - 1874) and Lewis (1800 - 1845), and three daughters - Polly, Sally, and Elizabeth. Lewis married Lydia Busey Carson (1798 - 1883) and became a farmer in Anderson County. Polly married Thomas Grace, an attorney, in 1808. Sally married Francis Long in 1809. Elizabeth married Leonard Young in 1816. About 1827, Stephen moved to Anderson County buying two tracts of land. He became crippled and needed Benjamin to run the farm.

Benjamin Franklin (1800 - 1874) married Sarah Husband (1816 - 1896) on September 9, 1839. They had nine children and although he could neither read nor write, his children went to school and when they were grown, he gave them each a farm. Their children were Lewis who married Lydia Oliver, Stephen who married Mary Shely, Elizabeth (1843 - 1858), Barnett who first married Eliza June Huffman and then Jennie Hazlewood, Sarah who died young of T.B., Benjamin who married Kate Petty, Thomas who married Betty Noel, Lydia Frances who married Ben Tindal, and Matilda who died young.

Front: Mary Franklin, Bruce Worley Franklin, Ruby Franklin, Ibra Evan Franklin. Back: Zack Franklin, Samantha Franklin, Mary Shouse (Gillis), Stephen Franklin and Ollie Franklin

Stephen Franklin, son of Benjamin and Sarah Franklin, was born in 1841. As his parents before him, he grew up to be a farmer, and married Mary Shely, daughter of Peter Shely and Meriam DeWitt Shely. Together, they had nine children: William married Hattie Sutherland, Zack married Samantha Johnson, Annie Married Ryley Brumley, Claude died young, Ben died young, Mary died young, Sarah died in infancy, Holmes married Florence Sparrow, and Lizzie married Everett Ackerman.

Zack Worley Franklin was born June 30, 1870 to Stephen and Mary Franklin. He also was an Anderson County farmer. He married Samatha Alice Johnson, on January 23, 1896. They had eight children: Ibra Evan who first married Ruby Gillis and secondly Betty Prather and finally Ruth Catlett, William Truman died as an infant, Ollie Townsend married Mary Pearl Buntain, Mary Elizabeth married Tullie Morgan, Ruby B. who married John Willie Perry, Bruce Worley married Edith Young, Virginia Alice who married Ernest Brown, and Bonnie Charlotte who married Raymond Carlton.

Zack Franklin died July 31, 1945 and is buried with his wife in the Old Lawrenceburg Cemetery. His father and mother, Stephen and Mary Franklin are buried in the Shely Graveyard in Anderson County. *Submitted By: Billy Joe Hume.*

LEWIS FRANKLIN

LEWIS FRANKLIN (1843 - 1910) married Lydia Oliver (1839 - 1912) and they were the parents of three children: Alice Franklin Sullivan, Kate Franklin, and Johnny B. Franklin.

Johnny B. Franklin (1878 - 1929) married Laura May Franklin (1883 - 1957) in 1899. She was the daughter of Benjamin Franklin (1851 - 1936) and Katherine Petty Franklin (1859 - 1932). She had nine brothers and sisters: Ezra Franklin, Petty Franklin, Charlie Franklin, Willie Franklin, Leora Franklin Sparrow, Estel Franklin Benett, Ben Franklin, Coolie Franklin, and Cheslie Franklin. Johnny and Katherine were the parents of nine children: Elmer, Myrtle Franklin Catlett, Olive, Roy, Kenneth, Ben, Lydia Franklin Watts, Harold, and Johnny Floyd.

Johnny Floyd Franklin was born on 4-2-1903 in Anderson County and died 7-25-1981 in Anderson County. He married Nancy Ethel Gregory on 1-25-1931 in Lawrenceburg. She was born on 1-27-1909 in Lawrenceburg and is the daughter of Everett Lewis Gregory and Lula May Gillis. They were the parents of ten children: Hollis; Betty Joyce Franklin Hutcherson; Anna Beele Franklin Glass; Johnny Keith; Vivian Arlene Franklin Beasley; Donald Everett; Thelma Lee married 1st James Thomas Smith - two children - Diana Smith Koonce and James Steven Smith - 2nd Wendell Bruce; Alma Jean Franklin Gaines; Sherri Denise Franklin Hahn; and Phillip Garrett.

Everett Lewis Gregory (1886 - 1968) was the son of Elijah Lewis Gregory and Sara Elizabeth Lynch. He married Lula May Gillis (1891 - 1911) in 1908. She was the daughter of William Vaught Gillis (1875 - 1917) and Mary Williams Gillis (died 1938). She had five brothers and sisters: Elmo Gillis, Robert Gillis, Walter Gillis, Nanny Gillis, and B. Gillis. Everette Lewis and Lula May were the parents of ten children: Paul, Doris Gregory Dailey, Carl, Floyd, Audrey Gregory Gritton, Willie, Ruby, Elizabeth Gregory Keeling, Margie Gregory McHenry, and Nancy Etyel Gregory Franklin.

Elijah Lewis Gregory married Sara Elizabeth Lynch and they were the parents of six children: Everett Lewis, Dale, Annie Gregory Hopkins, Claude, Ethyl Gregory Brown, and Ida Gregory Sparrow. *Submitted By: James Steven Smith.*

GAINES

GAINES The Gaines family was established in Kentucky by two brothers, Thomas and Richard Gaines, settled in Franklin County (later Anderson County) about 1818. Thomas and Richard were sons of Robert Gaines and Elizabeth Long. Thomas married Mildred Rowe and had three children. Richard married Malinda Sanders on 6-22-1818 and had two known children, Robert Samuel Gaines and Gabriel Hansford Gaines.

Robert Samuel Gaines was born on 10-17-1821. He married Eliza Jane George on 9-21-1846. Eliza was the daughter of Dudley George and Lucretia Major. She was born on 2-2-19. Robert S. Gaines and Eliza Jane George had thirteen children: William (married Sallie Mountjoy), David (moved to St. Louis), James (married Ann Mary Thomas), Mary (died at age seven), Lazarus (married Amanda Louise Smith), Martha (married Thomas Hawkins), Fannie (died at age twenty without marrying), Robert (married Lelia Searcy), Samuel (died in infancy), Arthur (died in infancy), Ada (married William Marrs), John (married Imogene Tinsley Gaines), and Boone (married Imogene Tinsley). Robert S. Gaines died in 1870. Eliza inherited her father's farm at his death in 1871. She lived there until her death on 3-11-1918.

Frank and Katie Gaines, 1946

Lazarus Beckinridge Gaines was born on 10-8-1854. He married Amanda Louise Smith (daughter of Fielding W. Smith and Sarah M. Carpenter of Oldham County) on 12-9-1875 and had four children: Oscar (married Mary Yager), Lelia (never married), Frank (married Katie Dunn), and Beulah (never married). Lazarus was injured in a saw mill accident about 1890. A wooden board struck him in the head and a steel plate was inserted to repair the damage. As a result, Lazarus was unable to provide for the family. Amanda moved the family to Oldham County so that her relatives could help the family make ends meet. Lazarus died on 5-17-1915. Amanda died on 2-7-1944.

Frank Breckinridge Gaines was born on 6-18-1882 in Anderson County. He married Katherine Elizabeth Dunn (Katie) on 2-27-1906 in Louisville. Katie was the youngest of eight children of Michael Dunn and Mary Ellen Fahey of Hardin County. Frank was a street car conductor for the city of Louisville. When street cars were phased out, he became a bus driver. Frank and Katie had eight children: Jaunita (married Walter Willman), Lillian (married Henry Kelting), Frank (married Josephine Duncanson), Catherine (married Joseph Redelberger), Angela (married Kenneth Lord), Robert (married 1st Amy Lee Stocking and 2nd Shirley Foley Gibson), and Darleen (married Ernest Diemer). Frank and his family lived on Queen Avenue in Louisville, just three doors down from Churchill Downs. Frank died on 4-19-1954. Katie died on 5-16-1959. *Submitted By: Darryl J. Diemer*

JOHN GASH

JOHN GASH married Mattie Overstreet. They were the parents of six children: Claude married Laura Hurst; Forrest married Jula Phillips; Ada (not married); Elva (not married); Jim married Geanva Rice; and John Dudly married Corinne Sweeney.

Claude Gash was born on 1-23-1881 in Mercer County, KY. He married Laura Maude Hurst. They were the parents of four children: Stella May married J. W. Cole; Hansford married Faye Sweeney; Jake married Carrie Ruth; and J. B. married Eleanor Cox. Claude died in December 1963 in Anderson County and Laura passed away on 8-8-1937.

J. B. Gash was born on 7-25-1915 in Mercer County. He married Eleanor Cox on 12-12-1935. She was born on 12-1-1916 in Lawrenceburg. She is the daughter of William Thomas Cox and Effie Wilson Cox. J. B. and Eleanor are the parents of two children: Mecia, born 1939, married Dickie Crutcher; and William Stewart I, born 1940, married Mary Joyce Adkins - four children - William Stewart II, David Bruce, Charles Edward and Chaundra Lynn.

William Thomas Cox "Daddy Cox" was born on 10-15-1893 in Lawrenceburg. He was the son of Jimmy Doyle Cox and Elizabeth McMurray Cox. He married Effie D. Wilson on 10-1-1914. She was born on 7-1-1890 in Lawrenceburg. She was the daughter of Billy Wilson and Sadie Walker Wilson. She had five brothers and sisters: Mammie Bell, Clyde Lucien, Taylor, Mary Walker, and Catherine. Billy Wilson came to America from Ireland at the age of 21. He came straight to Anderson County, where he married and raised his family on a farm on Fox Creek Road. Only Effie, also called Momma Cox, married. The other five children remained on the family farm and took care of each other. The old two-story white house is still standing. In 1955, after the deaths of Katherine and Mammie, the other three moved into town and bought a small house. When Taylor and Clyde died, Mary was left alone. The same with Momma Cox when Daddy Cox died on 5-13-1967. Mary and Momma Cox spent their last years together. Momma Cox died on 10-20-1980 and Mary in 1984.

Daddy and Momma Cox were the parents of two children: Eleanor Wilson Cox (who married J. B. Gash) and Sadie Elizabeth Cox (who married Ray Brown).

Jimmy Doyle Cox married Elizabeth McMurray. They were the parents of three children: William Thomas Cox (who married Effie Wilson); Minnie Bell (who married Charlie Morris); and Frances Elizabeth Cox (who married Carl McGaughey). *Submitted By: Chaundra Gash*

WILLIAM H. GAMMON

WILLIAM H. GAMMON, the son of Earl T. Gammon (1900 - 1973) and Laura E. Milburn Gammon (1909 - 1966), was born on 10-28-1920 in Washington County, KY. He has five brothers and sisters: Elmer (1928 - 1980); Martin, born 1916, married Polly Hays; Margie, born 1925; Buela, born 1922, married Bob Shagwood; and Pauline, born 1926, married John Bradshaw.

William H. Gammon married Marie B. Hays on 6-22-1936 in Danville, KY. She was born on 7-4-1920 in Boyle County, KY. She is the daughter of Louis J. Hays (1899 - 1967) and Elsy R. Bandy Hays (1901 - 1974). She has one sister, Hazel T., who married Clarence Brooks.

William H. and Marie are the parents of two children: June P., born 6-5-1939, married Bobby T. Denny; and William R., born 12-27-1947 in Boyle County. He married Linda G. Gillespie on 4-25-1968 in Lexington, KY. She was born on 10-25-1947 in Fayette County, KY. She is the daughter of Robert S. Gillespie and Betty L. Cooper Gillespie.

William R. and Linda are the parents of three children: Shane, born 9-26-1968; twins, Cherry and Terry, born 1-29-1973. All were born in Fayette County. The family lives in Anderson County.

Robert S. Gillespie, the son of August Gillespie (1898 - 1975) and Elizabeth Ham Gillespie (1900 - 1980), was born on 3-22-1928 in Fayette County. He married Betty L. Cooper on 8-4-1945 in Fayette County. She was born on 7-14-1927 in Fayette County. She is the daughter of James R. Cooper (1906 - 1951) and Violet C. Conclin Cooper (1908 - 1981). She had two brothers: Charlie (who died an accidental death) and Buddy (who died at birth).

Robert and Betty are the parents of three children: Linda; Bobby, born 1949; and Jana, born 1965, married Mark Sparks - one child, Drew. Robert is a plumber and Betty is a secretary. They live in Harrodsburg, KY. *Submitted By: Sherry Gammon.*

THOMAS EDWARD GASH

THOMAS EDWARD GASH was born in 4-9-1836 and died on 8-5-1908. He married Una Mae Sea on 10-28-1856. She was born on 2-19-1839 and died on 3-19-1917. They had a son named Thomas Neal Gash born on 2-6-1859 in Anderson County. He was a Baptist minister and died on 1-19-1940. He married Nannie Etherington on 10-13-1880. Nannie was born on 3-23-1861 in Anderson County, the daughter of Marvin Chester Etherington (1839 - 1909) and Lizzie Jane Reynolds (1841 - 1901). Nannie died on 11-25-1938.

Thomas Neal and Nannie Gash were the parents of eight children: Ethel married Ollie Ragan; Herbert (below); Arthur married Alice Shely; Chester Francis married Mary Alice Shouse; Una married Dave Rogers; Nettie married Richard Overstreet; Zyphlia married Oscar Adkins; and Mary married Wilmer Duncan.

Herbert Gash was born on 8-16-1883 in Lawrenceburg and died 5-27-1951. He married 1st Nell Shields, 2nd Nellie Sutherland on 8-17-1927. Herbert was the father of seven children: Thomas Neal married Ruby Crossfield; Wallace married Ada Brown; Clyde married Evelyn Gash; Mitchell married Jean Gash - one son, Gary; Ruby Charlotte (1934 - 1973) married Paul Nutgrass - two children - David and Linda; Nancy married Bobby Hyatt - three children - Tammy, Todd, and Meredith; and Wilmer Carl "Woody" married Wanda Joyce Chilton, the daughter of John Chilton and Corinne Satterly - two daughters - Tabitha Marshea and Tiffany LeShea.

Nellie Sutherland Gash was born on 4-27-1903 in Anderson County. She is the daughter of Howard Sutherland and Mary Anne Whitehouse. Howard Sutherland was born on 3-17-1872 in Anderson County and died on 1-19-1940. He married Mary Anne Whitehouse on 9-14-1901. Mary Anne, the daughter of John Henry Whitehouse (1850 - 1919) and Talitha Moffett (1854 - 1924), was born on 9-30-1874 in Anderson County and died on 12-23-1959. Howard and Mary Anne were the parents of seven children: Nellie; Elbert married Blanche Curtsinger - seven children - James, Dorothy, Dorris, Joyce, Chester, Linda Lou, and Betty Sue; Georgia; Paralee married Charlie Whitehouse - two sons - Howard Curtis and Jerry Lyons; Ruby married R. C. Dennis - two children - Donald and Judy; Margaret married J.R. Curtsinger - three sons - James Ray, Bobby, and Edward; and Nettie.

Howard Sutherland was the son of Hozie Sutherland and Leaky Jane Brown. Hozie Sutherland was born on 9-13-1820 and died on 4-14-1899. He married Leaky Jane Brown on 7-3-1869. She was born on 11-29-1825 and died on 2-7-1896. They were the parents of two sons - Howard and Johnny. *Submitted By: Tiffany Gash.*

TRAVIS GEORGE

TRAVIS GEORGE and his wife, Sarah Watkins, moved to Kentucky and settled on Hammonds Creek. Travis and Sarah had four children: Dudley (married Lucretia Major), Patsy (married Nathan Watson), William, and Sarah (married Salathael Cole). Travis died before 1810.

Dudley George was born on 12-14-1791 in Virginia. He was a Private in the Kentucky Mounted Infantry during the war of 1812 and was present at the Battle of New Orleans under General Andrew Jackson. On 1-14-1826, Dudley married Lucretia Major, daughter of Littleton Major and Polly Payne. Dudley and Lucretia had four children: Mary, William, Eliza (married Robert S. Gaines), and David (never married).

Dudley was an early member of the Anderson County Board of Internal Improvement. He was an active member of the Old Salt River Baptist Church and served on the building committee of the church's meeting house that was erected in 1842. Lucretia died in 1838.

On 11-13-1842, Dudley married Mariah Walker, daughter of Ronald and Polly Walker. There were no children born from this union. Polly died in 1864.

Dudley died on 1-31-1871 at the age of 79. He was buried in a little family graveyard, located on his farm near Lawrenceburg. Dudley's daughter, Eliza Gaines, was his only living child and she inherited his entire estate. *Submitted By: Lillian G. Kelting*

JACOB CREATH GIBBS, M.D.

JACOB CREATH GIBBS, M.D., born on 4-30-1822 in Franklin County, KY moved to Glensboro, KY in 1847 and began his medical practice.

On 2-3-1850, he married Mary Ann Munday. They continued to live in Anderson County until each one passed away. They had 14 children but only 10 lived to be adults. Two of the adults lived in Anderson County until they died.

Dr. Gibbs built the first frame house west of Lawrenceburg in Anderson County. The above Picture shows the family home. Standing in front of the house from left to right are: Dr. J.C. Gibbs, his wife, Mary Ann Gibbs; a daughter, Ella, who married W.O. Moffett. They had four children: Rose, Mary Catherine, Elva and Belva, two of whom are still living, namely the twins, Elva Moffett Blandford who lives in Dayton, Ohio and Belva Moffett, the only grandchild now living in Anderson County. Next to Ella is her twin brother, Ezra, who married Mary Moffett. They had four children but one still survives - Minnie Gibbs who now lives in Lexington, KY. Next in the picture is Minnie Stinnett who had no children. She lived in the New Liberty neighborhood. Then we come to Salathiel Cole Gibbs who married Nancy Moffett, a cousin to W.O. and Mary Moffett. They had four children but only one is still living, namely, Mrs. Elouise Ledford who lives in Louisville, KY. The deceased are Onita Gibbs Perry, Rollin Gibbs, and Owen Cole Gibbs. Onita lived in Glensboro until her death in December 1986.

Slathe became a doctor and continued to live in Glensboro until his death in 1971. Dr. Gibbs was a very compassionate doctor. He always responded to every call regardless of what pay he would receive; sometimes it was eggs or hens, maybe a ham for delivering a baby or frequently nothing. His life was one of service to others. He continued to practice medicine until he was quite old.

The Gibbs children not in the picture are Lucy Buntain who lived in Texas; Lillie McGaughey in Mt. Eden, KY; Emma Gudgel in Shelbyville, KY; W. Sneed Gibbs in Shelbyville, KY; Ida Glass in Anchorage, KY; and Jo Ann Bickers in Louisville, KY. Most of the folks lived a very active life and lived to be in their 80s or 90s.

The Gibbs family was very active in church and in public schools. Farming was an important pursuit of most of them. Many of them raised tobacco.

The descendants still living have wonderful memories of the happy days spent in Anderson County at church picnics, fishing, horseback riding, playing baseball, gathering wild flowers, going to the Lawrenceburg Fair and just being together. *Submitted By: Minnie Gibbs.*

CHARLES LEON GIBSON

CHARLES LEON GIBSON was born on 5-23-1922 in Anderson County. He married Doris Marie Driscoll on 4-24-1948. She was born on 4-25-1930 in Mercer County. They are the parents of three children: Joyce Gibson Dean was born on 11-30-1948. She has two children - Stephanie Lee Giles, born 11-30-1967, and Chad Allen Dean, born 10-5-1973.

Donald Leon Gibson was born on 9-15-1950. He has four children - Michelle Denise Gibson, born 3-12-1969, Eric Reid Gibson, born 9-7-1974, Jodie Lynn Gibson, born 3-12-1985, and Charles Jared Gibson, born 5-29-1986.

Edward Merl Gibson was born on 4-10-1954. He has two daughters - Melissa Susan, born 3-16-1982, and Jennifer Marie, born 5-6-1984.

Charles Leon and Doris Marie Gibson also have one great-grandchild, Quinnan Marie Bond, born 11-12-1987. She is the daughter of Stephanie Giles Bond. *Submitted By: Charles Gibson.*

ANCIL GARVICE GIBSON

ANCIL GARVICE GIBSON and Garnett Burgin Gibson are lifelong resident of Anderson County. They married November 3, 1940 at the home of the bride. He was farming and she was teaching school. He is the son of Russell Porter and May Eva Cole Gibson. She is the daughter of Tyler Preston and Truman Frances Case Burgin. They lived on the Mays Road when Geraldine was born October 5, 1941 and Reuben Carroll was born December 6, 1942.

In January of 1943, Garvice was drafted and served in the army during World War II for nearly three years. He came home December 22, 1945. They moved to Owensboro, KY for about two years where Garvice worked in a hardware store. They bought 25 acres of the Burgin farm on Anderson City Road and built a house where they have lived ever since.

Garvice and Garnett Gibson

Both were educated in one room schools. Among teachers remembered are Miss Annie Wash, Miss Rachel Baxter, Mrs. Corrine Gash, Mrs. Hazel Gash, and Mrs. Grace McKee. He graduated from Western

Anderson High School and she graduated from Kavanaugh High School. She went to Eastern University for two years and graduated from Georgetown College, Georgetown, KY.

Geraldine married Russell Gene Harrod and resides in Lawrenceburg. They have two boys and one grandchild. Reuben Carroll married Shirlene Driscoll and they reside in Louisville. He has four children and one grandchild.

Garvice was a self-employed truck driver, delivering limestone to farmers in Anderson and adjoining counties. Later he owned and operated Gibson Fertilizer and Spreader Service in Lawrenceburg until his retirement. Garnett continued her teaching career in one room schools for eight years and when they were consolidated, she went to Alton School and taught there until her retirement in 1974, a total of 31 years.

In early years, Garnett went to Goshen Baptist Church. She remembers when the church was filled with Bro. W. D. Moore preaching. Many of the members were relatives and they would go home with each other for Sunday dinner and spend the afternoon. Garvice grew up in Mt. Pleasant Baptist Church where his parents and grandparents attended. He remembers revival meetings when the people couldn't all get inside the church. Now they are regular attendants at Sand Spring Baptist Church. He is a Deacon and she is clerk and Sunday School Teacher. She is Anderson Baptist Associational Clerk, member of Fox Creek Homemakers and Retired Teachers Association. *Submitted By: Garnett Gibson.*

RUSSELL PORTER GIBSON

RUSSELL PORTER GIBSON (1893-1980) and Mary Eva Cole Gibson (1897 - 1973) were married on December 1, 1915 and lived most of their life on their farm located on the Mays Road. He moved to Anderson County from Mercer County when they married and she lived all her life in Anderson County. She attended Rutherford School. She was the daughter of Charlie and Gracie Cole.

Porter was the son of William James Gibson (1869 - 1945) and Mary Ann Overstreet Gibson (1873 - 1920). Porter had one brother, Owen Gibson, and three sisters, Maymie Carter, wife of Lester Carter, Bessie Carter, wife of Willis Carter, and Lennie Hawkins, wife of Ben Hawkins.

Mary Eva had one sister, Gertie, who died at the age of five in 1904, and one brother, Marvin, born in 1908. He lives in Owensboro, KY.

Mr. and Mrs. Porter Gibson

Porter and Mary Eva are the parents of three children. Ancil Garvice married Garnett Burgin in 1940 and they are retired and live on Anderson City Road. They are the parents of Geraldine Harrod, Lawrenceburg and Reuben Carroll of Louisville. Venie Gladys married Clay Cornelius in 1948 and they live in Louisville, KY. They have two daughters, Brenda Cornelius and Paula Price. Charles Wayne never married and lives at the homeplace on Mays Road.

Porter and Mary Eva were longstanding members and regular attendants of Mt. Pleasant Church. They were buried in the Lawrenceburg Cemetery. *Submitted By: Garvice Gibson.*

JOHN W. GILES

JOHN W. GILES was born in Woodford County, the fourth son of nine children to the late Peter K. and Eva O'Nan Giles. He attended Woodburn School in Woodford County and as a young man he worked with horses for Senator Johnson N. Camden of the Hartland Farm. From 1935 to 1938, he worked for Kentucky Utilities Company.

In 1837, he married Christine Perry, daughter of the late Ollie T. and Minnie Monroe Perry, and came to Lawrenceburg where in 1938 he worked on the building of the Fox Creek Rural Electric lines. He then started his woodworking shop.

John and Chris have four children: Larry, a Kentucky State Trooper; Pamela Sweasy, a secretary in the State Vocational Education Department; John L., a technician for Mago Construction Company; and Ginger Haydon, who is branch manager for the Kentucky Retirement Systems. They have nine grandchildren and three great-grandchildren.

John is noted for his tobacco cutting abilities and he introduced the "spear" to tobacco farmers in Anderson County on the farm of J.L. Sherwood in the early 1940s.

John and Christine Giles

In 1966, he was elected Mayor of Lawrenceburg, after serving eight years as city councilman under Mayor Tom Ripy. He served three terms as mayor, during which time Twentieth Century Fox filmed the movie "Flim Flam Man" here, a sidewalk was laid to the fairgrounds, cable T. V. came to town, the ambulance service was started, ground was broken for a new business: Florida Carpet and Tile, plans were laid for West Park Shopping Center, the paperwork was done and grant money received for a new sewage treatment plant as his term ended in 1981. He is now semi-retired and working in his shop.

Chris is a 1934 graduate of Lawrenceburg City High School, a charter member and past president of the Lawrenceburg Business and Professional Women's Club and a 1982 retiree of the Kentucky Department of Human Resources. The Giles are members of the First Christian Church where Chris is an active member of two missionary circles. *Submitted by: John and Chris Giles.*

WILLIAM DUDLEY GOODLETT

WILLIAM DUDLEY GOODLETT was the third child and second son of James Robert (1882 - 1932) and Martha Florence Moore (1885 - 1967). He was born on the hill across Salt River overlooking Glensboro, Kentucky. He graduated from Lawrenceburg High School. After graduating from Bowling Green Business College, he took a bookkeeping job at a coal camp in Leatherwood, Kentucky at a time when the last few miles into the city were by mule back. His tenure in that job was brief. He returned to Lawrenceburg and in June, 1937, he married Jean Conrad McKay (1918), the daughter of Orion Cox (1878 - 1955) and Lillian Mae Trent McKay (1886 - 1972). To this marriage four children were born: Robert Dudley "Sandy" (1941), Orion McKay "Mac" (1947), Myra Cox (1949), and William Conrad (1957).

After serving as a seaman in the Navy in World War II, Mr. Goodlett had his own insurance agency, and from 1960 - 1980 worked in the Insurance Department for the Commonwealth of Kentucky. He

died on 5-4-1981, and is buried with his father, mother, and two brothers in the Lawrenceburg Cemetery. *submitted By: Robert D. Goodlett.*

JAMES ROBERT GOODLETT

JAMES ROBERT GOODLETT was born 6-10-1882 in Mercer County, Kentucky. He was the eldest child of John Thomas (1852 - 1931) and Virginia Campbell Robinson Goodlett (1862 - 1891).

As a child his family moved across Cheese Lick into the Ballard-Rutherford section of Anderson County. He was educated in the county schools and in 1904 was awarded a State Teaching Certificate by the Board of Public Instruction.

On 6-16-1908, he was married by Brother W.D. Moore to Reverend Moore's daughter, Martha Florence (1885 - 1967). To them were born Virginia Moore Fallis (1910 - 1985), Robert Vincent (1913 - 1973), William Dudley (1915 - 1981), and John Campbell (1922 - 1967).

After teaching school, cashiering at the Farmer Bank of Glensboro and being a bookkeeper at the Lawrenceburg National Bank, Mr. Goodlett served as a deputy county clerk under Harry Wise and J. N. Crook. In 1917, he was elected County Clerk and served in that capacity until his death on 12-21-1932. He and his wife are buried in the Lawrenceburg Cemetery.

Mr. Goodlett was a member of the Sand Spring Baptist Church where he was a member of the Board of Deacons and Sunday School Superintendent. He was also a Mason. *Submitted By: Robert Goodlett.*

JOHN GREER

JOHN GREER was born on 9-26-1941 in Louisville, KY. He is the son of J. Marcus Greer (1904 - 1963) and Ave Maria Cruch Greer. John married Donna Helm on 4-20-1963. She was born on 11-4-1940 in Lebanon, KY. She is the daughter of Clarence Helm and June Maxine Langford Helm. She has one sister and two brothers: Sharon, Larry, and Bobby.

John and Donna are the proud parents of four children: Susie Greer, born 10-25-1964, married Mark Prater; Kim Greer, born 3-21-1968; David Greer, born 1-7-1970; and Andy Greer, born 11-25-1973. All the children were born in Louisville, KY with the exception of Andy who was born in Versailles, KY.

The Greer family is of the Catholic faith and currently resides on Mary Elizabeth Lane in Anderson County. John and Donna Greer are the owners of the McDonald's Restaurant located in West Park Shopping Center. Besides managing the restaurant, the Greers are very active in the community. *Submitted By: Andy Greer.*

RICHARD GREGORY

RICHARD GREGORY (1763 - 1814) married Helena Voorhies (1772 - 1823). Richard and Helena owned a farm in Shelby County. They sold this farm and bought 90 acres at Pleasant Hill. They became Shakers. Richard worked as a shoe cobbler. He is buried at Shakertown. After his death, Helena took her children and moved to Washington County.

They had a son named Seneca Gregory born in 1804 in Shelby County. He married Rhoda Bell - 8-17-1831. She was the daughter of John B. Bell. Her brother, James Bell, was a surveyor of Anderson County from 1866 - 1868, Deputy Clerk from 1862 - 1866, and County Judge from 1866 - 1868

Seneca and Rhoda had a son, Elijah Lewis, who married Lizzie Lynch on 1-18-1877 in Anderson County. Elijah Lewis and Lizzie Gregory had a son named Everett Louis born 2-14-1886 in Anderson County. He died on 11-27-1964 in Anderson County. He married Lula Mae Gillis and Mary F. Williams Gillis.

Everett Louis and Lula Mae Gregory were the parents of ten children: Nannie Ethel married Floyd Franklin - ten Children; Margie Rose (1911 - 1982) married Rexford McHenry - two children; Ida Elizabeth married Elmer Keeling - five children; Mary Ruby (1915 - 1958) one child; William Louis (1917 - 1989) married Frances Shea Hall; Aubrey Alice married Gilbert Gritton - two children; Floyd Everett married Jean McHenry - two children Carl Ray; Paul Gerald married Betty Lewis - three children; and Doris Marie married Emmett Dailey.

Carl Ray Gregory was born 10-27-1925 in Lawrenceburg. He married Arlene Bruner - 6-7-1947 in Anderson County. She was born 9-20-1928 in Anderson County and is the daughter of Elmo Bruner and Nina Brown Bruner. She has one sister, Lucille Elizabeth, who married Robert Duncan - three children. Lucille is currently Circuit Clerk for Anderson County. Carl and Arlene Gregory are the parents of two sons: Glen Clark and Phillip Nolan married Carol Grubbs.

Glen Clark Gregory was born on 8-4-1950 in Anderson County. He married Sandra Kay Toll - 7-3-1970. She was born 9-12-1951 in Anderson County and is the daughter of C.C. Toll Jr.. and Jewel F. Hulette Toll. Clark and Sandra are the parents of two children: Kimberly Renee, born 1973, and Stacy L., born 1979.

Charles C. "C.C." Toll Jr. was born 10-9-1918 in Anderson County and died 4-16-1986. He is the son of Charles C. Toll and Pearl Jackson Toll. He married Jewel F. Hulette - 10-19-1945. She was born on 6-24-1924 in Franklin County and is the daughter of Clarence Bain Hulette (1893 - 1969) and Elizabeth Moor Hulette (1896 - 1972). They were the parents of four children: Patricia Ann married Thurman G. Reed; Sandra Kay; Charles Vernon married Cynthia Martin; and Debra Lynn. Charles C. Toll Sr. (1878 - 1947) was the son of Charles R. Toll (1841 - 1903) and Margaret Tucker Toll (1844 - 1919). Charles C. Toll Sr. married Pearl Jackson (1882 - 1969). She was the daughter of Joe Jackson and Maggie Hanks. Charles C. and Pearl Toll were the parents of eleven children: Karl (1905 - 1972) married three times - two children; Katherine, born 1905, married John Dadisman - two children; Sadie Mildred (1906 - 1921); Cletis, born 1908, married Herbert McCown; Lucille, born 1911, married William DeGraff - one child; Harold Jackson (1914 - 1948) married Jean Mountjoy - two children; Charles C. Jr.; Maxine, born 1916, married J. W. Catlett; Etta, born 1920, married Marvin Moffett - two children - 2nd marriage to Marvin Noel; Benjamin R., born 1923, married Louise Gritton - two children - 2nd marriage to Ceulah; and James, born 1926, married Price Green - three children. *Submitted by: Kim Gregory.*

GUDGEL

Like many others, the spelling of this family name has undergone many changes. One Andrew Gottshall, immigrant to Pennsylvania, was a son of Fredrick and Mary Gottshall, Germany. The Gottshall's (Gotchal, Gudshal, Gudgell, Gudgel) were found early in Virginia and in what is now Kentucky before the beginning of the nineteenth century.

The family was well established in Anderson County by 1830 and by 1850 many sons and daughters of the early pioneers had settled there.

Andrew Gudgel was a member of our first grand jury and was one of the first constables of the town. One Thomas Gudgel served in the Mexican War. Martin Van Gudgel was a Lieutenant in the Kentucky Calvary and also served as Sheriff in 1867.

A small community about six miles west of Lawrenceburg was known as Gudgel, taking its name from the influential family established there. Gudgel post-office, Edward Gudgel first post-master, continued from 1895 - 1907. J. W. Gudgel was elected as school superintendent in 1892. There is a Gudgel graveyard off the Rice Road in Anderson County.

One Elijah Gudgel and his wife, Lydia Bell, were early members of the Lawrenceburg Baptist Church. They reared nine children and at Elijah's death in 1866, he owned a 103 acre farm at Fox Creek. Both Elijah and Lydia are buried in the Gudgel cemetery on Rice Road.

In 1857, Jacob M. Gudgel (1833 - 1896), son of Elijah, married Frances M. Griffey (1835 - 1903). This marriage produced six children: John William, Benjamin Thomas, Edward F., Margaret Bell, Annie, and Allie L.

Allie (1875 - 1899) attended Lone Oak and Griffey School, was a member of the Fox Creek Christian Church, and in 1896 married Clara H. Hawkins. They resided on Route 62 and later at Fox Creek. One child, Samuel Madison, was born to them. Allie died at the early age of 24 and Clara at 84. Both are buried at Fox Creek.

Samuel Madison Gudgel and Verna Hutchinson Gudgel

Samuel Madison Gudgel (1899 - 1940) attended Griffey School and in 1918 married Verna E. Hutchinson, daughter of James Rabe and Margaret Bunton Hutchinson. They lived at Alton next to the Alton Cemetery on the Frankfort Pike.

Besides farming, Samuel also engaged in all kinds of contract work with Ernest Hatchell. They emptied coal cars and delivered for a Mr. Wheat, who also ran a drug and grocery store at Alton Station. Pond cleaning, horse and stock trading, and Gudgel's Garage at Alton were some of their other ventures.

Three children were born to Samuel and Verna:
Norman Earl - (1925) who still resides in Lawrenceburg and is retired from Schenley Distillery.

James Garland - (1922 - 1953) 1940 Kavanaugh High School Graduate.

Majorie Eloise Collins Yount - (1928 - 1965)

Samuel died at the age of 41 and was buried at Fox Creek. Verna was a devoted member of the Alton Christian Church and later remarried Willie Cole. She retired from Schenley Distillery in 1963 and died in 1970. Verna was buried in the Alton Cemetery.

The Gudgel family has scattered to surrounding counties and states over the years and at this writing (1989) there is but one family remaining and that is my father, Norman Earl Gudgel. Despite this small number, I feel the Gudgel family has played a very important role in the growth and development of Anderson County. *Submitted By: Linda Carol (Gudgel) Finnell.*

ELIJAH GUDGEL, born in 1797, is most likely the son of Jacob Gudgel and Drucilla Driskell of Woodford County, Kentucky. Elijah married Lydia "Millie" Bell in 1819 in Mercer County, Kentucky. They soon moved to Anderson County where Elijah owned land around Glensboro. This land was sold and he bought more on what is now Rice Road. Elijah's brothers were: Andrew (married Elizabeth ?); Jacob (married Elizabeth ?); John (married Cynthis ?); and Joel.

The children of Elijah and Lydia Bell Gudgel were: Amanda (June 13, 1820 - December 25, 1893) married Woodford Crossfield. She died of a stroke; Martha (1824 - 1852) married Richard Henry Crossfield in 1843; Lydia Ann married A. C. Herndon; Elizabeth married ? Brown; William married Elizabeth Bledsoe; Susan married Thomas A. Bass; Jacob married Frances Griffy; Elijah; Sarah; and Armenta married John W. Bickers.

Lydia Bell Gudgel is buried in a family graveyard on the Rice Road, on the property of Connie Carlton. Where Elijah is buried no one knows.

Any person who is a direct descendant of Lydi Bell Gudgel is eligible to join the Sones of the American Revolution or the Daughters of the American Revolution. *Submitted By: Mrs. Willie Crossfield.*

JEREMIAH VARDEMAN HAHN, son of William Hahn and Sophia Crow, married in Nelson County, Kentucky , on 22 October 1840, to Louisa Calvert, born 1829, daughter of Richard Calvert and Elizabeth Dadisman. They had six known children:

1) William Hahn, born 1841.

2) Richard H. Hahn, born 1843, married 16 May 1867, in Anderson County, Kentucky, to Mary F. Bowman.

3) Robert Harrison Hahn, born 1845, married 1) Elizabeth C. ?. 2) on 31 November 1911, in Anderson County, to

  Alice Barnett.

3) Cynthia Ann Hahn, born 7 May 1846, married 1) 23 January 1865, to Wade Campbell, who died 2 Jan 1869. She married 2) 22 March 1870, in Nelson County, to John Foster Bond.

5) Samuel Mack Hahn, born 23 June 1848, married Elizabeth Calvert, daughter of Jefferson Calvert and Frances Bond.

6) Jordan Hahn, born 3 June 1850, married first, on 8 January 1870, in Anderson County, Kentucky, daughter of William H. Bently and Phidelia C. Toles. She died 17 January 1888. Jordan married second, on 23 December 1888 to Emma Searcy, and died 28 February 1923, in Nelson County. Fourteen known children, five from the first marriage, and nine from the second, all born in Anderson County.

  a) George Hahn, born 2 Sept 1873
  B) Fida Hahn, born 31 Jan 1878, married Lebon Merritt Case.
  C) Robert Hahn, born Feb 1880
  d) Edward Hahn, born 25 Mar 1885
  E) Louis W. Hahn, born 19 Aug 1887
  F) William Hahn, born 5 September 1889
  G) Lize Hahn, born 2 June 1891
  H) Corie Hahn, born 1 September 1893, married ? Newton
  I) Mollie Hahn, born 14 Oct 1895. Married ? Richardson.
  J) Lottie Hahn, born 1897
  K) Allie Hahn, born 17 May 1899
  L) Myrtle Hahn, born 23 September 1901
  M) Mattie Hahn, born 28 February 1904
  N) Grace Hahn, born 12 Aug 1907
Submitted By: William R. Walls,

WILLIAM HAHN was born in 1785, in the area that was later to become Bullitt County, but was then a part of Nelson County, Kentucky Territory, Virginia, a son of German immigrants. His parents were Peter Hahn and Mary Schmitt, who married 23 July 1763, in Pennsylvania. William married 14 July 1814, in Bullitt County, KY, to Sophia Crow. He died in Anderson County, KY in November of 1859. Deed Book N, page 239, in Anderson County, dated 26 October 1867, listed his heirs as: Sophia Hahn, (wife) of Anderson county; Jeremiah Vardeman Hahn, (son) and his wife Louisa, of Anderson County; Hadon E. Hahn, (son) and his wife Catherine, of Anderson County; Mary Ann Loper/Soper, (daughter) and her husband Robert Loper/Soper, of Anderson County; Dillard Hahn, (son) and his wife Bettie, of Daviess County; and William Hahn, (son) and his wife Mary, of Washington County.

1) Christopher Hahn, born 1815 - 1820, married in Nelson County, KY on 23 May 1838 to Lucy Gatewood.

2) William Hahn (Jr.), born 1817 - 1818, married in Anderson County, KY on 4 April 1842 to Mary Ann Disman/Dusman.

3) Unknown daughter, born 1815 - 1820, may have died before 1830.

4) Jeremiah Vardeman Hahn, born September 1820, married Louisa Calvert.

5) Mary Ann Hahn, born 1823 - 24, married Robert H. Loper/Soper.

6) unknown son, born 1820 - 1825, may have died before 1830.

7) Samuel C. Hahn, born 1821 - 1826, married in Nelson County, KY on 2 February 1849 to Elizabeth

Calvert, daughter of Garrett Calvert and Diana Glass.

8) Norman S. Hahn, born 20 November 1828, died 17 January 1899, married Millie Ann Yocum, daughter of Henry Yocum, Jr. and Malinda King.

9) Dillard Hahn, born circa 1830, married Bettie ?.

10) Hadon E. Hahn, born June 1832, married in Anderson County, KY on 22 September 1853 to Catherine Dedman.

11) Dudley Hahn, born circa 1834, no further information. *Submitted By: William R. Walls.*

HANKS Around 1800, four Hanks brothers (George, Turner, Chichester, and Pittman) migrated to Kentucky from Virginia, settling in what is now Anderson County. Their homesteads were generally a few miles south and southeast of the present city of Lawrenceburg. Mrs. Lydia Bond in her book "Memories and Reveries" described them as strong men, rugged of constitution, robust and active, and generally living to an advanced age.

Turner (1784-1858) married Nancy Holman (1801-1864) and they had six children, two of whom were Mary Jane (1826 - 1890) and Francis Marion (1828 - 1891). Francis Marion married Cynthia Sutherland (1838 - 1871) with one of their sons being William Johnson Hanks (1860 - 1912).

In 1897, W. J. Hanks wedded Mary Jane Bond (1873-1951). Mary Jane was a descendent of William Bond and John Bond, early Kentucky and Anderson County pioneers, and the granddaughter of Mary Jane Hanks, mentioned above, and Medley Bond, son of John Bond. W.J. and Janie Hanks had six daughters. Mrs. Hanks was left a widow before the birth of her last child and was held in high esteem for her ability to cope with operating her farm and raising and educating her children. She was dearly loved and respected throughout her life by all who knew her. These daughters were:

1) Stella (1899 - 1981) married Raymond G. Smith (1892 - 1952) children - Roberta Hanks (1921 - 1966) married Myrle Roehm Children - Sharon and Robert M. Paul Jenson (1931 - 1972) married Dortha Case son - Terry.

2) Anna Frances (1901 - 1966) married Thomas Porter Smith (1896 - 1958). Son - William Johnson married Nancy Toll, children - Sheila and Thomas Hanks.

3) Gertrude Bond, 86, married Carl E. Hutchinson (1902 - 1985) Children - Dorothy E. married Glen D. Cummins, Margaret Jane married William G. Paasch. Children - Jane Garth, Robert Douglas, Joe Bond, Michael Atkins, and Stephen Ray.

4) Beulah (1905 - 1967) married J. William Nevins (1903 - 1987) children - Mary Nancy (1926 - 1985) married Floyd Gritton Jr. children- Judith, Marc Nevins, Sally Jane, Nancy June. Eleanor Anne married Gordon Jenkins, children - Anne Lewis and Mary Ruth. Bonnie Moss married J. P. Hatchett, children - Julie and William Hanks. Willie Frances married Gary Scott, children - Melissa and Robby

5) Katherine (1907 - 1988) married Reuben Jamerson (1905 - 1986), children Reuben Jr. married Ruby Hyatt, children - Kathy and Brenda Katherine Louise married David Drury, daughter - Nancy Ray.

6) Willie J., 76, married Thomas Beasley (1910 - 1975)

These sisters lived within or near Lawrenceburg all their lives, educating their children in the Lawrenceburg and Anderson County schools. They were lifelong members of the Sand Spring Baptist Church. Gertrude and Willie J. are still regular attendants. All were excellent cooks with a family dinner as something to behold. Mr. and Mrs. Hanks have three generations of descendents scattered over the eastern United States, in various occupational pursuits. Those still residing in Lawrenceburg are Gertrude Hutchinson, Willie J. Beasley, W. J. Smith, Anne Jenkins, Louise Drury, Tom Smith, Anne Morris, Nancy Sawyer, Anne Marie and Bradley Holt, and David Sawyer.

All of the deceased members of this Hanks Branch, except Nancy Gritton, are buried in the Lawrenceburg Cemetery. *Submitted By: W. J. Smith.*

HANKS ancestors came from Scotland, lived in Virginia, then came to Anderson County, KY. George Hanks lived on the Potomac River, joined the Confederate Army, killed at Yorktown.

William Hanks I died 1704. Will was probated 1705, Richmond County, VA. Three children lived, William II, Luke and John. Luke had two sons, Alexander and Turner, one daughter, Lucretia. Turner (1737 -1794) married Sarah (?). They had six sons, Pittman, Chichester, Luke, Raleigh, Turner and George, two daughters, names unknown.

Turner (1781 - 1858) married Nancy Holman, 1820. They had four sons, two daughters. One son, Reuben Anderson (1827 - 1915) married Valeria Driskell, 1854. Their son, Dandridge (1858 - 1944) married Nannie Nevins 1884. They had eight children, Valeria, Robert, Nevins, Virginia, Clyde, Franklin, Norris, and Magdalene. Lived in a large two-story house on Wildcat Road.

After Valeria's death, Reuben Anderson married Virginia Coke, 1860. They had three sons and five daughters. James Carlton (1863 - 1944) married Lina Bennett 1892). They had one daughter, Bonnie 1904. Thomas Francis (1871 - 1935) married Edith Brown, no children. Reuben Anderson II (1875 - 1920) married Marcie Labraly 1906, One daughter, Virginia, married Paul Zec - one daughter, Barbara.

The five daughters: Valeria (1865 - 1951) married Russell S. Martin, 1922, two sons, R. S. and Bernill. Nancy Ella (1867 - 1918) married James Gee, 1885, one daughter, Ruby. Bessie (1873 - 1945) married Tom Ledridge (1896 - ?), one son, Lynn, married Lena Utterback, no children. May (1879 - 1957) married Forrest Moore, 1905, no children. Virginia C. (1879 - 1906) single.

Charlton and Lina's daughter, Bonnie, married Lethan Waller, 1922. They had two daughters, Virginia, 1923, and Nina, 1927. Nina married Charles Tucker, 1951. They had two children, son, Randolph married Virginia Curd and they have one son, Lethan, 1988. All the Tuckers live in Louisville, except their daughter, Bonnie, who married Dr. Jeff Echelberger, 1988. They live in Germany where Jeff is practicing dentistry and attending school.

Virginia married Charles Klink, 1943. One son, Keith, a pharmacist, married Patricia Keitz. They have one son, Brian, who graduated from Anderson County High School in May 1990. And a daughter, Laura, 6th grade Anderson Middle School. Klink's Drug Store, 115 Main Street, opened November 1947 in the Hanks Building, which was originally owned by her great uncle, Thomas F., and her Grandfather, James Charlton, from their heirs.

After the deaths of Thomas F.'s parents, he bought the old R.A. Hanks home, an old colonial house, also on Wildcat Road, for any of his brothers or sisters who wished to live there. Charlton died there in 1944, and Bessie died there 1945. The old homestead then was bought by Clyde, a half-brother. His wife, Margaret, and daughter, Elise, still live there.

All the Klinks live in Lawrenceburg, as does Ginny's mother, Bonnie Waller. Bonnie's father was a charter member of Sand Spring Baptist Church. *Submitted by: Bonnie Hanks Waller.*

WALKER THOMAS HANKS (1885 - 1949) was the son of Turner P. Hanks (1858 - 1926) and Mildred Hawkins Hanks (1858 - 1909). He married Susie Stratton, the daughter of John Stratton and Mary Sanders Stratton. Walker Thomas and Susie were the parents of nine children: Marion married Selena - two children, Selena and Richard; J. T. married Floetta - two children, Judy and Johnny; Louise married Montgomery Wilson, two children, Marion and Billy; Melburn (below); Margie married Thomas Peach - six children - Don, Ronnie, Jerry, Debbie, Beverly, and Johnny; Mary Jasper married Bob Cook; Mildred married Woodrow Phillips -

three children - Patty, Janet, and Woody; Eva married George Lynn - two children, Rita and Larry; and Irene married Dillard Gibson - two daughters, Linda and Lois Ann.

Melburn Hanks was born on 12-8-1904. He married Alice Ray Phillips in 1934. She was born on 10-31-1904 and is the daughter of Cecil Phillips and Alice Birdwhistell Phillips. Melburn and Alice have three children: Louise married J. C. Stratton - two sons, James Robert and George; Carolyn married Davis McMichael - four children - Tammy, Eric, Marty, and Candy; and James M. married Edith M. Robinson - three children - Marcia, Stacey, and Jamie. Melburn and Alice reside in Lawrenceburg. Melburn retired from Seagram's Distillery after over forty years, but he still does a little taxidermy for a hobby.

Cecil Phillips (died 1951) was the son of Jim Phillips and Hattie D. Elliott Phillips. He married Alice Birdwhistell, the daughter of Ezra Birdwhistell and Annie Nevins Birdwhistell. Alice died in 1967. They were the parents of four children: Beulah - one daughter, Dorothy; Mattie D. married Ollie Carter - one son, Alan; Anna Ruth married Russell Overstreet - three children - Elizabeth, Russell, and Wilda; and Alice Ray. *Submitted By: Stacey Hanks.*

ALLAN S. AND JEAN HANKS are lifelong residents of Anderson County. Jean was born in Anderson County to Edgar R. and Lillie Hawthorne Franklin. She has one brother Glen W. Franklin of Boulder, Colorado.

Allan was born in Anderson County to James C. and Sadie Houchin Hanks. He has two brothers and one sister: Carl of Louisville, KY; Paul of Lawrenceburg; and Helen Monroe of Lawrenceburg.

They both attended Kavanaugh High School where Allan graduated in 1942 and Jean in 1944. Allan joined the Air Force on September 15, 1942, and served until September 20, 1945. During this time, he completed 23 combat missions over enemy occupied territory.

Allan and Jean were married at the Sand Spring Church parsonage by Reverend Roy A. Hamilton on June 30, 1945. They are the parents of two children. Douglas Ray, a sales coordinator for Universal Fasteners, is married to the former Sandy Baumstark. They have one son, Lucas Carl, 10.

Allan and Jean Hanks

Glenda Carol, is married to David Bogie, a plant manager at General Cable Corporation. They have two daughters, Deanna Hanks 19 and Alana Dawn 14.

After returning from service, Allan accepted a job with the Anderson County Health Department. His next job was a short period of employment as Probation Officer for the Twelfth Judicial District of Kentucky.

He joined the Anderson National Bank on September 20, 1948 and served in various capacities until his retirement on December 31, 1986. He became President of the bank in 1974. While in banking, he was elected chairman of the board in 1978 of the Kentucky Bankers Association and President in 1981.

Allan also served as a Member of the Federal Reserve Bank of St. Louis, Louisville Branch, for six years and six years on the Board of Trustee's at the King's Daughter Memorial Hospital in Frankfort, KY.

Allan and Jean are both members of the Sand Spring Baptist Church. Allan's hobbies are fishing and golfing. Jean's hobbies are reading, cross stitching, and crocheting. *Submitted By: Allan S. Hanks.*

DANDRIDGE F. HANKS

DANDRIDGE F. HANKS (1858 - 1944) was the only child of Reuben Anderson Hanks (1827 - 1915) and Valeria Driskell Hanks (1832 - 1858). Valeria Hanks died while in childbirth and in doing this research, information was found that a twin also died at birth. His father remarried to Virginia "Jennie" Coke (1839 -1916) in 1860. She was the only mother D.F. had. They had seven more children: J. C., R.A. Jr., Mrs. R. S. "Lee" Martin, Mrs. James Gee, Mrs Bessie Ledridge, Mrs. Forrest "Mae " Moore, and Miss Virginia Hanks (all deceased).

D. F. Hanks married Nancy "Nannie" Nevins (1863 - 1929). She was the daughter of John M. and Mary E. Nevins. They were the parents of eight children: Valeria L. (1885 - 1919) married John Benjamin Stratton (1885 - 1960), the son of John Corbin and Mollie Sanders Stratton, on 12-12-1906 in Anderson County. They were the parents of five children: John Benjamin Jr. (deceased), Edna Earl (married Charlie Smith and lives in Anderson County), Vurley Summers (deceased - married Onis Jordan Brown and later Harvey Sea), Eugene Clinton (1914 - 1983) married Mattie Evelyn Robinson, and John Franklin (married 1st, Lillian K. Gortney, 2nd, Juanita Coke).

Robert Roach Hanks (1887 - 1959) married Lucy Moore (1887 - 1974). Lucy was the daughter of Reverend W. D. Moore and Alice Vincent Hedger Moore. They had three children: Robert Harold (deceased), Edyth May Hanks Edwards, and Charles Truett. All attended Lawrenceburg High School and Edyth May and Charles live in Lawrenceburg.

Clyde Hanks married Margaret Hawkins. They had three children: Elise (lives in Anderson County), R. A. (living in Danville, KY), and Edwin (deceased).

Virginia Hanks married C. F. Marlowe of Anderson County. They had two children: Mary Alpha Marlowe Cammack (living in Lawrenceburg) and C. F. Marlowe Jr. (living in Frankfort).

Nevins Hanks married Flora Burford of Anderson County. They were the parents of one son, Allen Burford Hanks (living in Anderson County).

Norris Hanks married John Cinnamon of Mercer County. They had five children: Nell Cinnamon Lawrence (living in Williamstown, KY), Kenneth (deceased), Betty Lou Cinnamon Sanford (living in Mercer County), Mary Nevins Cinnamon Warford (living in Anderson County) and Gene C. Cinnamon (living in Lawrenceburg.)

Franklin Hanks married Harlan Gaines of Anderson County. They are the parents of two children: Keith (Anderson Co.) and Nancy Gaines Goff (Florida). Magdalene Gaines is the only surviving child of D. F. and Nannie Nevins Hanks.

Lots of Hanks' are still in the county and all are kin to each other. The D. F. Hanks Family Reunion is held each year on the 4th of July and usually has 75 or more attending. *Submitted by: Mrs. Marvin Edwards.*

PAUL WICKLIFFE HANKS

PAUL WICKLIFFE HANKS and Elizabeth Crossfield Hanks were married on November 4, 1950 ,at First Baptist Church. To this union were born two sons, George Wickliffe and Brent Coleman. George married Charlene Beasley and they have two sons, Ryan Wickliffe and Cory Todd. Brent married Traci Frederick and she has two girls, Tara Brook and Tabby Gail.

Paul is the son of James and Sadie Hanks and is a graduate of Kavanaugh High School. He joined the Navy in 1950. Paul is retired from Kentucky Utilities after 35 years of service. He is a member and past member of Anderson Lodge, member and past President of the Rotary Club, and a member of the Chamber of Commerce. He is a member and deacon and substitute Sunday School teacher of First Baptist Church. He was also a volunteer with the Lawrenceburg Fire Department for 25 years.

Paul and Elizabeth Hanks

Elizabeth is the daughter of Myrtle and Geobel Crossfield and a graduate of Lawrenceburg High School and Bethel Woman's College. She is a Sunday School teacher and very active in First Baptist Church. She has been City Clerk for the past twenty years.

Paul and Elizabeth Hanks have been residents of Lawrenceburg and Anderson County all of their lives. *submitted by: Elizabeth Hanks.*

JASPER WALKER HANKS

JASPER WALKER HANKS was the great grandson of Turner Hanks (1784 - 1858) who came to Anderson County, Kentucky, from Virginia in the early 1800's. His grandfather was Francis Marion Hanks (1828 - 1891) who was named after the great Revolutionary War hero. Walker's father was Turner Pittman Hanks (1858 - 1926).

Walker was born in 1885. In 1907 ?, he married Susie Mae Stratton, daughter of John and Mary Sanders Stratton. They had nine children.

Their first son was named Francis Marion (deceased). Marion married Selena Terhune from Harrodsburg. Their children are Selena Chilton and Rick Hanks, both of Lawrenceburg. Grandchildren are Carl Samples, Kenneth Chilton and Missy Hanks. One great-grandchild, Carrie Samples.

Margaret Louise was Walker and Susie's first daughter. Louise married Montgomery Wilson (deceased) of Anderson County. They had two sons, Marion Hanks Wilson and William T. Wilson. Two grandsons, Jeff and Keith Wilson.

James Melburn "Meb" married Alice Ray Phillips of Anderson County. They have three children - Louise Stratton of Salvisa, Carolyn McMichael and Jimmy Hanks of Lawrenceburg. Their grandchildren are James Robert and Kevin Stratton of Salvisa; Eric, Tammy, Marty, and Candy McMichael,;Marcia, Stacy, and Jami Hanks all of Lawrenceburg. Great grandchildren are Ben, Cara, and Shana Stratton and Steven and Matthew McMichael.

Next came John Turner (deceased). J.T. married Flo Etta Riddle of Switzer and had three children - Dolores Carol (deceased), Judy Crawford and John Turner Hanks II of Lawrenceburg. They have four grandchildren - Chris and Jared Crawford and Emily and John Hanks.

Margie Mae married Thomas F. Peach (deceased) of Anderson County. They had three sons and one daughter - Donald and Ronnie Peach of Lawrenceburg and Jerry Peach and Debra Francis, both of Florida. Margie has eight grandchildren - Kim, Scott, Jennifer, Ken, Rhonda, Stephanie, and Natalie Peach and Tiffany Francis. Two great grandchildren - Nathan and Matthew.

Mildred Lyen married Woodrow Phillips of Anderson County and they have three children - Patty Tracy, Janet Goodlett and Woody Phillips all of Lawrenceburg. Their grandchildren are Phillip and Chuck, Tracy, Laurie, Shannon, and Page Goodlett, and Sarah and Karla Phillips.

Mary Jasper married Bob Cook of Anderson County. Their children are Beverly Campbell of North Carolina and Johnny Whitehead of Lexington. Their grandchildren are Damien, Shea, and Bradley Whitehead.

Eva Kathleen married George Lynn (deceased) of Houstonville. They had two children - Rita Kay Lynn Summers (deceased) and Larry Walker Lynn of Pikeville. Eva has four grandchildren - Scott, Moore, Christopher, Lincoln, and Leigh Brittany Lynn.

Edna Irene is the baby of the family and the only one to move from Anderson County. Irene married Dillard Gibson of Harrodsburg and has lived there all her married life. They have two daughters - Lois Ann Adams of Frankfort and Linda McCrystal of Harrodsburg. Their grandchildren are Eric and Troy Adams and Katie Hanks McCrystal.

As you can see, many of Walker and Susie Hanks' family still live and work in Anderson County. There are 83 direct descendents. *Submitted by: Selena Hanks Chilton,*

BOBBY GENE AND BETTY LOWE HATTER

BOBBY GENE AND BETTY LOWE HATTER moved to Lawrenceburg from Casey County on August 15, 1970. Betty was born at Monticello, KY., the third of seven children born to Walter and Dortha Doss Lowe. Walter was the son of John Nathan and Louisa Jones Lowe. Dortha was the daughter of Edwin and Amelia Thornton Doss.

Bobby was born in Casey county, KY. in the Walltown community, the fifth of ten children born to Charles and Lillie Wall Hatter. Charles was the son of Ransom and Rosa Napier Hatter. Lillie was the daughter of Willie and Martha Sims Wall.

Bobby and Betty both attended the Walltown Elementary School in Casey County which was a two room schoolhouse. Betty attended Middleburg High School until she and Bobby were married. They were married February 24, 1962 in Liberty, KY. by Judge W. R. Wilkinson. Betty was 16 and Bobby was 18 years old.

Bobby enlisted in the Army National Guard in January, 1963. He served six months of active duty. His basic training was served at Fort Knox and the remaining four months at Fort Sill, Oklahoma.

They moved to Indianapolis, Indiana, in May, 1965 and lived there two years while Bobby worked at Hall-Neal Furnace Company before returning to Casey County. Bobby and Betty both worked for Liberty Sportswear before moving to Lawrenceburg. Bobby worked at Sikes Carpet for almost 3 years. Betty worked at Union Underwear in Frankfort for 2 years. They both have worked at the Sylvania Lamp Plant in Versailles for 16 years.

Bobby and Betty have two sons, Jacky - born April 23, 1963 and Robby - Born August 15, 1964. Jacky is married to a lifelong Anderson County resident, the former Judy Lee Perry who has two children by a previous marriage, Jackie Curtis (Curt) Bowen, Jr. - age 17 and Jeremy Lee Bowen - age 14.

Robby is married to the former Peggy Gil Jeffers who has a daughter by a previous marriage: Jennifer Rae Jeffers - age 8. Robby and Peggy have a son, Casey Lynn Hatter - age 2. Peggy's family is from Hodgenville, but she was born in Germany when her father was serving in the U. S. Army.

Batty Lowe and Bobby G. Hatter - Jacky Ray and Robby Lynn Hatter

Bobby likes to hunt, fish, and do anything outdoors. Betty prefers all kinds of crafts and doesn't like to camp, fish or anything outdoors. She does enjoy being a Girl Scout leader for Troop 754.

Before moving to Lawrenceburg, Bobby and Betty were members of the Walltown Christian Church. They transferred their membership to the Corinth Christian Church where Bobby served as deacon. Bobby, Betty, Jacky, and Robby all transferred their membership to the Anderson Christian Church after it began meeting at the Emma B. Ward School. Shortly after transferring their membership, Bobby began playing rhythm guitar for the Firm Believers Gospel Quartet. They don't travel with them anymore. They enjoy staying at their home on Jenny Lillard Road, where they have lived since August, 1971.

DUDLEY M. HAWKINS

DUDLEY M. HAWKINS was born October 1821, in Franklin County, KY, where he grew up. He was a son of Roddy and Elizabeth (Jones) Hawkins, who came to Franklin County from Orange County, Virginia. Dudley M. Hawkins came to Anderson County, KY, when he married Miss Susan Jane Thacker, daughter of Samuel P. Thacker and wife, Elizabeth McGaughey, December 26, 1844. He bought a tract of land on Hammonds Creek at the crossing of Camdenville Pike, from his half-brother, Edwin E. Hawkins. Dudley M. had a water operated grist and saw mill here, which he and his family operated for about 50 years. They were the parents of nine children. They are as follows: 1) Elizabeth Jane Hawkins (1845 - 1910) married James S. Long and had these children: Bessie J. (1867 - 1891) married Harrison H. Cinnamon; William A. Long (1870 - 1891); Susan Mary (1876 - 1902) married Ezra J. Bailey ; Hallie (1884 - 1918) married H. L. Rainey; Hattie D. (ca. 1887 - 1959) married Ends, C. Siers. 2) John William Hawkins (1848-1853). 3) Mary Ann Hawkins (1850-1929) married three times, 1st ,Solomon M. Hedden, 2nd, James S. Coke, 3rd Henry Clay Melear, but no children; 4) Baby Hawkins (July 1852 - August 1852); 5) Samuel Hutson Hawkins (1853 - 1927) married Mary L. Mothershead and had a daughter, Clara Hawkins, who married 1st, Allie Gudgel, 2nd Clarence Young - and had a son, Clarence Hawkins (March 1882 - June 1882); 6) Dudley James Hawkins (1856 - 1923) married Mary Am Amsden and had - Amos B. Hawkins, married Beulah Wilson - Helen Wright, married Ollie C. DeWitt - Clarence Lester Hawkins, married Bonnie Brown; 7) Infant Boy Hawkins (March 1859 - 1938) married Maggie L. Cole (1867 - 1890) and had Paul Hawkins who died young. Married 2nd to Sarah Frances Barnes and had - Sadie Flora (1895 - 1975), infant (born and died August 1896) and Ollie Hawkins (1898 - 1966) married Thelma S. Powell, married last, our mother, Stella Sherwood.

Dudley M. and Susan J. Thacker Hawkins

Alvin H. Hawkins was just sixteen years old, when he started working for Presley Watts, who ran a blacksmith shop in the neighborhood. He worked for Mr. Watts (Uncle Pres, as most people called him) for a number of years. He also worked as a blacksmith for some of the distilleries in Anderson County. After he first married he started a blacksmith shop of his own on Hammonds Creek. He also ran the saw and grist mill and about the turn of the century, he built a General Store at the west end of the Hawkins Bridge over Hammonds Creek. There was a post office in this store, called Grafton and our father was the postmaster during the years of 1900 to 1905. Our mother, Stella Sherwood, taught the Munday School for the years of 1909 - 1910 and at the close of the 1910 school year she married our father. We are the last of the grandchildren and still live in the house our Grandfather built.

WILLIAM HAWKINS

WILLIAM HAWKINS' will was written 12-31-1789, and probated 10-20-1799, in Orange County, Virginia. He married Elizabeth Wall and they were the parents of the following: William Jr., Reuben, Elisha, Arculus, John and Mary (who married Adam Markspile).

Reuben Hawkins married Rebecca Edwards, daughter of Uriah Edwards and Mildred Head Edwards, in August 1778 in Virginia. Reuben died in August 1812 in Orange County, VA. Rebecca Edwards was born May 1762, and died 7-27-1840 in Franklin County, KY. They were the parents of the following: Elizabeth, William B., Elisha, Roddy, Arculus, Reuben Jr., Lucy, Moses, Uriah E., Milly, Benjamin S., and Sally.

Roddy Hawkins was born ca 1785 and died 6-15-1841, in Franklin County, KY. He married 1st, Miss Alice Chamberlain on 3-31-1803, in Orange County, Va. He married 2nd, Miss Elizabeth Jones on 2-28-1817, in Orange County, VA. She died on 10-4-1839, in Franklin County, KY. The following children were borne by his first wife: Francis, Edwin E. and Susan M. (who married Norman Greene). The following by his second wife: Dudley M., William W., Roddy Hutson, and Reuben Arculus.

HAWKINS

HAWKINS Record forebearers on the Hawkins side of the family start with Benjamin Hawkins (1738 - 1806) who, in 1768, married Nancy Ann Boin (1749 - 1832). They were the parents of the following ten children: Sarah, Andrew, Jane, Abraham, Frances, Elizabeth, Frank, John, Lucy, and Benjamin.

Andrew Hawkins (1771 - 1858) married Malinda Shelton (1784 - 1820) in 1808 and together were the parents of: Sheridan Bone, Pendleton, Alphea, Livingston, Shelton Cauter, and Granville B., Malinda died in 1820, after which Andrew remarried to Nancy Thompson in 1822. Their children were: Marion, Benjamin L., and Price.

Sheridan Bone Hawkins (1809 - 1875) married Mary Ann White (1809 - 1892) in 1832. They had the following eleven children: Ferdinand Erastus, Eromulus Remus, Onesimus Dekalb, Florelle Hervie, Anteria Rosaline, Jasper Reoleous, William Shruseberry, Ballard D. Wilton, Avia Revia, Granville Bourbon and Oscar Dunruth.

Sheridan Bone Hawkins became quite prosperous in farming and distilling, and before he died in 1875, had become owner of extensive land holdings in the Gilbert Creek section of Anderson County.

Ballard D. Wilton (1859 - 1912), known by the nickname "Bunk", married Capitolia Elizabeth Bond (1859 - 1942) in 1877. Capitolia was a daughter of Preston Bond who was well-known and respected throughout Anderson and adjoining counties as a teacher and a Methodist circuit riding minister. He acquired many acres of land surrounding the Bond homesite and bordering on the Harry Wise Road. Part of his holdings included the land on which the famous Panther Rock promontory and cave are located.

Ballard D. W. Hawkins and Capitolia Bond were parents of the following eight children: Linda Belle (1878 - 1971), Joseph Hurd (1881 - 1949), William Arthur (1883 - 1953), Bolivar Bond (1887 - 1937), Leva Ann (1890 - 1965), Mary Alva (1893 - 1894), Edward Bryan (1896 - 1965), and John Herman (1903 - 1974).

This family lived in a home overlooking the Kentucky River at a point midway between where Gilbert's Creek flows into the river and the location

Back Row, Left to Right: William Arthur and Minnie Myrtle Hawkins. Front Row, left to right: Their Children, Dorothy Belle, Nellie Myrtle, and Wilton Arthur. Back row, left to right: J. Hurd, William Arthur, Bolivar Bond, Edward Bryan, and John Herman Hawkins. Seated Lady is Capitolia Elizabeth Hawkins, mother of the five men.

down river of the old Sward's Ferry. Ballard D. Wilton spent most of his adult life involved in the operation of Hawkins Bros. Distillery located on Gilbert's Creek.

William Arthur Hawkins married Minnie Myrtle Chilton (1894 - 1980) on 3-28-1915. Her parents were Joseph Nelson Chilton (1865 - 1937) (son of Elliot H. Chilton (1814 - ?) and ? Frost) and Mertie Hawkins Chilton (1866 - 1956) (daughter of Eromulus Remus Hawkins (1853 - 1904) and Mary Jane Duncan Hawkins (1854 -?)).

Joseph and Mertie Chilton were the parents of the following nine children: Sue Emma (1887 - 1981), Owen Taylor (1889 - 1956), Blonie Jane (1891 - 1961), Annie Belle (1892 - 1893), Minnie Myrtle (1894 - 1980), Virgie Frances (1896 - 1931), Joe Earl (1898 - 1941), Huntley Hawkins (1900 - 1966), and Benjamin Thomas (1904 - 1950).

William Arthur and Minnie Myrtle were the parents of three children: Dorothy Belle, born 7-12-1919; Nellie Myrtle, born 1-25-1921; and Wilton Arthur, born 10-1-1922.

During the prohibition and depression years, when work was difficult to find in the Gilbert's Creek section of the county, William Arthur Hawkins moved his family to Ft. Wayne, Indiana, where he found work with the Pennsylvania Railroad Company. Following the repeal of prohibition, he moved his family back to Lawrenceburg, residing for a number of years on Bell St. and working at the Old Joe Distilling company at McBrayer, a small community in the southern section of the county. For a short time, in 1941 - 1942, he operated a creamery station on Woodford Street. Following the outbreak of World War II, he went to work at Ripy Brothers Distillery in Tyrone where the distillery's total output was devoted to producing alcohol for use in powering torpedoes for the U.S. Navy. Still later in life, he became part owner and operator, with his two daughters, of Hawkins Grocery on Main St. In Lawrenceburg.

The oldest daughter, Dorothy Belle, married David Leslie Carter of this county by whom she had one son, David Arthur, born in 1942. Following a divorce, she then married Medley O. Houchin of this county by whom she had one daughter, Patricia Ann, born in 1948. Dorothy, her husband, her children and three grandchildren now reside in Santa Clara, California. Nellie Myrtle married Freeman R. Boggess of this county. The marriage ended in divorce a few years ago, and Nellie now resides in Lawrenceburg. Wilton Arthur served four years in the armed forces during World War II and graduated from Carnegie

Institute of Technology with an Engineering Degree. He now lives in Montclair, New Jersey, having founded in that state in 1954, a company, Chemplast, Inc. which became one of the country's leading processors of the well-known plastic, Teflon. He is married to Thelma "Teddy" Drusilla Duncan Hawkins. *Submitted By: Wilton A. Hawkins.*

CARL AND MYRTLE ANN HAWKINS were

both born in Anderson County and lived all their lives there, except four years when Carl was in the Air Force. He was stationed in Texas, Wyoming, and England from February 1952 to January 1956.

Carl was the first son born to Ben and Linnie Gibson Hawkins who lived near the banks of Gilberts Creek. They had two more sons, James Allen and J.B. The three brothers still live on Harry Wise Road, only a few miles from where they were born.

Myrtle Ann was born on Walker Lane, north of Lawrenceburg, but moved to the Harry Wise Road area at a very young age. She has an older brother, Thomas, and a younger brother, Delbert West. They are the children of Robert and Elberta Chapman West also of Anderson County.

Carl and Myrtle Ann both attended Sand Spring School and Myrtle Ann attended Anderson County High School.

After Carl returned home from the Air Force, he and Myrtle Ann were married at Sand Spring Baptist Church by Reverend Melvin Torstrick. They continued to farm the family farm as Carl and his brothers had done before he went to the service. They also rented some neighboring farms. They went to part time farming when they purchased Dawson Feed and Supply from J.W. Dawson, January 1, 1970. Now he farms part time with his brother and son.

Carl and Myrtle Ann are the parents of three children. Sandra is married to James Ritchey and is a registered nurse at St. Joseph Hospital in Lexington. They have one daughter, Mary Ann Ritchey. They live on Harry Wise Road in Anderson County.

Brent farms his own farm on Harry Wise Road and also farms, with Carl and James, some land they own together. He works part time at the store with his parents. He also works for Elliott Security in Lexington.

Darren is still in high school. He works part time at the store with his parents. He is very interested in trains, especially the old steam engines. He is a member of the Bluegrass Railway Museum in Versailles, KY.

The Hawkins family have lived in the same area all of their lives and are members of the Sand Spring Church where they have attended all of their lives. Carl is a deacon at the aforementioned church. *Submitted By: Myrtle Ann Hawkins.*

DUDLEY JAMES HAWKINS, the son of Dudley

M. and Susan Jane Thacker, was born 3-12-1856 and died 1-26-1923. He married Mary A. Amsden on 9-19-1882 in Anderson County, KY. Mary was born 10-30-1863 and died 9-15-1937. They were the parents of six children: 1) Amos Burns Hawkins, born 12-12-1883, married Buelah Wilson (1888 - 1957) on 11-24-1909. They had two children - Raymond Wilson (married Miss Abbott and had one son, Raymond Jr.) and Mary Lucretia (married John Dudley Connelly - two children, John Dudley II and Jerry Lee).

2) Helen Wright Hawkins (1885 - 1945) married Ollie Cleveland DeWitt (1885 - 1952) on 8-13-1911. They had five children: William Gilbert married 1st Ruby Birdwhistell - one daughter, Margaret Wright DeWitt; Roy Milton married Geneva Perry - two children, Lrue Ann and Donnee Kay; Mary Virginia married 1st, Edgar Huffman - one son, Larry, 2nd, Ray Evans - two sons, Phillip and Lewis DeWitt Evans; Mildred Wright married William Oscar Sutherland - two sons, William Carroll and David Cleveland; and Charles Edgar.

3) Clarence Lester Hawkins (1887 - 1962) married Cordie Riley (1896 - 1982) on 10-15-1914. They had

the following children: James Clarence (1916 - 1945) married Margaret Katherine Casey - one daughter, Dorothy Mae; Juanita Francis married Charles F. Peyton - two daughters, Bette Frances and Charlene; William (died as an infant); Paul Stewart married 1st, Doris Brown - two daughters, Marie and Patsy Lue - 2nd, Lavon Lewise - one son, Paul Lewise; Zula Belle married Adolph Darnell - two children, Clarence Wayne and Maryline Mae; Floyd Arnold married Bettie Ruth Searcy - one daughter , Ann Elizabeth; Dudley Leon married Norma Jean Crossfield - one son, Troy Brent (1962 - 1982); Irvine Thomas married Clara Louise Pickard - three children Irvine Thomas, Jr., George Micale, and Carlene Rose; Maurice Elwood married Edna Mae Carlton - five children - Judy Carlene, Edna Darlene, James Carlton, Keith Allen, and Maurice Dwayne; Earl Burton married Evelyne Stratton - four children - Kenny, Kathy Jane, Donna, and Louise; Mary Catherine married Henry Louis Thurman - two sons, Bobby Louis and Timmy Joe; Garland Gene married Betty Jane Thomas - one daughter, Vickie Lynn; and Ronald Lyen.

4) Estelle H. Hawkins (1891 - 1984) married John Wyatt Flynn (1879 - 1964). They had the following children: Mildred Brunelle married Thomas Berry Casey (1906 - 1953) - four children - Harold Thomas, Raymond Stewart, Mary Carolyn and Charles Edward; Sylvia Maybelle married William Lee Pence - two children - Donnie Lee and Deborah Marie; Martha Alice married Joseph Patrick Brown - six children - Nancy Patricia, Douglas Andrew, Terry Joseph, Sandra Catherine, Gregory Allen, and Edward David; Harold Blaine married Leona Princess West - four children - Barbara Gail, Pamela Kay, Harold B., and Karen Denise; Bernard Ray married Lillie Maxine Warford - three children - Bernard Wayne, Troy Keith, and Rebecca Raynelle; John Winston married Betty Jean Peach - two sons, Gary Winston and Mark Lynn; Kermitt Truman married Mary Ida McMurray - one daughter, Susan Renee; Edwin Curtis married Billie Jean Fraley; Shirley Jean married Donnie Gail Riley - four children - Donnie Glenn, Donald Kay, Doris Jean, and Paula Marie; James Quentin (1935 - 1940); and John Michael.

5) Nancy Belle Hawkins, born 11-30-1897, married James Dudley Boggess on 12-23-1926. They had two children: James Dudley Jr. married Margaret Lee Bohannon - three daughters - Dandra Lee, Cynthia Denise, and Pamela Sue; and Mary Helen married Fredrick B. Rakutt - two sons, James Warren and John Paul.

6) Alton Davis Hawkins (1903 - 1980) married Bonnie Craig Brown on 9-1-1934. they had two children: Nancy Alda married 1st, Johnie Morgan McQueary (1933 - 1961) no children - 2nd, Donald Cheville; and Davis married Betty Doris Simpson - two children - Stewart Davis and Derris Alan.

NELSON WRIGHT HAWKINS, the only son

born to Hugh C. and Nell T. Hawkins, on July 8, 1928, at Ninevah in Anderson County, Kentucky. The family history of the Thacker, Hanks, and Coke, who are ancestors of Nell Thacker Hawkins, can be found on pages 207, 191, and 188 of the "History of Anderson County 1780-1936" by Lydia K. Bond. Nell Thacker Hawkins was born at McBrayer in Anderson County, Kentucky, on September 12, 1896, and died January 2, 1976. Hugh Cleveland Hawkins was born in Franklin County, KY on November 16, 1892 and died February 3, 1966. Both are buried in the Hebron Cemetery in Anderson County.

Nelson Hawkins married Eileen Nicholson, who was born October 23, 1930 and died December 23, 1971, and buried in the Lawrenceburg Cemetery in Anderson County. They had one child, Sharon Darline Hawkins, born September 19, 1950. Nelson Hawkins then married Dorothy Shouse Robinson and they had one child, Melissa Jean Hawkins, born April 2, 1957. Dorothy Robinson had two children, James C. Robinson and Stewart C. Robinson, who were reared by Nelson Hawkins and Dorothy

Robinson Hawkins. They were divorced in 1969. Nelson married Ann Webb Thomas of Frankfort, Kentucky, in Franklin County on April 20, 1973. They made their home in Frankfort, KY, where he was employed by the State of Kentucky. Ann Thomas Hawkins has two children, Jack K. Thomas and Linda Thomas, and two granddaughters, children of Jack and Brinda Thomas of Frankfort, KY.

Sharon D. Hawkins married Wythe C. Morris Jr. of Wytheville, Virginia on August 14, 1971. One child was born to them, Justin H. Morris, on December 3, 1980. They make their home in Wytheville, VA. They are teachers in the Wythe County, VA school system.

Melissa J. Hawkins married Larry Garrity of Anderson County on August 14, 1976 and have two children, Joshua Garrity, born May 8, 1978, and Travis Garrity, born May 31, 1980. They were divorced in 1983. Melissa Garrity married David Noble of Frankfort, KY on July 27, 1985, and they make their home in Lawrenceburg. Joshua and Travis Garrity make their home with them. Melissa is employed by the State of Kentucky in Frankfort and David is employed by the General Electric Plant in Frankfort. *Submitted By: Nelson Hawkins.*

DR. ROBERT W. HENSLEY, a native of Clay

County, Kentucky, is the son of Dr. Hiram and Lula Wilson Hensley. He is a graduate of Kentucky Weslyan College and the University of Louisville School of Dentistry. After graduating in 1934, he began the practice of dentistry in Lawrenceburg.

Mary Elizabeth Cox and Dr. Hensley were married December 22, 1934. They have a daughter, Linda Lou, wife of Dr. James P. Fields of Nashville, Tennessee and grandchildren, Timothy Austin Fields, married to Jo Garner of Nashville, and Amy Elizabeth Fields who is a nurse and residing in Arizona. Linda is a graduate of Lawrenceburg High School and Transylvania College. She received a master degree in Religious Education from Perkins School of Theology, Southern Methodist University, in Dallas, Texas.

Dr. and Mrs. Robert W. Hensley

Dr. Hensley entered the military service in 1942 and served four years in the Army United States Dental Corp. Two years of this period, he was assigned to the 178th General Hospital in Reims, France, and was discharged as a Major in 1946. For 52 years Dr. Hensley practiced dentistry. He is a life member of the Kentucky State Dental Association and also a member of Pierre Fauchard Academy. He served four years on the City School Board and twelve years as a City Councilman. He is an active member of the Lawrenceburg United Methodist Church, serving as teacher, board member, trustee, and finance chairman. He has been a Rotarian since 1934, received his 50 year pin in Masonry and is a member of Scotish Rite, Oleika Shrine, and Civil War Round Table.

Dr. Hensley worked as a volunteer dentist in Haiti in 1975 and on the Island of St. Vincent in 1984. He received an award for Outstanding Citizen of Anderson County in 1984.

Mary Elizabeth Cox Hensley is a native of Lawrenceburg and daughter of Judge John T. Cox and Leva Ann Hawkins Cox. She is a graduate of Lawrenceburg High School and attended Fugazzi Business College. Mary is a member of the Lawrenceburg United Methodist Church, Women's Division of Christian Service, Lawrenceburg Women's Club, and Lawrenceburg Business and Professional Women's Club. She has a brother, J. T. Cox and sister Mildred Cox Hodson.

Mary has been a partner in the Mrs. Cox Shop in downtown Lawrenceburg since 1965. The business, which was formerly owned by their mother, Mrs. John T. Cox, is now operated by Mary Hensley and Mildred Hodson.

The Hensleys, better known as Mary and Doc, reside on North Main in their home which was built in 1948. Their comment "We love our town and our roots are deep with family and friends connections." *submitted By: Dr. and Mrs. Robert W. Hensley.*

HERNDON The earliest known Herndons in America were three brothers that came from Wales to settle in Fauquier County, Virginia.

In Alexandria, Virginia, a marriage was found for John Herndon, Jr., son of John and Mary Herndon, this marriage being with a Miss Nutt. John Herndon, Jr. died after the birth of his son, Alvin Nutt Herndon, and the widow subsequently became Mrs. Mountjoy. There were a number of children from her 2nd marriage, among the older ones being William and Edward Mountjoy, who in 1813 came with Alvin, to what is now Anderson County. The three brothers took up land adjoining the other near Alton.

Alvin Nutt Herndon and his Virginia bride, Susan Holtzclaw, built a spacious log house near a generous spring, which met both farm and household needs. The couple planted near the homestead, a large orchard. The Herndon Orchard became a neighborhood attraction. Neighbors, school children in particular, were free to help themselves to apples, pears, peaches, chickasaw plums, cherries, and quince. Purchasers also traveled many miles to visit this farm to obtain fruit.

Alvin was described as being tall and sparsely built, with the strong domestic characteristics of a Welshman, a great love for home and family. This sentiment extended to all his relationships, to whom he was known as "Uncle Herndon" and his wife as "Aunt Suckie." Susan is said to have been the opposite of her husband. In stature, she was as short as he was tall and as plump as he was spare.

Alvin engaged in farming, teaching, and surveying. He was at one time justice of the peace, at another time sheriff, and in 1851 was elected to the legislature, where in the lower house, he was appointed chairman of the committee of Religion and Morals. In the State Militia, he held the commission of Major, but was never called on active duty during his enlistment.

Alvin Herndon manifested keen interest in politics, holding a number of political offices. He was appointed Commissioner of Revenue in 1827. He was an early member of the county Court and was influential in securing funds for early roads. He also helped to furnish plans for Seller's (Bond's Mill) Wooden Bridge.

Alvin and Susan had the following eight children: Presley Fisher (below); John Chapman; William Travers; Nancy (married Anthony Long); Sarah (married Rowsey Herndon); Elizabeth (married William Thomas); Susan (married Lewis James); and Lucy (married John Major).

Presley Fisher Herndon married Marcy Jane Roach and by this marriage had three sons: Daivd William; Alvin Gideon; and John Chapman. The wife died and Presley married 2nd, Elizabeth Jane Cole and they had three children: Susan Mary (married Elijah "Lit" Catlett); Lucy Agnes (married Lewis Young); and Thomas Dudley (married Lula Stevens).

David William Herndon, the oldest son of Presley Fisher, was in the service of the Confederacy under General John Morgan. After the war, he married Mary Thurman and set up housekeeping at the homestead of his grandfather Roach. They had six children: Four boys and two girls.

Alvin Gideon Herndon, the 2nd son of Presley Fisher, married Mildred Catlett. On their farm west of Alton Station, they raised thirteen children. *Submitted by: Jane Walker Wyatt Puhr.*

HERNDON The Herndon Family got its beginnings in England, probably Kent, England. William Herndon born around 1649. He married Catherine Diggs, daughter of John Diggs, the governor of Virginia in 1655. Children of record are: Edward, James, and William.

James Herndon (1683 - 1744) married Mary George. They had four sons: William, Edward, Joseph, and John.

Edward Herndon (1709 - 1743) married Ann Collins. They had four sons: Edward, William, Reuben, and John. All of these descendents who moved to Anderson County.

William (1737 - 1796) married Frances White. They lived in Prince William County, Virginia, where he was a prosperous farmer and did Revolutionary War service. They had twelve children.

John (1773 - around 1820), son of William and Frances, married Lydia Wood on 10-31-1798 in Virginia. They had nine children.

Haywood Herndon (1799 - 1835), son of John and Lydia, married Susannah Jackson on 4-29-1820 in Shelby County, KY. They had eight children; two of the girls are traced to Anderson County. Lucy Herndon married Josiah Martin on 3-27-1839. Their son, Joseph Howard Martin, married Georgia CaHill, daughter of Caleph CaHill and Ophelia Munday. Georgia was a sister to Sarah Ellen CaHill, wife of Alvin Herndon Perry.

Lydia Frances, daughter of Haywood Herndon, married John Young Perry on 11-24-1841. Their children can be found under the descendants of "William Jackson Perry". *Submitted By: Paula Perry Mitchell*

BURDETTE HUFFAKER is a fourth generation American. His great-grandfather came form Germany to Pennsylvania in 1732. His grandfather moved to Wayne County, Kentucky, in 1799. In Shearer Valley, in Wayne County, Burdette Huffaker was born on a farm, 25 December 1860. He farmed until 1888 when a freak freeze in July destroyed his crops and he lost his farm. He took a job teaching at Mill Springs in Wayne County. He married Annette Helen Hicks on 1 Jan 1890, in Wayne county, Kentucky. She was born 31 March 1859 in Wayne County.

Burdette and Helen then moved to Denver, Colorado, Burdette worked on the railroad, Helen worked in a mill. They bought a farm, but one year later, sold out and returned to Wayne County.

In 1900, Burdette, having accepted a position as a

W.P., R.L., M.A. and J.B. Farris, Roy McBrayer, Helen Hicks-Huffaker.

Storekeeper-gauger for the Internal Revenue Service, was transferred to Lawrenceburg, Kentucky, to work the distilleries in Anderson County. In 1906, he built a home at 239 North Main Street. On the night of 11 January 1923, the regular guard at the Old Joe Distillery called to say he was sick and could not complete his shift, and asked Burdette to finish it for him. Burdette went to the distillery and relieved the guard. Around midnight, Burdette was called to come out of the office with his hands up. He came out with his revolver drawn, and seeing an armed man, fired one shot at him. Another thief who was behind Burdette then fired, killing Burdette with a shot in the back. Helen, in a precedent setting suit, received a pension from the government which helped her for the rest of her life.

Burdette and Helen were members of the First Christian Church, (Disciples of Christ) in Lawrenceburg. They had four daughters: Leona Huffaker, born 29 October 1890 in Wayne County, married 20 September 1916 to Ezra McBrayer in Lawrenceburg, they had one son. Flonnie Evelyn Huffaker, born 18 April 1892 in Wayne County, married 30 May 1916 Alex Pearl Farris in Lawrenceburg. They had one daughter and three sons: Geneva Huffaker, born 8 June 1894, in Wayne County, married to Harold Victor Temple in Lexington, KY, they had no children, Dora Mae Huffaker, born 7 September 1900, in Wayne County, died of diphtheria on 10 January 1922, while teaching at Quicksand, Kentucky. She was single.

Burdette, Helen, Dora Mae, Leona, and Ezra are buried in the Lawrenceburg Cemetery.

RONALD WAYNE HODGES, the son of Julian Arthur Hodges (7-16-1924 - 5-8-1988) and Carrie Ernestine Shelton Hodges (born 3-30-1925), was born on 3-16-1948 in Ronceverte, West Virginia. Ronald has four brother and sisters: Shirley Jean married Sherrell Milliken; Donna Sue married Ronald Wayne Clark; Julian Arthur Jr.; Larry Allan; and one half-brother, Jerry Warner.

On 12-17-1971, in Smithfield, KY, Ronald married Donna Dean Webster. She was born on 7-7-1949 in Smithfield. She is the daughter of Virgil Lee Webster and Zella O'Nan. Ronald and Donna are the parents of two daughters: Angela Dawn and Stephanie Gayle.

When Ronald Wayne Hodges and Donna Dean Webster married, they moved to Lexington, KY to be closer to Ron's place of employment. While there they lived in an apartment complex and tried to get a loan to buy a house. Later they moved into another apartment in Lexington and applied for another loan. They were denied until their first child was born. They purchased a house in Lexington. Three years after Stephanie Gayle was born, they moved to Lawrenceburg. *Submitted By: Angela Hodges.*

MILDRED ANN COX HODSON, born 1928 in Anderson County, is the daughter of the late Judge and Mrs. John T. Cox. She has a sister, Mary Elizabeth Hensley, and a brother, J. T. She attended twelve years of school in Lawrenceburg, graduating in 1946. She is a graduate of Kentucky Wesleyan College and attended the University of Louisville graduate school. For may years she did heraldic research and art work under the business name, Studio of Heraldic Art. A former teacher in Louisville and Lawrenceburg, she is now a partner with her sister, Mrs. Robert Hensley, in The Mrs. Cox Shop. This retail apparel shop was started by her mother, Leva Ann Hawkins Cox. She is also the teacher/owner of Mickey's, a decorative painting shop.

Jeff, Lydia and Mildred Hodson

Mrs. Hodson is the mother of Robert Jefferson Hodson, born in 1952. Jeff is a graduate of Henry Clay High School, Lexington, and attended the University of Kentucky. He is in sales and promotion and lives in Orange County, California.

Lydia Anne Hodson Copeland, daughter, was born in 1954. She graduated from Henry Clay High School and George Washington University. She was America's Junior Miss in 1972. Lydia resides in Louisville and is a writer and producer.

Mildred has two grandsons: Robert Jeffery Hodson, New York, and Philip Ashton Copeland, Louisville.

A life-long Methodist, Mildred is the former president of the women's organization and a former Sunday School teacher. *Submitted By: Mildred Ann Cox Hodson.*

ALFRED HERMAN HOFFELD

ALFRED HERMAN HOFFELD was born in 1843, in Hanover, Germany, and educated in Germany where he received an MD Degree. He later opened Farmers Drug Company in Lawrenceburg. Dr. Hoffeld married Lucinda Case in 1894. At the age of 52, their first son, Alfred, was born. A daughter, Emily, was born in 1897 and Morris, born in 1906.

As a druggist, Dr. Hoffeld mixed prescriptions for all ailments. His cherry flavored cough syrup was a favorite of his granddaughter, Dorothy Hoffeld Atkinson, now living in Valdosta, Georgia. Besides caring for the ills of the family, he also doctored farm animals. The farmers especially appreciated the prescription they got to treat hogs. Many people didn't have the money to pay, so their names were recorded in a ledger.

In 1918, when the flu epidemic hit the area, Lucinda, in her kind caring way, waited on many of these families. A young dentist promised to make dentures for her when that day arrived that she would need them. Lucinda had cared for the dentist's family. True to his promise, he made the dentures.

Dr. Alfred Herman Hoffeld died in 1930 and Lucinda in 1942. They were known as the Hoffields or even Hawfields. Some of the Hoffeld family are still living in Lawrenceburg, others are scattered over the entire United States. *submitted By: Alfred Herman Hoffeld.*

ABRAHAM HOLT

ABRAHAM HOLT married Elizabeth Taylor. To this union were born five children: Sherman, Alice Holt Riley, Nora Holt Dennis, Maitie Holt Harley, and Silas.

Silas Holt was born on 5-10-1881, in Anderson County. He married Molly Florence Harley in 1900. She was born on 8-6-1883, in Washington County. She was the daughter of George Harley and Pal Riley Harley. She had four brothers: Grand, Amos, Joe, and Raymond. Silas and Molly were the parents of seven children: Mattie (1902 - 1989) married Stanton Peyton - five children; Mabel (born 1905) married Haskel Stratton - four children; Madge (1908 - 1978) married Obed Stratton - eight children; Janie (born 1911) married Horice Disponett - six children; Frank (born 1-12-1914) married Paige - one child; and Kenneth Holt. Silas Holt died in 1960 and Molly preceded him in death in the summer of 1950.

Kenneth B. Holt was born on 9-6-1924, in Anderson County. He married Rose Wooldridge on 4-12-1946, in Lawrenceburg, KY. She was born on 5-31-1927, in Anderson County. She is the daughter of Claude Wooldridge and Leeda Douthitt. Kenneth and Rose are the parents of five children: Wanda Faye Holt McNeese (born 1-22-1947) married seven times - two sons; Leida Carol Holt Owen (born 6-9-1950) married three times - two daughters; Robert Lewis Holt (born 6-9-1950) married once - divorced - two sons and two daughters; David Lee Holt (born 1-1-1953) married three times - divorced three sons and one daughter; and Kathy Diane Holt Wainscott (born 5-19-1957) married once - divorced - one son and four daughters.

Claude Woolridge was born in December 1894, in Anderson County. He was the son of Thomas Wooldridge and Melvina Scarbrough. He had brothers and sisters: Merit, Sarah, Birdie, Will, Jim, Grover Cleveland, and Thomas Jr. He married Leeda Douthitt, the daughter of J. Andrew Douthitt and Elizabeth Rogers. She was born on 9-10-1892 and died in 1971. She had seven brothers and sisters: Mildred, Jasper, Archbald, Fielding, Helen, William, and Otha. Claude and Leeda had five children: Lura, born 1913, married Paul Dick; Evelyn Frances, born 1914, married George Doss; Claude Andrew, born 1917, married Evelyn; Elmer Thomas, born 1919; and Rosa Lee. Claude Wooldridge died on 9-11-1974 in Woodford County. *Submitted By: Angie Wainscott.*

VERNON DEWEY HOLT

VERNON DEWEY HOLT, the son of Dewey Holt and Hallie Mae Cole Holt, was born on 3-29-1945, in Oneida, Kentucky. Vernon has one sister, Cleva, born 9-19-1942, who married Carmon Bingham on 2-9-1963. Vernon is a manager with the IBM Corporation.

On 6-11-1966 in Tyner, KY, Vernon married Winifred Gail McWhorter. she was born on 9-30-1948 in Oneida, KY. She is the daughter of Leonard Oak McWhorter and Nainnie Ruth Moore. She has one brother, Jeffrey Leonard McWhorter, who married Donna Gay.

The young couple left the hills of Easern Kentucky to move to Lexington, Kentucky in search of work. There they had: Christopher Vernon, born 8-7-1967; Matthew Allen, born 10-22-1971; Elizabeth, born 1-7-1975; and Jonthan David, born 3-21-1982.

In the spring of 1984, the family moved from Lexington to Lawrenceburg, KY. The oldest son, Christopher married Margaret Pearl Boblitt in 9-10-1988. The young couple is expecting a child in early July, 1990. *Submitted By: Elizabeth Holt.*

KENNETH P. AND SHIRLEY HOSKINS

KENNETH P. AND SHIRLEY HOSKINS are lifelong residents of Anderson County. Shirley was born January 17, 1936, and Kenneth was born on January 20, 1927. Shirley is the daughter of the late Curtis William and Ann Burke Headen. Her brother, Arnold C. Headen, resides in Lexington. Curtis died in 1987 and Ann died in 1978.

Kenneth is the son of Raymond Hoskins and the late Irma Lee Yeager Hoskins. His sister, Mrs. Arnold (Beulah) Sea, died in 1983. His step-brother C. T. Robinson, died in 1978 and his half-sister, Mrs. John (Wanda) Perry resides in Anderson County.

Shirley attended Gordon School, Waddy Grade School, Lawrenceburg Elementary and graduated from Anderson County High School. Kenneth attended Searcy School, Western High School and received a GED from Anderson County High School. He is a veteran of World War II serving in Germany. Places of employment have been Dean and Shirk Thread Factory, Kraft Foods, Edwards Sausage, and Veterans Hospital, Lexington, where he retired after 30 years of service. He has served as Councilman of Lawrenceburg for 1 term and as Mayor of Lawrenceburg for 3 terms. He is also a salesman for Adver-Tek Inc. Shirley has served as Church Secretary at First Baptist Church for 30 years.

Kenneth and Shirley Hoskins

Shirley and Kenneth are the parents of three children. Stephen, born in 1953, is a graduate of Georgetown College and Southern Baptist Theological Seminary, lives in Nashville and is manager of an apartment complex. He is married to the former Barbara White of Memphis. They have one son, Whitaker, born in 1989.

Philip, born in 1955, is a graduate of Georgetown College and Indiana University and is Parks and Recreation Director for the City of Owensboro. He is married to the former Janet Calhoun of Richardson, TX. They have two sons - Bryan, born in 1981, and Todd, born in 1983.

Their daughter, Leann, was born in 1961, and is a graduate of Georgetown College. She is married to Mark C. Warford. They have two daughters - Amanda, born in 1988, and Mary Ann, born in 1990. They reside in Anderson County.

Kenneth is a Trustee at First Baptist Church, is a member of the Rotary club, Alton Ruritan Club, Optimist Club, American Legion, VFW, DAV, Masonic Lodge #90, Eastern Star, Chamber of Commerce, Industrial Foundation, Bluegrass Area Development and Chairman of the Red Cross Bloodmobile Program.

Shirley is a member of the Eastern Star, Anderson Chapter of the American Cancer society and a Sunday School Teacher at First Baptist Church. Both are members of the Sanctuary Choir and other organization of the First Baptist Church. They have resided at 103 Saffell Street since 1959.

RAYMOND HOSKINS

RAYMOND HOSKINS, a resident of 309 Saffell Street, was born on August 26, 1896. He is the son of the late William Jesse and Mary Priscilla Beasley Hoskins. He was the youngest of eight children. Brother and sisters (all deceased): Jim, W. B., Clarence, and Harve Hoskins, Ess Mitchell, Alta Hardin, and Net Hatchett.

Farm life has been his only life, since his father was an avid farmer, coming from Virginia. He began his farming career at the early age of 16. He tilled the land with horse-drawn plows, mowing machines, and hay balers, and setting tobacco by hand. His father was instrumental in helping him buy his first farm of 66 acres on the Leathers Road in the western part of Anderson County.

Raymond Hoskins

He managed through the years to successfully adopt to the many and varied methods by being active in farm related organizations and civic clubs. He became a member of Farm Bureau in 1946, having served on the Board of Directors and has been recognized for his service. He is still a member.

He was elected a community committeeman from the Alton district and served many years in ASC (Agricultural Stabilization and Conservation).

During the peak of his farming career, he served on the Southern States Board of Directors and still is interested on how S. S. can help the farmer, Lawrenceburg, and Anderson County.

He joined the Alton Ruritan Club, shortly after its formation in 1960. He served on many committees and Board of Directors. His attendance record is one of the best in the club.

He is a member of the Beaver Creek Lodge and sometime ago received his 50 year membership service award.

Along with these civic and farm organizations, his church is vital to him. In 1945, he moved his membership from the Antioch Christian Church to the Lawrenceburg Christian Church. He is an active member of the Birdwhistell Sunday School Class. and has served many years as a deacon. He is now Deacon Emeritus.

He attended Searcy School in his youth, however his years of experiences in life account for wisdom.

He was married to the former Irma Lee Yeager and they had five children. Three died at an early age, leaving a daughter, Beulah Sea, who passed away in 1983, and a son Kenneth P. Hoskins who resides in Lawrenceburg. Irma Hoskins died in 1930. He married the former Katherine Sea Robinson, mother of C. T. Robinson. Katherine passed away in 1978 and C. T. passed away in 1986. Raymond and Katherine have one daughter, Wanda Perry who resides in Anderson County. He has nine grandchildren and 13 great-grandchildren and 3 great-great-grandchildren.

Now that he is in his twilight years, what are his feelings? PURE OPTIMISM! He remains vitally interested in all facets of life. He raises a garden, remains active in many civic organizations and church. He think this is a great country, city, and county with a rich, rich heritage.

What is his goal now in life? "To live another year, better than last."

CHESTER HOUCHIN

CHESTER HOUCHIN was born in Anderson County, Kentucky, on August 9, 1883. His parents were John William "Billy" Houchin (formerly from Mercer County, Kentucky) and Georgia Cook Houchin, who as a little girl came in a covered wagon with her parents from Virginia, to settle in the Salt River Church area, and later moved to Shelby County, Kentucky.

Tida Deane Carter was born November 30, 1886. Her parents, William B. Carter and Elizabeth Belle Bentley Carter lived in Shelby and Anderson Counties during their lifetimes.

Chester Houchin and Tida Deane Carter were married in Shelbyville, Kentucky, on October 4, 1906, and lived for many years on a farm they bought near Fox Creek, Kentucky. Later, they purchased and moved to a farm (her parents owned until her father's death) on the Glensboro Road, four miles west of Lawrenceburg, KY. In 1950, they sold both farms and then purchased a farm within a mile of Campbellsburg, Kentucky, in Henry County on the Carrollton Pike. They lived here until their deaths in 1963 and 1961, respectively.

To this union were born six children, five daughters and a son: Lucille and Luella (1914) twins; Georgia (1908); Sallie (1921); Edna (1925); and William Chester "W.C." (1926). Lucille and Sallie died in infancy.

Luella Houchin married Marvin Shely on December 22, 1934. They lived in Anderson County eight years; then moved to Louisville, Kentucky. Born to them were two sons and three daughters: Marvin Lee, Mary Lou, Joseph Wayne "Joe", Paula Ann, and Bettye. Marvin Shely died January 1, 1975, and is buried in the Fox Creek Cemetery. Marvin Lee Shely died October 2, 1987, and is buried in Fountain Inn, South Carolina.

Georgia Houchin married Paul C. Carter on June 10, 1939. To this union was born one daughter, Carolyn. They lived several years in Louisville, Kentucky, and later moved to the Chicago area.

Edna Houchin married Joseph Edwin Shouse on September 17, 1938. They lived several years in Anderson County and later moved to Louisville, Kentucky. Born to them were a daughter and two sons: Marilyn, Joseph "Joe", and William "Bill".

William Chester "W.C." Houchin married Mary Lee Inabnit on May 24, 1946. They lived in Anderson County for a while, and later moved to Louisville, Kentucky, and then to Finchville, Kentucky. To this union were born two sons: William Alan and Howard Clyde. *Submitted By: Edna Houchin Shouse.*

M. JACKSON HOUCHIN

M. JACKSON HOUCHIN was born 12 -3-1860 and Emma Z. Routt was born 9-10-1860. They were both members of large families - both the Houchin and Routt families consisted of thirteen children each. They were married in 1884. They married life was spent on farms in Anderson and Mercer Counties. They were parents of three daughters: Ruby Alice (1886 - 1966), Eva Myrtle (1888 - 1983), and Edith Earl (1902 - 1933).

Ruby married J.M. "Coy" Chilton. They were the parents of six children: Emma J. (Mrs. Curtis Chapman) deceased 1976; Huntley Chilton of Anderson County; Nellie (Mrs. Robert Stratton) of Mercer County; Frances (Mrs. Earl Robinson) of Mercer County; Earl M. Chilton of Mercer County; and John H. Chilton of Anderson County.

Eva married Clarence Chapman. They were the parents of four children: Durwood Gillman Chapman, deceased 1972; Elberta (Mrs. Robert T. West) of Anderson County; Lena (Mrs. Vernon Hostetter) of Mount Holly, North Carolina; and Floradell (Mrs. Harold Cunningham) of Anderson County.

Mr. and Mrs. "Jack" Houchin

Edith married H. Guy Bowen. They were the parents of four children: Onita (Mrs. William C. Morgan) of Anderson County; Frances (Mrs. Vernon Thornsburg), deceased 1972; Herbert K. Bowen of Anderson County; and M. Allen Bowen of Mercer County.

Edith Bowen died in 1933, when her children were small and the children lived with the Houchins for three years.

Mr. and Mrs. Houchin lived the latter part of their life in Anderson County, near the present intersection of Old 127 and the 127 By-pass, just north of the Bonds Mill Road. They both died in 1936, within a period of three weeks, after having been married for more than 50 years. Mr. and Mrs. Houchin and their three daughters are all buried in the Hebron Cemetery.

The grandchildren of this couple still have many pleasant memories of visits in the home of "Granny" and "Daddy" Houchin. *Submitted By: Onita B. Morgan.*

RUSSELL B. HOWARD

RUSSELL B. HOWARD, the son of Kenoyd B. and Lani Miller Howard, was born on 5-15-1951 in Russell, Kentucky. Russell has one brother and four sisters: Jack; Mary Edna married David Hamilton; Sara Lou married Larry Moore; Bonnie married Jerry Bryant; and Roseanna married Joseph Marcum.

On 2-1-1970, Russell married Gloria Jean Baer, the daughter of James Ruben and Ann Mae Hall Baer. She was born on 10-12-1951 in Ashland, Kentucky. She has one brother and four sisters: Violet Mae married Donald Davidson; Francis Eleanor married Fred Davis; Judith Florence married June Stidham; Barbara Allen married Donald Brunty; and James married Pamela Meadows.

Russell and Gloria Jean Howard have two daughters: Kristie Lynn (born 4-17-1973 in Ironton, Ohio) and Tammy Ann (born 2-26-1978 in Ironton, Ohio).

The Howard family has been living in Lawrenceburg, Kentucky since January of 1988. They attend Freewill Baptist Church. *Submitted By: Kristie Howard.*

HOUCHIN

HOUCHIN The Houchin ancestors first came to this country from Norfolk County, England, in 1629. The Houchin family that settled in southern Kentucky was of the family of John Houchin of Amherst County, Virginia. They came to Kentucky, moving to Mercer County in 1827. The change made John Houchin a resident of Anderson County.

One of John's sons, Steven, born in 1818 and died in 1899, was married to Ann Bond. After her death, Steven married Mary Scearce on December 1, 1859. Children born to this marriage were Jack, Reuben Matterson, Thomas Edward, and Minerva Ellen. After the second wife died, Steven married Jane Hawthorne and had four sons: Wesley; John; Coleman; and Medley.

Susie, Aileen and Reuben Houchin

Reuben Matterson was born June 24, 1864. He married Susie Routt (1866 - 1901) daughter of Francillo and Esther Coke Routt. Their children were Warren Routt (1889 - 1975), Sue Esther (1892 - 1980), and Minnie (1894 - 1976). Warren married Lena Oliver (1893 - 1940). They had three children, James Carlton (1908 - 1911), Lewis Routt (1911 - 1954), and Elizabeth Mollie Houchin Beals (1940 - 1972), and Warren Stanley. He married Verda Gould. Their children are Jenny and Bryan. Evelyn married Clellan McMurry. One son was born to them, James Warren. He married Mary Catherine Sparrow. They have three children: James Douglas; Melissa Dawn; and Steven Warren. Douglas married Nancy Wilson. After Warren's wife died, he married Emma Bell Hawkins.

Sue Esther married Raymond C. Crossfield. They have three children: Mary Esther; Minnie Bell (1918, lived 18 days); and William Matterson (1920 - 1944). He was killed in action in France during World War II.

Mary Esther married C. B. Brown. They have one son, William Burton. He married Sharon Greer and they have two children: Jeffrey Scott and Amber Dawn.

Minnie married Sim H. Anderson of Lancaster. They have no children.

After the death of Reuben's first wife, he married Susan Mary Thacker (1873 - 1966). She was the daughter of Rufus E. Thacker and Sarah Frances Crossfield Thacker. They had three children: Mary Frances (1903 - 1905); Matt (1908 - 1936); and Aileen, who married Ray McAnly, a native of Boyle County. They have two children: Mary Belle and Robert Lee. Mary Belle married Thomas E. Christerson. They have three children: Susan Anne; Steven; and John. Susan married John Brown of Hazard and they have two children: David Michael and Laura Catherine. Steven married Lisa Smith of Huntington, West Virginia. Robert Lee married Mary Jane Duncan and they have two children: Robert Douglas and Janeen Kaye.

Reuben Houchin was a farmer and livestock trader in his early years. In 1904, he bought and operated a general store at Ripyville. Later, he bought a health resort, Elixner Springs, in Casey County. He died in 1935 at the age of 70 and was buried on the family lot in the Hebron Cemetery in Anderson County, along with his two wives, two sons and infant daughter.

ROBERT LEONARD AND ANN STRATTON HUDNALL came to Anderson County to set up housekeeping right after Leonard came home from service in World War II with the 106th Infantry, 27th Division in the South Pacific. Leonard was born March 13, 1926 and raised in Franklin County. His parents, Shadie Reed and Katherine Corbin Hudnall, moved from Paris, KY to Frankfort. Shadie's parents, John Calvin and America Jane Hudnall, lived in Paris and raised seven children.

Leonard is the second oldest of five children; brother John, and sisters Adra, Betty and Ethelee. He attended school at Elkhorn and Frankfort High in Franklin County. His father was a grocer and car salesman; his mother worked at the shoe factory in Frankfort for many years and was a housewife.

Ann Stratton was born September 23, 1924 at Sinai, KY and was raised in Anderson County. She is the daughter of George W. and Mabel Cunningham Stratton. George's parents, John Morton and Mamie Stratton, were born and raised in Anderson County. They were carpenters and housewives.

Ann is the oldest of nine children; brothers Floyd, George, Bruce (deceased), William, Ralph, Glenn and Edward Leon (deceased) and one sister, Bonnie Jane Schell.

Robert L Hudnall Sr., Ann Atratton Hudnall, Robert L. Hudnall, Jr., Jana Thurman Hudnall, Robert Jason Hudnall, Ronald Lynn Hudnall, Karen Peach Hudnall, Melamie Jane Hudnall, Jonathan Lynn Hudnall.

Ann and Leonard were married August 28, 1943 in Frankfort. They have two sons. Robert Leonard Jr. was born July 12, 1944 and is married to the former Jana Thurman. Robert is employed at Rand McNally in Versailles and also owns and operates Robert's Frames in Lawrenceburg. They have one son, Robert Jason, age 23, who is attending the University of Kentucky and working for IBM. Ronald Lynn was born May 26, 1949 and is married to the former Karen Peach. Ron works at IBM in Lexington and raises and shows hackney ponies. They have two children, Melanie Jane, age 16, senior at Anderson High, and Jonathan Lynn, age 13, eighth grade at Anderson Middle School.

Ann has been retired for three years from Webster Electric where she worked for 32 years. She is now busy with her flowers, visiting old friends, piecing quilts and doing things she likes at home.

Leonard worked for the Bluegrass Parkway for several years and then went to work for the Kuhlman Corporation in Versailles for 20 years. He retired October 8, 1989. He will now try to get the little jobs done he never had time to do and work their horses.

They have been residents of 209 Village Drive since December 1971 when they moved from a farm they owned at Rutherford. They are members of Mt. Pleasant Baptist Church, but mostly attend First Baptist Church in Lawrenceburg. *Submitted By: Robert L. Hudnall, Sr.*

HUGHES The 1850 Spencer County Kentucky Census shows that Joseph Hughes and his wife, Lucinda Taylor Hughes, were living with her father, Zackariah Taylor, and his family. Joseph and Lucinda lived in Spencer County all their lives. He was a farmer. They had five sons: John, Zackariah, George, Thomas (died at six months), and Joseph.

Their second son, Zackariah Jefferson Hughes, was born on 4-16-1853. He married Susan Mary Shields on 9-21-1874, in Spencer County. She was born on 6-16-1855, and was the daughter of Joseph Shields and Susan Self. Zackariah and Susan had eight children born between 1875 and 1896: Effie Pearl, Clarine, Herman, Bessie, Fred Hale, Marie, and Captola. Zackariah Hughes died on 12-11-1927, and his wife, Susan, died on 1-31-1933.

Fred Hale Hughes was born on 2-26-1895, in Nelson County, KY. He was a merchant and he married Emma Lee Wagner. She was born on 8-17-1892 in Nelson County. She was the daughter of Louis Wagner (1841 - 1903) and Catherine Montgomery Wagner (1849 - 1919). Fred Hale and Emma Lee lived all their lives in either Nelson or Anderson County. They were the parents of four children: Geneva, born 1911, married Allen Cammack; Herman; Odoa (1914 - 1967) married Earl Mitchell; and Lillian, born 1922, married Francis Holdhouser. Fred hale died on 1-18-1932 and Emma Lee on 2-28-1962. They were both buried in New Liberty Christian Church Cemetery near the Nelson-Anderson County line.

Herman Hughes was born on 9-14-1912 in Sinai, KY. He married Emma Mae Stratton on 2-12-1945, in Harrodsburg, KY. She was born on 10-14-1921, in Sinai and is the daughter of Samuel Boaz Stratton and Rosa Mae Camic. Herman and Emma Mae have three children: Jody Earl, born 5-24-1946, married Cathy Ann Brickler; Billie Diane, born 11-1-1948, married Larry Trueman Gabhart; and Rosemary, born 12-30-1958, married Donnie Sutherland. Herman Hughes passed away on 3-8-1986, and was laid to rest in Lawrenceburg.

Samuel Boaz Stratton, the son of James Dogad Stratton (1863 - 1947) and Lydia Meridas Caldwell Stratton (1867 - 1956) <see James Dogad Stratton Article>, was born on 3-19-1902, in Anderson County. He married Rosa Mae Camic on 11-14-1920. She was born on 4-16-1898, and is the daughter of James Nathan Camic and Emmie Pinkston Camic. Samuel Boaz and Rosa Stratton are the parents of four children: Emma Mae, William (1923 - 1935), Samuel Jr. married Faye, and James Raymond married Jonelle Ross. *submitted By: Amy C. Hughes.*

EDWARD HUGHES In 1719, Edward Hughes was living in Northumberland County, Virginia. He and his wife, Elizabeth, in 1751, bore a son, one William Hughes, who married Mary "Polly" Foster Hughes. They lived in Prince William County, Virginia, and he was later killed on a business trip to Washington. William and Mary "Polly" Hughes had a son, William, born in 1791. This young William, while living in Prince William County, married Elizabeth Bowen, and they had one son, James. Elizabeth Bowen died, and William later moved to Nelson County, KY.

In Kentucky, William met and married Sarah Elizabeth Sweasy, of Nelson County, (in old Sweasy family Bible). Both William and Elizabeth (b.1807 - d. 1897) are buried in the Penny's Chapel graveyard. They were the owners of some 400 acres of land in Nelson County, but gradually sold off that land and in 1834 moved to Anderson County where he bought 469 acres. They lived there the rest of their lives.

William and Elizabeth were proud parents of ten children: Grayson, (1831 - 1909); Susan (1832 - 1902) married 1st, William Black in 1850, and 2nd., Esq. John Hyatt; Varlorus (1833 - 1916) married Mary E. Terrell; LaFayette (1835 - 1910) married Lutitia Johnson in 1857; Sarah (1836 - 1880) married 1st, William T. Skinner and moved to Texas (Skinner died after a companion put poison in his coffee over payment of a cattle sale in Arkansas.) 2nd, Oliver Keith; Nancy (1838 - 1901) married Isaac Johnson in 1861 (Johnsonville was named after him.); John M. married Nancy Ellen in 1860; Levenia married George Eaton, Woodford County; Joseph Toliver (1844 - 1909) married Joicy Crossfield; and Fannie (born 1846) died young. After the death of her husband, Elizabeth Sweasy Hughes maintained her own household at their homestead for several years. She later lived with her son, Joseph, but died at the home of her daughter, Mrs. Susan Hyatt.

Joseph Toliver Hughes was a soldier in the Civil War on the Confederate side, (his brother-in-law was a captain on the Union side.) in Company H 6th Kentucky Calvary, listed on the Civil War statue in the Courthouse yard. The men that were killed, the men that were wounded and the men that survived, are listed there. After the war, Mr. Hughes was active in local government and helped to get the statue. He was also active in the local school system as a census taker. The Hughes School was named for him. He also ran a country store which contained the Cora Post Office. At the time of his death, he was Deputy County Clerk. Joseph married Joicy Crossfield on September 11, 1867, in Anderson County. She was the daughter of Morgan Good and Katherine Samuel Crossfield. Joseph and Joicy were the parents of seven children: Fannie married John Ed Sweeny; Elizabeth married a Cranfill; Nannie E. married a Wilhout; Susan Mary (below); Louella (born 1-3-1880); William Morgan (born 10-30-1883) married Nancy Whitehouse; and Hattie married Dr. Robert Birdwhistell (he was a veterinarian). They had two sons, Dr. Ray Birdwhistell and Dr. Ralph Birdwhistell. Ray has two daughters, Jill and Nan. Ralph and his wife, Myram, have three sons, Reece, Kirk, and Scott. Joseph and Joicy Hughes are both buried in the Fox Creek Cemetery and two daughters, Nannie Wilhout and Susan Mary, are buried nearby.

Susan Mary Hughes (nicknamed by her husband Suky) married John E. Brown at Orr, KY (now Glensboro). They had five children: 1) Marion C. (1896 - 1967) married Martha Boyer. They had one son, John B. Marion who was a WWI soldier and taught at UK for 30 years as a professor of math. His son is now professor of chemistry at the University in Granville, Ohio. 2) Blanche (1900 - 1983) married Wyatt Shely and they had two sons, Forest and Robert (deceased). Before his death, Robert was married to Annenell Birdwhistell, and they had one son, Brent. Forest and Roberta Hale have five children: Jackie, Debbie, Bill, Karen and Carla. 3) Joe Hughes Brown (1901 - 1988) married Alpha Butner; they had one son, Wendall (deceased). For most of their lives Joe and Alpha built a new home on that site. 4) Nina (1903, still living) married Elmo Bruner and they have two daughters, Lucille Elizabeth and Arlene Mae Bruner. (below) 5) Olete Ruth (1910 - 1962) married Willard Gillis and they had two children, Beverly married Robert Stivers and their children are Karla and Brian. Gary Gillis married Mary Lee Slaughter, from Versailles and they have three children, Gary Willard, Barbara, and David Bertram.

Lucille Elizabeth Bruner (named after all the Elizabeths in the family) married Robert Duncan. They lived a mile apart (in the community where all the Hughes heritage surrounded Lucille) from each other as they were growing up and later married during the WW II in an Army Chapel in Alexander, LA. They have three daughters: Angelene married Larry Ferguson of Knoxville, TN; Patricia Elaine; and Cheryl Ann married Stephen Wyatt of Benton, KY. Besides being Circuit Court Clerk since June, 1963, Lucille's hobbies are first of all, husband and family, living parents, a little photography and poetry, along with a little travel.

Arlene Bruner married Carl Ray Gregory at Shiloh Christian Church. They have two sons: Glen Clark married Sandy Toll and have two daughters, Kimberly and Stacy. Philip Gregory married Carol Grubbs of Louisville, KY. *Submitted By: Lucille Duncan.*

HUME Probably the first Hume to set foot on Anderson County soil was John W. Hume. born in Virginia circa 1814, he was the son of Jessie and

Elizabeth Hume. John W. was orphaned at the early age of five years old. In 1837, he married Susannah Bond, daughter of Anthony Bond, who appears in the McKee-Bond edition of the History of Anderson County. Born to this union were: Eliza (Tipton); Mary (Shelborn); George W. Hume; Martha (Ryan); and Elizabeth (Brooks). Shortly after Susannah Bond Hume died, John W. married Susannah's sister, Nancy in 1851. By this marriage, John Lewis Hume was born in 1858. John W. Hume would marry two more times before he died around 1906. He was a farmer and one of the first settlers in the Birdie community. In 1900, at the age of 86, he became the Postmaster there. Only the foundation now remains of the building that served as a Post Office and a home to John W. Hume.

John Lewis Hume continued to farm the land on which his father had reared six children. On February 5, 1878, John Lewis Hume wed Ann Edna Haden and in November of that same year their only child, Joseph Edgar Hume was born. John Lewis had built for his wife a home made of logs that were cut from the land that gave them life. In the Fall of 1921 on a November afternoon, John Lewis Hume died on a ridgetop about 300 yards from the house he built years before. For 15 years after her husband's death, Ann Haden Hume lived in that same home and on a hot September day in 1936, she died there alone. It was two days later that some of her grandsons discovered her fate.

Joseph Edgar Hume married Ann Elizabeth Brown, daughter of Joseph H. Brown and Susan Redom, on November 4, 1896. A well-known and popular minister in Anderson County of that time, Jordan T. Ragan, performed the ceremony. Into that union was born: Joseph Allie Hume; Gracie (Hockhalter); Sadie (Perry); Earl Hume; Elbert Ray Hume; and twin sons, Elmer and Edgar Hume. Sadie, Earl, and Elmer still reside today in Anderson County. Like the Hume families before them, Joe and Annie built a home for themselves on that same land. As if to continue tradition, Joe and Annie died on their Birdie Farm, November 1930 and May 1947, respectively

A large portion of this same farm is owned today by Elmer Hume, son of Joe and Annie Hume. On a quite hillside near the site of the Post Office and home of John W. Hume, lies the resting bodies of several members of this family in the Hume Cemetery. At the present time, Elmer and his son, Billy Joe, raise tobacco, hay, and livestock as did their parents before the, This makes Billy Joe the fifth generation of the Hume family to farm the same land as John W. Hume did around 150 years ago. *Submitted By: Billy Joe Hume.*

BILLY JOE HUME, a lifelong native of Anderson county, was born December 9, 1948 , He is the first child of Elmer Hume, born January 25, 1923, and Helen Perry Hume, born May 21, 1929 and died June 12, 1959. (See Hume Family article).

In his early years, Billy Joe grew up in the Birdie community where he attended Marlowe Grade School. Later his family moves to Lawrenceburg and he graduated from Lawrenceburg Elementary School. He went to Anderson County High School where he graduated with honors. He then moved to Richmond where he attended Eastern Kentucky University.

In May of 1967, he began employment with Boulevard Distillers and Importers and he remains employed there today. He also is a farmer and operates a small business. His hobbies include genealogy work, fishing, and he has hunted big game extensively over the North American Continent. He is also a member of the Sons of Confederate Veterans, Anderson County Historical Society, Foundation for North American Wild Sheep, various conservation and outdoor organizations which include life memberships with National Rifle Association and the North American Hunting Club.

On November 22, 1967, Billy Joe married Jane Carol McNabb, the daughter of Andrew Forrest McNabb and Cora Mae Pulfrey McNabb. Jane was born July 7, 1950. She attended elementary schools in Franklin County and attended Franklin County High School. After her marriage, she became employed at Texas Instruments in Versailles and since October 1985, she has been employed at Heritage Hall Nursing Home in Lawrenceburg. She enjoys antiques and cooking.

From Billy Joe and Jane's union were born three children: Melinda Jean, born December 2, 1971; Joseph Aaron, born January 9, 1975; and Dustin Ryan, born November 14, 1976. All three children attend schools in the Anderson county school system. Billy Joe has one brother, John Mark Hume who is currently with IBM in Charlotte, North Carolina. Jane has four brothers: Ronald, Michael, Donnie, and Danny all of Frankfort, KY. She has one sister, Brenda McNabb, of Frankfort also.

The Humes have resided at 212 Forrest Drive in Lawrenceburg since 1970. The entire family are members of the Corinth Christian Church. One of Billy Joe's hopes and wishes was to see this book written and published. He and his family sincerely dedicates what work he has done toward this publication to the future generations of Anderson County and to the County's growth. *Submitted By: Billy Joe Hume.*

HUBERT HUNTER and Della Sherrow were married in 1925, in Jessamine County, KY. The Hunters came to Anderson County, Ky in a horse and buggy. They made their first home at Lock Five.

When Hubert Hunter was 16 he joined the United States Corps of Engineers as a deck hand on a boat called the *Kentucky*. As years went by, he became the pilot on the *Kentucky* for sixteen years. From there, he went to work on the dredge boat cleaning out the Kentucky River.

He then met Della Sherrow, married her, and took up housekeeping at their first home at Lock Five, as Lock Keeper.

There are many stories that could be told about things that happened on the river. The logged rafts came down the river on the way to Frankfort to the saw mill. The logs had to be locked through by man power because the gates were not operated by electricity until 1965. Mr. Hunter often locked through paddle boat jiggs. These show boats traveled up and down the river entertaining people. There were also the coal barges. Gulf gasoline was hauled up and down the river on a boat called the *John J. Kelly.*

Hubert and Della Sherrow Hunter

The lock and dam were built October 1st, 1885. It was the last dam built by slaves.

There was a beach on the lower end of Lock Five. There has been as many as 1500 people of the beach in the 1940's and 1950's. It was a big place for swimming and fishing.

In 1945, Hubert Hunter celebrated his 45th birthday. He had as guests as Lock Five, about 500 people of Anderson County. Hubert Hunter, Louis Sherwood, and Walter Major cooked fish outdoors in a large kettle for all of his guests. One of his guests was Happy Chandler.

Hubert and Della Hunter made their home at Lock Five for 35 years. He then retired and moved to Woodford Street, in the city of Lawrenceburg.

The Hunters had three children, Pauline H. Edwards, Carrie Wilson, and Donnie Hunter.

Pauline H. Edwards resides in Harrodsburg, Kentucky. She has one son, Bill Edwards, who is married to Debra Sanders. Bill has three children, Elizabeth Ann, Clint, and Josh. They too reside in Harrodsburg, Mercer County, Kentucky.

Carrie Wilson is married to Lonnie Wilson. Carrie has one son, Tommie Milburn, who is married to Sandy Phillips. They have two children, Ryan and Kris. They reside in Anderson County, KY.

Donnie Hunter is married to Dottie Carter. They have two children, Grant and Paula. Grant is married to Mary Beth Shingleton. Paula is married to Randy Glisson. They all reside in Anderson County, KY.

Both Hubert and Della Hunter are deceased. Hubert was born in 1900 and died in 1960. Della Hunter was born in 1907 and died in 1957. *Submitted By: Carrie Wilson.*

JULIAN T. AND GENEVA RAY HUTCHINSON were married at St. Peter Church in Lexington, KY on 6-27-1923 Geneva was the daughter of William C. and Martha Ann Sewell Ray of Lawrenceburg, KY. Julian was the son of Charles C. and Bridget Reynolds Hutchinson of Bourbon and Fayette Counties. Charles's father and mother came to Bourbon County in 1859. His father, William D. was from Washington, D.C. His mother, Laura Munday, was from Zanesville, Ohio. The Hutchinson and Munday families came to America in the 1600's. Julian's mother's parents came to Kentucky in 1847, from Roscomman, Ireland. They were John and Mary Gannon Reynolds.

Julian T. and Geneva Ray Hutchinson

Julian and Geneva lived most of their life in Lexington. They owned the Mack Drug Company in the 1930's. Julian was a Registered Pharmacist. Geneva was educated in Anderson county and Miller's Business College. They had twelve children. Joseph E., Mrs. George (Martha) Talbott, John William, Mrs. Fred (Catherine) DeFelice, Mrs. Daniel (Mary Frances) Fister, Genevieve, Julian Jr., Blanche Horseman, Robert P., Thomas A., and Charles E. Hutchinson. They had one son, Charles Richard, who died at the age of six months. The couple were members of Christ the King Cathedral in Lexington. Julian died on 12-12-1962 and Geneva on 8-11-1989. They are buried in Calvery Cemetery, Lexington. *Submitted By: Michael Ray.*

HARVEY HUTTON, the son of James Orr Hutton (1823 - 1907) and Mary Katherine Short Hutton (1844 - 1922), was born on 4-6-1884, in Lawrenceburg, KY. Harvey was a farmer in the county and died there on 4-8-1964. He married Mary Jane Hughes on 1-28-1906 in Lawrenceburg. Mary Jane, the daughter of John Hughes (1850 - 1936) and Minerva Ann Davis (1854 - 1903), was born on 6-5-1884, in Madison County, KY and died on 6-9-1954, in Anderson County.

Harvey and Mary Jane Hutton were the parents

of ten children: Bertha (1907 - 1979) married Jessie Medley; John (8-1908 - 12-1908); Lucille (1910 - 1989) married Willard Mitchell; Katherine, born 1912, married Dillon Montgomery; Elizabeth (1914 - 1981) married Estill Reed; Theodore, born 1915, married Mary Peyton; Fred (1917 - 1983) married Loraine Hellard; Guy E. (below); Sadie (2-1922 - 3-1922); and Jane, born 1924, married Stanley Perry.

Guy E. Hutton was born on 10-17-1919 in Lawrenceburg and died on 12-5-1969, in Lexington, KY. He married Loraine Peyton on 10-5-1948, in Franklin County, KY. Loraine was born on 3-31-1931, in Shelby County, KY and died 9-12-1987 in Franklin County. She was the daughter of Willie Peyton (1909 - 1989) and Jennie Richards Peyton, born 1914. She had four brothers and sisters: Mary, born 1929, married Jim Clark; Ralph, born 1934, married Geraldine Baxter; Lillian, born 1937, married Joe Mills; and Dale, born 1954.

Guy and Loraine had two daughters: Donna, born 1949, married Kenneth Peach - three children - Stephanie, Melissa, and Jennifer; and Judy, born 1952, married Bobby Mefford - two sons - Derrick and Chad. *Submitted By: Melissa Peach.*

LEWIS HYATT

LEWIS HYATT was born in Virginia and came to Anderson County. In 1818, he built a house on lot #15 on the north side of the Anderson County Courthouse, in Lawrence (name later changed to Lawrenceburg). It was a two-story house with about ten rooms, and it was called Hyatt's Tavern. He married Meredith (?). They were the parents of three children: Mary Ann, born circa 1816, married James B. Oliver; Sarah born circa 1817, married Patrick O'Brien; and John.

John was born on 11-6-1834, in Anderson County. He married his first wife, Sarah Cornett, on 3-22-1856 in Anderson County. They had two children: John P. (1857 - 1859) and Mary (1858 - 1859).

John Hyatt remarried in 1859 to Malinda Ann Waterfill (1834 - 1874). She was the daughter of Jessie Carter Waterfill (1813 - 1905) and his wife, Frances Routt Waterfill (1812 - 1894). Malinda Hyatt is believed to have been buried in the Old Salt River Baptist Church Graveyard in Stringtown, KY. John and Malinda were the parents of six children: Sarah Fannie (1860 - 1936); Lulie (1862 - 1863); William Jess (1864 - 1918); Molly (1866 - 1954); James Calvin (below); and Daniel (1871 - ?). John Hyatt died on 1-30-1910 in Anderson County.

James Calvin Hyatt was born on 5-19-1869 in Anderson County and died on 4-1-1946. He married Mary Elizabeth Franklin (1870 - 1944) on 10-19-1887. She was the daughter of James (1844 - 1916) and Gabrieller Franklin (1850 - 1941).

Vernon Hyatt was born 10-21-1891 in Anderson County to James Calvin and Mary Elizabeth Hyatt. He married 1st, Sallie Morris (1896 - 1925). No children. He married 2nd, Edna Ruby Dennis on 8-16-1936. She was born on 4-14-1920 in Washington County. She is the daughter of William Thomas Dennis and Mollie Brothers Dennis. Vernon and Edna were the parents of ten children - Dudley and Allen; Harold Lewis (1940 - 1949); Clarence, born 1942, one son - Joey; Mary Jane, born 1941, two children - Vicki and Curtis; Lulia Bell, born 1946, Bobby Allen, born 1950, one son - Bobby; Dorothy Carol, born 1952, one daughter - Mellissa; Vernon Jr., born 1954; and Linda Sue, born 1958. Vernon Hyatt Sr. died on 9-17-1989.

Betty Frances Hyatt was born on 1-7-1937, in Anderson County. Her first marriage was to Charles Louis Best and they had four sons: Charles Thomas, born 1954, one son - Jason; Bobby Louis, born 1956, two children - Robbie and Michelle; Allen Wayne, born 1957, two children - Misty and Connie Wayne; and Carl Anthony, born 1967.

Betty married second to Carl Trent (1-7-1918 - 1-4-1981). They had one child, Carla Frances, born 3-8-1974 in Woodford County.
Submitted By: Carla Trent.

MARY MARGARET COLLINS JACKSON

MARY MARGARET COLLINS JACKSON was born on 2-28-1936 in Hazard, KY. Mary Margaret Collins Jackson is the daughter of Earl Collins (2-11-1909 - 3-4-1974) and Margaret Baker Collins (born 11-11-1911). They were married in Scott County, KY on 11-29-1934. Earl and Margaret Collins were the parents of two children: Mary Margaret and Dr. Bill Collins. Bill was born on 1-8-1938 in Hazard, KY. He married Martha Layne Hall on 7-3-1959 in Shelby County. she was born on 12-7-1936 in Shelby County. Earl and Margaret were both school teachers in Perry, Woodford, and Jefferson Counties.

Mary Margaret Collins Jackson and Grandchildren

Mary Margaret Collins married James R. Jackson on 6-1-1979 in Jessamine County. He was born on 4-30-1936 in Burgin, KY. James is a member of the Lexington Model Airplane Club. Mary Margaret is a member of the Frankfort Chapter of D.A.R. and both are members of Lex Singles Square Dance Club.

Mary Margaret Collins is the mother of four children: David McGohon, born 5-13-1955; Mark McGohon, born 6-15-1959; Robert McGohon, born 10-5-1961; and Nancy McGohon, born 3-23-1965.

Mary Margaret moved to Anderson County with her husband in February of 1989. They reside on Dan Street in Lawrenceburg.

Mary Margaret's ancestors were in Anderson County as early as 1827. Some include: Robert Collins and his wife, Mildred (Rev.) (Old Carl Wilson Farm); Thomas Collins and Mary Ann Bourne (War of 1812) (old Garret Farm, Hwy 151); Robert Elliott Collins and Permelia Lane; Edward and Rhoda Lane (Rev.) (Lane's Mill Road); Garland Lane and Elizabeth McBrayer (War of 1812) (Ninevah); James McBrayer and Naomi Hendricks; James McBrayer and Jane Montgomery (parents of above) came to Kentucky in 1782. *submitted By: Mary Margaret Collins Jackson.*

STANDLEY JEFFERIES

STANDLEY JEFFERIES, the son of Landon and Linda Jefferies, was born on 6-9-1899 in Anderson County. He married Lillian Burke on 1-5-1916 in Anderson County. She was born on 2-8-1901 in Anderson County. She was the daughter of Will and Judith Burke. Standley and Lillian were the parents of three sons: Kenneth (1919 - 1988) married Paulean Jefferies; James; and Coleman (born 1927) married Glenda Jeffries. Standley Jeffries died on 3-10-1966 in Louisville, KY and Lillian Jefferies died on 12-16-1981 in Louisville.

James Jeffries was born on 2-6-1921 in Glensboro, KY. He married Kathleen Grubbs on 7-28-1954. She was born on 5-4-1936 in Anderson County. She is the daughter of Gilbert Grubbs and Bertha Sea Grubbs. James and Kathleen are the parents of two daughters: Patricia (born 1956) married Ronald Eugene Grigsby - three children - Junior, Sue Ann, and Dale; and Vivian (born 1953) married Allen Noris Ritchey. James Jeffries died on 3-4-1982 in Frankfort, KY.

Gilbert Grubbs, the son of Clyde and Lucy Grubbs, was born on 9-12-1913 in Anderson County. He married Bertha Sea on 10-2-1936. She was born on 9-22-1915 in Anderson County, the daughter of John and Cora Sea. Gilbert and Bertha were the parents of nine children: Kathleen; David (born 1946) married Lucy Grubbs; Martha (born 1946) married Jerrie

Boblit; Caralen (born 1947) married Jimmy Natherly; Mary (born 1948) married Gary Terrell; Eugene (1949 - 1951); Marcella (born 1953) married Jerrie Devine; Debbie (born 1955) married Roger Richardson; and Daniel (born 1959). Gilbert Grubbs died on 12-13-1970 in Lexington, KY. *Submitted By: Junior Grigsby.*

EDWARD JEFFRIES

EDWARD JEFFRIES, the son of Willis Jeffries, was born on 12-25-1873. He married Lula Shely. She was born on 11-22-1875 and was the daughter of Thomas Shely. Edward was a sheriff of Anderson County in the 1930's. He was also a veterinarian and school teacher. Ed and Lula were the parents of four children: Roy (1902 - ?) married Zelma Gritton - he was buried in Mercer County; Atwood (1907 - 1984) married Ethel Lawrence - he was buried in the Lawrenceburg Cemetery; Margie, born 9-28-1910, married John W. Carlton; and Ralph T. (below). Ed died on 6-8-1946 and Lula died on 3-26-1963. Both are buried in the Shely Graveyard in Anderson County.

Ralph Thomas Jeffries was born on 12-11-1912 in Anderson County. Ralph has been a carpenter in Anderson County and has been married three times. He married 1st Margie A. Hardin on 5-31-1950 in Anderson County. She was born on 2-7-1912 in Anderson County. She was the daughter of John W. Hardin (1886 - 1966) and Alta F. Hoskins Hardin (1889 - 1971). Ralph and Margie had three children: William Ralph (below); Eva Marie, born 5-8-1932, married 1st Charles Pierce, 2nd Marvin Haeberlin; and Frances Doris "Louise", born 10-9-1934, married 1st Richard Colston, 2nd Gene Giles. Margie Hardin Jeffries died on 11-15-1950 in Anderson County. She was buried in the Friendship Church cemetery.

Ralph remarried on 6-14-1952 to Pearl Briscoe. they had no children. Ralph and Pearl were divorced. Then Ralph married Jean Searcy on 2-15-1963 in Anderson County. She was born on 3-26-1931 and is the daughter of Wade Hamilton Searcy. They had one daughter, Emma Loula, born on 5-20-1964. She married Gary Waldridge. Ralph and Jean reside in Anderson County.

William Ralph Jeffries was born on 5-7-1931 in Anderson County. He married Ida Roberts Chowning on 10-23-1953 in Anderson County. She was born on 3-20-1932 in Nelson County, KY and is the daughter of Lester Chowning (1896 - 1972) and Addie E. Bennett Chowning. William and Ida are the parents of seven children: Theresa Marie, born 8-7-1954, married John Thomas Tindall; Regina Gayle, born 8-24-1955, married 1st Ronnie Bast, 2nd Jimmy Campbell, 3rd Allen Taylor; Marjorie Beryle, born 5-12-1957, married Robert Lewis Best; Ruth Ellen, born 5-22-1959, married Richard Allen Soard; Tina Louise, born 3-7-1962, married Ricky Wayne Doss - divorced; William Scott, born 2-25-1964, married Elizabeth Ann Brown; and Melissa Gay, born 4-2-1967, married Patrick Howard Cox. *Submitted By: John Tindall.*

ED JENKINS

ED JENKINS was born on 11-14-1885 in Springfield, Kentucky. He was the son of Ervan Jenkins (1860 - 1930) and Betty Bryant (1859 - 1916). He was a farmer and died on 10-9-1962 in Willisburg. On 12-4-1903, he married Elsie Dora Armstrong. She was born on 8-10-1885 in Bardstown, KY and died on 6-5-45 in Willisburg. Ed and Elsie were the parents of seven children: Purdom married Hazel Jenkins; Ophia married Claude Wells; Everett married Helen Jenkins; George (below); Vallis (1914 - 1918); Truman married Grace Jenkins; and Reba married Cecil Coulter.

George Wilson Jenkins was born on 3-9-1911 in Willisburg, KY. He died on 4-30-1987 in Anderson County. On 5-17-1931, he married Alta Mae Shewmaker. She was born on 11-6-1910 in Willisburg. She was the daughter of Marvin "Dee" Shoemaker and Arzella Thompson. She died on 11-30-1986 in Anderson County. George and Alta were the parents of seven children: Kathleen married (?) Carlton; Carolyn (1933 - 1933); G. W. (below); Teddy married Sharon Jenkins; Brenda married Hurburt Clark;

Ronne J. (1947 - 1987); and Janet married Charles Lake.

G. W. Jenkins was born on 10-21-1940 in Franklin County. He married Shirley Ann Drury. She is the daughter of William Fredrick Drury (1915 - 1945) and Margaret Grace Wilham. Shirley has two sisters and one brother: Mary J. married Roy O. Carter; Emma J. married Ray Caldwell; and William O. (1935 - 1979) married Mary A. Davenport. G. W. and Shirley are the parents of seven children. They are: Ronnie, Nathan Bowen, Danette married Timothy Byrd, Melissa, Lori married Donald Corn, G. W. II "Chucky", and April. Shirley and all her children were born in Lawrenceburg. *Submitted By: Chucky Jenkins.*

WILLIAM JEWELL, son of William and Ann Tabitha Jewell was born September 1774 in Maryland. He came to Kentucky before 1800 and married Margaret Pantier, daughter of Philip and Susannah Pantier, April 15, 1795 in Mercer County, KY. Philip Pantier served with the Lincoln County, VA (now KY) Militia in 1782. In 1819, William Jewell bought a tract of land in Franklin County (now Anderson County), KY on Salt River about a mile above Anderson City, Kentucky. His older brother, Basil Jewell, owned a farm in Anderson County, on Hammonds Creek, where he was living when he died in 1842.

After the death of his first wife, William Jewell married Mrs. Eleanor Cromwell, in 1831 daughter of Rhodaham Petty in 1831, who was his neighbor. He was still living on Salt River when he died in 1848. His children, all born to his first wife, are as follows:

1) Elizabeth Jewell born 1797, married Nathaniel Cox and they moved to Morgan County, Illinois, ca 1820, where they continued to live raising a large family.

2) Susannah Jewell born 1799, married Edward M. Sherwood and they made their home on Salt River in Anderson County. They are the ancestors of the Sherwood family in Anderson County.

3) Sarah Jewell born 1802, married Henry Miller and they were living in Morgan County, Illinois in 1850.

4) Tabitha Jewell born 1806, married James I. Daviess and they were also living in Morgan County, Illinois.

5) William Jewell born 1809, died young.

6) John P. Jewell born 1811, married Martha Ann Casson, daughter of Isaac Casson. John P. died 1843 or 1844 in Anderson County, KY, leaving a wife and three small children.

7) Martha Ann Jewell born 1814, married William Stephens. She died in 1841 and left a daughter, Elizabeth Stephens who was in Morgan County, Illinois in 1850. *Submitted By: Hugh Hawkins.*

FLOYD LYNDELL JOHNSON, the son of Floyd Lyndell Johnson and Elenor Sue McCoy, was born on 5-19-1952 in Louisville, Ky. He has three brothers and one sister: John Allen married Lis Underwood - three children - Lavenus, Johnason, and Hason; David Ryan married Kathy Marshall - one daughter - Melissa; Susan Marie married Raymond Perkins - three daughters - Beverly Jo, Hope, and Katrina; and Charles Robert married Kathy Thacker - three children - Rose, Jessica, and Joseph.

Floyd married Janet Mae Peach on 12-31-1972 in Anderson County. She was born on 7-28-1954 in Shelby County, KY. She is the daughter of Walter Everett Peach (1923 - 1987) and Virginia Fay Barnett (1928 - 1978). Janet has nine brothers and sisters: Everett married Jean Hawkins - three children - Katrina, Henry, and Bradley; Darlene married Ray Searcy - two children - Sue and Ray; Marlene married Willis Hawkins - two children - Willis and Elizabeth; Terry married Carol Hurst - one son - Terry; Margaret Ellen married Henry Reynolds - two children - Krista and Jeremy; Donna married Bill Leigh - two children - Christopher and Jennifer; Darrell - two children - Tonya and Darnell; Mike

married Darlene H. (?); and Doren Doyle married Ellie Hunter - two children - Roger and Justin.

Floyd and Janet are the parents of three children: Floyd Jr., Margaret Ellen (1975 - 1978), and Sharon Lynn. *Submitted By: Sharon Johnson.*

EZEKIEL LOWRY KAYS was born February 1, 1870 in Anderson County and died July 31, 1959. He was the son of James William and Sarilda Hendricks Kays. Lowry came from a long line of farmers.

On March 3, 1892 in Anderson County, Lowry married Lora Anna Stratton. She was born April 14, 1874 in Anderson County and died July 5, 1968. She was the daughter of David Crockett and Sarah Cole Stratton.

Lowry and Lora had eight children; Madie (stillborn), Elmer (born 1895, died 1897), William Jesse (who married Emma Frances Peyton), David Leslie (who married Elmer Anderson), Amos (born 1903, died 1907), Onie Edna (who married Robert Lowe), Naomi Goldie "Noma" (who married Charles Curtis Fallis, and S. Lenora (who married Alvin L. Gregory).

Lowry's father, James William Kays Jr., was the son of James William and Lucretia King Kays. He was born December 1844 in Anderson County and died in 1935. On May 24, 1866 in Anderson County, James Jr. married Sarilda Richey Hendricks, the daughter of Ezekiel Lowry and Mary Jane Strange Hendricks. Sarilda was born February 14, 1844 in Woodford County, KY and died September 30, 1918 in Anderson County. They had 12 children; James Burton (who married Mary Lee Stratton), Druie Porter (who married Ora Sharp), Ezekiel Lowry, Lena River (who married John Strange), Charles Milton (who married Laura B. Stratton), Mary Jane (who married William E. Robinson), William Ezra (who married Stella Powell), Edgar (born 1879, died 1881), Chester (who married Bula Morrow), John Holly (who married Gladys Lucille Venable), Clyde Evert (who married Blanche Edwards), and Ida (who married Wallace Rogers).

The Kays family came to Kentucky in the early 1700's. There have been Kays' in the area since before the county was formed. There are many descendants of this family still living in Anderson County today. *Submitted By: Denise Wilder.*

ALLEN BECKMAN "BECK" LAFOE was born on January 19, 1902 in Woodford County; he was the son of Thomas Lafoe (1871 - 1948) and Pearl Jett Lafoe (1875 - 1912) and was the oldest of four children. Two sisters: Mary Bush (1905 - 1979) married Lindsay Watkins and Irene Ruby (1907) married Sam Roberts; one brother, John Jett (1909 - 1944) married Jannie Hatchell.

Beck's first marriage of January 15, 1920 was to Mary Belle Shouse (1905 - 1955), daughter of Samuel Shouse and Martha Sargracy Shouse and they were the parents of nine children.

Emma Louise (1921) married Virgil Howe in 1937. Two daughters: Brenda Ann Howe Pratt and Donna Carol Howe Wood.

Allen B. Lafoe, Jr. (1924) married Kathleen Nicholson in 1945. Four children: Gene Allen, John Lee, Dianne Frances Lafoe Rose and Paul Douglas.

Donald Gilbert (1927 - 1930)

Mary Elizabeth (1930) married Robert Atkins in 1950. Three children: Joseph Allen, Cathy Marie, and Karen Elizabeth Atkins Wagoner.

Patricia Ann (1933) married James Ward in 1953. Three sons: Michael Keith, Thomas Allen, and James Newton.

Charles Bradford (1935) married Christine Beckham in 1958. Two children: Deborah Anne Lafoe Slatten and Charles Beckham.

Della Joyce (1938) married Ronald Rose in 1956. Two daughters: Mary Pearl Rose Hallahan and Patricia Nell Rose Martinez. Teresa (1941) married Vernon Ray Chadwell in 1963. Five children: Vernon Ray, Jr., Kimberly Anne, Lori Lee, Sharon Kaye, and Mary Jo.

Allen Beckham "Beck" and Elizabeth Lafoe

David Marshall (1943) married Pamela Simpson in 1966. Two children: David Anthony and Carrie Elizabeth.

On July 8, 1957, Beck's second marriage was to Elizabeth Belle Foster (1922), daughter of John P. Foster (1895 - 1974) and Katie M. Lippert Foster (1897 - 1975). One daughter from this marriage, Katherine Pearl, born and died August 26, 1961.

Mr. Beck, as he was best known, was a resident of Anderson County a number of years and known by many people. Three of his ten children were born in Anderson County.

He spent most of his life working and living on the Kentucky River in Anderson and Woodford Counties. He learned to know what to expect from the river in all stages; whether it was at poll stage or flood level, and had a respect for it at both levels.

Before the bridge was built at Tyrone, he operated the ferry at Clifton between Anderson and Woodford Counties for B.F. Hughes. In 1946, he purchased the business from Mr. Hughes and for twenty years was owner and operator of Clifton Boat Livery.

After selling the boat dock in Woodford County, Beck and Elizabeth opened a business on Court Street in Lawrenceburg known as Lawrenceburg Marine. It was during this time that Mr. Beck was commissioned a Kentucky Admiral by Gov. Wendell H. Ford. In 1976, Beck retired within a few months of being age 75 and the business was sold to a son, Charles "Brad" Lafoe which at this date (1989) is still in operation. When he died November 2, 1988, he was survived by his wife, Elizabeth F. Lafoe, eight children, 23 grandchildren, 25 great grandchildren, 3 great great grandchildren, and one sister. *Submitted By: Elizabeth F. Lafoe.*

LAWRENCE Some members of this pioneer family came into what is now Central Kentucky as early as 1776. An article published in the Washington County Historical Series lists a deposition given by John McMurray in 1815. McMurray says that in the year 1776 that he and 11 others were piloted from Harrodsburg by William McAfee to the waters off the Rolling Fork River. Among those named in the deposition were Samuel Lawrence, John Lawrence, David Lawrence, Solomon Lawrence, and their brother-in-law, James Cloyd.

In the year 1780, William Lawrence was one of 500 pioneers who signed a petition to the Virginia Legislature regarding the issuance of land grants which often interfered with land claims of the established settlers. (Register of Kentucky Historical Society 1912).

Lincoln County marriage bonds record the marriage of Sarah Lawrence to William Crow in November of 1781. Sarah was the daughter of James Lawrence, a Danville silversmith. The 1801 will of James Lawrence shows that he was the father of the above listed David, John, Samuel, Solomon, William and Sarah Lawrence Crow. It further shows him to be the father of Elizabeth Lawrence Arbuckle, Janet Cloyd; also Isaac, Joseph and Robert Lawrence.

The Lincoln County survey book lists a survey of 780 acres for William Lawrence joining his settlement right (usually 400 acres). This indicates that William was in the county by 1778.

The will of William Logan names his daughter Mary Lawrence. She appears to have been the wife of William Lawrence. Deed and other records show that William and Mary had several children. Among them were William Lawrence Jr. and Samuel Lawrence. William Jr. married Annie Arbuckle in 1810. Samuel Lawrence married Fanny Arbuckle.

Deed records show that William Lawrence Sr. owned 340 acres near Danville. This land was sold and the family bought land on Logan's Creek near Stanford. Mary died in 1800 and William Sr. then married Jane Barnett. William bought land in Washington County prior to his death in 1806.

William's son, William Jr. remained in Lincoln County until 1810 when he and Annie moved to Franklin County. Annie was the daughter of Samuel Arbuckle. William Jr. and his father-in-law were instrumental in the founding of Lawrenceburg. Deed records of Franklin County show 22 land transactions involving William Jr.

John Lawrence, uncle of William Jr. also owned land in Franklin County where his will appears in the 1813 records. John owned land in several counties.

William Lawrence Jr. was a man of considerable means. He was a builder and owned a brick yard, a hotel, and a tavern. In this tavern was posted a sign "Don't Give Up the Ship." These were the famous words of Captain James Lawrence, Commander of the Chesapeake.

We must remember that Anderson County wasn't created until 1827. It was created from parts of Washington, Franklin, and Mercer Counties. Thus anyone wishing to do genealogical research prior to that time should consult Lincoln, Mercer, Franklin, and Washington County records.

Anyone wishing additional information of the Lawrences and Arbuckles may consult my book, "A KENTUCKY PIONEER FAMILY — THE LAWRENCES AND THEIR KIN", or they can contact James R. Lawrence, 1388 Cedar Grove Road, Deatsville, KY 40013. *submitted By: James R. Lawrence.*

THOMAS JEFFERSON LEATHERS

THOMAS JEFFERSON LEATHERS was born January 3, 1859 and died July 15, 1936. He was better known as Tom Jeff, short for Thomas Jefferson. He married Fannie Ensor and they had three sons and one daughter. The sons were Arvin, Grover Ray, and Smither. The daughter was Nora who married Richard Phillips. Arvin had one son, Ray Johnson and a daughter, Sarah Francis. Grover Ray married Otha Blockson. They had one son, Thomas Richard and two daughters, Ruby and Virginia. Smither had a daughter, Helen, and a son, Thomas Smither. Nora had three sons, Sidney, Allen Thomas, and Richard Jr. She had two daughters, Fannie Mildred and Jessie Mae.

Tom Jeff's father, Alfred was an abolitionist at the time of the Civil War. He had the house built and made his home at the present Waterfill Art Flowers on Highway 62. It was an "underground railroad station" and at that time had a secret ladder that led into a hidden room in part of the attic space. Runaway slaves hid there. There was also a secret passage to use for a quick get-a-way through the kitchen to a

tunnel that led some distance from the house. Alfred was the son of Nicholas, one of two brothers who came from Liverpool, England as a very young man. The two, Nicholas and Barnebas, first stopped in Virginia but soon moved into Kentucky to settle in the part of Anderson County around Friendship Church area, the intersection of Kays Road and Leathers Road and the area between them.

T.J. Leathers (on left) and family members - Funeral of Fanny Leathers

Tom Jeff was an educator and was Superintendent of schools in Anderson County at the time that Western High School was founded. Mr. Ezra Sparrow, one of the best teachers at that time, taught the first classes in 1925 - 1926 in an old storebuilding nearby while the four-room frame building with a central hall running from front to the back was being built on parts of the farms owned by Ray Leathers and Richard Blockson. Mrs. Rhoda Kavanaugh, who was principal of the only county high school, gave Tom Jeff encouragement and said she thought that the children in that part of the county deserved a chance to go beyond "grammar" school. Since very few families were financially able to board their children and send them to high school in Lawrenceburg, Tom Jeff worked faithfully to achieve this goal. By the fall of 1926 the building was completed and served the youth until it was replaced by the modern brick building.

Tom Jeff lived to see the first graduating class of 1929 as well as several more including the graduation of one of his grandchildren and namesake, Thomas Richard, in 1933. Tom Jeff is also remembered as an active member of the First Baptist Church in Lawrenceburg and a faithful worker in Sunday School.

He is buried with his wife and all his children in a family plot in the Lawrenceburg Cemetery. *Submitted By: Ruby Leathers Evans.*

ROBERT (BOB) NEWTON LOCKHART

ROBERT (BOB) NEWTON LOCKHART and Myrtle Irene Toll were lifelong resident of Anderson County. Robert, the eldest son of John T. and Mildred (Neal) Lockhart, was born on the family farm near Ninevah in 1874 and lived there for over 80 years. Myrtle Irene, daughter of Charles C. and Margaret (Tucker) Toll, was born in 1876 at the Toll farm on the Wildcat Road.

Bob Lockhart and Myrtle Toll were married in 1900. Their four children were born in the log cabin on the back of the farm near the Jenny Lillard Road. They later built a "new" house just off the Ninevah-Clifton Road. The children were: Frank Peak (1902 - 1946); Lenora Agnes (1904 - 1980); Margaret Lee (1907 -), Mrs. Irvin Sims; and Mildred Louise (1911 -), Mrs Charles Boggess.

Frank was a bachelor and lived as a farmer on the family farm his entire life.

Agnes graduated from Eastern State Teachers College and taught in county grade schools for over 30 years. She began her teaching career at Fairview, and later taught at Rutherford, Glensboro, Ninevah and Tyrone. After her retirement from teaching, she worked for the state in Frankfort.

Margaret earned a teaching certificate from Eastern State Teachers College and taught in grade schools

Robert Newton Lockhart and Myrtle Irene Toll

throughout the county. She reared five children after her marriage to Irvin Sims, and then continued her teaching career as the 5th grade teacher at Sand Spring School until her retirement in 1969.

Mildred married Charles Boggess. After a few years outside the county, they returned to rear their five children on farms on the Lock 5 Road and later on Hammonds Creek Road.

During their 38 years, Bob and Myrtle Lockhart were typical of the basic stock of Anderson County - life was lived on the farm and attending their church, Ninevah Christian, making occasional trips to Lawrenceburg to get things they couldn't produce on the farm, and seldom traveling elsewhere. Myrtle died on the farm in 1938. Bob moved to Lawrenceburg in the late 1950's and lived on Saffell Court until his death in 1962. Both are buried in the Lawrenceburg Cemetery, as are Frank and Agnes. *Submitted By: Wesley Sims.*

JOHN T. LOCKHART JR.

JOHN T. LOCKHART JR. was born in 1838 in Henry County, where he worked as a carpenter before marrying Mildred R. (Neal) Campbell and moving to Anderson County in 1872. Mildred Neal was born in Anderson County in 1840, married E. P. Campbell of Henry County and moved there in 1858.

On moving to Anderson County, they acquired a farm in the Ninevah area, where they reared their three sons and Mildred's son from her previous marriage.

Their children were: Robert (Bob) Newton, 1874 - 1962, a farmer and father of Margaret (Mrs. Irvin) Sims, Mildred (Mrs. Charles) Boggess, Lenora Agnes, 1904 - 1980, and Frank Peak, 1902 - 1946.

William Thomas (Dudley), 1877 - 1960, a railroad employee who moved to Henry County, and father of Adele.

Joseph Elisha (Lish), 1878 - 1953. A farmer and father of Joseph Thomas of Iselin, New Jersey and Martha Jean of Park Hills, Kentucky.

James P. Campbell, 1863 - 1909, Mildred's son, a farmer and father of Frances (Mrs. Klien) Campbell Vowels and Willie Campbell.

John and Mildred lived on their farm near Ninevah for the remainder of their lives and are buried in the Lockhart family cemetery on the back of the farm. *Submitted By: Wesley Sims.*

McALISTER

McALISTER Any history of Anderson County should include the McAlisters who came to Kentucky shortly after it became a state. Six generations of one line of the descendants of Bartlett McAlister have lived in Anderson, members of three generations remain in Kentucky, and others still call it home.

Bartlett, his wife Elizabeth (Betsy) Robinson McAlister, and their son, Allen, came to the section which was later called Anderson County, from Westmoreland County, Virginia. He had acquired extensive holdings on Gilbert's Creek where he built his home. He died and was buried at the "home place".

Col. Allen N. McAlister married Frances Egbert. He bought a considerable tract of land lying between Ripyville and Gilbert's Creek upon which he erected a distillery and a mill of the primitive type and operated both successfully until after the Civil War. He built his home near McCall's Spring, but all trace of the home and the family cemetery have vanished. One of his daughters was Eliza Jane.

Eliza Jane McAlister married John Howard Carr on Christmas Eve, 1857. Their daughter was Frances Lisbeth.

Frances Lisbeth Carr married James Thompson Bailey and lived at McBrayer in a big, old farmhouse which she referred to as "my only home". After his death in 1920, "Miss Fannie', as she was known to all her friends, and their only child, John Mitchell, ran the farm. She taught English at Lawrenceburg High School until her retirement in 1937. A dedicated teacher, she was determined that her students would learn literature, correct grammar, spelling, and word usage which they did. She died in 1949 shortly before her 82nd birthday.

John Mitchell "Mitch" Bailey II married Mary Elizabeth Toll, the only child of Dr. James Leslie and Julia Morton Sweasy Toll. Mitch was a rural mail carrier and an avid sportsman. They remained on the farm with their children, Frances Lisbeth, and John Mitchell III until 1939, when the entire family including Miss Fannie's companion of some 25 years, Miss Susie Hayden, moved into Lawrenceburg. The following year Mitch died.

Frances Lisbeth Bailey married Robert Curtis Baxter and had three daughters: Susan Ellen (1949 - 1965), Kay Tinsley, and Jill Whitton. She later married James David Carr and moved to Maryland where she worked for the federal government until her retirement in 1987. They now live in North Carolina. John Mitchell Bailey III, better known as Mitch, married Martha Jane Skaggs and lives in Shelbyville. Mitch taught school and coached for more than 30 years and now spends every spare moment on the golf course. Their children are John Mitchell IV, who lives in Arizona and Lisa Jane (Mrs. Dale Shuck) who lives in Virginia.

Kay Tinsley Baxter (Mrs. Ben Gleaton) is an army wife and lives in Vine Grove. Jill Whitton Baxter has made a career in the communications industry. She lives in Pennsylvania.

Benjamin Jay Gleaton, Jr., was born in Germany and David Curtis Gleaton was born at Fort Benning, Georgia. The seventh generation descendants of Bartlett McAlister, neither is a native Kentuckian but both have spent the majority of their lives here and call it home. *Submitted By: Frances B. Carr.*

HARVEY S. McBRAYER was born on 2-31-1854 in Lawrenceburg, KY. He married Mattie A. Wash on 3-14-1878 in Lawrenceburg. She was born on 5-3-1860 and died on 8-12-1942. They had a son, Lucien A. McBrayer, born 9-12-1884 in Lawrenceburg. Harvey S. McBrayer died on 9-25-1938.

Lucien A. McBrayer married Mary Cunningham on 12-25-1915 in Lawrenceburg. She was born on 11-12-1896 in Woodford County and was the daughter of Sammuel Cunningham and Louise Meyers Cunningham. Lucien and Mary had a son, Harvey Samuel McBrayer on 1-2-1917 in Lawrenceburg. Lucien died on 12-30-1953 and Mary died on 11-28-1977.

Harvey Samuel McBrayer served aboard a ship during World War II in the Merchant Marines. After the war, he was employed at Universal Fasteners until he retired at age 65. He married Agnes Collins on 1-10-1940 in Lawrenceburg. She was born on 7-21-1919 in Lawrenceburg and is the daughter of James D. Collins Sr. and Nannie Rachel McBrayer Collins. Harvey and Agnes are the parents of two daughters: Janice McBrayer, born 1942, married Darrell Clark; and Mary Elizabeth McBrayer, born 1949, married David Clark. Darrell and David are brothers.

James David Collins Sr., the son of Ezra Freeman Collins (1843 - ?) and Martha Redden Collins (1846 - 1923), was born on 6-16-1882 in Lawrenceburg. He married Nannie Rachel McBrayer on 12-14-1911 in Lawrenceburg. She was born on 4-22-1883 in Lawrenceburg. She was the daughter of John C. McBrayer and Mary A. Dawson. James and Nannie were the parents of six children: Hazel Collins married P. D. Boone; J.D. Collins married Martha Brandenburg; Eleanor Collins - never married; Agnes Collins McBrayer; Ellis Collins married Marguerite Martin; and Dane Collins married Betty Cunningham. *Submitted By: Chad Clark.*

ROY L. McBRAYER AND JANE MURPHY.
Roy was born 30 July 1919, in Lawrenceburg, Kentucky. His mother, Leona Huffaker, born 29 October 1890, in Wayne County, Kentucky. Moved with her parents to Lawrenceburg, Kentucky about 1900. She married on 20 September 1916 to Ezra McBrayer. Ezra's father was John C. McBrayer who lived at "Ripplewood" in Anderson County. Ezra worked for the Anderson National Bank as a book-keeper, teller, and cashier. Leona died 1 August 1919, two days after Roy was born. Ezra and Roy moved into the home of Roy's grandparents, Budette and Helen Huffaker, who lived at 239 North Main Street, Lawrenceburg, Kentucky. Burdette was killed in 1923, and Ezra died, unexpectedly, in 1925. Leona's sister, Flonnie, with her family of Alex Farris, and four children, then moved in with Flonnie's mother.

Roy progressed through the Lawrenceburg School systems, graduating from the Lawrenceburg High School in 1937. He received his Bachelor of Science degree from the University of Kentucky, August 1941 where he was a member of Delta Chi Fraternity. He immediately went into the Marine Corps during World War II, serving from January 1942 to January 1946 in the South Pacific Theater. He rose to the rank of Captain, earning 3 Battle Stars and 2 Presidential Unit Citations.

Roy married Jane Humphry of Bloomfield, Kentucky, and accepted a position with Jane's father in the hardware business in Bloomfield. In 1950, he was recalled to the Marines during the Korean Conflict, still a Captain, and was assigned to the Training Division in Carolina and Virginia. He returned to the hardware business in Bloomfield, where he worked until he sold out in 1985. From 1966 to 1976, Roy also served as the Mayor of Bloomfield. He obtained and oversaw the installation of a city wide sewer and water system.

In 1971, Roy joined the United States Coast Guard Auxiliary, working on the Ohio River and later, Taylorsville Lake, after it was opened to boating. He rose to the rank of Division Captain. Roy and Jane had no children.

PHILLIP McCORMICK JR., the son of Phillip McCormick (1915 - 1969) and Dora Harvey McCormick, was born on 5-17-1949 in Lexington, KY. He has one brother, Larry McCormick, who married Claudina Klinker McCormick.

Phillip met Jeanie Umberger while she was in college. They fell in love but the illness of Jeanie's mother kept them from being married. Jeanie was born on 10-21-1949 in Wytheville, Virginia. She was the daughter of Orville Umberger and Mable Sage Umberger (1927 - 1974). She had one brother and one sister: Jerry Umberger married Beth Turner; and Pattie Umberger married Jim Stanley.

Phillip and Jeanie were married on 6-13-1971 in Ashland, KY. They moved to Frankfort, KY. Jeanie found work with Investor's Heritage Life Insurance Company and Phillip found work with the Kentucky State Police Crime Lab. While living in Frankfort, they had their first child, Stacy Lynn McCormick, born on 1-23-1975. They decided to move to Anderson County, because it was close to Frankfort. While living in Anderson County, they had their second child, Shelly Jean McCormick, born on 11-22-1976.

After having Shelly, scientists detected a disease in Jeanie's heart. Being a strong and proud person, Jeanie didn't let this stop her. She led an active life with the church and her family. Unfortunately, her life came to an end on 11-1-1988. Her heart just gave out. She will be greatly missed. *Submitted By: Stacy McCormick.*

McBRAYER The first generation of McBrayers in America was a William McBrayer who came from Scotland. His grandson, also William, was one of the trail blazers led across the mountains from Virginia by James Harrod in 1775. His description of the blue grass led his parents to emigrate to Lincoln County, one of the three original counties in Kentucky. In 1795, this William moved to what was then part of Franklin County, now Anderson County. There has been a William McBrayer in most every generation since, now the 10th generation. Louise and Agnes McBrayer, twins, unmarried, the eighth generation are now the only McBrayers of this branch still residing in Anderson County. Their father, William Stewart McBrayer, (7-6-1886 - 10-26-1952) lived all of his life in Anderson County. He was born and spent his childhood on a farm near Clifton, called Indian Territory, later moving nearer Lawrenceburg on the Ninevah Road. The house built by his father, John C. McBrayer, in the early 1900's, still stands and has been owned by some of the John C. McBrayer heirs until just recently. William was married to Ramsey Fidler (3-20-1887 - 2-24-1982) who was also a native of Anderson County, and whose family were early settlers. They had five children: Preston Blakemore McBrayer (12-31-1909 - 5-8-1978); Stewart Fidler McBrayer (born 12-7-1910) married to Eleanor McGinnis and live in Shelbyville, KY; Louise McBrayer (born 3-11-1912); Agnes McBrayer (born 3-11-1912); Garey McBrayer Pennington (born 7-22-1916) lives in Frankfort, KY.

Blakemore married Virginia Driscol - three sons: William Ronald, born 5-4-1938, resides in West Palm Beach, FL; Jerry D., born 6-24-1940, resides in Georgetown, KY; and Gary Blakemore McBrayer, born 3-4-1949, resides in Greensboro, NC. William Ronald McBrayer married Norma Adkins - two children: William Patrick McBrayer, born 6-18-1961, and Barbara Ellen McBrayer, born 11-2-1970. Gary Blakemore McBrayer was married to Marcia Smith - three children: Kelly Brooke, born 10-23-1977; Jennie Diane, born 5-30-1981; and Jason Andrews, born 8-24-1984. Stewart McBrayer and Eleanor McGinnis McBrayer have two children: William Stewart McBrayer, born 1-24-1947 - Charlotte, NC - married Laura Cunningham - one daughter, Kelly Elizabeth, born 7-4-1983; and Jennie Ruth McBrayer, born 2-3-1952 married to George Lynch - Elizabethtown, KY - two sons: Eric William Lynch, born 4-23-1980, and Michael Stewart Lynch, born 3-12-1982.

Garey McBrayer Pennington married to Owen Wilmoth - one daughter, Eleanor Owen Wilmoth, born 8-10-1938. After Owen Wilmoth's death, Garey married Charles Pennington. Eleanor Owen was married to Terrett Teague. She has two sons: Terrett McBrayer Teague, born 9-12-1968, and Addison Emery Teague, born 2-13-1972. They live in Columbia, MO. *Submitted By: Garey M. Pennington.*

WESLEY TAYLOR McCOUN known as W. T., whose parents were Leslie B. McCoun married to Loretta Drury. They had four children being: Leslie Jr. (died at ten days), Wesley Taylor, Bobby Allen, and Donald Gene. Leslie's parents were Taylor Scott McCoun married to Blanche Montgomery. They had two sons and four daughters. They owned and farmed land on McCoun's Ferry Road in Mercer County.

Loretta Drury McCoun's parents were Wesley Moton Drury married to Anna Skelton. They had six children.

W. T. attended Anderson County schools and graduated from Kavanaugh High in 1948. Following high school he went to work for Charley E. McGinnis at Lawrenceburg Supply Company. In 1950 and 1951, he was inducted into the U.S. Army and trained at Fort George G. Meade, Maryland, for the 3rd

Armored Calvary Regiment. After discharge from the Army, married Lillie Catherine (Kitty) Boggess. They have three children: Lynn married Larry Drury, Wesley Scott married Pat Willis, and Jennifer Ann married John H. Taylor. The grandchildren are Paul Taylor, Russ Allen, and Crystal M. Drury; Wesley Scott, Thomas Matthew McCoun, Jennifer Hopper Riley; Adam Lee and Paul Taylor.

W. T. and Kitty McCoun

Kitty's parents were Vernon John Boggess, married to Mary Jane Cox. They had two daughters, Lillie Catherine and Patsy Ann. Patsy married Joseph Kelly Hawkins. They had three children - Patrick Kelly, Kimberly Kathryn, and John Lee.

In 1964, the Lawrenceburg Supply Co. was bought by Philip N. Goin and William M. Horn of Frankfort. W. T. continued working there as manager. Because of increasing volume of business and interest of the area, a larger building was needed. In December 1972, a new building was completed. The old building, which was built in 1907 was torn down to enlarge the parking area. The company celebrated open house and dedicated this building to William Cavel Harris for his long and faithful service since 1923.

In 1987, the opportunity came and W. T. purchased an interest in the company and became a partner.

The Lawrenceburg Supply Company is one of the community's oldest businesses, dating back to the turn of the century when it was founded as Tyrone Lumber Company by the late William A. Bottoms. Charles E. McGinnis was a son-in-law of Mr. Bottoms. The firm now includes about a dozen employees and the prospects for growth are good. When not at the office, W. T. enjoys his grandchildren and puttering around his farm on Wildcat Road. *Submitted By: W. T. McCoun.*

McDONALD The earliest ancestor that is known in the McDonald family is Charles McDonald Sr. His parents died in their mid 40's, when both Charles and his brother, Albert, were very young. Charles McDonald Sr. was born in Frankfort, Kentucky on 5-12-1913 and died on 7-15-1973. Charles Sr. married Hallie Hale (1915 - 1976) on 4-12-1925. She was the daughter of Allen Hale and Mildred Moorson. She had five brothers and sisters: Ethel, Lena, Aileen, Clarence, and Buddy. Charles Sr. and Hallie were the parents of ten children. They are as follows: Charles Jr. (below) ; Nora married Clyde Kring - three children - Scott, Betty, and Kenny; Mary married James Bailey - five children - James Jr., Donna Michelle, Rhonda, and Vicky; Margaret married Billy Graves - four children - Sharon, Regina, Debbie, and Terry; Carolyn married Jack Early - five children - Ralph, Teresa, Ronnie, Cathy, and Timmy; Jeanette married Vernon Coleman - three children - Nancy, Nikki, and Cathy; Mildred married Eddy Greene - three children - Vikki, Buddy, and Joe; Brenda married Sidney Adams - one daughter, Missy; David married Glenna Long - one child, Chris; and Rita married Donnie Cook - two sons, Keith and Tommy.

Charles McDonald Jr. was born on 11-25-1926, in Frankfort. He lived in Frankfort until his marriage on 2-23-1950. He married Thelma Perry, a native of

Anderson County. At this time, they decided to live in Anderon County so that they could farm and raise a family. Thelma is the daughter of Leslie Perry (1892 - 1982) and Alberta Cooper Perry (1901 - 1931). She had eight brothers and sisters: Coleman (1920 - 1924); Hansel married Elizabeth Wells; Sylvia married Joe Goins; Thomas married Mina Brown; Gerald married Shirley Cunningham; Albert V. married Sue Cox; Betty married Jimmy Wright; and Linda married Jimmy Henderson.

Charles and Thelma raised five children: Linda married Stanley Searcy; Michael married Rita Stratton - two children - Leah and Hannah; Becky married Jim Morgan; Steve; and Karen married Rob Wood. *Submitted By: Leah McDonald.*

ALLIE McGAUGHEY - July 28, 1891 - May 19, 1964 married Margaret Ann "Maggie" Bercaw - July 15, 1894 - October 23, 1978.

Allie and Maggie were married August 24, 1912.

As a very young man, Allie rode a bicycle from Tyrone to Alton Station to learn to be a telegraphist. He was a telegraph operator at the Tyrone Depot for several years.

Allie and Maggie McGaughey

In 1913, he and his dad, Turner McGaughey, started Boone Way Garage. This was his true calling that lasted 50 years.

Allie and Maggie worked hard and were good citizens of Anderson County. They left a loving legacy of 3 daughters, Catherine, Garnett, and Beatrice. Five grandchildren, Carolyn, Cindy, Nancy, Turner, and Mark; and 3 great grandchildren, David, Jayne, and Brandon. *Submitted By: Beatrice Williams.*

HERBERT McGAUGHEY was born in Osborn, Ohio to Herbert and Helen Boswell McGaughey, 3-7-1925. He graduated from Kavanaugh High School in Lawrenceburg, KY. Herbert had two brothers and a sister. His brother, Bill McGaughey, also graduated from Kavanaugh High School. Herbert served in the Navy in World War II. He worked for the City of Dayton, Ohio as a welder for 30 years.

Herbert married Myrtle Louise Rowland on April 6, 1948, in Lexington, Fayette Co., KY. They have five sons: Allen Michael McGaughey; Mearl Taylor McGaughey; Paul Douglas McGaughey; Robin Lawrence McGaughey; and Mark Rowland McGaughey. Herbert and Louise have eight grandchildren.

Herbert and Louise McGaughey

For nine years, Herbert and Louise were foster parents to about 23 children.

Louise was born in Midway, KY on 8-1-1928 to Virgil Taylor Rowland and Myrtle Searcy. She moved with her parents to Tyrone, KY in 1940.

After retiring in 1977, from the City of Dayton, Herbert and Louise lived in Florida for a number of years before returning to Ohio and Kentucky.

Herbert and Louise attend the Heritage Baptist Church at Alton, Ky in Anderson County.

Herbert and Louise McGaughey reside on Dove Drive in Lawrenceburg, KY.

JOHN ALVIN AND HAZEL McGAUGHEY have lived most of their married life in Anderson County, except for two years they lived on a farm in Franklin County. John Alvin the youngest of four children of John and Margaret Thurman McGaughey. Eunice, a brother, worked at R. C. Trent's department store for years and was married to Minnie Wiley of Mercer County. They had five children: Charles (deceased), Louise lives in Frankfort, KY, Cordelia lives in North Carolina, Paul (deceased), and Carl lives in Frankfort.

Sister Rose, married Herbert Hawkins and he operated a blacksmith shop at Alton. They had four girls: Evelyn married Dean Vincent; Olga married Hanks Houchin (deceased); Margaret married Forest Marshall (deceased), and Bertha (Billie) married Kirk Fique (deceased).

Sister Iva Mae married Andrew McCray (deceased) and they had two girls: Mary Lee - never married and lives with Iva Mae. Rose married Sidney Florance and had three boys. They all live in Lexington.

Left to Right: John Alvin McGaughey Jr., Elaine Corn, John Alvin Sr., Hazel McGaughey, Wilma Flygstad, Leslie McGaughey.

Hazel was the oldest of nine living children of Henry and Lutie Ockerman Duncan. She has four sisters: Wiola, Hallie, Linda and Betty Frances; four brothers, Leslie, Joe, Howard, and Emmett.

Hazel was born in Carlisle, KY in Nicholas County. Her grandparents lived at Alton. She came to visit them and meet John Alvin McGaughey. She attended Kavanaugh High. On 3-24-1934, they were married and have farmed all their life. They bought a farm on the Bonds Mill and McBrayer Road and lived there 30 years, raising tobacco and operated a graded dairy. They have four children and all live in Anderson County: Elaine, Wilma, John Jr., and Leslie Joe. Elaine is married to Maurice Corn. Wilma is married to Dale Flygstad. John Jr. is married to Shirley Chilton and Leslie Joe is married to Barbara Gastineau. They have 17 grandchildren and 30 great-grandchildren. They have been members of Sand Spring Baptist Church since 1941 and Elaine, John Jr., and Leslie Joe are still members but Wilma is a member of Anderson Christian Church.

Elaine has three girls and two boys: Patricia, Susan, and Marla, Larry and Michael. Wilma has three girls and three boys.: Donna, Diane, Denise, David, Dennis, and Dale Jr. John Jr. has one girl, Karen, and one boy, Steven Joe. Leslie Joe had two boys and two girls: Craig, Joseph, Gloria, and Kimberly.

After the children married, farming became harder as they grew older. They sold nearly all the cows except a few and started drawing Social Security. At the end of the year, they filed their income tax and after a certain amount, Uncle Sam took dollar for dollar. John Alvin threw up the red flag and said, "That's enough, I quit farming. I worked a long time as a tenant giving half. I don't have to do that now, so I'm through." They had Glen Birdwhistell sell the farm, sold the rest of the livestock, farm machinery, etc. They bought a home in Lawrenceburg on Highland and have been there for fourteen years. On 3-24-1990, they celebrated their 56th wedding anniversary. *Submitted By: Hazel McGaughey.*

ORION COX "MAC" McKAY,

the eldest of Hugh Lacy McKay (1854 - 1888), and Myra Belle Cox (1857 - 1915), was born on 3-7-1878, at the home of his grandfather, Dr. Oridn Noel Cox (1829 - 1903), at Cox's Creek, Kentucky, in Nelson County. His maternal and paternal ancestors were pioneer families in Nelson County, having migrated from Washington, Pennsylvania, and St. Mary County, Maryland, in the late 1700's. His great-great-great-great grandfather, Colonel Issaac Cox, Jr. established Cox's Station in 1780.

After being educated at the Male and Female Institute in Bardstown, Kentucky, he went into the dry good business and later a livery business in that city. In the early 1900's he decided to move to Lawrenceburg. Upon arrival he was able to buy a partnership in the large livery stable owned by Mr. W. B. Morgan. With the popularization of automobiles and the decline of the livery business, Mr. McKay became a storekeeper gauger. In his later years, Mr. McKay became the county treasurer and Master Commissioner for Anderson County.

On St. Valentine's Day in 1907, Mr. McKay married Miss Lillian Mae Trent (10-30-1886 - 9-26-1972). The wedding took place at the home of her mother, Minnie McMurray Trent (1862 - 1938), and father, Christopher Chinn Trent (1843 - 1915), on Woodford Street. Mrs. McKay was educated in the Lawrenceburg school and graduated from Campbell-Hagerman College in Lexington, Kentucky. She taught school and for many years was an antique dealer. Mrs. McKay was active in Lawrenceburg society being an officer at various times in the DAR, Lawrenceburg Women's Club and the the Pierian Club.

To this marriage were born: Hugh Trent (1-22-1908), Nellie Bell (died shortly after birth in 1910), Lillian MaeGriggs (11-27-1912 - 3-16-1965), and Jean Conrad Goodlett (8-31-1918). Hugh McKay was a 1930 graduate of the Naval Academy. He lost a ship, the *Cassin* at Pearl Harbor, and retired from the Navy after being Commander of the Naval Shipyard in Garden City, New York. He married Marion Mannheart and they had two sons: Dr. Hugh Trent of Sacramento, California and Douglas McMurry of San Francisco. Lillian Mae attended the University of Kentucky and married Orvis Griggs. Mr. Griggs was an employee of the Orkin Exterminating Company in New Orleans, Louisiana and Richmond, Virginia. They had two sons: Dr. Thomas McKay, an ear, nose, and throat specialist in Huntsville, Alabama and Gene Conrad, a restauranteur, also in Huntsville. Jean Conrad attended Georgetown College and married William Dudley Goodlett in June 1937.

Mr. McKay was a staunch Democrat and Baptist, having entered the church at Cox's Creek Baptist Church, and was a Mason. He died at his home on South Main Street on 1-10-1955. He and Mrs. McKay are buried in the Lawrenceburg Cemetery. *Submitted By: Robert D. Goodlett.*

WILLIE B. McKEE

was born on 3-29-1913 in Lawrenceburg. He is the son of Charlie McKee and Jennie Taylor. He served in World War II from 1942 to 1945 in the army. He did guard duty, worked on stoves, and worked in the mess hall. After the war, he went to work. He washed cars at what is now White's Car Wash.

Willie married Mary B. Gray in 1940. She worked for the Hawkins family before she married. Mary B. was the daughter of Charlie and Susan M. Gray. She passed away in 1975.

Mary B. Gray had one son before her marriage to Willie B. McKee. His name is James Gray, born 2-11-1938 in Anderson County - he has three daughters, Kim, Stephanie, and Sue.

Willie and Mary were the parents of five children: William McKee, born 4-20-1942, married Janis Bean - two children -Shawana and William; Lois McKee, born 2-7-1950, - one daughter, Stacy McKee; Bonnie McKee, born 4-4-1952, married Olivet Williams - four children - Sharon, Tera, Ronnie, and Leron; Connie McKee, born 5-20-1953, one son, William; and Mary McKee, born 1-31-1954, married Sam Jackson - one son, Damon - divorced. All five children were born in Anderson County. *Submitted by: Stacy McKee.*

EDGAR CHARLES AND EDNA MAE McKENNEY

have spent most of their 55 years of married life in Anderson County.

Edna Mae, daughter of the late Coleman Luther Overstreet and Minnie Mae McCoy Overstreet, graduated from Kavanaugh High School, Lawrenceburg, and Good Samaritan School of Nursing, Lexington, Kentucky.

Edgar, son of the late Charles W. and Bessie Lee McKenney, spent his childhood years in Harrison County. He began his career of Morris Telegraphy with Southern Railroad, Lexington, Kentucky.

They were married in 1934 and have two children: a daughter, Shelby Jean and a son, Edgar Jr. Both children now live in Texas.

After working 42 years for Southern Railroad, Ed retired and they moved back to Lawrenceburg in 1970. *Submitted by: Mrs. Edna Mae McKenney*

JAMES L. MCMICHAEL,

listed in First Census of Kentucky in Lincoln County, in Franklin County in 1810 and 1820 Census, and 1830, when Anderson County formed, listed, as well, his two sons. In history of Anderson County, by Bond and McKee, there are references to him as well as his sons.

James L. and wife Ellen (?) were parents of 10 children: 1) Joseph M. married Jane McCoun 1820 in Mercer County; 2) Robert W . married Rachel Biles 11-8-1913 in Mercer County by Rev. John Penney; 3) James L., Jr. married Nancy M. Boston 1822; 4) John K. married Catherine Whalen 1813; 5) Margaret, unmarried; 6) Prudence, unmarried; 7) Joshua; 8) Fannie married James Boston (brother to Nancy) 1820 in Franklin County; 9) Elizabeth married Joseph Peyton 1811; 10) Sarah (Sally) married Milton Hanks 1823 in Franklin County. Information obtained from Anderson County Library; Wills of James L. and Margaret, and Kentucky Census Records.

James L., Jr. and Nancy Boston McMichael had 12 children: 1) Frances Jane married John B. Griffey 1851; 2) Robert Thomas married twice; 3) Joshua married Emma Oats; 4) James L. married Mary E. Smith; 5) Dixon G. married twice; 6) Benjamin H. married Mary Emiline Carter 1861; 7) Samuel married Elizabeth Alpin; 8) Thomas married; 9) John married Susan Ann (?); 10) Eliza Ann married James M. Searcy; 11) Joseph; 12) G. W. This information taken from Census Records; Griffey Genealogy; Marriage Bonds, Anderson County.

Robert H., two above, moved to Lexington in 1847, working as a clerk in a retail store, later establishing a store with McCorkle, known as McMichael and McCorkle. The site of the business is now part of the Festival Market in Lexington. He was listed in Who's Who in Kentucky. He is buried in the McMichael plot in the Lexington Cemetery together with his parents, children, and some brothers. His estate, Coolaven, was located at the end of West Sixth Street and is now a housing complex.

Benjamin H., six above, and his wife had five children: 1) Lewis T. married Alma Stratton (seven children); 2) Gilbert married Lida; 3) William, unmarried; 4) James R. married Ella Paxton, first cousin to James Cash Penny (two children); 5) John Edward married Kathryn Kramer (one child).

John Edward, five above, married Kathryn Kramer of a prominent German family in Louisville, and had one son, Robert Carl who married Zela Mae Jones. They had one daughter, Maisie Evelyn, preparer of this information.

The McMichaels migrated to Ireland in the 1600's to escape political persecution, and it is believed they came to Kentucky in the 1770's with the McCoun and McAfee families.

CHARLES McMICHAEL

The late Charles McMichael and Ella Medley were married August 5, 1933 in Lawrenceburg. He was the son of the late Lewis T. and Alma Stratton McMichael of Anderson County and life long resident of Anderson County. He has two surviving brothers, "B" and John, living in Anderson County. He worked for the City of Lawrenceburg as Water Plant Operator. An avid sportsman, he especially enjoyed fishing and hunting, as well as gardening. Ella is one of six children of the late Charles E. and Maude Casalow Medley of Mercer County. Three of her siblings, Jessie and Bessie, twins, and Bertha are deceased, Verna of Shelby County, KY and Worley of Anderson County survive. She worked at the distillery until it closed and loves her gardening and being a homemaker. She attends Sunday School and church regularly.

Their son, Davis Reed, graduate of Anderson County High School is employed by Quick Tool Manufacturing in Lexington. He married Wilma Carolyn Hanks, December 3, 1955, and they have four children. He is a golfer, as well as a gardener; and she, who is an Anderson County High School graduate, works at Austin Nichols Distillery, and enjoys crocheting, quilting, and gardening. Sons: Eric married Jean Shaken and they have two sons; Stephen and Matthew; and Martin, who married Kelly Louise Perry, also share their love of the outdoors in fishing and golfing, and both are active in church work. Their daughters are Tammy Kaye of Little Lamb Pre-School in Frankfort, and an outstanding athlete at Anderson County High School, where her sister Candido Ray (Candy) is a student and cheerleader.

JOHN G. AND NORA BROWN McMICHAEL

are life long residents of Anderson County. She was born in Woodford County, KY, the daughter of Norman Fred Brown and Mary Elizabeth Sharp. She has three brothers, two of whom are deceased, Wilbur and James, and Jesse Brown, who lives in Baltimore, Maryland, and a sister, Bonnie Beasley of Lawrenceburg. He was born in Anderson County, one of seven children of the late Lewis T. and Alma Jane Stratton McMichaels. His surviving brother, James Madison Bell, "B", lives in Anderson County, and his other siblings were William (Willie) and Charles of Lawrenceburg, Valeria Grubbs of Beech Grove, Indiana, Rhoda Lock of Acton, Indiana, and Lawrence of Beech Grove, Indiana.

He attended Salt River Grade School and worked for Kraft Foods for 31 years, and the Commonwealth of Kentucky for 10 years, having retired from both. He has an orchard and gardens on Bonds Mill Road. She attended Kavanaugh High School and has devoted her time to being a housewife, and doing handwork. They have two children, Mary Elizabeth (Betty) Heineman, and John Lewis McMichael.

Betty is married to Carl Heineman, CPA and realtor, and resides in Chattanooga, Tennessee, where she teaches music. She is a graduate of Georgetown College with Bachelors in Music Education and Trevecan Nazarene in Nashville with Masters of Education. She has taught in Michigan, Clark Air Base in the Philippines where she learned

John and Nora McMichael Golden Anniversary Reception, December 18, 1988. Sand Spring Baptist church.

to fly a single engine aircraft, Bad Kreuznach, West Germany, and Georgia. While teaching overseas she visited Russia, Istanbul, and Thailand. They have one daughter, Susan.

John Lewis, 1963 graduate of the University of Kentucky with a Bachelor of Science Degree in Civil Engineering, is Vice President of Vaughn and Melton, Engineers and Architects, with offices in Middlesboro, KY, Greenville, Tennessee, and Ashville, North Carolina. He is currently serving as Project Manager of the Cumberland Gap Tunnel Project, due to be completed in 1995. He is married and has two sons, Johnny and Danny of Harrogate, Tennessee, and one grandchild.

The McMichaels are members of Sand Spring Baptist Church and have resided on Bonds Mill Road for 47 years. Married in 1938, in Frankfort, they celebrated their 50th Anniversary in 1988 with a trip to Alaska in the summer, and a reception at Sand Spring Baptist Church on the anniversary, December 17, 1988.

JIM B. AND ARZELIA WHITE McMICHAEL,
life long residents of Anderson County, live on Bonds Mill Road where he is engaged in farming. They were married in 1940, and have no children. She is one of six children of the late Hugh William White and Eddie Johnson Boggess. Her siblings are Flora Mae Chaffin of Norwalk, California; John L. of Lexington; William S. of Lawrenceburg; Rose Frances Jordan of Fern Creek; and Houston S., deceased. He is one of seven children of the late Lewis T. and Alma Jane Stratton McMichael, and has a surviving brother, John G., living in Anderson County. They have 14 nieces, 16 nephews, 29 great-nephews and 9 great-nieces, all of whom are scattered in Kentucky, California, Oregon, Tennessee, Indiana, Washington, and Nebraska.

He attended Salt River Grade School and retired from Austin Nichols Distillery after 31 years. She worked at Old Joe and Bonds Mill, Barrett Sewing Factory and retired from Hoffman Distillery. They both attend Sand Spring Baptist Church, where she is a member of the Senior Adults, and was former member of Ladies Aid and Ladies Aid Quilters and Homemakers.

THOMAS H. McMURRY
was born April 15, 1834, in Boyle or Garrard County, Kentucky. When quite young he moved to Anderson County where he became a prominent farmer and stock trader. At the time of his death, he owned a farm in the Western part of the county.

He married three times. The first to a Miss Leather and the last to Miss Mary Bell, sister of Professor H. V. Bell. Apparently there were no children to either of these marriages. His middle wife was Latitia Elizabeth Routt Bond. Mrs. Bond had been married to Clairbourne Bond and a son, William C. Bond, born 10-3-1856.

To this union were born: Sara Bell Walker (1861 -1929), Minnie McMurray Trent (1864 - 1938), Tinsley J. (1866 - ?), Edward Lee (1869 - ?), and Frances E. (1871 - ?). All of these children were living at the time of his death.

Mr. McMurray served as justice of the peace for a number of years. Sometime in the 1870's he made a race for the democratic nomination for the General Assembly against Colonel William Neal. He was victorious but Colonel Neal bolted the nomination and defeated him in general election.

He was a member of the Christian Church and the Masonic fraternity. He died 12-26-1911.

After the funeral service at his son-in-law's home (Mr. C.C. Trent) the Anderson Lodge No. 90 F and A.M. took charge of the remains which were conveyed to the Lawrenceburg Cemetery. They were placed in a vault until a more suitable time for interment. Mr. McMurry's twin brother, Tim McMurry of Woodford County, preceded him in his death by 10 days. *Submitted By: Robert D. Goodlett.*

GEORGE D. McWILLIAMS, JR.,
was born March 14, 1922, in Lawrenceburg, KY. He attended elementary school and graduated from Lawrenceburgh High School in 1940.

George was a member of the Boy Scouts and attained the rank of Eagle Scout.

In 1940, George enrolled in Davidson College and attended there until the outbreak of World War II. In 1942, he enlisted in Aviation Cadets, Army Air Corps. He graduated from Navigator School, Hondo, Texas, on February 1944 as a 2nd Lieutenant.

George then entered service as a combat navigator in Europe with the 15th Air Force, flying bombing missions over France, Germany, Austria, Czechoslovakia, Poland, Hungary, Yugoslavia, Romania, Bulgaria, Albania and Greece. Later he served as Intelligence Officer with the 15th Photo Reconnaissance Squadron until the end of World War II.

Detached from the military, with rank of Captain, in December 1945.

George then enrolled in the University of Kentucky in the spring of 1946. In 1947 he met and married the former Ann Garst, a 1946 graduate of the University of Kentucky. He graduated in 1948 with a degree in accounting from the University of Kentucky.

From there, he went to work as an auditor for the Department of Revenue, Commonwealth of Kentucky. After two years, he started his own business of Income Tax Preparation in Lawrenceburg, KY. In February 1953 he was appointed Anderson County Treasurer, a position he still retains.

In 1958 he purchased Wilkes Bond Property and Casualty Insurance Agency and operated it until selling the business in 1975.

In 1960, George started McWilliams Real Estate after becoming a broker that year. He operated this business until selling it in the mid 1980's.

George McWilliams' civic activities include:

Member and past president of Lawrenceburg/ Anderson County Chamber of Commerce (1952). Member and past president of Lawrenceburg Rotary Club. He has been a member of First Baptist church sine 1931.

He married Ann Garst McWilliams, born and reared in Tazewell, Virginia. A Phi Beta Kappa graduate of the University of Kentucky, 1946. He has three children: John Garst, February 23, 1950; Robert Poteet, December 4, 1952 and James Marrs, January 11, 1957. He also has five grandchildren.

Ann has served as teacher of the old Lawrenceburgh High School and of Western High School. She served nine years as the Treasurer of the City of Lawrenceburg before accepting the position of Head Librarian at the old Woodford Street Library.

With help from Governor Wendell Ford, a lot of hard work by volunteers and a good board of directors, the present library on North Main was built. Ann served for 19 years as its director before retiring at the end of 1986.

Georges father was G. D. McWilliams, Sr. born in Lawrenceburg in 1893. Attended the University of Kentucky. Operated businesses which sold farm

supplies, buggies and Ford automobiles. Served on Lawrenceburg City Council.

His mother was a school teacher all her adult life until retirement. She was a graduate of Centre College. She was also a Sunday School teacher for many years at the First Baptist Church.

His paternal grandparents were J.P. McWilliams who moved to Lawrenceburg at age 15 from Woodford County, Ky., where he was born August 2, 1861. He was engaged in the mercantile business and farming. He served as Mayor of Lawrenceburg for 16 years. Mrs. Katie Hagerman McWilliams was the wife of J. P. McWilliams until her death at age 55 in 1925. She was the niece of the late Campbell Hagerman, president of Campbell Hagerman College, Lexington, KY. She was active in civic affairs.

His maternal grandparents were Robert H. Marrs born September 19, 1862, died February 9, 1936. He was in the merchantile business and also a farmer. Atha B. Marrs wife of R. H. Marrs, born August 14, 1864 died October 28, 1959, at age 95.

His paternal great-grandparents are John R. McWilliams who was born in Tyrone County, Ireland, in 1829 and died in Lawrenceburg January 7, 1909. He was a farmer.

C.V. "PAT" AND LILLIAN BLAKEMAN McGUIRE
met at McRoberts, Kentucky, and were married in Hazard on March 21, 1931. They came to Anderson County the following June.

Lillian was born and reared in Anderson County. She was the daughter of Thomas H. and Lillie Bowen Blakeman. She had two brothers - Gilbert Blakeman formerly of Frankfort, now deceased, and Lilliard Blakeman of Spencer County. Lillian taught school for 43 years, one year in McRoberts, Lethcher County, and the remaining years in Anderson County.

C. V. or "Pat", as he was known locally, was born in Tazewell County, Virginia. He was the son of John Henry and Sarah Frances Crockett McGuire. Pat was the second son of a family of nine children. One sister, Nina Mildred McGuire, has lived with Pat and Lillian for many years. Pat is remembered for his quick wit and ready sense of humor.

Pat and Lillian were the parents of one daughter, Jane Carolyn, born June 15, 1949. She graduated from Eastern Kentucky University in 1971. Jane was married to Glen Allen Gritton on March 27, 1969, and had two children: Brian Michael Gritton, born August 20, 1971 and Jennifer Leigh Gritton, born April 4, 1974.

Pat's occupation was mainly farming, yet he was involved in other business and in civic affairs. He was assistant mail carrier for Sinai Route One for many years; a member and past president of Anderson County Farm Bureau; Farm Bureau Insurance agent from 1949 - 1951; member and past master of Beaver Creek Lodge No. 335; member of Lawrenceburg Chapter of Royal Arch Mason No. 138; served on Anderson County Board of Education; was a director of Fox Creek RECC from 1958 to 1976; and was for several years chairman of the board of the Anderson County Public Library.

Pat and Lillian were members of Friendship Baptist Church. Lillian joined Friendship in the fall of 1916, shortly after the new church building was finished, and was baptized in Beaver Creek the first Sunday in November that year. Pat joined Friendship in August 1933 and was ordained as deacon on July 11, 1936. He remained a member and deacon until his death on March 29, 1981. *Submitted By: Lillian B. Mcguire.*

MAJOR
The Major family had its beginnings in America when Richard Major (born at Hursley Manor, Hampshire, England) moved to Virginia and settled near the Charles River about 1634. Richard's son, grandson, and great-grandson were all named George Major.

Samuel Major, a son of George Major III, was born in 1712. He married Elizabeth Jones (daughter of

Humphrey Jones) on 6-22-1735 at Christ Church in Middlesex County, VA. About 1749 the family moved to Culpeper County (today Madison County). The couple had 11 children: George (married Sallie Brooking), Richard (married Jane Dilliard), Sarah (married a Mr. Taylor), Lodowick (settled in Christian Co., KY), Samuel (married Mary Monroe), Eliza (married John Sampson and later Mr. Reynolds), Josiah, Jane (married William Chowning)., John (married Elizabeth Porter and later Euphrates Sleet), Francis (married Margaret Porter), and Humphrey. John and Francis Major settled in Woodford County, KY. Samuel Major died in 1799.

Richard Major was born in Middlesex County, VA on 3-24-1738. He married Jane Dilliard and had six children: Betsey (married a Mr. Cole), Frances (married a Mr. Realm), Littleton (married Polly Payne), Jane (married John Redd), Beverly, and Lucy (married Lynn Dear). Richard died in Culpeper in 1822.

Littleton Major was born in Culpeper about 1770. He moved to Kentucky about 1800 and settled in Rough and Ready (today Alton). Littleton married Polly Payne on 6-16-1804. Polly was the daughter of Littleton's first cousin, Lucy Taylor and William Payne. The couple had five children: Lucretia (married Dudley George), Eliza (married William Satterwhite), Almeda (married William Ashford Munday), John (married Lucy Herndon), and William (married Sarah Bunting). Littleton Major was impaneled as a grand juror for the first circuit court of Anderson County. He died about 1829. *Submitted By: Darlene G. Diemer*

CHARLES FOSTELL MARLOWE A giant has

fallen! So began the funeral address for Charles F. Marlowe, better known as "Mr. Charlie" or "Mr. Marlowe". Charlie Marlowe was born in the Birdie section of Anderson County on 12-22-1890. He was the youngest son of James Madison and Alpha Jane Ruble Marlowe. Other siblings include Ida Bell (Marlowe) Lane, Obidah K. "Obie", Tola (Marlowe) Willard, Jesse, Leveland, Virgil, twins, Vena and Verna (Marlowe) Hord, and Mayme (Marlowe) Jeffries. After working in St. Louis for a spell, Charlie came home and married Mary Virginia Hanks, daughter of Dandridge Franklin and Nannie Nevins Hanks. "Miss Gin" was born 4-15-1892 and was one of eight children. Her siblings were Valeria (Hanks) Stratton, Robert, Nevins, Clyde, Franklin, Norris, (Hanks) Cinnamon and Magdalene (Hanks) Gaines.

Charlie and Virginia were married on 12-17-1913 at the bride's parents' home in Stringtown, They were the parents of three children. Their only daughter, Mary Alpha, married Oscar Cammack from Ballard. They were the parents of Donna (Cammack) Freeman, Charles Lynn and Mary Jane Cammack all of Lawrenceburg.

Their oldest son, Charles Franklin, resides in Frankfort and married Margaret Crossfield from Lawrenceburg. They are the parents of two daughters — Anne (Marlowe) Shurling of Lexington, KY and Jayne L. Marlowe of Orlando, FL.

Charles and Virginia Marlowe

Their youngest son, James Maxwell, was born in 1921 and lived only five weeks.

In addition, Charlie and Virginia had four great-grandchildren. They are: Keith Martin Freeman, Versailles, KY; James Marlowe Freeman and Stephanie Lynn Cammack of Lawrenceburg; and Jayne-Margaret Shurling of Lexington.

Charlie and Virginia were life-long residents of Anderson County, living in many different places. Charlie had small grocery stores in many parts of the county with the last one being a partnership with J.E. Blackburn on the corner of Court St. and Waterfill Ave. He sold his interest in this grocery to Oscar Cammack and became a "traveling salesman" for Altsheler and Company, Louisville. In 1956, he left Altsheler and went to work for the Oscar Brown and Sons Wholesale Grocery in Lawrenceburg. He continued to work there until his death in 1964.

Charlie was a member of the Anderson Masonic Lodge #90 and the Royal Arch; Sand Spring Baptist Church where he was a deacon, choir member, and a Sunday School teacher of the Men's Bible class. For 29 years he was a director of the Baptist Training Union and president of the Anderson Association of Baptists and past president of the Regional Baptist Association.

Virginia worked in the grocery store with Charlie and was a housewife. She was also active in the Sand Spring Baptist Church where she was a Sunday School teacher in the Junior Department for many years and sang in the choir.

Because of Charlie's many years of being a "traveling salesman", he was well known throughout many counties. He was never too busy to stop and have prayer with someone who was sick or do a kindness for them.

Charlie died on 8-26-1964, and Virginia died on 8-5-1976. *Submitted By: Mary Alpha Cammack*

JOHN MEAUX, of French origin, was married to

Mary Agnes Bacon, probably in Virginia, where Mrs. Meaux is believed to have died before John and his two children, Sallie and Nathaniel Bacon, came to Kentucky.

The Meaux farm, with its many acres and spacious homestead, was near McCall's Spring and Hebron Presbyterian meetinghouse.

John Meaux was one of the few people in this area who was actually wealthy because of his property in slaves. His score or more of slave cabins resembled a village.

Several of the Meaux slaves were listed as members of the Hebron Church, and "Uncle George", who refused to leave even after freed by the Civil War, was buried in Hebron Cemetery. He died in 1894, having lived to be about 100 years old.

John Meaux was buried in the Providence Cemetery in Mercer County, where a handsome stone marks his grave.

Sallie Meaux was married to Matthew Bush, who in pioneer days purchased a large estate on what is now known as the Jennie Lillard Road.

Nathaniel Bacon Meaux was married to Elvira Driskell, a daughter of Dennis Driskell, a pioneer settler who lived in a spacious log house near the present intersection of old 127 and 127 Business. The place was later known as the Jack Houchin place and still stands.

Nathaniel Bacon Meaux, born in 1781, was 60 years old when he married the 18 year old Elvira. Though he had never seen military duty, he was generally known as "Captain" Meaux. He was considered "meticulous in business" giving and requiring receipts even for a 24-cent transaction. He served some time as county clerk of Mercer County.

The freeing of the slaves took the major part of Nathaniel's wealth. He felt that such action was very unjust. He died soon after the close of the war and was buried at Hebron.

Nathaniel and Elvira had four sons and four daughters:

1) Nathaniel Meaux, Jr., never married
2) Mary Agnes Meaux (Mrs. William W. White)

had several children, including Ora, Warren, James, and Philip.

3) Sarah (Sallie) Louis Meaux married Samuel Coke. Children were Perrah and Roy. She died at her home in Lawrenceburg and was buried at Hebron.

4) John Ezra Meaux married Mattie Betty and had two children: Itibird (Mrs. J. R. Hutchinson) and Beulah (Mrs. J. M. B. Birdwhistell II). The Hutchinsons had two children — Lois (Mrs. Roy Robinson), Anderson County, and William Ezra (now deceased). John Ezra and Mattie Meaux lived and died in Illinois. When they died, their two young daughters were sent to Anderson County to be raised by their aunts; Itibird with Lutie Meaux Smith and Beulah with Sallie Meaux Coke.

5) Dennis Driskell Meaux married Amanda Ellen Moseley, daughter of Armsted Moseley in 1885. They moved to Carthage, Illinois, where he died in 1936. Children were: Carlisle, Vivian, and Roy.

6) William Conner Meaux married Nina Lester in 1887. He died in Milton, Illinois. Children: Margaret, Gordon, John and Lester.

7) Lutie Meaux married J. W. Smith. No children.

8) Allie Kirby Meaux married John Jead. Children: Caldwell and William Jesse. They lived at the old home place many years and it came to be known as the Head place. She later married Guy Barnes.

The only descendents of the Meaux family now living in Anderson County are Lois Hutchinson Robinson and her family. She is the daughter of Itibird Meaux Hutchinson and lives in the same neighborhood as her Meaux ancestors did and near Hebron Cemetery where many of them are buried. Lois and her husband, Roy Robinson, still own 30 acres of the original Meaux farm. Each Meaux child was given a portion of the land and this 30 acres was given to Lutis Meaux Smith with whom Itibird Meaux made her home. *Submitted By: Roy Robinson.*

MIDDLETON FAMILY As of this writing, three

miles west on U.S. 62, from the Anderson County Courthouse, Lawrenceburg, KY, (1700 Fox Creek Road), an old log cabin still stands on the remaining 160 acres of the Middleton Family Farm. James Middleton pioneered with his family from Charlotte County, Virginia, in early 1800. He built a one-room log cabin on Salt River upon taking up settlement claim of 800 acres stretching from Salt River to Powell Taylor Road. When this cabin was destroyed by fire, he built the cabin on the site described above, with its limestone chimney at each end, two large rooms on the lower and upper level and a dog trot in the center, which was closed when the logs were covered with clapboard and later siding. See pictures as cabin looked in 1962. Closed stairs in one room and the dog trot leading to the upper rooms, with no opening between, provided separate quarters for boys and girls. The fireplace was the only means of heating and cooking. There is still a very active spring, which provided water and was used for keeping food cool. Also water was available from the hand-built limestone well in the front yard. Laundry was done in Fox Creek across the old turnpike. A hand-built limestone wall with its stile, across the front of the homeplace and once directly on the turnpike, and was where the horse-drawn vehicles could let passengers out. This old log cabin was the home of James Middleton and subsequently his son Daniel, until their death.

James Middleston (1780 - 1860) married Anne Wilcox, son (Wilcox) (1789 - 18—), daughter of Sarah "Sallie" Faulkner (1760 - 1831) and Daniel Boone Wilcoxson (1755 - 1837), the son of Sarah Boone (1724 - 1815) and John Wilcoxson (17— - 1782). It is said that John was killed by Indians in 1782, near Bryant's Station, KY, but this statement has not been confirmed. Sarah Boone Wilcoxson was the daughter of Squire Boone and sister of the great frontiersman, Daniel Boone (1734 - 1820). Daniel Boone Wilcoxson served as Lieutenant in the Revolutionary War in defense of Bryant's Station and in General Clark's expeditions. Sarah Faulkner was the daughter of

John and Joyce Craig Faulkner. Joyce was the daughter of Toliver and Mary Hawkins Craig. Their son, Lewis Craig, was the pastor of "The Traveling Church" that came to Kentucky from Virginia. James and Anne Middleton had ten children: Daniel Boone (1804); Jacob and Seth (twins - 1806); Artimesa (1808); Henry (1809); Hawkins Craig (1812); Lucrecia (1814); James Faulkner (1816); Parthina (1819); and Joseph Faulkner (1823). In 1834, James Middleton by his will, arranged with his first son, Daniel to become heir to his entire estate in turn for providing him and his wife, Anne a home during their natural lives. Daniel fulfilled his father's and mother's wishes.

Daniel Boone Middleton (1804 - 1882) married Anne Rice (1810 - 1890) and had ten children: Jesse Rice (1829), James (1831), Martha Anne (1833), Hawkins Craig (1838), William (1839), John (1842), Thomas O'Bannon (1844), Sarah Jane (1846), Henley (1848), and Daneil Wilcoxson (1853). Daniel Boone Middleton's will of 1870 bequeathed the log home, 90 acres and $600 to his wife, Anne, and son, John. The remaining land was divided equally between his children. John was hopelessly handicapped, at the age of seven, as a result of falling from a horse. Because of this, John's siblings deeded their share of property inheritance to him. As a source of income over the years, John sold all the land except 80 acres with the homeplace. The last ten acres were sold in 1907, to Powell Taylor. When John's mother became so she could not care for him and the house, she had a young girl, Mary A. "Mollie" Stratton, come live with them. Upon the death of John's mother, he married Mollie. See picture which was made on their wedding day. The little chair John is sitting in was his only way of getting around. The room on the end of the porch was a temporary arrangement for the little boy, standing behind the bride and groom, and his mother who worked there.

John Middleton (1842 - 1918) and Mary A. Stratton (1870 - 1955), had no children, John's will of 1901, bequeathed all his property to his wife, Mary, during her natural life. At her death, it was to revert to his nearest relative. It is believed that John wanted to remember his siblings and/or their heirs for the inheritance he acquired through them at the time of his father's death. Accordingly, when Mary died in 1955, the remaining 80 acres with the old log cabin was sold by the Middleton Heirs to the Lewis Sisters (Lorena Hill and Mary Elizabeth) of Arlington, Virginia, daughters of David Hill Lewis and Mary Evelyn Middleton Lewis, daughter of William Middleton and Mary Evelina Templeton Middleton.

The combined 20 children of James and his son Daniel all had productive and successful lives, worthy of being included in this history of the Middleton family; however, other than John, it is primarily confined to their parents.

The old log house is haunted with and occasional appearance of Anne Rice Middleton and her son John. Anne has not been seen since her picture was removed from over the fireplace mantel in her bedroom, but John still appears on occasions. His most surprising appearance was seen by four people, outside in broad daylight, as he passed by hurriedly in midair in his little chair. No doubt John is very happy that the old homeplace, they loved so dearly, is still in the Middleton Family.

Middleton Home - 1890

The Deed to the farm provides "excepted and reserved from said tract of land the old Middleton Family graveyard with the right of reasonable ingress and egress to and from US-62." This portion of the farm belongs to the Middleton Heirs and will not ever become a part of the farm under exchange of ownership. Unfortunately, only two markers are there, Sarah Middleton Ellison (1846 - 1876) and her infant daughter, Anne R. Ellison (1869 - 1870); however, many unmarked graves are identified by Kentucky Native Limestone, which includes James, Daniel, their wives and other members of their family. The last burial were that of John in 1918 and later a family member known only as "Little Doc".

It is appropriate to include Mr. Ollie J. Bowen, Anderson County Attorney at the time and attorney for the Plaintiffs in the settlement of John Middleton's estate. Mr. Bowen will always be remembered with sincere gratitude for his interest and long hours of faithful service locating the many Middleton Heirs. The Lewis sisters commend with their highest personal regards for the successful job so well done for all the Middleton Heirs. GOD BLESS YOU - OLLIE.

In 1967, the Lewis sisters purchased an adjoining 80 acres, which was originally part of the Middleton Family Farm. This land is divided by US-62, having 38 acres on the north and 42 acres on the south. An underpass allows livestock to cross. In 1989, the little white Victorian House was destroyed by fire. *Submitted By: M. Elizabeth Lewis.*

JOHN MOFFETT

JOHN MOFFETT Little is known of John Moffett, except that he filed marriage bonds in Anderson County in November of 1840. He wed Mary Briscoe, daughter of Williamson and Katherine (Eberley) Briscoe. Family folklore tells of four brothers who traveled west from Culepepper, Virginia, in the early 1800's. One of these brothers, believed to be John, settled in the Anderson County area. To this extent there are three other Moffett families that trace their roots back to this time in Kentucky. Perhaps the story is true. Regardless, John and Mary had five children by the time Mary died as a widower in October of 1852. Benjamin"Ben, Williamson "Wis", John Warner, James Polk, and Owen Moffett were their sons. The oldest child, Benjamin was only about 10 years old when his mother died. The children were raised by their grandparents.

During the Civil War, Benjamin and John Warner joined the Confederacy, while Williamson and James Polk joined the Union Army. Owen was too young to have participated in the war. They all survived the war.

Ben Moffett married Susan Mary Sutherland and they had 12 children: Katie, Muzi, Cleo, Jess, Lonzo, John Warner, Benjamin, Delbert, Bruston, Jeptha, Charlie, Thomas, and Clifford. Williamson Moffett married Susan Siers and they had a child by the name of Sallie Ben. John Warner Moffett married Susan Sherwood and they had seven children; John T., Lewis Cardwell "Collie", Willie (married Ella Gibbs), Lester, Mary Zella (married Ezra Gibbs), Lizzie (married Cliff Stevens), and Ira D. (married Ophelia Moore). James Polk Moffett married Martha Siers and they had 11 children; Mary, Jim, Charlie, Florence, Mehala, Aslie, Squire, Alice, Owen, John, and David. Owen Moffett married Nannie Gilman and they had two children; Nancy and Lewis.

My descendents are from the line of Ben and Susan and their son, John Warner "Pink" Moffett. In January of 1899, John married Bessie Brown, daughter of Byron and Sarah Brown. They had four children; Collie, Iva, Guy, and Wilbur. Collie Moffett married Katherine Franklin in 1919 and they had four children; Roy Bruston, Oneita, Gene, and Phyllis. Iva married Bill Moffett and they had three children; Mary, Juanita, and Garnett. Guy Moffett married Nellie Martin and they had two children; Linda Lou and Kenneth. Wilbur "Woody" married Birda Kays and they had three children; Georgia, Wilbur Jr., and Anne Moffett. Many of these people are still residents of Anderson County.

I descended from the late Roy Bruston. After graduating from Kavanaugh, he joined the Navy during World War II. He married Jeannette Slocum of Providence, Rhode Island. I was born in Rhode Island, but have always lived in Kentucky. I received a Bachelors Degree in chemistry from Union College in Barbourville, Kentucky. I married Carol Lynn Dougherty in 1972 and have lived in Kentucky since 1967. We now reside in Mercer County, with our two children, Richard Bruston and Jennifer Lynn. *Submitted by: John Warner Moffett.*

JOHN WARNER MOFFETT This picture was made on the side porch of the family home of Mr. and Mrs. John Warner Moffett. It was made in 1913. Mrs. Kitty Sherwood Moffett is on the left, next to her husband, John Warner Moffett. Next is a grandson, Melwood Stevens, and his mother, Lizzie Moffett Stevens. Next is a very dear friend, Mrs. Aileen Buford; then a Moffett daughter, Mrs. Mary Moffett Gibbs, and her youngest child, Minnie Gibbs. All of the above are now deceased except for Minnie Gibbs.

There were seven Moffett children, two daughters and five sons. They were John T., Lewis Cardwell, Lester, William O., Lizzie, Mary and Ira D.

W. O. Moffett married Ella Gibbs and they had four children: Rose, Mary Catherine, and twins, Elva and Belva. The twins, Elva and Belva, are still living. Elva M. Blandford lives in Dayton, Ohio and Belva lives in Lawrenceburg, KY.

Lizzie Moffett married Cliff Stevens and they had one child, Melwood, who is deceased.

Ira D. Moffett married Ophelia Moore and they had five children. Frances is deceased, but the other four live in Lawrenceburg, KY. They are Kitty Moffett Montgomery, Mary Lois Moffett Birdwhistell, Martha Moffett and Georgia Moffett.

Mary Moffett married Ezra Gibbs. They had four children: Oscar, deceased; Elizabeth Deming, deceased; Lena Ransdell, deceased; and Minnie Gibbs who lives in Lexington, KY. Mary, the mother died in 1914.

The Moffett family loves Anderson County as is shown by the fact that most of them continue to make Anderson County their home. *Submitted By: Minnie Gibbs.*

HARVEY MOODY married Mrytle Cave. They had four children: Leon Moody married Winnie (?); Vivian married Myron Duggan; Orene married Manuel Ice; and Finley Powell.

Finley Powell Moody married Myra Lee Roth. She was born on 9-12-1916 in Underwood, Indiana. She is the daughter of Clarence Roth and Cosby S. Petty Roth. She has three sisters and one brother: Virginia married Russel Hillerich; Wanda married Teddy Randall; Gayle married Granville Carroll; and Woodrow married Verna (?).

Finley Powell and Myra Lee Roth Moody have three children: Michael Lee married LaToka Curry, the daughter of Ernest Curry - four children - Michael, Dana, Tessa, and Jason; Vicki Lynn married Joe Gibson - two children - Jill and Brandi; and Don Powell married Mary Frances Clark.

Don Powell Moody was born on 8-13-1936 in Louisville, KY. He served in the Korean Was as a communications officer with the Untied States Air Force. He married Mary Frances Clark. She was born on 3-2-1927 in Louisville, KY. She is the daughter of Lester Ray Clark and Emily Jane Utterback. Don and Mary have one son, Mark Finley. He was born on 6-12-1973 in Louisville.

The Moody family has a military tradition. This family has served it's country well in times of war. The women even served their country by assembling equipment during these times. *Submitted By: Mark Moody.*

RUSSELL S. MOORE

RUSSELL S. MOORE was born on 11-25-1953 in Corbin, KY. He is the son of Russell R. Moore (1919 - 1989) and Beatrice Farmer Moore. He has five brothers and sisters: Diane Moore, born 1945, married Richard Harper; Gary Moore, born 1948, married Espie Moore; Carol Moore, born 1951, married Brad Berglind; Lisa Moore, born 1958, married Brian Ruholt; and James Moore, born 1963, married Carol Hedges. Russell R. Moore died from complications from his second open heart surgery. He was a navigator in World War II. He flew in a B-52 bomber. He was a teacher, principal, superintendent and a Kentucky Colonel.

Russell Stuart Moore married Beverly Anne Hablutzel in Erlanger, KY on 10-6-1973. She was born on 5-23-1954 in Cincinnati, Ohio. She is the daughter of Robert Charles Hablutzel and Elizabeth Jane Osborne Hablutzel. She has one sister and one brother: Cynthia J. Hablutzel, born 1948, married Wayne B. Miller; and Robert C. Hablutzel, Jr., born 1951, married Ellen Glasford. Robert Charles Hablutzel fought in World War II also. He was in the army. A story he tells is that they were walking through a village in France one time and a German shot him in the foot. He was sent back to the front. The soldiers were sent back on trains in box cars. They put as many soldiers in the cars as possible. Robert was in the front of the box car. As the doors were opened, the soldiers on the back started pushing forward. They pushed Robert and three other soldiers out on the tracks into the path of another train. Robert was the only one who survived. He was unconscious for two weeks, and he almost lost his left arm. He was sent home after that. Russell S. and Beverly Moore are the parents of two children: Aimee E. Moore, born 4-23-1975 in Covington, KY; and Ian S. Moore, born 3-10-1984 in Lexington, KY. The Moore family resides on Nevins Station Road in Anderson County. *Submitted By: Aimee Moore.*

WILLIAM DUDLEY MOORE

WILLIAM DUDLEY MOORE, only child of Hamilton G. Moore and Lucy Ann Searcy Moore, was born June 9, 1856.

Hamilton G. Moore, Mexican War Soldier, was the son of Arthur Moore and Nancy Plough, daughter of Revolutionary soldier, Daniel Plough, and Sarah Ann Driskell.

Lucy Ann Searcy was the daughter of Dudley Searcy and Sallie Morton, whose father, William Morton, had also served in the Revolution. They were all residents on Mortonsville in Woodford County until Sallie Morton Searcy and Lucy Ann came to Anderson County in 1849. The Village of Mortonsville is reported in the history of Woodford County as having been founded by Jeremiah Morton, a brother of William Morton.

William Dudley Moore was educated in the one-room school near his home, at the Lawrenceburg Seminary which survived for a short time, and at Georgetown College in Georgetown, Kentucky.

On January 21, 1881, he was married to a young widow, Mrs. Alice V. Hedger Williams, daughter of the Rev. J. T. Hedger and Mary Ann Routt. Rev. Hedger was one of the most popular Baptist ministers of this entire area. Alice's great grandfather was the Rev. John Rice who was if not the first - one of the first preachers ordained in Kentucky.

William Dudley Moore was ordained as a Baptist minister on May 26, 1886 at Salvisa in Mercer County.

Rev. J. T. Hedger and Dr. E. Y. Mullins participated in the ordination service. He pastored various churches in Anderson and Mercer Counties, which included more than 30 years at Shawnee Run Baptist Church in Mercer County and 30 years at Goshen Church in Anderson County where he was the pastor at the time of his death. Some of these pastorates were on a part time basis as was customary in early times. In addition to his pastorates he was one of the organizers of the Sand Spring Baptist Church near his home which in later years was to become one of the largest rural churches in Kentucky. Bro. Moore, his wife and three of his children became charter members of this church, moving their memberships from the Salvisa Baptist Church and the Goshen Baptist Church.

Bro. Moore's home in Ripyville was the site of perhaps 1000 marriages. The home, which is on the National Register of Historic Places, is still standing on the old Harrodsburg Road. The first couple married by Bro. Moore was E. H. Highbarger and Mrs. Mary Phebley, July 6, 1886. His last ceremony was that of Robert Spalding and Margaret Roark, July 27, 1935.

He was called upon by folks of many faiths to preach at funerals and a record was kept of around 1400 funerals that he conducted.

Bro. Moore did some extensive traveling during his ministry. He visited the Buena Vista Battlefield in 1904 where his father fought but his real thrill was in 1911 when he was able to take a three months tour of the Holy Land.

Rev. William Dudley Moore died August 5, 1935 from injuries received in an automobile accident on the way to preach a funeral. He was 79 years old.

Rev. W. D. Moore on trip to the Holy Land in 1911

Bro. Moore's funeral, held August 8, 1935, was attended by an estimated 4,000 people with 800 automobiles in the procession. The funeral was attended by 24 ministers of all faiths.

He was preceded in death by his devoted wife, Alice. They had been married 50 years. To them were born six children: Martha (Mrs. Robert Goodlett); Lucy (Mrs. Robert Hanks); Opelia (Mrs. Ira D. Moffett); Sallie (Mrs. Leonard Short); Forrest Moore and John F. Moore. Two other children, Mary Williams and Walker Williams, children of Mrs. Moore by her previous marriage, also blessed this happy home.

Grandchildren of William Dudley and Alice Hedger Moore now living in Anderson County are Kitty Moffett Montgomery (Mrs. J. B. Montgomery); Mary L. Moffett Birdwhistell (Mrs. Carl V. Birdwhistell); Martha Moffett; Georgia Moffett; Edyth May Hanks Edwards (Mrs. Marvin Edwards); and Charles Truett Hanks. Other grandchildren of Brother Moore and his wife are John Allen Moore and Joe Moore (both living in Atlanta, Georgia); and Jane Moore McKinney of Owensboro, KY. *Submitted By: Mary L. Moffett Birdwhistell.*

KISLE AND HELEN MONROE

KISLE AND HELEN MONROE are lifelong residents of Anderson County. Helen is the daughter of the late James and Sadie Houchin Hanks. James (Jim) was Deputy Sheriff for four years and then Sheriff of Anderson County from 1950 to 1954.

Helen has three brothers, Carl of Louisville, KY; Allan and Paul of Lawrenceburg, KY.

Kisle, the son of the late Oscar and Athena Royalty Monroe, was born in Anderson County and moved to Mercer County at age three. He moved back to Anderson County when he was eleven. He was working for the Southern Railroad when World War II began. Kisle one of two boys and three girls. Brother Harold of Anderson County; Sisters Mrs. Volney (Josephine) Elam and Mrs.. Julian (Irene) Birdwhistell of Anderson County; and Vora Hicks of Chattanooga Tennessee.

In 1940, Kisle and Helen were married by then pastor of Sand Spring Church Rev. M. D. Morton. They are the parents of two children. Paula, a graduate of the University of Louisville, lives in Louisville and is a math teacher at Southern High School. She is married to William Goins who works for UPS. They have two sons, Bill Jr. 22 and Greg 13. Mary Frances, a graduate of the University of Kentucky, lives in Jefferson County. She and her husband own a few acres and she works for Freda's Florist. Her husband, Robert Bruenderman, is part owner of Bruenderman Construction. They have two daughters, Randi 6 and Erin 3.

Kisle and Helen Monroe

Kisle and Helen both attended Salt River Elementary School and Helen went on to the Kavanaugh High School. In November 1942, Kisle was inducted into the army where he spent three years. After Basic Training he was sent to Africa as a replacement. There he was attached to the 540th Amphibian Engineers where he made six invasions through Sicily, Italy, France, and Germany until the end of the war in 1945.

After returning from overseas he began working for the railroad again, but after five years he and Helen bought a farm which he worked until he was forced to retire due to ill health. In the meantime, after the girls were in school, Helen went to work at Magnolia Mano Nursing Home. After it's closing she went to work for Ballards Drug Store where she worked for fifteen years. After leaving the farm they moved to 313 Carlton Drive in Lawrenceburg where they now reside. They are members of the Sand Spring Baptist Church where they attend regularly. *Submitted by: Mr. and Mrs. Kisle Monroe.*

ROBERT AND PATRICIA (CARTER) MOORE

ROBERT AND PATRICIA (CARTER) MOORE Of course, not every person with ties to Anderson County and affection for it lives there. Robert Moore and Patricia (Carter) Moore of Arlington, Virginia are two such people. Bob's father Elwood Moore and Pat's mother, Rae (Poulter) Carter were both born in Ashbrook section. Elwood on July 23, 1901, and Rae on June 13, 1909. Elwood was the son of Walter Moore and Maude Black and Rae the daughter of Ernest Poulter and Lola Bryant, all four of Anderson County. Walter was the son of James H. Moore and Amanda Gregory; Maude was the daughter of William H. Black and Octavia Vowels; Ernest was the son of Henry Poulter and Sarah Elizabeth Baxter; and Lola was the daughter of Douglas Bryant and Martha Ellen Noel.

The Moores go back to David Moore who married Elizabeth Boggess in 1801, while part of Anderson was still Franklin County. The Boggesses may be traced back through Fairfax County, Virginia to a coastal county of Northumberland, where they were living with the Dutch migration from the East, and many of them became Shakers. Amanda Gregory Moore's mother was Rhoda Bell of that Mercer and Anderson County family. The Bells came from Orange County, Virginia, as did so many settlers in Anderson and Mercer.

Maude Black Moore's grandmother Black was Susan Hughes of an Anderson County family that may be traced back to Prince William County, Virginia. Maude's mother's Vowels family first settled in the 1790's in Nelson County, from which they may be traced to St. Mary's County, Maryland in the late 1600's. Some of the Maryland names in the Vowels ancestry are Willett, Price, Beall, and Maddox.

Robert P. and Patricia C. Moore

The Poulters are another family who came to Anderson from Mercer by way of Washington County. They go back to the Virginia Counties of Orange and Culepepper. Families in their ancestry are Sanders, Hendren, Yates, Ransdell, and Petty. Before moving on to Anderson the Baxters came first to the Boonesboro area, having left their home near Baltimore, Maryland, with a brief stop in southern Pennsylvania. The Baxters have Moore, Royalty, Trent, and Sappington ancestors.

Among the Bryant's ancestors are McMicheals and Ploughs. Martha Ellen Noel's family came to Anderson from Washington. Her mother was Mary Trout and her grandmother Noel was Thurza Bowen. The Noels first settled in Essex County, Virginia, in the 1600's and can be traced to the 1500's in Leiden, Holland.

Rae Poulter's family moved from Anderson County to Lexington, where she met and married the late Forrest Carter from Boyle County. His Carters may be traced to the 1500's in Kempston, Bedfordshire, England, where the 400 year old family home is still standing.

Elwood Moore moved as a child with his parents to Chaplin and then, after he married Sarah Moores of Chaplin, eventually moved on the Bloomfield. There for about 25 years until his death he was in the grocery business.

So Bob and Pat, despite their Anderson County heritage, grew up away from there and about 50 miles from each other. It was only after Bob finished Air Force duty that their old University of Kentucky friends introduced them while Pat was teaching in Bardstown. They married in 1958 and left for graduate study at Harvard. The 31 years since have been spent in various cities and states. During most of the early years, Bob was teaching Russian in college, with time out for a doctorate at Cornell. For the last 13 years, they have lived in the Washington area. Bob works as a civilian for the U.S. Air Force Intelligence Agency in translation and publishing of Russian military writings. Pat works in the personnel office of a large east-coast bank. They both return to their home grounds in Kentucky at least once a year. *Submitted By: Robert P. Moore.*

RALPH G. MORGAN,

The family pioneer was Andrew Morgan of North Parnham Parish, Richmond County, Virginia. In 1730, he married Sarah Dawson, daughter of William and Elizabeth Stone Dawson. They had six children: David, Andrew, Daniel, Margaret, Benjamin and William.

William, born 1756, came to Nelson County, Kentucky in 1791 and settled in the Bloomfield-Chaplin area. William and his wife, Nancy, had eight sons and seven daughters: William (died before 1826), Peter (died before 1826), John, Daniel (married Elizabeth Redmon), James (married Mary Ann McHenry), Reuben (married Polly Popham), George, William C. (married Dorinda Prather), Mary (married a Middleton), Elizabeth (married Thomas Barker), Sarah Dawson (married John Redmon, Jr.), Lausanne (married John Woods, Jr.), Catherine (married Richard Bond) and Fanny Marie (married Henry Prather).

John Morgan, born in Virginia in 1779, married Sarah Jane Burrus, daughter of Samuel and Cathy Rucher Burris. They built their home west of Glensboro overlooking Salt River. Here they raised five sons and two daughters: Wilkes H. (married Martha Ann Faris), Sabra (married Rowan Coalter), Wade H. (married 1st Sarah E. Franklin, 2nd Mary A. Langford), John H. (married 1st Mahala E. Oliver 2nd Thompson Ann Wilson), Pittman, North (married Susan Mary Franklin), Margaret Jane (married Nathaniel Harris).

John H. Morgan married Mahala, daughter of John B. and Nancy Northern Redmon Oliver, in 1849. They had five children: Edgar B. (married Aileen Searcy), John C., Alonzo Culvin, Nancy Jane (died age 13) and James P. (died in infancy).

Mahala died in 1865. In 1867, John H. married Thompson Ann, daughter of Henry Jr. and Carrie Gains Wilson. They had five children: Florence (married Thomas Calvert), Wilkes Howell (married Elizabeth Barnette), Henry W. (married JoAnn Yocum), Ruby Alice (married Dr. Sidney Simpson).

Alonzo Culvin Morgan became a doctor and shortened his name to Dr. L. C. Morgan. He married Susan Mary, daughter of William and Hannah Voorhies Lake of Mercer County, KY. They had three children: John Edgar (married Mabel Darland), Lillian Neal (married Luther Adden), and Veal Coleman (married 1st Johnnie Bell Young) - They had one daughter, Jean Coleman (married Sidney Norton).

Veal Coleman married 2nd to Lela Florence, daughter of Edgar and Elmer Sanders Darlan of Mercer County. They had seven children: Ralph Gilbert, Mary Neal (married Coleman Clarke), Nancy Rae, Emma June (married Robert Gilbreath), Louis Baxter (married Madonna Collinsworth), Jack Donald (married 1st Margaret Shewmaker, 2nd Maria London), Dorothy Glada (married Louis Daugherty).

Ralph G. Morgan

Ralph G. Morgan married four times and has nine children: Ronald Lewis (married 1st Nelda Gandia, had a daughter, Cassandra who married Dave Docherty - two daughters, Kelly and Katey, -married 2nd Patricia Kay Lumbeck. They have a son, Kevin Hunt and a daughter, Lora Kay); Virginia Ann (married Robert Eugene Medley. They have three children: Richard Lynn, Bobbi Ann (married Larry Graves, they have two sons, Jared and Aaron Morgan), Diana Gayle (married Marty Hendrix); Jerry Lee (married Kathy Probus); Larry Gilbert; Ralph David; Vivian Jeanetta (married 1st Billy Carmen 2nd Roby Mullins 3rd Van Cunigan. Two daughters: Angela Nicole and Robyn Ann); John Neal (married Sherri Lee Yates. They have two sons, Christopher James and Joshua Neal); James Coleman (married 1st Beverly Emerson, they had one daughter, Kitty Coleman 2nd Becky Quinn).

In 1962, Ralph G. Morgan married Patsy, daughter of Russell and Dorothy Kenney Myers. They have one daughter, Cheryl Lynne (married Carey McGuire. They have two daughters, Erin Courtney and Sarah Lindsay).

Ralph Morgan was a supply truck driver in the Phillipines during World War II. After the war, he continued as a truck driver and a mechanic.

Since 1961, Ralph has been owner/operator of Morgans Marathon Service on Beaumont Avenue in Harrodsburg, KY. Over the years the service station had grown to include a grocery and hunting and fishing supply lines. *Submitted By: Ralph Morgan.*

EDWARD JACKSON MORRIS

married Ruth Irene Maule Morris on 8-15-1970 in Norfolk, Virginia. They have three children: James Jackson, Melissa Carol, and Gretchen Marie. Edward Jackson Morris is the only child of Eddie James Morris (1910 - 1975) and Mary Elizabeth Slaughter Morris (born 1915). Ruth Irene Maule Morris is the daughter of Francis Eugene Maule, Jr. (born 1917) and Irene Virginia Barrett Maule (born 1924).

Eddie James Morris was the only child of Homer W. Morris (1885 - 1952) and Ophelia Mothershead Morris (1882 - 1947) Mary Elizabeth Morris is the daughter of Henry Slaughter (1885 - 1920) and Mayme Poulter Slaughter (1890 - 1970). She has one sister, Louise Slaughter Rice.

Homer W. Morris was the son of Madison Garnett Morris (1856 - 1939) and Mattie Bickers Morris (1860 - 1907). He had one sister, Cora Morris Sweeney (1890 - 1970), and two brothers, Jackson Bickers Morris (died 1985) and William Burrus Morris (1895 - 1979). Ophelia Mothershead was the daughter of Clifton Mothershead (1837 - 1925) and Louisa Yancy Mothershead (1844 - 1916). She had four brothers and one sister: John William (1867 - 1953); Van (1870 - 1889); Aldridge (1871 - 1944); Forrest (1874 - 1942) and Mary (1886 - 1953).

Madison Garnett Morris was the son of Joseph Paul Morris and Melissa Holder Atkins Renfro. He had four brothers and sisters: Susan Elizabeth; Daniel Webster; Martha Alles; and Joseph Burrus. Mattie Bickers Morris was the daughter of Andrew Jackson Bickers and Harriet F. Thomas Bickers. She had seven brothers and sisters: Alma, Cora, Emma F., Elmonia R. York Bickers, James R. York Bickers, Beebe J., William H., and Bettie.

Clifton Mothershead was the only child of John and Mary Mothershead. Louisa Yancey Mothershead was the daughter of Robert Yancey and Martha Jordan Yancey.

The Morris's are descendents of both Robert Morris, who signed the Declaration of Independence, and Gonverneur Morris, a member of the Continental Congress. He was also a member of the committee that drafted the constitution. *Submitted By: Melissa Morris.*

MORTON

the first of the Morton's to settle in Anderson County was Reuben Morton (1797 - 1877), he was the son of William Morton (ca. 1760 - 1826) of Woodford County. William Morton was a son of John Morton (ca.1735 - 18070 a Revolutionary War veteran who came to Kentucky from Orange County, Virginia around 1787. Reuben Morton was born at Mortonsville in Woodford County and settled in Anderson County about 1830 near Gilbert Creek where he farmed and raised his family. He married Sarah Abbott, a daughter of William Abbott, on the 8th of July, 1840. They were members of the Hebron Church and are buried in the cemetery there. Reuben and Sarah Abbott Morton raised seven children: William H., Elizabeth C., Palmyra, Joseph W., James Parker, Margaret A., and Otha S.

James Parker Morton (1846 - 1914) married Therresa Hill (1852 - 1893) on the 2nd of June, 1870. Therresa Hill was the daughter of John and Margaret Ware Hill of Garrad County. James Parker and Therresa Morton raised five children: Minnie, Porter, Lewis, Joseph and Harvey. All but Minnie Morton are buried in the cemetery at the old Salt River Primitive Baptist Church at Stringtown.

Minnie Morton (1875 - 1951) married Louis Ballow, of Washington County, in 1891 and had two sons: Thomas Lee and Eddie. Louis Ballow died in 1903 at which time Minnie Morton Ballow moved to Louisville with her sons and remarried in 1906 to Thomas Pelley.

It is not known how many descendents of Reuben Morton reside in the county today, but many familiar and related names do still exist: Abbott, Beasley, Hahn, Moore, Mothershead, Mountjoy, McKee, and Searcy.

MOUNTJOY

Shortly after the Revolutionary War, two brothers, William and Edward Mountjoy, migrated from Virginia to Kentucky to make their home. They had been soldiers in the Revolutionary War, and Edward was complimented by General George Washington on his soldierly bearing. The brothers settled on land north of Lawrenceburg, married and had families. The names Edward and William Mountjoy are listed in the Anderson County Census Report of 1827.

One of their descendents, Thomas Mountjoy and his wife, Sarah, owned land on Hammons Creek two miles north of Lawrenceburg where they reared several children. One of their sons, William David Mountjoy and his wife, Melissa Herndon Mountjoy, settled on 249 acres of adjoining land. There in 1863 they built a colonial style home, facing the Lawrenceburg-Alton Turnpike. Trees on the farm furnished the lumber, which was sawed from hewn logs. An "everlasting spring" on the farm was known to run dry only once. In 1866, a Union Calvary Regiment, going home north, passed through the farm and the horses drank the spring dry.

David and Melissa Mountjoy had four children, two of whom, Sara and Thomas Coleman, died in infancy. On 11-28-1864, a son, Bailey Waller was born and on 2-2-1872, daughter, Mary Eliza was born. The children grew up on the farm and attended the country schools. Mary Eliza completed her education at the Birdwhistell Academy in Lawrenceburg.

B. W. Mountjoy (The man in the Black Derby.)

When Waller was fourteen and ready for higher education, his parents took him to Lexington and enrolled him in the University of Kentucky. In 1882, he graduated at age seventeen, the youngest man in his class with both a Bachelor of Arts and a Bachelor of Science degrees. He spoke of being pleased that John Fox, Jr. was class valedictorian, that his English teacher was James Lane Allen, and that J. W. McGarvey baptized him at age seventeen. All were well-known Kentucky authors. After graduation, he attended a Louisville Business College, and received a diploma.

Waller chose the field of merchandising for his vocation. Salesmanship was his forte and he was always happiest when meeting the public. He wore a black derby hat, and his business cards read "The Man in the Black Derby."

He held a sales position with the C. C. Trent Company, and Bacon's in Louisville, and for 12 years, the Famous Bar in St. Louis. He was House Furnishings buyer for L. S. Ayres Company, Indianapolis for sixteen years. After leaving that position, he became senior salesman for Borin Art Products and continued with this company until he retired 27 years later at the age of 80.

Mary Eliza, life-long resident of Anderson County, chose to remain single.

Bailey Waller married Miss Bertha Alice Caster, Indianapolis, and became the parents of three children: Bailey Waller, Jr. married Miss Marion Wagner, Palos Park, Illinois, and they have six children. He was senior engineer with Western Electric, Indianapolis; Bertha Alice married Joshua Dawson Grace, Anderson County, machinist and farmer, and they had two children; Jean Frances married Harold Jackson Roll, a State Policeman, the first to be killed while on duty. They had two children.

The house that David and Melissa Mountjoy built in 1863 was a Christian home, much lived in, where friends and relatives were always welcome. It remained in the Mountjoy family for 83 years. *Submitted By: Bertha Mountjoy Grace.*

VIRGINIA BEST MOUNTJOY,

has lived in Anderson County all her life. One of six children born to Roy T. and Lillie R. Wells. Her brothers and sister grew up in Anderson County. Two brother have since moved to Shelby County. Her father was the son of Tom and Anna Wells and was a farmer in Anderson County. Her mother was the daughter of Tom E. and Victory Drury and she was a homemaker and a mother.

Virginia attended schools in Anderson County - the first eight grades. She then attended the last four grades in Shelby County (Waddy High School) and graduated in 1945. After graduation, she went to work for the Commonwealth of Kentucky.

Virginia Best Mountjoy

She then married Winfrey R. Best in 1946. He was the son of Clive and Verna Best. He went to be with the Lord in 1972. In 1978, she married Jimmy R. Mountjoy, his father was Lin M. Mountjoy and his mother was Bonnie B. Mountjoy.

Virginia is the mother of Ray T. Best, born in 1952, and Becky Best White, born in 1957.

Virginia is the grandmother of four children, Travis, Ty, Jimmy and Sarah. Virginia resides at 1361 Fox Creek Road. *Submitted By: Virginia Mountjoy.*

GEORGE SANDFORD MUNDAY

married Sarah Hurst. They lived in Mercer County in 1850, 1860 and 1870. Census records list his occupation as being a Tailor. They had four known children. These children and their spouses are: Elizabeth Ann (Daniel Patterson), Kinoldon (male, no other information), George and Ophelia (Caleb CaHill).

A family story handed down through the generations goes like this. Sanford and Sarah were entertaining a guest when a terrible electrical storm came up. Sarah invited the guests to spend the night. She put the children to bed then went upstairs to get a feather tick for the guest to sleep on. Lightning struck the house setting fire to it and killing everyone in the house except Sarah and the children in the beds. Sarah put the fire out and laid out the bodies putting pillows under each of their heads. She sat up with them until morning when she could go for help and her hair turned white overnight.

Ophelia Munday married Caleb CaHill on 9-19-1866. Their children and their spouses are: Sarah Ellen CaHill (Alvin Herndon Perry), Georgia (Joseph Howard Martin), Artemesa "Mecia" (Jordan Thomas Ragan), Mary E. "Mollie" (Dawson Grace), Felicia (Theodore Alcorn), William Clay "Willie" (Ruby Young), Foster D. (Mamie ??), Laura D. (died in infancy), Maggie (James Mayberry), and Ada (1st Edward Woodrow, 2nd ??? Osborne). *Submitted By: Paula Perry Mitchell.*

GEORGE ALFRED MURPHY

was born on 10-29-1918 in Anderson County and died April 1974. He was the son of Ed Murphy and Laude Mae Harley Murphy. George married Nellie Racheal Norton on 2-5-1946. She was born on 3-9-1921 in Spencer County, KY and is the daughter of Ben Norton and Sarah Otis Goodlett Norton.

George and Nellie Racheal Murphy were the parents of nine children: Wayne Allen married Angeling - two daughters; Benny Alfred; Racheal married William O. Robinson - two sons; Geraldine (deceased); Sue married Clyde Ritchey - two children; Rodney married Wanda - two children; Edith Loraine married Michael Driskell - one child; Johnny Walker married Sheila Driskell - three children; and James Francis.

Benny Alfred Murphy was a New Years Baby. He was born on 1-1-1947 in Louisville, KY. Because both his parents were married before, he had one half-sister and two half-brothers on his father's side and one half-brother on his mother's side. He went to school through the ninth grade, then left home and moved to Dayton, Ohio where he met Constance Sue Neal. They moved back to Kentucky and married in 1967. She was born on 5-7-1947 in Dayton to Joseph Forrest Neal and Bertha Eva Thorpe. Because of the marriage break-up, she was moved around very often when she was young. When she was in second grade, she lived in Ontario, Canada. She returned and lived in Greene County Childrens Home until she entered the 7th grade, when she went to a foster home. She lived there until she completed 11th grade. She moved back with her mother, her senior year, and graduated in June of 1965.

Benny Alfred and Constance Sue were the parents of four children: Benny Alfred Jr. (1967 - 1968) buried in the Murphy Graveyard; Joseph Alfred, born 10-30-1969; and twins, Donald Ray and Judy Kay, born on 8-9-1973.

Benny Alfred Murphy died in a single car accident as a result of drinking and driving in January of 1975. The Murphy family resides on Waterfill Avenue in Lawrenceburg. *Submitted By: Judy Murphy.*

EZRA WILLIAM MURPHY

was born on 10-17-1890 in New York City. He was the son of John Patrick Murphy and Elizabeth O'Bryan Murphy. He had seven brothers and sisters: Ethel (1885 - 1967) married Joe Benson - two children, Oscar and Corrine; Ivy Jo (1888 - 1980) married Bill Slater - three children - Katherine, Jim, and Bob; Ada (1889 - ?) married John Schroyer - one daughter, Norma; Clel (1890 - 1986) married Johnson North - one daughter, Lorraine; Al (1893 - 1941) married Susie Stratton - one daughter, Elizabeth; Ben (1894 - 1947) married Daisy Mason - three daughters - Nellie, Mary, and Isobel; and Nannie (1898 - 1987) married Leslie Warford - four daughters - Ethel, Norine, Corine, and Lucille.

Ezra William Murphy married first Elizabeth

Warford. They had four children: Verna Ethel (1907 - 1921); Raymond A. (born 1916) married Blanche Thacker; Charles B. (1917 - 1974) married Betty Wiseman - three children - Gladys, Thomas and Charles; and James Leslie (born 1919) married Elizabeth Sparrow - four children - Dorothy, Eldon, Ruth, and Elaine.

Ezra William Murphy married Goldie Mae Tindall on 2-2-1927 in Lawrenceburg, KY. She was the daughter of Taylor Finley Tindall (1881 - 1948) and Lilly Jane Wayne Tindall (1888 - 1973). She was born on 12-13-1909 in Lawrenceburg. She had six brothers and sisters: Jim Henry (1905 - 1966) married Aderine Simpson - three children - Bill, Henry, and Rosa.; Charles Taylor (1907 - 1907); Edward William (born 1910); John Claude (1911 - 1988) married Nancy Wade - seven children - Claude, Annie, Lilly, James, Linda, Opal, and Harold; Mamie Lee (1914 - 1985) married John Sayre - three children - John, Betty, and Allen; and Lillian Irene (born 1925) married Bill Jordan - one daughter, Debbie.

Ezra William and Goldie Murphy were the parents of three children: John Thomas (1927 - 1979) married Ida Hawkins - four children - Daisy, Goldie, Blanche, and Kathy; Edward W.; and Edna Mae (1929 - 1967) married Park Blackwell - one daughter, Barbara. Ezra William died on 4-25-1972 and Goldie died on 12-6-1986.

Edward W. Murphy was born on 8-4-1929 in Lawrenceburg. He married Ina Blondella Baxter on 3-1-1947 in Lawrenceburg. They are the proud parents of three daughters: Linda Sue (born 1949) married Gordan Wayne Edington - one daughter, Lisa Dawn; Margaret Geraldine (born 1951) married 1st Paul Stephen Galliher - two daughters, Jane Michelle and Edna Renee Galliher - 2nd Joseph Samuel Farris; and Patricia Jean (born 1952) married 1st Freddy Brumley - one daughter, Tracy LeAnn Brumley - 2nd John Wesley Nunley - one daughter, Bethany Nicole Nunley.

Ina Blondella Baxter Murphy was born on 3-1-1929 in Lawrenceburg. She is the daughter of Leslie Baxter and Mary Armstrong.

Charles Leslie Baxter was born on 1-9-1871 in Mason County, KY. He was the son of Frank Baxter and Elizabeth McDowell Baxter. He married Mary Frances Armstrong on 6-20-1906 in Lawrenceburg. She was born on 4-4-1889 in Lawrenceburg and was the daughter of Tibitha Armstrong. Leslie and Mary were the parents of nine children: Everett Arvin (1908 - 1985) married Lizzie Hale - three sons - Arvin, Roy, and Kenneth; Charles Luther (1909 - 1966) married Doris Butler - four children - Minnie, Jeanette, Gary, and Margaret; Nettie Lee (born 1910) married Archie Satterly - two sons, Joseph and Tony; Elmer Wayne (born 1913); Margaret Ann (1922 - 1925); Lelia Sea (born 1924) married Clyde Stratton - three children - Bobby, Judy, and Kathy; James Vernon (1926 - 1972) married Christine Allison - nine children - Shirley, Jay, Wanda, Donnie, Mike, Earl, Glen, Betty and Joyce; Ina Blondella; and Edna Rose (1930 - 1931). Leslie died on 6-16-1941 and Mary died on 10-6-1957. Both are buried at Antioch. *Submitted By: Edie Galliher.*

WILLIAM AND FRANCES NICHOLLS, na-
tives of Nelson County, came to Lawrenceburg in September, 1936. For 26 years they owned and operated the Western Auto Associate Store on Main Street. Bill, as he was better known, served two terms as Mayor, 1946 - 1954. During that time he was instrumental in moving the city water plant from Salt River to the Kentucky River, which was badly needed. Now this modern facility furnishes water for most of Anderson County. He was elected Police Judge in 1962, and served in that capacity for ten years.

He was active in community affairs having belonged to the Rotary Club and Chamber of Commerce. He and Ollie C. Clavert (deceased) opened one of the first subdivisions in Lawrenceburg in 1940, Village Drive, between Highland and Walnut

Streets. He and his wife Frances built their first home that same year. After his retirement he devoted most of his time to his hobby of refinishing old trunks. They are scattered all over Anderson and surrounding counties as well as other states.

Frances has been very active in the community also, having been President of the Lawrenceburg Women's Club three terms and presently as one of the trustees; past President and organizer of Parent Teachers Association, she also served on the State Board; member of Anderson County 4-H Council and 4-H Leader; President of Anderson County Democratic Womens Club and 4th District Director; worked with Red Cross Blood Moblie until the past few years; and organized the Women's Club "Bingo Ladies" for Heritage Hall nursing home.

Bill and Francis are the parents of two children. Wilson, a graduate of the University of Kentucky, lives in Paris and is co-owner of Springland Farm. He is married to the former Barbara Taylor and they have two children, Mary Frances - 21 and Bill - 19, both students at Morehead State University.

Judy, a graduate of St. Catherine, Springfield, Kentucky, is married to John C. Ryan of Lebanon, an attorney in Frankfort where they reside. They have four daughters, Jennifer - 21, employed by Farmers Bank; Kimberly - 19, a student at Eastern Kentucky University; Roby - 8; and Kelli - 6, both attending Good Shepherd Grade School.

Bill and Francis are both members of St. Lawrence Catholic Church, each having served as President of the Church Council.

Bill passed away on July 10, 1989 at the age of 89. *Submitted by: Frances Nicholls.*

C. DARRELL OSBORNE was born on 10-7-1952
in Versailles, KY. He is the son of Cecil Osborne and Louise Ashcraft Osborne. He has four sisters and one brother: Darlene, born 1954, married Ricky Bramblett in 1972 - three daughters - Crystal, Karissa, and Kalena; Kimberly, born 1963; Eric, born 1965, married Susan Kline in 1989; Carla, born 1967; and Darby, born 1969.

Darrell Osborne married Pamela Bolin on 11-25-1972 in Trenton, Georgia. She was born on 5-2-1948 in Barbourville, KY. She is the daughter of Leslie Bolin (9-5-1906 / 7-18-1989) and Mary Payne Bolin (2-7-1909 /4-30-1975). She has six sisters: Margaret, born 1933, married Ralph Arnett - two children - Cheryl and Mark; Mary Sue, born 1934, married Tom McDermott - four children - Bridget, Michelle, Michael, and Joseph; Arbadella, born 1936, married W. Scott Owens - four children - Renee, Kim, Shawn, and Robert; Vivian "Boosh" (1938 - 1978) married Gerald H. Miller Sr. - two children - Marion "Kelly" and Gerald, Jr.; Carolyn, born 1944, married Ronald Wagoner - four children - Rae, Carol, Erin, Jennifer, and Valarie; and Leslie, born 1946, married Gene Mackey - three children - Christopher, Sarai, and Elizabeth.

Darrell and Pamela Osborne are the proud parents of two daughters: April, born 8-5-1975, and Amanda, born 4-29-1977. Both attend Anderson County Schools.

The Osborne family moved to Anderson County in 1979 from Lexington, KY. Darrell is a building contractor. *Submitted By: April Osborne.*

RUSSELL J. OVERSTREET, a Lawrenceburg
businessman, was born on July 30, 1915 in Lathrop, Missouri. He was the son of the late James Lewis and Elizabeth David Dailey Overstreet.

Originally from Mercer County, Kentucky; his parents decided to move back to Kentucky in 1923 with their four children: Lois, Loraine, Francis, and their only son, Russell.

At 13 Russell nearly died with a ruptured appendix. His parents were never able to pay for his operation. As years went by Russell never forgot and finally paid for the operation himself. There after, he struggled to be a self-reliant pillar that stood within the community and his family.

He never knew his grandfather, Steven Johnson Overstreet, but was fortunate enough to have known his grandmother, formerly Susan Margaret Hutton. She and Steven lived in Anderson County before Steven's death. Steven is buried in the Hebron Cemetery in an unmarked grave located on the right side of the cemetery behind William J. Overstreet and wife Martha B. and beside a Cox according the the caretaker of the cemetery. Susan moved to St. Joseph, Missouri after Steven's death and lived to be 101 years old and is buried there along with all her children except James Lewis, Russell's father.

On August 4, 1934, Russell married Annie Ruth Phillips, the daughter of the late Cecil Thurman and Alice Ophelia Birdwhistell Phillips, at the home of Rev. H.H. McGinty on South Main Street in Lawrenceburg.

Russell and Annie Ruth both worked at the Bond Mill Distillery until Russell was laid off. They had to move five times within one year, finally he had to seek work in Louisville collecting money for magazines, Ben Lyen offered him a job with C. D. Lyen and Company where he worked until 1964 when he established Overstreet Plumbing and Heating which he operated out of his home on Fairview Ave. until he was forced to retire due to ill health in 1980.

Russell J. and Annie Ruth Overstreet, Russell T. Wilda, Ray and Elizabeth.

Annie worked at the Lawrenceburg Grade School as a cook and worked at the Anderson Grill on Saturday's and Sunday's until she went to work at J.C.H. Brown's Distillery where she retired after 25 years of service.

Russell served in the United States Navy during World War II and was honorably discharged from the United States Naval Personnel Separation Center, Great Lakes, Illinois on the 2nd day of November 1945.

Russell and Annie Ruth were the parents of Elizabeth, Wilda Ray and Russell Thurman. They were all born in Anderson County and reside there.

Russell's family was the center of attraction in his life. Not one holiday would pass without a huge meal and all of his children, grandchildren, and great-grandchildren gathering and joining in the joyous occasion.

He had a great passion for the young and old. He watched over his father morning and night to see to his needs. Russell was always there for the elderly and the people with young children anytime, day or night, even in the dead of winter. He was one of the most honored and respected men that ever graced the streets of Lawrenceburg. Russell died on July 1, 1983 at his home on Fairview. *Submitted By: Brenda Overstreet*

BRENDA PARRISH, the daughter of Clarence
Wesley Parrish and Louise Vela Kirsch Parrish, was raised in Cox's Creek, KY where her family had resided since the 1800's. In her second year of high school her family moved to Bardstown, KY. She attended Nelson County High School for two years and Bardstown High School for two years. It was in high school that she met Francis Larry Donahue.

Together they had two children: Mark Donahue and Kyle Wesley Donahue. Brenda and the two children reside in Lawrenceburg. She has four brothers and sisters: Jimmy Parrish married Joann Parrish; Norman Parrish married Kathy Parrish; Marilyn Parrish married Donald Jones; and Kathy Parrish married Yancy Parrish.

Larry Donahue resides in Bardstown. He has four brothers and sisters: Jane Donahue Durbin; Linda Donahue; Nolin Donahue; and Pascal Donahue. *Submitted By: Mark Donahue.*

JOHN KIRK PEACE was born on 11-5-1951 in Hodgenville, KY. He is the son of Herbert E. Peace (9-17-1928 - 12-3-1985) and Mary E. Davenport Peace (born 8-17-1928). He has two brothers: Don Glenn Peace, born 9-14-1949, married Rose Mary Norfleet; and Timothy Herbert Peace, born 4-29-1962, married Belinda Sue Routte.

John Kirk Peace married Vicki Lee Hoover on 6-6-1971 in Lexington, KY. She was born on 5-31-1950 in Louisville, KY. She is the only child of Robert L. Hoover (born 12-17-1923) and Florida Bertha Young Hoover (born 7-10-1926).

John Kirk and Vicki Lee Peace are the parents of two sons: Robert G. Peace, born 7-1-1970, and John Emanuel "Jay" Peace, born 7-31-1974. Both were born on Wildcat Road in Anderson County.

Robert L. Hoover served in the U.S. Army during World War II. While on duty in Italy, he was baptized in the freezing Boltona River. He served in Italy and France. He was also a POW in Germany. He earned a Purple Heart, he had a piece of shrapnel from a bomb go through his back, missing all his organs. It went all the way through and landed in his front pocket. He also got grazed on the back of his head with a bullet, but it didn't do much damage. (He still has the shrapnel and the bullet.) *Submitted By: Jay Peace.*

DANIEL PEACH, born 1765, married Elizabeth Gibson on 10-25-1793 in Fauquier County, Virginia. She was the daughter of William and Hannah Settle Gibson. It was in Fauquier County that seven children were born to Daniel and Elizabeth: Hannah (1794 - 1833) married James Bennett. She and her husband died soon after the birth of their third child. Their young children were raised by Elizabeth Gibson Peach; Catherine "Kitty" (1797 - 1853) never married; Theresa (1799 - ?) married Anthony Hunn, a well-known doctor - two sons and one daughter ; Susan (1808 - ?) married Lawrence Vanarsdall - ten children - after the death of her husband she apparently left the area; George Henry (1813 - 1889) ; Sanford (1814 - 1845) married Elizabeth Carnes - three children - they also lived with their grandmother after Sanford died; and William (below).

The Peach family lived in Fauquier County for 20 years before starting their journey to Kentucky in 1814. Together the Peachs and Gibsons traveled from Virginia to Kentucky. The Peaches settled in Lincoln County, KY while the Gibsons made their home in Garrard County, KY.

It is not known whether Daniel Peach died in Virginia or perhaps shortly after arriving, as the first records in Kentucky on this family show Elizabeth Gibson Peach as head of the household in the year 1815.

William Peach (1802 - 1877) married Lydia Ann Nailor on 7-6-1830 in Lincoln County. There were born to them in this county, 13 children: Alexander (died young); William (1832 - 1875 — murdered) married Margaret Utley - six children - Mary, James, Fox, Betty, Anna, and Andrew; Lydia Ann (1834 - ?) married William Vandiver; Maryetta (1836 - ?) married Peter Gibson - one son, George; Fountain (1838 - 1864 Civil War); George (1840 - 1862); Elizabeth (1842 - ?) married Cyrus Gibson; Samuel (1844 - 1926) married Nancy Marlow - five children - Susan, Ida, Holly, Maude, and Amos; Catherine (1846 - ?) married F. M. Smalley; Thomas Daniel (1848 - 1931) married Liza Jane Pulliam - eight children; Angeline (1850 - ?) married Thomas Murphy; Peter; and Josephine.

William and Lydia Ann died in Lawrenceburg exactly four months apart. The year was 1877. The descendant of William and Lydia Ann have lived in the town of Lawrenceburg for more than 100 years. *Submitted By: Melissa Peach.*

DANIEL PEACH was born in 1765 in Virginia and died in 1814. He married Elizabeth Gibson (1774 - 1853) in Fauquier County, VA. She was the daughter of William Gibson and Hannah Settle. Daniel and Elizabeth were the parents of seven children: Hannah married James Bennett; Catherine; Theresa married Anthony Hunn; William married Lydia Ann Nailor; Susan married Lawrence Vandarsdall; George Henry (below); and Sanford married Elizabeth Carnes.

George Henry Peach was born on 12-6-1813 in Fauquier County, VA and died in Ohio County, KY. On 8-27-1832, he married Catherine Compton (1819 - 1842). She was the daughter of Burris Compton and Ann Dismuke. They had a son named Thomas William. He was born in 1841 in Lincoln County, KY and died on 8-11-1919. On 6-22-1864, he married Josephine Egerton (1837 - 1897). They had a son named Vardeman.

Vardeman Peach was born in 1865 in Anderson County and died in 1949 in Anderson County. On 4-4-1893, he married Visa Barnett (1873 - 1939). She was the daughter of John and Jelila Barnett. Vardeman and Visa had a son, Roscoe, on 3-12-1903 in Sinai, KY. Roscoe married Audie Ward in 1932. She was born on 1-19-1906 in Mercer County and died on 1-1-1981 in Frankfort, KY. She was the daughter of Frank Ward (1863 - 1917) and Liza Hume (1868 - 1949). On 6-14-1944, they had a son, Al, in Sinai. Al married Mary Mitchell on 6-7-1969. . On 3-7-1975 in Frankfort, KY, Al and Mary Peach had a son named Tim. Mary is the daughter of John Mitchell and Ethel Gibson.

John Mitchell served in World War II from 1942 - 1945, he served in the 1st Army in the 4th Infantry Division under Lt. General Courtney H. Hedges. His Division was forced to surrender due to low ammunition on 12-16-1944 to German soldiers. He was taken as a POW. During his time as a POW, he suffered many hardships. He only managed to survive due to an old guard who had been a POW in World War I. This guard knew that when the American forces came the prisoners would be killed. The guard hid John Mitchell's group in an old movie theatre nearby in Hamburg, Germany.

For his time in service, John Mitchell received three Bronze Stars and the Blue Field Rifle Medal for expert rifleman. He also won the European Operation Ribbon for his time spent in Europe. *Submitted By: Tim Peach.*

VARDEMAN PEACH, was born in 1868 in Anderson County. He died in 1949. On 4-4-1893, Vardeman married Visa Barnett (1873 - 1939), the daughter of John and Jellie Barnett. They were the parents of six children: James Peach, born 1895 - never married; Minnie, born 1897, married Wallace Peach; John Will; Josie (1902 - 1970) married William Ward - three sons - Edward, William, and Roy; Roscoe, born 1903, married Frances Ward - six children - Onis, Roscoe, Dorthy, Betty, Albert, and Alberta; and Lou Tish, born 1904, married James Case - three daughters - Cora, Mary, and Virginia.

John Will Peach was born in November of 1899 in Anderson County and died on 3-11-1982 in Anderson County. He married Zorilla Ward in September 1921 in Indiana. She was born on 8-5-1903 and died on 1-22-1978 in Anderson County. She was the daughter of Thomas W. Ward and Ophelia Adams Ward. John Will and Zorilla Peach were the parents of nine children: Ruby, born 1922, married Sidney H. Drury - four children - Linda, Sidney, Connie, and Paul; Thomas, born 1923, married Henrietta Cornish - six children - Bobby, Jerald, Jerry, Scottie, Peggy, and Anthony; Raymond, born 1925, married Lillian Faye Drury - two children - Brenda and Gilbert;

Forest, born 1928, married Ortha R. Cornish - one child, Maxy; Charles (below); John, born 1933, married Marlene Drury - three children - Johnny, Terri, and Dennis; Donnie, born 1936, married 1st Linda Barnett, 2nd Linda Parsons - two children - Mellisa and Robin; Betty Rose, born 1938, married Aaron Barnett - two children - Kenneth and Vickie; and Barbara, born 1941, married Kenneth Montgomery - three children - Rita, Kenneth, and Janet.

Charles Peach was born 2-16-1931 in Anderson County. He married Janice Stratton on 3-4-1950. Charles and Janice are the parents of four daughters: Judy Diane, born 1950, married 1st Harold Wayne Stockton - two sons, Douglas Wayne and David Martin - 2nd Paul Polly; Charlene, 1953, married 1st Johnny Brown - two children, Roger and Susan - 2nd Paul Cornish; Martha, born 1960, married Danny Robinson - two children - Mandy and Tori Lee; and Marilyn, born 1957, married Bobby Shryock - one daughter, Amy.

Janice Stratton Peach was born on 4-14-1936. She is the daughter of Obed Kenneth Stratton (1907 - 1989) and Madge Beatrice Holt Stratton (1908 - 1978). She has seven brothers and sisters: Lenora, born 1928, married Bill Drummond - two sons - David and Steve; Jane Irene, born 1929, married Ernest Wood - five children - Ernest, Scotty, Terry, Jeff, and Lisa; William Dudley, born 1931, married Joyce Sea - four children - Sandy, Wayne, Anthony, and Tamara; Daniel Michael, born 1941, married Betty Mae - two daughters - Rhonda and Jennifer; Geraldine, born 1943, married Winston Drury - two children - Jackie and Obad; and Kenneth Bronston, born 1934, married Jo Royalty. *Submitted By: David M. Stockton.*

THOMAS DANIEL PEACH, the son of William and Lydia Ann Nailor, was born on 5-8-1848 in Lincoln County, KY. There he married Liza Jane Pulliam on 6-30-1878 She was born on 5-9-1858 in Washington County, KY. She was the daughter of Edward Pulliam. They were the parents of eight children: Thomas Hudson (below); Lydia (1881 - ?) married M. T. Peyton; Alma (1883 - 1911); John (1885 - 1950) married Alma Brown - ten children - Ella, Clara, Catherine, Lela, Dorotha, Thomas, Mildred, Pauline, John, and Onita; twins, Nettie (1887 - ?) married Bevoni Puckett - one son, Earl, and Lettie (1887 - ?) married Jesse Peach; Alice (1891 - 1970) married Victory Puckett; and Mell (1896 - 1966) married Ida Peak - three children - Ethel, Jerome, and Michael.

Thomas Hudson Peach was born on 5-17-1879 in Anderson County. He married Susie Kate Searcy in Lawrenceburg. She was born on 2-27-1884 in Anderson County to William and Lucy Brown Searcy. Thomas and Susie had ten children: Lucy, born 1906, married Herbert Neal - one daughter - Mary; William (1908 - 1979) married Lillie Sea - four children - Edna, William, Lillian, and Virginia; Vernon (1910 - 1981) married Ora Sea - two children - Vernon and Shirley; J. B., born 1911, married Willard Sea - two children - Mildred and James; Mattie, born 1914, married Ben Bruner - one child, Alvie; Annie, born 1918, married Clinton Sea - six children - Barbara, Gilbert, Margaret, Sadie, Calbert; Herman (below); Katherine, born 1920, married Hubert Sparrow - five children - Ezra, Mary, Barbara, Allen, and David; Susie, born 1922, married Eddie Burge; and Nettie, born 1926. Thomas Hudson Peach died on 12-6-1945 and Susie Peach died on 7-17-1957, both died in Lawrenceburg.

Herman Peach was born on 5-11-1916 in Anderson County. He married Ethel Whobrey Peach on 10-2-1937 in Lawrenceburg. She was born on 8-31-1917 in Grayson County and died on 9-30-1985 in Anderson County. She was the daughter of Alfred Whobrey and Mary Conder Whobrey. Six children were born to Herman and Ethel. They were: Jimmie, born 1939, married Brenda Gash - two children - Kelly and Kevin; Herman Lee, born 1941, married Becky Drury - three children - Debbie, Ricky, and Susan; Kenneth (below); Linda, born 1946, married Ralston Puckett - three children - Connie, Tony, and David; Rita, born 1948, married Bobby Fields - three children - Barbara, Herman, and Bobby - divorced; and Billy, born 1950.

Kenneth Peach was born on 1-4-1945 in Anderson County. He married Donna Gail Hutton on 8-10-1973 in Lawrenceburg. She was born on 6-29-1949 in Frankfort and is the daughter of Guy Hutton and Loraine Payton Hutton. Kenneth and Donna are the parents of three children: Stephanie, born 1968, married Roy Alves in 1986 - one son, Ryan; Jennifer, born 1971,; and Melissa, born 1974. *Submitted By: Melissa Peach.*

WILLARD AND MAUDIE SPARROW PEACH were lifelong residents of Anderson County. They owned a farm on Fairmont Road for many years.

Willard was born July 17, 1889. He was the son of Peter and Mary Leathers Peach. He was the great-grandson of Daniel and Elizabeth Gibson Peach who came to this area from Virginia in 1814.

Maudie was born November 4, 1892. She was the daughter of Lewis and Nannie Richardson Sparrow. She was the great-granddaughter of Henry Sparrow and Lucy Shipley Sparrow.

Willard and Maudie Sparrow Peach on 50th Wedding Anniversary

Willard and Maudie were married January 19, 1909. They were the parents of seven children: one son, Herbert Harrison died at birth; Vurvie Ellen married Robert Brown. They had one son, William Thomas, one daughter, Mary Frances Henson, and raised one granddaughter, Diane Poole. Vurvie lives at 549 South Main St. Robert and William are both deceased; Ernest married Annie Searcy. They had one son, Bobby, and three daughters, Christine, Margaret, and Daphna. Ernest, Annie, and Christine are deceased; Marjorie is married to Walter Brown and they live on North Main Street. She has three daughters, Edna Mae, Rosetta, and Onita. Onita is deceased; Mattie was married to the late J. B. Robinson. She lives in Louisville. They had two daughters, Betty Jean and Virginia; Leslie and his wife, Lucille, live in Louisville. He is retired from G.E. He has three sons and three daughters; and Jesse is Leslie's twin brother. He was married to the late Frances Casey and they had five daughters and one son. The son died at birth. Jesse is also retired from G.E. and now lives in Shelbyville.

Willard and Maude were married for 57 years. They were members of the New Liberty Christian Church. Maudie died February 3, 1966 from cancer. Willard died May 15, 1971 at the home of his daughter, Vurvie Brown. *Submitted By: Diane Poole.*

WILLIAM JACKSON PERRY married Catherine Young in 1817 and thus began a long and prosperous linage of Perry descendants. They reared eight children but perhaps their first child, John Young Perry, was responsible for more of the Perry offspring than any other. John Young Perry was born December 29, 1817 and passed from this world on October 14, 1880. He married Lydia Herndon on November 24, 1841 and she bore him fifteen chil-

dren. These children and their spouses are William B. (Sarah E. ?), Lewis Gideon "Bob" (Mary Emma Palmer), Lucy J. (Brice Willard), John (Sarah DeWitt), Sarah (Matt Melear), Alfred (died as an infant), Thornton (Margaret Briscoe), Preston (Sarah Alice Siers), Henry Thomas (Malinda Burke), Benjamin (Jennie Cinnamon), Alvin Herndon (Sally Cahill), George McClelland (1st Mary Ann Cinnamon, 2nd Rhoda Espy Cinnamon, 3rd Bertha Proctor), James (Elceria Tipton), Merriett, Susan (Thomas Houchin). Thornton Perry killed his brother-in-law , Matt Melear, with an axe. Story has it that Thornton was sent to Eastern Kentucky to work on a chain gang. There he was believed to have been in a fight in which he was scalded to death. John Young Perry and his wife Lydia are buried on the old Josiah Martin Farm on the Hammonds Creek Road.

Henry Thomas Perry, son of John Y. and Lydia Perry, was born February 3, 1857 and died January 28, 1925. He married Malinda C. Burke, daughter of William F. Burke and Marilis Bond, on October 14, 1880. Henry and Malinda Perry's children and spouses include Susan Mary (Charles Catlett), Rosa (Murf Thurman), Lemon Thomas (Mary Holmes), Jesse (Grace Phillips), Sally (Charles Abrams), Mona (Hollie Brown), Julia (Hollie Searcy), John Willie (Ruby Franklin), Claude (Anna Robinson), Roscoe (Eva Catlett), Emma (none). Henry Perry was an Anderson County farmer and was left to raise several young children as Malinda Burke Perry died in 1904 when their youngest child was only three years old.

John Willie Perry and Ruby Franklin Perry

John Willie Perry, son of Henry and Malinda Perry, married Ruby Franklin, daughter of Zack Franklin and Samantha Johnson, on December 22, 1926. John was a farmer also, and for years operated the Anderson County Home for the Aged. The County Home, or Poor House as it was called then, was located near the intersection of highways 44 and 395 near Glensboro. In May of 1955, John and Ruby moved to the present location of the County Home (Sunset Hill) and operated it until John died in July of 1957. John Willie was known to spin a tall tale or two and was well liked in the community. The children of John and Ruby Perry along with their spouses are Alice Kathleen (died young), Helen Jean (Elmer Hume), Arnold Cole (Jo Ann Vowels), John Allen (Wanda Hoskins), Nancy Roberta (Ralph Bowen), William Ronald (Brenda Young). Currently in 1989, these children remain in Anderson county. Arnold "Buck" is a farmer, John Allen is the present Property Valuation Administrator, Nancy is employed at the Wild Turkey Distillery, and William "Ronnie" is a local barber. Helen passed away in 1959 and rests in the Lawrenceburg Cemetery. *Submitted By: Billy Jo Hume.*

WILLIAM JACKSON PERRY married Catherine Young on 2-28-1817. They had eight children. These children and their spouses are: John Young Perry (Lydia Frances Herndon), Sarah A. (John Gordon), Berry (Polly Searcy), Mary, George W., Christopher (Francis L. Lucas), Elizabeth (Alfred Gowen), and William (Sarah Payne Crook).

John Young Perry married Lydia Frances Herndon

on 11-24-1841. They had fifteen children. These children and their spouses are: William (Sarah "Judy" Sires), Lewis Gideon "Bob" (Mary E. Palmer), Lucy J. (Brice Willard), John (Sarah DeWitt), Sarah C. (1st Matt MeLear, 2nd Joe Rucker), Alfred (died at six months), Thornton Perry (Margaret Briscoe), Preston (Sarah Alice Siers), Henry T. (Malinda C. Burk), Benjamin (Mahula Jane Cinnamon), Alvin Herndon (Sarah Ellen CaHill), George B. McClellan (1st May Ann Cinnamon, 2nd Rhody Espy Cinnamon, 3rd Bertha Proctor), James B. (Ellera Tipton), Merrit, and Susan (Thomas Houchin).

Berry Perry married Polly Searcy. Family story handed down was that Berry was a big man. They said he had hands as big as a ham. They had seven children: John, George, Alford, Sarah, William, Charles, and Nancy.

Sarah married John Gordon. They had seven children: Jim Berry, John Jr. (Miranda Snider), Jasper (Icie Pulliam), Mary E. (John Abrams), Malissa (Buck Brown), Mason H., and Hider. Mason and Hider both married but the wives names are not known to the writer of this history.

Elizabeth married Alfred Gowen. They had one known child, a daughter, Amanda.

William married Sarah Payne Crook. They had five children. William (died as a small child), Celesta (Lewis Dudley Gowens), Cecil (Garret W. D. Reed), James Madison "Wax" (Myrtle Rogers), and Jesse. *Submitted By: Paula Perry Mitchell.*

ALVIN HERNDON PERRY married Sarah Ellen CaHill on 11-24-1886. They had five children. These children and their spouses are: Annie Thomas (Vester "Doc" Searcy), Floyd Granson (Radie E. Searcy), Ezra Lee (Minnie Earl Wilson), Jordan Hubert, and Julian Bishop (Lillie Mae Young).

Alvin farmed all of his life and was quite a good fiddle player. Annie played the guitar and together they kept the family entertained.

Julian Bishop "B-Tom" married Lillie Mae Young on 1-20-1926. J. B. farmed all his life and was a good carpenter. He was a deacon of the Pigeon Fork Baptist Church from 1936 until his death in 1977. In 1926, J. B. and Lil were selected as housekeepers and caretakers of the church and the grounds until their retirement in 1974. Their children and their spouses are: Paul Thomas "P. T." (Lela Powers) and Herman Gilbert (Margaret "Peggy" VanMeter.)

John and Wanda Perry

P. T. was quite an athlete. A basketball star for Waddy High School he once made a basket the length of the court. After serving in the army he played baseball for the Red Sox organization in Oneonta, New York, Melford, Delaware, and Roanoke, Virginia from 1948 - 1951. P. T. and Lela were married on 3-3-1949. In 1951 they moved back to Kentucky to raise the family. They have two daughters, Cynthia Louise and Paula Lynne.

Cindy is a graduate of Cumberland College and Eastern Kentucky University. Cindy is a music teacher in Garrard County.

Paula is a Certified Dietary Manager utilizing her abilities in the health care field. She is married to

Stephen Mitchell, a photographer for the last six Kentucky governors. They reside in Frankfort where both are employed.

Herman and Peggy were married on 12-21-1963. They have two children: Sarah Anne and David Julian "Chip" Perry. Both children are attending college. *Submitted By: Paula Perry Mitchell.*

ARNOLD AND JOANNE PERRY are lifelong residents of Anderson County, Kentucky.

Arnold or "Buck", as he is known by most people, is the son of the late John Willie Perry and Ruby Franklin Perry and was born in Anderson County on June 2, 1931. He is the third of six children, sisters - Alice Kathleen Perry died at the age of four months, Helen Hume Perry died in 1959 at the age of 30 and Nancy Perry Bowen; brothers - John and Ronnie, all live in Anderson County.

Arnold attended grade school in the county. Arnold served two years in US Army from October 5, 1954 to October 5, 1956. He was stationed at Fort Knox, Kentucky and Fort Hood, Texas.

Joanne was born in Anderson County on April 8, 1932. She was the daughter of Frances Campbell Vowels and the late Klien Vowels. She was the youngest of three children. She had two sisters, Mary Vowels Koger and Martha Vowels Crutcher, both live in Anderson County.

Arnold and Joanne Perry

Joanne attended Lawrenceburg Elementary, and was a member of the first class to graduate from Anderson County High School (class of 1950), after the consolidation of Lawrenceburg and Kavanaugh High Schools.

Before entering the service, Arnold and Joanne were married on September 25, 1954. Arnold has farmed all of his life and Joanne is a housewife.

Arnold and Joanne are the parents of two children - Klien age 31 is employed at General Cable and is married to Peggy Redding of Franklin County. Klien and Peggy have two children, Kristen age 8, and Travis age 6.

Anne age 26 is employed at the Anderson National Bank and is married to Dennis Stidham.

Arnold and Joanne have been residents of 411 North Main Street for 34 years. Arnold is a member of the Corinth Christian Church and Joanne is a member of the Lawrenceburg First Baptist Church.

E. PAUL PERRY, son of Delbert and Mary Zella Briscoe Perry, was born in Anderson County on June 8, 1924. He attended and graduated from Anderson City School. He worked on the farm until entering the U.S. Navy in 1944.

After returning home from the Navy, he worked at Dean and Sherk, later named American Effird Mills, in Lawrenceburg. While working there he met Mary Lucille Hatchett. They were married April 27, 1946.

E. Paul and Lucille have two children, Charles Allen Perry of Lexington, KY and Ernie Wayne Perry of Chesapeake, Ohio.

Paul became a Christian and member of the Corinth Christian Church in September 1939, and was very active in this congregation. In 1951, the decision was made to go full time in the Christian

Ministry. He, Lucille, and Charles moved to Grayson, Ky, where Paul became a full time student at Kentucky Christian College. He had begun preaching two Sundays per month at the Pleasant Hill Christian Church in January 1951. In January 1952, he accepted a call to preach at the Mayo Christian Church in Mercer County the other two Sundays per month and also the fifth Sundays.

In May 1955, E. Paul graduated Summa Cum Laude from Kentucky Christian College and near the same time received a GED High School Diploma from Prichard High School, Grayson, KY. The family moved back home at Alton Station and lived there while preaching at Pleasant Hill and Mayo through 1955, and a three year ministry at the Fairview Christian Church in Washington County.

E. Paul and Lucille Perry

Other ministries have been: Chaplin Christian Church (Chaplin, KY), Syria Christian Church (Orleans, Indiana), Henry Christian Church (Eminence, KY), Oak Grove Christian Church (Beckley, West Virginia), Antioch Christian Church (Mount Sterling, KY), and Salyersville Christian Church (Salyersville, KY).

In addition to the above ministries, Brother Perry has preached and worked in over 100 evangelistic meetings throughout Kentucky and other states including Indiana, Ohio, West Virginia, North Carolina, Missouri, Virginia, and Hawaii.

Other areas of ministry and service: served on faculty and dean of the following Christian Service Camps - Blue Grass Christian Assembly, Wonder Valley, Camp Calvary, and Howell Mill Christian Assembly; served in Naval Reserve; received the Community Leader of America Award; awarded plaque of appreciation for service rendered from the Limestone Crusaders in Indiana and the Salt River Christian Men's Fellowship in Kentucky; served two terms as Vice-President of the Kentucky Christian College Alumni Association and one term as President of the Association; has served many terms as member of the Council of Fifty of the College; and listed in the 1978 edition of Who's Who in Religion.

In the spring of 1986, the Perrys accepted a call to the ministry of the Graefenburg Christian Church in Graefenburg, KY. They bought a home in Lawrenceburg on Meriwether Drive. So E. Paul and Lucille are again living back in Anderson County, Kentucky, preaching and ministering in Shelby County. *Submitted By: E. Paul Perry.*

KLIEN PERRY, son of Arnold and Joanne Vowels Perry, was born 4-19-1957. (See Perry Article.) He attended grade school at Saffell St. Elementary, junior high at Anderson Jr. High School, and senior high at Anderson County High School. He worked with his dad on the farm and started employment with General Cable Company in Anderson County on 12-15-1975 and remains employed there.

On 9-1-1979, Klien Perry married Peggy Jo Redding. Peggy was born on 2-22-1958 in Franklin County and is the daughter of Billy Redding. Peggy attended Holmes St. Grade School, Elkhorn Elementary School and Franklin Co. High School. She became employed for the Kentucky State Government

Klien, Peggy, Kristin and Travis Perry

in 1976. She remains employed there today in the Department of Purchasing.

Klien and Peggy have two children, Kristin Nicole age 9 and Travis Klien age 7. They reside at 1118 Dudley Street in Lawrenceburg. Klien's hobbies and interests are church, family, hunting and fishing. Peggy enjoys reading, sewing, and cooking. They attend Heritage Baptist Church in Anderson County. Klien has one sister, Mrs. Dennis (Anne) Stidham, and she resides in Anderson County. Peggy has three sisters and one brother. Her brother is Ricky Redding and he lives in Frankfort, KY. Two sisters, Mrs. Jerry (Jonna) Howard and Jill Redding, live in Frankfort also. Her other sister, Mrs. Randy (Susan) Peyton, lives in Lawrenceburg. *Submitted By: Klien Perry.*

JOHN A. PERRY is the son of the late Ruby Franklin Perry and John Willie Perry. (See Franklin and Perry articles) He was born 9-7-1938, and grew up in Glensboro and Birdie vicinity of the county. He was educated in the Anderson County school system graduating in 1956. He attended and completed Louisville Barber School in 1958, and apprenticed and continued to work in Georgetown. In 1961, he returned to Lawrenceburg and operated the Barber Shop on Main Street for nine years. In 1970, he was appointed by Judge Hollie Warford to fulfill the unexpired term of Prentice Martin as tax commissioner. He has held this position to the present. In 1974, he became a partner in Birdwhistell and Perry Realty and Auction Company, and is currently engaged in this business. He and Glen Birdwhistell also own and operate a farm in Fox Creek and enjoy raising registered Angus cattle.

Wanda Hoskins Perry is the daughter of Raymond Hoskins, and the late Sara Katherine Sea. She was born 2-23-1939 in the Sinai vicinity of the county, but grew up on the Frankfort Road and the Alton vicinity. She graduated in 1957, and attended Georgetown College and Kentucky State College. She taught 6th grade at Alton Elementary for two years and was a substitute teacher for several years.

left to right: Jordan Perry, Alvin Herndon Perry, Ezra Perry, Annie Thomas Perry, Sarah Ellen Perry, Floyd Perry (on horse).

She and John married 12-20-1958. They have one son, Timothy Allen who is Assistant Vice President at the Lawrenceburg National Bank and have two grandsons, Christopher Adam Allen, age 12 and Timothy Brian, age nine. They have one daughter, Mary Katherine "Kathy" Adams who works for the

American Red Cross in Honolulu, Hawaii and two granddaughters, Ashlyn Brooke, age two and Courtlyn Adair, one month, (see Adams article).

In 1972, Wanda became deputy in the tax office after the retirement of Pearl Martin. She holds this position to the present. *Submitted By: Wanda Perry.*

KEN AND RITA PHILLIPS were both born and raised in Anderson County. Ken is the only child of Lister Carl and Martha Drury Phillips. Rita is the third child of Theodore and Mary Peyton Hutton. She has a sister, Barbara Ann Thacker and a brother, Allen Hutton. Ken was born on July 2, 1946, and lived during his childhood at McBrayer near Seagram's Distillery. Prior to his entering high school his parents moved to Stringtown, just across the road from Rita's grandparents, Frank and Ruth Peyton.

Rita was born on August 22, 1948, and, like Ken, attended Sand Spring School and Anderson High School. After Rita graduated from high school in 1966, she worked briefly for the State Government before joining the Sylvania Glass Plant in Versailles. She worked there while Ken attended Georgetown College. He graduated in May of 1968, with a degree in Business Administration.

Ken and Rita were married on July 12, 1968. While Rita continued to work at Sylvania, Ken accepted a position with the U.S. Treasury Department, Bureau of Alcohol, Tobacco and Firearms in Lawrenceburg, Indiana. He commuted to work there until mid-December when he was drafted into the U.S. Army. He spent time at Fort Knox, Kentucky, Fort Holabird, Maryland, and Fort Hood, Texas , before leaving for a year in Vietnam. While there, Ken worked in military intelligence with the First Infantry Division in Lai Khe and with the 7th Psychological Operations Batallion in Da Nang.

Ken, Rita, Jason and Ben Phillips

Rita came home from Fort Hood and went to work for John Willie Carlton in the County Clerk's office on January 1, 1970. She worked there for Clerk Carlton and later Clerk Julian Birdwhistell for seven years.

After returning from the service, Ken resumed work with the federal government in Frankfort. He has continued to work for BATF in either Frankfort or Louisville since.

In January 1978, Rita became a secretary for Dale Wright and Ray Edelman in Lawrenceburg. While employment was initially part-time, is subsequently became full time. She presently works for Ray Eldelman, at 140 South Main Street. Also Rita worked for a number of years as Secretary to the Lawrenceburg-Anderson County, KY Joint Planning Commission.

Ken and Rita are the parents of two sons, Jason Neil Phillips, born on December 7, 1972, and Benjamin Kent Phillips, born on February 6, 1977. Both have been active in Scouts and both play drums in the band; both are honor students and have been very active in academic competition, as well as other school activities.

Ken served as president of the Lawrenceburg Lions Club in 1977-78, as well as various other offices in local, district, and state levels. Rita has been active

for a number of years in the local chapter of the national sorority, Beta Sigma Phi. Both Ken and Rita spend a lot of their free time on projects of the ACHS Band Boosters and the ACHS Academic Boosters.

Ken, Rita, Jason and Ben are all members of the Sand Spring Baptist Church. Since 1971, they have resided at 407 Carlton Drive in Lawrenceburg. *Submitted By: Rita Phillips.*

STANLEY PHILLIPS was born in Mercer County on 6-18-1922 to David and Mattie Kurtz Phillips. He lived most of his childhood in the Braxton area of Mercer County. The other children of David and Mattie Phillips were: Alvin, who died at birth; Dave; Raymond; Carl; and Albert; and daughters: Sarah, who married H. R. Hall; Ruth, who married Raymon Grider; Lena, who married Lee C. Sims; and Lela, who died at the age of seven of diphtheria.

Frances Elizabeth West was born to Robert and Annie Martin West on 2-20-1921, and grew up on the Dawson Ferry Road in Anderson County. Her brothers included: Lester Thomas, who died at birth; Earl; Robert Taylor; Joe; and Elzie West. Sisters included: Genevieve (Mrs. Earl) Gregory; Rose (Mrs. Chester) Sutherland; Leone (Mrs. Harold) Flynn; and Nora (Mrs. Harold) Knight.

Stanley Phillips and Frances Elizabeth West were married on 6-18-1938 by the Rev. M. D. Morton at the Sand Spring Baptist Church parsonage. They are both members of Sand Spring Baptist Church, reside on Harry Wise Road and have lived in that vicinity most of their married lives.

Seated: Stanley, and Frances Phillips with children: Mary, John, Mattie Stanley Jr., Ruth and Marvin. June 18, 1988 50th Wedding Anniversary

They are the parents of six living children and one who died at birth. Sons include Stanley Jr., who married Frankie Sue Lollis and now resides in Hayes, Virginia; John Robert, who is married to Martha Gregory; and Marvin Ray, who is married to Sue Ann Driskell Freeman. Both John and Marvin live in Anderson County. Daughters include Frances Lucille, deceased; Mary Elizabeth (Mrs. James Allen) Hawkins; Mattie Catherine Cheek, both of Anderson county; and Ruth Ann (Mrs. Garry Delbert) Carpenter of Lancaster, KY.

The Phillipses have ten grandchildren; Brenda Hawkins Suttles, Linda Faye Hawkins Carmickle, Wayne Kent Hawkins, Donna Marie Phillips, Michael Scott Phillips, Tina Marie Phillips Paris, Steven Neal Phillips, Alan Derek Phillips, Kelly Francine Cheek, and Phillip Weston Carpenter. They also have two great-grandchildren, Amber Marie Carmickle and Christopher Brandon Carmickle.

Mrs. Phillips is a housewife, however, she worked for a while at the thread factory and the button company.

Mr. Phillips, a former city policeman, is retired from Boulevard Distillery where he is fondly remembered by many who worked with him for his concern of others. He is a member of the Stringtown Ruritan Club and works when needed for Huddleston Funeral Home. In addition to public work, he has farmed most of his life.

Submitted By: Mattie Cheek.

RAYMOND I. AND CATHERINE UTTERBACK PLEASANT were educators in Lawrenceburg's black community. Raymond was born in 1890, the eldest of three sons of Carlton and Lucy Berry Pleasant. One of 16 children, Catherine was born in 1888 to Thomas and Amanda Meaux Utterback. The elder Mr. Pleasant was a mortician in the city. After graduating from Cincinnati School of Embalming, his son joined him in this endeavor.

Both Mr. and Mrs. Pleasant were graduates of Kentucky State College in Frankfort. He was in the Class of 1932, the second graduating class after the institution became a college. She graduated in 1936, a member of the class considered by many to be the most outstanding in the history of the institution. They both also received their high school diplomas from the High School Department of Kentucky State.

Catherine Pleasant - Raymond I. Pleasant

Mr. Pleasant's first teaching position was at Georgetown School in Anderson County, where he was followed by his wife. She served there over 30 years, until the one room school was closed. Her first job was in London, KY at a salary of $25.25 per month. They were required to keep their marriage a secret until the stipulation that female teachers could not be married was lifted. Both taught for years before receiving their college degrees. They would teach during the school year and attend college during the Spring Quarter and Summer School.

Mr. Pleasant was principal of the Lawrenceburg Colored School when it was located in the Grove. He also served as principal of several schools throughout the state including one in Morganfield.

The Pleasants were active in the social and religious affairs of the community. He was a trustee of the Second Christian Church and she was a staunch member of Evergreen Baptist Church. Mr. Pleasant died in 1941 and his wife survived until 1966 and did not remarry. Included in their family were four children: Lucille Harris Lynem, Santa Ana, California; Thomas Pleasant, Indianapolis, Indiana; Rhea Pleasant Hubbard, Santa Ana, California; and Naomi Pleasant Barkley, Cincinnati, Ohio. Other descendents include five grandchildren, five great-grandchildren, and three great-great-grandchildren. All live out of state. As a memorial to their parents, the children donated the Pleasant family home and the adjacent lot to the Evergreen Baptist Church as a location for their new church.

Both of these educators touched the lives of Lawrenceburg's black students and stories of Professor Pleasant and Miss Katie are still a part of the folklore of this community. Children who never knew them can relate to the tales as if they happened last week. Their devotion to education overcame the lack of equipment materials, adequate textbooks, electricity, and indoor plumbing by providing their students with a sense of pride and a desire to learn about things at hand and those in far away places. *Submitted By: Gertrude Cunningham.*

JAMES "JIM" STERLING POPE, a grandson of Martha Belle Ware Crossfield, was born in Omaha, Nebraska in 1914. He was the son of Charles J. Pope (1868 - 1840) and Ada Ware Pope (1882 - 1960). Charles came to Oklahoma Territory circa 1893 and was one of the early settlers of Kiowa County, Oklahoma Territory in 1902. He had a grocery store across the street from Squire M. Ware's Harness and Implement store. During the next few years the Ware girls did their shopping at Pope's Grocery and in time Ada and C. J. were married in 1905. C. J. and Ada had three children, two who died young with James being the sole survivor. C. J. was a hoisting engineer at Omaha, Neb. and in 1921 the family moved to Tyrone, Texas County, Oklahoma and farmed acreage with his brother Henry Pope and Ritchie Ware Pope (a sister of Ada). In 1929 - 30, the Pope families relocated in Baca County, Colorado where they farmed the remaining years of their lives. Jim entered military service during WW II in 1942 in the Corps of Engineers, U. S. Army. His stateside service was at Ft. Belvoir, Virginia where he was cadre at the Training Center, then an instructor at the Engineering School and later a draftsman in the 241st Eng. Battalion at Ft. Belvoir. In the summer of 1944, he was transferred to the 1769th Engineer Survey Liaison Detachment which soon went to the Southwest Pacific Area and was assigned to Headquarters, Sixth Army. His overseas tour of duty was in New Guinea, Leyte, Luzon and Japan. He returned to the U. S. in 1946 and was discharged at Ft. Logan Colorado as a T/Sgt. That same evening he and Fannie P. Fairchild of Washington, D. C., a daughter of Edward Lamar and Mary Blackmon Fairchild of Lauderdale County, Mississippi, were married in Denver, Colorado.

Jim and Fannie soon returned to Washington where they lived the next twelve years. They had one son, Michael Jay Pope, who was born in 1949 in Washington, D.C. In 1957, the family moved to St. Louis, MO where they were both employed by the Defense Mapping Agency - Aerospace Center (DMAAC). Jim's career was in mapping as a cartographer with the U. S. Army Map Service, U. S. Geological Survey, and DMAAC and Fannie's was as a mathematician and as a geodesist at U. S. Coast and Geodetic Survey and at DMAAC.

Jim's advanced collegiate work earned him a B. S. in Geography at Washington University, a M.S. in Cartography at St. Louis University, and a Ph. D. in History at St. Louis University. Fannie is a graduate of George Washington University with a B.A. in education with a mathematics major. Their son "Mike" graduated from Missouri University - Columbia as a geologist. His university work was interrupted by military service in 1971 - 1972 as a paratrooper assigned to Headquarters, 82nd Airborne Division. At the completion of his service he was discharged as a sergeant.

Jim retired in 1975 and Fannie in 1978. They have just moved to Boone County, MO where Mike and his family live. *Submitted By: James S. Pope*

JOHN BEN PRICE SR. was born on 11-6-1917 in Mercer County. He was the son of Willie Price and Evie Carmickle. He married Edna Beatrice Riley on 12-21-1940. She was born on 1-20-1924 in Mercer County. She is the daughter of George W. Riley and Frances Montgomery Riley.

They had six sons and one daughter: John Ben Jr., born 1941, married Sherlene Riley; David Carroll, born 1943, married Judy Leathers; Glenn Owen, born 1946, married Jane Freeman; James Robert "Bobby", born 1948, married Pat Dossett; Ronald Wayne, born 1951, married Arlene Driskell; Gary Michael "Mike" (below); and Donna Jean, born 1959, married Tim Shulte. John Ben Price Sr. passed away on 1-10-1987.

Gary Michael "Mike" Price was born on 8-12-1953 in Haggin Memorial in Mercer County. He met and married Virginia Mae Stratton on 8-20-1971 in Harrodsburg, KY at Cumberland Church. She is the daughter of Johnny and Murtie Stratton. They are the parents of three children: Twana Michelle, born 1-24-1973; Chasidy Marie, born 12-6-1977; and Gary Michael II, born 5-28-1979.

John Morton Stratton Jr. was born on 3-9-1905 in Anderson County. He was the son of John Morton Stratton Sr. (1861 - 1950) and Mammie Stratton (1873 - 1960). John married Murtie Wilson on 1-27-1931 in Mercer County. She was born on 5-11-1915 in Anderson County. She is the daughter of Murt Wilson (1882 - 1954) and Madie Harley Wilson (1893 - 1966). John and Murtie were the parents of 13 children: Elijah, born 1932, married Margie Davis; Jay, born 1934, married Jennie Crawford; Evelynn, born 1936, married Earl Hawkins; William, born 1938, married Phyllis Bingham; Cricket, born 1939, married James Carmickle; Elizabeth, born 1941, married Bruce Rogers; Sara, born 1942, married Wayne Doss; Roberts, born 1943, married Betty Tison; Joyce, born 1945, married Howard Douglas; Louise (May 1948 - December 1948); Goodloe (1949 - 1967); Gilbert, born 1952, married Mildred Reed; and Virginia. *Submitted By: Michelle Price.*

ROBERT PROPHET was born on 7-15-1935 in Shahala, Pennsylvania. He is the son of Robert L. Prophet (9-20-1901 - 1-28-1974) and Margaret Hobbes Prophet (9-19-1901 - 10-12-1987). He has two sisters: Charlotte Prophet, born 1921, married Stanley Tougher; and Florence Prophet, born 1923, married George Marshall.

Robert married Marylyn Kuss on 9-27-1953 in Pennsylvania. She was born on 5-9-1935 in New York, New York. She is the daughter of Helmut Kuss (1-18-1898 - 9-11-1973) and Mary Friedrich Kuss (born 5-6-1908 in Germany). She has one brother, Alfred Kuss, born 1949, who married Sarina.

At the age of five, Robert and his family moved to Barryville, New York. In 1946, he moved to SusqueShanna, Pennsylvania. Seven years after his marriage to Marylyn, they moved to Sherman, Texas. All of their children were born there. They lived in Texas for 14 years, then his employer, I. B. M. , transferred him to Anderson County.

Robert and Marylyn are the parents of seven children: Laura, born 1-14-1954, married Ricky Lashley; Karen, born 4-20-1956, married Dana Rindall; Allen, born 11-11-1961, married Christina Senson; Robert (born and died 2-10-1970); Baby (born and died 11-6-1972); Sue, born 1-28-1971; and Michael Robert, born 8-1-1973. The Prophet family currently resides in Anderson County. *Submitted By: Michael Prophet.*

JAMES ROBERT RAY was born on 2-20-1909 in Anderson County where he spent most of his life. He was the son of William C. and Martha Ann Sewell Ray. He married Elouise Gregory on 4-2-1939. Elouise Gregory was born on 4-10-1913. Also born in Anderson County, Elouise Ray still lives in Lawrenceburg on Versailles Road. Her parents were Chester and Ola Forston Gregory. James attended school in Anderson County and Elouise graduated from Lawrenceburg High School in 1931.

James worked at the local thread factory for 10-15 years and also did some farming; however, the majority of his life was spent as a respected carpenter who helped to build more than 150 houses in Anderson, Franklin, Woodford, and Fayette Counties. In 1931, James worked on the construction of the Tyrone Bridge. As a "common laborer" he worked 10 hours a day, six days a week and earned $2 to $2.50 per day. James collected prints and photographs of the bridge which reflected his interest and pride in his part of the construction of this Anderson County landmark. His first bridge photograph was given to him by Attorney Walter Patrick. In comments about his ties with the unusual construction, James proudly stated that he had "worked in every hole down there, except one...maybe two. I worked on footers and piers, and after the steel men finished, worked on the floor."

James was a member of the First Baptist Church in Lawrenceburg where he served for many years as a Trustee. He was always considered a dedicated church member who could be depended upon to do

whatever work needed to be done. From 1949 - 1960, James Ray served on the city council. During this time, much progress was made in the city of Lawrenceburg including the building of the Water Treatment Plant near Tyrone.

Elouise G. Ray and James R. Ray

James and Elouise had two children—Elaine Ray, who married Bill D. Davenport, and Michael Robert Ray who married Nancy L. Gaunce. The couple also had five grandchildren — David Michael, Melissa Ann, and Karen Ray Davenport, and Shawn Michael and Nancy Nicole Ray.

James' hobbies were fishing, working in the garden, and playing cards. But perhaps his greatest joy came from building and fixing things for his family, especially his grandchildren.

James Robert Ray died on 4-3-1986 and is buried in the Lawrenceburg Cemetery.

Grandaddy

He was tall and lean, never was he mean.
He had silver hair, and his skin was fair.
His eyes were crystal blue, and his heart was true.
I remember popping corn in an antique popper, and
collecting wheat pennies of dull faded copper.
He liked playing cards, going fishing, and working
in his garden.
But most of all he liked fixing and building things
that will never be forgotten.
He built many houses — large and small, but to me
my doll house was the grandest of them all.
One of my fondest memories is a treasure trunk he
built for me.
When he finished he asked - what color? I said
purple please Granddaddy.
He had an odd look on his face that day,
but he painted it purple anyway.
When I look at my trunk I always smile, for it's my
treasure with the most style.
As I grow older he becomes more dear to me,
and I thank God for such precious memories.
He was a good Christian, who shared God's love
I know he is happy in Heaven above.
Submitted By: Karen Ray Davenport Dadisman

MICHAEL ROBERT RAY has lived in Anderson County all of his life except for the time he was on active duty with the U.S. Air Force. He was born on 1-14-1943 to James Robert and Elouise Gregory Ray. He has one older sister, Elaine Ray (Mrs. Bill Davenport). He attended Lawrenceburg Elementary School and graduated from Anderson High School in 1961. In August of that year he began working for Kentucky State Government in the Department of Economic Security. Later he transferred to the Department of Finance as a computer programmer.

In 1964, Michael joined the Kentucky Air National Guard and spent four months in Texas for basic training. In January 1968 the Kentucky Air National Guard was called to active duty during the Pueblo crisis and he spent the next 18 months on active duty. A year of that time was spent at Elgin Air Force Base in Florida.

Michael returned home in July 1969 and resumed

his employment with state government in Frankfort. At this time he is a computer programmer/analyst in the Finance Cabinet.

Nancy, Nicole, Shawn, and Michael Ray

On 6-24-1972 at the First Baptist Church in Lawrenceburg, Michael R. and Nancy Lou Gaunce were married by Reverend Bob C. Jones. She is the daughter of William Edward and Clara Friedly Gaunce. Nancy attended Sand Spring Elementary School and graduated from Anderson High School in 1967. She enrolled in Morehead State University where she graduated in 1971 with a Bachelor of Science Degree in Vocational Home Economics. She returned to Lawrenceburg and was hired by the Anderson County Board of Education as a home economics teacher at Western High School. She obtained a Master of Science Degree from the University of Kentucky in August of 1977. She taught at Western from 1971 - 1980.

Nancy and Michael have both been active in the Anderson County Community Theater. Nancy was one of the original board members when the theater group was formed in 1983. Michael has served as a board member, president, vice-president and is currently serving as treasurer.

They have two children. A son, Shawn Michael, was born on 8-22-1978 and a daughter, Nancy Nicole, was born on 7-12-1980. The Ray family are active members of the First Baptist Church in Lawrenceburg where Michael has served as a Deacon since September 1987. They reside at 319 Forrest Drive. *Submitted By: Michael Ray*

WILLIAM C. AND MARTHA ANN SEWELL RAY were married 2-1-1894 in Lawrenceburg, KY. They lived most of their lives in Anderson County.

William was born in Russell County, Virginia on 5-28-1871. His parents were William R. and Louisa Browning Ray. They later moved to Anderson County. William R. Ray was the son of Barton and Rebecca Ray. Louisa was the daughter of Jacob and Margaret Browning.

Martha Ann Sewell Ray was born in Anderson County on 9-12-1873 and was the daughter of James Henry Sewell who was shot in Lawrenceburg during the Civil War.

William C. Ray and Martha Ann Sewell Ray

William and Martha Ray enjoyed the farm life. They were active members of the Lawrenceburg First Baptist Church. They had eight children.

Herman (married Irine Gardner), Leslie, Mrs. Al. L. (Blanche) Arnold, Mrs. William (Lula) Sampson, Mrs. Julian R. (Geneva) Hutchison, Mrs. Joseph C. (Adi Beatrice) Lochart, James R. (married Elouise Gregory), and Mrs. Cecil (Frances) Brothers. Herman died in a swimming accident 7-26-1920 in Fayette County at the age of 25. He had one son, Herman Jr. Leslie died at an early age of 2.

William C. Ray died on 1-12-1932. Martha Ann Sewell Ray died on 8-24-1955. They are buried in the Hebron Cemetery in Anderson County. *Submitted By: Michael Ray.*

REDMON The Redmon name is deeply rooted in Irish and English history. Wexford County, Ireland is still the home to many Redmons. There is a Redmon now serving in the British Parliament.

John, son of Thomas Redmon and Rebecca Settle of Philadelphia, PA, known as John Jr. bought 300 acres of land in Washington County, PA in 1784. (Recorded in the Court House in Washington, PA.) The land was on the Dunkard Fork of Wheeling Creek. This section of Pennsylvania was claimed by Virginia, Pennsylvania, and the Indians. John Redmon, Jr. sold his land September 3, 1789.

John Redmon, Jr. is listed with Capt. Grigsby's Militia Co. (later called Corn Stalk Militia 1792 - 1811) in Nelson County, KY in 1789. In October of 1789 in "Petitions from Kentuckians Nelson County, KY 10-24-1789:" Badness of roads, inconvenience in carrying produce to market; ask to establish a warehouse on Beach Creek at the mouth of Cartwrights Creek on the land of Richard Parker. Signed: John Redmon, Thomas Redmon, and John Redmon, Jr.

John Redmon, Jr. married Sarah Dawson Morgan (Sally) August 18, 1809. She was the daughter of William Morgan and Nancy Thrift Morgan of Virginia. They moved to Spencer County, KY after 1820. The will of John Redmon, Jr., dated May 30, 1833, Spencer County, KY, gave beloved wife Sally all his possessions and then to be divided among his children, five girls and one boy. John Redmon, Jr. was buried in Mount Moriah Cemetery in Shelby County, KY. The will was proved in September, 1833.

Annie Ruble Redmon and John Dawson Redmon

Widow Sally D. M. Redmon had a brother, John Morgan and his wife, Jane Burris, living in Anderson County. She moved with her children to her farm on Crooked Creek, Anderson County. Dawson Northern Redmon married ann Maria Shaddock in 1854. Another house, built close-by was to be their home until death. Ann Maria in 1895 and Dawson Northern in 1906. Only three of their nine children survived him; Margaret Martin, Sarah (Sally) Redmon, and John Dawson Redmon.

Dawson Northern Redmon and Francis Munday Catlett were appointed overseers of the Mount Vernon, Crooked Creek Turnpike. The road runs from Mount Vernon Baptist Church in Shelby County, KY to Lawrenceburg, county seat of Anderson County. There was a Redmon School House. The Redmon home was where Dawson held singing schools. Corinth Christian Church was built in 1870. It was church home to the Redmon family. In 1970, a comprehensive church history was written by life member, Miss Myrtle Perry, retired Anderson County

school teacher. Dawson Redmon's wife had been a school teacher. Their son, Thomas Northern Redmon, twin brother of John Dawson Redmon, taught several terms in Anderson County schools before his death at an early age.

John Dawson Redmon, surviving son of D. N. Redmon, married Annie Ruble December 27, 1899. He was a farmer and landowner of Anderson County. They attended Fox Creek Christian Church where Mr. Redmon was a deacon and Sunday School teacher. They had 5 children. They were educated in the Anderson County schools and Kentucky colleges; Guy Lillard (deceased), Martha Ann (Mattie) (deceased) teacher and librarian, Lois (widow of Earl F. Metcalf) teacher and librarian, Naomi (widow of Thomas Shouse Brown), and Bronston R. (lieutenant and pilot in World War II). He is married to Jean Hall Stewart.

MARK EDWARD RICE was born on 2-25-1955 in Bloomington, Illinois. He is the son of Joseph Earl Rice and Shirley Mae Feese. He had one sister and two brothers: Hallie Teretha married Ed Short; Joseph Dwayne (1955 - 1980), and David Randall.

In Edinburgh, Indiana, he married Debra Sue Terry on 10-9-1973. She was born on 10-9-1955 in Shelby County, Indiana. She is the daughter of Fred Jr. Terry and Dolly Marie Weber. She has three sisters and one brother: Diana Lee married Terry Burton; Deloras Maxine married Larry Kent; Marlene Kay Terry; and Fred Terry Jr.

Mark and Debra Rice are the parents of one son, Brian Edward. He was born on 1-23-1974 in Johnson County, Indiana. The Rice family lived in Edinburgh, Indiana until they moved to Anderson County in 1985. Brian currently attends Anderson County High School.

RIPPEY-RIPY During the 1830's, three members of the Rippey family left County Tyrone, Ireland for the New World, leaving family and friends behind like many others. Earlier their ancestor, Dr. William Rippey (Rippi?), had made a similar journey from France through England and Scotland to Ireland. He was a Hugenot and although enjoying an extensive practice was compelled to leave France and all his property, hurriedly, in fact, between suns, on account of his religion. During WWII, ties with Ireland were renewed as Ernest W. Ripy, Jr. was stationed in County Tyrone at Five Mile Town. Later, Frank Ripy McWhorter would journey to Northern Ireland, providing the family with a narrative of his trip. Descendants of one brother of those early immigrants are still to be found there; the author of the sketch, Thomas B Ripy IV, and his parents enjoyed their hospitality as visitors in 1986. Handley Rippey and his wife, Susan, greeted us with enthusiasm in response to a phone call from Scotland. Handley, now deceased, took us on a tour and introduced us to family. He and his lovely wife, Susan, had us to dinner with their son, Brian. It was a wonderful chance to explore roots in a way that many can only imagine. Not only did we learn of family in Ireland, but we also found out that descendants of our ancestors are here in the States, Canada, Australia, and New Zealand. Later, his brother, Jimmy, would join us in a visit to the States. Jimmy has also found some French Rippis.

The three Rippeys who immigrated to the United States in the 1830's were James, John, and their sister, Eliza. The first to leave Ireland was James, who came to Anderson County via Philadelphia and Centerville, KY. The family retains copies of his naturalization papers, renouncing allegiance to Queen Victoria and pledging allegiance to the United States.

At some point he shortened the name to Ripy. According to family legend this may have been a result of the name proving too large for a sign painter painting his name on a store. In 1839, the year he was naturalized, his brother and sister joined him. James served as postmaster in Lawrenceburg and was a businessman. He married Artemesia Walker, a native Kentuckian and they had two children who survived to adulthood. The youngest, Thomas Beebe, was born in 1847. A well-known distiller, he married Sallie Fidler (affectionately known as Ma'am Ripy) and built a home on South Main (now the home of Dr. and Mrs. George Gilbert). They had ten children who survived to maturity. Thomas died in 1902, when his youngest child was about nine years old. Ma'am Ripy continued to live in the home, completed the raising of her family, living until 1948. By that time there were many grandchildren and great-grandchildren. For those too young to remember and those not yet born, she was a tiny lady, with a sharp mind and a keen sense of propriety. The family often gathered there. She sat in her chair to the right of the fireplace in the parlor, frequently cautioning her children and grandchildren to "Love One Another" as the Ripy men engaged in their favorite pasttime - argument. At Christmas, the family would gather there for dinner. There was a large punch bowl in the hallway filled with eggnog and a house full of people, filled with the joy of Christmas and love of family. The big house was a wonderful place for small people. Great-grandchildren always looked forward to visits, particularly when Uncle Ez's wife, Aunt Dodie, was there. She would take us to their bedroom and open the drawer to the bedside table, which always seemed filled with everything a child could want that parents were reluctant to provide, candy and that marvelous invention - bubble gum.

Ma'am Ripy as a girl

The Ripy family owned and operated a number of distilleries in and around Tyrone. The history of these plants was recounted in the earlier History of Anderson County. Sons of Thomas B. later built and operated the Old Hoffman Distillery and the Old Ripy Distillery, now known as the home of Wild Turkey Bourbon. Descendants of Thomas B. and Ma'am Ripy have, however, succeeded in other businesses and careers, including stone, road construction, teaching, transportation, medicine, and law. Scattered around the United States, Anderson County is still a special place for all of them. It is home for a few literally, and home in the hearts of many others. *Submitted By: Thomas B. Ripy IV.*

RIPY The Ripy family has been identified with Anderson County for over 150 years. Two brothers, John and James Ripy came to Anderson County from County Tyrone, Northern Ireland prior to 1840. A sister, Eliza Ripy, came with her brothers, and married Thomas B. Lyons of Shelby County, and was the mother of Jasper W., Robert, and Hamilton Lyons. The Ripys were Hugenots and during the reign of Louis IIV, their ancestors had to flee from France to Ireland for self-preservation.

James Ripy, (1811 - 1872) married Artemesia Walker (1811 - 1888) in 1839. Their children were James Porter Ripy and Thomas Beebe Ripy.

James Porter Ripy (1844 - 1922) served in Company H, 5th Kentucky Cavalry CSA, under General John H. Morgan. After the War Between the States, he married Miss Sarah Ellen Lillard (1846 - 1927). He acquired the Old Hickory Springs Distillery, and

after operating it for a number of years, sold it to Kentucky Distilleries and Warehouse Co. The children of James P. and Helen Ripy were the following: (1) James Beebe Ripy (1870 - 1951) was a graduate of K.M.I. and Washington and Lee University. In 1923, he married Flora A. Elkington. He had a position with the Louisville Bank and Trust Co. when he retired. (2) Marion Wallace Ripy (1873 - 1965) graduated from the law college of Washington and Lee University, and practiced law in Lawrenceburg, Louisville, and New York City. He married Charlotte Millett Jacobi in 1921. (3) Hardie B. Ripy (1875 - 1942) graduated from Washington and Lee University, and was an employee of the Internal Revenue Service in Washington, D.C. He married Ethel Gist in February 1898, and they had one child, (3a) Margaret Ripy (1899 - 1969). Margaret married George Elgin Morrison in 1922 and they had two children, (3aa) George Elgin Morison, Jr. (1923 - ?) who died in an auto-train accident in Florida, and his widow resides in Winterhaven, Florida; and (3ab) Ethel Kathleen Morison, born in 1927 and resides in Venice, Florida. (4) Col. Francis "Frank" Lillard Ripy (1878 - 1929) who earned his law degree from the University of Louisville and practiced law in Lawrenceburg. He was a Lt. Col., 88th Division, Infantry, World War I. He married Mrs. Elizabeth Hazelrigg Hall in 1923. (5) Helen Ripy (1883 - 1960) graduated from Beaumont College, Harrodsburg, Kentucky. In 1916, she married Thomas Afton McWhorter from Texas. They had two children, Frank Ripy McWhorter, the author of this article, born in 1918 and Thomas Osborne McWhorter (1920 - 1978), both taken from Texas to Lawrenceburg to be born. (5a) Frank received a B.S. Degree from the University of Texas. He served as a Captain in the Army Air Corps during WW II and in the Air Force during the Korean War. Frank retired from the Legal Department of Tenneco Inc. after 34 years, in 1983. He married Elizabeth Morrow in 1941. They have two children, (5aa) Robert Frank McWhorter, born in 1950, who has a BBA Degree from the University of Houston and his J. D. Degree from the Oklahoma City University Law School. He practices law in Houston. He has one son, Jason Adam McWhorter, born 1971, now attending Concorida Lutheran College in Austin, Texas, (5ab) Marian Helen McWhorter Wiley, born November 11, 1954, attended Southwestern University at Georgetown, Texas, has taught handicapped children and is married to Edward Rippy Wiley. They have one daughter, Christina Virginia. (5b) Thomas Osborne McWhorter graduated from the U.S. Naval Academy in 1941 and served in the Navy until 1953 when he resigned, took a reserve commission of Commander. He entered the Law School of the University of Texas, receiving his J.D. Degree in 1955. He practiced law in Houston until his death. At that time, he was Chancellor General of the National Society of Sons of the American Revolution. He had two sons, Thomas Duvall McWhorter and James Barry McWhorter, and one daughter, Anne Stuart McWhorter Fanelli, who resides in Memphis, TN.

Thomas Beebe Ripy (1847 - 1902) was educated at K.M.I. and at Sayre Institute in Frankfort. When only 21 years of age, he purchased an interest in the Walker, Martin and Company Distillery at Tyrone, and later built a more modern plant on that site. In 1874, Mr. Ripy was married to Miss Sallie Fidler (1856 - 1948). Their ten children who lived to maturity are: T. B. Ripy, Jr., Ernest Whitney Ripy, Ezra Fidler Ripy, James Catlett Ripy, Forest Ripy, Susan Wallace Ripy Johnson, Artemesia Ripy Gaines, Robert Ripy, Roger Allen Ripy, and William Ripy. *Submitted By: Frank Ripy McWhorter.*

ROACH The family name of Roach is widespread in the United States and Britain. It is of French origin (Roche), and its prevalence in Ireland and England dates to the migration of French Protestants, or Hugenots, in the religious reforms of the 16th century. Most of those in the U.S. came from Ireland.

Bailey Roach came to Anderson County from

Madison County, Kentucky about 1850. He taught school in what used to be called the Palmer Precinct, and later ran a general store in Glensboro, and then a mill at Anderson City.

He married Letitia Herndon in 1858 and they reared a large family. The family's homeplace was a farm 1 1/2 miles south of Lawrenceburg on Hwy. 35, which they had purchased from the pioneer McBrayer family.

Of the ten children born to Bailey and Letitia Roach, four died before reaching adulthood. Bailey was killed in 1902 when a horse he was riding fell on him. His widow continued to live on the place and operate the farm for another 30 years. She died in 1935, and is buried in the family cemetery on the farm, as are her husband and five of her children.

The six sons and daughter who survived to adulthood:

1) Allen Roach (1859 - 1955) who never married.

2) David William Roach (1860 - 1945), married Cleora Cox (1871 - 1931) their children are Lutye Mae (1891 - 1953), Carey Burton (1893 - 1930), and William Bennett (1901).

3) Coleman Herndon Roach (1870 - 1962) married Bessie Dunn; their children are Waller, Herndon, Wallace, and Wilbur.

4) Nannie Roach (1873 - 1934) married Edgar Cole, moved to Oklahoma in 1906. Their children: Mabel, Charles, Wallace, John, Minnie, and Lula. All now (1989) deceased, except Mabel (Mrs. Harry Zeck) of Wellington, Kansas.

5) Mary Roach (1875 - 1944) married Rev. Arthur Tharp, Christian minister; his pastorates in Kentucky and Indiana; both buried in Greenwood, Indiana.

6) Lula Roach (1880 - 1964) married Burton Cole (1881 - 1983) their children: Julian (1902 - 1984); J. W. (1905); Mary Louise Ransdell (1911 - 1988); Carroll (1916 - 1987); and Robert (1922). *Submitted By: Bennett Roach.*

ALONZO ROARK was born on 1-20-1912 in Clay County, KY. He is the son of William Roark and Laura Holland Roark. He has seven brothers and sisters: Lily married Roy Schaffer; John married Dorthy; and twins, Sadie married Garnett Robinson and Ben (who died at birth).

Alonzo Roark married Elsie Rae Chilton in 1939. She was born on 3-28-1915 in Mercer County, KY and died on 6-19-1987. She was the daughter of Fred Chilton and Minnie Robinson Chilton. She had five brothers and sisters: Horace married 1st Sadie, 2nd Ruth; Allie Bell married Tom Coke; Melvin married 1st Margaret Cubert, 2nd Margaret Cottrell; Everett married Inez; and Kathryn married R. V. Jefferies.

Alonzo and Elsie Rae were the parents of one son, Bobby Louis. He was born on 9-4-1939 in Salvisa, KY. He is a builder in Anderson County. On 9-29-1962, he married Marcia Kathleen Hart in Little Rock, Arkansas. She was born on 3-28-1943 in Little Rock. She is the daughter of Joseph Edward Hart (1910 - 1973) and Ona Burgin Hart (1909 - 1963). Mr. and Mrs. Hart both died of cancer. Marcia has four brothers and sisters: Carol Ann married John Campbell Gilliland; Joseph Edward Jr. married Marjori Kremers; Wallace Fredrick (1939 - 1980) married Sharon Wetzel; and Cynthia Jane married Alan W. McMillen.

Bobby and Marcia are the parents of five children: Sheila Rae; Robert Lewis married Wendy Sue Shutz; Sharon Renee; Grant Stewart; and Jennifer Lynn. The Roark family currently resides on Woodlake Drive in Anderson County. *Submitted by: Jennifer Roark.*

ROBERT AND RACHAEL ROBINSON farmed in Mercer County. He died on 3-14-1945 and she died on 7-8-1937. They had several children who all lived and died in Kentucky.

One son, Roy Robinson, was born in August, 1897. He married Verna Currens, the daughter of Ben and Luella Currens. Verna was born on 8-7-1895. They were married in 1916 in Salvisa. Roy and

Verna farmed both in Mercer and Anderson Counties. Both were members of the Claylick Methodist Church in Mercer County. In later years they moved to Lexington where Roy worked as a carpenter with his brother. At retirement age, they returned to Mercer County. He died on 3-3-1980 and she died on 8-12-1976. They were the parents of four sons and three daughters: Adelene married A. J. Kieghtley - two daughters, Janet and Alta Mae; Eugene (below); J. D. married Ethel; Evelyn married W. R. Riley - two children, Regina and Lynn; Roberta married Becham Sea - two children, Gregory and Francis; Randall married Dolly - four children - Eddie, Jude, Steven, and Reggie; and L. H. married Carolyn - two children, Sylvia and Lynn.

Eugene Robinson was born on 10-21-1921. He married Martha Cottrell in 1940. She was born on 8-12-1923 and is the daughter of Clarence Cottrell and Ethel Baker Cottrell. Eugene and Martha have always lived in either Mercer or Anderson County. Eugene served in World War II from 1942 - 1946. He was in a Tank Division at Normandy Beach and fought on the front lines during the war. They are the parents of two sons and five daughters: Doris married Clarence Goodpaster - four children - Sherry, Kenny, Jimmy, and Len; Patsy - one daughter, Kelley Chapman; Leroy married Melinda Ripy - two sons, Rodney and David; Betty married John Thompson - three children - Marti, Kristi, and Brad; Edith married Jimmy Hanks - three children - Marcia, Stacey, and Jamie; Larry - one son, Justin; and Pam. Their youngest, Pam, was killed in an automobile accident in 1980.

AMOS AND SARAH ROGERS.

It all began in Mercer County where Andrew Jackson Rogers was born in 1810. He had a son, Joel M. Rogers, born in 1860. He married Lucretia L. Jordan. They had three sons: Wallace, Ova, and Amos.

Amos married Sarah R. Kays, daughter of Mary Lee and James Burton Kays of Anderson County. Amos and Sarah had 13 children — nine sons and four daughters. Two sons (twins) died in infancy. The children are Virginia, Robert, Earl, Glen, Roy, and Hazel (twins), Joel B., Sue, James, Jean, and Connie.

Virginia married Emmett Cammack (deceased). They had four children: Joanne Deavers, Wanda Hammond, Larry, and Rilda Craig. Robert married a lady from Frankfort. Earl married Pearl Stratton. Glen married Louise Phillips. They had two sons: Glen Jr. and Donnie Joe. Roy married Lucy Stratton. They had seven children: Jeffery, James, Michael, Roger, Timmy, Patricia Sweasy, and Sandra Hargis. Hazel remains unmarried. Joel B. remained unmarried. Sue married Robert Perry III. They had two children: Robert IV and Beth. James married Charlene Mayne. They had one son, Carlie. Jean married Richard DeBell. They had two daughters: Laurie and Richelle. Connie married Wanda Rucker. He had two sons: Larry and Gary, and a daughter, Teresa, by previous marriage. He and Wanda had a daughter, Catherine.

Amos and Sarah Rogers

Amos was educated in the schools of Mercer County. When he and Sarah married, they lived for a brief time in Mercer County making farming their occupation. Later, they moved to Anderson County and purchased the J. N. Walker farm on the Bonds Mill-Goshen Road. This was considered the family home place where all the children grew up. The family lived here for 42 years.

The children were educated in the schools of Anderson County. They attended Hickory Grove Elementary School and Western, Kavanaugh, and Anderson High Schools.

The family farm joined the Goshen Baptist Church property. This church was an integral part of the lives of the Rogers family. Every Sunday found part or all of this family making their way to and from the Goshen Baptist church.

Interestingly, all seven sons served in the armed forces of our country. Five of them were serving during the Korean War, and one served during peacetime. Earl was wounded in action in Sicily while serving during World War II. Miraculously, all returned home safely.

Amos was a member of the Beaver Creek Masonic Lodge. In 1968, after selling the home place, he moved to a smaller farm on the edge of Lawrenceburg. He and Sarah lived there along with their son, Joel B., until their deaths in 1978 and 1980. *Submitted By: Alma Jean Rogers DeBell.*

VIRGIL TAYLOR ROWLAND

came to Tyrone, Anderson County, Kentucky in 1940 when he came to work for J.T.S. Brown Distillery at Tyrone.

Virgil's grandfather, Joseph Rowland was born about 1846 in Harrison County, Kentucky, and he married Alice Jane Honaker January 13, 1869 in Robertson County, Ky. Virgil's father, Luther Taylor Rowland was born to Joseph and Alice Jane December 28, 1879 in Robertson Co., Ky. Luther married Mary Lillie Cooper, and they had one son, Virgil Taylor Rowland born on October 19, 1906 in Midway, Woodford County, Kentucky.

Virgil Rowland and Myrtle Rowland

Virgil married Myrtle Searcy of Anderson County, Ky. on March 3, 1924 in Versailles, Woodford County, Ky. They had four children: Myrtle Louise born August 1, 1928, married Herbert McGaughey; Marion Luther born June 3, 1932; Paul Edward born and died December 6, 1943; and Connie Sue born October 16, 1945, married William P. Farris.

Virgil attended Midway High School where he played football. He farmed in Woodford Co., Ky. before coming to Tyrone. He retired early from J. T. S. Brown (now known as Boulevard Distillery) due to an accident at work in July of 1964. Virgil died January 28, 1984 and is buried in the Lawrenceburg Cemetery.

Myrtle Searcy Rowland was born July 8, 1907 in Anderson County, KY. to John Wilkerson Searcy and Sue H. Brumley. Myrtle had four sisters: Gertis Laura, Nannie Jane, Annabel, and Susie. She attended the McGinnis Elementary School in Anderson County, Ky. Myrtle died November 14, 1966 and is buried in the Lawrenceburg Cemetery.

In the 1950's, Myrtle and Virgil owned and operated a general store in Tyrone, KY. called Rowland's Grocery.

CLIFFORD AND BONNIE ROYALTY

have been residents of Anderson County since moving here from Mercer County in 1958.

Connie Clifford Royalty was born July 2, 1936 in Mercer County, Kentucky to Elmer Elwood and Mary Will Brown Royalty. He is the eldest of three children. His brother, Donald Wayne, lives in Harrodsburg and sister, Brenda Carol Stiglic, lives in Mercer County. His grandparents were Samuel S. and Addie Robinson Royalty and Herman and Margaret Thompson Brown. He was reared on a farm and attended McAfee and Salvisa grade schools and graduated from the last class at Salvisa High School in 1955. He served nine years in the Kentucky National Guard. After completing high school, he worked for Edwards Sausage Company for ten years and since 1966 has been employed by International Business Machines in Lexington, KY.

On June 16, 1956, he married Bonnie Jean Riley. Bonnie was born January 7, 1936 to William Russell and Virgie Myrtle Ellis Riley. She is the youngest of five children. Her sisters are Marie Carter of Lawrenceburg, Dorothy Sparrow and Edna Mae Phillips of Salvisa, KY. One brother, William R. Riley, Jr., lives in Jeffersontown, KY. Her grandparents were William M. and Anna Taylor Riley and Marion F. and Alice Caldwell Ellis. Bonnie attended grade school at Salvisa, graduated from Salvisa High School in 1954 and Campbellsville Jr. College in 1956. For several years she did substitute teaching in Mercer and Anderson County school systems. Since 1978 she has been Church Secretary of the Sand Spring Baptist Church in Lawrenceburg.

Clifford and Bonnie have three children. Kevin Dale was born April 11, 1957. Kevin attended grade and high school in Anderson County. He enrolled at the University of Kentucky in 1975 on a voice scholarship. He graduated with a degree in Music Education in 1980. He taught Public School Music in Anderson County for two years before entering the Southern Baptist Theological Seminary in Louisville where he received a masters degree in Religious Education. He presently is Associate Pastor, Minister of Music and Youth at First Baptist Church, Sebree, Kentucky. He is married to Jana Renee Forker and has a son, Slade.

Steven Scott was born July 4, 1960. He is a graduate of Anderson County High School, attended the University of Kentucky and graduated from Georgetown in 1983 with a degree in accounting. He is presently employed as Senior Staff Accountant at Southern Baptist Seminary in Louisville. He is married to Glenda Dawn Morrell of Lawrenceburg. They live in Louisville.

Andrea Dawn was born June 18, 1966. She is also a graduate of Anderson County High School and graduated in 1988 from Georgetown College with a BA degree in Psychology. She is not married and is presently employed as an Admissions Counselor for Georgetown College in Georgetown, KY, where she resides.

Clifford and Bonnie are active members of Sand Spring Baptist Church. Clifford has been a deacon of that church since 1965. They reside at 102 Park Lane in Lawrenceburg. *Submitted by: Bonnie Jean Royalty.*

ROBERT DOW SADLER ,

was born on 7-14-1948, in North Springs, Tennessee. He is the son of Robert P. Sadler and Mazel Clark Sadler. They live in Tennessee. He has two sisters: Donna Poke Sadler, born 1942, married Herald Johnson - two children; and Joy Bell Sadler, born 1945, married Robert Wilson - four children.

Robert D. Sadler moved to Ft. Lauderdale, Florida to live with his sister, Joy Sadler Wilson, when he was 23. He met Cynthia Ann Wilson. Soon after, they were married. While living in Florida, they had two children: Troy Dow Sadler, born 11-6-1973, and Karen Renee Sadler, born 1-5-1975. In 1987, Robert changed jobs and the family came to live in Anderson County.

Cynthia Ann Wilson Sadler was born on 12-20-1953 in Ft. Lauderdale. She is the daughter of James E. Wilson Jr. and Johnnie Woodcock Wilson. They live in Ohio. She has two brothers and one sister: Larry L. Wilson, born 1949, married Phyllis J. Powell; Robert K. Wilson, born 1950, married Jill; and Jill S. Wilson, born 1969. *Submitted By: Karen Sadler.*

SALE FAMILY, In the year 1800, Samuel Sale and his wife, Elizabeth, came from Virginia and settled near the source of Buchannon's Creek, about four miles southeast of Ripyville. They had nine children: Clayton, Stephen, James, Ira, Samuel, William D., Lucy, Mary and Nancy. In 1826 the pioneer, Samuel Sale, died. After the death of the father, William D., the youngest son, his mother and a sister, remained on the farm. On April 20, 1829, William D. was married to Miss Catherine Cardwell. They had five sons and three daughters and they continued to live on the ancestral farm until William's death in 1860. Then his son, W. Cardwell Sale, on the death of his mother in 1878, and his sister, Maggie, continued to live in the homestead, which he purchased from the other heirs. Two other brothers, S. T., and W. Henry lived in the same neighborhood for many years; one brother, James, moved to Missouri, and another brother, John, died in the Confederate Army. One sister, Nannie, married Will Baker, and another sister, Mary D. married John Sherwood.

The Sale family lived on the ancestral farm over 90 years. Most of the family members mentioned in this history are buried in the family cemetery on the farm. A portion of the farm and the old homestead are now owned and occupied by Dr. D. F. Dahlen, a local dentist, and his family.

Most of the descendants of the Sale family now living in Anderson county are the descendants of Kitty Sherwood Moffett and Alla Sale Case. Miss Betsy Sale of Mercer County is the granddaughter of the late Fauster Sale and the daughter of the late Forest Sale, a former All-American, University of Kentucky basketball player. *Submitted By: Mary L. Moffett Birdwhistell.*

JOHN LEWIS SAYRE, and Violet M. Tomlinson were married on 6-12-1930. To this union were born two children: William Edward "Bill", born 4-12-1932, married Juanita Durr; and Jim, born 10-28-1935, married Mary Sparks.

John Lewis, the son of William E. Sayre (1879 - 1953) and Bessie Brown Sayre (1887 - 1975), was born on 4-24-1912 in Anderson county, KY. He had seven brothers and sisters: Loyd, Earl, Aaron, Asa, Grandville, Roberta, and Virginia. William E. Sayre was the son of James Sayre and Molly Norton Sayre. Bessie Brown Sayre was the daughter of John Brown and Leora Grubbs Brown.

Violet May Tomlinson Sayre, the daughter of Edward Tomlinson and Katherine Donevan Tomlinson, was born on 2-5-1914 in Indianapolis, Indiana. She had four brothers and one sister: John E., James, Paul, Clarence, and Grace.

John farmed and worked at the local thread mill for many years until the plant moved. He was then employed by Lawrenceburg Transfer until he retired in 1974. His hobbies were fishing and horseshoe pitching.

Violet, a housewife, enjoys caring for all types of farm animals and fishing. She still lives on Salt River Road where they resided for over 40 years. *Submitted By: Jim Sayre.*

JIM SAYRE, and Mary Sparks were married on 6-22-1956. To this union were born two sons: James L. "Bo", born 2-6-1959, married Darla Kaye Rowe - two children, Lisa Kaye and Adam Chistopher. David Barton "Bart", born 8-28-1960, married Suzanne Shryock - two children, Brian Caleb and Kelly Nicole.

Jim, the son of John Lewis Sayre and Violet Mae Tomlinson Sayre, was born on 10-28-1935 in Anderson County. He has one brother, William Edward,

born 4-12-1932, and married to Juanita Durr. Jim attended school at Lawrenceburg Elementary and Anderson High.

Mary Alice Sparks, the daughter of Sherman B. Sparks and Carrie Kirkland Sparks, was born on 8-17-1940 in Versailles, KY. She has one brother and one sister: Irene B., born 7-27-1942, married Robert Scrogham; and Sherman B., born 2-2-1944, married Linda Reynolds. Sherman B. Sparks is the son of Frank Sparks and Mellie Litteral Sparks. Carrie Kirkland Sparks was the daughter of Robert Hart Kirkland and Bessie Baker Kirkland. Mary attended school in Fayette County, KY.

Mary is employed by Charm-kins Day Care Center in Alton. She enjoys travel and her grandchildren. She is a former Sunday school teacher and formerly employed at Hoffman Distillery.

Jim is employed by Lawrenceburg Transfer. He served two years with the U. S. Army Signal Corps in East Africa. He enjoys travel, his grandchildren, and studying U.S. History. He is a member of the Madison County Civil War Round Rable. He also portrays Abraham Lincoln in churches, schools, community meetings, and has won several contests. Jim looks so much like Abe Lincoln that his grandson, Adam, once thought his "Pa" was on the five dollar bill.

Jim and Mary are active members of the Ninevah Christian Church where Jim is an Elder. They reside at 1495 Alton Station Road. *Submitted By: Jim Sayre.*

WILLIAM E. SAYRE, was born in 1879, and died in 1953. He was the son of James Sayre and Molly Norton Sayre. He married Bessie B. Brown. She was born in 1887, and died in 1975. She was the daughter of John Brown and Leora Grubbs Brown. Bessie was a typical farm housewife, caring for the children and often helping with farm chores.

William and Bessie were the parents of eight children: Loyd, Roberta, Aaron, Virginia, John, Earl, Asa, and Grandville.

William was a farmer and preacher most of his life. In the early 1920's, he and his oldest son, Loyd, drove a Model "T" to Detroit, Michigan, to make their fortune. They were employed by Hudson Motor Company. Soon, they found housing and moved the family to Detroit. Only a short time passed before they discovered the big city was not for them, and returned to Anderson County. They lived out the remainder of their lives in Anderson County. William and Bessie are buried in the Old Lawrenceburg Cemetery. *Submitted By: Jim Sayre.*

LEONARD EDGAR SANFORD SEA,, the son of Leonard Hamilton and Mary Catherine Robinson Sea, was born 8-23-1875, and died 11-1-1942.

His father, "Len", operated a general store and the Seaville Post Office at the place known as Addie Springate's Home. He lived there and reared his children. Len and Cass and young children, William Walker, John Harvey, and Mary Ada are buried at the Darnell Cemetery in Anderson County.

Edgar had two sisters, Ida Belle and Addie Lee. He married 9-13-1894, Lena Reeves Jenkins (4-19-1880 - 5-1-1969) daughter of James Irvin and Sarah Louisa Griffin Jenkins. Irvin was the manager of his large farm. Part of the highlight of his farm to his grandchildren was tapping sugar trees used to make syrup, sugar and candy. His wife was reared by her "mammy" after her mother died when she was a very small girl. After "finishing school" in the summer, she and mammy went on the boat on the Mississippi River where her father, Napoleon Boneparte Griffin was clerk. She was the only child and was called Sallie. The Jenkins are buried in the Tressler Cemetery near Bohn.

Irvin and Sallie's children were Nannie Wheeler, Martha Jane Howerton, Addie Norton, Christopher and James. Two boys died in youth, Daley and Elmo.

Edgar and Lena's children were Mrs. James Frank Bowen (Margie Lee), Mrs. William Satterly (Lillian Marie), Mrs. Clarence Robinson (Sarah Catherine

Standing: Edgar Sea and Lena Jenkins Sea. Sitting: Nancy Case Robinson, Leonard H. Sea, Leonard.. Cornish, Mary Catherine Robinson Sea, William Merritt Sanders, Virgil Sanders, Ida Sea Sanders, James Springate, and Addie Sea Springate taken in 1894

who later married Raymond Hoskins) and Cecil Ray Sea who married Lettie Satterly. A daughter, Martha Bell, died as a baby and was buried in the Darnell Cemetery.

Their grandchildren are: Mary Reeves (died at birth), Mildred Paulina, Mable Irene, James Frank, Jr., and William Edgar Bowen, Mary Lena, Paul Sea and Frances Marie Satterly, Clarence Truman Robinson and Wanda Joyce Hoskins, Juanita Gayle and Donnie Ray Sea.

Great grandchildren Linda Joyce and Danny Eugene Corley, Brenda Carlene, James Carl, Jr., Carroll Bowen, Sandra Gayle, Gerry Dale, Mildred Ann and Starlette Lee Stine; James Frank, III, Steven Ray, Jackie Curtis Bowen; Barbara Carolyn, William Edgar, Jr., Kishell Brown and Wendell Gaylord Bowen; Michael Lynn, Sharon Dale and Robin Ann Davenpoprt; Carolyn Jean, Paul Sea, Jr., and Frances Marie Satterly; Ronald H., Suann Marie, and Rita Gayle Merriman; Beverly Renee and Sonja Lynette Sea.

Edgar S. and Lena J. Sea and Lillian Satterly are buried at the Bethel Baptist Church in Mercer County. Margie Bowen and Catherine Hoskins are buried at the Lawrenceburg Cemetery in Anderson County and Cecil Ray Sea is buried in the Springhill Cemetery in Harrodsburg, Mercer County. Edgar and Lena Sea and their children have left a great heritage to their descendants. May they honor and appreciate it. Serving their country in war were: their son, Cecil Ray Sea, and grandsons, James Frank Bowen, Jr., William Edgar Bowen, Clarence Truman Robinson, Jr., and Paul Sea Satterly. Danny Eugene Corley served a year in Vietnam and James Carl Stine, Jr., in Korea. All returning home safely. *Submitted By: Pauline Bowen Devine.*

JOHN WILKERSON SEARCY, was born June 15, 1872, in Anderson County, Ky. to John Penney Searcy and Jane Mariah Huffman. His brothers and sisters were William Henry (Ike), Hollie, and Eliza.

John married Sue H. Brumley in Anderson County, KY. They had five daughters: Gertie Laura born August 12, 1905, married Herbert Jack Lloyd, died December 3, 1981, buried in the Lawrenceburg Cemetery; Myrtle born July 8, 1907, married Virgil Taylor Rowland, died November 14, 1966, buried in the Lawrenceburg Cemetery; Nannie Jane born February 20, 1910, married Charlie Redman, died October 30, 1983, buried in the Lawrenceburg Cemetery; Annabel born March 16, 1912, married Carl William Robinson, died October 13, 1969, buried in the Hebron Cemetery; and Susie born August 2, 1917, died February 24, 1920.

John was a stonemason and a caretaker of land below the present Ky. Utility Plant in Woodford Co., KY. He died February 6, 1929.

John's parents, John Penny Searcy and Jane Mariah Huffman were married August 29, 1871 in Anderson County, KY. His father, John Penney, was born in Anderson County, KY to John H. Searcy. John Penney was a blacksmith. He died May 24, 1916, in Tyrone. His mother, Jane Mariah was born May 10, 1850, in Mercer Co., KY. to Will Huffman. Jane died February 25, 1929, in Tyrone.

John Wilkerson Searcy and Sue H. Brumley Searcy

Sue Searcy was born March 7, 1882 in Carrollton, Carroll Co., KY. to John Brumley and Sarah Frances Harlow. Her brothers and sisters were John Owen, Lizzie, and Mary Lee (or Lou); half brothers and sisters were Robert Harrison, Mitchell, William Madison, Carrie Bell, Cordie Jane, and Charlotte. She died at the home of her daughter, Nannie Jane Redman, in Tyrone on August 4, 1955.

It is believed that Sue's father, John Brumley, was born in Carroll Co., KY, and had a brother named Owen; married in Worthville, Carroll Co., KY.; and was killed in a distillery approximately in 1885. John married Sarah Frances Harlow. Sarah was born in Franklin Co., KY. to Robert (Vol) Harlow and Mary Elizabeth Warner. Sarah's brothers and sisters were George, Simpson, Sue, and Jeff. Sarah died at her home in Tyrone, June 1, 1928, at the age of 68. Records show Sarah's father as being born in KY. or Virginia; and her mother as being born in Owen Co., KY.

JAMES CLEVELAND SEARCY, JR.,

was born on 5-30-1924, in Anderson County. He was the son of James Cleveland Searcy, Sr. and Mary Thrailkell Searcy. He married Susan Mary Stratton on 5-18-1942. She was born on 4-8-1928, in Anderson County. She is the daughter of William "Stanley" Stratton (3-20-1894 - 9-20-1937) and Susan Betsy Disponett (10-18-1892 - 1-8-1973).

James Cleveland, Jr. and Susan Mary Searcy had five children: 1) James Winston, born 2-16-1944, married 1st Sandra Gritton - four children - Sean, Brad, Lisa, and Lynn - divorced; 2nd, Sandra Giles - divorced; 3rd, Jamie Ellis - first child due in February 1990. 2) Larry Gale, born 7-26-1947. 3) Jackie Dale, born 9-8-1950, married 1st, Karen Ruth Sea - two sons, Anthony and Travis - divorced; 2nd, Sherrie Ellis - one daughter, Heather. 4) Stanley Harrison (below). 5) Robert Allen, born 2-6-1955, married 1st, Vicki Lee Smith - one child, Shane - Divorced - 2nd, Theresa Kincer - one daughter, Kayla. James Cleveland Searcy, Jr. died on 9-21-1979.

Stanley Harrison Searcy was born on 5-30-1952, in Oldham County. He married Linda Gail McDonald on 4-30-1971, in Lawrenceburg, KY. She was born on 4-3-1952, in Frankfort, KY. She is the daughter of Charles McDonald and Thelma Perry McDonald. They are the parents of two daughters: Leslie Daniele, born 6-21-1974, and Carrie Lane, born 11-25-1981.

Charles Thomas McDonald, Jr. was born on 10-25-1926, in Anderson County. He is the son of Charles McDonald Sr. and Hallie Hale McDonald. He married Thelma Mintie Perry on 2-26-1950, in Anderson County. She was born on 7-22-1925, in Anderson county. She is the daughter of Leslie Perry (1897 - 1982) and Alberta Cooper Perry (1901 - 1938). *Submitted By: Leslie Searcy.*

SEARCY,

It is thought that the Searcys came from the city of Cericy. It is believed that they left France in the late 1500's due to religious wars. They went to Nottingham, England. In the mid 1700's they arrived in Jamestown, Virginia. From there some made their way to the Carolinas while others made the journey to Kentucky.

Two of the men traveling with Daniel Boone were Searcys. They fought many Indian battles on the journey to Kentucky. They also helped Daniel Boone establish the Fort at Boonesborough.

Charles Searcy, the son of Berry Searcy and Frances A. Spoonemore Searcy, was born on 1-15-1858, in Lawrenceburg, KY. He married Lula Shouse on 6-11-1891. They were the parents of ten children: Lola Alice (1892 - 1977) married Edward Lewis; Katie (born 1894) married John Darham; Phillip W.; Goldie (1902 - 1989)(married James Harley; Marry Liz (1904 - ?) married Leroy Hennessey; Ethel (born 1907) married Joseph Oates; Herrison (born 1909) married Edith Simpson; Hardy (born 1910) married Dorthy Chidres; Jessie (born 1912) married Thorton Losey; and Agnes (born 1914) married James Mallaley. Charles Searcy died on 12-3-1918 and is buried in Ashbrook, KY.

Phillip W. Searcy was born on 5-10-1897, in Lawrenceburg. He married Lora Goodlett on 9-8-1914, in Lawrenceburg. She was born on 8-13-1894 in Lawrenceburg and she is the daughter of John J. Goodlett (1858-1911) and Sara Lay Goodlett (1872 - 1927). Phil and Lora were the parents of seven children: J.C. (1918 - 1978) married Virginia Thompson - one son, Keith; Vincent (born 1915) married Lucille Nowlin - one daughter, Cathy; Marshall; Gilbert (born 1921) married Dortha Shryock - two children - Gil and Donna; Harold (born 1923) married Annie Ledridge - one son, Paul; Earl Ray (born 1925) never married; and Betty Lou (born 1932) married Bob Gillis - two children, Robby and Cora. Phil Searcy died on 5-30-1981 in Louisville and Lora Searcy died on 3-23-1986, in Louisville.

Marshall Searcy was born on 5-6-1919, in Lawrenceburg. He married Jessie Mae Monroe on 9-3-1946, in Lawrenceburg. She was born on 7-24-1930, in Taylorsville, KY. She is the daughter of Albert Monroe and Lizzie McGaughey Monroe. She has one sister and one brother: Pat married Tommy Sims - three children - Ann, Buddy, and Faye; and Bobby married Nancy Smith - one child, Chris.

Marshall and Jessie are the parents of three children: William (born 1947) married Myra Nevins - two children, Suzanne and Dale; Kenneth Ray; and Marsha Jane (born 1954) married Larry Jackson - one child, Meaghan.

Kenneth Ray Searcy was born on 11-21-1950, in Lawrenceburg. He married Judith Ann Peach on 2-16-1974, in Jellico, Tennessee. They have one daughter, Tonya Leigh, born 9-26-1974, in Versailles, KY. Judith Ann Peach Searcy was born on 1-25-1956 in Frankfort, KY. She is the daughter of Coleman Peach and Agnes Gritton.

Coleman Peach, the son of John B. Peach and Alma Mae Brown Peach, was born on 7-12-1930, in Spencer County, KY. He married Agnes Gritton on 9-30-1950, in Bloomfield, KY. She was born on 8-25-1931, in Anderson County. She is the daughter of O.H. Gritton and Margie White Gritton. She has six brothers and sisters: Dot married J.P. McMichael; Bud married Drucilla Casey; Jerry married Brenda Rucker; O.H. Jr. married Juanita Thompson; Linda married Bic Baxter; and Larry married Linda Elliott. Coleman and Agnes are the parents of four children: Terry married Kathy Drury - one child, Shelly; Martin; Judith; and Stephen married Sheila - one child. *Submitted By: Tonya Searcy.*

SHARP,

In 1750, Matthew Sharp left his plantation to his eldest sons, John and Adam Sharp. (Will Book, 1745 - 1756, Augusta County, Virginia). John and Adam Sharp sold 350 acres, left to them by their father. Many people changed the spelling of their names about that time. (Sharp was previously spelled Shaup.)

John Sharp married Anne Dooley (1792) (Marriage Bonds of Bedford County, VA). Their sons were (1) Solomon, (2) Noah, (3) Samson, (4) Lott, (5) John. The elder John received a grant of 2230 acres in KY. He did not claim this land himself, but left it to his son, Solomon and his heirs. (Bedford County Court Records). Solomon came to KY with his uncle, Abraham Sharp, and married a cousin, Catherine Sharp (1794) (Mercer County, KY Marriage Records). Solomon died in 1847. Many of their descendents are buried in the New Providence Presbyterian Church Cemetery, Mercer County.

Abraham, Adam, James, and John Sharp (Veterans of the Revolution) received grants in KY (over 5000 acres) (Grants south of Green River, Lincoln County, KY Entries).

Noah (2) married Jane Dooley (1792) (Marriage Records of Bedford County, VA). In 1804, he bought land on the KY River in Franklin County (now Anderson County) next to his cousin, Abraham Sharp. This land is known as the Noah Sharp Farm. Noah, Abraham and his son, Francis, operated the largest ferry on the KY River (near Lock 5). Noah died in 1823, leaving the farm to his eldest son, Job.

Fred and Hazel Sharp - 50th Wedding Anniversary

Job married a cousin, Elizabeth, and continued in the partnership of the ferry and lived on the farm, leaving it to his children; Jane, James, and Elizabeth. James died in 1873 and Elizabeth in 1877. Both are buried in the Sharp Family Cemetery.

James and his wife, Mary, lived on the farm. They raised 2 sons, George and Philip (never married).

George married Eliza Smiley. They reared nine children on the farm: (1) Nell McKendrick, (2) William, (3) James, (4) Lucy Wooldridge, (5) Mary Brown, (6) Nora Sims, (7) Philip, (8) Fred, who still lives on the farm, (9) Stacy Sims, who lives nearby. Children (1) through (7) are deceased. George died in 1949, and Eliza in 1953. Both are buried in the Lawrenceburg Cemetery.

Fred (8) married Hazel Brown; reared 2 children (Philip and Freda) on the farm. Freda (Lexington) married Steve Demers (children - Matthew and Rachel).

Philip married Phyllis Hahn. They have 2 sons, Ronnie (Air Force) and Destry (Navy). Philip bought an adjoining farm (originally part of the Sharp holdings) (1971) and lives there. He bought the Noah Sharp Farm (1987) and farms both places.

Other grandchildren of George and Eliza Sharp, presently residing in Anderson County are Anna Parrish, Margaret Cole, George Sims, Freddie Sims, Bonnie Beasley, and Nora McMichael. Parts taken from a book by Anne E. Montgomery (descendent of Abraham Sharp.) *Submitted By: Nora McMichael.*

JAMES HUBERT SHELTON,

one of the children of Tom and Dessie Harley Shelton, was born 12-15-1912, in the western part of Anderson County. Sylvia Pauline Phillips, was born 4-1-1922, in Anderson County. Hubert and Pauline were married 1-26-1935.

It is not clear whether Tom, Hubert's father, approved of their marriage. On their wedding night, Hubert and Pauline stayed with Hubert's family. In the middle of the night, Tom decided to get out of bed, go out on the porch with his shotgun and fire a round. Tom wanted everyone to know that he was still in charge.

During their many years of marriage, before Hubert's death on 12-16-1977, they lived and worked in Anderson County. At one time, Hubert had three jobs: working at Booneway Garage in Stringtown; raising a tobacco crop; and full-time employment at Seagram's Distillery, Bonds Mill. He retired in 1976 with over 30 years of employment with Seagram's. Pauline, a housewife, worked very hard raising the family and taking care of the home.

In 1953, the family's house burned to the ground. Relatives and friends helped the young family get on their feet again.

They had six children, Junior, Elizabeth, Mary, Martha, James and Donnie. James Hubert, Junior was the first born, 3-6-1936. He lived only a few weeks and died of pneumonia. He is buried at the Darnell Cemetery.

Elizabeth Mae was the second child, born 6-11-1937. She married Billy Grubbs, son of Martha and Arthur Grubbs of Anderson County. They have three children, Karen, Kimberly, and Kelli. Karen has two children, Beth and Jamie. Elizabeth and Billy have lived most of thier married life in Richmond, KY where both have worked for Eastern Kentucky University.

Mary Frances was born 8-27-1939. After graduation from high school, she worked several years in Louisville before meeting her future husband, Charles Ratchford. They were married and have two daughters, Christy and Lisa. Their home is in Jeffersonville, Indiana.

Hubert Shelton Family - Front: Donnie, Mary, Bobby. Back: Elizabeth, Hubert, Pauline, Ann

Martha Ann was the fourth child born to Hubert and Pauline, 5-28-1941. After high school, she married Bronson Proctor, son of Jim and Geneva Proctor of Anderson County. They have four sons: Darryl, Rodney, Mark, and Jason. Darryl has one son, Travis. Rodney has three children, Amanda, Kendra, and Jeremy. Ann and her children reside in Lawrenceburg.

James Robert, "Bobby", was born 2-23-1944. Upon graduation from high school, he served two years in the army, of which one was in Vietnam. He married Connie Perkins, the daughter of Dewey and Gladys Perkins of Anderson County. They have one daughter, Stacy, and reside in Mt. Washington, KY.

Donnie Ray was the last child of Hubert and Pauline, born in 5-1-1945. He made the army his career, serving one year in Vietnam. He married Dianne Hopkins and they have one son, Bart. They reside at Ft. Belvoir, Virginia.

Pauline still lives in Lawrenceburg. She and her children remain close. They continue to carry on family traditions, especially at Christmas. *Submitted By: Elizabeth Grubbs.*

SHELY, The Shely name has been a familiar one in Anderson County for many years. Oral history suggests that the first of this family arrived in America as a ship stowaway from Germany. In 1903, Tyler Gilbert Shely was born in Anderson County to Ernest Desha Shely and Effie Dee Jones Shely. Their home was in the Sinai area of the county. His mother died

when he was seven years old but he never forgot that her last words to him were "Gilbert, be a good boy". (In later years, he related this experience many times from the pulpit when emphasizing the importance of each individual's Christian influence and example.)

Gilbert had two brothers and one sister. Wyatt (1901 - 1976), a lifelong resident of Anderson County, was a well-known teacher and historian. Vivian Shely Blakeman (1905) lived most of her life in Franklin County, KY and now resides in Greenville, SC. Melvin (1908) has maintained the family roots by raising his family and remaining in the Sinai community all his life.

Gilbert attended grade school in Anderson County and graduated from Berea Normal School and Berea College. He received his Master of Theology Degree from Southern Baptist Seminary in 1940.

The Reverend Shely was ordained a Baptist minister in 1930, and pastored Friendship (12 yrs.) and Goshen Baptist Church (4 yrs.) in Anderson County, Shawnee Run Baptist Church (23 yrs.) in Mercer County, and Clear Creek Baptist Church (3 yrs.) in Woodford County.

In 1936, Gilbert married Sally Crook, the daughter of James Henry "Cutter" Crook and Ollie Bell McGaughey Crook. (Bro. Shely liked to joke about the "preacher" who married the "crook".) Sally was born in the Penny's Chapel area of Anderson County in 1915, and was a 1934 honor graduate of Kavanaugh High School, furthered her education at Southern Seminary and in later years, trained to be a psychiatric aide. She was employed at Kentucky State Hospital in Danville for 18 years as an aide and occupational therapist. Throughout their years in the ministry, Brother Shely and Sally were highly regarded as inspirational servants of God, humble teachers and Christian examples in their church and community.

Gilbert and Sally were the parents of five children, Dee and Gilbert, Jr., born in Anderson County, and Sara Evelyn, Dixie, and Oneta, born in Mercer County.

Dee (Mrs. Ronald) Johnston and her husband live in Stephens City, VA and she is Director of Purchasing at O'Sullivan Corp. in Winchester. They have four children, Steven, Michael, Kevin, and Russell, and six grandchildren.

Tyler Gilbert "Bub" Shely, Jr., married to the former Phyllis McGaughey, lives in Immokalee, FL and is principal of Immokalee High School. They have three children, Tyler Gilbert "Ty" Shely III, Eugenia, and Ivan Del.

Evelyn (Mrs. Charles) Matherly and her husband live in Mercer County where she is Office Supervisor at the KU E. W. Brown Power Plant. She has two children, Kathleen Everman and Thomas Drury, and a granddaughter.

Dixie Donnell lives in the last homeplace of her grandparents, "Cutter" and Ollie Crook, in Alton and is employed in the Professional Unit at Electronic Data Systems in Frankfort. She has two daughters, Tracey and Melissa Donnell.

Rev. Gilbert and Sally Shely

Oneta (Mrs. Barry) Brandenburg and her husband live in Anderson County where she is employed in the Transportation Department at Florida

Tile. They have two children, Joseph Adams, III, and Shannon K. Brandenburg, and a granddaughter.

Brother and Mrs. Shely retired to their home in Harrodsburg in 1968, where he remained active for many years in the radio ministry and served as interim pastor for several churches. He also continued to conduct numerous weddings and funerals until stricken by illness in 1984. He died at his home on July 19, 1987. Mrs. Shely still resides at their residence in Harrodsburg. *Submitted By: Evelyn Matherly and Dee Johnston.*

WYATT SHELY, The Wyatt Shely family resided in the Western Section of Anderson County, and in Lawrenceburg, Kentucky, for most of Wyatt's life. Wyatt was the son of Ernest Desha Shely and Effie Dee Jones Shely. He was born in 1901, and died in 1976. He was the brother of Rev. Gilbert Shely, Melvin Shely and Vivian Shely Blakeman. He was married to Blanche Brown in April, 1922, and to this marriage two sons were born. Robert (Bobby) Edward Shely was born in 1930 and died in 1955. He was married to Annelle Birdwhistell and they had one son, Brent. Forest Franklin Shely was born in 1924, and is a practicing physician in Campbellsville, Kentucky. He is married to Roberta Hale of Springfield, Kentucky and they have five children: Jacuqe, Deborah, William, Karen, and Carla. There are eight children who call Dr. Chely "Granddaddy".

Wyatt was a graduate of Berea Normal School and Berea College. He was valedictorian of the 1931 graduating class of Berea College. After graduation from college, he taught for a short time in Mercer County, and then returned to his native Anderson County where he taught until his retirement. Most of his teaching years were spent at Western High School. He was also very active in Friendship Baptist Church and was very instrumental in "coaching" young preachers in the ministry. He affectionately referred to them as his "sons" and on his death-bed he wrote to each of them a very inspiring and loving farewell.

Wyatt and Blanche Shely about 1950

For many years, Wyatt wrote a weekly column for The Anderson News. This was called "Our Heritage", because of the interest and concern he had about the heritage of Anderson County. He also wrote several Church histories including, "This Is Friendship", "This Is Goshen", and an untitled history of the First Baptist Church of Lawrenceburg that was finished, but not bound, at the time of his death. He also wrote numerous articles for the Western Recorder and other publications.

Blanche Shely, wife of Wyatt, was the daughter of John and Susan Brown. She was a faithful and devoted wife, and supported her husband in his school, church and community activities. She followed him in death and both are buried in the Friendship Church Cemetery.

Marvin Shely and his wife, Addie Yeager Shely, still reside in Western Anderson County. They have had three children, Maurice Raymond, Tony Dixon - now deceased, and Patsy McIlroy. There are several grandchildren. Vivian Shely Clakeman, widow of Gilbert Blakeman, now resides in Greenville, South Carolina, near her son, Don and his wife, Betty. Another son, Dan, lives in Atlanta, Georgia. *Submitted By: Forest F. Shely M. D.*

EDWARD M. SHERWOOD, was born March 5, 1797, in Talbot County, Maryland, the son of Moses and Margaret (Valliant) Sherwood. The family left Maryland sometime after 1800, stopping in Ohio for a year or two, but in 1810 were living in Clark County, KY. In 1813, Moses Sherwood and his son, Edward M., enlisted for a short duration of service in the War of 1812. In 1818, we find Moses Sherwood with a family of eight living in Gallatin County, Illinois and they are: Edward M.; John; Hugh B.; Mary, who later married J. J. Kanady; Thomas; and Washington Sherwood. In 1820, Edward M. Sherwood came back to Franklin (now Anderson County) County, KY to marry Susannah Jewell, daughter of William and Margaret (Pantier) Jewell. He took his bride back to Illinois where they lived for sometime, but in 1825, they were back in Franklin Co., KY. In 1834, they bought a farm on Salt River, about a mile above Anderson City, KY, where they continued to live the remainder of their lives. Edward's parents, brothers, and sisters remained in Illinois. Edward and Susannah's children are as follows: 1. Margaret Sherwood (1820 - 1848) married Jackson Siers. They had Susan Siers, wife of Jackson Burge, and Margaret Siers, wife of Calvin Morgan; 2. John Sherwood, Sr. (1822-1823); 3. John Sherwood, Jr. (1824 - 1863) married Mary D. Sale. They had Susan Catherine Sherwood, wife of John Moffett - Thomas Sherwood, Albert Sherwood, married Clementine Busey - and S. D. Sherwood;

John Sherwood and Albert Gallatin Sherwood

4. William J. Sherwood (1826 -1849) died of Typhoid Fever; 5. Hugh Sherwood (1829 - 1849) died of Typhoid Fever; 6. Mary Sherwood (1831 - prior to 1868) married Lewis S. Walker. They had Susan B., John, and Sallie Walker, who married William B. Wilson; 7. Martha A. Sherwood (1833 - 1882) married William G. Cole. They had James Edward, Presley F. (married Nettie B. Pickers), John William (married Annah Russell Bond), Mary Belle (married William H. Crossfield), Lula A. (married James T. Cox), Thomas Merritt, and Louis Edgar (married Nancy Roach); 8. Smith Sherwood (1836 - 1863) served in the Civil War for the South; 9. Thomas Sherwood (1838 - 1854); 10. Susan Tabitha Sherwood (1840 - 1887) married Marion Clay Young; 11. Albert Gallatin Sherwood (1843 - 1914) served in the Civil War for the South. He married Mary Catlett and had - Smith, James (married Lillian Sullivan), William (married Rosa Munday), John, Allie, Ester, Stella (married Alvin H. Hawkins), Clarence, Clifford (married Anna Gee). He was a veteran of World War I. His son, Allen, was in World War II and his grandson was in the Korean War, making six generations of Sherwood War Veterans), and Thomas Irvine Sherwood (married Irene Burga). *Submitted By: Hugh Hines Hawkins.*

SHERWOOD - GILLIS, John Sherwood was born in England. As an adult, he was very poor and lived in a house that contained over four other families. John received news that a ship was leaving England and was bound for Maryland. On arrival in Maryland, John married a woman, whose name has not been recorded. They conceived a child and named him Moses. Moses was thought to have been born somewhere between 1760 and 1765. Moses married

Margaret Valiant, the daughter of John and Mary Valiant.

Moses and his wife settled in Talbot County, Maryland. They had a son, Edward M. "Neddie", born in 1797. At the age of 18, Neddie left Talbot County and journeyed through Kentucky, settling in Estill, Fayette, and finally Anderson County. While in one of these counties, Neddie met and befriended a young woman named Susannah Jewell. She was born on 3-30-1799 in Anderson County, then Franklin County. She was the daughter of William Jewell. As their love for each other grew, so did the attraction between them. "Neddie" and "Sukey" married on 1-16-1820. Soon after their marriage, Neddie received news that his father had died.

Neddie and Sukey were the parents of 11 children: Margaret (1820 - 1848) married Jackson Siers; John Sr. (1822 - 1823); John Jr. (1824 - 1863) married Mary D. Sale; William J. (1826 - 1849) unmarried; Hugh (1829 - 1849) unmarried; Mary (1831-1868) married Lewis S. Walker; Martha A. (1833 - ?) married William G. Cole; Smith (1836 - 1863) unmarried Confederate soldier; Thomas (1838 - 1854); Susan Tabitha (1840 - 1887) married Marion Clay Young; and Albert Gallatin. Neddie died on 9-12-1855, in Anderson County and Sukey died on 11-14-1872. Both are buried in the Sherwood Graveyard in Anderson County.

Albert Gallatin Sherwood was born on 7-11-1843, in Lawrenceburg and died on 11-9-1914. He met and married Mary Catlett on 10-17-1867. She was born in September of 1851, and was the daughter of George Washington Catlett (1804 - 1870) and Nancy Cole Catlett (1813 - 1900). They bore a child, Clifford Troops Sherwood, born 4-27-1889.

Clifford married Anna Bryant Gee. She had a gold pocket watch that has been passed down from generation to generation. This couple conceived a son, Emery Allen Sherwood. He was born on 7-11-1922, in Anderson County. Emery Allen married Mary Virginia Bryant on 2-1-1946. She is the daughter of Winford Bryant (1910 - 1969) and Mary Hazel Cummins Bryant (born 7-30-1911). She was born on 9-9-1928, in Anderson County. They have a son, Allen Wayne, born on 2-20-1947, in Anderson County. He married Linda Sue Gillis. She was born on 8-11-1948, in Frankfort. She is the daughter of Charles E. Gillis and Margie Richardson Gillis. They are the parents of two sons: Bryan Kent, born 2-20-1972 and Chad Allen, born 7-10-1975. Allen and Linda are divorced.

Charles E. Gillis was born on 8-26-1920, in Anderson County. He is the son of George Edward Gillis (1875 - 1961) and Maggie Rena Johnson Gillis (1885 - 1944). He married Margie Richardson on 9-6-1947. She was born on 6-3-1927 in Estill County. She is the daughter of Clell Richardson and Maggie Harris Richardson. They are the parents of three children: Linda Sue; Charlene, born 1953, married Jerry Goodlett - two children, David and Dawn; and Charles Edward Jr., born 1962, married Kim Smith - one child, Chris. *Submitted By: Chad Sherwood.*

THOMAS SHIFFLET, was born in France about 1766. Came to America as a French Soldier. Served in the American Revolutionary War. Became an American citizen and made his home in Albermarle County., VA. Was married to Elizabeth Lamb, born 1768, of Orange County, VA. in 1788. He was present at Yorktown when the British surrendered in 1781.

Thomas and Elizabeth had 12 children. The sixth one being Fontaine. In 1802, the family moved to Madison Co., KY where Thomas died 1823, and is buried with his wife, Elizabeth.

Fontaine Shifflet born 1800, in Virginia. Married Lucy Martin born 1847, Madison County. She died in 1895, and Christopher died 1910. Both are buried in Madison County. They raised eight children. The second one was Owen.

Owen Shiffet born 1872, Estill County. Died 1899, and buried in Madison County. He married Eliza

Brown, born 1875, in Madison County. She died 1956, in Mercer County and is buried in Anderson County. They had four children.

After the death of Owen, Eliza moved to Mercer County and settled with her four children.

William was born 1897, in Madison County and died in 1965. First married to Ramie Nichols who died 1926. Second marriage to Eunice Masters who died 1973. They are all buried in Anderson County.

W.B. Shifflet ca. 1916 - Lawrenceburg Water Works

William and Ramie had three children: 1) Alvin Shifflet born 1921, died 1967, buried in Anderson County. Was married in 1945 to Lois Smith, Mercer County. They had two children, Connie and Vickie, who live in Salvisa, KY.

2) Irvine Shifflet, born 1922, Mercer County. Married Inis Wooldridge 1945. She was born in Louisville and reared in Anderson County. They have one son, Irvin, born 1946 in Franklin County. He attended Anderson County schools until the age of 10 when they moved to Lexington, KY. He married Jeri Wagner and they have two sons, Brian Scott, born 1976, and Kenny Allen, born 1978.

3) Theresa Shifflet born 1924, died 1969, buried in Anderson County. Married Garald Carter. They had two children. David resides in Lawrenceburg. Carol lives in Versailles.

In William's second marriage to Eunice there were two children: 1) Wilbert Shifflet, born 1928, died 1981, buried in Anderson County, married Alpha Shouse. They had one son, William O. Shifflet. Second marriage was to Ortha Cornish. They had four children: Judy Shifflet Dollins of Florida, Larry, James, and Owen Shifflet live in Frankfort.

2) Juanita Shifflet married Paul Stapp. There were three children by a previous marriage: Sandra, Tony, and John live in Versailles.

William B. Shifflet lived in the Claylick area before moving to Stringtown, where he lived until his death. He was employed at the Lawrenceburg Water Company until ill health forced him to retire. *Submitted By: Inis M. Shifflet.*

LUDLOW BERRY SHOUSE, was born December 16, 1895, in Anderson County, Kentucky. He spent most of his life here while he attended his elementary school in Anderson City, in what was known as The Red Round School. He also attended Kavanaugh High School in Lawrenceburg.

He entered the United States Army in 1918, and served 11 months in Europe. He arrived back in the States, July of 1919.

Ludlow's father, Ezra Shouse, was married to Nannie Thompson. They had two children: Ludlow and Mrs. Floyd (Gippie) Shely, deceased. At the age of four, Ludlow's mother died and his father remarried Vada Grubbs, and to this marriage were born seven children: Harry Shouse, deceased; Mrs. Chester (Mary Alice) Gash, Lexington, KY; Ollie Shouse, Tuscon, Arizona; Capterton Shouse, Lexington, KY; Ruby Shouse Fuecha, Lexington, KY; Della Shouse and Donald Shouse of Louisville, KY.

Ludlow married the former Bertha Mae Searcy of Louisville, KY on August 31, 1919 in Jeffersonville, Indiana. Bertha was the oldest daughter born to Edward and Georgia Coomes Searcy, both deceased.

She was born in Bloomfield, KY on August 5, 1901. Bertha attended elementary school at The Big Springs School in Nelson County, KY. Her family later moved to Louisville, where her mother died in 1918.

Bertha had five sisters and one brother: Mrs. Arthur (Ruby) Brumley; Mrs.. Charles (Carrie) Byers; Mrs. William (Evelyn) Brumely; Michael Reno Searcy; Christine Searcy; and Mrs. George (Edith) Crouch, all of Dayton, Ohio.

Ludlow and Bertha Shouse

Ludlow and Bertha made their home in Glensboro, KY. From this marriage were born six children: Mrs. James (Dorothy) Casey; Mrs. Stanley (Georgia) Casey, Lawrenceburg; Sterling Shouse; Stewart Shouse, Louisville; Mrs. Jessie (Joyce) Duncan, deceased; Mrs. Robert (Nancy) Hutcherson, Frankfort, KY.

Mr. and Mrs. Ludlow Shouse attended and were members of the Glensboro Christian church for many years. Ludlow was the song leader for 25 years, and Bertha was a Sunday School Teacher for 20 years.

Ludlow and Bertha have 14 grandchildren: James Carroll Robinson; Stewart Collins Robinson; Melissa H. Noble; Forest Wayne Casey; Elaine S. Genote, Linda S. Boaz; Stewart Shouse; Kathy Lewis Edlin; Debra Joyce Alfred, Todd Duncan, Paul Douglas Trent, Denise T. Morrow, Krista Jean Ray, and Melaine Ann Malone. 25 great-grandchildren: James Timothy Robinson; Tina Marie Robinson; Jimmy Stewart Robinson; Joshua Keid Garrity; Travis Lyn Garrity; Jeffery Wayne Casey; Martin Sean Casey; Kevin Coke; Sherry Coke; Stacy Coke; Shad Boaz; Craig Boaz; Kelly Shouse; Berry Shouse; Fred Gassett III; Justin Morgan Ray; Carrie Ellen Ray; Christopher Morrow; Racheal Trent; and Marlene Malone. Two great-great-grandchildren: Jeffery Steven Casey and Brook Deshay Robinson.

Mr. and Mrs. Ludlow Shouse farmed until 1960, when they sold their farm and moved to Lawrenceburg. In 1963, Ludlow and his oldest daughter, Dorothy, bought and operated a business on College Street until his death on January 12, 1974. He is buried in the Lawrenceburg Cemetery.

Bertha remarried Walker J. Parker of Lexington, KY on November 10, 1975. They reside at 100 Saffell Ct. in Lawrenceburg.

FRANCES MARION AND RACHAEL (FLETCHER) SIMS entered Anderson County from Casey County about 1911. Traveling with their 10 children, their first night in Anderson County was spent a couple of miles north of the county line at McCall's Spring, a common stopping point for the wagon borne travelers of the day. They settled on a farm on the Kentucky River at the end of the old Harry Wise Road.

Nine years later, they moved to another farm, also on the Kentucky River, on the Ninevah-Clifton Road. Frances Marion passed away in 1926. Rachael continued to live on the family farm till her death in 1933. Both are buried in the Sand Spring Cemetery.

The children were: A baby who died at birth in 1884, and a son, Edgar, 1885-1886. Both are buried in Casey County near Kings Mountain.

Maude (1887-1934) married Albert Brown in 1911 and lived near New Castle, Indiana; mother of Eliza-

beth, Clifford, Richard, Josephine, Carlton, Alice, Irene, George, and Francis Marion.

William Lucas "Willy" (1889 - 1950) married Martha Holman and father of Cecil Sims.

James "Jim" Washington (1891 - 1973) married Leda Houchin in 1915 and father of James Washington Jr., Christine, Harold Houchin "Houchie", Author Thomas "Tommy".

Francis Marion "Frank" (1893 - 1972).

Goodloe Allen (1896 - 1977) married Nora Lee Sharp in 1923 and father of Goodloe Allen Jr., Allen Washington, Raymond Wilson, and Frankie M.

Henry Howard (1897 - 1973) married Bessie Lula Quisenberry and moved to Woodford County; father of Paul Darter, Mary Magdalene, Henry Howard Jr. "Jug", Bobby Carl, Levie Doris, Jo Ann, Minnie Elizabeth, James Thomas, and France Leon.

Irvin, Howard, Parker, Maude, ?, Gordloe, Ethyl, Jim or Willie, Frank and Granny Sims, seated c. 1930.

Irvin Wesley (1899 - 1978) married Margaret Lee Lockhart in 1934 and father of Wesley Newton, Myrtle Elizabeth, Roberta Lee, Ethyl Agnes, and Mildred Frances.

Nannie E. Sims (1901 - 1918).

Parker Davis (1903 - 1978) married Nora Hyatt in 1936 and father of Phillip and Gary.

Jim and Goodloe were lifelong county farmers. Frank served in Europe during World War I and returned to become co-proprietor, with Parker, of the infamous Sims Poolroom and restaurant on Main Street in Lawrenceburg. Parker also served in the State Legislature and later worked for IBM in Fayette County. Irvin was a farmer and later a building contractor. The sons were all ardent outdoorsmen who collectively claimed to have caught more fish than were known to exist in the county.

From the ten children of Frances and Rachael Sims, their descendents now exceed 150. *Submitted By: Wesley Sims.*

IRVIN WESLEY SIMS AND MARGARET LEE LOCKHART Irvin Wesley Sims, the 10th of 12 children of Frances Marion and Rachael (Fletcher) Sims, was born near Kings Mountain in Casey County in 1899. His first recollection of Anderson County was McCall's Spring, where the family spent their first night on arrival about 1905. The Sims family lived on a farm on the Kentucky River at the end of the Harry Wise Road until 1920. They then moved to a Kentucky River farm on the Ninevah-Clifton Road. As a young man, Irvin went west several summers and worked on farms in Iowa. He also worked in Detroit in the auto industry for a time.

Margaret Lee Lockhart was born on the family farm just off Ninevah-Clifton Road. She attended Kavanaugh High School (class of 1926), traveling the 12 mile round trip each day by horse and buggy. She earned a Teaching Certificate from Eastern State Teachers College and began her teaching career in 1928 at Ninevah.

Irvin and Margaret were married on March 31, 1934. Margaret suspended her teaching career while five children were born. Irvin farmed as a sharecropper with the resultant somewhat nomadic life. The family moved 11 times before purchasing the old Woods Home and settling on South Main Street in

1954. Irvin began a construction business in 1948 and later started the Sims and Stockton Construction Company in partnership with Clayton and Harold Stockton. After his retirement from construction in 1966, he became an active participant in the competition for biggest "mater" or other garden/orchard object of the week in the Anderson News window. He also found plenty of time for his other favorite activity - communing with nature, fishing pole in hand.

Margaret and Irvin Sims, 1973

Margaret returned to teaching in 1950 at Sand Spring Elementary School, where over 500 county youngsters received their 5th grade education in her classes before her retirement in 1969. After attending the Ninevah Christian Church for 40 years, she became a member of Sand Spring Baptist Church, where she taught the Senior Ladies Sunday School Class for over 30 years. The Senior Citizens bus rarely makes a trip without her.

Irvin and Margaret's five children were: Wesley Newton, 1935 - : a career Army Aviator; married Sally (Pendergast) of Bremerton, Washington; now a resident of Washington State and employed by the University of Washington; they have two children - Wesley Jr., and Sherry Ann.

Myrtle Elizabeth, 1937 - : (Mrs. Ed Sparkman) was a career employee with the State Office Of Vocational Rehabilitation in the Department of Education. She lives on West Broadway in Lawrenceburg.

Roberta Lee, 1939 - : (Mrs. J. B. Crafton) a career teacher with the Bullitt County school system in Shepherdsville; now resides in Mount Washington. They have two sons: Ronald Lee and Michael Dale.

Ethyl Agnes, 1940 - : (Mrs. Reese Letcher) works for the State Department of Education in Frankfort and resides in Lawrenceburg on Meriwether Drive.

Mildred Frances, 1944 - : (Mrs. Thomas Blair) after a career as a Navy Wife, they now live on Jennifer Drive, and she works for the Anderson Public Library. They have two sons: Mark Thomas and Wesley Scott.

Irvin died in 1978 and is buried in the Lawrenceburg Cemetery. Margaret continues to reside in their home on South Main Street. *Submitted By: Wesley Sims.*

JAMES A. SIMPSON, was born in Anderson County on August 6, 1854, and died in Nelson County on July 16, 1920. He was the son of Lloyd Simpson and Lucinda Franklin, the daughter of Claiborne Franklin and Elizabeth Sparrow. James A. was a farmer and a member of the Christian Church.

Frances A. Whitehouse was born in Anderson County, September 20, 1851, and died in Nelson County, March 30, 1906. She was the daughter of John Whitehouse and Laura Wyatt. She was a member of the Christian Church.

James A. and Frances E. were married, November 7, 1875, at the home of John Whitehouse. They resided in Anderson County until about 1888.

James A. and Frances were the parents of nine children.

They are:

Charles Simpson, born 1877, not married

Orvey Simpson, born July 7, 1878, married Donnie Burgin.

Betty M. Simpson, born July 29, 1879, married Walter Terrell.

Laura Simpson, born February 3, 1881, married James Sparrow.

Stanley Simpson, born 1882, married Mary L. Thomas.

Clayborn Simpson, born April 1883, married Flora E. Conway.

Marion Simpson, born September 14, 1886, married Lula Bunch.

Jesse Simpson, born 1892, not married.

John Sherwood Simpson, born September 6, 1889, married Vangie Hawkins.

James A. and Frances are buried at the New Liberty Cemetery.

James A. Simpson married Julia Frances Catlett, widow of Edgar Hawkins on March 7, 1907. They are the parents of three children.

Herbert Simpson, born January 28, 1909, married Elizabeth Ritter.

Mabel Simpson, born October 20, 1910, married Hubert Arnold.

Elizabeth Simpson, born August 2, 1912, married Marvin Sexton.

All children are deceased, except Elizabeth who resides in Louisville.

LLOYD AND LUCINDA SIMPSON,

were born in Marion County, KY, and came to Anderson county in the 1840's from Mercer County. Lloyd was born in 1829, and Lucinda in 1824. Lloyd was a farmer and a carpenter. Lucinda was the daughter of Claiborne Franklin and Elizabeth Sparrow.

Lloyd and Lucinda were married in January of 1852, in Anderson County, KY, and lived in the Willow Creek area.

They were the parents of six children. They are: Elizabeth Simpson, born February 1, 1853, married 1st Dennis Casey, 2nd, James Murphy; James Andrew Simpson, born August 6, 1854, married 1st, Frances Whitehouse, 2nd, Julia Catlett Hawkins; Louisa Simpson, born January 11, 1856, and died August 6, 1865; George Simpson, born November 7, 1857 married 1st Delpha Burgan, 2nd, Sally Nutgrass; Mary E. Simpson, born 1865, married John Spratt.

Lloyd and Lucinda were buried in a family cemetery on Willow Creek. Due to the construction of Taylorsville Lake, the Corps of Engineers moved the remains to Valley Cemetery, Taylorsville, Kentucky, in 1979. *Submitted By: Glenna Simpson.*

LOYD SIMPSON,

was born circa 1829, in Marion County, Kentucky. He was living in Anderson County, Kentucky, by 1850, where the Federal Census listed him as a "farm laborer" in the household of Claibourne Franklin, who later became Loyd's father-in-law. He married in January of 1852, to Lucinda Franklin, born 1824, in Marion County, Kentucky, a daughter of Claibourne Franklin and Elizabeth Sparrow, and a granddaughter of Harry Henry Sparrow, Jr. and Lucy Shipley Hanks.

Loyd and Lucinda owned their own farm by 1860, and beside farming, Loyd was also engaged in the occupation of carpentry. They remained in Anderson County, both dying sometime after 1880, and both are buried in the Willow Creek Cemetery in Anderson County. During the construction of the Taylorsville Lake, their remains were removed to the Taylorsville Cemetery.

There were six known children born to Loyd and Lucinda Simpson:

1) Elizabeth Simpson, born 1 Feb 1853, died 1930, married ? Spratt, Dennis Case, and James Murphy. No Children.

2) James A. Simpson, born 6 August 1854, died 16 July 1920, married 7 November 1875 to Frances E. Whitehouse.

3) Louisa Simpson, born 11 January 1856, died 6 August 1865, buried in Willow Creek Cemetery.

4) George Washington Simpson, born 7 November 1857, married 23 January 1879 to Delphia Burgan

(three children), married second, to Sally Nutgrass, (one child). The three children of the first marriage were:

a) Perry Landon Simpson, born 1879, married Susan H. Rogers and had nine children: Philadelphia Virginia; Charlie; John Truman; Mary Elizabeth; Effie Catherine; P.L.; a son who died young; Leona; and Otis.

b) William Edward Simpson, born 1889, left Kentucky

c) Malinda Ellen Simpson, born 13 September 1891, married Rome Gardie Case, son of Lebon Merritt Case and Fida Hahn. Six children: daughter, died as infant; Alberta, married Prentice B. Walls; William Elmo, lives in Seattle, Washington; Leroy, died young; and Leb Merritt.

5) Mary E. Simpson, born 2 July 1859, died 31 October 1880, married Isaac Burgin.

6) Nancy Jane Simpson, born 1865, died 27 August 1951, married John Spratt. *Submitted By: William R. Walls.*

FRANCES MARION AND RACHAEL (FLETCHER) SIMS

entered Anderson County from Casey County about 1911. Traveling with their 10 children, their first night in Anderson County was spent a couple of miles north of the county line at McCall's Spring, a common stopping point for the wagon borne travelers of the day. They settled on a farm on the Kentucky River at the end of the old Harry Wise Road.

Nine years later they moved to another farm, also on the Kentucky River, on the Ninevah-Clifton Road. Frances Marion passed away in 1926. Rachael continued to live on the family farm until her death in 1933. Both are buried in the Sand Spring Cemetery.

The children were: A baby who died at birth in 1884, and a son, Edgar, 1885 - 1886. Both are buried in Casey County near Kings Mountain.

Maude (1887 - 1934) married Elmer Stanforth and mother of John Franklin, Geneva, and Anthony Thomas. Then married Elmo Boston and mother of Nannie, Lewis, and Rachel.

Ethel (1888 - 1971) married Albert Brown in 1911 and lived near New Castle, Indiana; mother of Elizabeth, Clifford, Richard, Josephine, Carlton, Alice, Irene, George, and Francis Marion.

William Lucas "Willy" (1889 - 1950) married Martha Holman and father of Cecil Sims.

James "Jim" Washington (1891 - 1973) married Leda Houchin in 1915 and father of James Washington, Jr., Christine, Harold Houchin "Houchie", Author Thomas "Tommy".

Francis Marion "Frank" (1893 - 1972).

Goodloe Allen (1896 - 1977) married Nora Lee Sharp in 1923 and father of Goodloe Allen Jr., Allen Washington, Raymons Wilson, and Frankie M.

Henry Howard (1897 - 1978) married Bessie Lula Quisenberry and moved to Woodford County; father of Paul Darter, Mary Magdalene, Henry Howard, Jr. "Jug", Bobby Carl, Levie Doris, Jo Ann, Minnie Elizabeth, James Thomas, and Frances Leon.

Irvin Wesley (1899 - 1978) married Margaret Lee Lockhart in 1934 and father of Wesley Newton, Myrtle Elizabeth, Roberta Lee, Ethyl Agnes, and Mildred Frances.

Nannie E. Sims (1901 - 1918).

Parker Davis (1903 - 1978) married Nora Hyatt in 1936 and father of Phillip and Gary.

Jim and Goodloe were lifelong county farmers. Frank served in Europe during World War I and returned to become co-proprietor, with Parker, of the infamous Sims Poolroom and restaurant on Main Street in Lawrenceburg. Parker also served in the State Legislature and later worked for IBM in Fayette County. Irvin was a farmer and later a building contractor. The sons were all ardent outdoorsmen who collectively claimed to have caught more fish than were known to exist in the county.

From the ten children of Frances and Rachael Sims, their descendents now exceed 150. Submitted By: Wesley Sims.

JAMES HENRY SMITH,

was born in October 1840, and died in 1920, in Anderson County. He married Mary Elizabeth Crossfield on 5-11-1865, in Anderson County. She was born 1-7-1843, in Anderson County and died in 1930. She was the daughter of Woodford (1816 - 1890) and Amanda Gudgel Crossfield (1820 - 1893).

James Henry and Mary Elizabeth had a son named William Henry Smith. He was born on 3-30-1866, in Anderson County and died in 1938. He married Martha Lee York, the daughter of William York (1842 - 1928) and Sara Elizabeth Crossfield York (1843 - 1873) She was born on 8-9-1866, in Anderson County and died in 1930. They were the parents of six children: Elizabeth Smith Young, Carrie Smith Young, Walter H. Smith, Sarah Eddie Smith, James Dudley Smith, and Mabel W. Smith Milburn.

James Dudley Smith was born 2-7-1910 in Anderson County. He married Ruth Agnes Young on 12-20-1936, in Anderson county. She was born on 11-11-1918 in Anderson County to Charles Vaughn Young and Beulah Barnes Young. They were the parents of two children: James Thomas Smith married Thelma Franklin - two children - Diana Smith Koonce and James Steven Smith; and Cheri Lynn Smith Lynn.

Charles Vaughn Young (1898 - 1963) was the son of Lewis Young and Lulie Herndon Young. He married Beulah Barnes in 1918. She was born in 1898, in Anderson County and died on 10-8-1965. She was the daughter of Butler Barner and Sara Duncan Barnes. They were the parents of four children: Paul Young, Edith Young Franklin, C. V. Young, and Ruth Agnes Young Smith.

Lewis Young (1855 - 1899) married Lulie Herndon (1856 - 1889). They were the parents of five children: Grace Young Thompson, Charlie Young, Oscar Young, Mattie Young, and Chester Vaughn Young. *Submitted By: James Steven Smith.*

JAMES J. SMITH,

was born on 3-4-1947, in Louisville, Kentucky. He is the son of James L. Smith (9-23-1923 - 10-12-1979) and Mary Down Smith (4-7-1928 - 1-6-1967). His parents were married on 5-6-1946, in Owensboro, KY. He has three sisters and one brother: Peggy Sue, born 6-20-1949; Linda Hasile, born 5-10-1953, married Terri Higdon in 1975 - two children, Terry, born 1980, and Jennifer, born 1983; Patricia Ann, born 4-30-1955, married Jerry Waldridge - two children, Jamie, born 1974, and Jerry, born 1976; and Timothy Robert, born 12-13-1957.

James J. Smith married Gayle K. Casteel on 8-21-1965, in Louisville. She was born on 7-4-1947, in Louisville. She is the daughter of Harvey Casteel and Verdia Hayes Casteel. Her parents were married on 6-11-1944, in Louisville. She has three sisters and one brother: Patricia A., born 10-20-1945, married Robert E. Colligan in 1965 - three children - Jinella, Bobby, Brian; Joyce C., born 6-8-1952, married William Bill Saylor in 1970 - three children - Lindsay, Tonya, Roger; Brenda Fay, born 1-14-1955, married Wayne R. Miller in 1975 - three children - Billy, David, Kristy; and Michael C., born 10-5-1957.

James and Gayle Smith are the parents of four children: James Robert, born 9-30-66, married Lorrisa

Meril Doughery on 8-1-1987, in Lawrenceburg - one daughter, Lisa, born on 6-7-1989; Joseph Michael, born 5-7-1969; Stephanie Pauline, born 12-9-1971; and Amy Kay, born 3-14-1974. All the children were born in Louisville, except Joseph Michael. He was born in Fort Know, KY. *Submitted By: Amy Smith.*

J. CONWAY SMITH, and Sally Jo Payne were born and raised in Lebanon, KY. They met and married in 1933. Conway had just begun his career with Kentucky Utilities Co., after completing two years at the University of Kentucky where he majored in electrical engineering. Their first daughter, Connie, was born in Lebanon the following year. The family moved to Greensburg, KY in 1937, where they had their second child, a son whom they named after Sally's father, Sam Payne. Conway and his father-in-law built their home in Greensburg from the basement up, completing it just in time for their son's arrival. Two years later they had their last child and second daughter, Betty.

The family moved to Lawrenceburg in the fall of 1946, living for about a year on Broadway Street across from the Witherspoon farm. Conway had worked in Greensburg as the sole representative of Kentucky Utilities, doing everything but collecting bill money, and worked out of his home. The move to Lawrenceburg was a promotion to Local Manager, where he now had an office on Main Street, a secretary, and one service man. The family's next move was to Woodford Street, to a big white house that had several fireplaces, and a wood stove in the kitchen. Conway took a bucket, shovel, pick, and wheelbarrow and proceeded to dig a basement under the house for a coal stoker furnace.

J. Conway and Sally Smith Family

Conway was always dedicated to his family, his job, his church, and his community. He was very active in many civic endeavors, and held membership and office in the Rotary Club and Chamber of Commerce. His most memorable endeavors for his son were the swimming pool project and his efforts in getting various industries to locate plants here. Conway's presence and influence in the community was significant, and this short history can only touch on them. Conway and Sally supported three children through college, only the youngest not receiving a college degree.

Connie received a masters degree in education, married, taught school, and raised a family consisting of a son, William, and a daughter, Sally. She was divorced from her first husband, was later remarried, and the family then moved to Ann Arbor, Michigan. She divorced again, and not being able to find the job she needed, proceeded to organize and open a new high school for exceptional students. The school flourished with her as dean. She later received her doctorate from the University of Michigan shortly before her retirement at the age of 53. She still lives in Ann Arbor, is now writing, and conducting seminars on women's studies around the United States.

Sam received a Bachelor's degree in engineering, married his high school sweetheart, Jane Brown, and raised a family consisting of two sons, Greg and Conway. They have lived in Louisiana, Alabama,

Texas, and Kentucky. Sam presently is a computer programmer at IBM in Lexington, while Jane presently is working as receptionist at Florida Tile Corp. The two boys are now grown, and Sam and Jane presently reside on Djeddah Drive in Lawrenceburg.

Betty spent one year at Eastern State University, married and raised a family consisting of three sons, Martin, David, and Clay, and one daughter, Gretchen. Betty presently works as a secretary at Assumption High School. Betty, her husband, and the two youngest children reside at their home in Jefferstown, KY where they have lived for many years.

Conway and Sally died about five months apart in 1984. *Submitted By: Sam P. Smith.*

VERNON AND EVELYN SPARKS, and sons Mike, Ralph, and Alan became residents of Anderson County in 1962, when Vernon was transferred to the local Kraft Plant to help with the new whey operation.

The family quickly settled into the life of the community. Mike enrolled in the junior class at Anderson High. Ralph was a seventh-grader and Alan a third grader and they played Little League Football. All became involved in activities of Lawrenceburg United Methodist Church.

While Vernon fulfilled his obligations to Kraft, Evelyn enjoyed a brief association with Mrs. John T. Cox and family in the ladies ready-to-wear store downtown.

In 1963, Evelyn, who had a background in newspaper work, left The Mrs. Cox Shop to become linotype operator at the Anderson News. She changed positions several times before her retirement in 1986, when she was reporter/photographer and feature writer. During her career, she witnessed many changes, among them the demise of the linotype and the advent of off-set printing.

In 1978, Vernon became a disabled Kraft employee due to problems following by-pass surgery in 1976. He had 30 years of service and held the J.L. Kraft Jade Award.

Vernon has remained active in his church where he has served as Chairman of the Board, Sunday School Superintendent, teacher and trustee. He is an Army veteran, holds a BS degree from Mississippi State University, is a former member of The Committee of 101 at U.K., and a former Rotarian. He is Past Master of the Masonic Lodge, Past Worthy Patron of the Order of Eastern Star and past president of the Lions Club of Alexandria, Tennessee.

When a Cub Scout pack was formed in Alexandria, he became Cub Master and Evelyn a Den Mother.

Describing themselves as a "team", they have supported each other in their work-related and civic activities., while being very much involved with their sons' projects. Mike and Ralph worked at Model Market and played varsity basketball and football. Alan played trombone in the band. They graduated from Anderson High in 1964, 1968, and 1972, respectively, and now live with their families in Frankfort, Cincinnati, and Burgin. Mike is an Air Force veteran and electronic technician with Sears. Ralph is an entrepreneur, and Alan is with Kentucky Utilities at Dix Dam.

Evelyn is a lay delegate to The Kentucky Annual Conference of the United Methodist Church, past president of United Methodist Women, former Sunday School teacher and church financial secretary. She is past president of the Anderson County Unit of The American Cancer Society and is crusade chairperson. She is Past Worthy Matron of The Eastern Star, past P.T.A. President, former church pianist, and is a Kentucky Colonel.

All are Mississippi natives, except Alan who was born in Tennessee.

In 1970, the family moved to 1014 Mac Avenue, Lawrenceburg, which is the retirement home of Vernon and Evelyn. *Submitted By: Mrs. Sparks,*

CLAYTON "BROWNIE" SPAULDING, was born in 1890 in Woodford County, one of four chil-

dren born to John Spaulding and Nancy Simpson Spaulding. His father died at an early age and his mother had a hard time raising and keeping the children together. As a young man, he lived with a family in Woodford County. To make a living, he cut wood out of the river cliffs and carried it to the house during the day and would keep a fire all night for the loggers floating their logs down the river to the saw mill. For this he was paid .25 per person.

He married Minnie Waller and they had three children: Nellie, born 1911, married J. E. Sparrow (deceased) and they had seven children. She now lives in Lexington; Robert, born 1915, married Margaret Roark. They had nine children and live in Troy; and Johnny (deceased), born 1919, married Ruby Cosby. They had three children and live in Shelbyville.

Their mother died of pneumonia when Johnny was a small child. Then in 1925, he married Ruth Mae Brown. She helped raise these three children and had six of her own.

Mary Elizabeth "Betty", born 1927, married Kenneth Stinnet. They had three children, Charles, Velma, and Nelson and live in Lawrenceburg.

Clayton Spaulding and Ruth Mae Brown Spaulding - 1925

William Glenn, born 1929, married Marie Drury. They had one daughter, Paula Kay, and live in Anderson County.

Myrtle Hazel, born 1932, married Robert Drury. They had three children, Wanda, Carson, and Tony and live in Mercer County.

Jessie Leroy, born 1934, married Ailene Kinder. They had two children, Harrison and Tommy and live in Mercer County.

Allen Eugene, born 1936, married Geraldine Waldridge. They had three children, Sharon, Ricky, and Todd and live in Anderson County.

Clayton lived and worked in and around the Anderson and Mercer County line. He worked on the W.P.A. Road Construction and as a farmer and carpenter in and around Anderson County. After his retirement he lived on the Claylick Road until his death in 1963. His wife, Ruth, moved to Lawrenceburg and lived on Main Street and Court Street until her death in 1983. *Submitted By: Betty Stinnett.*

SPENCER, The Spencers originally came to this country from England, settled in New York, Fort Springs, Woodford County, Kentucky, and then in Alton, Kentucky.

William C. Spencer, Jr. is the son of William Spencer and Russell Fallis of Mercer County. He is the third generation of Spencers to own and farm the 525 acres farm on Clifton Road at Kentucky River. He lives in the house built in 1840 that he was born in on 7-14-1926. William C. Spencer, Jr. has three sisters: Jane Champion, Fort Wright, Kentucky; Peggy Cheak, Owensboro, Kentucky; and Ann Richard, Lawrenceburg, Kentucky. He attended Lawrenceburg Graded School, City High, where he was Captain of the basketball and football teams, and attended Eastern University and University of Kentucky. William C. Spencer, Jr. served in the Marine Corp from 1945 to 1946. He is a Mason and member of the American Legion. William C. Spencer, Jr. married Jean Carlton on 10-8-1949. They have four children: William C. Spencer, III, Nashville, Tennessee; Robert (Bob) Young Spencer; Nancy Buhling; and John Fallis Spencer, all of Lawrenceburg. They have ten grandchildren.

Jean Carlton Spencer is the daughter of John Willie and Marjorie Carlton, and was born on 4-17-1933, in Anderson County. She attended Lawrenceburg Graded School, Sand Spring Graded School, and Kavanaugh High where she was a cheerleader. She served three terms as President of the Lawrenceburg P.T.A. and served on the District Board. Jean Carlton Spencer was Anderson County's Master Homemaker. She was co-owner and manager of a dress shop called "The Hayloft" on Main Street from 1973-1982. Her hobbies include decorating their 150 year old home and making crafts. Jean Carlton Spencer has two sisters: Twyla Trisler, Harrodsburg, KY and Judy Bailey, Frankfort, KY, and she has two brothers: William Bert Carlton (deceased), and Edward Lynn Carlton, Lawrenceburg, KY.

Billy and Jean are members of the First Christian Church where Jean has taught Sunday School and Billy has served as Deacon, Elder, and Trustee. *Submitted By: Billy and Jean Spencer.*

SPENCER, The Spencer family came from England in the early 1600's. Gerard Spencer, Jr. was born in 1614 in England, the son of Gerard Spencer, Sr. and Alice Whitbread. He was baptized at St. Mary's Church in Stotfors, Bedfordshire, England, on April 25, 1614. He with his three older brothers, William, Thomas, and Michael, came to New England in 1632, and settled in Massachusetts. Gerard married Hannah Pratt on December 22, 1637. They had 11 children: John, Hannah, Alice, Mebitable, Thomas Sr., Samuel, William, Nathaniel, Rebecca, Ruth, and Timothy. Gerard died in 1685 in Hartford, Connecticut.

Thomas Spencer, Sr. was born in 1648, in Lynn, Mass. and died at Saybrook, Conn. on February 3, 1699. He married 1st, Elizabeth Bates, daughter of James Bates and Ann Withington, and 2nd, Elizabeth Waller. He had a total of seven children: Gerard, Hannah, Thomas Jr., Caleb, Sarah, Mary, Elizabeth.

Thomas Spencer, Jr. was born in April 1679, in Saybrook, Connecticut, and died in 1758, at Groton, Connecticut. He married Anna Douglas on September 3, 1702. She was the daughter of Deacon William Douglas and Abigail Hough. They had six children: Temperance, Ann, Thomas III, Rebecca, Consider, and Jabez.

Thomas Spencer III was born in Saybrook, Connecticut on February 26, 1708, and died there in 1764. He and his wife, Deborah, had seven children: Michael, Thomas IV, Deborah, Ann, Phoebe, Elisha, and Beulah.

Thomas Spencer IV was born in Saybrook, Connecticut, on January 16, 1736, and died in Winstead, Connecticut, on May 1, 1807. He served in the Revolutionary War. On April 10, 1760, he married Phobe Grinnel, daughter of George Grinnel and Mary Post Bull, in Connecticut. They had nine children: Phoebe, John, Chloe, Thomas V. Grinnel, Charlotte, Candace, Sylvia, and Hulda.

John Spencer was born in Saybrook, Connecticut, on October 18, 1762, and died in Verona, New York, on February 14, 1826. He married Abrigail Marshall on February 14, 1793, in Connecticut. She was the daughter of Abner and Hannah Marshall. They had 11 children: Julius; Almeda (married ? Carter); George Grinnel (below); Harlow (died at the age of 23); Sylvia (married Jason Merrell); William Scott; Laura (married ? Green); Orpha (married ? Miscock); John; Franklin Augustus; and Riley.

George Grinnel Spencer was born in Winchester, Connecticut, on November 17, 1796, and died in Fayette County, KY on January 10, 1872. He married Amelia Phelps, daughter of Jedediah Phelps and

Deborah Crowell, on September 11, 1821. They had four children: Harlow, George W. (below), Charles, and Franklin.

George Washington Spencer was born on September 8, 1825, in Verona, NY. He came to Fort Spring, KY with his family in 1832, at the age of 7 years. He married Elizabeth Cook, daughter of James Dingle Cook and Frances Wallace, in January of 1855, in Fort Spring. George was a carpenter and moved to Alton, Ky. in Anderson County in 1860. He died in Alton on December 8, 1899. They had ten children: Laura, Ida; Mary; William Young; Sallie; John Cook; Robert Lee (below); Jefferson Davis; Joseph; and Everett Earl (married Allie Lyen Hiner).

Robert Lee was born on January 16, 1868, in Alton, once known as Rough-and-Ready. He was a carpenter, like his father before him. Following the purchase of a new fairgrounds site in 1911, he was given the contract for erection of an amphitheater and other buildings. It was ready for the 1912 fair. The amphitheater, one of the largest and most complete in Central KY, was destroyed by fire in 1961. Robert Lee also built scores of dwelling houses, worked on warehouses, and was foreman on construction jobs at JTS Brown's Distillery. He also helped with the Bond's Mill Distillery and Kavanaugh Gym. On January 2, 1902, he married Carrie Hermid Dedman (1883 - 1937), They had five children: George Philip; Davis Earl; Robert Lee Jr.; Frank Linden (died in infancy); and Mrs. Juanita Spencer Gentry. Robert Lee died on December 11, 1968. *Submitted By: George Philip Spencer.*

M. KENT STEVENS, except for the four years he spent in Richmond while attending Eastern Kentucky University, Kent Stevens had lived in Anderson County all of his life.

The oldest of three children born to Melvin L. and Helen S. Stevens, Kent, his sister, Janet, and brother, Bruce, grew up in the Van Buren Community. His father, the son of Ben and Rose Dadisman Stevens, was an employee of the General Electric Corporation, in Louisville. He died in an automobile accident in August of 1963. His mother, the daughter of Truman and Mae Stinnett, was an employee of the Van Buren State Bank before becoming a homemaker and mother.

Kent attended Western School for 12 years, graduating in 1969. Along with his parents, he gives credit to many of his former teachers for having encouraged him to continue his education. Among those mentioned were current Anderson County residents, Robert Turner, Helen Turner, Louise Puckett, Lillian McGuire, Ada Burgin, Rudy Case Evans, Helen Crossfield, Ada Gash, Robert "Sandy" Goodlett, and Albert Peach.

M. Kent Stevens family

Kent received his B.S. Degree from Eastern Kentucky University in December 1973, his M.A. Degree from Eastern in 1976 and his Rank I Degree from Eastern in 1983.

Since January 1974, Kent had been employed by the Anderson County Board of Education. In August of 1984, he became the 5th principal of Western/Anderson School, a position he holds at the present time.

Kent is married to the former Deborah Cornett, daughter of Mr. and Mrs. E. B. Cornett, Jr. She is a 1970 graduate of Anderson High School and 1974 graduate of Georgetown College. Deborah teaches first grade at Saffell Street Elementary School. Kent and Deborah along with daughters, Katharine Anne, born June 14, 1979 and Ellen Elizabeth, born July 30, 1985, reside in Lawrenceburg, KY.

JOHN STINNET, was a farmer in Anderson County. At a youthful age, he married Edith Grant. She was a housewife and helped on the farm. She gave birth to a son and named him, Morris McKinely Stinnett.

Morris M. Stinnett also pursued the occupation of farming. He married Daisy Gill Stinnett on 2-11-1917. He died in Lawrenceburg and is buried in the Hebron Cemetery. Daisy currently resides in Alton. Morris and Daisy had several children including a son, Kenneth Carl Stinnett.

Kenneth Stinnett was an experienced carpenter. He also worked as a factory worker. He married Mary Elizabeth Spaulding on 12-22-1943. She was born on 11-1-1927, the daughter of the late Charles Clayton Spaulding and Ruth Mae Brown Spaulding. Mary works at Kentucky Overall Service. They are the parents of three children: Charles Stinnett married Betty Wright; Velma Stinnett married Junior Penn; and James Stinnett.

James Nelson Stinnett was born on 7-25-1950. He fought in the Vietnam War. After he came home, he married Rita Ann Burgin on 2-16-1974, in Lawrenceburg, KY. Rita was born on 10-14-1953, in Lebanon, KY. She is the daughter of Harvey Milton Burgin and Katherine Eugene Steff Burgin. James worked at several factories and now works at Square D in Lexington, KY.

James and Rita are the parents of two daughters: Jamie Ann, born 10-9-1974, in Harrodsburg, KY; and Amanda Lee, born 12-30-1981, in Frankfort, KY. *Submitted By: Jamie Stinnett.*

KENNETH STINNETT, was born in Madison County, KY on July 8, 1921. He was the oldest of nine children born to Morris Stinnett and Daisy Gill Stinnet. He got his schooling in Madison County until they moved to Anderson County in about 1940.

He married Mary Elizabeth "Betty" Spaulding in 1943 and they had three children: Charles Kenneth, born in 1945, married Betty Wright and now lives in Harlan, KY.

Velma Mae, born in 1947, married J. R. Penn Jr. and lives in Anderson County. And James Nelson, born in 1950, married Rita Burgin and lives in Lawrenceburg, KY.

Kenneth and Betty Stinnett

Kenneth worked as a farmer, then as a carpenter and as a janitor and night watchman at Kentucky Overall Service. He is now unable to work and is retired.

He and Betty live on Woodford Street in Lawrenceburg. *Submitted By: Betty Stinnett.*

JOHN STRUTTON, from Amherst County Virginia, served in the War of Independence, and for that service, he was awarded 100 acres of land. this land was supposedly in Mercer County, KY. Although he was unable to make the trip, he sent two of his sons in his place. Between the years 1815-1823, John Jacob and William Strutton made their way to Kentucky in covered wagons. Unfortunately on the way, "Bill's" wagon broke down and his family stopped to fix it. The brothers were to meet up again in Kentucky. Bill and his family never made it. Many family members believe that they were attacked by Indians.

John Jacob Strutton (1790 - 1873) married Elizabeth Sorrel (1793 - 1878) in 1809 in Spotsylvania County, VA. She was the daughter of John Sorrel. They tell stories about the day that Elizabeth was to be buried. During her lifetime, John would not let her be baptized. As the story goes, the hearse doors came open and the casket slid into Cheese Lick Creek. Folks back then believed that this was Elizabeth's way of being baptized.

John and Elizabeth raised nine children: Letitia Ann (married John Mahan); Levi B. (below); John Dogad (married Almira Brown); Richard "Dick" (married Melissie Riley); Elizabeth (married John Riley); Catherine "Kitty" (married George Sutton); Jacob (married America Young); William Byrd (married Mildred Hawkins); and Judy (she was the first to be buried in the Stratton Family Graveyard. At the time, it was just a vegetable garden. She died as a child.)

John Strutton always said, "I left a fortune in Virginia". When they came to Kentucky they drove hogs, like cattle, and carried as many possessions as was possible and practical. John was a farmer and he owned and operated a mill. He was proud and a strong man. One of his greatest prides was a beautiful horse which turned the mill stone. This was during the Civil War days, and on one such day some guerillas came there and took his horse out of the mill and rode away. Years later, one of the old mill stones was brought to the homeplace of a great grandson and placed at the end of the walk. It gave boys who came courting a boost when they helped the girls into their buggies.

Levi B. Stratton, son of John and Elizabeth Strutton, married Mary Driskel on January 4, 1838, in Mercer County, KY. They had nine children: Roxy Ann (married Perry Carrol); Sarah Margaret "Sally" (married James Clancy); David Crockett (married Sarah G. Cole); Bernard O. (married 1st, Agnes Munday; 2nd, Eugenia Jane Coubert); William Wilsher "Salter" (married 1st, Elizabeth Temples; 2nd, Lucy Catherine Couvert); Levi Jr. "Coon" (married Parthenia Robinson); Elijah Butler "Kaby Lige" (married Lucy Mildred Riley Stratton); Gabriel P. (married Frank M. Stratton), Levi Stratton was said to be a horse doctor. He was also a Civil War soldier. He served with the 9th Kentucky Calvary Co. K in the Union Army, along with his son David. *Submitted By: Denise Wilder.*

KENNETH BRONSTON "BUD" STRATTON,

born on 5-26-1934, in Anderson County, was the fourth child of Obed and Madge Stratton. He grew up in the Ballard and Sinai communities, attended church at Goshen and Mt. Pleasant, and attended Ballard, Royalty, and Western Schools. He later completed high school through American School of correspondence.

Kenneth, namesake of his uncles Randolph Bronston Holt and Kenneth Holt, has been a lifelong resident of Anderson County except for his U.S. Army service, from January 1954, to December 1955. Together with his brother, Billy, and later alone, he was a distributor for Broughton Dairy from 1960 - 1978. He owned and operated Stratton's Restaurant from 1978 - 1982 and joined Lawrenceburg IGA Foodliner as Department Manager in September 1983.

Kenneth has always been a sports enthusiast and, for many years, was involved in softball and participated in the Alton Ruritan League. He is a member of VFW.

Jo and Kenneth Stratton - October 14, 1988, Retirement Reception.

Kenneth and Jo Royalty married on 12-30-1952. The oldest of three children of Eugene Royalty (12-1-1911 - 5-31-1973) and Hazel Ann Monroe Royalty (11-18-1912-1-17-1984), Jo was born in Mercer County on February 24, 1935. She attended schools in Mercer County for 11 years and graduated from Anderson High School in 1953. She was a member of Salvisa Baptist Church until her marriage, when she joined Mt. Pleasant Baptist Church. Jo's brothers are Jackie Royalty, Lexington, and Glenn Royalty, Louisville.

Jo is active in many organizations, including Professional Secretaries International and the National and State Association of Parliamentarians. She attained the Certified Professional Secretary rating in 1964 and the Professional Registered Parlimentarian status in 1983. She retired from Kentucky State Government on 11-1-1988, after 34 years service in such positions as Executive Secretary, Administrative Assistant, Branch Manager, and Executive Assistant to Cabinet Secretary.

Jo and Kenneth, who have no children, live at 1086 Hazel Drive, Lawrenceburg. Jennifer Royalty, daughter of Jo's brother Jackie, lives with them; Jennifer's sister Jacquelyn also spend time with them. *Submitted By: Jo Stratton.*

OBED KENNETH STRATTON, (6-12-1907 - 4-2-1989, son of James Dogad Stratton and Madge M. Caldwell Stratton) and Madge Beatrice Holt (6-23-1908 - 5-7-1978, daughter of Silas Daniel Holt and Mollie Florence Harley Holt) were married on 3-12-1927, by the Reverend Mr. Fletcher Payton.

They lived at various addresses in Anderson County until 1947, when they bought and moved to the Herman Satterly property (formerly the Bowen farm). They moved to 517 Woodford Street, Lawrenceburg, in 1973. After Madge's death, Obed moved to 109 Franklin Street, where he lived until his death. Madge completed eighth grade; Obed completed eighth grade and attended Kavanaugh. Board of Education records show that he was a good student.

Obed and Madge Stratton

Obed and Madge were members of Goshen Baptist and Mt. Pleasant Baptist Church until they moved to Lawrenceburg, when they joined First Baptist Church. Obed was an avid instrumentalist and was most outgoing. He often said that he went out to have a good time, to see and be seen, and that otherwise, he may as well stay home. Another fre-

quent comment was that if he saw someone who wasn't smiling, he gave him one of his smiles, and then they both had one. Madge's life centered around her family. She knew all of her children, their spouses and her grandchildren intimately and was able to relate to each of them in a special way.

Obed and Madge had eight children: Lenor Stratton Drummons, Jane Irene Stratton Wood, William Dudley "Billy" Stratton, Kenneth Bronson "Bud" Stratton, Janice Florence Stratton Peach, James Silas Stratton, David Michael Stratton, and Geraldine Stratton Drury.

Madge died of Myelfibrosis, a blood disorder, and congestive heart failure. Obed suffered from severe pulmonary emphysema. His death was attributed to an "apparent cerebral vascular accident/ incident". Both are buried in the Lawrenceburg Cemetery. *Submitted By: Jo Stratton.*

JAMES DOGAD AND LYDIA M. CALDWELL STRATTON, were married on April 8, 1886. They lived most of their married life on Bear Creek in Sinai, KY. They had 187 acres and grew crops for feeding their animals and for their use, for food in the winter months. Jim operated a mill for many years.

Jim was born in Mercer County on February 26, 1863, and died September 11, 1947, and was the son of John Dogad and Alimira Brown Strutton. He was the 13th child of 14 children. His brothers were Frank, George Washington, William Jackson, Augustine "Gus"., Joseph Newton, John Corbin, Napolean Bonaparte "Polander", Elijah Butler "Lige", Jacob Granville "Dump", Alona Parker, Thomas Jefferson "Charlie", Abraham Lincoln, and a sister, Sara. Jim's saying was "there were 13 boys and a sister for each."

Lydia M. "Lyd", born March 30, 1867, and died January 21, 1956, in Anderson County, KY, not far from the farm where she spent her married life, was the daughter of John W. and Nancy Holt Searcy Caldwell. She had one brother, Merritt Caldwell and two sisters, Sarah Belle Ellis and Alice Caldwell; and five half-brothers and a sister.

Jim and Lyd were members of the Goshen Baptist Church and Lyd was an active member. She enjoyed going to church on Sunday morning and visiting the rest of the day. She was a strong Republican and a very dominate, strong willed woman, while Jim was an easy going man who often read his Bible and sang or hummed. He was a Democrat. They are buried in the Goshen Church Cemetery. They had eight sons and five daughters. Their sons were John D., James A.D., Willie S., Robert Bruce, Obed K., L.Z., and Samuel B. Sr. Samuel is the only child living and he and his wife, Rosie, live in the Ballard community. Their daughters are Effie Taylor, Nannie Shouse, Ruth Peyton, Sarah Disponett Gordon, and Lenore. Their children stayed in the area for the early years. Later some of them moved to nearby towns or Lawrenceburg.

Jim sent his sons Obed and L.Z. to the field with

Front: Obed Stratton, Lyd, Jim, Ms. Moore, L.Z. Stratton. Back: Sarah Disponett Gordon, Ruth Peyton, Nannie Shouse, John Stratton, Effie Taylor, James A. D. Stratton, Willie S. Stratton, Samuel B. Stratton, Jr., Bruce Stratton James Dogad Stratton and Lydia M. Caldwell Stratton.

some beans to plant in the corn. They became tired of this and dumped the beans in the stump of a tree. Days later Jim came in with a switch and told the boys "Sons, your sins have found you out". The beans had come up in the stump of the tree. So, it is old the boys paid for their "sins".

Through the years the family celebrated Jim and Lyd's birthday each year, when each family would come and bring a basket of food. These groups grew of friends and relatives, as well as children, and their families began to attend. They were held at the old homeplace on Bear Creek for all those years. The Old Homeplace burned a few years after Lyd passed away and the land now belongs to C.B. Brown. These family reunions are still a part of the family as the Sunday before Labor Day is the day the reunion is held at the Alton Ruritan Building in Alton, Kentucky. In 1956, when Lyd passed away, she had 58 grandchildren, 97 great-grandchildren and 22 great-great-grandchildren, that has been 33 years ago and that number has probably tripled in greats and great greats. The average attendance is near two hundred. Jim and Lyd have left a large legacy of much talent, many of them doctors, lawyers, detectives, dentists, executives - too many to try and mention them all. A family to be proud of! *Submitted By: Jean Stratton Tharp*

L.Z. AND OPAL NAOMI PEACH STRATTON,

were natives of Anderson County, KY. L.Z., the 13th child and eighth son of James Dogad and Lydia M. Caldwell Stratton, was born July 26, 1909, in Sinai, KY on Bear Creek. His brothers were John D., James A.D., William S., Robert Bruce, Obed K, L.N. (died at birth) and Samuel B., Sr. (the only surviving child.) He and his wife, Rosie Camic Stratton live in the Ballard community. Sisters were Effie Taylor, Nannie Shouse, Ruth Peyton, Sarah Disponett Gordon and Lenore. Opal, one of six children, was born July 6, 1910, to George T. and Annie Lee Harley Peach in the Mount Pleasant area of Anderson County. Two sisters, Verlie Monroe Springate and Estelle Langley Perone, are deceased and brothers, Wilburn of Harrodsburg, Goodloe of Cardville and Homer of Louisville, survive.

L.Z. and Opal were married December 24, 1928, in Anderson County by Reverend Dudley Moore. They were farmers and owned a small farm on Highway 62, across from the old Wash farm. They told of the lean years after the depression and how difficult is was just to "get by". He worked with the WPA when the Western High School was being built and bridges in that area. On the Family Birth Chart, he was listed as L. Zeminous but did not use it as he went by L.Z. While on the WPA job, his boss told him he would have to have a name and at that time Alf Landon was campaigning for office, so he became Landon Z. and through the years has conducted his business in this name.

Since farming at this time was hard and meager, they decided to try to better raise their family by making the move to Louisville. They made that move in January 1940, and L.Z. worked at Fort Knox, the bag plant in Charleston, Indiana, and at the International Harvester Plant. While working at the I.H. Plant he had the opportunity to take a job driving a school bus for Jefferson County Board of Education and continued to work both jobs as they were hoping to build them a house. They bought an old house and some acreage in the south end of Louisville and still having their love for the country, they had cows and chickens and planted a large garden each year. Opal canned and preserved everything she could for the winter months. She baby-sat for several years, sold butter and eggs, still hoping for their new house. This hope became a reality in the summer of 1950. Opal's father died when she was 10, leaving her mother with six small children and problems in feeding and keeping them together. Opal "stayed out" with people to earn a little money but mostly for a home. She told of staying with the

McMichael family on North Main Street in Lawrenceburg for some time.

L.Z. and Opal Stratton's last picture together 1979 - Christmas

L.Z. continued to drive the school bus for 27 years. He was a carpenter and did remodeling work. He had a severely crippled hand and arm due to being cut while cutting wood on a cut-off saw in 1929. This did not hinder him in his work since he could use his tools as well as anyone.

They had little formal education but had pride and courage and desire to better their lives and give their children the best they could. Opal was determined that none of her children would ever be hungry and they gave their children a happy and secure life, while teaching them morals and the fundamentals of life, such as education and not being afraid to work at whatever they wanted to be.

Anderson County was always "home" to them and they wanted to come back there to live someday - their wish was granted as they are interred in the Lawrenceburg Cemetery along with their third child, Bessie Pauline "Duck" Trageser. Opal died January 3, 1981, of a heart attack and L.Z., ill himself, could never adjust to her loss; this added to the diagnosed report that their only son, George Dudley, had cancer. George passed away March 20, 1983 and L.Z. died April 25, 1983. They have three more daughters: Alma Jean Tharp, Opal Merlene "Goldie" McDaris and Flora Marie Mason, all of Louisville. They have sixteen grandchildren and fourteen great-grandchildren.

Opal and L.Z. were Baptists and members of Auburndale Baptist Church. They had been a part of the church in its beginning. L.Z. helped to build the church and the parsonage. Two of their daughters and their families are members of the church now. *Submitted By: Jean Stratton Tharp.*

WILLIAM STANLEY STRATTON,

was born on 3-20-1894, in Anderson County and died 9-20-1937. He was the son of Benoni Stratton and Eugenia Jane Cubert. He had four brothers and sisters: Godfrey Hunter (1895 - 1954); Nell Stratton Coffey; Charles Fisher; and Maggie Pearl. He also had six half brothers and one half-sister from his father's first marriage. They were: Ezra, Goodloe, Leroy B., Holly, Jesse, Chester and Laura.

William Stanley Stratton married Susan Betsy Disponett on 7-24-1921, in Anderson County. Betsy was born on 10-18-1892, and died 1-8-1973. She was the daughter of John J. Disponett and Anna Lee Jordan. She had three brothers: David, Peter, and James.

William Stanley and Susan Betsy Stratton were the parents of six children: Evelyee (below); Clevia married Lowell Riley - five children - Donnie, Connie, William, Lowell, and Brenda; Lucy married Roy Rogers - seven children - Jeff, Patrisha, Roger, Time, Sandra, Jimmy, and Mike; Susan married J.C. Searcy - five children - Winston, Larry, Jackie, Stanley, and Robert; Maggie married Bruce Stratton - seven children - Barbara, Ricky, Wanda Carol, Steve, Coy, Kay, and Peggy; and William Stanley Jr. married Betty Bruner - four children - Stanley David, Diane, Gary Thomas, and Brian.

Evelyee Stratton was born on 1-19-1927, in Lawrenceburg, KY. She married Earl Goodlett (1916 - 1983) and they had ten children: Mildred Ann married James Earl Dennis - seven children - James Ray, Annie, Johnny, Joey, Mary, Ronnie, and Jennifer; William R. married Bonnie Durr - three sons - Drew, Darin, and Donald; Floyd married Dianne Atkins - two sons - Michael and Kevin; Judith Faye married Wilson Wash Jr. - two daughters - Charlene and Angela; Joyce Stinnett Sutton Smith married Eric Smith - she has two children, Marsha and Sean; Shirley Scott Maddox married John Maddox - she has two daughters, Tammy and Dianna Scott; Earl Ray married Mildred Turner; Debra Gayle married Johnny Carrier - one son, Jason; Barry married Julie Sparrow; and Charles married Susie Vaughn - two daughters - Crystal and Stacey. *Submitted By: Dianna Scott.*

WILLIAM CLAYTON STOCKTON,

was born on 7-16-182?, and was a direct descendant of Commodore Robert Fields Stockton and Richard Stockton, one of the signers of the Declaration of Independence. In his early years, William Clayton Stockton was a teacher and then fought in the Mexican War in 1847. He was in the Battle of Buena Vista. When peace was declared, he joined a party of men that crossed the plains to California. After he returned home, he married Lydia Bailey and settled down to raise a family. They married on 7-29-1858, in Anderson County. Lydia Bailey was born on 7-30-1836, in Franklin County and died on 2-14-1915, in Anderson County. She was the daughter of Abraham Bailey Jr. and Eliza Hickman Bailey. They were the parents of nine children: Sarah Elizabeth married John T. White - four children - Pearl, John, Lily, and James; George married Catherine Stigers; Mary Florence married John Lancaster; Ida Mae married Judge J. Odelle; John; James; Harriett "Hallie"; Horace - never married; and Davis Doyle. William Clayton Stockton died on 7-23-1909. His obituary stated that "Mr. Stockton was a man of sterling integrity with the highest of ideas and sacredness of the rights of the American people. He has many friends and no enemies."

David Doyle Stockton was born on 9-22-1875, in Anderson County and died on 12-9-1960. He married Jesse Belle Stockton (1893 - 1928) on 9-27-1916. She was the daughter of Preston Hardin Stockton and Louisa Anne Armstrong Stockton. They were the parents of five children: Lenwood Doyle married Adra Johnson; Anacelia Darr married Harlan Heilman - four children - James Albert, Mary Susan, Jessye Anne, and William Clayton; William Clayton married Marie Hokensmith, then Beulah Atkins - three children - Walter Clayton, Karen Sue, and William Mark; Bertha Algean married Mortimer Litwen - one daughter, Carol Stockton; and Harold Allison.

Harold Allison Stockton was born on 12-17-1924, in Anderson County. He married Anelle Stine on 9-11-1948, in Lawrenceburg. She was born on 7-11-1933, in Washington County. She is the daughter of James Roy Stine and Estelle Drury Stine. Born to this union were two children: Harold Wayne, born 7-20-1949, and Mary, born 7-26-1958. Harold Allison and Anelle Stine Stockton currently reside on Humston Drive in Lawrenceburg.

Harold Wayne Stockton married Judy Diane Peach. They have two sons: Douglas Wayne, born 4-26-1971, and David Martin, born 2-8-1974. Harold Stockton remarried to Sherrill Stockton and they reside on Carlton Drive in Lawrenceburg. *Submitted By: David M. Stockton.*

DONALD AND EVELYN SULLIVAN,

are lifelong residents of Anderson County. Evelyn, the daughter of the late Willie and Nell Hill, was born at Avenstoke in Anderson County and the youngest of five children; two brothers, Edward of Frankfort and Earl of Fern Creek and two sisters, Irma of Jeffersontown and Gladys of Taylorsville.

In about 1845, Evelyn's great-grandparents, Russell and Kathryn Hill set out from Virginia for Kentucky and settled in Anderson County. Russell got in a dispute and several men followed him to his home and killed him. Kathryn remarried Billy Brown, who was once taken prisoner by the Indians, possibly somewhere near Avenstoke.

Donald, the son of the late Jesse and Ethel Sullivan, was born in Woodford County, moved to Anderson County when he was 12 years old. Donald is the third of 10 children: Brothers; James (deceased in 1930), Elwood (Florida), Kenneth (Waddy), Harold and David (Anderson County), Joseph (Frankfort), Douglas (Fern Creek), and sisters, Elsie and Sue of Frankfort.

Donald and Evelyn both attended Avenstoke School and Anderson High School. He and Evelyn were married at the Pigeon Fork Church Parsonage by the Rev. Charles Tipton.

Donald served two years in military service with 16 1/2 months spent in Korea with the 3rd Infantry Division. After returning from overseas, he engaged in full time farming, which he is still employed.

Evelyn, a State Employee, started working in Driver License and is presently employed with the State Police Personnel in Frankfort.

Donald and Evelyn Sullivan

Donald and Evelyn are the parents of two children. Gary 33, is a graduate of Anderson County High School and Vocation School and lives in Shelby County and works for the State Police in Frankfort as a KEWS Technician. He is married to the former Deborah Perry of Shelby County and they have two children - a son, Andrew, 6, and a daughter, Brenna, 20 months.

Teresa, 30 is a graduate of Anderson County High School, lives in Anderson County and is presently employed with the Revenue Cabinet in Frankfort. She is married to David Burns and they have a daughter, Kathleen - 3 months.

The Sullivans have been residents of Avenstroke for 34 years. Members of Pigeon Fork Baptist Church for many years, where they are regular attendants every week. *Submitted By: Donald and Evelyn Sullivan.*

LARRY AND JUDY SUTHERLAND,

are lifelong residents of Anderson County. Larry was born in Franklin County on December 19, 1951, the son of Ellie Leon and Juanita Francis Carlton Sutherland. He has two brothers, Gary and Danny, also of Anderson County. They lived in the community of Birdie on Crooked Creek Road.

Larry attended Glensboro and Marlow Elementary Schools and Anderson County High School, graduating in 1970. Larry is a farmer and an employee of Boulevard Distillery in Lawrenceburg.

Judy was born in Franklin County on February 23, 1952, the daughter of Gilbert Dora and Corine Camic Cubert. She has one brother, Jerry, also living in Anderson county. They live in the community of Ripyville.

Judy attended Lawrenceburg and Sand Spring Elementary Schools and Anderson County High School, graduating in 1970. Judy is a homemaker and an employee of Boulevard Distillery.

Larry and Judy were married July 6, 1971, in

Sevier County, Tennessee. They have two children: Christopher Wayne, born in Fayette County on February 27, 1973, and Kimberly Renee, born in Franklin County on February 21, 1978.

The Sutherland's are members of the First Baptist Church in Lawrenceburg. *Submitted By: Judy Sutherland.*

SUTHERLAND, In 1684, three brothers came to America from Aberdeen, Scotland, on the Earl of Perth New Jersey Expedition. One brother stayed in Virginia, and the other two started north to Maryland. One of these made it there, but the other one stopped somewhere along the way. The Sutherlands in Anderson County are descendant of the brother who went to Maryland.

John Sutherland, the son of William and Elizabeth Travis Sutherland, married a woman by the name of Prater. They had seven sons and two daughters: Baily, Arjalon, Howard, Micajah, Hosea, David, Asa L., Maydalin and Nancy. John Sutherland died in 1823 in what is now Anderson County.

Howard, born in 1792, in Pendleton, SC, married Patsy Paxton in Fayette County, Ky in 1818. Howard served as a soldier in the War of 1812. Howard and Patsy both died in the 1840's. They had one son, Howard, born in 1822 in Franklin County, KY. Howard Sr. remarried to widow Martha Sutherland after Patsy died. She had four children by her first marriage: Sanderson, Elizabeth, Thomas H. and William B.

Howard Sutherland Jr. married Elizabeth Derissa Sutherland, the daughter of Enos and Martha Sutherland (Martha was Howard's step-mother), on May 12, 1846. They had ten children: Thomas Hosea, Sarah, Evangelist "Van", John, Hezekiah, Dolly, Samuel, Gabrilla, Tilby, and James.

ROBERT BRUCE SWEENEY, Sometime between 1850 and 1860, Robert Bruce Sweeney came to Anderson County, Kentucky, with his aunt, Mary Sweeney Champion and her husband, Davis. Robert Bruce was born in Washington County, September 27, 1843. His mother, Susan Sweeney Hamilton (Mrs. Thomas Hamilton), died in January 1874, and is buried in the family graveyard on a hill above Ballard Road, not far from the Sweeney homeplace.

Robert Bruce was well-known and respected throughout Anderson County. He contributed much to education as a teacher and as Superintendent of Anderson County Schools from 1880 to 1886. At the time of his death, October 2, 1907, he was a U.S. Revenue Officer.

He married Martha French Powell, May 6, 1868. She was the daughter of Joel Pace and Nancy Hawkins Powell who moved from Madison County, Kentucky, after 1828, to what later became known as the Sweeney homeplace. They reared nine children on this farm which remained in the Sweeney family until 1987.

The nine Sweeney children were:
Myrtie 1869 - 1965 (Mrs. Burrus Morris), mother of Martha Bruce (John) Boggess and foster parents of Blanch Caldwell (Mrs. Roy York).
Virginia "Virgie" 1871 - 1946
Charles 1873 - 1944, a doctor, husband of Lizzie Robinson.
Nancy 1875 - 1965 (Mrs. J. B. Black).
John Edwin 1877 - 1962, husband of Louella Hughes 1880 - 1904 and Alice Sparrow 1886 - 1952 and father of Corinne (Mrs. John D. Gash) and Bruce, husband of Blanche Wash.
Clinton 1879 - 1927, husband of Mary Phillips and foster parents of Hulan Farmer.
Susan 1881 - 1972, (Mrs. Forest Mothershead and foster parent of Gee Lancaster.)
Ethel 1883 - 1970 Mrs. Harrison Baxter and foster parents of Alice (Mrs. Manson Duncan).
Joel Bruce (J.B.) 1891 - 1987, husband of Cora Morris.
Robert Bruce and Martha also reared a foster daughter, Mae Kimp (Mrs. Roger McMurry).

Of the nine children, six of them were teachers in Anderson County. Also, the three grandchildren were teachers. Martha Bruce taught 45 years in Anderson County, Corinne taught five years in Anderson County and 30 years in Mercer County, and Bruce taught, coached, and was a principal in Anderson, Nelson, and Shelby Counties.

John Edwin worked for Black and Blackburn in Van Buren and McWilliams Hardware, later Marrs Hardware, in Lawrenceburg. Clinton and J.B. owned and operated a mill in Fox Creek until it burned and a feed store in Lawrenceburg. Later J. B. owned and operated dairy farms, was a cattle dealer, extensive landowner, and after the age of 70, began a career in house building that was to continue until he was past the age of 90. At the time of his death at age 95, he was still managing his properties and business affairs.

The Sweeney family has also been active in Christian Churches in Anderson County. Robert Bruce and Martha were charter members of the Shiloh Christian Church, as were both their mothers. Robert Bruce served the church as elder, Sunday School superintendent, and teacher. Their children will be remembered by many for their service to the Lawrenceburg Christian Church.

The Sweeney family

An old newspaper article titled "A Tribute From an Old Friend" had this to say about Robert Bruce Sweeney at the time of his death. "He ever had a smile and pleasant word for all, and if trouble came to his neighbors, he was ever ready to lend a hand." I, his great-granddaughter, feel this is a legacy he left his children.

RICHARD D. SWEETS, was born on 11-21-1949, in Louisville, KY. He is the son of John R. Sweets (3-26-1914 - 5-9-1983) and Yuleen Huff Sweets. Richard has one brother, Garry W. Sweets, born 1-26-1957, who married Karen Russell.

Richard Sweets married Alice N. Halbrook on 3-10-1973, in Leitchfield, Grayson County, KY. She was born on 12-13-1949, in Greenwood, Leflore County, Mississippi. She is the daughter of James Porter Halbrook Jr. and Nelwyn Nason Halbrook. She had three brothers and one sister: Jimmy Halbrook (1942 - 1947) buried in Belzoni, Mississippi; Richard O.H. Halbrook, born 1946, married Donna Bell; Steve Halbrook, born 1947, married Marsha Quarterman; and Melissia Halbrook (1954 - 1976) buried in Belzoni, Mississippi

Richard and Alice Sweets are the proud parents of four children: Darrel C. Sweets, born 8-23-1974, in Elizabethtown, KY; Jeremy N. Sweets, born 6-12-1978, in Nashville, Tennessee; Alice D. Sweets, born 8-2-1981, in Versailles, KY; and Toby R. Sweets, born 1-22-1989, in Lexington, KY.

The Sweets are members of the Church of Christ. They currently reside on Alton Road in Anderson county. *Submitted By: Darrel Sweets.*

JOEL THACKER , first came to Kentucky in the early 1800's. from Amherst Co., VA. He was the son of Pettis and Mary Thacker of Amherst County, VA, where he had married Sarah Burford, daughter of William Burford, on May 3, 1797. Joel Thacker was living in Mercer County, KY, when he bought 347 acres of land from John Lightfoot on Salt River in

Anderson County. Sarah (Burford) Thacker died in 1839 in Anderson County. They were both buried on their farm in Anderson County on Salt River. Their children are as follows:

1) Lewis Thacker (ca 1798 - 1870) md. Jane McGaughey (ca 1805 - 1865), daughter of Arthur and Elizabeth (Hockensmith) McGaughey in 1819, buried on their farm on Enterprise Road. Parents of thirteen children. Son, Arthur, was killed in 1847 at Buena Vista in the Mexican War.

2) Samuel P. Thacker (1801 - 1863) md. 1823 to Elizabeth McGaughey (1805 - 1870) (a sister of Jane). They are buried in Munday Graveyard and the parents of six children.

3) Alfred Thacker (1802 - 1886) md. 1827 to Rose Ann McGaughey (1808 - 1883) daughter of Daniel McGaughey. They are buried in Munday Graveyard. Four children.

4) Frances Thacker (ca1805 - 1856) md. ca 1825 to Daniel McGaughey, Jr., son of Arthur McGaughey. Were the parents of ten children.

(Most of the McGaughey's living in Anderson County descend from this couple.)

5) Lenarius Thacker (ca1808 - 1839) md. 1828 to Nancy Rogers, daughter of Andrew and Polly (Kenady) Rogers. Lived in Owen County, KY, where he died. Left six daughters.

Nancy Thacker md. Thomas Jefferson Leathers and moved to Morgan Co., Ind., where they lived. Left children.

7) Mary "Polly" Thacker (1814 - 1851) md. 1830 to James Munday (1804 - 1879) . Lived in Missouri when they died. Left issue.

8) Sarah Thacker md. Napoleon B. Griffin (1816 - 1899) January 26, 1836 in Anderson County. They had children.

9) Asa Thacker (ca 1818 - ca 1848) md. in 1840 to Amanda Holman, daughter of Daniel and Rebecca Holman. Amanda and her three children, after Asa's death, moved to Indiana.

10) Francis Marion Thacker (ca1821 - 1894) md in 1840 to Susannah McMichael. Md. 2nd to Sarah A. Thompson (1831 - ?) daughter of John S. Thompson, in 1850. He had children by both wives, ten in all.

11) Rhoda Thacker md. Rufus M. Elliott, 1841. In 1850 were living in Woodford County, KY with four children, that had been born in Missouri.

(Most of the Thackers, now living in Anderson County, descend from F.M. Thacker.)

RUFUS E. THACKER

RUFUS E. THACKER , The Thacker family came to this country from England, some of them settling in Virginia and then coming to Anderson County about the time of its founding in 1827. Samuel, Joel and Lewis Thacker were listed as residing here in 1827. Francis M. Thacker and Susan McMichael were married in 1840. They had three sons, Thomas, J.D., and Rufus E., and two daughters, Lucy T. Moore and Evaline T. Munday.

Rufus (1846 - 1911) married Sarah Frances Crossfield (1851 - 1910) daughter of Richard Henry and Martha Gudgel Crossfield, on December 26, 1872. They moved to a farm near Glensboro. At that time the village was called Camden or Camdenville. After the establishment of the post office, the name was changed to Orr, in honor of an early settler. In 1904 the name was changed to Glensboro.

Children born to Rufus and Sarah Frances were Susan Mary (1873 - 1966); Henry E. (1874 - 1955); Aileen (1877 - 1952); Martha Bell (died at age six); Cordie Ella (1884 - 1963); Lula Frances (1893 - 1975). They raised their children on the farm and they attended the one room school at Glensboro. There was a mill at Glensboro operated by an undershot wheel, and the water supply was so abundant that grinding could be continued almost throughout the year. A roller mill was built in 1896. Farmers took their grain to be ground into flour and meal. There was also a carding factory erected in 1868 that carded wool for farmers raising sheep. This was in operation until 1896.

Susan Mary married Reuben M. Houchin in 1902. They had three children: Mary Frances (1903 - 1905), Matt (1908 - 1936), and Aileen. She married Ray McAnly. They have two children, Mary Belle and Robert Lee McAnly.

Henry married Zella Crossfield of Mercer County. Their children were Lena C. (1904 - 1911) and Raymond Everett (1907 - 1952). After Zella's death in 1913, Henry married twice more.

Aileen married George C. Burford. Their children were Gertrude (1897 - 1969) and Rufus (1901). Gertrude married Homer T. Lyen. They had a daughter, Betty Aileen. Rufus married Florence Horton. Their children are Martha Jane, Homer Clark and Mary Ellen.

Susan, Aileen, Cordie, Henry, and Lula Thacker

Cordie married Kirby S. Duncan. They have one son, Charles Walton (1911 - 1975). He married Katherine Parker.

Lula married Foree Boston. They were divorced in 1933. She later married Dillard Hill of Madison County. She had no children.

Shortly before 1900 the Thacker family moved to Ripyville, a small village four miles south of Lawrenceburg, buying the farm that was owned by John Ripy for whom Ripyville was named. Mr. Thacker was a farmer all of his life. Mrs. Thacker fell and broke her hip, an injury from which she did not recover. She died May 13, 1910. Mr. Thacker married Miss Ida Parker. About six months later he was killed when the two-horse wagon he was driving was struck by a train at the Duncan Crossing on the Pump House Road on November 23, 1911.

Mr. and Mrs. Thacker and the deceased families of Aileen, Henry, and Cordie are buried in the Lawrenceburg Cemetery. Susan's family is buried in the Hebron Cemetery, and Lula was buried in the College Hill Cemetery in Madison County. *Submitted By: Aileen McAnly.*

SARAH FRANCES (CROSSFIELD) THACKER

SARAH FRANCES (CROSSFIELD) THACKER, the third daughter of Richard Henry and Martha Crossfield, was born on 6-29-1851 on the family plantation near the head of Fox Creek. She and Rufus E. Thacker were married on 12-26-1872. Rufus Thacker, the first son of Marion and Sarah Thacker, was born in 1847. Five children were born of this union as listed: Susan M. in 1874; Henry E. on 12-5-1875; Alleen circa 1877; Corda (date not known); and Lula circa 1882. Rufus was a farmer in Anderson and he and Sarah Frances spent the remainder of their lives in Anderson County. Sarah Frances died on 5-13-1910 and is buried in the Crossfield graveyard across Fox Creek from the homestead where she was born. In early 1911, Rufus married Ida Bell Parker. There were no issues from this union. Rufus was hit by a Passenger Train #1 of the Southern Railroad on 11-11-1911, as he was crossing the tracks of that railroad. His death resulted that day from the accident. *Submitted By: James S. Pope.*

THRASHER

THRASHER The Thrasher family was transplanted to Lawrenceburg and Anderson County in March 1970.

Kenneth Jackson (Jack) Thrasher (9-8-1930 - 5-12-1984) was born in Cumberland County, KY. He

attended Greensburg High School and graduated from Western Kentucky University in 1959 with a bachelor of science degree in agriculture. He became a manager trainee for Southern States Corp., Inc. at Georgetown,KY in July 1959; continued training at Lexington before going to Richmond, KY as assistant manager in January of 1960, and on to Ashland, KY in December of 1960 as manager. He managed stores in Beckley, West Virginia and Grayson, KY before becoming Southern States Regional Feed Supervisor in Huntington, West Virginia and then at Lexington, KY. In 1970, Jack, with two partners, built a Southern States franchise store and moved to Lawrenceburg, KY.

Jack had moved to Franklin, KY in 1953, after serving in the Korean War. He was the son of Taft Thrasher and the late Mellie Capps Thrasher (1907 - 1978). He had three sisters, Winnie Bell Thrasher Eastridge, Campbellsville, KY; Mary Thrasher Rhea, Franklin, KY; and Earline Thrasher Williams, Nashville, TN. Two brothers preceded him in death - Earl A. Thrasher and Billy Thrasher.

On 9-8-1957, Kenneth J. Thrasher and Bettie June Eldridge were united in marriage at the South Main Street Church of Christ in Franklin, KY. June was born in Robertson County, TN on 6-2-1935 to Sam T. Eldridge (1908 - 1983) and Ruby N. Welty Eldridge (1913). She had a brother, Charles M. Eldridge (1931 - 1978).

June graduated from Franklin-Simpson High School in 1953. She worked for Dr. J.J. Kelly in Franklin, Ky from 1953 through July 1959, except for a time in 1955, when she attended Bowling Green Business University at Bowling Green, KY.

Left to Right: Front: Jobee, June, Jerry Back: Jeff, Jack Thrasher

After Jack graduated from Western Kentucky University, he and June moved from Franklin to Georgetown, KY in July of 1959. Born to Jack and June Thrasher were three sons: Kenneth Jeff Thrasher (1962) at Beckley, West Virginia; Jerry Alan Thrasher (1965) at Ashland, Ky; and Jobee Sam Thrasher (1968) at Huntington, West Virginia.

Jeff, Jerry, and Jobee Thrasher completed their secondary education in the Anderson County School system at Lawrenceburg, KY. All three were active in band, sports, and church work.

Jeff Thrasher graduated with a Bachelor of Science degree in Chemistry from Western Kentucky University, received his Master of science degree in Chemistry from Purdue University, West Lafayette, Indiana, and is employed as a research scientist with Eli Lilly Pharmaceutical Co., in Indianapolis, Indiana. Jeff is a member of the American Chemical Society.

Jerry Thrasher received his bachelor and master degrees in electrical engineering from the University of Louisville. He has been awarded membership in "Eta Kappan Nu" and in "Tau Beta Pi". He is employed as an electrical engineer at IBM in Lexington, Ky.

Jobee Thrasher is attending Western Kentucky University where he is a senior, majoring in agriculture. He is a member of the Agriculture Business Club, member of the Agronomy Club (Respresentative), member of the Agriculture Department Student Council, Western Kentucky University Church of Christ Student Center, Assistant Youth Group director for Greenwood Park Church of Christ in Bowling Green, KY. *Submitted By: June Thrasher.*

ROBERT MARTIN THOMPSON, and Volita Ruth Cox were married December 23, 1950 at the Methodist parsonage in Salvisa, Kentucky by Rev. Hugh Delaney, Pastor of the the Claylick Methodist Church.

Robert and Volita are the parents of three children: Debra Charlene, September 29, 1954 - Frankfort, KY., married Arthur Cunningham; Vickie Sue, December 16, 1957 - Lexington, SC, married David Neal Brooks; and Ruth Ann, March 13, 1961 - Lawrenceburg, Ky., married "J" Hamon.

Robert was educated by the public school systems of Mercer and Anderson counties. He attended school at: Hebron (Anderson County); Short and Salvisa Elementary Schools (Mercer County); Sand Spring Elementary and Kavanaugh High School (Anderson County). He graduated in the class of 1948 from Kavanaugh High School.

Robert also attended the University of Kentucky and Kentucky State University.

Volita was educated by the public school systems of Shelby and Anderson Counties. She attended school at: Hickory Grove and Ballard, (Anderson County); Waddy (Shelby County); Searcy, Royalty, and Western Elementary and High School (Anderson County). She graduated in the Class of 1950 from Western High school (Anderson County).

Robert and Volita were reared on the farms of their parents. After their marriage they continued farming with Robert's parents until Robert entered the US Navy, January 9, 1952, during the Korean Conflict.

Robert received basic training at Bainbridge Naval Training Center, Bainbridge Maryland. He received advanced training at the school for Machinist's Mates at the Great Lakes Naval Training Center, Great Lakes, Illinois. Upon graduation Robert was assigned to duty aboard an aircraft carrier, USS Wright (CVL 49), ported at US Naval Air Station, Quonset Point, Rhode Island.

After the Korean Conflict, Robert was released from active duty, September 8, 1953, at the Philadelphia Navy Yards, Philadelphia, Pennsylvania.

Having completed his tour of duty Robert and Volita returned to farming in Anderson County, Kentucky, He did custom farm machinery work in partnership with his father until 1964.

In 1964, Robert and Volita sold their farm and moved to 423 South Main, Lawrenceburg, Kentucky.

Robert became active in community functions and in 1978 was elected to the Lawrenceburg City Council (1978 - 1986).

Robert serves as Treasurer for the City of Lawrenceburg (January 1986 -).

Robert was selected Anderson County's Outstanding Citizen in 1987. He is or has served as president of the Anderson County Chamber of Commerce (1986 -), Chairman of the Hebron Cemetery Board, Chairman of the Administrative Board of the Claylick United Methodist Church, Executive Board of the Bluegrass Area Development district, and Secretary/Treasurer of the Lawrenceburg/Anderson County Industrial Foundation.

Robert is a programmer for IBM, Lexington, KY. He has been an employee of General Electric (Appliance Park) Louisville, Kentucky; and Universal Button Company, Lawrenceburg, Kentucky.

Volita is a housewife and is supportive of Robert and the Community Activities.

Robert was born September 8, 1929 at the home of his parents on the Mercer County side of the Claylick Road.

Robert's parents were Berryman Robert Thompson, December 19, 1906 -, and Viola Magdalene Etherington, August 2, 1909 -.

Robert M. and Volita Thompson

Robert has two sisters: Nina Margaret, February 20, 1932 - married Bruce Poulter; and Juanita Magdalene, May 18, 1940, married O.H. Gritton Jr. Both reside in Lawrenceburg, KY.

Robert's paternal grandparents were John Martin Thompson, January 13, 1879 - January 20, 1963 and Margaret Sue "Sabe" Chilton , June 11, 1884 - October 24, 1973.

Robert's maternal grandparents were Robert Etherington, September 9, 1873 - November 10, 1942 and Nina Lee Stratton March 2, 1878 - August 15, 1948.

Volita Ruth Cox was born July 13, 1930 in Anderson County, Kentucky.

Volita's parents were John Thomas Cox, June 29, 1903 - January 18, 1989 and Thelma Florence Ward, August 4, 1910 - Lawrenceburg, Ky. John Cox is buried in the Highview Cemetery, Nelson County, Kentucky.

Volita has two brothers: Leon Thomas Cox, September 13, 1925, Nelson County, KY. married 1. Roxie Ockerman and 2. Wilanna Barnes Hood; and Ralph Coleman Cox, April 20, 1933 - Lawrenceburg, KY., married Onita Cox; and one sister: Donna Rhea, January 10, 1945 - Lawrenceburg, KY., married Daniel Tipton.

Volita's paternal grandparents were Robert L. Cox, 1868 - 1946 and Cora Jane McGinnis, 1869 - July 8, 1912.

Volita's maternal grandparents were Newton Laurel Ward, October 25, 1881 - January 13, 1963 and Emily Tranquil Miller Adams, March 16, 1882 - February 28, 1962. *Submitted By: Robert Martin Thompson.*

BERRYMAN ROBERT THOMPSON, "B.R.", and Viola Magdalene Etherington, were married November 29, 1928 by Rev. W. D. Moore, pastor of the Sand Spring Baptist Church. They affectionately refer to each other as "Baby".

B.R. and Viola are the parents of three children: Robert Martin Thompson, September 8, 1929, married Volita Ruth Cox; Nina Margaret, February 20, 1932, married Bruce Poulter; and Juanita Magdalene, May 18, 1940, married O.H. Gritton, Jr. All reside in Lawrenceburg, Ky.

B.R. attended the Hebron one room school.

Viola attended the Alexander one room school and Kavanaugh High School.

Prior to retiring B.R. and Viola lived on a farm near the Anderson - Mercer County line in the Claylick Community of Anderson County. After retiring they moved to 555 South Main Lawrenceburg.

They attend the Claylick United Methodist Church where they have served as Sunday School teachers for many years and members of various committees and the Administrative Board.

B.R. was born December 19, 1906 in Anderson County, Kentucky.

B.R.'s parents were John Martin Thompson (1-13-1879 - 1-20-1963) and Margaret Sue Chilton "Sabe" (6-11-1884 - 10-24-1973). (Married 1905.)

B.R. has one brother - George Davis Thompson, December 8, 1910. George resides in Lawrenceburg, Kentucky with his wife Olive Attwood McMurray.

B.R. and Viola Thompson

B.R. 's paternal Grandparents were Silas Myers Thompson, (10-18-1839 - 12-1-1914) and Martha Belle Robinson. They are buried in the Hebron Presbyterian church Cemetery, Anderson County Kentucky.

B.R.'s maternal Grandparents were Berryman Rial Chilton (9-24-1855 - 5-31-1933) and Elizabeth Bell Robinson (11-4-1858 - 4-26-1898). They are buried in the Hebron Presbyterian church cemetery, Anderson county Kentucky.

Viola Magdalene Etherington was born August 2, 1909, in Anderson County, Kentucky.

Viola's parents were Robert Etherington (9-9-1873 - 11-10-1942) and Nina Lee Stratton (3-2-1878 - 8-15-1948). (Married July 15, 1896). Buried in the Sand Spring Cemetery, Anderson County, KY.

Viola had six brothers - John Heart Etherington (5-30-1897 - 9-12-1965); Hiram Bronston (8-11-1900 - 1-30-1923); Robert Overton (1-31-1906 - 9-9-1980); Willard Aubrey (1-25-1908 - 8-19-1988; Carl Beryl (4-7-1917 - Anderson County, KY.) Clyde Darrel (4-7-1917 - 4-7-1917); and five sisters - Pearl Thelma (5-19-1899 - 12-23-1959); Nannie Lee (5-20-1903 - 10-6-1925); Mary Bird (4-30-1911 - Jefferson County, Ky); Mattie Bell (11/13/1913 - Anderson County, KY.); and Nina Moore (8-14-1923 - Jefferson County, KY.)

Viola's paternal Grandparents were Hartwell Etherington (10-12-1829 - 11-17-1905) and Hettie Thomason (7-12-1842 -). They are buried in the Etherington Cemetery near Ballard in Anderson County, Kentucky.

Viola's maternal Grandparents were John Corbin Stratton (1-17-1846 - 8-28-1921) and Elizabeth "Mollie" Sanders (9-30-1848 - 3-20-1915). John and Elizabeth were married August 2, 1870. They are buried in the Sand Spring Church Cemetery in Anderson County, Kentucky. *Submitted By: Robert Martin Thompson*

JOHN MARTIN THOMPSON, January 13, 1879 - January 20, 1963, and Margaret Sue "Sabe" Chilton, June 11, 1884 - October 23, 1973, married November 1905.

John and Sabe were the parents of two children: Berryman Robert "B.R.", December 19, 1906 and George Davis, December 8, 1910; both live in Lawrenceburg, KY.

John and Sabe lived and raised their family on this Anderson County farm near the Mercer County line. They were members of and regularly attended the Claylick United Methodist Church. They and their sons, B.R. and George, were musically talented and sang gospel quartet music for church services, funerals, singing conventions etc. throughout Central Kentucky.

John and Sabe are buried in the Hebron Presbyterian Church Cemetery, Anderson County, Kentucky.

John's parents were Silas Myers Thompson, October 18, 1839 - December 1, 1914 and Martha Belle Robinson. Silas owned considerable acreage in Anderson County. Each of his children inherited a small farm at his death. Silas served on the side of the Union during the Civil War and was in the Battle of Perryville. Silas and Martha are buried in the Hebron Presbyterian Church Cemetery, Anderson County, Kentucky.

John had one brother - George Michael Thompson, January 21, 1882 - November 22, 1968, married Nannie Lee Hawthorne; and four sisters Cordia, December 18, 1874 - May 21, 1907, married Will Drury; Myrtle, January 9, 1877 - April 19, 1954, married R.A. Wilham; and Martha Belle, 1884 - 1970, married Tom Hawthorne. All are buried in the Hebron Presbyterian Church Cemetery, Anderson County, Kentucky.

Debra, Robert, J.M., B.R., and Mrs. J.M. Thompson

Sabe's parents were Berryman Rial Chilton, September 24, 1855 - May 31, 1933 and Elizabeth Bell Robinson, November 4, 1858 - April 26, 1898. Berryman's second wife was Cynthia Sutterfield, February 28, 1855 - July 31, 1927. They are buried in the Hebron Presbyterian church Cemetery, Anderson County, Kentucky.

Sabe had one sister Minnie M. Chilton married Charles B. Homan; and four brothers - Thomas Clinton "Bud" Chilton, December 12, 1879 - November 27, 1943, married Floella Hervie Bond; John Myers McCoy Chilton, October 11, 1881 - October 24, 1963, married Ruby Alice Houchin; Fred Rial Chilton, June 30, 1886 - October 9, 1959, married Minnie Cronley Robinson; and Warren Davis "Took" Chilton May 21, 1890 - June 2, 1941, married Nena Wade.

Sabe's paternal grandparents were: Aylette Haws Chilton (1-13-1814 - 1891) and Susan Frost (1820 - 1896) Aylette's second wife was Louisa Frost.

Sabe's Paternal great-grandparents were: George Chilton (10-13-1785 - 4-7-1862) and Eleanor Cinnamon (2-10-1787 - 2-18-1852). *Submitted By: Robert Martin Thompson.*

WILLIAM OSCAR THOMPSON

was born on 11-1-1882. He was the son of Edward Thompson (1855 - 1930) and Mary Davis Tenley Thompson (1862 - 1929). William Oscar married Eula Dee Brown on 6-29-1904. She was born on 3-14-1884. She was the daughter of Buck H. Brown (1858 - 1936) and Melissa Gorden Brown (1861 - 1938). William Oscar and Eula Dee were the parents of two sons: Gilbert and Hollis. William Oscar died on 1-5-1964 and Eula Dee died on 7-22-1965.

Hollis Raymond Thompson was born on 6-9-1907 in Anderson County. Hollis married Ethel Charlotte Hawkins on 1-19-1941. She was born on 7-8-1914 in Anderson County. She is the daughter of Chester Hawkins and Addie Bowen Hawkins. Hollis and Ethel had four children: Charlotte (born 1942) married Bobby Robinson; William (born 1944) married Jane Mohalland; Marilyn; and Joy (born 1952) married Johnny Spencer. Hollis died on 12-12-1984.

Marilyn Dee Thompson was born on 10-11-1948 in Frankfort. She married Harry Lee Robinson on 4-14-1966 in Harrisonville, KY. Harry was born on 5-15-1946 in Mt. Eden, KY. He is the son of Merritt Richard Robinson (1917-1989) and Iva Lee Cook Robinson. He has nine brothers and sisters: Bobby (born 1939) married Charlotte Thompson; Mildred (born 1942) married Robert Bently; Gary (born 1944); Sharon (born 1947) married Marvin Sammons; Brenda (born 1948) married Henry Adams; Angels (born 1954) married Charlotte Dearman; and Ricky (born 1956) married Rose. Marilyn and Harry are the parents of three children: Tamara Twainette, born 3-

11-1969; Richard Raymond, born 9-27-1973; and Timothy Lee, born 11-17-1978.

Chester Hawkins, the son of George Hawkins and Nancy Catherine Bacie Hawkins, was born in 1881 in Anderson county. He married Addie Charlotte Bowen on 1-10-1906. She was born on 10-19-1887 in Anderson County. She was the daughter of Elijah Bowen (1842 - 1921) and Charlotte Royalty Bowen (1849 - 1929). Chester and Addie were the parents of three children: Enda married Paul York; Mary Lois married Harold Hanks; and Ethel Charlotte. Chester died on 11-6-1943 in Anderson county and Addie died on 9-11-1986 in Scott County. *Submitted By: Richard Robinson.*

WILLIAM KELLY THOMPSON,

was born on 2-10-1945 in Hodgenville, Kentucky. He is the son of Chester Lee Thompson and Sarah Jane Hubbard Thompson. Kelly had two brothers: Donald Lee (1933 - 1952) and David Allen who married Sue Fister - four children - Nathan, Emily, Jeffery, and Sarah.

Kelly Thompson met Glenda Fay Yarbrough and married her on 8-23-1968. She was born on 10-10-1944 in Nelson County, KY. She is the daughter of Ural Glenn Yarbrough and Marian Lucille Hampton Yarbrough. Glenda has one sister and one brother: Sarah Kay married Larry Hall. They have two children, Larry and Larissa. Byron married Carolyn (?). They have two daughters, Kristen and Lauren. They are now divorced.

Kelly and Glenda moved to Massachusetts after their marriage and later moved back to Kentucky, to Anderson County. They have two children - Benjamin Kelly, born 5-7-1974 and Carolyn Sue, born 6-1-1978. Both children were born in Georgetown, KY. The Thompson family built a home on Woodspoint Drive and live there today. *Submitted By: Benji Thompson.*

BENNIE TAYLOR TINDALL,

was born on 3-22-1884. He married Lille Ann Wayne on 5-3-1905. She was born on 6-24-1889. Bennie was a stonemason in Anderson County and Lillie Ann was a feedstore owner. They were the parents of seven children: William Thomas (below); Edward married Aderine Riley Tindall; Goldie married Exra Murphy; Charles; Mamie married Lloyd Sayers; Irene married William Burton; and James Henry married Aderine Riley. After the death of James Henry Tindall, Aderine married Edward. Bennie died on 11-17-1952 and Lillie Ann on 3-19-1973. She is buried in the Lawrenceburg Cemetery.

William Thomas Tindall was born on 9-20-1906 in Anderson County. On 12-5-1927, he married Nancy Elizabeth Ingram at the Anderson County Courthouse. She was the daughter of Oscar Ingram and Mertle J. Morris Ingram. They were the parents of seven children: William Jr. (below); Lillie Belle, born 6-12-1931, married Lois York; Bennie (1936 - 1944); Harold, born 6-6-1937, married Minnie Farmer; Claudie, born 3-18-1941, married Elaine Spencer; Opal, born 4-13-1944; and Linda, born 6-8-1946. William Thomas died on 8-25-1985 and his wife preceded him in 1-28-1976.

William Tindall Jr. was born on 11-18-1928 in Anderson County. He married Emmie Gaines on 9-11-1948. She was born on 10-2-1931 in Owen County, Ky and was the daughter of James T. Gaines (1886 - 1956) and Ona F. Gaines (1897 - 1975). William and Emma are the parents of two children: James William, born 10-17-1950, married Marlene Fay Artist; and John Thomas (below). William and Emmie Tindall reside on Eagle Drive in Lawrenceburg.

John Thomas Tindall was born on 1-24-1956 in Anderson County. He married Theresa Marie Jefferies on 11-30-1973 at Fellowship Baptist Church in Anderson County. She was born on 8-7-1954 in Nelson County and is the daughter of William Ralph Jeffries and Ida Chowning Jeffries. John T. and Theresa M. Jeffries are the parents of two children: John William, born 7-19-1974; and Jennifer Renee, born 9-13-1979. Both were born in Mercer County.

They reside on Versailles Road in Anderson County. *Submitted By: John Tindall*

JAMES COLEMAN AND SADIE SEA

TINSLEY were married July 18, 1970 at Friendship Baptist Church by the Rev. Don Walker. James is the son of Cordelia Huffman Tinsley Dennis and the late J.C. Tinsley. He has two sisters, Mary Lois Tabscott of Lexington and Betty Ann Bennett, Lawrenceburg (deceased) and two half brothers, David Dennis, Lawrenceburg, and Kelvin Dennis, Springfield.

James attended Western High School and served in the U.S. Army during the Vietnam War. He was employed by Universal Fasteners for six months prior to joining the Army. In 1969, he began working at GTE Sylvania in Versailles, KY. James is a member of the Anderson County Volunteer Fire Departments, Station Five.

Left to Right: Sadie, Julie, James, and Justin Tinsley

Sadie is the daughter of Annie L.sea and the late Gilbert Clinton Sea. She has one brother, Gilbert Sea, Lawrenceburg, and one sister, Margaret Woodside, Lawrenceburg. Sadie graduated from Western High School in 1962. She was granted a B.S. degree from Eastern Kentucky University in 1966. She completed a Fifth Year Program at Georgetown College in 1986. She is currently working toward her Rank I Certification from Georgetown College. She began her teaching career in 1966 in Jefferson County, Ky. After four years, she returned to Anderson County. She began teaching 3rd grade at Western School in 1970. Her hobby is cake decorating.

James and Sadie have two children; Justin Coleman was born March 23, 1972. He is a senior at Anderson County High School. He is a defensive linebacker for the Anderson County Bearcats. He is also a Junior Volunteer Fire Fighter and loves horseback riding.

Julie Coleman was born January 15, 1977. She is a seventh grade student at the Middle School. Julie's hobbies are horseback riding and clogging. She is currently a member of the Mi-Stlye Cloggers of Versailles, KY.

The Tinsley's live at 1211 Hickory Grove, Lawrenceburg. They also raise tobacco on their farm near Salt River, on the Bond's Mill Road.

CHARLES TOLL,

the son of Charles C. Toll Jr. (1948 - 1986) and Jewel F. Hulette Toll, was born on 12-29-1965 in Frankfort, Ky. He has a sister, Sandy Toll.

Charles married Cindy L. Martin on 7-6-1984. She was born on 6-22-1964 in Madisonville, KY. She is the only child of Mutt W. Martin (1945 - 1983) and Loyce A. Blackwell Martin (born 1947).

Charles and Cindy Toll are the proud parents of three children: Heath Martin, born 12-26-1973 in Madisonville (Charles adopted Heath when he married Cindy.) ; Ashley Toll, born 7-13-1982 in Frankfort, KY; and Charlsie, born 2-20-1986 in Frankfort.

Charles, Cindy, and their three children currently reside on Alton Station road in Anderson County. *Submitted By: Heath Martin.*

DR. JAMES LESLIE TOLL,

One of the civic-minded and respected men of the first half of the 20th

Century was Dr. James Leslie Toll, who was the mayor of Lawrenceburg from 1913 - 1921 and again from 1929 - 1945, a total of 24 years. One of the serious problems faced by the city during the summer of 1930 was the lack of city water because of the severe drought. At the time, water for Lawrenceburg came from Salt River and the water level became dangerously low. That led the council to begin planning to get the city's water from the Kentucky River.

Dr. Toll was born in the Sinai area of Anderson County in 1874, the third son of James Pole and Arietta Champion Toll. He had four young sisters, all of who married Anderson Countains and lived their lives here: Verna, who married Wilkes Bond; Mary, whose husband was Frank Baxter; Nora, who married Homer Baxter; and Mabel, whose husband was Lindsay Baxter.

During the years he attended Louisville Medical College, he taught school in various Anderson County schools for six moths each year and went to college the other six months of the year. After his graduation in 1897, he began practicing medicine at Salvisa, moving to Lawrenceburg in 1904. While living in Salvisa, he married Julia Sweasy and their only child Elizabeth was born. Elizabeth later married Mitchell Bailey and after his death, Dudley Walker. She had two children: John Mitchell Bailey III and Frances Bailey Carr. Julia died in 1920 and Dr. Toll was remarried in 1922 to Fred Fillmore. their two children were: Nancy, whose husband in W. J. Smith, and Leslie, who married Donn Hollingworth. Two of Dr. Toll's grandchildren call Lawrenceburg home: Thomas H. Smith and Shelia Smith McFarland.

Many men in the medical profession in Kentucky considered Dr. Toll as an excellent diagnostician. He had a wide practice in Anderson County and into parts of Mercer and Franklin Counties. In addition to his medial and civic duties, he was active in the Lawrenceburg First Christian Church, both as an elder and as chairman of the Board of Trustees that built the building on South Main Street where the church is presently housed. One of his avocations was singing, often being one member of a quartet that sang for funerals in the small county churches.

Dr. Toll died in October of 1952. *Submitted by: Nancy T. Smith.*

TONEY - According to what has been passed down by word of mouth from the late Reuben Winters, Mariah Townsend was brought from Africa to New Orleans, Louisiana on a slave ship. Mr. Booker, a farmer from Washington County, Mississippi, bought her and made her a personal servant to his wife, Cora Booker. Mariah Townsend married and had a daughter, Jane. Jane was freed at the age of 12.

Jane married Felix Hall, a homesteader from Washington County, Miss. They had two children, Cora and Marian (1891 - 1952) who married Peter Dumas. Jane was a seamstress.

Cora Hall was born on 3-3-1889 in Washington County, Miss. and died 4-16-1946. She married Archie Winters (1882 - 1942) on 2-10-1911 in Belzoni, Mississippi. Archie was the son of Harry and Mary Winters. Archie and Cora were the parents of one son, Reuben Hall, born on 1-13-1913 in Belzoni. Reuben married Attie White, the daughter of George and Katie Phillips White, on 10-10-1940 in Mississippi. They were the parents of eight children: Carl (1941 - 1973) married Ruby Winters - four children - Carl, Gregg, Gina, and Reuben; Dorothy Ann married Charley Gross - one child, Terran; William; Essie (below); Felix Hall married Landress Winters; Charles Reuben; Gwendolyn Patrick; and Gregory Patrick.

Essie Winters was born on 10-14-1946 in Belzoni. She married Roy Howard Toney on 8-6-1968. He was born on 10-25-1943 in Columbia, Mississippi. He is the son of Maxie Toney and Rouells Brown. Roy and Essie moved from the state of Mississippi to Wisconsin, where they had their first child. Ladonis Toney was born on 11-8-1969 in Sparta, Wisconsin. She is currently attending Tougloo College, Tougaloo,

Mississippi. The family later moved to Colorado and then back to Kentucky, where their son, Kwasi Du'Bois, was born on 4-19-1974 in Bowling Green, KY. He is currently attending Anderson County High School.

The Toney family now lives in Anderson County where Roy is a soil conservationist and Essie is a teacher. *Submitted By: Kwasi Toney.*

GEORGE LEROY TRACY, was born in April 1910 and died on 3-20-1978 in Harrodsburg, KY. He was the son of Eugene Tracy (1876 - 1971) and Nora Milton Tracy (1881 - 1951). He had five brothers and sisters: William (1900 - 1913); Edna (1902 - 1972) married Ralph Catlett; Rebecca (1903 - 1969) married Willis Green; Jowitt (born 1906) married Gladys Brown; and Charles (1908 - 1980) married Pearl Tracy.

George Leroy Tracy married June Slaughter. She was born on 6-1-1910 in Anderson County and is the daughter of J.W. Slaughter (1877 - 1971) and Nancy Carrol Slaughter (died 1959). George Leroy and June were the parents of two sons, Carroll and John (born 8-10-1943). June currently resides on Nevins Station Road in Anderson County.

Milton Carroll Tracy was born on 12-13-1940 in Harrodsburg. He married Ann Overstreet on 3-12-1961 in Anderson County. She is the daughter of Fred Davis Overstreet (born 12-6-1905 - Mercer County) and Zoe Anna Rue (9-7-1908 - 7-28-1982).

Carroll and Ann are the parents of two children: Lanny, born 3-26-1962, married Beverly Lowe in 1987 - Bluefield, West Virginia; and Carol, born 11-23-1973 in Mercer County. Carroll Tracy died on 1-19-1984 in Boyle County. He is buried in Anderson County. The Tracy family currently resides on Nevin Station Road. *Submitted By: Carol Tracy.*

CHRISTOPHER CHINN TRENT, was the oldest dry goods merchant in Lawrenceburg at the time of his death. Born in Washington County, Kentucky, on 12-5-1843, he was one of the youngest children of James and Mary Trent. His siblings were James M. (1830 - 1970), John R. (1833 - 1908), Martha, Mary E., Eliza, Lucy, Paul, and Thomas F. (?). The parents and some siblings are buried in Antioch Christian Church Cemetery in Washington County.

On 4-6-1865, he married Miss Kate Parsons of Washington County. A short time after his marriage he engaged in a general merchandise business in the county. To this union were born: James W. (1866 - 1868), Edgar (1867 - 1875), Oscar (1870 - 1950), Paul Victor (1871 - 1912), Chris Lee (1873 - 1874), and Ada Trent Ragan (1875 - 1951) (no children). Mrs. Ragan was a school teacher and principal of Butler School in Pendleton County, Kentucky. Kate died 6-3-1878, and she and the children who died in childhood are buried at Antioch Christian Church Cemetery.

On 2-11-1879, he was united in marriage to Miss Nannie Hall. They had no children, and she died on 10-21-1880. She is buried at Antioch Christian Church Cemetery.

In 1880, the Republicans of Washington County prevailed on him to become a candidate for the Kentucky General Assembly. He was elected and became the first Republican ever elected to the Legislature from that county.

In 1882, he gave up his seat in the Legislation and moved to Lawrenceburg where he began the general dry goods business in which he was active at the time of his death. On 8-28-1884, he married Miss Minnie McMurry, daughter of Thomas H. and Lucinda Elizabeth Bond (nee Routt) McMurry. To this union were born: Raymond C. (1885 - 1942), Lilian Mae McKay (1886 - 1972), and Charles Stanley (1890 - 1950).

Mr. Trent was a member of the Lawrenceburg City Council for several terms. In 1907, he was the Republican nominee for the Legislature. He was a member of the First Christian Church. He died on 8-6-1915, and was buried in the Lawrenceburg Cemetery. *Submitted By: Robert Goodlett.*

JAMES OSCAR TUCKER, was the son of William Tucker Jr. and Ona Miles Polle Tucker. He was born on 5-27-1909. He had ten brothers and sisters: twin girls (died at birth - 1940); Emmet, born 1906; Delbert, born 1914; Baby (stillborn - 1917); Clarence, born 1919; Anthony Hall; Charles Edward, born 1923; Samuel Shasteen; and Cratcha.

When James Oscar was in the 5th grade, he quit school to help take care of his brothers and sisters because his father died. Without his help the family wouldn't have made it. When he was about 21, he met Katherine C. Blair.

James Oscar was a very good baseball player and was asked to try out for the Cincinnati Reds Team. He went and was offered a position! He gave it up to marry Katherine.

James Oscar Tucker married Katherine C. Blair (she was only 13 at the time). She was born on 3-25-1917. She was the daughter of Bill Blair and Mattie Sprugeon Blair. When she was young, her father left her mother. He remarried and had three daughters who live in Lexington. By the time Katherine really got to know her father, he was put in a TB Hospital in Versailles, KY and soon died with TB.

James Oscar and Katherine Tucker were the parents of eleven children: Bobby Gene (died young); James Olson (1933 - 1980); Billie Tucker Bowers; Doris Ann (died young); Zelma Tucker Carter; Joseph Lee; Danny Rogers; Garnett Earl (1946 - 1963); Kathy Tucker Belcher; Yvonne Tucker Toles; and Charles Gail.

They lived on a large farm in Versailles on Dry Ridge Road. It was a beautiful home. Right after Christmas in the late 50's, the house burned. That day everyone was in school, but the little ones. The women were in the kitchen. Over Christmas, Katherine Tucker, had candles up and down the bannisters and the little ones thought they were beautiful. The children took some of the candles to an upstairs closet. They lit three candles and their eyes just danced as they watched the flames flicker.

Katherine called for the children to come downstairs and they blew out two candles. They left the other for later, because there were no more matches. The children no sooner got downstairs to eat, than the whole upstairs was on fire. They all managed to survive, but nearly everything was lost.

The family moved to a 308 acre dairy farm on Green Wilson Road in Anderson County. James Oscar also started his own Construction Company. James Oscar Tucker died of a heart attack and complications of a wreck on 9-5-1970. His wife died of an aneurysm of the brain on 11-3-1979.

Garnett Earl Tucker was born 3-10-1946 in Versailles. He married Hazel Doss on 10-21-1963 in Jellico, TN. Hazel was born on 11-25-1946 in Lawrenceburg. She is the daughter of Jimmy Doss Sr. and Louise Peyton. Garnett is the father of three daughters: Tina, born 1964; Diane Tucker Butler, born 1968; and Stacy, born 1975.

Jimmy Doss Sr. was born 4-5-1904 and died 7-19-1976. He was the son of Matt Doss and Hattie Carrier Doss. He had five brothers and sisters: Pearl Doss; Robert, died 1988; Matt Jr., died 1971; Zeek; and Clarabelle Doss James, died 1980. Jimmy married Louise Peyton, the daughter of John Peyton and Mary Woods Peyton. Louise was born on 8-25-1916 in Lawrenceburg. She has ten brothers and sisters: Herman; Myrtle Peyton Snow (dec.); Sara Peyton Snow; Bill Peyton (dec.); Della Peyton Curley; Ida Peyton Mitchell; Jeneva Peyton Whitehouse; Shirley Peyton McDonald (dec.); Chester; and Debbie (died at birth).

Jimmy and Louise were the parents of five children: Sara Ann Doss Haden (1931 - 1989); Jimmy Jr. (1939 - 1986); Bobby Lewis: Mary Jo Doss Hopper; and Hazel Doss Tucker. *Submitted By: Stacy Tucker.*

ROBERT BOWLING TURNER, educational administrator, was born 9-13-1913 in Wabash, Indiana. He was of English heritage, the son of Benjamin

R. and Charlotte Reeves Turner. As a small child, the family moved to New Albany, Indiana where his parents had grown up. He graduated from New Albany High School in 1932, having played both basketball and football.

He was granted an athletic scholarship to Indiana University, where he reported in late August of 1932. At the end of one week, friends from New Albany who were attending Georgetown College, Georgetown, KY, came to Bloomington. They asked him to come with them to Georgetown for a weekend visit. He went with them and liked the town, campus, and college so well, he never returned to I.U.

He ran track, played football and basketball for the Georgetown Tigers, graduating in 1936, with an A.B. Degree. He later earned a M.A. Degree and Rank I from the University of Kentucky.

Robert accepted a position as coach and teacher at Chaplin High School in Nelson County, staying for a year. He came to Western Consolidated School in 1937, where he remained as a coach and teacher until entering the Navy. He entered the Navy as an Ensign in 1943. He served in the American Theater, European Theater of Operations and Asiatic-Pacific Theater, until retirement in 1946. Following this he returned to Western School as the principal and remained here until his retirement in June 1980.

Robert was a member of the Anderson County Sportsman Club, Charter member of the Kentucky Athletic Hall of Fame, the Retired Officers Club, DAV, Anderson County American Legion Post, Beaver Creek Lodge #335, NEA and KEA Teachers Association, Indiana National Guard, and a member of Fairmount Church of Christ.

On December 2, 1939, he married the former Helen Mitchell Blockson. They were the parents of two daughters: Mrs. Charles (Charlotte) Vaughn and Mrs. Mac (Sharon) Goodlett. Both daughters followed their parents in the teaching profession. Charlotte and Charles are the parents of one son, Charles Robert Vaughn.

Robert B. Turner passed away on February 18, 1989. *Submitted By: Helen Turner.*

THE VAUGHN FAMILY has lived in Anderson County since 1896. Samuel Vaughn was the second of six children. He was the son of John Paul Vaughn. He lived most of his life in Anderson County. At one time, he bought a farm in Shelbyville, KY, sold it, and moved back to Woodford Street in Lawrenceburg. He lived there until he died in 1952.

Paul Wilbur Vaughn was one of the five children of Samuel and Mayme Vaughn. Paul W. Vaughn lived in Anderson County his entire life. He was born in 1895. He attended school at Kavanaugh and played on one of their first basketball teams. He was a veteran of World War I having served in the Navy. As a a young man, he worked for the Southern Railway Company. After leaving this job, he worked at the Distilling Company at Bond's Mill. He was transferred from the Old Joe Distilling Company when they were purchased by Austin Nichols where he retired. He and his wife died in 1982.

Mary Louise Roach Vaughn lived in Harrodsburg and met Paul Wilbur Vaughn while he was working for the Southern Railway Co. Mary Louise's family was from Mississippi. Her mother, Ann Irene Williams Roach, married Benjamin Franklin Roach in 1906. He graduated from Old Central University which later became EKU. He was county attorney for Mercer County. Ann's mother would come to Kentucky from Mississippi on the train to visit. The last trip she made was for her 100th birthday. She made the trip alone by train. She was 13 years old when the Civil War began. She told stories about the war. One was about Union Soldiers who rode their horses through the southern mansions slashing the pictures and portraits with their swords.

Paul Vaughn, the son of Paul Wilbur Vaughn and Mary Louise Roach Vaughn, has lived in Anderson County since birth. He attended Lawrenceburg Grade School and Anderson High School. After graduating from high school, he attended and graduated from Eastern KY University in 1960.

After graduation, he joined the Kentucky National Guard for six months of active duty. He then served six years as a reserve. While on active duty, Paul graduated from finance school at Fort Benjamin Harrison in Indianapolis, Indiana. When released from active duty with the guard, he started to work full time at the Lawrenceburg National Bank. He has worked part-time at the bank since June 1955. Currently he is the Executive Vice-President, Senior Trust Officer, and has been serving on the board since 1975.

In 1962, Paul married Eva Kidwell Vaughn. She teaches in the Anderson County School System. They have one son, Paul Thomas. He is a policemen in Lawrenceburg. *Submitted By: Paul Vaughn.*

JOHN PAUL VAUGHN, was born in Estill County, Kentucky on February 25, 1845. After serving in the Confederate Army, Company H, 4th Infantry (Orphan Brigade), he came to Anderson County. In 1869, he married Mary Alise (Molly) sharp and they farmed the Noah Sharp farm. He resided there until his death on October 5, 1913.

John and Molly were the parents of six children: H.K. (Hez), Samuel Sales, Anna Belle, Margaret Carol, Oran, and Elizabeth Zarelda.

H.K. married a Miss McMichael and they had two children, Mary and Howard.

Samuel married Mayme Bond and their children were: Anna Elizabeth, Paul Wilbur, Vernon Bond, Charles Samuel, and Thomas Rice.

Oran and Jessie Vaughn had three children: John, Jennie, and Ruby.

Anna married Edgar Hollis and they had one son, Robert.

Margaret married Grover Folsom Harmon and their two children were Mary Virginia and Pauline Vaughn. Mary Virginia died in infancy and Pauline married Joseph McKay Howard. They have two children: Molly Sharp Feist and Thomas McKay Howard.

KLIEN AND FRANCES VOWELS, were born and reared in Anderson County. Klien worked at Wardsville and Frances at Ninevah. He is the second son of Richard and Mary Frances Vowels. He has a brother, Tom and a sister, Elizabeth. Frances is the daughter of James and Minnie Neal Campbell. She has a younger brother, William. Klien and Frances both attended one room schools in Anderson County. Klien at Wardsville and Frances at Ninevah. Later they attended Kavanaugh High School. He graduated in the class of 1915 and she in 1921.

Klien grew up on a large farm and after graduating loved farm life and chose farming as his vocation. He raised tobacco, corn, wheat, also hay for his beef and dairy cows, along with sheep and hogs. Frances was employed at the Home Telephone Company until the Home and Bell Telephones consolidated in 1927.

Klien and Frances are the parents of three daughters: Mary, Martha, and Joanne. All are graduates of Lawrenceburg City High and members of First Baptist Church. Mary owns and operates the Trading Post at Stringtown and married Harold Brown, a veteran of WWII. He helped, when not working on their farm where he died in 1984 suddenly while cutting wood. They were the parents of three children: Beverly, graduate of ACHS, married Allen Chambers - one son, Chris; Mitchell, graduate of ACHS, farms and helps Mary in Stringtown grocery when not in crops.; and Mary Frances, graduate of ACHS, married Vince Jordan, works for the state and she at Winn Dixie. Mary later married Dillard Koger, a veteran of WWII and employed at Square D and now retired.

Martha attended business college in Louisville and was employed as bookkeeper at the Old Joe

Klien and Frances Vowels

Distillery. She married Paul H. Crutcher, Jr., a vet of WWII and employed at Chevrolet Garage in Frankfort. After retiring he farmed his and Martha's farms and died suddenly on her farm while baling hay in 1988. They have three children: Marcus, Ann, and Jonathan. Mark married Cindy Welch, she taught music and sold real estate - now they are the proud parents of a baby girl, Lean Michelle; Ann married David Roe, employed at Rand McNally and she at the state; and Jonathan, a junior at ACHS.

Joanne married Arnold (Buck) Perry, a vet of WWII. They farm and raise beef cattle on their farm. They are the parents of two children, Klien and Anne. Klien graduated from ACHS and is employed by General Cable. He married Peggy Redding, a graduate of Frankfort H.S. and employed at the State. They have two children, Kristin and Travis, both attend grade school. Anne an ACHS graduate, is employed at the Anderson National Bank. She married Dennis Stidham, an employee at Sylvania.

Klien and Frances were married in Frankfort by Rev. Hampton Adams on 4-12-1928 and have always lived on their farm on North Main Street in Lawrenceburg. Klien died on 2-5-1962 in the barn lot suddenly while feeding the cows of a heart attack. He was a member of the Fairmont Christian Church and she at the First Baptist Church, where she attends Sunday School and Church every Sunday. *Submitted By: Frances Vowels.*

DAVID WAINSCOTT, The son of Jacob Wainscott and Luvisha Simpson Wainscott, was born in 1883 in Anderson County. He married Ora McGaughey. She was born in 1886 in Anderson County, the daughter of Leon McGaughey and Mary Jane Durgin McGaughey. David and Ora were the parents of 11 children: Beatrice (Perry) Wainscott (deceased) married Mattie Watts; Mary Lou Wainscott married Andy Hyatt; L.E. Wainscott (deceased) married Margaret Morris; Jesse Wainscott married Jenny Tinsley; David Wainscott Jr. married Evelyn Jordan; Ora Belle Wainscott married Billy Wiley; Woodrow Wainscott married Erma Foster; Guy Wainscott married Arntea Disponnett; Jimmy Wainscott married Ann Doss; Edward Wainscott married Elizabeth Giles; and Leonda Wainscott. David Wainscott died in 1947 and Ora died in 1982.

Leonda Wainscott was born on 12-11-1924 in Anderson County. He married Pauline Rogers on 4-23-1948. She was born on 7-1-1928 in Harrodsburg, KY. She is the daughter of Ova M. Rogers and Ophilia May Robinson Rogers. Leonda and Pauline had seven children: Larry Brent Wainscott (7-19-1949 / 8-23-1949); Michael Leon Wainscott (born April 1951) married Jeanne Kirby - two children, Lori and Justin; Glenn Jeffrey Wainscott (born 7-21-1955) married twice - five children by 1st marriage - Angela Gwen, Alissa Lynn, Aaron Kelly, Amanda Rose, Ashley Nicole - one son by 2nd marriage, Jonas; Don Kelly Wainscott (born and died 1959); Marcus Brian Wainscott (born 5-19-1965) married once - divorced - one son, Adam; Gregory David Wainscott (born 11-26-1966) married Sherri Mansfield; and Darren Bradley Wainscott (8-8-1971 - 11-3-1989). Leonda Wainscott died on 12-29-1976.

Ova M. Rogers, the son of Joel C. Rogers and

Lucretia McKinney Rogers, was born in Mercer County. He had two brothers: Amos Rogers and Wallace Rogers. He married Ophilia May Robinson, the daughter of Charlie Robinson and Loulie Hendrix Robinson. She was also born in Mercer County. She had eight brothers and sisters: Major Robinson, John Robinson, Delbert Robinson, Howard Robinson, Bradley Robinson, Nell Robinson married Gene Richardson, Clara Robinson married Robert Taylor, and Sue Robinson married Howard Whitage.

Ova and Ophilia were the parents of five children: Louise Rogers (born 1923) married Woodrow Humphrey - one daughter; J.C. Rogers (deceased); Pauline Rogers Wainscott; Elsie Rogers (born 1930) married Archie Gayle; and Mildred Rogers (deceased) married Garnett Semonis. Ophilia passed away in 1935 in Mercer County and Ova in 1975 in Anderson County. *Submitted By: Angie Wainscott.*

BENJAMIN RILEY WALDRIDGE, born 12 Dec 1866 in Washington County, Kentucky, son of Peter Waldridge, Jr., and Manerva Yocum, married in Anderson County, Kentucky on 19 August 1892 to Lucy Frances Barnett, born 30 July 1871 in Anderson County, daughter of Charles Barnett, Jr. and Elizabeth Strange. Ben spent most of his adult life engaged in farming, and in later years ran a small grocery store from one room of his house. He died in Anderson County on 30 August 1950, Lucy died there on 30 August 1951. Both are buried in the Fairview Christian Church Cemetery in Washington County. Fifteen children, all born in Anderson County:

1) Edna R. Waldridge, born 2 May 1893, married John Mobley.

2) Annie Jane Waldridge, born 24 Sept 1894, married Jasper Newton Walls, son of Frank G. Walls and Perlina Mobley. She died 3 May 1970 in Jefferson County, Kentucky and was buried in the King's Baptist Church Cemetery in Bullitt County, Kentucky. Ten children.

3) Noah Webster Waldridge, born 30 Mar 1896, married Minnie M. Goodlett.

4) Hattie Elizabeth Waldridge, born 13 Dec 1897, married Theodore S. Breeding.

5) John Harrison Waldridge, born 13 Nov 1898, married Arletta Husband.

6) Charlie Frank Waldridge, born 2 August 1899, married Hazel Blanche Husband.

7) Benjamin Waldridge, born circa 1901, died circa 1903.

8) Vennie Waldridge, born circa 1903, died of pneumonia at 2-3 months of age.

9) Herbert H. Waldridge, born 13 June 1904, married Lula M. Milburn.

10) Peter Hurdle Waldridge, born 1906, never married.

11) Homer E. Waldridge, born 1907, married Verlie O. Leathers.

12) Marvin B. Waldridge, born 1909, married in Anderson County on 8 Jan 1938, to Evelyn Faye Leathers, born 1922, daughter of Walter L. Leathers and Mattie D. Walls.

13) Verlie May Waldridge, born 1912, married William Drury and John Bragg.

14) Wilbert Waldridge, born 1914, married Ruth Langford.

15) Samuel Waldridge, born circa 1916, died young.

Verlie and Marvin are all that remains of the above fifteen children, most of the other are buried in the Fairview Christian Church Cemetery. *Submitted By: William R. Walls.*

PETER WALDRIDGE, JR., was born in Kentucky, probably in Garrard County, in 1819, a son of Peter and Fanny Waldridge, who had migrated to Kentucky from Virginia a few years earlier. He married first, in Garrard County, on 15 December 1840 to Matilda Matthews and remained in that county until after the 1850 Census, their four children were born

there and most likely Matilda died there. He was in Washington County by 1860, where he married second on 5 April 1860 to Manerva Yocum, born June 1837 in Lincoln Co., KY, daughter of Hardin Yocum and Lucinda Wells. They were listed on the 1900 Anderson County Census, where Manerva stated she was the mother of 14 children, nine of them were then alive. We do not know if she was including her four step-children or not, but either way, we have found only 12 children for Peter Waldridge, Jr.:

1) Mary F. Waldridge, born 1841 in Garrard County.

2) Anderson Ellis Waldridge, born 1843 in Garrard County, died of "Camp Diarrhea" while serving in the Civil War. Buried in the Antioch Christian Church Cemetery in Washington County.

3) Peter Fleming Waldridge, born 12 January 1845 in Garrard Co., married in Washington Co. in 1865 to Mahala Frances Yocum, born 1842, daughter of Henry Yocum III, and Martha Ann Wells. He also served in the Civil War, and died 30 August 1904. Mahala died in 1922, both are buried in the Fairview Christian Church Cemetery. They had nine children.

4) Elizabeth Waldridge, born 1849 in Garrard County, married in Washington County on 5 October 1867 to Thomas Montgomery.

5) Mariah J. Waldridge, born 1861 in Washington Co., married Bruner Darnell.

6) Paralee Waldridge, born 1863, married Fry Barnett.

7) Henry Mason Waldridge, born 1 Dec 1865, married Nancy Eller Brown.

8) Benjamin Riley Waldridge, born 12 December 1866, married Lucy Frances Barnett.

9) Matilda Waldridge, born 1868, married Jeff David.

10) Anna Belle Waldridge, born 1872, married Leslie Barnett.

11) Milton Waldridge, born 1879, married Eliza Brown.

12) John Samuel Waldridge, born 1881, married Emma Leathers and Estelle Kinder. *Submitted By: William R. Walls.*

HORACE WITHERSPOON WALKER SR.,
the son of William Walker and Elizabeth Carr Walker, was born on 10-15-1908 in Anderson County. He married Hattie Evangelene Crossfield on 8-20-1927. She was born on 5-12-1909 in Anderson County. She is the daughter of Ernest Crossfield and Sara E. Carter Crossfield. She has one brother, Geobel Crossfield.

Horace W. and Evangelene are the parents of three children: Horace Witherspoon Jr.; Delora Evalee, born 1934, married Robert Mefford; and James Nelson, born 1937, married Barbara.

Horace Witherspoon Walker Jr. was born on 3-20-1929 in Louisville, KY. He married Judy Faye Sparrow on 1-11-1963. She was born on 6-8-1942 and died on 12-11-1989. She was the daughter of the late Henry Ray Sparrow and Oneda Morris Sparrow. They had six children: Elizabeth Ann, born 1951, married Randell W. Taylor of South Dakota - two sons, Rusty and Greg; Jana Vee, born 1952, married David Downing - three sons - Troy, Eric, and Marc; Randall Crie, born 1956, married Ann Elise Morrow - divorced; Ronald Eugene, born 1958, married Lori; Kevin Ray, born 1965, married Pamela Ray; and Krista Janeen, born 1971.

Henry Ray Sparrow was the son of Charles Pierce Sparrow and Maudie May Sparrow (1897 - 1982). Oneda Morris Sparrow is the daughter of Robert Lee Morris (1896 - 1955) and Mary Ellen Case Morris (1899 - 1967). *Submitted By: Rusty Taylor II.*

OSCAR YOUNG WALKER (1870 - 1940), the
son of Leonidas and Susan Mary Young Walker, married Valerie Aylmer Catlett (1871 - 1938), the daughter of Elijah and Susan Mary Herndon Catlett. They had seven children: Nora Wallace (below); Susan Mary; Justus David (married Beatrice Gravitt);

Leon Catlett (married Lillian Barnes) They had one daughter, Shirley Jane Walker. She married Charles Martin. They had three children - "Lee", Jill, and Scott; Thomas Dudley (married 1st Madeline Bish 2nd Elizabeth Toll Bailey); Georgia Frances (marr William James Alexander) one son, William Jar Alexander Jr. - She died in childbirth; and Pres Herndon (married Alma Goodlett). Susan M Walker was Deputy County Clerk for 29 years. died of a stroke when she was being sworn in Circuit Clerk on January 2, 1963. Oscar Young Wal er was deputy sheriff of Anderson County for 8 years and also as sheriff.

Oscar Young Walker

Nora Wallace Walker (1895 - 1963) married Joseph Stewart Wyatt (1900 - 1950), the son of J.D. Wyatt and Susan Mary Cooper Wyatt, on December 12, 1925. They had one daughter, Jane Walker Wyatt. She married on December 2, 1946 to Warren Frank Puhr. They had two children: Terry Warren and Barry Walker. *Submitted By: Jane Walker Wyatt Puhr.*

WALKER The Walker's were among the earliest settler's in Anderson County, having come to the county in 1796 when it was still a part of Franklin County. They are the forebearers of many old and distinguished names in Anderson County. The old Walker cabin, built in 1796 is on the present Jenny Lillard Road and was owned in 1988 by Morris Hyatt. The Walker's owned this property from 1796 to 1952.

The history begins with "Old" Randol and Elizabeth Harris Walker who were born in Richmond County, Virginia and who migrated to Kentucky with their seven children in 1786. They originally purchased property in Woodford County and upon selling this property moved to the present Anderson County in 1796. Their children were:

John - born 1766, probably Northumberland County, Virginia. In 1792, he married Betsy Stott. He took office as Sheriff of Franklin County in 1824, and it has been commonly said that his son, Jordon, then Deputy Sheriff, tied the rope around Beauchamp's neck on 7-7-1827 when he was hung for the murder of Soloman P. Sharp. John and Betsy were the parents of: (1) Jordon H. Walker, born 1792, who was county clerk from 1833 to 1844, and who then became the second County Judge of Anderson County, an office he kept until his death in 1862. 2) Randol Walker, born 1796, married 1st Malinda Mizner, and upon her death married 2nd Eliza Matthews. He was Deputy Sheriff of Anderson County from 1833 to 1841. He represented the county in the State Legislature in 1848. 3) Lucinda, born 1794, married Hardin Haynes. 4) Katherine, married James Mizner. 5) Harriett married Joseph Mizner. 6) Arameus married David George. 7) Elizabeth 8) John Jr. 9) James S. 10) Lewis.

Randol, Jr. - born 1777, Northumberland County, VA. In 1796, he married Polly Hobblitt in Woodford County. They moved to Anderson County in 1796 and were the parents of the following: 1) Maria, born 1798, married Dudley George. 2) Randol, III, born 1808, married Sarah Boggess. 3) Artemesia, born 1811, married James Ripy, who was one of the founders of the Ripy Brothers Distillery. 4) Sarah, born 1816, married John McDonald Walker. 5) Monroe, born 1826, married Vienna McMichaels. 6) Merit, married Jane Minter. 7) Lucretia, married Jeremiah [...]ey. Their son, James Monroe Posey was Judge of [...]derson County.

William - BD unknown, settled in Jennings, In[...]na.

Nancy - BD unknown, married ? Patterson and [...]ved to Fayette County.

Elizabeth - born 1774, married David Egbert.

Sarah "Sally" - BD unknown, married James Frazier.

Mary "Fannie" - BD unknown, married Vincent Boggess.

The Walker's, Frazier's and Boggess' owned property which ran from the present Walker Lane to the Kentucky River. There is an old Boggess Cemetery on Lock Lane. There is a Frazier cemetery and two Walker cemeteries on Hwy 62 between Lawrenceburg and the Kentucky River.

Walker's, Scott's, Frazier's, Boggess' and Egbert's were all members of the Old Salt River Baptist Church shortly after it was formed in 1798.

During the Civil War, the Walker farm was inhabited by Leonidas "Lon" Walker and his wife, Susan. Lon was a son of Randol and Malinda. The farm is close to the Kentucky River, at what was then one of the easiest places to cross. Family legend has it that troops from both North and the South camped on their property many times, taking everything. One of the last armies that came through were told that there was nothing left. The women were baking bread, which the soldiers took from the oven. Legend also has it that upon being pressured to join the Army, Lon paid a slave $5.00 to go in his behalf. This was not an uncommon practice. *Submitted By: Pat Walker.*

RANDOLPH "OLD RANDOL" WALKER ,

was born on September 15, 1741 in Richmond Co., VA, the son of John and Alice Walker. He married Elizabeth "Betsy" Harris. They settled in Woodford County, VA, where they purchased property in 1790, two years before Kentucky became a state. They had seven children: John (below); Randol, Jr. (born March 14, 1777 - Virginia) married Mary "Polly" Hoblet, daughter of Michael and Catherine Hoblet) Eight children; William (married Rebecca Gill); Nancy (married ? Patterson); Elizabeth (born May 21, 1774 - Virginia) married David Egbert; Sarah "Sally" (married James Frazier); and Mary Frances "Fannie" (married Vincent Boggess). Betsy died sometime between the years of 1796 - 1801. Randolph then remarried to Lucy Haydon, the widow of John Haydon. Randolph died in 1822 in Jessamine County, KY. He was a deacon at Mt. Pleasant Baptist Church in Jessamine County.

John Walker was born on January 13, 1766 in Virginia. He married Elizabeth "Betsy" Stott on January 10, 1792 in Woodford County, KY. They had ten children: Jordan H. (1792 - 1862) married Susan A. Burrus; Randolph (below); Lucinda (born 1794) married 1st Hardin Haynes; Katherine (married 1st James Mizner in 1821, 2nd Spencer Tinsley in 1836; Hariett (married Joseph Mizner in 1825); Arameus (married David George); Elizabeth; John Jr. (1805 - 1837); James S. (1803 - 1852) married 1st Malinda ?, 2nd Florinda Skelton; and Lewis (married 1st ?, 2nd Mary Sherwood). John Walker, Sr. was sheriff of Franklin County in 1824 and died in a cholera epidemic on June 12, 1833 in Anderson County.

Randolph "Randol" Walker (1796 - 1863) married 1st Malinda Mizner (1802 - 1832), daughter of John and Linda Mizner, on January 31, 1822 in Franklin Co., KY. They had five children: John McDonald (1822 - 1877) married Sarah Walker; Elizabeth (1825 - 1849) married William F. Leathers; William Wallace (1826 - 1833); Amanda (1829 - 1854); and Leonidas (below). Randol married his 2nd wife, Elizabeth "Eliza" Matthews, the daughter of Jeremiah and Katherine Matthews, on December 16, 1834. They had eight children: Aldridge J. (born 1836); William

L. (born 1838) married Nancy J. ? - four children; Mortimer (born 1838) married Laura McClanahan - two children; Susan M. (1841 - 1915) married George W. Scott - four children; Jeremiah M. (1842 - 1855); Henry Harrison (1847 - 1883) married Alice Edwards - four children; George Washington (1848 - 1909) married Ellen Ripy; and Randol. Randol, Sr. served as Deputy Sheriff of Anderson County in 1833, 1835, 1837, 1839, and 1841. He represented the county in the State Legislature in 1846.

Leonidas Walker (1831 - 1902) married Susan Mary Young, daughter of Berry and Martha Young, on March 26, 1857. They had 14 children: Mary Elizabeth (1859 - 1877) unmarried; John W. (1861 - 1908) married Katie Marshal; Martha Jane (1862 - 1935) unmarried; Buddy (1863 - 1864); Lew Ella (1864 - 1865); James Derry (1866 - 1938) married Lulie Belle Pile; twins, Sarah Emma (1867 - 1942) unmarried and Ezra Randol (1867 - ?) married Pearl Mountjoy; Oscar Young (1870 - 1940) married Lee Catlett; Lucy Ellen (1871 - 1949) unmarried; twins, Lister (1873 - 1930) unmarried and Laura (1873 - ?) unmarried; Susie Lou (1875 -?) unmarried; and George Scott (1877 - ?) unmarried. All of those who remained unmarried lived on the farm which belonged to the Walkers from pioneer days until the death of George Scott Walker in 1952. *Submitted By: Jane Walker Wyatt Puhr.*

FRANK G. WALLS,

born April 1876, son of John William Walls and Mary Ann Yocum, married in Anderson County, KY on 17 April 1892 to Perlina Ann Mobley, born 16 June 1872 in Anderson County, daughter of Edmond Mobley and Martha Ann Kays, and a sister to Stuart Allen Mobley. Frank bought the family farm from his father, shortly before the latter's death, and persued farming most of his life. He died in Jefferson County, KY on 20 November, 1936, and was buried in the Antioch Christian Church Cemetery, near his father. Perlina died 22 Feb 1933 in Anderson County, and was buried in the Fairview Christian Church Cemetery in Washington County. Eight children, all born in Anderson County:

1) Jasper Newton Walls, born 15 March 1893, married 3 October 1912 in Anderson County, to Annie Jane Waldridge, born 24 September 1894 in Anderson County, daughter of Benjamin Riley Waldridge and Lucy Frances Barnett. He died in Jefferson County, KY on 28 April 1952, and was buried in the King's Baptist Church Cemetery in Bullitt County. Ten children: Arthur V.; Martha F.; Prentice B.; Raymond C.; Hubert R.; Alma E. P.; Harry B.; Homer S.; William T.C.; and Kathryn J.

Frank G. Walls, Perlina Ann Mobley Walls, and their first five surviving children - 1907 -08.

2) Bessie May Walls, born 2 February 1895, married 12 October 1913 in Anderson County, to Erastus Wells, born 25 May 1888, died 1970, son of Thomas Wells and Annie Darnaly. Bessie died in Anderson County on 12 September 1978. She and her husband are buried in the Lawrenceburg Cemetery. Eleven children: Velma; Clinton; Clifton; Ruby A.; Sally; Orbey; Cletus; Dorothy; Curtis; Gertie; and Onita.

3) Mattie Dove Walls, born 3 March 1896, married in Anderson County on 4 January 1913 to Walter Lee Leathers, born 13 March 1895, son of William and

Nancy Leathers. She died in 1964 and Walter died in 1970, both are buried in the Fairview Christian Church Cemetery. Five children: Levi; Randle; Evelyn F.; Trecy; and Roland.

4) unknown child, possible twin, born and died before 1900 census.

5) unknown child, possible twin, born and died before 1900 census.

6) William Dudley Walls, born 26 May 1903, married Gertrude Hazelwood. He died in 1981 and was buried in Fairview. Two children: Pauline and William.

7) Margie Pearl Walls, born 6 December 1906, married 1) Lester Walls, son of Thomas S. Walls, and 2) George Henderson . She died in Jefferson County, KY and is buried in the Resthaven Memorial Park Cemetery. Several children by first husband, but only four survived: Christine; Juanita; Kenneth B.; and Lester, Jr.

8) Homer Green Walls, born 14 November 1909, married Sylvia Satterly. He is buried in the Jeffersontown Cemetery in Jefferson County, KY. Seven children: Helen; David M.: Virginia L.; Robert; Doyle; Jerry W.; and Susan. *Submitted By: William R. Walls.*

JOHN WILLIAM WALLS,

was born in Casey County, KY on 18 June 1826, a son of Elias Walls and his unknown first wife. He enrolled in Stanford, Lincoln County, KY on 21 May 1846 and served as a private in Captain Daughtery's Second Regiment of Kentucky Infantry in the Mexican War. He was discharged in New Orleans, Louisiana on 10 June 1847, returned to the Lincoln County area and married, on 10 July 1847, to Margaret Ann Yocum, born 25 April 1831, daughter of Henry Yocum III and Martha Ann Wells. Sometime within the next three years, John and Margaret moved to Washington County, KY and settled in the area that was given to Anderson County, before 1900, and has since been known as "The Cut-off" by some of the older residents. Margaret Ann Yocum Walls died 28 February 1859, of "unknown causes", and was buried in the Antioch Christian Church Cemetery in Washington County. John married second, in Mercer County, KY, on 21 January 1860, to Mary Ann Yocum, born 6 August 1841, also a daughter of Henry and Martha Yocum.

He enrolled at Camp Dick Robinson, in Garrard County, on 25 September 1861 and was mustered into the United States Army as a second Lieutenant on 2 January 1862 at Camp Harrod in Mercer County, where he was assigned to Captain Hannibal Downey's Company, the 19th Regiment of Kentucky Infantry, to serve in the Civil War. He was promoted to first Lieutenant on 12 August 1862 at Cumberland Gap, Tennessee, but due to ill health, he resigned and was discharged at Young's Point, Louisiana on 5 March 1863, before his unit took part in the famous "Battle of Vicksburg".

John William and Mary Ann Yocum Walls

On 1 January 1866, John bought 120 acres, on Beaver Creek, from W.T. Hedges and was engaged in farming the remainder of his long life. On 22 March 1894, he sold one-half acre, for $7.50, to the Anderson County School Board for the construction of a school house. The Kays School was erected on the half-acre. John sold several other small parcels of land to his son, Frank, shortly before his death. He died in Anderson County, KY on 19 April 1914, of "Senile Heart Failure", and was buried in the Antioch Christian Church Cemetery. Mary Ann Yocum Walls died 25 September 1913, of "General Dropsy" and was buried in the same cemetery. There were three children from his first marriage and ten more from the second. Those 13 children were:

1) Margaret E. Walls, born 22 November 1849 - died 21 September 1919, married 4 September 1868 to John Yocum, Jr. and moved to Carroll County, KY.

2) Sarah J. Walls, born 31 January 1853, married the widower Colman R. Curtsinger and moved to Missouri.

3) Jincy Ann Walls, born 1854 - 55, married Arthur Humphrey and moved to Carroll County, KY.

4) John Henry Walls, born 1860, married 1st Mary E. Monroe, 2nd Racheal Catherine Baxter, 3rd Eliza ?. He died in Bullitt County, KY in 1925.

5) Rosey Ann Walls, born May 1864, married 16 March 1883 to James H. Yocum.

6) Margaret F. Walls, born 4 June 1866, married the widower William Alonzo Goodlett on 22 July 1888. She died 19 February 1901 and was buried in the Antioch Christian Church Cemetery.

7) Martin M. Walls, born 22 May 1868, died 28 February 1870, buried at Antioch.

8) William Grant Walls, born 1 August 1870, died of "Lock-Jaw" on 19 February 1888, buried at Antioch.

9) Thomas S. Walls, born 21 October 1872, married Eliza Leathers. He died in Spencer County, KY on 25 July 1903, of Typhoid, buried at Antioch.

10) Sophia Ann Walls, born 25 August 1874, married 7 May 1892, in Anderson County, KY on 12 January 1947, and was buried in the Valley Cemetery.

11) Frank G. Walls, born April 1876, married Perlina Ann Mobley.

12) Mary Love Walls, born 7 June 1880, married 4 September 1897 to Samuel J. Barnett. She died on 17 June 1951, in Anderson County, and was buried in the Antioch Christian Church Cemetery.

13) Lillie Dove Walls, born 14 April 1883, married 28 December 1896 to James L. Leathers. They moved to Illinois. *Submitted By: William R. Walls.*

NEWTON LAUREL WARD, and Emily Tranquil Miller Adams were married August 11, 1901.

Newt and Tran farmed and reared their family in the western section of Anderson County and adjoining Washington County near Fairview. For a short period of time they moved to DeKalb, Illinois, where they were employed. They returned to their farm in Anderson County, Kentucky and lived out their lives near Fairview. They are buried in the Mt. Freedom Baptist Church Cemetery in Washington County.

Newt and Tran were the parents of five daughters: Margaret Z., June 23, 1903 - June 30, 1903; Cora Elizabeth Annfield, March 17, 1905 - 1941, married Robert Darnell; Hester A., July 23, 1907 - resides in Lawrenceburg, KY., married Cecil Wells; Thelma Florence, August 2, 1910 - resides in Lawrenceburg, KY., married John T. Cox; and Alma Rhea, May 6, 1913 - 1985) married 1. Silva Stoner and 2. Dillard

Koger; and two sons: Woodrow Ward, April 14, 1918 - May 20, 1982, married Gertrude Cornish; and Bernice Edward Ward, September 19, 1921 - 1937, buried in Fairview Cemetery.

In addition to their own children, Newton and Tranquil reared two of their nieces - Francis Coleman Ward, August 12, 1901 - April 22, 1928, married Roscoe Peach; and Zorilla Margaret Ward, August 5, 1903 - January 22, 1978, married John Peach. Francis and Zorilla were the daughters of Tom Ward, March 4, 1879 - November 1, 1909 and Ophelia Adams, March 3, 1880 - January 1, 1905.

Newton Laurel Ward (October 25, 1881 - January 13, 1963) was the son of Newton Ward and Margaret Durr.

Newton's brothers and sisters included: Tom Ward (March 4, 1879 - November 1, 1909); Lee Ward, George, Tom, Jake, Addie (married Grover Rays) and Wrendy (married ? Mastin) and half - brothers, Jim and Bob Kyler.

Emily Tranquil Miller Adams (March 16, 1882 - February 28, 1962) was the daughter of Dr. Robert Adams and Zorilla Sims.

Tranquil's sisters were: Ophelia (March 3, 1880 - January 20, 1905) and Florence (married John Pinkston); and brothers: Bob Adams, Frank Adams, and Dr. Willie Adams. *Submitted By: Robert M. Thompson.*

JOHN RICHARD WARD, was born on 8-5-1863 in Anderson County and he died on 12-5-1935. He married Sarah Catherine Hume on 6-5-1888 in Anderson County. They were the parents of one son, John Worley Ward.

John Worley Ward was born on 10-22-1902 in Anderson County and he died on 11-14-1955 in Anderson County. He is buried in the Sand Spring Cemetery. He married Gracie Florine Gaines on 2-18-1928 in Anderson County. She was born on 7-21-1909 in Anderson County. She is the daughter of Thomas Samuel Hume and Virginia Hanks. John Worley and Gracie Florine Ward had four children: Sarah Frances (1928 - 1946) married Marvin Morris in 1946; Margaret Ann (1931 - 1938); George Allen; and Eldon Ray, born 1936, married Dorthy Jamison in June 1960 - three daughters - Anita, Jan, and Deana.

George Allen Ward was born on 11-14-1933 in Anderson County. He married Alice Louise Curtsinger on 4-13-1963 in Lexington, KY. She was born on 1-11-1946 in Jefferson County, KY. She is the daughter of Gilbert Curtsinger and Mattie Louise Masters Curtsinger. George Allen and Alice Louise Ward are the parents of four children: John Allen, born 1964, married Darlene Spencer in 1986 - one son, John Martin; Marvin Keith, born 1966; April Rose, born 1972; and Sara Louise, born 1974.

Gilbert Thomas Curtsinger was born on 4-22-1915 in Anderson County. He is the son of James Curtsinger and Calpurni Brown Curtsinger. Gilbert married Mattie Louise Masters on 12-2-1941. She was born on 8-17-1922 in Louisville, KY. She is the daughter of George Masters (1887 - 1957) and Ina Lee Buress (1889 - 1938). She has 11 brothers and sisters: James Franklin married Georgia - six children - Evelyn, Glenda, Jimmy, Frank, Leonard, and Regina; William Norman (1913 - 1985) married Alice - three children - Norman, Donald, and Virgil; Carl Edwards (1915 - 1981) married Marion - one daughter, Edith; Arthur Earnest (1917 - 1924); Dorthy Edna married J.L. Hatfield - two daughters - Ina Mae and Shirley; Chester Leroy (1921 - 1970) married Dorothy Walthrop - six children - Alma, Sandy, Robert, Terry, Loui, and Ricky; Victor J. (1925 - 1976) married Dorothy Warren - three children - Dennis, Mark, and Jannette; Rosie Lee (1930 - 1938); Eugene (1932 - 1981) married Lena Keith; and Ruth Gloria married Calvin Conover. Gilbert and Mattie Louise Curtsinger were the parents of six children: Alice Louise; George Allen (1948 - 1973); Gilbert Ray married Candy Teresa Hawkins - two children - Toby

and Gina; James Calvin married Jackie Stratton - two sons - Jeff and Jason; Daniel Lee married Rita Satterly - two children - Lee and Ashley; and Jerry Len married Rhonda Hawkins - two children - Alicia and Bryon. *Submitted By: Sara Ward.*

JULIA ANN CROSSFIELD WARE, the second daughter of Richard H. and Martha Crossfield, was born on 2-18-1849 near Fox Creek. Shortly after the close of the Civil War she married Henry Nathan Ware, a cousin of her stepmother, Elizabeth Ann Crossfield, on 12-3-1868. Henry Nathan Ware, a native of Garrard County, was a descendant of Kentucky pioneers, Dudley and Polly Ware, who are recorded as settlers in Lincoln County as early as 1787. Soon after their marriage they moved to Garrard County where they farmed during the next decade. They later moved to Lincoln County to a farm near Hall's Gap and then to the town of Rowland, near Stanford, Lincoln County where Henry engaged in real estates activities.

Eight children were born to this union as noted: Drusilla Sterling in 1869; Burton Squire in 1871; Susan Mary in 1873; Lillian Bell in 1875; Richard Henry in 1882; Charles Crossfield "C.C." in 1886; and Julia Ann on 12-12-1892. Charles Crossfield Ware became the most prominent of Henry and Julia's children. He received his higher academic training at Transylvania College and graduated from the College of the Bible at Lexington in 1907. After serving pastorates in Mississippi, Texas, Arkansas, Louisiana, and Kentucky, he became state secretary of the Christian Church of South Carolina and then missions secretary for the North Carolina Disciples of Christ at Winston Salem, N.C. for 37 years. He authored 19 published books. Of these books are "Life of Barton Warren Stone", 1932 and "Kentucky's Fox Creek", 1957. Henry Nathan Ware died in September 1928 and his wife, Julia Ann, died on 1-12-1913. Both are buried at Lebanon, KY. *Submitted By: James S. Pope.*

MARTHA BELLE CROSSFIELD WARE, the fourth daughter of Richard Henry and Martha Crossfield, was born on 3-13-1854. She married Squire Martin Ware (a cousin of her stepmother, Elizabeth) of Garrard County on 11-7-1875. They moved to Garrard County and remained there until 1878 when they moved to Montgomery County, Missouri with the family members of Squire's parents. By 1880, they were living near Moundville, Vernon County, MO and in 1883 moved to Crowley County, Kansas where they were near neighbors to the William H. and Susan Mary York family. In April 1889, Squire with his brother, Alexander A. Ware, made the "run" in the Oklahoma "opening". Both of the brothers "claimed" adjoining homesteads ten miles west of Stillwater in Payne County. That fall the family moved to Stillwater where they remained until 1902. Squire was elected one of the commissioners in Payne County in 1892. That same year he served as president of the first Payne County Fair. Squire and "Belle" had ten children as follows: Tilden H. (1876 - 1902); Harry C. (1878 - 1930); Maudie (1880 - 1949); Ada (1882 - 1960); Ernest (1884 - 1957); Roy Martin (1886 - 1935); Nancy Elizabeth (1888 - 1979); Glessie Belle (1890 - 1967); Ritchie C. (1895 - 1940); and Clifford R. (1898 - 1949). Belle Ware died of cancer on 8-13-1898 and was buried in the Stillwater Cemetery. In 1902, the remaining family moved to Gotebo, Kiowa County, Oklahoma Territory where most of the children reached adulthood. The third daughter, Nancy Elizabeth Ware, was probably the most prominent child of the Squire M. Ware family. She began her college training at the Christian College at Eugene, Oregon in 1911. After graduation, she was ordained a minister of that denomination and served in pastorates in Lincoln County, Nebraska. In 1926, she married Ransom Doolan, a carpenter, and some ten years afterwards they moved to Brighton, Colorado where she occupied the pulpit at the Christian Church. In 1974, the Doolans moved to Fullerton,

Orange County, California where she was quite active in establishing the Christian Church at that city. During her later years at that place she was lovingly referred to as the matriarch of the congregation. She died there at the age of 92 in 1979. Belle's husband, Squire, died at Cordell, Oklahoma on 3-22-1912 and was buried at that place. *Submitted by: James S. Pope.*

H. MARSHALL WARFORD,

was a lifelong resident of Anderson County. He was the oldest of 12 children born to Hollie W. Warford and Stella Overstreet Warford. His father was a farmer and in 1966, became County Judge of Anderson County for 14 years. He died 6-26-1986. His mother a homemaker with 12 children, lovingly teaching and bringing out each of their personalities.

Marshall graduated from Kavanaugh High School in 1942, after which he went to Kodiaka, Alaska, to help build the first air strip there. He served with the C. Bee's that were attached to the United States Navy. When he returned home from Alaska he went to work in the Dravo Shipyard in Wilmington, Delaware, there he met his wife to be Lenora (Billie) Stewart Warford, daughter of Mr. and Mrs. Lewis Stewart, Wilmington, Delaware. When the shipyard closed, Marshall and Billie returned to Lawrenceburg and made their home here.

Billie, worked as a nurse for Dr. R. N. Lawson for several years, also the Commonwealth of Kentucky in the Revenue Department. She also worked for the Anderson County Senior Citizens and later became self-employed.

Marshall and Billie have two daughters, Marsha Lewis Warford Proctor working for the State Fire Marshall's Office. She is married to J. Paul Proctor, living in Lawrenceburg with their two children, a daughter, Trish Lee Proctor - age 13, a son, Bryan Marshall Proctor - age 9.

Tammy Lee Warford Greer, their second daughter, married Paul D. Greer and is living in Lexington, Kentucky. She is a Registered Nurse at the Central Baptist hospital. They had two children, a son, Terrence Alan Greer - age 5, a daughter, Marissa Daniella Greer - age 2.

Marshall worked for Fox Creek R.E.C.C. for 28 years, Superintendent of the Old Masons Home, Shelbyville, Kentucky, and served our Commonwealth as manager of the Bluegrass Parkway until his death.

Marshall was a faithful member of Claylick Methodist Church, served as Chairman of the Board and teacher of the Men's Class. He was also a very active member in the community. He served as Treasurer of the Anderson County Public Library, also the Anderson County Public Library Construction Corporation. He was a Mason for 30 years, a member of the Rotary Club, Assistant Fire Chief of the Voluntary Fire Department, President of Kavanaugh High School Association and State Electrical Inspector.

Marshall, a man dedicated to God, his family, and friends is missed. He died 5-29-1980. *Submitted By: Billie Warford.*

HOLLIE WITHERSPOON WARFORD,

was born 11-15-1901 to John L. and Maude Doak Warford, on the Gaines farm, Highway 44 near Lawrenceburg. His father was a bricklayer and a farmer, who while Hollie was young worked for a contractor in Cincinnati. When Hollie was four his mother died. Hollie, his sister, Katie, and a brother, Herman, were placed in a Catholic Orphanage in Cincinnati. A brother, Andrew, died as infant.

Later, his father and the children returned to Anderson County to live. As a youngster, Hollie lived on the Jim Head, Frank Searcy and Ben Hawkins farms. He helped with the farm work, and learned masonry from his father. He attended Stingy School near Gilbert's Creek and the Short School on McCoun's Ferry in Mercer County.

While growing up, three special women helped raise Hollie and were like "mothers" to him. They were Mrs. Nan Hawkins, Mrs. Gert Searcy, and Mrs. Matt Bond Wiley.

As a teenager, Hollie moved to the farm of Mrs. M. B. Overstreet below Claylick Church. There, he met Stella Gertrude, Mrs. Overstreet's granddaughter. Stella was born 11-15-1906, the daughter of William Thomas and Margaret Bixler Overstreet. A sister, Ella Belle (Mrs. Luther Baxter) also lives in Lawrenceburg. Stella attended Hebron School near McCall's Spring.

Hollie and Stella Warford

Hollie and Stella were married 1-3-1923. They bought a place near Claylick, and began raising their family. Their children were: Marshall, Hollie Jr., David, Lawrence, John, Jane, Robert, Nancy, Alton, and Walter. Two sons, Allen and Norman, died as infants. 21 grandchildren, 15 great-grandchildren, two step-grandchildren, four step-greatgrandchildren, and many in laws complete the family.

In addition to farming, Hollie worked on construction of Route 127 through Anderson County and did masonry work. He owned and operated a truck for many years, hauling cattle, wheat, and tobacco to markets, and bringing back hogs and goods to local businesses.

During the 1960's, he was Compliance Officer for the State Department of Transportation.

The Democratic Party also benefited from Hollie's hard work. He was elected Magistrate of the 1st District for eight years, 1945 - 1953. He served as Anderson County Democratic Chairman for many years, led political campaigns, and helped many local people obtain state employment.

Governor Edward T. Breathitt appointed Hollie to fill the unexpired term of John Birdwhistell as County Judge. Hollie took the oath January 1, 1966 at the age of 64. The voters accepted his campaign pledge that he was "Always ready to serve the people of Anderson County" and he was elected in 1967, re-elected in 1969, 1973, and in 1977 as County Judge-Executive.

Hollie was a member of the Claylick United Methodist Church where he served on the board and was in the Methodist Men. Stella is also a member of Claylick, a member of the board and W.S.C.S. organization.

Hollie was active in Anderson Lodge No. 90 F. and A.M., serving many years as Tiler, and was a 50 year Mason. He was a member of the Lions Club, holding various offices, and being presented a Lifetime Membership in 1980. He was a member and director of the Anderson County Farm Bureau, and longtime "burgoo maker." Hollie was a charter member of the Stringtown Ruritan Club, and was a board member of the Hebron Cemetery.

In the years 1982 - 1986, Hollie was an employee of the Kentucky legislature during regular and special sessions. They and Anderson County lost a dear friend when Hollie died at the age of 84 on June 26, 1986.

BEN WASHINGTON,

the son of Lewis and Molly Washington, was born in Virginia. He married Martha McCauly of Lawrenceburg. She was the daughter of Bill and Mary McCauly. Ben and Martha were the parents of three children: Mat married Lizzie Creech; Lewis (below); and Maebell married Steve Brown.

Lewis Washington was born on 11-3-1888 in Alton, KY. He married Lucille Pleasant. She was born on 12-23-1911 in Anderson County. She is the daughter of the late Eddie Pleasant and Genevia Brown Pleasant. Lewis and Lucille had four children: Ann, born 1936; Pearl, born 1937, married Thomas Allen - one daughter, Melissa, who married Melvin Yates (They have one daughter, Katianna Yates.); Rose, born 1941, married Merle Cunningham, Sr. - four children - Merle Jr., Stacie, Jeneen, and Elizabeth; and Geneva, born 1949, married Harold Howard - one daughter, Alisha. Lewis Washington died on 7-1-1974 in Frankfort, KY.

Eddie Pleasant, the son of Dudly Pleasant and Rosie Hayden Pleasant, was born on 1-24-1883 in Ninevah, KY. He married Genevia Brown. She was born on 1-23-1886 in Ninevah. She was the daughter of Ben Brown and Mattie Lytle Brown. Eddie and Genevia were the parents of 14 children: George, born 1905, married Jenetta Rice - one daughter, Mildred Ann; Matthew Pleasant, born 1907, married Lillian - one son, John Kelly; Emma Rose (1909 - 1984) married Lubert Booker; Eddie Sterling (born and died 1909); Lucille; Levegia, born 1913; Hubert, born 1915, married Evelyn - one child, Ollie; Cornelius (1919 -1988) married Rose - two children, Cornelius Jr. and Lolitha; Melvin (1923 - 1968) married 1st Lucille, 2nd Maggie - four children - Milton, Melvin, Novis and Maggie; Sterling, born 1924, married Alma - one daughter, Brenda; Darnell, born 1925, married 1st Ollie; 2nd Flora Anna - seven children - Ronald, Barbara Ann, Ollie, Stephanie, Steven, ? Georgetta, and Darnell Jr.; Vernice, born 1927, married Lambert Bruce - two children - Sara and Jonny; Kenneth, born 1929, married Joyce - two sons, Kenneth and Matthew; and Benjamin (1921 - 1924). *Submitted By: Jeneen Cunningham*

WILLIAM JESSE WATERFILL

had a large family to provide for. During the Civil War, he elected to stay home as a Captain in the Home Guard. (Several Waterfills lost their lives or were injured fighting for the South.) After the War, William Jesse was referred to as Captain Waterfill by members of his family and the community.

In 1885, Captain Waterfill built this home for his family on 107 acres of land one mile east of Lawrenceburg on what is now Versailles Road. This brick house had nine rooms, two baths, linen closets, and a large, lovely attic, with a ceiling peak of 18 feet. The children and grandchildren used the attic as a recreation room for roller skating, playing pool, dress-up, and so on. This house is presently being restored by Bill May and his wife for their home. Mr. May is a professional restorer of older homes, usually for rental properties, but not in this case.

Captain Waterfill was a businessman of many talents. He owned a store in Tyrone. He was a dealer in "Drygoods, Groceries, Hardware, Saddlery, Harness, Coal and Lime." A bill dated 1891 showed that he also dealt in lumber and millwork. He built many houses along Waterfill Avenue in Lawrenceburg for rental purposes. His daughter-in-law, Sadie Clay Waterfill, complained that no sooner than she and her husband, Will, settled in one of these houses, it was sold, and they had to move into another.

Of course, the lumber and millwork were used to build the Captain's home, and the bricks were made "on the place." He built a wharfhouse on the river at Tyrone and was considered "one of Tyrone's best friends."

In 1881, Captain Waterfill, operating with the Waterfill-Dowling Co. and with T.B. Ripy as a partner, built the Clover Bottom Distillery at Tyrone. This distillery, which began operation in 1882, was also known as the Anderson County Distilling Company and the Pilgramage Distilling Company. It had the Register Number 418. Another large distillery at Tyrone was the T. B. Ripy Distillery Company, Register No. 112. In 1885, four years after No. 418 was built, T. B. Ripy, and original partner, bought out Waterfill and Dowling. (It later became Kentucky Distilleries and Warehouse Company when it was sold in 1899.)

The Waterfill House

The Waterfills had long been in the distilling business. Waterfill and Frazier whiskey, which was on the market until 1972, had a label that gave the date "since 1810". The Waterfills apparently began distilling in Tyrone in the early 1800's. There were some 50 small distilleries in Anderson County between 1817 and 1870, when outside interests began to move in.

If a still could produce a gallon of whiskey a day, people called it a distillery. The Waterfill-Frazier Distillery is the mid to late 1800's involved two Fraziers, Robert and Grant, and three Waterfills, including Captain Waterfill.

After the Clover Bottom Distillery was sold to T. B. Ripy in 1885, Mr. Dowling bought the Waterfill-Frazier Distillery. Waterfill-Frazier whiskey continued to be made, even after the distillery was moved to Mexico in 1917 to escape the Prohibition years. After Prohibition, the distillery was moved up into Texas where they continued producing Waterfill-Frazier whiskey. It was also made in Bardstown, Ky by several different distilling companies even through the Prohibition years. The labels read "made with pure spring water for medicinal purposes." Of course, it could only be bought when prescribed by a doctor, and it was priced accordingly.

Another Waterfill, James Monroe Waterfill, was involved with the T.L.S. Brown and Sons Inc. Distillery built at Tyrone in 1890. The Getz Whiskey Museum in Bardstown has a large — 5 feet by 8 feet — blow-up of a picture of this distillery in the 1900's.

In 1890, Captain Waterfill bought 50 acres of land on the Kentucky River near Panther Rock, where a "magnificent spring gushes from beneath the rock." This was purchased with the expectation of building and operating another distillery there.

Panther Rock is located down the Harry Wise Road . In 1773, so the story goes, Elijah Scearce, a hunter and trapper out of Fort Harrod, was saved from death at the hands of Indian Chief Arrowhead by a panther, who disposed of the chief in the middle of the night. The next morning, Mr. Scearce found Chief Arrowhead dead at the base of the rock and buried him there. Hence - "Panther Rock."

In 1891 - 1892, however, Captain Waterfill became involved with W.A. Bottom, of the Bottom and Gee Lumber Company of Tyrone, in the building of the Warbott Hotel and Opera House on Main Street in Lawrenceburg. (The name Warbott is a combination of Waterfill and Bottom.)

The Opera House seated 560 on the main floor and 300 in the gallery and cost $37,000.00 to build. Opening performance was 5-3-1892. Captain Waterfill died four months later on 10-28-1892. The Warbott Hotel and Opera House burned down in 1898. So, Captain Waterfill did not get his distillery built on Panther Rock. All but ten acres of that land was sold. That remaining ten belongs to his great-granddaughter.

Captain Waterfill's widow, Louisa Adeline Waterfill, continued to make a home for her children and grandchildren during the remaining 32 years of her life. She also offered room and board to Anderson County boys, in exchange for chores around the place. The boys wanted to be closer to Lawrenceburg to complete their educations at Kavanaugh High School. They were known by his family as "Grandma's Boys" and included Ezra Sparrow, Manson Morgan and Ollie Brown.

"Grandma" Waterfill died in 1923, and is buried alongside her husband, Captain Waterfill, in the Lawrenceburg Cemetery. *Submitted By: Mary Jane Griffith.*

WILLIAM JESSE WATERFILL, was the grandson of David and Mary Carter Waterfill. Louisa Adeline Waterfill was the daughter of John McGinnis (8-7-1790 - 1-12-1858) and Sally Riley (3-26-1799 - 10-29-1840).

John and Sally McGinnis were married on 7-13-1815. These families were among the pioneer families who were living in Anderson County prior to 1812. The population of Anderson County consisted of approximately 300 sturdy people at that time.

On the Fourth of July in 1860, Louisa Adeline McGinnis and William Jesse Waterfill were married. Jesse Waterfill had been born on 12-1-1837, 28 days before his future bride was born, 12-29-1837. They were both 23 years old on their wedding day.

Mr. and Mrs. Waterfill became the parents of the following eight children: Genetta C. Waterfill (5-22-1861 / 11-11-1861); Alice V. Waterfill (4-2-1863 / 1948); Erminore P. Waterfill (4-16-1868 / 5-1-1945); Sallie B. Waterfill (5-2-1871 / 3-12-1959); James Bryan "Jim" Waterfill (1874 / 2-12-1953); Thomas Edward "Ed" Waterfill (1-11-1878 / 12-2-1939); and Pearl Waterfill (1880 / 1975).

Jesse Waterfill and Louise Adeline McGinnis Waterfill

Their first surviving child, Alice V. Waterfill, graduated from Daughters College in Danville (now the Beaumont Inn). She married Dr. Charles A Leathers. Dr. Leathers was an 1879 graduate of K.M.I., and in 1882, the medical school of the University of Louisville. Dr. Leathers gave up most of his medical practice after he bought the Lawrenceburg Drug Co. in 1902. In 1905, he was elected president of the State Pharmaceutical Association. In 1907, he purchased the first privately owned automobile in Anderson County. Dr. Leathers died in 1923.

Dr. and Mrs. Leathers had one child, Ruby Leathers, born in 1855. Ruby married A. C. Williams, Jr. Mr. Williams was associated with his father-in-law in the Lawrenceburg Drug Co.

The family lived on Main Street across from the drug company. Alice wrote a great deal of poetry for all occasions. Many of her poems were published in the local paper and the Courier-Journal. Ruby worked in Trent's Department Store for many years. She enjoyed people, playing bridge and life in general. Ruby died 2-2-1961.

The second surviving child (two others had died in infancy) was John William "Will" Waterfill. In 1893, Will married Sadie Clay, who was born in Paris, KY in 1872, the daughter of Elizabeth Forman and Isaac Cunningham Clay. Will and Sadie had three children.

The first was Robert William Waterfill, born 5-18-1897. Robert was a 2nd Lt. in the Army and served in France during World War I. He earned a degree in mechanical engineering from the University of Kentucky in 1921. After that, he moved to New York City where he worked for all but the last 10 years of his life.

He was a pioneer in the field of air conditioning, working first with Carrier Air Conditioning Corp. and then with Buensod-Stacy Air conditioning Corp. He was a vice-president of both of these firms. They installed air conditioning in such buildings as the Rockefeller Center and the White House, m e theaters and department stores.

Robert married Eleanor Sparton in 1946. They had two children, Betty Carol, born in 1952, and Dorothy Jane, born in 1957. The family moved to Charlotte, North Carolina, in 1961, where Robert worked as a consultant with the Buensod Division of Aeronic Corporation. During those years, he received a Fellow Award from the American Air Conditioner Society for his contribution to the field of air conditioning. Robert died 3-20-1971.

Their daughter, Betty, married Steve Stone in 1980. They live with their two young sons in Salisburg, North Carolina, where Steve is a controller for a large food chain. Betty teaches adult English Classes. The other daughter, Dorothy, still lives in Charlotte, where she works as a public relations director for a local business.

Will and Sadie's second child was Elizabeth Clay Waterfill, born 7-25-1898. After attending Hamilton College in Lexington, Elizabeth married James Carroll Pickett, a farmer in Finchville, Ky, near Shelbyville. Their son, James Carroll Pickett, Jr., was born in 1924. Jim attended Swanee Military Academy in Tennessee, before graduating from the Finchville High School in 1942. During World War II, he served as the pilot of a B-24 bomber over Germany. During this period he was married to Mary Harmon.

Jim and Mary had two sons, Jamie and John. Jamie is a teacher-writer who lives in Los Angeles, Ca. John is a farmer-carpenter living on the family farm with his family.

In 1962, Jim married Avonelle Glowatch after his divorce from Mary. He was head of the Kentucky Air National Guard in Frankfort before becoming associated with the L. and N. Railroad Company in Louisville as a pilot. Later, he became a vice-president of the L. and N. Railroad Industrial and Real Estate Company in Richmond, Virginia. He retired to Finchville in 1986, where he is engaged in farming and real estate.

Elizabeth Waterfill Pickett still lives in Finchville. She is 92 years old.

The youngest child of Will and Sadie is Mary Louise Waterfill, born on 9-28-1900. After attending Oxford College in Miami, Ohio, and Eastern State Teachers College in Richmond, KY, Mary Louise married Elbridge Broaddus Noland, a farmer in Richmond. Elbridge later worked as the cashier at Easter Kentucky University in Richmond.

Mary Louise and Elbridge had one child, Mary Jane Noland, born 10-5-1929. After graduating from the University of Kentucky in 1951, Mary Jane married Thomas Eli Baldwin, III, a farmer in Richmond. Tom graduated from Mrs. Kavanaugh's Preparatory School in Lawrenceburg in 1942. After attending Princeton University for a year, he served in the Army in Europe during World War II. He graduated from the University of Kentucky in 1951. Tom died of cancer on 9-6-1956.

Mary Jane married Dr. Richard M. Griffith in 1959. Dr. Griffith died of injuries suffered in an automobile accident in 1969. Their one child, David Harris Griffith, was born in 1965. David, a recent graduate of the University of Kentucky now lives with his mother in Lexington. Mary Louise Waterfill Noland died 12-6-1954. Elbridge Broaddus Noland died 7-23-1973.

In 1908, Will and Sadie, their children, his sister

Sallie, her family, his father-in-law "Grandpa" Clay and a young cousin "John Willie" Waterfill homesteaded in Nara Visa, New Mexico. Although the others soon returned to Lawrenceburg, the Will Waterfills remained there until 1912. In 1928, Will and Sadie lived for a year in Homestead, Florida - the year a hurricane killed 600 residents of Miami. Upon their return to Lawrenceburg, they lived on Woodford Street until his death in 1945. Sadie Waterfill died in Louisville, KY in 1962.

The Jesse Waterfill's third child, Sallie, was born in 1871. She married Bryon Allin of Harrodsburg. They had one child, Jesse Allin. Jessie studied piano at the Boston Conservatory of music and taught piano in Lawrenceburg before attending business school. She worked as a secretary for the superintendent of the Ormsby Village Orphanage at Anchorage, KY for many years. Her mother, Sallie, suffered from Parkinson's disease for many years, and Jessie cared for her while continuing her job. Jessie was a talented amateur photographer and won a number of awards. Sallie Waterfill Allin died in 1959. Jessie Allin died at Anchorage in 1964.

The Waterfill's fourth child, James Bryon Waterfill, married Sallie Searcy. They lived across Woodford Street from Will and Sadie Waterfill. They had no children, although Sallie had three children from a previous marriage. These two Waterfill brothers, Will and Jim, operated a very successful dry goods and grocery store on Main Street in Lawrenceburg in the late 1800's and 1900's. It was known as The Waterfilll Brothers Company. Mr. Florian Bond was one of the incorporators of this company. He was married to the Waterfill brothers' sister, Pearl.

After the Waterfills closed their store, Jim became a bookkeeper for the old Citizens Bank, later Citizens and Union Bank of Lawrenceburg. He also worked as a bookkeeper for a Frankfort Distillery. Jim Waterfill died in 1961.

The fifth child was Thomas Edward Waterfill. He married Ethel Allen. They had five children — Frances, who married Lem Searcy; Dorothy Gorman; Malcom; Allen, unmarried; and Martha Jean, who married Paul Harris. Ed Waterfill's granddaughter (Frances's daughter), Bonnie Vineiquerra, lives in Melbourne, Florida, with her husband, Louis. Ed was a bookkeeper who worked in Lawrenceburg, Paris and later Indianapolis, Indiana. Ed Waterfill died on 12-2-1939.

The last child of Jesse and Louisa Waterfill was Pearl Waterfill. She married Florian Bond, and after the Waterfill Bros. Company was closed, they moved to Muskogee, Oklahoma, where Florian owned and operated a drugstore for many years. The Bonds had one son, John, who graduated from the University of Oklahoma. He became a partner in the Manhattan Construction Company of Muskogee. The Manhattan Company constructed buildings in many states, including the Corning Glass Works in Danville, KY and the Western Kentucky University Coliseum in Richmond, KY. When John Bond retired, he and his wife, Marium, moved to Little Rock, Arkansas. His mother, Pearl Waterfill Bond, moved there with them. Pearl died there in 1975. John Bond died in 1985. His second wife, Frances, lives in Little Rock. He had no children.

William Jesse and Louisa Adeline Waterfill are buried in a beautiful lot marked by a tall obelisk at the back of the Lawrenceburg Cemetery. Along with them are buried four of their children, Alice, Will, Sadie, and Jim and their spouses, and five grandchildren, Ruby Leathers, Jessie Allin, Robert Waterfill, Martha Harris, and Allen Waterfill. James Carroll Pickett, Sr., the husband of Elizabeth Waterfill Pickett, is also buried there. *Submitted By: Mary Jane Griffith.*

WATERFILL'S have been in the Anderson County area for over 150 years. David and Mary Carter Waterfill were living in Anderson County prior to 1812 on land referred to as "The Waterfill Plantation". They had four children: Pamala, Jesse, Janetta, and David.

Mary Carter Waterfill was apparently widowed young as permission for Jesse's marriage in 1833 was given by his mother, and not his father.

In 1843, Mary sold 77 acres of her land to Turner Hanks, reserving the Salt River Meeting House and an acre of attached land for a cemetery. In 1848, her will divided the remaining holdings between her four children and Jesse (1813 - 1905) got the Plantation where he was residing.

Jesse and his wife, Renor Route (daughter of William Route and Malinda Parker) had ten children: Malinda (married John Hyatt); Jane (married Daniel M. Yocum); Sarah Francis (married Jim Martin); Martha (married John Hammond); John (died in the Civil War); William (died in the Civil War); James Monroe (married Floris Allen and then Susie Highbarger); Permelia (married John Utterback); David (married Sylvia Yocum); and Beatrice (married Richard Tipton). The eight oldest children are listed in the 1850 census for Anderson County.

The youngest son, David, and his wife, Sylvia Yocum, had ten children. Daniel Mitchell Waterfill was next to the youngest.

Dan and Nora Mizner Waterfill and the living children in 1939.

Daniel Mitchell married Nora Mizner, the great granddaughter of Joseph Mizner and daughter of Joseph Leslie Mizner. The eldest Joseph Mizner and his brothers, John, James, and Jeremiah, were prominent citizens of Anderson County in the early 1800's. they all used the simple signature: J. Mizner.

Daniel and Nora had 11 children: Flora Murl (married Donald Hill and then Marvin Klein); David Leslie (married Alowese Thomas); Ruth Ellen; Martha Mona (married Earl Sellers); Daniel Mitchell Jr.; Sylvia Frances (married Edward Willis); Everett Bell (died in childhood); Virginia Pauline (married Joseph Lamkin); Billy Mizner (died in childhood); Jane Marilyn; and Jerry Ethan (married Joy Alexander and then Elizabeth Scott).

Everett and Billy are buried in the old churchyard at Salt River Baptist Church along with Jesse and other early Waterfill pioneers of Anderson County. Luella Perry and Geneva Hoskins, two granddaughters of David, still live in Lawrenceburg. James M. Waterfill, the only living grandson of Jesse, lives in McBrayer. *Submitted By: Martha Waterfill Sellers.*

EDMUND (1783 - 1859) AND ALPHA LANE WATTS,

came to Kentucky from Virginia with their parents around 1785 - 1788. It is thought that he might have been the son of John Watts who was on a Woodford County tax list in March, 1970. The Watts settled on Benson Creek. Their farm consisted of 285 acres in the 1840's and at one time, they owned at least 11 slaves. Alpha survived her husband. She appears in the Anderson County Census of 1860 with property worth $8,000. It is assumed that Edmund and Alpha Watts were buried in Anderson County.

Edmund's son, Buford (1805 - 1876), married Martha Young. Buford and his wife owned land near Benson Creek. Part of this land may have been given to him by his father, Edmund. It is thought that he and his wife are buried in the Watts Cemetery on the former Wesley T. Watts farm in Anderson County.

The present owner of this land states that he has heard there are two family cemeteries on his land, but he has never located the older one.

Wesley T. (1842 - 1912), son of Buford Watts, was married to Nannie J. Kurtz. He was crippled and held prisoner of war while serving in the Confederate Army. Wesley T. and his wife owned a farm on Benson Creek and raised their family there. He and his wife are buried in the Watts family cemetery on the farm.

Clarence Edward Watts (1873 - 1954), son of Wesley T., was a schoolteacher and farmer who also served a term as Anderson County Coroner. Clarence and his wife, Effie Gray, set up housekeeping on Benson Creek on the Watts family farm in 1895 living in the house known as the "Morning Place". They later bought land and built a house on Benson Creek about three miles from the "Homeplace". Several years later, they moved back to the "homeplace". They moved from there to Alton Station. A story was handed down to Clarence of someone being killed by an Indian and then buried under an oak tree on the Watts farm so he couldn't be scalped.

C. E. Watts was the father of nine children: Verne O., who was stationed in Russia during World War I; Marion Rupert, who also served during World War I; Thelma Glynn, schoolteacher, (Mrs. R. G. Lee); Gladys Blanche (Mrs. June Maddox); Enid, schoolteacher (Mrs. Albert McCourt); Clarice (Mrs. Elmer Maddox); Wilbur; Lillian May (Mrs. Ralph Botkins); and John Wesley, who was employed by the Federal Government. *Submitted By: Enid Watts.*

ROBERT AND ELBERTA WEST,

Elberta was born in Mercer County, but moved to Anderson County at the age of one. The daughter of the Late Clarence and Eva Houchins Chapman, she had one brother Gilman Chapman (deceased) and two sisters, Mrs. Vernon (Lena) Hostetter of Mt. Holly, North Carolina and Mrs. Harold (Floradell) Cunningham of Anderson County.

Robert, the son of the later Robert and Annie Martin West, was born at Clifton and moved to Dawson Ferry Road at the age of 9. He has three brothers, Earl of Louisville, Joe of Smithfield, and Elzie of Anderson County; and five sisters, Mrs. Harold (Nora) Knight of Dalton, Georgia, Mrs. Chester (Rose) Sutherland of Elizabeth, Indiana, Mrs. Earl (Genevieve) Gregory, Mrs. Stanley (Frances) Phillips, and Mrs. Harold (Leona) Flynn of Anderson County.

Robert and Elberta were married on March 31, 1934 by W. D. Moore at his home in Ripyville.

Robert and Elberta West

Robert was a farmer until a few years ago, and they have lived on the Harry Wise Road for the past 45 years.

Robert and Elberta are the parents of three children: Thomas lives in Lancaster and is married to Ann Snyder and has three children, Marty of Ohio, Rodney of Danville, and Michele of Lancaster. He has one grandchild, Arron Culley West of Danville; Myrtle Ann lives in Anderson County and is married to Carl Hawkins. They have three children, Mrs. James (Sandra) Ritchey, Brent and Darren Hawkins and one grandchild, Mary Ann Ritchey, all of Anderson County; and Delbert lives in Burgin and is married to Jane Barker and has one son, Delbert Ashley West of Frankfort.

The Wests are members of the Sand Spring Baptist Church.

WESLEY OLIVER WHITE

WESLEY OLIVER WHITE was born on 4-30-1875 in Anderson County. He married Margaret White. She was born on 9-8-1879 in Anderson County. They were the parents of five children: Joseph T. White (died September 1981) married Pauleen Krutsinger; Constance L. White (died 4-27-1977) married Ben R. Bond; Cecil Wesley White (below); Deulah Blanche White married Clifford Ernst; and Waller White married Norma White.

Cecil Wesley White was born on 5-12-1909 in Tyrone. He married Lalah Gillis on 9-8-1940. She was born on 10-11-1919 in Fayette County, KY. She is the daughter of Holly Hugh Gillis and Nancy Ellen Royalty Gillis. They had three children: Bobby White married Freddy - one child; Nancy White married Mike Mathews - two children; and Connie White married 1st David Lee Holt - two children - married 2nd David Cottrell. Cecil White died on 7-21-1981 in Florida. Lalah White currently resides in Anderson County.

Holly Hugh Gillis married Nancy Ellen Royalty. She was born on 12-27-1884 in Washington County, KY. They were the parents of two daughters; Ollie Ellen Gillis, born 6-6-1918, married Frank Clegg; and Lalah Gillis White. *Submitted By: Dave Holt.*

WILLIAM STANLEY WHITE

WILLIAM STANLEY WHITE was born on 10-21-1927 in Anderson County. He is the son of Hugh William White (1887 - 1967 drowned in Salt River) and Eddie J. Boggess (1888 - 1953). He married Lucille Lancaster on 3-24-1951. She was born on 6-23-33 in Woodford County, the daughter of Emerson Burgess Lancaster (1902 - 1964) and Rosa Fox (1908 - 1986). They were the parents of three children: Larry Wayne (below); Ricky married Betty White - two children - Houston C. and Lee; and Donna married Tad Young - three daughters - LaShannon Dawn, Renee D., and Cecilia Young.

Larry Wayne White was born on 5-16-1952 in Versailles, KY. On 10-1-1971, Larry married Beverly Carleen Mefford. She was born on 2-26-1952 in Frankfort, KY. She is the daughter of Robert Paul Mefford Sr. and Dolores Evalee Walker. Beverly has one brother, Robert Paul Mefford Jr., who married Judy Ann Hutton Byrd. He has one son, Joshua Shane, and two step-sons, Derrick Hutton and Chad Byrd.

Larry Wayne and Beverly Carleen Mefford White are the proud parents of one daughter, Desiree Michelle, born at Woodford Memorial Hospital in Versailles on 5-4-1974. She currently attends Anderson County High School. *Submitted By: Desiree White.*

RICHARD THOMAS WHITAKER

RICHARD THOMAS WHITAKER, the son of Thomas Jefferson Whitaker and Anna Pauline Ford Whitaker, was born on 8-12-1951 in Shelbyville, Kentucky. Richard has one brother, Jeff, who married Robin Bohanon.

On 4-11-1970, Richard married Beverly Jean Meeks in Shelbyville. She was born on 5-20-1948 in Shelbyville. She is the daughter of James Rogers Meeks and Virginia Jones Meeks. Beverly has a brother and a sister: Eddie married Yvonne Quior; and Kristy married George Hawkins.

In 1970, after their marriage, Richard and Beverly Whitaker moved to Anderson County. They have one daughter, Shea, who was born on 4-18-1975 in Woodford County. Richard also has one son, Troy Allen, who was born on 4-2-1965 in Shelbyville, KY. *Submitted By: Shea Whitaker.*

RONALD VENON WHITAKER

RONALD VENON WHITAKER, the son of Venon E. Whitaker and Ethlyn Boyd Whitaker, was born on 5-14-1944 in Baltimore, Maryland. He has one brother and two sisters: Robert Terrell married Mavis Jean Stacey - three children - Robert, Anthony, Krista; Deanna married James Paul Foster; and Janet Lee married Thomas Ward - one child, Devon.

On 8-30-1969, in Fairlea, West Virginia, Ronald married Sandra Lee Walton. She is the daughter of Hazle Copenhaven Walton and Colleen June Bennett Walton. Sandra was born on 2-20-1948 in Ronceverte, West Virginia. She has five brothers and sisters: Opie Edward married Sandra N. Stone - two children, Russell and Robin; Patricia Ann "Dede"; Michael Shawn married Tina Bennett; Jeffery Scott married Deanna O'Brien - one daughter, Jennifer; and Darla Renee.

Sandra spent all her elementary and high school years in the same school system, as opposed to Ronald who attended several schools. His father was in the field of education, so they moved a great deal. They even stayed a time in Anderson County. After graduation from high school, Sandra came to Georgetown, Kentucky to attend college. She then met and married Ronald Whitaker. They later moved to Lexington where their two children, Ronald Boyd and Lisa Paige, were born.

Shortly after Lisa was born, they began to think about moving from Lexington and began to look around for a community outside Fayette County with a good school system. Ronald had fond memories of the years he lived in Lawrenceburg and still had friends and relatives living there, so they came here to look for a place to live. In July of 1980, they moved their family to their present home on Jenny Lillard Road. *Submitted By: Ronnie Whitaker.*

FREDRIC RILEY WHITEHOUSE

FREDRIC RILEY WHITEHOUSE is one of 12 children born to John and Nancy Ann (McCamish) Whitehouse. His father's home was on Crooked Creek in Anderson County, KY. He had an older brother that volunteered in the Civil War and died of yellow fever. Fredric was ten years old at the time the Civil War started.

Fredric Riley Whitehouse (10-8-1851 / 3-24-1924) married Luranah Brown (8-3-1861 / 3-26-1924) of Jackson County, Indiana. They lived in a log house on Pleasant Grove Ridge Road, Anderson County; and in 1894, they moved to a home on the Salt River Road near Glensboro. Fredric and Luranah had five children: 1. William Ambrose married Rose Jeffries - four children. 2. Nancy Jane married Morgan Hughes - four children. 3. Ida Mae married George H. Best - 11 children. 4. Ollie Thomas married Jessie Sparrow - one son. 5. Elmo Vance married Nina Shely - one daughter.

Fredric and Luranah died of natural causes within 30 hours of each other. Fredric died at 9 p.m. on March 24, 1924, and Luranah died the next night at 3 a.m. They were buried the same day, same grave, and separate coffins. The funeral procession consisted of a black hearse, drawn by big black horses, and a black man driver from the Taylorsville Funeral Home with one body; and the other one was a black hearse, drawn by big white horses, and a white man driver from the Cleveland Funeral Home, Mt. Eden, KY with the other body. It was a sad day, yet a memorable and beautiful sight to behold.

Fredric Riley Whitehouse and Luranah (Brown) Whitehouse

Fredric's wife, Luranah (Brown) Whitehouse, was born in the year 1861 when the Civil War started and her father, Samuel Brown, was drafted to go to the army. At that time, if you could find a substitute to go in your place and pay $25, you could be exempt from the draft. So Samuel sold a horse to get the $25 and someone went in his place. Later, he was drafted again and someone volunteered this time and his wife, Nancy Jane (Chaney) sold her new cooking stove to get the $25 required. He wasn't drafted again. That is what kept him out of the Civil War.

Samuel Brown (9-18-1833 / 11-9-1911) married Nancy Jane Chaney (10-12-1833 / 10-21-1880). They had nine children - Luranah, William, John, Abe, Julia, Almira, Edd, Sallie, and Durand. Samuel's wife, Nancy Jane Brown, died leaving a baby (Durand) just 18 months of age. There were several other children at home, the oldest girl about ten years old. So you see, Samuel had a lot of responsibilities. He re-married three years later but all the children are by his first wife.

Samuel Brown and his wife, Nancy Jane, are buried in Franklin County, KY on what is now the Roy Peach Farm, U. S. 127, near Frankfort.

Samuel Brown's father was Berry Brown. Berry was just a lad when his parents came by pack horse from Virginia to Kentucky in the early 1800's or perhaps earlier. He married Polly Bailey. They had eight children - Peyton, Susan, Obedience, George, Byron, Neil, Sophronia, and Samuel. Between the Brown family and Chaney family, there were four marriages. *Submitted By: Juanita Best Glass from hand written records of her mother Ida Mae Whitehouse Best (Mrs. George H. Best).*

IDA MAE WHITEHOUSE

IDA MAE WHITEHOUSE (10-8-1880 / 11-12-1977) is the daughter of Fredric Riley Whitehouse, the son of John Whitehouse. Fredric Riley Whitehouse (1851 - 1924) married Luranah Brown (1861 - 1924) the daughter of Samuel Brown, the son of Berry Brown from Virginia. John Whitehouse from Washington County, KY married Nancy Ann McCamish (1819 - 1899) from Breckinridge County, KY.

Ida Mae Whitehouse was born in a little log cabin on the Old State Road now known as Pleasant Grove Ridge. No paved highways then just dirt roads and horse and buggies. She is one of five children. Her siblings are William Ambrose (1879 - 1951), Nancy Jane (Hughes), Ollie Thomas, and Elmo Vance.

When Ida Mae was eight years old her parents moved to a farm on the Salt River Road not far from her original home. After her marriage to George Hudson Best, she was back on Pleasant Grove Ridge again.

One of Ida Mae's memories of her childhood was their "Hungry Jack Suppers" the family (five children) would have on Friday nights. This was an evening meal of corn bread and milk around the old fireplace. The children would sit on the floor. She also told of the pleasures of riding horses with her brother on their Salt River Farm.

George H. Best and Ida Mae Whitehouse Best

Ida Mae Whitehouse married George Hudson Best on 12-29-1909, at her home in Glensboro. They had 11 children - Lorine (Peak), Wilma Kathleen (Williams), Naomi, Cecil, Lucille (Shouse), Ellis, Joyce

Mae (Murphy), Geneva (Ruble), Minnie Mildred (Rucker), Juanita (Glass) and Geraldine Marie (Glass). (see article on George Hudson Best.)

When George Best died in 1961, Ida Mae found it necessary to live elsewhere. She chose to live with her daughter, Joyce Mae Murphy, and diedt here in 1977.

Ida Mae sold the farm in 1975 because the upkeep was more than she could manage.

Ida Mae and George were of the Christian faith. Before the children, they were not demonstrative of their love for each other, but a quiet, mutual devotion permeated in the home. This had its lasting effects on their children.

Ancestors: Ida Mae (Whitehouse) Best, Fredric Riley Whitehouse, John Whitehouse

Ancestors: Ida Mae (Whitehouse) Best, Luranah (Brown) Whitehouse, Samuel Brown, Berry Brown

Submitted By: Juanita Best Glass from hand-written records of her mother Ida Mae Whitehouse Best (Mrs George H. Best).

JOHN WHITEHOUSE

JOHN WHITEHOUSE (born @ 1819) was from Washington County, Ky and his wife, Nancy Ann McCamish (1819 - 1899) was from Breckenridge County, KY. They married in Washington County and shortly thereafter came to Anderson County, KY and made their home. They owned property on Crooked Creek.

John and Nancy Ann are buried a short distance from the old house on Crooked Creek. John has only a field stone as a marker and Nancy Ann has a tombstone and the lettering is plain. She was born 12-14-1819 and died 10-31-1899.

John and Nancy Whitehouse had 12 children: 1. William Thomas volunteerd in the Civil War, died of yellow fever and never got back home - no children. 2. Nancy Jane - died young; buried at Mt. Moriah Cemetery, Mt. Eden, KY. 3. Martha married Bluford Ritter - seven children. 4. Louise married John Frazier - eight children. 5. Fredric Riley married Luranah Brown - five children. 6. Augustus married Laura Sea - three children. 7. Sanford married Maggie Proctor - no children. 8. Vincent married Sarah Ritchey - seven children. 9. Amanda married 1st Dock Sutherland, 2nd Marshall Ritchey - seven children (triplets once and twins twice). One of the triplets lived and one of the twins lived. No children by Marshall. 10. Eliza Jane married Hoseah Sutherland. Eliza had no children but reared two sons by Hoseah's previous marriage. 11. John Henry married Tilithia Moffett - one daughter. 12. Mary Ann married Dan Holmes - five children.

John and Nancy Ann Whitehouse eldest son, William Thomas, volunteered in the Civil War. What little money he sent to his parents was kept in an old teapot in the tall grass on the hillside below the house as means of keeping the guerrillas from finding it. Nancy would walk by the teapot occasionally to assure the spout was downhill; and if not, she would take her foot and turn it downhill. She didn't want anyone to see her pick it up, yet she managed to get some savings into it. William Thomas contracted yellow fever and never got back home. His parents received $12.00 a month pension.

Back of the John Whitehouse home. Taken about 1968.

In 1982, Nancy Ellen Whitehouse, a daughter of Augustus Whitehouse (child no. 6) died intestate. She had no immediate family and the heirs of her estate went back to the descendants of her grandparents (1/2 to paternal side and 1/2 to maternal side), the paternal side being John and Nancy Ann Whitehouse. The attorney handling the estate asked Juanita Best Glass to research the Whitehouse descendants and report to him. Of course, Juanita knew there would be none of John's 12 children living but she felt confident she would find a first cousin (grandchildren of John and Nancy Ann Whitehouse) to Nancy Ellen living because her mother's sister (first cousin to Nancy Ellen) had died just seven months before. But she was wrong; there were no first cousins living as of 2-8-1982. This complicated matters because she now had to get names and addresses of first cousins once removed. Juanita's research showed that John and Nancy Ann Whitehouse had 37 grandchildren and 94 great-grandchildren; and there were 63 of the 94 great-grandchildren living on 2-8-1982. She was successful in ascertaining and locating all the 63 paternal heirs-at-law (first cousin once removed) of Miss Nancy Ellen Whitehouse. *Submitted By: Juanita Best Glass from hand-written records of her mother, Ida Mae Whitehouse Best (Mrs. George H. Best) and her own research.*

BOBBY WILDER

BOBBY WILDER , was born on 12-3-1956 in Versailles, KY and has lived all his life in Anderson County. He is the son of William Lee Wilder and Dorothy Fallis Wilder Hoskins. Bobby has one brother, Larry Wayne, who married Lisa Merton of Indiana. They have two children: Charles Michael and Nicole Clarice. Bobby also has one sister, Debra Lynn, who married Gary Sutherland. They have two children: Crystal Michelle and Gary Michael. Both Wayne and Debbie reside in Anderson County. After his parents divorce, Bobby lived with his mother in Lawrenceburg. She remarried to Wilmer Hoskins and had two more children: Kimberly Jo, who married David Wilcher - They have one son, David Leon Jr. "DJ"; and Bradley Todd Hoskins, both of Lawrenceburg.

William Wilder remarried to Roselene Tingle and they had two children: William Davis, who married Kim Bryant of Shelby County - They have one daughter, Marissa Pearl; and Patricia "Pattie" Annette, who married Jimmy Fishback - he has a son by a previous marriage, Anthony Michael Fishback. William and Rosie were divorced. He then married Freda Sue Wadkins Chapman on 11-20-1985. Freda passed away in the summer of 1986. Bill later married Glenda Sue Hughes Darnell and they currently reside in Harrodsburg, KY.

Bobby started working at the Lawrenceburg Post Office as a city postal carrier soon after he graduated from Anderson County High School in 1974. On 7-16-1985, Bobby married Denise Marie Rowe. They now reside in Stringtown. She is employed by the Anderson County Chamber of Commerce as office secretary. They are expecting their first child in February.

Denise was born on 2-24-1965 in Sedalia, Missouri. She is the daughter of Frank David Rowe and Patricia Eileen Jeffries Rowe. Denise moved to Lawrenceburg with her family in 1972, when her father, who worked for Kraft, Inc. was transferred here. Frank and Pat Rowe are currently living in Mosheim, TN where he is employed by Dairymen, Inc. Denise attended Anderson County Schools and graduated from Anderson High School in 1983. She has five brothers and sisters: Donna Sue married Dan Pursley - They have three sons, Kurtis Allen, Kendall Ryan, and Kyle Derrick. They live in Nevada, Missouri; David Alan married Marlene Barnett of Breathitt Co. They reside in Lawrenceburg; Dale Lee married Gwen Thomas Coffman of Arkansas - They have three children, Daryl Lee, Desiree Lynette, and Darcia Louise. They currently live in

Holland where Dale is in the Air Force; Darla Kaye married Bo Sayre of Anderson County - They have two children, Lisa Kaye and Adam Christopher; and Darren Wayne married Pamela Shofner. They reside in Indiana.

Bobby and Denise Wilder - February 1986

Bobby's father, William Wilder, is the son of the late Stanley Burton and Nancy Pearl Green Wilder. Stanley was born 4-7-1913 in Jessamine County, KY and died 4-18-1981 in Tennessee. He was the son of Robert Jefferson and Minnie Frances Grow Wilder. Nancy Pearl was born 11-12-1911 in Mercer County, KY and died 2-25-1969. She was the only child of James Andrew and Bessie Harris Purvis Green.

Bobby's mother, Dorothy Fallis Wilder Hoskins, is the only daughter of the late Charles Curtis and Noma Goldie Kays Fallis. Curtis was born in December of 1904 in Anderson County and died 3-10-1979. He retired with 50 years of service with Southern Railroad. He was the son of Charles Lewis and Nancy Cordonia Norton Fallis. Noma was born 8-17-1909 in Anderson County and died 9-22-1984. She was the daughter of Ezekiel Lowry and Lora Anna Stratton Kays. Dorothy has one brother, Charles Curtis Fallis, Jr. "C. C." of Lawrenceburg.

Denise's father, Frank David Rowe, was born on 6-29-1930 in Eugene, MO. He is the son of the late Everette Matthew Rowe (1910 - 1971) and Louise Delilah Williams Rowe. Frank has one sister, Shirley Ann Rowe Jones of Kansas City, MO.

Denise's mother, Patricia Eileen Jeffries Rowe, was born on 11-22-1930 in Brumley, Missouri. She is the daughter of Ottie Harrison Jeffries and the late Lora Bell Fredrick Jeffries. She has one brother, William Ottie Jeffries of Camdenton, MO. After the marriage of Frank and Pat Rowe, Ottie Jeffries married Louise Williams Rowe. They reside in Camdenton, MO. *Submitted By: Denise Rowe Wilder.*

CARRIE WATSON WILLIAMS

CARRIE WATSON WILLIAMS was born in Anderson County, 5-16-1900. Daughter of Virgil Alexander Watson and Kittie Hawkins Watson. Paternal Grandmother was Enfield McBrayer Watson. Great-grandfather was James H. McBrayer, prominent farmer and citizen of the county. Maternal grandmother was Amanda Joiner Hawkins. Amanda was a sister to Harvey Joiner, well-known artist and portrait painter who had studios in Courier Journal Building in Louisville for many years.

Carrie W. Williams

Carrie graduated from Kavanaugh High School and attended the University of Kentucky. She taught school in Anderson and Woodford Counties.

She married Christopher E. Williams of Birmingham, Alabama in 1926. Has one son, E. Keith Williams, Account Executive, W B R C - TV, Birmingham.

Carrie has four grandchildren and four great-grandchildren.

A widow since 1950, she is currently living in Birmingham, Alabama. She still owns the family farm on Ninevah Road, and it is operated by Wendol K. Smith. *Submitted By: Carrie W. Williams*

RANDELL F. WRIGHT.

It is said that the Wright family came from Denmark and in 1812 made their way to the United States. As far back that is known on the Wright family is Frank Wright and his wife, Olive. They had a son, Harland, born in Chelsee, Iowa in 1910. On 12-9-1933 in Bradgate, Iowa, Harland married Muriel Olson. Her mother and father were Nel and Carrie Olson. Her mother died in 1959 and her father died in 1952. Muriel had a brother, Raymond, who died in 1953. Muriel was born in South Dakota on 12-10-1910.

Harland and Muriel had four children: Paul (born 1-25-1928), Diana (born 1-27-1930), Farrel (below), and Harlowe (born 1-1-1936).

Farrel (born 11-10-1934) married Sheryl Cruichshank, the daughter of James Cruichshank and Faye Bass Kilbourn. They were the parents of three children: Randall, Sandy, and Shannon. They lived in Humbolt, Iowa.

Farrel and Sheryl divorced and she went to live in Kentucky. The children went to live with their mother. A few years later Randall went to live with his father in Iowa. After graduating from high school, Randall married Linda Kearney. They moved to Kentucky and there had three children - Kristie, David, and Sarah Wright.

Seven years later, Linda and Randall divorced. The three children went to live with their mother in New Hampshire. Linda later met and married Bill Hamilton, and had two more children - William Kelly and Krystal Lynn.

In the meanwhile, Randall met and married Peggy Robinson, who was born and raised in Lawrenceburg, KY. They moved from Frankfort, KY to Lawrenceburg. In 1989, Kristie came to live with her father. *Submitted By: Kristie Wright.*

WOOLRIDGE.

Coming from England at an early age, the Wooldridge men were found in the Revolutionary War and their descendants have gained admission into the Daughters of the American Revolution (DAR). This family, both in Kentucky and other states, have been well represented in Civic, political and religious affairs.

The Wooldridge family were numbered among the first settlers in Woodford County, having come from Virginia, and were very prominent in the early affairs of the county.

John Wooldridge, born in 1678 likely in Virginia, was married to Martha (family name unknown) were progenitors of most Wooldridges in the United States today, having five sons and one daughter. John became one of the most respected and prosperous men in Chesterfield County, Virginia.

One son, Robert, married Magdalene Sallee, died in 1794 in Chesterfield County, Virginia. He left a will to Magdaleen and four sons, Captain Thomas Wooldridge, Captain Elisha Wooldridge, Captain Robert Wooldridge Jr., and William Wooldridge. Robert owned extensive land acreage in addition to the Wooldridge Coal Pits in Chesterfield County, Virginia. Son, Elisha, born 7-16-1752, married Hannah Wooldridge, born 11-10-1761.

Elisha and Hannah came to Woodford County, Kentucky and acquired extensive land acreage and settled there. They had nine children though several dying in childhood. One son, Robert Turner Wooldrige, came to Anderson County, married Jane Guinn and settled at Tyrone in 1847, where only three houses stood. They had nine children, John Merrit, William, Elisha, Grant, Thomas, Robert Jr., Caroline, and Mary.

Thomas Jr. (born 4-22-1898) married Delia Akins (born 12-31-1898) on 11-3-20. Thomas died 6-30-1920. Their children were Virginia, Lillard, Inis, and Melvina.

Thomas and Delia Wooldridge

Virginia married John P. McGuire of Houston, Texas, now living in Louisville. Their children are Donna, Larry, and Ricky. Donna married Nolan McDaniel: children; Craig, April, and Keith. Ricky married Debbie Dumas; children Jennifer, Eric, and Sara.

Lillard Wooldridge died in 1958. Inis married Irvine Shifflet. They have one son, Irvine Jr. who married Jeri Wagoner and have two sons, Brian and Kenny.

Melvina married Bernard Elkins and they have two daughters, Vicky and Sharon. Vicky married Thomas Yonders; children are Thomas, Jr. and Melissa. Sharon married Frank Embry and has one daughter, Stacy.

Grover Wooldridge married Maude Dean and had two daughters, Catherine and Mary. A second marriage to Jesse Carrier and had a daughter, Melissa. A third marriage to Delia Akins Wooldridge resulting in children, Florence, Hazel and Phillip.

Florence married G. B. Coovert; children Linda and Marshall. Hazel married Harry McCoy; children, Harry Jr. (Butch), Rhonda, Jeffery and Beverly. Phillip married Nellie Brooks and have a daughter, Phyllis.

The Wooldridge clan became very prominent in Woodford County, a community was named for them and there is a Wooldridge Lane in Versailles today. Earlier Wooldridges intermarried with families of Major, Moss, Hawkins, Trabue, and Thompson. Some of the Wooldridge family settled in the Ninevah section of Anderson County and some in Frankfort and Franklin County. *Submitted By: Virginia Wooldridge McGuire.*

JOSEPH SEWELL YATES

and Minnie Rea Woods Yates have lived in Lawrenceburg only 11 years, but have family connections with the town from the past. They moves here from Frankfort in 1978.

Joe is a native of Danville, Ky and as a child lived in Danville, Harrodsburg, Lawrenceburg, and Cloverport. His parents were the late Cale Benton Yates and Josephine Setters Yates. His brothers and sisters are: Frank; Bill, who married a Lawrenceburg native (Park Smith); MaryAnna, Mildred Y. Dietz, C.B. Jr.; John; and Beulah. Frank, Bill, MaryAnna, and Beulah are deceased. Mr. Yates Sr. was manager of the telephone company in Lawrenceburg from 1931 to 1934. Joe served in the U. S. Army Signal Corps in Japan from 1946 to 1948. He has been with Bell Telephone Company for 37 years.

Rea is a native of Harrodsburg. Her father was the late Lewis Witherspoon Curry Woods, member of a pioneer Harrodsburg family, and her late mother was the former Minnie Alice Wilder, a native of Lawrenceburg. The Wilders, Elijah Edwin and Fannie Blair, resided at 237 North Main in Lawrenceburg and moved to Harrodsburg in 1919. Rea developed a deep affection for Lawrenceburg early in her life from all the stories her mother told about the town and its people. Rea is the youngest of four children: two brothers, Lewis Jr. and Jack, and one sister, Sarah W. Bottom, all of Harrodsburg.

Joseph Sewell Yates, Minnie Rea Woods Yates August 19, 1950, Harrodsburg, KY. Wedding Day

The Yateses were married in 1950 at the Harrodsburg Methodist Church. They have since lived in Harrodsburg, Lexington, Frankfort, New Castle, Princeton, and Lawrenceburg. They have two children: Joe Jr., 37, and Alice Catherine, 35. Joe is an attorney in New Castle and is married to the former Phyllis Jeanne Haag. They are the parents of Zachery Graham Yates, 14, and Olivia Rea Yates, 4. Alice is married to Todd Saffell Lemley, son of a Lawrenceburg native, the late Frankie Smith Lemly. They own and operate a horse-boarding farm near NoneSuch.

Joe and Rea are both 1949 graduates of Harrodsburg High School and are lifelong Methodists. They reside in the former Jerome Tartar house, 501 South Main Street. *Submitted By: Joe and Rea Yates.*

YOCUM

The Yocum family traces their linage back to the very early settlement of Kentucky. In 1776, Mathis Yocum was with James Harrod at Fort Harrod in Mercer County, KY. Mathias was a descendant of Hendrick Yocum. Hendrick was born in Germany and came to New Amsterdam, New York on the ship "Beaver" in 1661. Mathias, after leaving the early settlements of Mercer County, settled in that part of Washington County, KY that became Anderson County in 1827. From him, a long line of descendants can be traced. Mathew Yocum, Sr. (son of Mathias) was born in 1770. He married Selvey Coulter. She was the daughter of Thomas Coulter. Mathew, Sr. died in 1837. Mathew Yocum, Jr. was born in 1801. He married Mary Birch Mitchell. She was the daughter of Daniel Mitchell and Jennie Berry Mitchell. He died in 1887. Daniel Mitchell Yocum was born in 1836. He married Mary Jane Waterfill. She was the daughter of Jesse Waterfill and Irene Routt Waterfill. He died in 1926. David Alfred Yocum was born September 30, 1870 at Leather's Store, Anderson County, Kentucky. He married Edith Lois Barnette. She was the daughter of Dr. James Berry Barnette and Rhoda Alice Vowels Barnette of Wardsville, Anderson County, Kentucky. He died April 15, 1953. They had four children: The late Dr. Earl Vance Yocum of Ashland, Kentucky; the late Hilary Vaught Yocum of Miami Springs, Florida; David Barnette Yocum of Winter Haven, Florida; and Alice Yocum Pelsor of Harrodsburg, Kentucky. *Submitted By: Suzanne Pelsor Mesta.*

BARTLETT YORK,

son of John and Nancy York, was born on June 26, 1792 in Orange County, Virginia. He married Agnes Susan Paxton, In Virginia, 1817. She was a daughter of James Paxton. Agnes was born in 1796 and died August 21, 1887 in Anderson County, KY at the age of 91 years.

Bartlett and Agnes York were the parents of 12 children: John B. (1818 - 1839); James R. (1820 - 1905); Elizabeth (1821 - 1822); Frances (born 1824 in Franklin County, KY); Ann Maria (1825 - 1838); Mary Jane (born 1827 in Anderson County); Benjamin (born 1829 in Anderson County); Susan (born 1831 in Anderson County); Samuel (born 1833 in Anderson County); Armstead (born 1835 in Anderson County. He was a soldier for the Confederacy in the Civil War.); William H. (below); and John T. (born 1842 in Anderson County).

Bartlett York, a soldier in the War of 1812, lived in Jessamine County, KY before he came to Anderson County where he died on December 2, 1853. Both he and his wife are buried in the Christian Church Graveyard, Fox Creek, KY.

William H. York was born in 1840 in Anderson County and he married 1st Susan Mary Crossfield in November of 1865 in Anderson County. She died at Hutchinson, Kansas on April 14, 1888 and was buried there. They had the following children: Martha Lee (1866 - 1930); James R. (1868 - 1958); John (1870 - 1894); Lesley (1871 - infant); Annie (1873 - 1954); Margaret (1877 - 1958); Mary Agnes (1879 - 1968); Alice (1881 - 1952); Walter (below); and Ethel (1887 - 1918). All were born in Anderson County with the exception of Ethel, who was born in Kansas.

William remarried to widow Susan Prewitt of Paris, KY in 1890. In 1862, William enlisted in the 5th Kentucky Cavalry of the Confederate Army and served until the end of the war. William H. entered the Confederate Soldier's Home, Pewee Valley, KY in July 1921. He died on January 25, 1929 and was buried there at the age of 89 years.

Walter York was born in 1883 and married Ermin Morris on April 30, 1905 in Anderson County. She died on April 11, 1968 at the age of 83 years. They had five children: Paul (1907 - 1967); Roy (below); Thelma (1911 - 1988); Wanda (born 1915 in Anderson County); and Lois (born 1917 in Anderson County). Walter died on September 1918 at the age of 35 years. Both he and his wife are buried in the Fox Creek Cemetery in Anderson County. *Submitted By: Roy York.*

ROY YORK and Gladys Blanch Caldwell York were married on January 4, 1936 at the First Christian Church Parsonage in Lawrenceburg. To this union were born 2 children: James Walter "Jimmy" (married Vicki Shelburn) They have two children,

Richard Ellis and Charlotte Ann. Richard (married Elizabeth Wash). They have one son, Roy Lewis and live in Georgetown. Charlotte (married Clyde Murray). They have one daughter, Kara Michelle and live in Frankfort; and Robert Burris "Bob" (married Cathy Hardin). They have two daughters, Melinda and Jennifer. They live in Louisville.

Roy York, the son of Walter H. York and Ermin Morris York was born April 22, 1909, in Anderson County, KY. He had four brothers and sisters: Paul (1907 - 1967); Thelma (1911 - 1988); Wanda (born in 1915); and Lois (born in 1917). Walter York died in 1918 when Roy was only nine years old. He lived on the family farm until his marriage to Blanche. They then moved to Lawrenceburg, where they reside today.

Roy went to work for Fox Creek Rural Electric in 1938, helping to survey lines to the rural sections of Anderson County. In 1940, he was promoted to manager. He held this position until his retirement in 1974. Roy was also involved in a number of community organizations. He was President of the Chamber of Commerce for one term, President of the Kentucky Association of Rural Electric Cooperatives for one term, and served on the 1st East Kentucky Board of Directors until they made a point to put all Directors instead of having managers and directors to serve the board. He also served as one of the Directors of the Beaver Lake Inc. He served as chairman for a number of years, during the development of the area around Beaver Lake. In 1941, he joined the Masonic Lodge and served as Mastor a few years later. He also joined the Royal Arts Masons and served one term as high priest. He also served as Chairman of the Board and Elder of the First Christian Church.

Gladys Blanche Caldwell York, the daughter of Charles Caldwell and Betty Satterly Caldwell, was born on May 3, 1917. She had four brothers and sisters: Early; Bill; J.S.; and Audrey. Blanche's mother died when she was four years old and she went to live with her grandmother until she was 11 years old. At which time, she went to live with Mr. and Mrs. Burris Morris, who lived out on Fox Creek Road. She lived here until her marriage to Roy York.

Blanche, a member of the First Christian Church with her husband, served many years as a Sunday School teacher. She also served as Den Mother for the Cub Scouts. Both she and her husband are members

of the Eastern Star. He has served as a patron and she as a matron. *Submitted By: Roy York.*

JOSEPH YOUNG was born 7-17-1798 and died 9-14-1887. He married twice the first being Martha Railenback the mother of his five children. The second being Mary, whom he married late in life.

Joseph is mentioned many times in early minutes of Pigeon Fork Baptist Church. He served on the building and cemetery committees.

Joseph's children and their spouses are: David William (Susan Bowler), Bennett (Sarah Ann Haden), Lawrence (Sarah Ann Sedars), Lucy (Joeseph Shannon), and Permelia Ann (James Ryan).

Joseph Breckenridge Young

David William Young married Susan Bowler on 2-9-1852. They had eight children. These children and their spouses are: Cynthia Ann Brown (John Thomas Ruble), John J. (Nancy Jane Tinsley), Carrie (8-28-1873 - 11-28-1907), Sarah "Sallie" (Major Travis), William Thomas (Nora Jeffers), Lucy Katherine (John Neal Cinnamon), Joseph Breckenridge (Lucy Ann Frain), Mary Elizabeth Young.

Joe B. married Lucy Ann Frain on 1-12-1881. They had six children. These children and their spouses are: David William (1st Beatrice Lacefield, 2nd Rebecca Lowe Ingram), Annie Kate (George Lacefield), Lillie Mae (Julian Bishop Perry), Clarence Harrison (died in infancy), Jessie B. (Lucille Burton), Clara Frances (Paul C. Miller).

Joe B. farmed all of his life. He also served as magistrate of Anderson County. *Submitted By: Paula Perry Mitchell.*

CLIFFORD J. MARTIN, The pioneer, Edward Martin was born in Ireland in 1803. His bride-to-be, Lydia Mathis was also born in Ireland in 1803. The two families left Ireland in 1820 and came to America.

They made their way to Virginia where Edward and Lydia were married. Soon after their marriage, Edward and Lydia Martin moved to Kentucky where they settled in the Hammonds Creek area of Anderson County. During the War Between the States, Edward was arrested and taken to Louisville and put in prison. Lydia decided that wasn't right, so she rode a horse from Anderson County to Louisville and, as they said "outtalked the generals" and brought Edward home.

They raised six sons: George, John, Allen, William, Louis, and Frank; also four daughters: Kate, Liza, Margaret, and Josephine. William T. Martin, son of Edward and Lydia Martin was born Jan. 11, 1840. He married Miranda Hedger, daughter of J.T. Hedger. They had eight children - George (died at age 14), Susie (never married), Allen (died when two years old), Edward (married Bert Waterfill, daughter of Joe Waterfill), William Thomas (married Affie McBrayer), John B. (married Annie Smith), Jasper (married Maggie Brown), James A. (married Minnie K. Smith, daughter of Jeff Smith of Fulton, KY).

James A. and Minnie K. Martin had five children, three of whom died in infancy. Willie (married Lizzie Hawthorne, daughter of Jim Hawthorne) and Clifford J. (married Margaret E. Fallis, daughter of Cleve and Olive Key Fallis).

Clifford J. and Margaret E. Martin had one daughter, Marguerite Anne. She is married to Ellis Dawson Collins, son of James D. and Nannie McBrayer Collins. They are the parents of one daughter, Marilyn Louise (married to Lloyd Horne of Paintsville, KY), who has two sons - Michael Shain and Dustin Scott.

Clifford J. Martin was educated in the schools of Mercer and Anderson Counties and was a graduate of the Sweeney Automotive School in Kansas City. He operated a service station in the Stringtown community from 1932 until his death in 1983. During World War II his wife, Margaret, kept the service station open while he worked as a radio technician at the Lexington Blue Grass Army Depot at Avon, KY.

He was the first chairman of the Stringtown Water District which he helped organize in 1950.

After the war, he returned to his service station. His son-in-law, Ellis Collins, joined him in the business and a line of appliances, radios and televisions were added. Later fishing tackle and bait were brought in and the service station became more like a general store or a bait shop. In his late 70's, age and ill health took their toll and he died in 1983 at the age of 78. *Submitted by: Margaret E. Martin*

Joseph Hanks (Dick) Crook and James Henry (Cutter) Crook.

Lucille, Cheryl, Robert, Elaine Angelene Duncan Ferguson, Larry Ferguson, Phil Gregory, Arlene Gregory, Carl Gregory, Mrs. Elmo Brimer (Nina)

FAMILY TREE

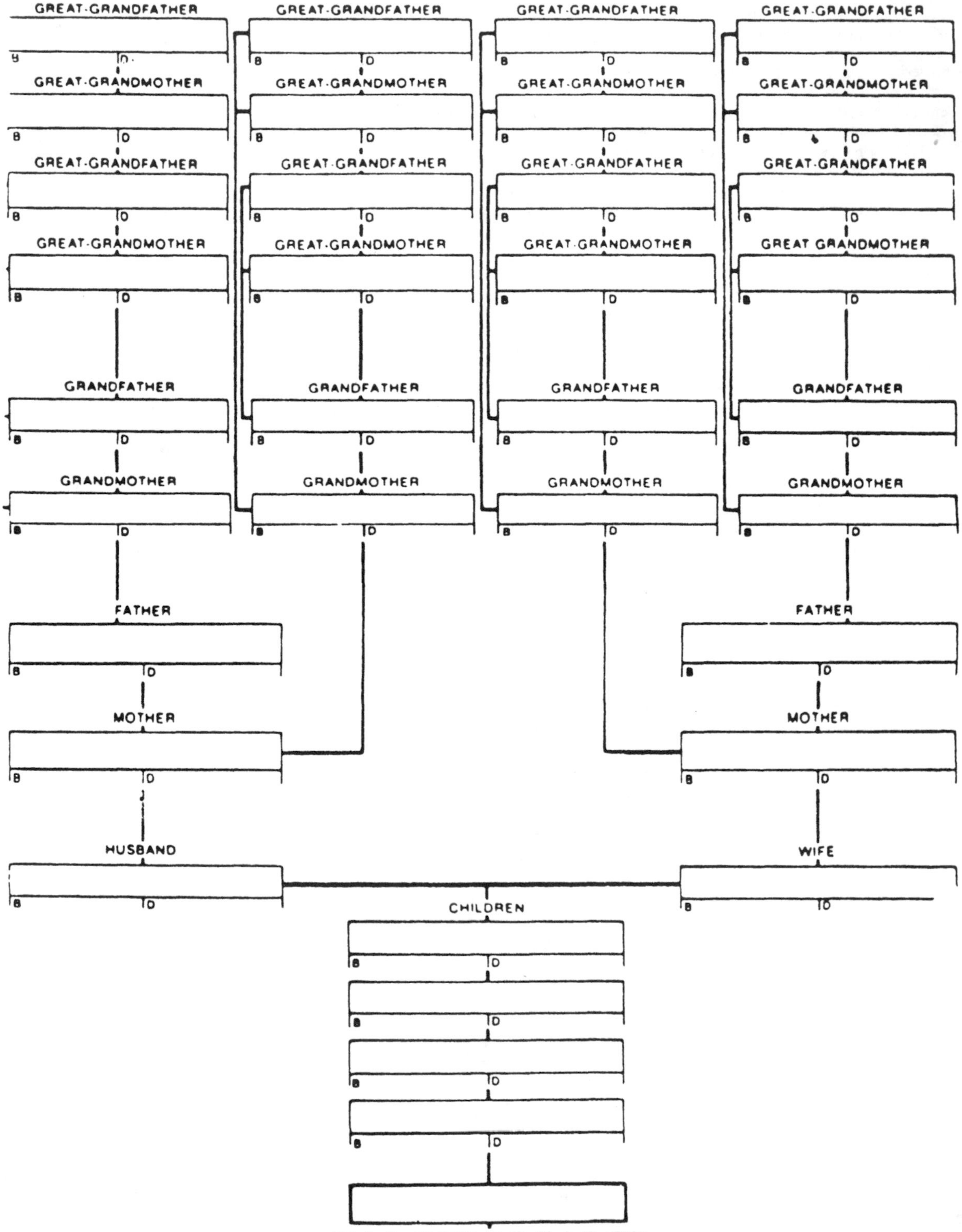

GREAT-GRANDFATHER	GREAT-GRANDFATHER	GREAT-GRANDFATHER	GREAT-GRANDFATHER

B · · · D

GREAT-GRANDMOTHER	GREAT-GRANDMOTHER	GREAT-GRANDMOTHER	GREAT-GRANDMOTHER

B · · · D

GREAT-GRANDFATHER	GREAT-GRANDFATHER	GREAT-GRANDFATHER	GREAT-GRANDFATHER

B · · · D

GREAT-GRANDMOTHER	GREAT-GRANDMOTHER	GREAT-GRANDMOTHER	GREAT-GRANDMOTHER

B · · · D

GRANDFATHER	GRANDFATHER	GRANDFATHER	GRANDFATHER

B · · · D

GRANDMOTHER	GRANDMOTHER	GRANDMOTHER	GRANDMOTHER

B · · · D

FATHER		FATHER

B · · · D

MOTHER		MOTHER

B · · · D

HUSBAND		WIFE

B · · · D

CHILDREN

B · · · D

B · · · D

B · · · D

B · · · D

FAMILY NAME

FAMILY RECORD

NAME	BIRTH		DEATH	
	Date	Place	Date	Place

McCALL'S SPRING
Formerly Cove or Lillard Spring

The McAfee bros., James McCoun, Jr. and Samuel Adams, first white men to explore this area, 1773. Cove Spring and Cove Spring Branch in Franklin Co. boundary line, 1794. Maj. Gen. E. Kirby Smith, CSA, and troops camped here on their way to join General Bragg Oct. 9, 1862. Only known time Spring's supply was exhausted.

Printed in the USA
CPSIA information can be obtained
at www.ICGtesting.com
JSHW060053150824
68134JS00032B/2726

9 781681 624464